.

Villainage in England

ESSAYS

IN

ENGLISH MEDIAEVAL HISTORY

BY

PAUL VINOGRADOFF

PROFESSOR IN THE UNIVERSITY OF MOSCOW

THE LAWBOOK EXCHANGE, LTD.
Clark, New Jersey

ISBN 978-1-58477-477-8

Lawbook Exchange edition 2005, 2019

The quality of this reprint is equivalent to the quality of the original work.

THE LAWBOOK EXCHANGE, LTD.
33 Terminal Avenue
Clark, New Jersey 07066-1321

*Please see our website for a selection of our other publications
and fine facsimile reprints of classic works of legal history:*
www.lawbookexchange.com

Library of Congress Cataloging-in-Publication Data

Vinogradoff, Paul, Sir, 1854-1925.
    Villainage in England: essays in English medieval history / by
Paul Vinogradoff.
        p. cm.
    Originally published: Oxford: Clarendon press, 1892.
    Includes index.
    ISBN 1-58477-477-0 (cloth: alk. paper)
      1. Villainage—England—History—To 1500. I. Title.

HC254.V52005
305.5'633 '09420902—dc22   2004048672

Printed in the United States of America on acid-free paper

Villainage in England

ESSAYS

IN

ENGLISH MEDIAEVAL HISTORY

BY

PAUL VINOGRADOFF

PROFESSOR IN THE UNIVERSITY OF MOSCOW

Oxford
AT THE CLARENDON PRESS
1892

𝔒𝔵𝔣𝔬𝔯𝔡

PRINTED AT THE CLARENDON PRESS

BY HORACE HART, PRINTER TO THE UNIVERSITY

PREFACE

A FOREIGNER'S attempt to treat of difficult and much disputed points of English history requires some justification. Why should a Russian scholar turn to the arduous study of English mediaeval documents? Can he say anything of sufficient general interest to warrant his exploration of so distant a field?

The first question is easier to answer than the second.

There are many reasons why we in Russia are especially keen to study what may be called social history — the economic development of nations, their class divisions and forms of co-operation. We are still living in surroundings created by the social revolution of the peasant emancipation; many of our elder contemporaries remember both the period of serfdom and the passage from it to modern life; some have taken part in the working out and putting into practice of the emancipating acts. Questions entirely surrendered to antiquarian research in the West of Europe are still topics of contemporary interest with us.

It is not only the civil progress of the peasantry that we have to notice, but the transformation and partial decay of the landed gentry, the indirect influence of the economic convulsions on politics, ideas, and morality, and, in a more special way, the influence of free competition on soil and people that had been fettered for ages, the passage from 'natural husbandry' to the money system, the substitution of rents for labour, above all, the working of communal institutions under the sway of the lord and in their modern free shape. Government and society have to deal even now with problems that must be solved in the light of

history, if in any light at all, and not by instinct groping
in the dark. All such practical problems verge towards
one main question : how far legislation can and should act
upon the social development of the agrarian world. Are
economic agencies to settle for themselves who has to till
land and who shall own it ? Or can we learn from Western
history what is to be particularly avoided and what is to
be aimed at ? I do not think that anybody is likely to
maintain at the present day, that, for instance, a study of
the formation and dissolution of the village community in
the West would be meaningless for politicians and thinkers
who have to concern themselves with the actual life of the
village community in the East.

Another powerful incitement comes from the scientific
direction lately assumed by historical studies. They have
been for a long time very closely connected with fine
literature : their aim was a lifelike reproduction of the
past ; they required artistic power, and stirred up feelings
as well as reflective thought. Such literary history has a
natural bent towards national tradition, for the same reason
that literature is attracted by national life : the artist
gains by being personally in touch with his subject ; it is
more easy for him to cast his material into the right mould.
Ancient history hardly constitutes an exception, because
the elements of classical civilisation have been appropriated
by European nations so as to form part of their own past.
What I call literary history has by no means done all its
work. There is too much in the actions of men that
demands artistic perception and even divination on the part
of the historian, to allow this mode of treatment to fall into
decay. But nobody will deny that historical study is extending more and more in the direction of what is now
called anthropology and social science. Historians are in
quest of laws of development and of generalisations that
shall unravel the complexity of human culture, as physical

and biological generalisations have put into order our knowledge of the phenomena of nature.

There is no subject more promising from this point of
view than the history of social arrangements. It borders
on political economy, which has already attained a scientific standing; part of its material has been fashioned by
juridical doctrine and practical law, and thereby moulded
into a clear, well-defined shape; it deals with facts recurring again and again with much uniformity, and presenting
great facilities for comparison; the objects of its observation
are less complex than the phenomena of human thought,
morality, or even political organisation. And from the
point of view of the scientific investigator there can be no
other reason for taking up a particular epoch or nation, but
the hope of getting a good specimen for analysis, and of
making use of such analysis for purposes of generalisation.

Now I think that there can be no better opportunity for
studying early stages of agrarian development than that
afforded by English mediaeval history. The sources of
information are comparatively abundant in consequence
of the powerful action of central authority; from far back
in the feudal time we get legal and fiscal documents to en-
lighten us, not only about general arrangements but even
about details in the history of landed property and of
the poorer classes. And the task of studying the English
line of development is rendered especially interesting because it stands evidently in close connexion with the
variations of the same process on the continent. Scan-
dinavian, German, French, Italian, and Spanish history
constantly present points of comparison, and such differences as there are may be traced to their origins just
because so many facts are in common to start with. I
think that all these considerations open a glorious vista for
the enquirer, and the interest excited by such publications
as those of Fustel de Coulanges proves that the public is

fully alive to the importance of those studies in spite of their dry details.

What could I personally undertake to further the great objects of such investigation? The ground has been surveyed by powerful minds, and many controversies show that it is not an easy one to explore. Two main courses seemed open in the present state of the study. A promising method would have been to restrict oneself to a definite provincial territory, to get intimately acquainted with all details of its geography, local history, peculiarities of custom, and to trace the social evolution of this tract of land as far back as possible, without losing sight of general connexions and analogies. How instructive such work may become may be gathered from Lamprecht's monumental monograph on the Moselland, which has been rightly called by its author 'Deutsches Wirthschaftsleben im Mittelalter.' Or else, one might try to gather the general features of the English mediaeval system as embodied in the numerous, one might almost say innumerable, records of the feudal period, and to work back from them into the imperfectly described pre-feudal age. Such enquiry would necessarily leave out local peculiarities, or treat them only as variations of general types. From the methodical point of view it has the same right to existence as any other study of 'universalities' which are always exemplified by individual beings, although the latter are not made up by them, but appear complicated in every single case by additional elements.

Being a foreigner, I was driven to take the second course. I could not trust myself to become sufficiently familiar with local life, even if I had the time and opportunity to study it closely. I hope such investigations may be taken up by scholars in every part of England and may prosper in their hands; the gain to general history would be simply invaluable. And I was not sorry of the necessity of going by the second track, because I could hope to achieve something useful even if I went wrong on many points. Every year brings publications of Cartularies, Surveys, Court-rolls ; the importance of these legal and economic records has been duly realised, and historians take them more and more into account by the side of annals and statutes. But surely some attempt ought to be made to concentrate the results of scattered investigation in this field. The Cartularies of Ramsey, Battle, Bury St. Edmunds, St. Paul's, the Hundred Rolls, the Manorial Records of Broughton and King's Ripton, give us material of one and the same kind, which, for all its wealth and variety, presents great facilities for classification and comparison[1]. I have seen a good many of these documents, both published and in manuscript, and I hope that my book may be of some service in the way of concentrating this particular study of manorial records. I am conscious how deficient my work is in many respects ; but if by the help of corrections, alterations, additions, it may be made to serve to some extent for the purpose, I shall be glad to have written it. I may say also that it is intended to open the way, by a careful study of the feudal age, for another work on the origins of English peasant life in the Norman and pre-Norman periods.

One pleasant result the toil expended on mediaeval documents has brought me already. I have come into contact with English scholars, and I can say that I have received encouragement, advice, and support in every case when I had to apply for them, and in so large and liberal a measure as I could hardly hope for or expect. Of two men, now dead, I have to repeat what many have said before me. Henry Bradshaw was the first to lay an English

---

[1] Miss Lamond's edition of Walter of Henley did not appear until the greater part of my book was in type. I had studied the work in MS. So also I studied the Cartulary of Battle Abbey in MS. without being aware that it had been edited by Mr. Scargill Bird. Had Mr. Gomme's Village Communities come to my hands at an earlier date I should have made more references to it.

MS. cartulary before me in the Cambridge University Library; and in all my travels through European libraries and archives I never again met such a guide, so ready to help from his inexhaustible store of palaeographical, linguistic and historical learning. Walford Selby was an invaluable friend to me at the Record Office—always willing and able to find exactly what was wanted for my researches.

It would be impossible to mention all those from whom I have received help in one way or another, but I should like to speak at least of a few. I have the pleasant duty of thanking the Marquis of Bath for the loan of the Longleat MS. of Bracton, which was sent for my use to the Bodleian Library. Lord Leigh was kind enough to allow of my coming to Stoneleigh Abbey to work at a beautiful cartulary in his possession, and the Hon. Miss Cordelia Leigh took the pains of making for me some additional extracts from that document. Sir Frederick Pollock and Mr. York Powell have gone through the work of reading my proofs, and I owe to them many suggestions for alterations and improvements. I have disputed some of Mr. Seebohm's opinions on mediaeval history; but I admit freely that nobody has exercised a stronger influence on the formation of my own views, and I feel proud that personal friendship has given me many opportunities of admiring the originality and width of conception of one who has done great things for the advancement of social history. As for F. W. Maitland, I can only say that my book would hardly have appeared at all if he had not taken infinite trouble to further its publication. He has not only done everything in his power to make it presentable to English readers in style and wording, but as to the subject-matter, many a friendly suggestion, many a criticism I have had from him, and if I have not always profited by them, the blame is to be cast entirely on my own obstinacy.

PAUL VINOGRADOFF.

CONTENTS

—+—

Contents.

SECOND ESSAY.

The Manor and the Village Community.

INTRODUCTION.

WHEN the time comes for writing a history of the nineteenth century, one of the most important and attractive chapters will certainly be devoted to the development of historical literature. The last years of a great age are fast running out : great has been the strife and the work in the realm of thought as well as in the material arrangement of life. The generations of the nineteenth century have witnessed a mighty revival of religious feeling ; they have attempted to set up philosophical systems as broad and as profound as any of the speculations of former times ; they have raised the structure of theoretical and applied science to a height which could hardly have been foreshadowed some two hundred years ago. And still it is to historical study that we have to look as the most characteristic feature of the period. Medieval asceticism in its desperate struggle against the flesh, and Puritanism with its sense of individual reconciliation with God, were both more vigorous forms of religious life than the modern restorations of faith and Church, so curiously mixed up with helplessness, surrender of acquired truth, hereditary instincts, and utilitarian reflection. In philosophy, Hegel's metaphysical dialectic, Schopenhauer's transformation of Kant's teaching, and the attempts of English and French positivism at encyclopaedical science may be compared theoretically with Plato's poetical idealism or with the rationalistic schools of the seventeenth and eighteenth centuries. But it would be difficult to deny, that in point of influence on men's minds, those older systems held a more commanding position than these : Hegel seems too arbitrary and phantastical, Schopenhauer too pessimistic, positivism too incomplete and barren as to ultimate problems to suit the practical requirements of philosophy ; and people are already complaining of the decay of philosophical study. In science, again, the age of Darwin is certainly second to none, but it has to share its glory with the age of Newton, and it may be reasonably doubted whether the astronomer, following in the footsteps of Galileo and Kepler, was not actuated by even greater thirst and pride of knowledge than the modern biologist or geologist. It is otherwise with regard to history.

Progress of historical methods.

Students of science are wont to inveigh against the inexact character of historical research, its incoherence and supposed inability to formulate laws. It would be out of place here to discuss the comparative value of methods and the one-sided preference given by such accusers to quantitative analysis ; but I think that if these accusers were better acquainted with the subject of their attacks, or even more attentive to the expressions of men's life and thought around them, they would hardly dare to maintain that a study which in the short space of a century has led to a complete revolution in the treatment of all questions concerning man and society, has been operating only by vague assumptions and guesses at random. An investigation into methods cannot be undertaken in these introductory pages, but a general survey of results may be attempted. If we merely take a single volume, Tocqueville's Ancien Régime, and ask ourselves whether anything at all like it could have been produced even in the eighteenth century, we shall have a sense of what has been going on in the line of historical study during the nineteenth. Ever since Niebuhr's great stroke, historical criticism has been patiently engaged in testing, sifting, and classifying the original materials, and it has now rendered impossible that medley of discordant authorities in which eighteenth-century learning found its confused notions of Romans in French costume, or sought for modern constitutional ideas as manifest in the policy of the Franks. Whole subjects and aspects of social life which, if treated at all, used to be sketchily treated in some appendix by the historian, or guessed at like a puzzle by the antiquarian, have come to the fore and are recognised as the really important parts of history. In a word, the study of the past vacillates no longer between the two extremes of minute research leading to no general results and general statements not based on any real investigation into facts. The laws of development may still appear only as dim outlines which must be more definitely traced by future generations of workers, but there is certainly a constant progress of generalisation on firmly established premises towards them.

What is more striking, the great change in the ways and results of history has made itself felt on all the subjects which surround it. Political economy and law are assuming an entirely new shape under the influence of historical conceptions: the tendency towards building up dogmatic doctrine on the foundation of abstract principle and by deductive methods is giving way to an exact study of facts in their historical surroundings, and to inquiries into the shifting conditions under which the problems of social economy and law are solved by different epochs. As a brilliant representative of legal learning has ironically put it, it would be better for one nowadays to be convicted of petty larceny than to be found deficient of 'historical-mindedness.' The influence of historical speculation on politics is yet more definite and direct: even the most devoted disciples of particular creeds, the most ardent advocates of reform or reaction dare not simply take up the high standing ground of abstract theory from which all political questions were discussed less than a hundred years ago: the socialist as well as the partisan of aristocracy is called on to make good his contention by historical arguments.

It may be urged that the new turn thus taken is not altogether beneficial for practical life. Men of fanatical conviction were more likely to act and die for the eternal truth revealed to them, than people reflecting on the relative character of human arrangements. But can one get blissfully onesided by merely wishing to be so? And is it not nobler to seek knowledge in the hope that it

[margin note: Growing influence of history on kindred subjects.]

will right itself in the end, than to reject it for the sake of being comfortable? However this may be, the facts can hardly be denied: the aspiration of our age is intensely historical; we are doing more for the relative, than for the absolute, more for the study of evolution than for the elucidation of principles which do not vary.

Sketch of the literary development of social history as a necessary introduction to its treatment.

It will not be my object to give a sketch of the gradual rise of historical study in the present century: such an undertaking must be left to later students, who will command a broader view of the subject and look at it with less passion and prejudice than we do now. But Lord Acton's excellent article[1] has shown that the task is not quite hopeless even now, and I must try, before starting on my arduous inquiry into the social history of the middle ages in England, to point out what I make of the work achieved in this direction, and what object I have in view myself. Quite apart from any questions of detail which may come under consideration as the treatment of the subject requires it, I have to say in what perspective the chief schools of historians present themselves to my view, in what relation they stand to each other, to show how far they have pushed the inquiry, and what problems still remain unsolved. Such a preliminary sketch must not be carried out with a view to criticism and polemics, but rather as the general estimate of a literary movement in its various phases.

Late recognition of the value of social history.

It is a remarkable fact, that the vast importance of the social side of history has been recognised later than any other aspect of that study. Stating things very broadly, one may say that it was pushed to the fore about the middle of our century by the interests and forces at play in actual life: before 1848 the political tendency predominates; after 1848 the tide turns in favour of the social tendency. I mean that in the first half of the century men were chiefly engaged in reorganising the State, in trying to strike a balance between the influence of government and the liberties of the people. The second half of the century is

[1] English Historical Review, No. 1.

engrossed by the conflict between classes, by questions of economical organisation, by reforms of civil order. Historical literature, growing as it was in the atmosphere of actual life, had to start from its interests, to put and solve its problems in accordance with them. But it is no wonder that the preceding period had already touched upon a number of questions that were fated to attract most attention in later research. The rise of the Constitution, for instance, could not be treated without some regard being paid to the relative position of classes; it would have been out of the question to speak of political feudalism without taking into account the social bearing of the system. And so a sketch of the literary treatment of social questions must begin with books which did not aim directly at a description of social history.

I shall not detain the reader over the work achieved in the seventeenth and eighteenth centuries. The learning of a Selden or of a Madox is astounding, and a student of the present day has to consult them constantly on particular questions; but they never had in mind to embrace the history of their country as a whole. Facts are brought into a system by Coke, but the system is strictly a legal one; undigested historical knowledge is made to yield the necessary store of leading cases, and, quite apart from the naive perversion of most particulars, the entire view of the subject is thoroughly opposed to historical requirements, for it makes the past an illustration of the present, and regards it as planned on the same lines. There is no lack of books setting forth historical proof for some favourite general thesis or arranging facts according to some general idea, but such attempts were distinguished by unbounded imagination and by endless sacrifices of fact to the object of the writer's devotion. The curious literary by-play to the struggle of political party which Aug. Thierry[1] has artistically illustrated in France from the writings of Boulainvilliers and Dubos, Mably and Lézardière, could

Characteristics of the work done in the seventeenth and eighteenth centuries.

---

[1] In his Considérations sur l'histoire de France.

certainly be matched in England by a tale of the historical argumentation of Brady[1], or Petyt[2], or Granville Sharp. Nothing can be more eloquent in a sense than the title given by this last author to his book on the system of frankpledge :—" An account of the Constitutional English Polity of Congregational Courts, and more particularly of the great annual court of the people, called the View of Frankpledge, wherein the whole body of the Nation was arranged into the regular divisions of Tythings, Hundreds, etc. :—the happy effect of that excellent institution, in preventing robberies, riots, etc., whereby, in law, it was justly deemed 'Summa et maxima securitas:'—that it would be equally beneficial to all other nations and countries, as well under monarchical as republican establishments ; and that, to the English Nation in particular, it would afford an effectual means of reforming the corruption of Parliament by rendering the representation of the people perfectly equal, in exact numerical proportion to the total number of householders throughout the whole realm[3]."

Historical research, in the true sense of the word, was indeed making its first appearance in the eighteenth century, and it was more fruitful in England than in any other country, because England was so far ahead of the Continent in its political condition : the influence of an intelligent society in political affairs had for its counterpart a greater insight into the conditions of political development. But the great English historians of the eighteenth century were looking to problems in other fields than that of social history. Robertson was prompted by an interest in the origins of that peculiar community called Western Europe, so distinctly dismembered in its component States and so closely united by ideal and material ties ; Gibbon could see the shadows of the old world in which the new world was living ; both had been attracted to research by an

---

[1] History of Boroughs.

[2] Ancient Rights of the Commons of England.

[3] Quoted by Palgrave, English Commonwealth, i. 192, from the second edition of 1786. The first appeared in 1784.

admirable sense of influences deeper and stronger than nationality, or State, or class, and both remained indifferent to the humbler range of English social history. Hume took his stand on England, but he had to begin with a general outline and the explanation of the more apparent changes in State and Church.

In this way current notions on our questions remained Black- towards the close of the eighteenth century still undis- stone's Commen- turbed by writers of a high order. We may take as a fair taries. sample of such current notions Sir William Blackstone's historical digressions, especially those in the second volume of his Commentaries[1]. There is no originality about them, and the lack of this quality is rather an advantage in this case : it enables us through one book to glance at an entire literature. I may be allowed to recall its most striking points to the mind of my readers.

The key to the whole medieval system and to the constitution emerging from it is to be found in feudalism. 'The constitution of feuds had its original from the military policy of the northern or Celtic nations, the Goths, the Huns, the Franks, the Vandals, and the Lombards, who poured themselves into all the regions of Europe, at the declension of the Roman Empire. It was brought by them from their own countries, and continued in their respective colonies as the most likely means to secure their new acquisitions, and to that end large districts or parcels of land were allotted by the conquering general to the superior officers of the army, and by them dealt out again in smaller parcels or allotments to the inferior officers and most deserving soldiers.' 'Scarce had these northern conquerors established themselves in their new dominions, when the wisdom of their constitutions, as well as their personal valour, alarmed all the princes of Europe. Wherefore most, if not all, of them thought it necessary to enter into the same or a similar plan of policy. And thus, in the

---

[1] The first edition of the Commentaries appeared in 1765. I have been using that of 1800.

compass of a very few years, the feudal constitution, or the doctrine of tenure, extended itself over all the western world.'

'But this feudal polity, which was thus by degrees established over all the Continent of Europe, seems not to have been received in this part of our island, at least not universally and as a part of our national constitution, till the reign of William the Norman. This introduction, however, of the feudal tenures into England by King William does not seem to have been effected immediately after the Conquest, nor by the mere arbitrary will and power of the Conqueror, but to have been gradually established by the Norman barons, and afterwards universally consented to by the great Council of the nation.' 'The new polity therefore seems not to have been *imposed* by the Conqueror, but nationally and freely adopted by the general assembly of the whole realm.' 'By thus consenting to the introduction of feudal tenures, our English ancestors probably meant no more than to put the kingdom in a state of defence by establishing a military system. But whatever their meaning was, the Norman interpreters ... gave a very different construction to this proceeding, and thereupon took a handle to introduce, not only the rigorous doctrine which prevailed in the duchy of Normandy, but also such fruits and dependencies, such hardships and services, as were never known to other nations.' 'And from hence arises the inference, that the liberties of Englishmen are not (as some arbitrary writers would represent them) mere infringements of the king's prerogative, but a restoration of the ancient constitution, of which our ancestors had been defrauded by the art and finesse of the Norman lawyers, rather than deprived by the force of the Norman arms.'

The structure of the component parts is (for Blackstone) as ancient as the constitution of the whole. The English manor is of Saxon origin in all its essential characteristics, but the treatment of the people within the manor underwent a very notable change in consequence of the Norman invasion. In Saxon times the common people settled on folkland were immersed in complete slavery. Their condition was improved by the Conquest, because the Normans admitted them to the oath of fealty. And the improvement did not stop there : although the peasantry held their plots only by base tenure and at the lord's will, the lord allowed in most cases a hereditary possession. In this way out of the lord's will custom arose, and as custom is the soul or vital principle of common law, the Courts undertook in the end to protect the base tenure of the peasantry against the very lord whose will had created it. Such was the rise of the copyhold estate of modern times.

Blackstone's work is a compilation, and it would be out of the question to reduce its statements to anything like consistency. The rationalistic mode of thought which has left such a peculiar stamp on the eighteenth century, appears in all its glory in the laying out of the wise military polity of feudalism. But scarcely has our author had time to show the rapid progress of this plan all round Europe, when he starts on an entirely new tack, suggested by his wish to introduce a historical justification of Constitutional Monarchy. Feudal polity is of late introduction in England, and appears as a compact between sovereign and subjects; original freedom was not destroyed by this compact, and later infringements of contractual rights by kings ultimately led to a restoration and development of ancient liberties. In the parts of the treatise which concern Private Law the keynote is given throughout by that very Norman jurisprudence on which such severe condemnation is passed with regard to Public Law. The Conquest is thus made to appear alternately as a source of danger, struggle, and hardship from one point of view, and as the origin of steady improvement in social condition from another. In any case the aristocratic cast of English life is deduced from its most ancient origins, and all the rights of the lower orders are taken as the results of good-humoured concession on the part of the lords of the soil and of quiet encroachment against them.

Revolution in Historical literature. The Romantic school. Statements and arguments in Blackstone's style could hold water only before that great crisis in history and historical literature by which the nineteenth century was ushered into the world. The French Revolution, and the reaction against it, laid open and put to the test the working of all the chief forces engaged in historical life. Government and social order, nationality and religion, economic conditions and modes of thought, were thrown into the furnace to be consumed or remoulded. Ideas and institutions which had towered over centuries went down together, and their fall not only brought home the transitory character of human arrangements, but also laid bare the groundwork of society, which however held good in spite of the convulsions on its surface. The generation that witnessed these storms was taught to frame its politics and to understand history in a new fashion[1]. The disorderly scepticism of the eighteenth century was transformed by Niebuhr into a scientific method that paved the way by criticism to positive results. On the other hand, the Utopian doctrines of political rationalism were shattered by Savigny's teaching on the fundamental importance of tradition and the unconscious organic growth of nations. In his polemic with Thibaut, the founder of the historical school of law enters a mighty protest against wanton reform on the ground of a continuity of institutions not less real than the continuity of language, and his ' History of Roman Law during the Middle Ages' demonstrated that even such a convulsion as the Barbarian Invasion was not sufficient to sweep away the foundations of law and social order slowly formed in the past. Eichhorn's ' History of German Public and Private Law' gave detailed expression to an idea which occurs also in some of Savigny's minor works—to the idea, namely, that the

---

[1] ' Es war eine Zeit, in der wir Unerhörtes und Unglaubliches erlebten, eine Zeit, welche die Aufmerksamkeit auf viele vergessene und abgelebte Ordnungen durch deren Zusammensturz hinzog.' Niebuhr in the preface to the first volume of his Roman history, quoted by Wegele, Geschichte der deutschen Historiographie, 998.

German nations have had to run through their history with an engrained tendency in their character towards political dismemberment and social inequality. This rather crude attempt at generalising out some particular modern features and sanctioning them by the past is of historical interest, because it corresponds to the general problem propounded to history by the Romantic school : viz. to discover in the various manifestations of the life of a nation its permanent character and the leading ideas it is called to embody in history.

The comparative soundness of the English system had arrayed it from the very beginning on the side of Conservatism against Revolution, and Burke was the first to sound the blast of a crusade against subversive theories. No wonder the historical discoveries on the Continent found a responsive echo in English scholarship. Allen[1] took up the demonstration that the Royal power in England had developed from the conceptions of the Roman Empire. Palgrave[2] gave an entirely new construction of Anglo-Saxon history, which could not but exercise a powerful influence on the study of subsequent periods. His book is certainly the first attempt to treat the problems of medieval social history on a large scale and by new methods. It deserves special attention[3].

The author sat down to his work before the Revolution of 1830, although his two volumes were published in 1832. Sir Francis Palgrave.

[1] Enquiry into the Rise and Progress of the Royal Prerogative, 1831.

[2] History of the English Commonwealth, 1832 ; Normandy and England, 1840.

[3] I do not give an analysis of Hallam's remarkable chapters on England in his work on the Middle Ages (first edition, 1818), because they are mostly concerned with Constitutional history, and the notes on the classes of Saxon and Anglo-Norman Society are chiefly valuable as discussions of technical points of law. Hallam's general position in historical literature must not be underrated ; he is the English representative of the school which had Guizot for its most brilliant exponent on the Continent. In our subject, however, the turning-point in the development of research is marked by Palgrave, and not by Hallam. Heywood (Dissertation on Ranks and Classes of Society, 1818) is sound and useful, but cannot rank among the leaders.

He shares the convictions of very moderate Liberalism, declares in favour of the gradual introduction of reforms, and against any reform not framed as a compromise between actual claims. Custom and tradition did not exclude change and development in England, and for this reason the movement towards progress did not tear that people from the inheritance of their ancestors, did not disregard the mighty agency of historical education. In order to study the relative force of the elements of progress and conservatism in English history, Palgrave goes behind the external play of institutions, and tries to connect them with the internal growth of legal principles. It is a great, though usual, mistake to begin with political events, to proceed from them to the study of institutions, and only quite at the end to take up law. The true sequence is the inverse one. And in England in particular the Constitution, with all its showy and famous qualities, was formed under the direct influence of judicial and legal institutions. In accordance with this leading view Palgrave's work begins by a disquisition on classes, forms of procedure and judicial organisation, followed up by an estimate of the effects of the different Conquests, and ultimately by an exposition of the history of government. We need not feel bound by that order, and may start from the conclusion which gives the key to Palgrave's whole system.

The limited monarchy of England is a result of the action of two distinct elements, equally necessary for its composition. It is a manifestation of the monarchical power descended both in principle and in particular attributes from the Roman Empire. If this political idea had not been at work the kingdoms of the barbarians would have presented only loose aggregates of separate and self-sufficient political bodies; on the other hand, if this political idea had been supreme, medieval kings would have been absolute. The principles of Teutonic and of Roman polity had to work together, and the result was the medieval State with an absolute king for its centre, and a great independence of local parts. The English system differed from the continental in this way, that in England the free judicial institutions of the localities reacted on the central power, and surrounded it by constitutional limitations, while the Continent had to content itself with estates of a very doubtful standing and future. It is easy to see in this connexion how great an importance we must assign to the constitution of local Courts: the shires, hundreds, and townships are not mere administrative divisions, but political bodies. That the kingdom formed itself on their basis, not as an absolute but as a parliamentary monarchy, must be explained in a great measure by the influence of the Norman Conquest, which led to a closer union of the isolated parts, and to a concentration of local liberty in parliament.

But (such is Palgrave's view) the importance of Conquests has been greatly overrated in history. The barbarian invasion did not effect anything like a sudden or complete subversion of things; it left in force and action most of the factors of the preceding period. The passage from one rule to another was particularly easy in England, as most tribes which occupied the island were closely related to each other. Palgrave holds that the Britons, Anglo-Saxons, Danes, and Normans all belong to one and the same Teutonic race. There were, of course (he allows), Celtic elements among the Britons, but the greater part consisted of Belgian Kymrys, whose neighbours and kin are to be found on the Continent as Saxons and Frisians. The conquest of the island by bands of seafaring Saxons did not lead by any means to the wholesale destruction and depopulation which the legendary accounts of the chronicles report. The language of the Britons has not been preserved, but then no more has the Celtic language in Gaul. The Danish and Norman invasions had even less influence on social condition than the Saxon. It is only the Roman occupation that succeeded in introducing into the life of this island important and indestructible traits.

If we look at the results of all these migrations and ethnographical mixtures, we have first to notice the

stratifications of English society according to rank. It is
settled definitely enough in the Saxon period on an
aristocratic basis. In the main, society consists of eorls and
ceorls, noblemen and serfs. The difference does not consist
merely in a diversity of legal value, social influence and
occupation, but also in the fact that the ceorl may economically and legally be dependent on the eorl, and afterwards
on the thane. How did this aristocratic constitution arise?
Social distinctions of this kind may sometimes originate
in the oppression of the weak by the strong, and in
voluntary subjection, but, as a rule, they go back to conquest.
There is every reason to believe that the Anglo-Saxon conquerors, who were very few in number, became the privileged class of the new States, and reduced the Britons to
serfdom ; a corroboration of this assumption may be found
in the fact that the services of Celtic and Saxon peasantry
are extremely alike.

It is more difficult to trace the influence of different races
in the agrarian system, of which the township or manor is
the unit. It is by comparing it with the forms in its immediate neighbourhood that one gets to understand its origin.
The Roman organisation of husbandry and ownership on
the basis of individualism is too well known to be described.
In marked contrast with it stands the Celtic community,
of which survivals were lingering for a long time in Ireland
and Wales. Here the land is in the ownership of tribal
groups : rights of individuals and families expand and
collapse according to the requirements and decisions of
the entire tribe ; there is no hereditary succession, but
every grown-up clansman has a claim to be endowed with
a plot of land, and as a consequence of this, all land in
separate possession is constantly liable to be divided by
the tribal community. The Anglo-Saxon system is an
intermediate stage between Roman individualism and
Celtic communalism. No wonder that the Saxons, who
at home followed a system closely resembling the Celtic,
modified it when they got acquainted with Roman forms
and entered into their Roman inheritance in Great Britain.

The mixed organisation of the township was the result of the assimilation.

Such are in the main those conclusions of Palgrave which have a direct bearing on the questions before us. It is easy to perceive that they are permeated by certain very general historical conceptions. He is greatly impressed by the ' Vis inertiae ' of social condition, and by the continuity of historical development arising from it. And so in his work the British population does not disappear without leaving any traces of its existence ; the Roman dominion exercises a most conspicuous influence on important aspects of later condition— on central power, feudalism, and agrarian organisation : the most recent of the Conquests—the Norman invasion—is reduced to a comparatively secondary share in the framing of society. The close connexion between Palgrave's ideas and the currents of thought on the Continent is not less notable in his attempts to determine the peculiarities of national character as manifested in unconscious leanings towards certain institutions. The Teutonic system is characterised by a tendency towards federalism in politics and an aristocratic arrangement of society. The one tendency explains the growth of the Constitution as a concentration of local self-government, the other leads from the original and fundamental distinction between a privileged class and a servile peasantry to the original organisation of the township under a lord.

There can be no question as to the remarkable power displayed in Palgrave's work, or as to the value of his results. He had an enormous and varied store of erudition at his command, and the keenest eye for observation. No wonder that many of his theories on particular subjects have been eagerly taken up and worked out by later scholars. But apart from such successful solutions of questions, his whole conception of development was undoubtedly very novel and fruitful. One of Palgrave's main positions—the intimate connexion between the external history of the Constitution and the working of private law in the courts—

opened a wholly new perspective for the study of social history. But naturally enough the first cast turned out rather rough and distorted. Palgrave is as conspicuous for his arbitrary and fanciful treatment of his matter, as for his learning and ingenuity. He does not try to get his data into order or completeness, and has no notion of the methods of systematic work. Comparisons of English facts with all kinds of phenomena in the history of kindred and distant peoples sometimes give rise to suggestive combinations, but, in most cases, out of this medley of incongruous things they lead only to confusion of thought. In consequence of all these drawbacks, Palgrave's attempt only started the inquiry in most directions, but could not exhaust it in any.

Romanists and Germanists.

The two great elements of Western civilisation—Roman tradition and Teutonic tendencies—were more or less peacefully brought together in the books of Savigny, Eichhorn, and Palgrave. But in process of time they diverged into a position of antagonism. Their contrast not only came out as a result of more attention and developed study; it became acute, because in the keen competition of French and German scholarship, historians, consciously and unconsciously, took up the standpoint of national predilection, and followed their bias back into ancient times. Aug. Thierry, while protesting against the exaggerations of eighteenth-century systems, considered the development of European nations almost entirely as a national struggle culminating in conquest, but underlying most facts in the history of institutions. He began, for the sake of method, by tracing the conflict on English ground where everything resolved itself to his eye into open or hidden strife between Norman and Saxon[1]. But William the Bastard's invasion led him by a circuitous way to the real object of his interest—to the gradual rise of Gallo-Roman civilisation against the Teutonic conquest in France : historical tendencies towards centralised monarchy and municipal bourgeoisie were connected by

[1] Histoire de la conquête de l'Angleterre par les Normands.

him with the present political condition of France as the abiding legacy of Gallo-Roman culture[1].
Men of great power and note, from Raynouard[2] and B. Guérard[3] down to Fustel de Coulanges[4] in our own days, have followed the same track with more or less violence and exaggeration. They are all at one in their animosity towards Teutonic influence in the past, all at one in lessening its effects, and in trying to collect the scattered traces of Romanism in principle and application. The Germans did not submit meekly to the onslaught, but went as far as the Romanists on the other side. Löbell[5], Waitz[6], and Roth[7]—to speak only of the heads of the school—have held forth about the mighty part which the Teutons have played in Europe ; they have enhanced the beneficial value of Germanic principles, and tried to show that there is no reason for laying to their account certain dark facts in the history of Europe. The Germanist school had to fight its way not only against Romanism, but against divers tenets of the Romantic school as represented by Savigny and Eichhorn, of which Romanists had availed themselves. The whole doctrine was to be reconsidered in the light of two fundamental assumptions. The foundations of social life were sought not in aristocracy, but in the common freedom of the majority of the people : the German middle class, the 'Bürgers,' who form the strength of contemporary Germany, looked to the past history of their race as vouching for their liberty; the destinies of that particular class became the test of social development. Then again the disruptive tendency of German national character was stoutly denied,

[1] Histoire du tiers état.
[2] Histoire du droit municipal.
[3] Prolégomènes au polyptyque de l'abbé Irminon.
[4] Histoire des institutions de la France; Recherches sur quelques problèmes d'histoire.
[5] Gregor von Tours und seine Zeit.
[6] Deutsche Verfassungsgeschichte.
[7] Geschichte des Beneficialwesens, 1856 ; Feudalität und Unterthanenverband, 1863.

and all the historical instances of disruption were demon-strated to be quite independent of any leaning of the race. In the great fermentation of thought which led indirectly to the unification of Germany, the best men in the country refused to believe that Western Europe had fallen to pieces into feudalism because Teutonic development is doomed to strife and helplessness by deeply engrained traits of character[1]. German scholarship found a most powerful ally in this period of its history in the literature of kindred England: German and English investigators stood side by side in the same ranks. Kemble, K. Maurer, Freeman, Stubbs, and Gneist form the goodly array of the Germanist School on English soil.

Kemble. Kemble's position is, strictly speaking, an intermediate one: in some respects he is very near to Eichhorn and Grimm; although his chief work was published in 1849, he was not acquainted with Waitz's first books. But Kemble is mostly in touch with those parts of Eichhorn's theory which could be accepted by later Germanists; other important tenets of the Romantic School are left in the shade or rejected, and as a whole Kemble's teaching is essentially Germanistic. Kemble's 'Saxons in England' takes its peculiar shape and marks an epoch in English historical literature, mainly because it presents the first attempt to utilise the enormous material of Saxon Charters, in the collection of which Kemble has done such invalu-able work. With this copious and exact, but very onesided, material at his disposal, our author takes little notice of current tales about the invasion of Great Britain by Angles and Saxons. Such tales may be interesting from a mytho-logical or literary point of view, but the historian cannot accept them as evidence. At the same time one cannot but wish to try and get certain knowledge of an historical fact, which, as far as the history of England is concerned, appears as the first manifestation of the Teutonic race in its stupendous greatness. Luckily enough we have some

---

[1] Roth is very strong on this point.

means to judge of the invasion in the names of localities and groups of population. Read in this light the history of Conquest appears very gradual and ancient. It began long before the recorded settlements, and while Britain was still under Roman sway. The struggle with the Celts was a comparatively easy one ; the native population was by no means destroyed, but remained in large numbers in the lower orders of society. Notwithstanding such remnants, the history of the Anglo-Saxon period is entirely Teutonic in its aspect, and presents only one instance of the general process by which the provinces of the Empire were modified by conquerors of Teutonic race.

The root of the whole social system is to be found in the Mark, which is a division of the territory held jointly by a certain number of freemen for the purposes of cultivation, mutual help and defence. The community began as a kinship or tribe, but even when the original blood ties were lost sight of and modified by the influx of heterogeneous elements, the community remained self-sufficient and isolated. The whole fabric of society rested on property in land : as its political divisions were based on the possession of common lands, even so the rank of an individual depended entirely on his holding. The Teutonic world had no idea of a citizen severed from the soil. The curious fact that the normal holding, the hide, was equal all over England ($33\frac{1}{2}$ acres) can be explained only by its origin ; it came full-formed from Germany and remained unchanged in spite of all diversities of geographical and economical conditions.

The transformation of medieval society is, for Kemble, intimately connected with the forms of ownership in land. The scanty population of ancient times had divided only a very small part of the country into separate holdings. The rest remained in the hands of the people to supply the wants of coming generations. The great turn towards feudalism was given by the fact that this reserve-fund lapsed into the hands of a few magnates : the mass of free people being deprived of its natural sphere of expansion was forced to seek its subsistence at the hands of private lords (loaf-givers). From the point of view of personal status the same process appears in the decrease of freedom among the people and in the increase of the so-called Gesíð. According to Teutonic principles a man is free only if he has land to feed upon, strength to work, and arms to defend himself. The landless man is unfree; and so is the Gesíð-cundman, the follower, however strong and wealthy he may be through his chief's grace. The contrast between the free ceorls tilling their own land and the band of military followers, who are always considered as personally depen-dent—this contrast is a marked one. From the first this military following had played an important part in German history. Most raids and invasions had been its work, and sometimes whole tribes were attracted into its organ-isation, but during the first period of Saxon history the free people were sufficiently strong to hold down the power of military chiefs within certain bounds. Not so in later development. With the growth of population, of inequali-ties, of social competition, the relations of dependency are seen constantly gaining on the field of freedom. The spread of commendation leads not only to a change in the distribution of ranks, but to a dismemberment of political power, to all kinds of franchises and private encroachments on the State.

I may be excused for marshalling all these well-known points before the public by the consideration that they must serve to show how intimately these views are con-nected with the general principles of a great school. The stress laid by Kemble on property in land ought to be noticed especially : land gets to be the basis of all political and social condition. This is going much fur-ther than Palgrave ever went ; though not further than Eichhorn. What actually severs Kemble from the Ro-mantics is his estimate of the free element in the people. He does not try to picture a kind of political Arcadia in Saxon England, but there is no more talk about the rightless condition of the ceorls or the predominance of aristocracy.

The Teutonic race towers above everything. Although the existence of Celts after the Conquests is admitted, neither Celtic nor Roman elements appear as exercising any influence in the course of history. Everything takes place as if Germanic communities had been living and growing on soil that had never before been appropriated. Curiously enough the weakest point of Kemble's doctrine seems to lie in its very centre—in his theory of social groups. One is often reminded of Grimm by his account of the Mark, and it was an achievement to call attention to such a community as distinct from the tribal group, but the political, legal, and economical description of the Mark is very vague. As to the reasoning about gilds, tithings, and hundreds, it is based on a constant confusion of widely different subjects.

Generally speaking, it is not for a lawyer's acuteness and precision that one has to look in Kemble's book: important distinctions very often get blurred in his exposition, and though constantly protesting against abstract theories and suppositions not based on fact, he indulges in them a great deal himself. Still Kemble's work was very remarkable: his extensive, if not very critical study of the charters opened his eyes to the first-rate importance of the law of real property in the course of medieval history: this was a great step in advance of Palgrave, who had recognised law as the background of history, but whose attention had been directed almost exclusively to the formal side— to judicial institutions. And Kemble actually succeeded in bringing forward some of the questions which were to remain for a long time the main points of debate among historians.

The development of the school was evidently to proceed K. Maurer. in the direction of greater accuracy and improved methods. Great service has been done in this respect by Konrad Maurer[1]. He is perhaps sometimes inclined to magnify

[1] Ueber angelsächsische Rechtsverhältnisse, in the Munich Kritische Ueberschau, i. sqq. (1853).

his own independence and dissent from Kemble's opinions, but he has undoubtedly contributed to strengthen and clear up some of Kemble's views, and has gone further than his predecessor on important subjects. He accepts in the main Kemble's doctrines as to the Mark, the allotment of land, the opposition of folkland and book-land, and expounds them with greater fulness and better insight into the evidence. On the other hand he goes his own way as to the Gesíðs (Gefolgschaft), and the part played by large estates in the political process. Maurer reduces the importance of the former and lays more stress on the latter than Kemble [1]. Altogether the German scholar's investigations have been of great moment, and this not only for methodical reasons, but also because they lead to a complete emancipation of the school from Eichhorn's influence.

Freeman. As to the Conquests, Germanist views have been formulated with great authority by Freeman. A comparison of the course of development in Romance countries with the history of England, and a careful study of that evidence of the chronicles which Kemble disregarded, has led the historian of the Norman Conquest to the conclusion, that the Teutonic invaders actually rooted out most of the Roman-ised Celtic population of English Britain, and reduced it to utter insignificance in those western counties where they did not destroy it. It is the only inference that can be drawn from the temporary disappearance of Christianity, from the all but complete absence of Celtic and Latin words in the English tongue, from the immunity of English legal and social life from Roman influence. The Teutonic bias which was given to the history of the island by the Conquest of Angles and Saxons has not been altered by the Conquest of the Normans. The foreign colouring imparted to the language is no testimony of any radical change in the internal structure of the people: it remained on the surface, and the history of the island remained

---

[1] K. Maurer is very near Waitz in this respect.

English, that is, Teutonic. Even feudalism, which appears in its full shape after William the Bastard's invasion, had been prepared in its component parts by the Saxon period. In working out particulars Freeman had to reckon largely with Kemble's work and to strike the balance between the conflicting and onesided theories of Thierry and Palgrave. Questions of legal and social research concern him only so far as they illustrate the problem of the struggle and fusion of national civilisations. His material is chiefly drawn from chronicles, and the history of external facts of war, government, and legislation comes naturally to the fore. But all the numberless details tend towards one end : they illustrate the Teutonic aspect of English culture, and assign it a definite place in the historical system of Europe.

Stubbs' 'Constitutional History,' embracing as it does Stubbs. the whole of the Middle Ages, is not designed to trace out some one idea for the sake of its being new or to take up questions which had remained unheeded by earlier scholars. Solid learning, critical caution and accuracy are the great requirements of such an undertaking, and every one who has had anything to do with the Bishop of Oxford's publications knows to what extent his work is distinguished by these qualities. If one may speak of a main idea in such a book as the Constitutional History of a people, Stubbs' main idea seems to be, that the English Constitution is the result of administrative concentration in the age of the Normans of local self-goverment formed in the age of the Saxons. This conclusion is foreshadowed in Palgrave's work, but what appears there as a mere hypothesis and in confusion with all kinds of heterogeneous elements, comes out in the later work with the overwhelming force of careful and impartial induction. Stubbs' point of view is a Germanist one. The book begins with an estimate of Teutonic influence in the different countries of Europe, and England is taken in one sense as the most perfect manifestation of the Teutonic historical tendency. The influx of Frenchmen and French ideas under William the Conqueror and after him had

important effects in rousing national energy, contributing
to national unification, settling the forms of administration
and justice, but at bottom there remained the Teutonic
character of the nation. The 'Constitutional History'
approaches the question of the village community,
but its object is strictly limited to the bearing of the
problem on general history and to the testimony of
direct authority. It starts from the community in land as
described by Cæsar and Tacitus, and notices that Saxon
times present only a few scattered references to communal ownership. Most of the arable land was held
separately, but the woods, meadow, and pasture still
remained in the ownership of village groups. The township with its rights and duties as to police, justice, and
husbandry was modified but not destroyed by feudalism.
The change from personal relations to territorial, and
from the freedom of the masses to their dependency, is
already very noticeable in the Saxon period. The Norman
epoch completed the process by substituting proprietary
rights in the place of personal subordination and political
subjection. Still even after conquest and legal theory had
been over the ground, the compact self-government of the
township is easily discernible under the crust of the manorial system, and the condition of medieval villains presents
many traces of original freedom.

Gneist.

Gneist's work is somewhat different in colouring and
closely connected with a definite political theory. Tocqueville in France has done most to draw attention to the
vital importance of local self-government in the development of liberal institutions; and Stubbs' history goes far
to demonstrate Tocqueville's general view by a masterly
statement as to the origins of English institutions. In
Gneist's hands the doctrine of decentralisation assumes
a particular shape by the fact that it is constructed on a
social foundation; the German thinker has been trying all
along to show that the English influence is not one of
self-government only, but of aristocratical self-government.
The part played by the gentry in local and central affairs

is the great point of historical interest in Gneist's eyes.
Even in the Saxon period he lays stress chiefly on the
early rise of great property, and the great importance of
'Hlafords' in social organisation. He pays no attention
to the village community, and chiefly cares for the landlord. But still ever. Gneist admits the original personal
freedom of the great mass of the people, and his analysis
of the English condition is based on the assumption, that
it represents one variation of Teutonic development: this
gives Gneist a place among the Germanists, although his
views on particular subjects differ from those of other
scholars of the same school[1].

Its chief representatives have acquired such a celebrity The Mark
that it is hardly necessary to insist again, that excellent system.
work has been done by them for the study of the past.
But the direction of their work has been rather one-
sided; it was undertaken either from the standpoint of
political institutions or from that of general culture and
external growth; the facts of agriculture, of the evolution
of classes, of legal organisation were touched upon only as
subsidiary to the main objects of general history. And
yet, even from the middle of the century, the attention
of Europe begins to turn towards those very facts. The
'masses' come up with their claims behind the 'classes,'
the social question emerges in theory and in practice, in
reform and revolution; Liberals and Conservatives have to
reckon with the fact that the great majority of the people
are more excited, and more likely to be moved by the
problems of work and wages than by problems of political
influence. The everlasting, ever-human struggle for power
gets to be considered chiefly in the light of the distribution of wealth; the distribution of society into classes and
conditions appears as the connecting link between the
economical process and the political process. This great
change in the aspect of modern life could not but react
powerfully on the aspect of historical literature. G. F. von

[1] See especially his Englische Verfassungsgeschichte.

Maurer and Hanssen stand out as the main initiators of
the new movement in our studies. The many volumes
devoted by G. F. Maurer[1] to the village and the town of
Germany are planned on a basis entirely different from
that of his predecessors. Instead of proceeding from the
whole to the parts, and of using social facts merely as a
background to political history, he concentrates everything
round the analysis of the Mark, as the elementary organisation for purposes of husbandry and ownership. The Mark
is thus taken up not in the vague sense and manner in
which it was treated by Kemble and his followers; it is
described and explained on the strength of copious, though
not very well sifted, evidence. On the other hand, Hanssen's
masterly essays[2] on agrarian questions, and especially on
the field-systems, gave an example of the way in which
work was to be done as to facts of husbandry proper.

Nasse.

Nasse's pamphlet on the village community[3] may be
considered as the first application of the new methods
and new results to English history. The importance of
his little volume cannot easily be overrated : all subsequent
work has had to start from its conclusions.

Nasse's picture of the ancient English agricultural
system, though drawn from scanty sources, is a very
definite one. Most of the land is enclosed only during
the latter part of the year, and during the rest of the
year remains in the hands of the community. Temporary enclosures rise upon the ploughed field while the
crop is growing ; their object, however, is not to divide the
land between neighbours but to protect the crop against
pasturing animals ; the strips of the several members of
the township lie intermixed, and their cultivation is
not left to the views and interests of the owners, but

[1] Einleitung in die Geschichte der Hof-, Dorf-, Mark- und Städteverfassung in Deutschland, 1 vol. ; Geschichte der Frohnhöfe, 4 vol.; Geschichte der Dorfverfassung, 1 vol. ; Geschichte der Markenverfassung, 1 vol.;
Geschichte der Städteverfassung, 4 vol.
[2] Collected in 2 volumes of Agrarhistorische Untersuchungen.
[3] Zur Geschichte der mittelalterlichen Feldgemeinschaft in England, 1869.

settled by the community according to a general plan. The meadows are also divided into strips, but these change hands in a certain rotation determined by lot or otherwise. The pasture ground remains in the possession of the whole community. The notion of private property, therefore, can be applied in this system only to the houses and closes immediately adjoining them.

Then the feudal epoch divides the country into manors, a form which originated at the end of the Saxon period and spread everywhere in Norman times. The soil of the manor consists of demesne lands and tributary lands. These two classes of lands do not quite correspond to the distinction between land cultivated by the lord himself and soil held of him by dependants ; there may be lease-holders on the demesne, but there the lord is always free to change the mode of cultivation and occupation, while he has no right to alter the arrangements on the tributary portion. This last is divided between free socmen holding on certain conditions, villains and cottagers. The villains occupy equal holdings ; their legal condition is a very low one, although they are clearly distinguished from slaves, and belong more to the soil than to the lord. The cottagers have homesteads and crofts, but no holdings in the common fields ; the whole group presents the material from which, in process of time, the agricultural labourers have been developed.

The common system of husbandry manifests itself in many ways : the small holders club together for ploughing ; four virgates or yardlands have to co-operate in order to start an eight-oxen plough. The services are often laid upon the whole village and not on separate householders ; on the other hand the village, as a whole, enters into agreement with the lord about leases or commutation of services for money.

Each holding is formed of strips which lie intermixed with the component parts of other holdings in different fields, and this fact is intimately connected with the principle of joint ownership. The whole system begins to break up in the thirteenth century, much earlier than in France or Germany. As soon as services get commuted for money rents, it becomes impossible to retain the labouring people in serfdom. Hired labourers and farmers take the place of villains, and the villain's holding is turned into a copyhold and protected by law. Although the passage to modern forms begins thus early, traces of the original communalism may be found everywhere, even in the eighteenth century.

Maine.

Nasse's pamphlet is based on a careful study of authorities, and despite its shortness must be treated as a work of scientific research. But if all subsequent workers have to reckon with it in settling particular questions, general conceptions have been more widely influenced by Sir Henry Maine's lectures, which did not aim at research, and had in view the broad aspects of the subject. Their peculiar method is well known to be that of comparing facts from very different environments—from the Teutonic, the Celtic, the Hindu world; Maine tries to sketch a general process where other people only see particular connexions and special reasons. The chapters which fall within the line of our inquiry are based chiefly on a comparison between Western Europe and India. The agrarian organisation of many parts of India presents at this very day, in full work and in all stages of growth and decay, the village community of which some traces are still scattered in the records of Europe. There and here the process is in the main the same, the passage from collective ownership to individualism is influenced by the same great forces, notwithstanding all the differences of time and place. The original form of agrarian arrangement is due to the settlement of a group of free men, which surrenders to its individual members the use of arable land, meadows, pasture and wood, but retains the ownership and the power to control and modify the rights of using the common land. There can be no doubt that the legal theory, which sees in the modern rights of commoners mere encroachments upon the lord, carries feudal notions back into too early a period.

The real question as conceived by Maine is this—By what means was the free village community turned into the manor of the lord ? The petty struggles between townships must have led to the subjugation of some groups by others; in each particular village the head-man had the means to use his authority in order to improve his material position ; and when a family contrived to retain an office in the hands of its members this at once gave matters an aristocratical turn. In Western Europe external causes had to account for a great deal in the gradual rise of territorial lordship. When the barbarian invaders came into contact with Roman civilisation and took possession of the provincial soil, they found private ownership and great property in full development, and naturally fell under the influence of these accomplished facts ; their village community was broken up and transformed gradually into the manorial system[1].

Maine traces economic history from an originally free community ; Nasse takes the existence of such a community for granted. The statements of one are too general, however, and sometimes too hypothetical, the other has in view husbandry proper rather than the legal development of social classes. Maurer's tenets, to which both go back, present a very coherent system in which all parts hold well together ; but each part taken separately is not very well grounded on fact. The one-sided preference given to one element does not allow other important elements to appear ; the wish to find in the authorities

---

[1] I do not mention some well-known books treating of medieval husbandry and social history, because I am immediately concerned only with those works which discuss the formation of the medieval system. Thorold Rogers, History of Agriculture and Prices, and Six Centuries of Work and Wages, begins with the close of the thirteenth century, and the passage from medieval organisation to modern times. Ochenkovsky, Die wirthschaftliche Entwicklung Englands am Ende des Mittelalters, and Kovalevsky, England's Social Organisation at the close of the Middle Ages (Russian), start on their inquiry from even a later period.

suitable arguments for a favourite thesis leads to a confusion
of materials derived from different epochs. These defects
naturally called for protest and rectification; but the
reaction against Maurer's teaching has gone so far and
comes from such different quarters, that one has to look
for its explanation beyond the range of historical research.

Reaction-
ary move-
ment.

Late years have witnessed everywhere in Europe a
movement of thought which would have been called
reactionary some twenty years ago [1]. Some people are
becoming very sceptical as to principles which were held
sacred by preceding generations; at the same time elements likely to be slighted formerly are coming to the front
in great strength nowadays. There have been liberals and
conservatives at all times, but the direction of the European mind, saving the reaction against the French Revolution and Napoleon, has been steadily favourable to the
liberal tendency. For two centuries the greatest thinkers
and the course of general opinion have been striving for
liberty in different ways, for the emancipation of individuals, and the self-government of communities, and the
rights of masses. This liberal creed has been, on the
whole, an eminently idealist one, assuming the easy per-
fectibility of human nature, the sound common sense of
the many, the regulating influence of consciousness on
instinct, the immense value of high political aspirations for
the regeneration of mankind. In every single attempt at
realising its high-flying hopes the brutal side of human nature has made itself felt very effectually, and has become all
the more conspicuous just by reason of the ironical contrast
between aims and means. But the movement as a whole

---

[1] Is it necessary to say that I am speaking of general currents of thought
and not of the position of a man at the polling booth? An author may
be personally a liberal and still his work may connect itself with a stream
of opinion which is not in favour of liberalism. Again, one and the
same man may fall in with different movements in different parts of his
career. Actual life throws a peculiar light on the past: certain questions are
placed prominently in view and certain others are thrown into the shade by
it, so that the individual worker has to find his path within relatively narrow
limits.

was certainly an idealist one, not only in the eighteenth
but even in the nineteenth century, and the necessary repressive tendency appeared in close alliance with officialism,
with unthinking tradition, and with the egotism of classes
and individuals. Many events have contributed of late
years to raise a current of independent thought which
has gone far in criticising and stemming back liberal
doctrines, if not in suppressing them. The brilliant
achievements of historical monarchy in Germany, the
ridiculous misery to which France has been reduced
by conceited and impotent politicians, the excesses of
terrorist nihilism in Russia, the growing sense of a
coming struggle on questions of radical reform — all
these facts have worked together to generate a feeling
which is far from being propitious to liberal doctrines.
Socialism itself has been contributing to it directly by laying
an emphatic stress on the conditions of material existence,
and treating political life merely as subordinate to economic
aims. In England the repressive tendency has been felt
less than on the Continent, but even here some of the
foremost men in the country are beginning, in consequence
of social well-known events, to ask themselves : Whither
are we drifting? The book which best illustrates the new
direction of thought is probably Taine's 'Origines de la
France Contemporaine.' It is highly characteristic, both in
its literary connexion with the profound and melancholy
liberalism of Tocqueville, and in its almost savage onslaught on revolutionary legend and doctrine.

In the field of historical research the fermentation of
political thought of which I have been speaking has been
powerfully seconded by a growing distrust among scholars
for preconceived theories, and by the wish to reconsider
solutions which had been too easily taken for granted. The
combined action of these forces has been curiously experienced in the particular subject of our study. The Germanist school had held very high the principle of individual liberty, had tried to connect it with the Teutonic
element in history, had explained its working in the society

described by Tacitus, and had regretfully followed its decay in later times. For the representatives of the New School this 'original Teutonic freedom' has entirely lost its significance, and they regard the process of social development as starting with the domination of the few and the serfdom of the many. The votaries of the free village community have been studying with interest epochs and ethnographical variations unacquainted with the economic individualism of modern Europe, they have been attentive in tracing out even the secondary details of the agrarian associations which have directed the husbandry of so many centuries, but the New School subordinates communal practice to private property and connects it with serfdom. We may already notice the new tendency in Inama-Sternegg's Wirthschaftsgeschichte[1]: he enters the lists against Maurer, denies that the Mark ever had anything to do with political work, reduces its influence on husbandry, and enhances that of great property. The most remarkable of French medievalists—Fustel de Coulanges—has been fighting all along against the Teutonic village community, and for an early development of private property in connexion with Roman influence. English scholarship has to reckon with similar views in Seebohm's well-known work.

Seebohm.

Let us recall to mind the chief points of his theory. The village community of medieval England is founded on the equality of the holdings in the open fields of the village. The normal holding of a peasant family is not only equal in each separate village, but it is substantially the same all over England. Variations there are, but in most cases by far it consists of the virgate of thirty acres, which makes the fourth part of the hide of a hundred and twenty acres, because the peasant holder owns only the fourth part of the ploughteam of eight oxen corresponding to the hide. The holders of virgates or yardlands are not the only people in the village; their neighbours may have more

[1] The last great German work on our questions, Lamprecht, Deutsches Wirthschaftsleben im Mittelalter, is nearer Maurer than Sternegg.

or less land, but there are not many classes as a rule, all
the people in the same class are equalised, and the virgate
remains the chief manifestation of the system. It is plain
that such equality could be maintained only on the
principle that each plot was a unit which was neither to be
divided nor thrown together with other plots. Why did
such a system spread all over Europe? It could not de-
velop out of a free village community, as has been
commonly supposed, because the Germanic law regulating
free land does not prevent its being divided ; indeed, where
this law applies, holdings get broken up into irregular
plots. If the system does not form itself out of Germanic
elements, it must come from Roman influence ; one has
only the choice between the two as to facts which prevail
everywhere in Western Europe. Indeed, the Roman villa
presents all the chief features of the medieval manor. The
lord's demesne acted as a centre, round which *coloni*
clustered—cultivators who did not divide their tenancies
because they did not own them. The Roman system was
the more readily taken up by the Germans, as their own
husbandry, described by Tacitus, had kindred elements to
show—the condition of their slaves, for instance, was very
like that of Roman coloni. It must be added, that we
may trace in Roman authorities not only the organisation
of the holdings, but such features as the three-field partition of the arable and the intermixed position of the strips
belonging to a single holding.

The importance of these observations taken as a whole
becomes especially apparent, if we compare medieval
England with Wales or Ireland, with countries settled by
the Celts on the principle of the tribal community : no
fixed holdings there ; it is not the population that has to
conform itself to fixed divisions of land, but the divisions
of land have to change according to the movement of the
population. Such usage was prevalent in Germany itself
for a time, and would have been prevalent there as long
as in Celtic countries, if the Germans had not come under
Roman influence. And so the continuous development

of society in England starts from the position of Roman provincial soil.

The Saxon invasion did not destroy what it found in the island. Roman villas and their labourers passed from one lord to the other—that is all. The ceorls of Saxon times are the direct descendants of Roman slaves and coloni, some of them personally free, but all in agrarian subjection. Indeed, social development is a movement from serfdom to freedom, and the village community of its early stages is connected not with freedom, but with serfdom.

Seebohm's results have a marked resemblance to some of the views held by the eighteenth-century lawyers, and also to those held by Palgrave and by Coote, but his theory is nevertheless original, both in the connexion of the parts with the whole, and in its arguments: he knows how to place in a new light evidence which has been known and discussed for a long time, and for this reason his work will be suggestive reading even to those who do not agree with the results. The chief strength of his work lies in the chapters devoted to husbandry; but if one accepts his conclusions, what is to be done with the social part of the question? Both sides, the economic and the social, are indissolubly allied, and at the same time the extreme consequences drawn from them give the lie direct to everything that has hitherto been taken for granted and accepted as proved as to this period. Can it really be true that the great bulk of free men was originally in territorial subjection, or rather that there never was such a thing as a great number of free men of German blood, and that the German conquest introduced only a cluster of privileged people which merged into the habits and rights of Roman possessors? If this be not true and English history testifies on every point to a deeper influence exercised by the German conquerors, does not the collapse of the social conclusion call in question the economical premises? Does not a logical development of Seebohm's views lead to conclusions that we cannot accept? These are all perplexing questions, but one thing is certain ; this last review of the

subject has been powerful enough to necessitate a reconsideration of all its chief points.

Happily, this does not mean that former work has been
lost. I have not been trying the patience of my readers
by a repetition of well-known views without some cogent
reasons. The subject is far too wide and important to
admit of a brilliantly unexpected solution by one mind or
even one generation of workers. A superficial observer
may be so much struck by the variations and contradictions,
that he will fail to realise the intimate dependence of every
new investigator on his predecessors. ' The subjective side
of history,' as the Germans would say, has been noticed
before now and the taunt has been administered with great
force: 'Was Ihr den Geist der Zeiten heisst, das ist im
Grund der Herren eigener Geist, in dem die Zeiten sich
bespiegeln.' Those who do not care to fall a prey to
Faust's scepticism, will easily perceive that individual peculiarities and political or national pretensions will not account
for the whole of the process. Their action is powerful indeed :
the wish to put one's own stamp on a theory and the
reaction of present life on the past are mighty incitements
to work. But new schools do not rise in order to pull
down everything that has been raised by former schools,
new theories always absorb old notions both in treatment
of details and in the construction of the whole. We may
try, as conclusion of our review of historical literature, to
notice the permanent gains of consecutive generations in
the forward movement of our studies. The progress
will strike us, not only if we compare the state of learning
at both ends of the development, but even if we take up
the links of the chain one by one.

The greatest scholars of the time before the French
Revolution failed in two important respects : they were not
sufficiently aware of the differences between epochs ; they
were too ready with explanations drawn from conscious
plans and arrangements. The shock of Revolution and
Reaction taught people to look deeper for the laws of the
social and political organism. The material for study was

Results attained by conflict between successive theories.

not exactly enlarged, but instead of being thrown together without discrimination, it was sifted and tried. Preliminary criticism came in as an improvement in method and led at once to important results. Speaking broadly, the field of conscious change was narrowed, the field of organic development and unconscious tradition widened. On this basis Savigny's school demonstrated the influence of Roman civilisation in the Middle Ages, started the inquiry as to national characteristics, and shifted the attention of historians from the play of events on the surface to the great moral and intellectual currents which direct the stream. Palgrave's book bears the mark of all these ideas, and it may be noticed especially that his chief effort was to give a proper background to English history by throwing light on the abiding institutions of the law.

None of these achievements was lost by the next generation of workers. But it had to start from a new basis, and had a good deal to add and to correct. Modern life was busy with two problems after the collapse of reaction had given way to new aspirations : Europe was trying to strike a due balance between order and liberty in the constitutional system ; nationalities that had been rent by casual and artificial influences were struggling for independence and unity. The Germanist School arose to show the extent to which modern constitutional ideas were connected with medieval facts, and the share that the German element has had in the development of institutions and classes. As to material, Kemble opened a new field by the publication of the Saxon charters, and the gain was felt at once in the turn given towards the investigation of private law, which took the place of Palgrave's vague leaning towards legal history. The methods of careful and cautious inquiry as to particular facts took shape in the hands of K. Maurer and Stubbs, and the school really succeeded, it seems to me, in establishing the characteristically Germanic general aspect of English history, a result which does not exclude Roman influence, but has to be reckoned with in all attempts to estimate definitely its bearing and strength.

The rise of the social question about the middle of our century had, as its necessary consequence, to impress upon the mind of intelligent people the vast importance of social conditions, of those primary conditions of husbandry, distribution of wealth and distribution of classes, which ever, as it were, loom up behind the pageant of political institutions and parties. Nasse follows up the thread of investigation from the study of private law towards the study of economic conditions. G. F. v. Maurer and Maine enlarge it in scope, material, and means by their comparative inquiry, taking into view, first, all varieties of the Teutonic race, and then the development of other ethnographical branches. The village community comes out of the inquiry as the constitutive cell of society during an age of the world, quite as characteristic of medieval structure, as the town community or 'civitas' was of ancient polity.

The consciousness that political and scientific construction has been rather hasty in its work, that it has often been based upon doctrines instead of building on the firm foundation of facts—the widely spread perception of these defects has been of late inciting statesmen and thinkers to put to use some of those very elements which were formerly ignored or rejected. The manorial School—if I may be allowed to use this expression—has brought forward the influence of great landed estates against the democratical conception of the village community. The work spent upon this last phenomenon is by no means undone; on the contrary, it was received in most of its parts. But new material was found in the manorial documents of the later middle ages, the method of investigation 'from the known to the unknown' was used both openly and unconsciously, comparative inquiry was handled for more definite, even if more limited purposes. Great results cannot be contested: to name one—the organising force of aristocratic property has been acknowledged and has come to its rights,

But the new impetus given to research has caused its
originators to overleap themselves, as it were. They have
occupied so exclusively the point of view whence the
manor of the later middle ages is visible that they have
disregarded the evidence which comes from other quarters
instead of finding an explanation which will satisfy all
the facts. The investigation 'from the known to the
unknown' has its definite danger, against which one has
to be constantly on one's guard : its obvious danger is to
destroy perspective and ignore development by carrying
into the 'unknown' of early times that which is known of
later conditions. Altogether the attempt to overthrow some
of the established results of investigation as to race and
classes does not seem to be a happy one. And so, although
great work has been done in our field of study, it cannot be
said that it has been brought to a close—'bis an die Sterne
weit.' Many things remain to be done, and some problems
are especially pressing. The legal and the economical side
of the inquiry must be worked up to the same level ;
manorial documents must be examined systematically, if
not exhaustively, and their material made to fit with the
evidence established from other sources of information ; the
whole field has to be gone over with an eye for proof and
not for doctrine. A review of the work already done, and
of the names of scholars engaged in it, is certainly an
incitement to modesty for every new reaper in the field, but
it is also a source of hope. It shows that schools and
leading scholars displace one another more under the
influence of general currents of thought than of individual
talent. The ferment towards the formation of groups
comes from the outside, from the modern life which sur-
rounds research, forms the scholar, suggests solutions.
Moreover, theoretical development has a continuity of its
own ; all the strength of this manifold life cannot break or
turn back its course, but is reduced to drive it forward in
ever new bends and curves. The present time is especially
propitious to our study : one feels, as it were, that it is
ripening to far-reaching conclusions. So much has been

done already for this field of enquiry in the different countries of Europe, that the hope to see in our age a general treatment of the social origins of Western Europe will not seem an extravagant one. And such a treatment must form as it were the corner-stone of any attempt to trace the law of development of human society. It is in this consciousness of being borne by a mighty general current, that the single scholar may gather hope that may buoy him against the insignificance of his forces and the drudgery of his work.

FIRST ESSAY.

THE PEASANTRY OF THE FEUDAL AGE.

CHAPTER I.

THE LEGAL ASPECT OF VILLAINAGE. GENERAL CONCEPTIONS.

IT has become a commonplace to oppose medieval Medieval serfdom to ancient slavery, one implying dependence on serfdom. the lord of the soil and attachment to the glebe, the other being based on complete subjection to an owner. There is no doubt that great landmarks in the course of social development are set by the three modes hitherto employed of organising human labour: using the working man (1) as a chattel at will, (2) as a subordinate whose duties are fixed by custom, (3) as a free agent bound by contract. These landmarks probably indicate molecular changes in the structure of society scarcely less important than those political and intellectual revolutions which are usually taken as the turning-points of ancient, medieval, and modern history.

And still we must not forget, in drawing such definitions, that we reach them only by looking at things from such a height that all lesser inequalities and accidental features of the soil are no longer sensible to the eyesight. In finding one's way over the land one must needs go over these very inequalities and take into account these very features. If, from a general survey of medieval servitude, we turn to the actual condition of the English peasantry, say in the thirteenth century, the first fact we have to meet will stand in very marked contrast to our general proposition.

Import-
ance of
legal treat-
ment.
The majority of the peasants are villains, and the legal conception of villainage has its roots not in the connexion of the villain with the soil, but in his personal dependence on the lord.

If this is a fact, it is a most important one. It would be reckless to treat it as a product of mere legal pedantry[1]. The great work achieved by the English lawyers of the twelfth and thirteenth centuries was prompted by a spirit which had nothing to do with pedantry. They were fashioning state and society, proudly conscious of high aims and power, enlightened by the scholastic training of their day, but sufficiently strong to use it for their own purposes ; sound enough not to indulge in mere abstractions, and firm enough not to surrender to mere technicalities[2]. In the treatment of questions of status and tenure by the lawyers of Henry II, Henry III, and Edward I, we must recognise a mighty influence which was brought to bear on the actual condition of things, and our records show us on every page that this treatment was by no means a matter of mere theory. Indeed one of the best means that we have for estimating the social process of those times is afforded by the formation and the break up of legal notions in their cross influences with surrounding political and economic facts.

Defini-
tion and
termin-
ology of
villainage
at Com-
mon Law.
As to the general aspect of villainage in the legal theory of English feudalism there can be no doubt. The 'Dialogus de Scaccario' gives it in a few words : the lords are owners not only of the chattels but of the bodies of their *ascriptitii*, they may transfer them wherever they please, 'and sell or otherwise alienate them if they like[3].' Glanville and Bracton, Fleta and Britton[4] follow in substance the same doctrine, although they use different terms. They appro-

---

[1] Thorold Rogers, History of Agriculture and Prices, i. 70 ; Six Centuries of Work and Wages, 44. Cf. Chandler, Five Court Rolls of Great Cressingham in the county of Norfolk, 1885, pp. viii, ix.

[2] Stubbs, Seventeen Lectures, 304, 305 ; Maitland, Introduction to the Note-book of Bracton, 4 sqq.

[3] Dial. de Scacc. ii. 10 (Select Charters, p. 222). Cf. i. 10 ; p. 192.

[4] Glanville, v. 5 ; Bracton, 4, 5 ; Fleta, i. 2 ; Britton, ed. Nichols, i. 194.

priate the Roman view that there is no difference of quality between serfs and serfs : all are in the same abject state. Legal theory keeps a very firm grasp of the distinction between status and tenure, between a villain and a free man holding in villainage, but it does not admit of any distinction of status among serfs : *servus, villanus,* and *nativus* are equivalent terms as to personal condition, although this last is primarily meant to indicate something else besides condition, namely, the fact that a person has come to it by birth[1]. The close connexion between the terms is well illustrated by the early use of *nativa,* nieve, 'as a feminine to *villanus.*'

These notions are by no means abstractions bereft of practical import. Quite in keeping with them, manorial lords could remove peasants from their holdings at their will and pleasure. An appeal to the courts was of no avail : the lord in reply had only to oppose his right over the plaintiff's person, and to refuse to go into the subject-matter of the case[2]. Nor could the villain have any help

Treatment of villainage in legal practice.

[1] Bracton, 5 ; Britton, i. 197. Pollock, Land-laws, App. C, is quite right as to the fundamental distinction between status and tenure, but he goes too far, I think, in trying to trace the steps by which names originally applying to different things got confused in the terminology of the Common Law. Annotators sometimes indulged in distinctions which contradict each other and give us no help as to the law. The same Cambridge MS. from which Nichols gives an explanation of *servus, nativus,* and *villanus* (i. 195) has a different etymology in a marginal note to Bracton. 'Nativus dicitur a nativitate—quasi in servitute natus, villanus dicitur a villa, quasi faciens villanas consuetudines racione tenementi, vel sicut ille qui se recognoscit ad villanum in curia quae recordum habet, servus vero dicitur a servando quasi per captivitatem, per vim et injustam detentionem villanus captus et detentus contra mores et consuetudines juris naturalis' (Cambr. Univers. MSS. Dd. vii. 6. I have the reference from my friend F. W. Maitland).

[2] Placita Coram Rege, Easter, 14 Edw. I, m. 9 : 'Willelmus Barantyn et Radulfus attachiati fuerunt ad respondendum Agneti de Chalgraue de placito quare in ipsam Agnetem apud Chalgraue insultum fecerunt et ipsam verberaverunt, vulneraverunt et male tractaverunt, et bona et catalla sua in domibus ipsius Agnetis apud Chalgraue scilicet ordeum et avenam, argentum, archas et alia bona ad valenciam quadraginta solidorum ceperunt et asportaverunt ; et ipsam Agnetem effugaverunt de uno mesuagio et dimidia virgata terre de quibus fuit in seysina per predictum Willelmum que fuerunt de antiquo dominico per longum tempus ; nec permiserunt ipsam Agnetem morari in predicta villa de Chalgraue ; et eciam quandam sororem ipsius

as to the amount and the nature of his services [1] ; the King's
Courts will not examine any complaint in this respect, and
may sometimes go so far as to explain that it is no business
of theirs to interfere between the lord and his man [2]. In
fact any attempt on the part of the dependant to assert
civil rights as to his master will be met and defeated by the
'exceptio villenagii [3].' The state refuses to regulate the

Agnetis eo quod ipsa soror eam hospitavit per duas noctes de domibus suis
eiecit, terra et catalla sua abstulit. Et predicti Willelmus et Radulfus
veniunt. Et quo ad insultacionem et verberacionem dicunt quod non sunt
inde culpabiles. Et quo ad hoc quod ipsa Agnes dicit quod ipsam eiecerunt
de domibus et terris suis, dicunt quod predicta Agnes est natiua ipsius
Willelmi et tenuit predicta tenementa in villenagio ad voluntatem ipsius
Willelmi propter quod bene licebat eidem Willelmo ipsam de predicto tenemento ammouere.—Juratores dicunt . . . . quod predicta tenementa sunt villenagium predicti Willelmi de Barentyn et quod predicta Agnes tenuit eadem
tenementa ad voluntatem ipsius Willelmi.' Cf. Y. B. 12/13 Edw. III (ed.
Pike), p. 233 sqq., ' or vous savez bien qe par ley de terre tout ceo qe le vileyn
ad si est a soun seignour;' 229 sqq., 'qar cest sa terre demene, et il les puet
ouster a sa volunte demene.'

[1] Coram Rege, Mich., 3/4 Edw. I, m. 1: 'Ricardus de Assheburnham
summonitus fuit ad respondendum Petro de Attebuckhole et Johanni de
eadem de placito quare, cum ipsi teneant quasdam terras et tenementa de
predicto Ricardo in Hasseburnham ac ipsi parati sunt ad faciendum ei
consuetudines et servicia que antecessores sui terras et tenementa illa
tenentes facere consueverint, predictus Ricardus diversas commoditates
quam ipsi tam in boscis ipsius Ricardi quam in aliis locis habere consueverint eisdem subtrahens ipsos ad intollerabiles servitutes et consuetudines
faciendas taliter compellit quod ex sua duricia mendicare coguntur. Et
unde queruntur quod, cum teneant tenementa sua per certas consuetudines
et certa servicia, et cum percipere consueverunt boscum ad focum et mate-
riam de bosco crescente in propriis terris suis, predictus Ricardus ipsos non
permittit aliquid in boscis suis capere et eciam capit aueria sua et non
permittit eos terram suam colere.—Ricardus dicit, quod non debet eis ad
aliquam accionen respondere nisi questi essent de vita vel membris vel de
iniuria facta corpori suo. Dicit eciam quod nativi sui sunt, et quod omnes
antecessores sui nativi fuerunt antecessorum suorum et in villenagio suo
manentes.'

[2] Note-book of Bracton, pl. 1237: 'dominus Rex non vult se de eis
intromittere.'

[3] It occurs in the oldest extant Plea Roll, 6 Ric. I ; Rot. Cur. Regis, ed.
Palgrave, p. 84 : 'Thomas venit et dicit quod ipsa fuit uxorata cuidam Turk-
illo, qui habuit duos filios qui clamabant libertatem tenementi sui in curia
domini Regis . . . et quod ibi dirationavit eos esse villanos suos, et non
defendit disseisinam . . . Et ipsi Elilda et Ricardus defendunt vilenagium et
ponunt se super juratam,' etc.

position of this class on the land, and therefore there can be no question about any legal 'ascription' to the soil. Even as to his person, the villain was liable to be punished and put into prison by the lord, if the punishment inflicted did not amount to loss of life or injury to his body[1]. The extant Plea Rolls and other judicial records are full of allusions to all these rights of the lord and disabilities of the villain, and it must be taken into account that only an infinitely small part of the actual cases can have left any trace in such records, as it was almost hopeless to bring them to the notice of the Royal Courts[2].

It is not strange that in view of such disabilities Bracton thought himself entitled to assume equality of condition between the English villain and the Roman slave, and to use the terms *servus*, *villanus*, and *nativus* indiscriminately. The characteristics of slavery are copied by him from Azo's commentary on the Institutes, as material for a description of the English bondmen, and he distinguishes them carefully even from the Roman *adscripticii* or *coloni* of base condition. The villains are protected in some measure against their lord in criminal law; they cannot be slain or maimed at pleasure; but such protection is also afforded to

Identification with Roman slavery.

---

[1] Maitland, Select Pleas of the Crown (Selden Soc. I), pl. 3: 'Quendam nativum suum quem habuit in vinculis eo quod voluit fugere.' Bract. Note-book, pl. 1041: 'Petrus de Herefordia attachiatus fuit ad respondendum R. fil. Th. quare ipse cepit Ricardum et eum imprisonauit et coegit ad redempcionem I marce. Et Petrus venit alias et defendit capcionem et imprisonacionem set dicit quod villanus fuit,' etc.

It must be noted, however, that in such cases it was difficult to draw the line as to the amount of bodily injury allowed by the law, and therefore the King's courts were much more free to interfere. In the trial quoted on p. 45, note 2, the defendants distinguish carefully between the accusation and the civil suit. They plead 'not guilty' as to the former. And so Bishop Stubbs' conjecture as to the 'rusticus verberatus' in Pipe Roll, 31 Henry I, p. 55 (Constit. Hist. i. 487), seems quite appropriate. The case is a very early one, and may testify to the better condition of the peasantry in the first half of the twelfth century.

[2] As to the actual treatment experienced by the peasants at the hands of their feudal masters, see a picturesque case in Maitland's Select Pleas of the Crown (Selden Soc.), 203.

slaves in the later law of the Empire, and in fact it is based in Bracton on the text of the Institutes given by Azo, which in its turn is simply a summary of enactments made by Hadrian and Antonine.   The minor law books of the thirteenth century follow Bracton in this identification of villainage with slavery.   Although this identification could not but exercise a decisive influence on the theory of the subject, it must be borne in mind that it did not originate in a wanton attempt to bring together in the books dissimilar facts from dissimilar ages.   On the contrary, it came into the books because practice had paved the way for it.   Bracton was enabled to state it because he did not see much difference between the definitions of Azo and the principles of Common Law, as they had been established by his masters Martin of Pateshull and William Raleigh.   He was wrong, as will be shown by-and-by, but certainly he had facts to lean upon, and his theory cannot be dismissed on the ground of his having simply copied it from a foreigner's treatise.

Villains in gross and villains regardant.   Most modern writers on the subject have laid stress upon a difference between *villains regardant* and *villains in gross*, said to be found in the law books[1].   It has been taken to denote two degrees of servitude—the predial dependence of a *colonus* and the personal dependence of a true slave. The villain *regardant* was (it is said) a villain who laboured under disabilities in relation to his lord only, the villain in gross possessed none of the qualities of a freeman.   One sub-division would illustrate the debasement of freemen who had lost their own land, while the other would present the survival of ancient slavery.

In opposition to these notions I cannot help thinking that Hallam was quite right in saying: ' In the condition of these (villains regardant and villains in gross), whatever has been said by some writers, I can find no manner of difference; the distinction was merely technical, and

---

[1] Stubbs, Constitutional History, ii. 652, 654; Freeman, Norman Conquest, v. 477; Digby, Introduction to the Law of Real Property, 244.

affected only the mode of pleading. The term *in gross* is appropriated in our legal language to property held absolutely and without reference to any other. Thus it is applied to rights of advowson or of common, when possessed simply, and not as incident to any particular lands. And there can be no doubt that it was used in the same sense for the possession of a villein.' (Middle Ages, iii. 173; cf. note XIV.) Hallam's statement did not carry conviction with it however, and as the question is of considerable importance in itself and its discussion will incidentally help to bring out one of the chief points about villainage, I may be allowed to go into it at some length.

Matters would be greatly simplified if the distinction could really be traced through the authorities. In point of fact it turns out to be a late one. We may start from Coke in tracing back its history. His commentary upon Littleton certainly has a passage which shows that he came across opinions implying a difference of status between villains regardant and villains in gross. He speaks of the right of the villain to pursue every kind of action against every person except his lord, and adds: 'there is no diversity herein, whether he be a villain regardant or in gross, although some have said to the contrary[1]' (Co. Lit. 123 b). Littleton himself treats of the terms in several sections, and it is clear that he never takes them to indicate status or define variation of condition. As has been pointed out by Hallam, he uses them only in connexion with

Littleton's view.

---

[1] Sir Thomas Smith, The Commonwealth of England, ed. 1609, p. 123, shows that the notion of two classes corresponding to the Roman *servus* and the Roman *adscriptus glebae* had taken root firmly about the middle of the sixteenth century. 'Villeins in gross, as ye would say immediately bond to the person and his heirs ... (The adscripti) were not bond to the person but to the mannor or place, and did follow him who had the mannors, and in our law are called villains regardants (sic), for because they be as members or belonging to the mannor or place. Neither of the one sort nor of the other have we any number in England. And of the first I never knew any in the Realme in my time. Of the second so fewe there bee, that it is not almost worth the speaking, but our law doth acknowledge them in both these sorts.'

a diversity in title, and a consequent diversity in the mode
of pleading.   If the lord has a deed or a recorded confession to prove a man's bondage, he may implead him as
his villain in gross; if the lord has to rely upon prescription,
he has to point out the manor to which the party and his
ancestors have been regardant, have belonged, time out of
mind[1].   As it is a question of title and not of condition,
Littleton currently uses the mere 'villain' without any
qualification, whereas such a qualification could not be
dispensed with, if there had been really two different
classes of villains.   Last but not least, any thought of
a diversity of condition is precluded by the fact, that
Littleton assumes the transfer from one sub-division to
the other to depend entirely on the free will of the lord
(sections 175, 181, 182, 185).   But still, although even
Littleton does not countenance the classification I am now
analysing, it seems to me that some of his remarks may
have given origin to the prevalent misconception on the
subject.

The 'villain regardant' of the Year Books.
Let us take up the Year Books, which, even in their
present state, afford such an inestimable source of information for the history of legal conceptions in the fourteenth
and fifteenth centuries[2].   An examination of the reports in
the age of the Edwards will show at once that the terms
regardant and *in gross* are used, or rather come into use, in
the fourteenth century as definitions of the mode of pleading in particular cases.   They are suggested by difference
in title, but they do not coincide with it, and any attempt
to make them coincide must certainly lead to misapprehen-
sion.   I mean this—the term 'villain regardant' applied to
a man does not imply that the person in question has any
status superior to that of the 'villain in gross,' and it does

---

[1] Section 182 is not quite consistent with such an exposition, but I do not
think there can be any doubt as to the general doctrine.

[2] I need not say that the work done by Mr. Horwood, and especially by
Mr. Pike, for the Rolls' Series quite fulfil the requirements of students.
But in comparison with it the old Year Books in Rastall's, and even more so
in Maynard's edition, appear only the more wretchedly misprinted.

not imply that the lord has acquired a title to him by some particular mode of acquisition, e. g. by prescription as contrasted with grant or confession ; it simply implies that for the purpose of the matter then in hand, for the purpose of the case that is then being argued, the lord is asserting and hoping to prove a title to the villain by relying on a title to a manor with which the villain is or has been connected—title it must be remembered is one thing, proof of title is another.   As the contrast is based on pleading and not on title, one and the same person may be taken and described in one case as a villain regardant to a manor, and in another as a villain in gross.   And now for the proof.

The expression 'regardant' never occurs in the pleadings at all, but 'regardant to a manor' is used often. From Edward III's time it is used quite as a matter of course in the formula of the 'exceptio' or special plea of villainage[1].   That is, if the defendant pleaded in bar of an action that the plaintiff was his bondman he generally said, I am not bound to answer A, because he is my villain and I am seised of him as of my villain as regardant to my manor of C.   Of course there are other cases when the term is employed, but the plea in bar is by far the most common one and may stand for a test.   This manner of pleading is only coming gradually into use in the fourteenth century, and we actually see how it is taking shape and spreading.   As a rule the Year Books of Edward I's time have not got it.   The defendant puts in his plea unqualified. 'He ought not to be answered because he is our villain' (Y. B. 21/22 Edward I, p. 166, ed. Horwood).   There is a case in 1313 when a preliminary skirmish between the counsel on either side took place as to the sufficiency of the defendant's plea in bar, the plaintiff contending that it was not precise enough.   Here, if any where, we should expect

---

[1] For instance, Liber Assisarum, ann. 44, pl. 4 (f. 283) : ' Quil fuit son villein et il seisi de luy come de son villein come regardant a son maneir de B. en la Counte de Dorset.'

the term '*regardant,*' but it is not forthcoming[1]. What is more, and what ought to have prevented any mistake, the official records of trials on the Plea Rolls up to Edward II always use the plain assertion, 'villanus . . . et tenet in villenagio[2].' The practice of naming the manor to which a villain belonged begins however to come in during the reign of Edward II, and the terminology is by no means settled at the outset; expressions are often used as equivalent to 'regardant' which could hardly have misled later antiquaries as to the meaning of the qualification[3]. In a case of 1322, for instance, we have

[1] Y. B. Hil. 5 Edw. II: 'Iohan de Rose port son [ne] vexes vers Labbe de Seint Bennet de Holme, et il counta qil luy travaille, etc., e luy demande.' *Migg.*: 'defent tort et force, ou et quant il devera et dit qil fuist le vilein Labbe, per qi il ne deveroit estre resceve.' *Devom.*: 'il covient qe vous disez plus qe vous estes seisi, ut supra,' etc. *Migg.*: 'il est nostre vileyn, et nous seisi de luy come de nostre vileyn.' *Ber.*: 'Coment seisi come,' etc. ? *Migg.*: 'de luy et de ces auncestres come de nos vileynes, en fesant de luy nostre provost en prenant de luy rechate de char et de saunk et redemption pur fille et fitz marier de luy et de ces auncestres et a tailler haut et bas a nostre volente, prest,' etc. (Les reports des cases del Roy Edward le II. London, 1678; f. 157.)

[2] I do not think it ever came into any one's mind to look at the Plea Rolls in this matter. Even Hargrave, when preparing his famous argument in Somersett's case, carried his search no further than the Year Books then in print. And in consequence he just missed the true solution. He says (Howell's State Trials, xx. 42, 43), 'As to the villeins in gross the cases relative to them are very few; and I am inclined to think that there never was any great number of them in England. . . . However, after a long search, I do find places in the Year Books where the form of alledging villenage in gross is expressed, not in full terms, but in a general way; and in all the cases I have yet seen, the villenage is alledged in the ancestors of the person against whom it was pleaded.' And he quotes 1 Edw. II, 4; 5 Edw. II, 157 (corr. for 15); 7 Edw. II, 242, and 11 Edw. II, 344. But all these cases are of Edward II's time, and instead of being exceptional give the normal form of pleading as it was used up to the second quarter of the fourteenth century. They looked exceptional to Hargrave only because he restricted his search to the later Year Books, and did not take up the Plea Rolls. By admitting the cases quoted to indicate villainage in gross, he in fact admitted that there were only villains in gross before 1350 or thereabouts, or rather that all villains were alike before this time, and no such thing as the difference between *in gross* and *regardant* existed. I give in App. I the report of the interesting case quoted from 1 Edw. II.

[3] Y. B. 32/33 Edw. I (Horwood), p. 57: 'Quant un home est seisi de son vilein, issi qil est reseant dans son vilenage.' Fitzherbert, Abr. Vill. 3 (39 Edw. III): '. . . villeins sunt appendant as maners qe sount auncien

'within the manor' where we should expect to find
'regardant to the manor[1].' This would be very nearly
equivalent to the Latin formula adopted by the Plea Rolls,
which is simply *ut de manerio*[2]. Every now and then cases
occur which gradually settle the terminology, because the
weight of legal argumentation in them is made to turn on
the fact that a particular person was connected with a
particular manor and not with another. A case from 1317
is well in point. B. P. the defendant excepts against the
plaintiff T. A. on the ground of villainage (*qil est nostre
vileyn*, and nothing else). The plaintiff replies that he was
enfranchised by being suffered to plead in an assize of
mort d'ancestor against B. P.'s grandmother. By this the
defendant's counsel is driven to maintain that his client's
right against T. A. descended not from his grandmother
but from his grandfather, who was seised of the manor of
H. to which T. A. belonged as a villain[3]. The connexion
with the manor is adduced to show from what quarter the
right to the villain had descended, and, of course, implies nothing as to any peculiarity of this villain's status, or
as to the kind of title, the mode of acquiring rights, upon
which the lord relies—it was ground common to both
parties that if the lord had any rights at all he acquired
them by inheritance.

Another case seems even more interesting. It dates Prior of
from 1355, that is from a time when the usual terminology the Hos-
had already become fixed. It arose under that celebrated Thomas
Statute of Labourers which played such a prominent and Ralph
part in the social history of the fourteenth century. One Crips.
of the difficulties in working the statute came from the
fact that it had to recognise two different sets of relations

demesne.' On the other hand, 'regardant' is used quite independently of
villainage. Y. B. 12/13 Edw. III (Pike), p. 133: 'come services regardaunts
al manoir de H.'

[1] Y. B. Hil. 14 Edw. II, f. 417: 'R. est bailli . . . del manoir de Clifton
. . . deins quel manoir cesti J. est villein.'

[2] See App. I and II.

[3] Y. B. Trin. 9 Edw. II, f. 294: 'Le manoir de H. fuit en ascun temps en
la seisine Hubert nostre ael, a quel manoir cest vileyn est regardant.'

between the employer and the workman. The statute dealt with the contract between master and servant, but it did not do away with the dependence of the villain on the lord, and in case of conflict it gave precedence to this latter claim ; a lord had the right to withdraw his villain from a stranger's service. Such cross influences could not but occasion a great deal of confusion, and our case gives a good instance of it. Thomas Barentyn has reclaimed Ralph Crips from the service of the Prior of the Hospitalers, and the employer sues in consequence both his former servant and Barentyn. This last answers, that the servant in question is his villain regardant to the manor of C. The plaintiff's counsel maintains that he could not have been regardant to the manor, as he was going about at large at his free will and as a free man ; for this reason A. the former owner of the manor was never seised of him, and not being seised could not transfer the seisin to the present owner, although he transferred the manor. For the defendant it is pleaded, that going about freely is no enfranchisement, that by the gift of the manor every right connected with the manor was also conferred and that consequently the new lord could at any moment lay hands on his man, as the former lord could have done in his time. Ultimately the plaintiff offers to join issue on the question, whether the servant had been a villain regardant to the manor of C. or not. The defendant asserts, rather late in the day, that even if the person in question was not a villain regardant to the manor of C. the mere fact of his being a villain in gross would entitle his lord to call him away. This attempt to start on a new line is not allowed by the Court because the claim had originally been traversed on the ground of the connexion with the manor[1].

The peculiarity of the case is that a third person has an interest to prove that the man claimed as villain had been as a free man. Usually there were but two parties in the contest about status ; the lord pulling one way and the person

---

[1] Y. B. Trin. 29 Edw. III, f. 41. For the report of this case and the corresponding entry in the Common Pleas Roll, see Appendix II.

claimed pulling the other way, but, through the influence
of the Statute of Labourers, in our case lord and labourer
were at one against a third party, the labourer's employer.
The acknowledgment of villainage by the servant did not
settle the question, because, though binding for the future,
it was not sufficient to show that villainage had existed in
the past, that is at the time when the contract of hire and
service was broken through the interference of the lord.
Everything depended on the settlement of one question—
was the lord seised at the time, or not? Both parties agree
that the lord was not actually seised of the person, both
agree that he was seised of the manor, and both suppose
that if the person had as a matter of fact been attached
to the manor it would have amounted to a seisin of the
person. And so the contention is shifted to this point:
can a man be claimed through the medium of a manor, if
he has not been actually living, working and serving in it?
The court assumes the possibility, and so the parties appeal
to the country to decide whether in point of fact Ralph
Crips the shepherd had been in legal if not in actual
connexion with the manor, i. e. could be traced to it
personally or through his relatives.

The case is interesting in many ways. It shows that the Results as
same man could be according to the point of view considered to 'villain
regardant'
both as a villain in regard to a manor, and as a villain in and 'villain
in gross.'
gross. The relative character of the classification is thus
illustrated as well as its importance for practical purposes.
The transmission of a manor is taken to include the persons
engaged in the cultivation of its soil, and even those whose
ancestors have been engaged in such cultivation, and who
have no special plea for severing the connexion.

As to the outcome of the whole inquiry, we may, it
seems to me, safely establish the following points: 1. The
terms 'regardant' and 'in gross' have nothing to do with
a legal distinction of status. 2. They come up in connexion with the modes of proof and pleading during
the fourteenth century. 3. They may apply to the same
person from different points of view. 4. 'Villain in gross'

means a villain without further qualification; 'villain regardant to a manor' means villain by reference to a manor. 5. The connexion with a manor, though only a matter of fact and not binding the lord in any way, might yet be legally serviceable to him, as a means of establishing and proving his rights over the person he claimed.

The astrier. I need hardly mention, after what has been said, that there is no such thing as this distinction in the thirteenth century law books. I must not omit, however, to refer to one expression which may be taken to stand in the place of the later 'villain regardant to a manor.' Britton (ii. 55) gives the formula of the special plea of villainage to the assize of mort d'ancestor in the following words : ' Ou il poie dire qe il est soen vileyn et soen astrier et demourrant en son villenage.' There can be no doubt that residence on the lord's land is meant, and the term *astrier* leads even further, it implies residence at a particular hearth or in a particular house. Fleta gives the assize of novel disseisin to those who have been a long time away from their villain hearth[1] ('extra astrum suum villanum,' p. 217). If the term 'astrier' were restricted to villains it would have proved a great deal more than the 'villain regardant' usually relied upon. But it is of very wide application. Britton uses it of free men entitled to rights of common by reason of tenements they hold in a township (i. 392). Bracton speaks of the case of a nephew coming into an inheritance in preference to the uncle because he had been living at the same hearth or in the same hall (in *atrio* or *astro*) with the former owner[2], and in such or a similar sense the word appears to have been usually employed by lawyers[3]. On the other hand, if we look in Bracton's treatise for parallel passages to those quoted from the Fleta

---

[1] Cf. Annals of Dunstaple, Ann. Mon. iii. 371 : ' Quia astrarius eius fuit,' in the sense of a person living on one's land.

[2] Bracton, f. 267, b.

[3] Bract. Note-book, pl. 230, 951, 988. Cf. Spelman, Gloss. v. astrarius Kentish Custumal, Statutes of the Realm, i. 224. Fleta has it once in the sense of the Anglo-Saxon heorð-fæst, i. cap. 47, § 10 (f. 62).

and Britton about the villain astrier, we find only a reference to the fact that the person in question was a serf and
holding in villainage and under the sway of a lord [1], and
so there is nothing to denote special condition in the *astrier*.
When the term occurs in connexion with villainage it
serves to show that a person was not only a bondman
born, but actually living in the power of his lord, and not
in a state of liberty. The allusion to the hearth cannot
possibly mean that the man sits in his own homestead,
because only a few of the villains could have been holders
of separate homesteads, and so it must mean that he was
sitting in a homestead belonging to his lord, which is quite
in keeping with the application of the term in the case of
inheritance.

The facts we have been examining certainly suppose
that in the villains we have chiefly to do with peasants
tilling the earth and dependent on manorial organisation.
They disclose the working of one element which is
not to be simply deduced from the idea of personal
dependence.

The territorial hold of villainage.

It may be called subjection to territorial power. The
possession of a manor carries the possession of cultivators
with it. It is always important to decide whether a bondman is in the seisin of his lord or not, and the chief means
to show it is to trace his connexion with the territorial
lordship. The interposition of the manor in the relation
between master and man is, of course, a striking feature and
it gives a very characteristic turn to medieval servitude.
But if it is not consistent with the general theory laid down
in the thirteenth century law books, it does not lead to
anything like the Roman *colonatus*. The serf is not placed
on a particular plot of land to do definite services under
the protection of the State. He may be shifted from one
plot within the jurisdiction of his lord to another, from
one area of jurisdiction to another, from rural labour to
industrial work or house work, from one set of customs

[1] Bracton, f. 190.

and services to another. He is not protected by his predial connexion against his lord, and in fact such predial connexion is utilised to hold and bind him to his lord. We may say, that the unfree peasant of English feudalism was legally a personal dependant, but that his personal dependence was enforced through territorial lordship.

CHAPTER II.

LEGAL theory as we have seen endeavoured to bring the general conception of villainage under the principles of the Roman law of slavery, and important features in the practice of the common law went far to support it in so doing. On the other hand, even the general legal theory discloses the presence of an element quite foreign to the Roman conception. If we proceed from principles to their application in detail, we at once find, that in most cases the broad rules laid down on the subject do not fit all the particular aspects of villainage. These require quite different assumptions for their explanation, and the whole doctrine turns out to be very complex, and to have been put together out of elements which do not work well together.

We meet discrepancies and confusion at the very threshold in the treatment of the modes in which the villain status has its origin. The most common way of becoming a villain was to be born to this estate, and it seems that we ought to find very definite rules as to this case. In truth, the doctrine was changing. Glanville (v. 6) tried in a way to conform to the Roman rule of the child following the condition of the mother, but it could not be made to work in England, and ever since Bracton, both common law and jurisprudence reject it. At the close of the Middle Ages it was held that if born in wedlock the child took after his father[1], and that a

Villainage by birth.

---

[1] Littleton, sect. 187. Cf. Fortescue, ' De laudibus legum Angliae,' c. 42.

bastard was to be accepted as *filius nullius* and presumed free [1]. Bracton is more intricate; the bastard follows the mother, the legitimate child follows the father; and there is one exception, in this way, that the legitimate child of a free man and a nief born in villainage takes after the mother [2]. It is not difficult to see why the Roman rule did not fit; it was too plain for a state of things which had to be considered from three different sides [3]. The Roman lawyer merely looked to the question of status and decided it on the ground of material demonstrability of origin [4], if such an expression may be used. The Medieval lawyer had the Christian sanctification of marriage to reckon with, and so the one old rule had to be broken up into two rules—one applicable to legitimate children, the other to bastards. In case of *bastardy* the tendency was decidedly in favour of retaining the Roman rule, equally suiting animals and slaves, and the later theory embodied in Littleton belongs already to the development of modern ideas in favour of liberty [5]. In case of *legitimacy* the recognition of marriage led to the recognition of the family and indirectly to the closer connexion with the father as the head of the family. In addition to this a third element comes in, which may be

---

[1] Littleton, sect. 188.

[2] Bracton, ff. 5, 193, b.

[3] I need not say that there were very notable variations in the history of the Roman rule itself (cf. for instance, Puchta, Institutionen, § 211), but these do not concern us, as we are taking the Roman doctrine as broadly as it was taken by medieval lawyers.

[4] Mater certa est. Gai. Inst. i. 82.

[5] See Fitz. Abr. Villenage, pl. 5 (43 Edw. III): 'Ou il allege bastardise pur ceo qe si son auncestor fuit bastard il ne puit estre villein, sinon par connusance.' There was a special reason for turning the tables in favour of bastardy, which is hinted at in this case. The bastard's parents could not be produced against a bastard. He had no father, and his mother would be no proof against him because she was a woman [Fitz. Abr. Vill. 37 (13 Edw. I), Par ce qe la feme ne puit estre admise pur prove par lour fraylte et ausi cest qi est demaunde est pluiz digne person qe un feme]. It followed strictly that he could be a villain by confession, but not by birth. The fact is a good instance of the insoluble contradictions in which feudal law sometimes involved itself.

called properly feudal. The action of the father-rule is modified by the influence of territorial subjection. The marriage of a free man with a nief may be considered from a special point of view, if, as the feudal phraseology goes, he enters to her into her villainage[1]. By this fact the free man puts his child under the sway of the lord, to whose villainage the mother belongs. It is not the character of the tenement itself which is important in this case, but the fact of subjection to a territorial lord, whose interest it is to retain a dependant's progeny in a state of dependency. The whole system is historically important, because it illustrates the working of one of the chief ingredients of villainage, an ingredient entirely absent from ancient slavery; whereas medieval villainage depends primarily on subjection to the territorial power of the lord. Once more we are shown the practical importance of the manorial system in fashioning the state of the peasantry. Generally a villain must be claimed with reference to a manor, in connexion with an unfree hearth; he is born in a nest[2], which makes him a bondman. The strict legal notion has to be modified to meet the emergency, and villainage, instead of indicating complete personal subjection, comes to mean subjection to a territorial lord.

This same territorial element not only influences the status of the issue of a marriage, it also affects the status of the parties to a marriage, when those parties are of unequal condition. Most notable is the case of the free wife of a villain husband lapsing into servitude,

[1] Bracton, f. 5: 'Servus ratione qui se copulaverit villanae in villenagio constitutae.' Bract. Note-book, 1839: 'Juratores dicunt quod predictus Aluredus habuit duos fratres Hugonem [medium] medio tempore natum et Gilibertum postnatum qui nunc petit, set Hugo cepit quamdam terram in uillenagio et duxit uxorem [uillanam] et in uillenagio illo procreauit quemdam filium qui ad huc superest. . . . Et bene dicunt quod . . . iste Gilibertus propinquior heres eius est, ea racione quod filius Hugonis genitus fuit in uillenagio.'

[2] Y. B. 30/31 Edw. I, p. 167 sqq.: 'Usage de Cornwall est cecy qe la ou neyfe deyt estre marier hors de maner ou ele est reseant, qe ele trovera seurte . . . de revenir a son *ny* ov ses chateux apres la mort de son baroun.' Bracton, f. 26, 'Quasi avis in nido.'

when she enters the villain tenement of her consort; her servitude endures as long as her husband is in the lord's power, as long as he is alive and not enfranchised. The judicial practice of the thirteenth century gives a great number of cases where the tribunals refuse to vindicate the rights of women entangled in villainage by a mesalliance [1]. Such subjection is not absolute, however. The courts make a distinction between acquiring possession and retaining it. The same woman who will be refused a portion of her father's inheritance because she has married a serf, has the assize of novel disseisin against any person trying to oust her from a tenement of which she had been seised before her marriage [2]. The conditional disabilities of the free woman are not directly determined by the holding which she has entered, but by her marital subordination to an unfree husband ('sub virga,' Bract. Note-book, pl. 1685). For this reason the position of a free husband towards the villainage of his wife a nief is not exactly parallel. He is only subject to the general rules as to free men holding in villainage [3]. In any case, however, the instances which we have been discussing

[1] Bract. Note-book, pl. 702 : ' Nota quod libera femina maritata uillano non recuperat partem alicuius hereditatis quamdiu uillanus uixerit.'

[2] Bract. Note-book, pl. 1837 : ' Nota quod mulier que est libera uel in statu libero saltem ad minus non debet disseisiri quin recuperare possit per assisam quamuis nupta fuerit uillano set hereditatem petere non poterit.' Bract. Note-book, pl. 1010: 'Et uillani mori poterunt per quod predicte sorores petere possint ius suum.' Fitzherb. Villen. 27 (P. 7 Edw. II.) : ' Les femmes sont sans recouverie vers le seignior uiuant leur barons pur ce que ils sont villens.' Cf. Bracton, f. 202.

[3] Another instance of the influence of marriage on the condition of contracting parties is afforded by the enfranchisement of the wife in certain cases. The common law was, however, by no means settled as to this point. Y. B. 30/31 Edw. I, p. 167 sqq. : ' La ou le seygnur espouse sa neyfe, si est enfranchi pur toz jurs ; secus est la ou un homme estrange ly espose, qe donk nest ele enfraunchi si non vivant son baroun, et post mortem viri redit ad pristinum statum.' Fitzherb. Vill. 21 (P. 33 Edw. III) : ' Si home espouse femme qe est son villein el est franke durant les espousailles. Mes quand son baron est mort el est in statu quo prius, et issint el puis estre villein a son fils demesne.' It is quite likely that gentlemen sometimes got into a state of moral bondage to their own bondwomen, and were even led to marriage in a few instances, but the law had not much to feed upon in this direction, I imagine.

afford good illustrations of the fact, that villainage by no means flows from the simple source of personal subjection; it is largely influenced by the Christian organisation of the family and by the feudal mixture of rights of property and sovereignty embodied in the manorial system.

There are two other ways of becoming a villain besides being born to the condition; the acknowledgment of unfree status in a court of record, and prescription. We need not speak of the first, as it does not present any particulars of interest from a historical point of view. As to prescription, there is a very characteristic vacillation in our sources. In pleadings of Edward III's time its possibility is admitted, and it is pointed out, that it is a good plea if the person claimed by prescription shows that his father and grandfather [1] were strangers.

There is a curious explanatory gloss, in a Cambridge MS. of Bracton, which seems to go back at least to the beginning of the fourteenth century, and it maintains that free stock doing villain service lapses into villainage in the fifth generation only [2]. On the other hand, Britton flatly denies the possibility of such a thing; according to him no length of time can render free men villains or make villains free men. Moreover he gives a supposed case (possibly based on an actual trial), in which a person claimed as a villain is made

Prescription.

---

[1] Fitzherbert, Vill. 24 (H. 50 Edw. III; P. 40 Edw. III, 17): 'Si home demurt en terre tenue en villenage de temps dount, etc., il sera villen, et est bon prescripcion et encountre tel prescripcion est bon ple a dire qe son pere ou ayle fuit adventiffe,' etc. I suppose *ayle* here to be a simple error for *ayl* or *ael*, grandfather.

[2] Cambridge Univ., Dd. vij. 6, f. 231: 'Nota de tempore quo servus dicere poterit quia fecerit consuetudines villanas racione tenementi non racione persone. Et sciendum, quod quamdiu servus poterit verificare stipitem suam liberam non dicitur nativus, set quam citius dominus dicere poterit villicus noster est ex auo et tritauo, tunc primo desinit gaudere replicacione omnimoda et privilegio libertatis racione stipitis, ut si A. primo ingressus villenagium tenuerit de F. per villana servitia, deinde B. filius A., deinde C. filius B., deinde D. filius C., et sic tenuerint in villenagium de gradu in gradum usque ad quartum gradum de F. et heredibus suis, ille uillanus inuentus in quinto gradu descendente natiuus dicitur.' I am indebted for this passage to the kindness of Prof. Maitland.

to go back to the sixth generation to establish his freedom[1]. It does not seem likely that people could often vindicate their freedom by such elaborate argument, but the legal assumption expounded in Britton deserves full attention. It is only a consequence of the general view, that neither the holding nor the services ought to have any influence on the status of a man, and in so far it seems legally correct. But it is easy to see how difficult it must have been to keep up these nice distinctions in practice, how difficult for those who for generations had been placed in the same material position with serfs to maintain personal freedom[2]. For both views, though absolutely opposed to each other, are in a sense equally true: the one giving the logical development of a fundamental rule of the law, the other testifying to the facts. And so we have one more general observation to make as to the legal aspect of villainage. Even in the definition of its fundamental principles we see notable discrepancies and vacillations, which are the result of the conflict between logical requirements and fluctuating facts.

Criminal law in its relation to villainage.
The original unity of purpose and firmness of distinction are even more broken up when we look at the criminal and the police law where they touch villainage. In the criminal law of the feudal epoch there is hardly any distinction between free men and villains. In point of amercements there is the well-known difference as to the 'contenement' of a free landholder, a merchant and a villain, but this difference is prompted not by privilege but by the diversity of occupations. The Dialogus de Scaccario shows that villains being reputed English are in a lower position than free men as regards the presumption of Englishry and the payment of the murder-fine[3], but this feature seems to have become

[1] Britton, i. 196, 206.

[2] Hale, Pleas of the Crown (ed. 1736), ii. 298, gives an interesting record from Edward I's reign, which shows that even the general theory was doubtful.

[3] Dial. de Scacc. i. 10. p. 193: 'Ea propter pene quicumque sic hodie occisus reperitur, ut murdrum punitur, exceptis his quibus certa sunt ut diximus servilis condicionis indicia.' On the other hand the Dialogus lays

obliterated in the thirteenth century. In some cases corporal punishment may have differed according to the rank of the culprit, and the formalities of ordeal were certainly different[1]. The main fact remains, that both villains and free men were alike able to prosecute anybody by way of 'appeal'[2] for injury to their life, honour, and even property[3], and equally liable to be punished and prosecuted for offences of any kind. Their equal right was completely recognized by the criminal law, and as a natural sequence of this, the pleas of the crown generally omit to take any notice of the status of parties connected with them. One may read through Mr. Maitland's collection of Pleas of the Crown edited for the Selden Society, or through his book of Gloucestershire pleas, without coming across any but exceptional and quite accidental mentions of villainage. In fact were we to form our view of the condition of England exclusively on the material afforded by such documents, we might well believe that the whole class was all but an extinct one. One glance at Assize Rolls or at Cartularies would teach us better. Still the silence of the Corona Rolls is most eloquent. It shows convincingly that the distinction hardly influenced criminal law at all.

---

stress on the fact, that if a villain's chattels get confiscated they go to the king and not to the lord (ii. 10. p. 222), but this is regarded as a breach of a general principle.

[1] Glanville, xiv. 1: 'Per ferrum callidum si fuerit homo liber, per aquam si fuerit rusticus.'

[2] Lighter offences committed by the lord could not give rise to prosecution, but the *persona standi in iudicio* was admitted in a general way even in this case. A curious illustration of the different footing of villains in civil and criminal cases is afforded by a trial of Richard I's time. Richard of Waure brings an appeal against his man and reeve, Robert Thistleful, for conspiring with his enemies against his person. He offers to prove it against him, 'ut dominus, vel ut homo maimatus, sicut curia consideraverit.' Reeves were mostly villains, and the duty of serving as a reeve was considered as a characteristic of base condition. The lord probably goes to the King's court because he wants his man subjected to more severe punishment than he could inflict on him by his own power. (Rot. Cur. Regis Ricardi, 60.)

[3] The lord had power over their property, but against everybody else they were protected by the criminal law.

Police in relation to villainage.

It is curious that, as regards police, villains are grouped under an institution which, even by its name, according to the then accepted etymology, was essentially a free institution. The system of frank pledge (*plegium liberale*), which should have included every one 'worthy of his *were* and his *wite*,' is, as a matter of fact, a system which all through the feudal period is chiefly composed of villains[1]. Free men possessed of land are not obliged to join the tithing because they are amenable to law which has a direct hold on their land[2], and so the great mass of free men appear to be outside these arrangements, for the police representation of the free, or, putting it the other way, feudal serfs actually seem to represent the bulk of free society. The thirteenth-century arrangements do not afford a clue to such paradoxes, and one has to look for explanation to the *history* of the classes.

The frankpledge system is a most conspicuous link between both sections of society in this way also, that it directly connects the subjugated population with the hundred court, which is the starting-point of free judicial

---

[1] Sometimes the system is used so as to enforce servitude. See Court Rolls of Ramsey Abbey. Augmentation Court Rolls, Edw. I, Portf. 34, No. 46, m. 1 d. (Aylington) : 'Adhuc dicunt quod Johannes filius Ricardi Dunning est tannator et manet apud Heyham, set dat per annum pro recognicione duos capones. Et quia potens est et habet multa bona, preceptum fuit Hugoni Achard et eius decennae ad ultimum visum ad habendum ipsum ad istam curiam, et non habuit. Ideo ipse et decenna sua in misericordia.' (This case is now being printed in Selden Soc. vol. ii. p. 64.)

[2] Bracton, 124 b : 'Quia omnis homo siue liber siue seruus, aut est aut debet esse in franco plegio aut de alicuius manupastu, nisi sit aliquis itinerans de loco in locum, qui non plus se teneat ad unum quam ad alium, vel quid habeat quod sufficiat pro franco plegio, sicut dignitatem vel ordinem vel liberum tenementum, vel in civitatem rem immobilem.' Nichols, Britton, i. 181, gives a note from Cambr. MS. Dd. vii. 6, to the effect that 'Villeins and naifs ought not to be in tithings, secundum quosdam.' This is certainly a misunderstanding, but it can hardly be accounted for either by the enfranchisement of the peasant or the decay of the frank-pledge. I think the annotator may have seen the passages in Leg. Cnuti or Leg. Henrici I, which speak about free men joining the tithings, or speculated about the meaning of 'plegium liberale.' There could be no thought of excluding the villains in practice during the feudal period. As to the allusion in the Mirror of Justices, I shall refer to it in Appendix III.

organisation. Twice a year the whole of this population, with very few exceptions, has to meet in the hundred in order to verify the working of the tithings. Besides this, the class of villains must appear by representatives in the ordinary tribunals of the hundred and the shire : the reeve and the four men, mostly unfree men [1], with their important duties in the administration of justice, serve as a counterpoise to the exclusive employment of 'liberi et legales homines' on juries.

And now I come to the most intricate and important part of the subject—to the civil rights and disabilities of the villain. After what has been said of the villain in other respects, one may be prepared to find that his disabilities were by no means so complete as the strict operation of general rules would have required. The villain was able in many cases to do valid civil acts, to acquire property and to defend it in his own name. It is true that, both in theory and in practice, it was held that whatever was acquired by the bondman was acquired by the lord. The bondman could not buy anything but with his lord's money, as he had no money or chattels of his own [2]. But

Civil disability of a villain as to his lord.

---

[1] See below, Essay I. chap. vi.

[2] Bract. Note-book, pl. 1256 : ' Et Ricardus dicit quod assisa non debet inde fieri quia predictus Iohannes dedit terram illam cuidam uillano ipsius Ricardi, et ipse uillanus reddidit terram illam domino suo sicut emptam catallis domini sui, et quod ita ingressum habuit per uillanum illum in terram illam ponit se super iuratam.' Liber Assisarum, ann. 41. pl. 4. f. 252, shows that the statute *de religiosis* could be evaded by the lord entering into his villain's acquest. 'Levesque d'Exester port un Assise de no. diss. vers le tenaunt et *Persey* pur Leuesque en euidence dit, que un A. que fuit villeine le Evesque come de droit de sa Eglise purchase les tenements a luy et ses heyres et morust seisie, apres que mort entra B. come fitz et heire, sur que possession pur cause de villeinage entra Leuesque.—*Wich.* Home de religion ne puit pas recoverer per assise terre si title de droit ne soit troue en luy, et ou le title que est trouue en Leuesque est pur cause de la purchace de son villein, en quel cas Leuesque ne fuit compellable de entre sil nust vola mes puit auer eu ses seruices, et le statute voit Quod terrae et tenementa ad manum mortuam nullo modo deueniant, per que il semble que nous ne possomus pas doner iudgement pur Leuesque en ceo cas. *Sanke* : de son villein ne puit il pas leuer ses seruices, ne accepter lesse par sa maine, car a ceo que ieo entend par acceptacion de homage ou de fealty per sa maine il serra enfraunchi, per quey necessite luy arcte dentre, et le statut nestoit pas fait mes de restreindre purchaus a faire de nouel, et non

the working of these rules was limited by the medieval doctrine of possession. Land or goods acquired by the serf do not *eo ipso* lapse into his lord's possession, but only if the latter has taken them into his hand [1]. If the lord has not done so for any reason, for want of time, or carelessness, or because he did not choose to do so, the bondman is as good as the owner in respect of third persons. He can give away [2] or otherwise alienate land or chattels, he has the assize of novel disseisin to defend the land, and leaves the assize of mort d'ancestor to his heirs. In this case it would be no good plea to object that the plaintiff is a villain. In fact this objection can be raised by a third person only with the addition that, as villain, the plaintiff does not hold in his own name, but in the name of his lord [3]. A third person cannot except against a plaintiff merely on the ground of his personal status. As to third persons, a villain is said to be free and capable to sue all

pas a defaire ceo qe fuit launcien droit dez eglises. Et sur ceo fuerent aiournes en common bank, et illonque le judgement done pur Leuesque sans difficultie,' etc. (See also the report of the same case in Y. B. Mich. 41 Edw. III, pl. 8. f. 21.)

[1] Bracton, f. 25 : ' Si ... stipulatus sit servus sibi ipsi, et non domino, id non statim acquiritur domino, quamuis illud (corr. ille) sit sub voluntate et potestate sua, antequam dominus apprehensus fuerit possessionem. Quod quidem impune facere poterit, si voluerit, propter exceptionem,' etc. Fitz. Abr. Vill. pl. 22 (Pasch. 35 Edw. III) : ' Si le villen le roy purchase biens ou chatteux le properte de eux est en le roy sauns seisier. Mes auter est de auter home, etc. Mes sil purchas terre le roy doit seisier, etc. car *Thorp.* dit que terre demurt terre tout temps, mes biens come boefs ou vache puit estre mange.'

[2] Bracton, f. 25 b : ' Sic constat, quod qui sub potestate alterius fuerit, dare poterit. Sed qualiter hoc cum ipse, qui ab aliis possidetur, nihil possidere possit ? Ergo videtur quod nihil dare possit, quia non potest quis dare quod non habet, et nisi fuerit in possessione rei dandae. Respondeo, dare potest qui seisinam habet qualemcunque, et servus dare potest,' etc. In case of an execution for debt due to the king the goods of the villain were to be taken only when the lord's goods were exhausted. Dialog. de Scacc. ii. 14. p. 229.

[3] Bracton, f. 190 : ' Et non competit alicui hujusmodi exceptio de villenagio, praeterquam vero domino, nisi utrumque probet, scilicet quod villanus sit et teneat in villenagio, cum per hoc sequatur, quod ad ipsum non pertineat querela sive assisa, sed ad verum dominum, et ideo cadit assisa quantum ad personam suam et non quantum ad personam domini.' Cf. Britton, i. 325.

actions[1]. This of course does not mean that he has any action for recovering or defending his possession of the tenements which he holds *in villainage*, but this disability is no consequence of his servile blood, for he shares it with the free man who holds in villainage; it is a consequence of the doctrine that the possession of the tenant in villainage is in law the possession of him who has the freehold. It may be convenient for a villain as defendant to shelter himself behind the authority of his lord[2], and it was difficult to prevent him from doing so, although some attempts were made by the courts even in this case to distinguish whether a person had been in possession as a dependant or not. But there was absolutely nothing to prevent a villain from acting in every respect like a free man if he was so minded and was not interrupted by his lord. There was no need of any accessory action to make his acts complete and legal[3]. Again we come to an anomaly: the slave is free against everybody but his lord.

[1] Britton, i. 199; Littleton, 189; Bract. Note-book. pl. 1025: 'Assisa venit recognitura utrum una uirgata terre cum pertinenciis in R. sit libera elemosina pertinens ad ecclesiam Magistri Iohannis de R. de R. an laicum feodum Gaufridi Beieudehe. Qui venit et dicit quod non debet inde assisa fieri quia antecessores sui *feoffati fuerunt a conquestu Anglie* ita quod tenerent de ecclesia illa et redderent ei per annum x. solidos. . . . . Iuratores dicunt quod terra illa est feodum eiusdem ecclesie ita quod idem G. et antecessores sui semper tenuerunt de ecclesia. . . Et dicunt quod idem Gaufridus est natiuus Comitis Warenne et de eo tenet in uilenagio aliud tenementum. Postea uenit Gaufridus et cognouit quod est uillanus Comitis Warenne. Postea concordati sunt,' etc.

[2] Example, Fitz. Abr. Villen. 16. The proper reply to such a plea is shown by Bract. Note-book, pl. 1833: 'Et Iohannes dicit quod hoc ei nocere non debet, quia quicquid idem dicat de uillenagio, ipsemet ut liber homo sine contradiccione domini sui terram illam dedit Iohanni del Frid patri istius Iohannis pro homagio et seruicio suo . . . Consideratum est quod predictus Iohannes recuperauit seisinam suam, et Richerus in misericordia.' Liber Assis. ann. 43. pl. 1. f. 265 gives the contrary decision: 'Lassise agarde et prise, per quel il fuit troue quil [le defendant] fuit villein al Counte. . . mes troue fuit ouster que le Counte ne fut unques seisie de la terre, ne onques claima riens en la terre, et troue fuit que le plaintif fuit seisie et disseisie. Et sur ceo, le quel le plaintif recouerer, ou que le brief abateroit sont ajornes deuant eux mesmes a Westminster. A que jour per opinion de la Court le briefe abatu, per que le plaintif fuit non sue,' etc.

[3] A different view is taken by Stubbs, i. 484.

Convention with the lord.

Even against his lord the bondman had some standing ground for a civil action. It has rightly been maintained, that he could implead his master in consequence of an agreement with him. The assertion is not quite easy to prove however, and has been put forward too sweepingly[1]. At first sight it seems even that the old law books, i.e. those of Bracton and his followers, teach the opposite doctrine. They deal almost exclusively with the case of a feoffment made by the lord to a villain and his heirs, and give the feoffee an action only on the ground of implied manumission. The feoffor enfranchises his serf indirectly, even if he does not say so in as many words, because he has spoken of the feoffee's heirs, and the villain has no other heirs besides the lord[2]. The action eventually proceeds in this case, because it is brought not by a serf but by a freed man. One difficult passage in Bracton points another way; it is printed in a foot-note[3].

[1] Digby, Real Property, 3rd ed. p. 128. I may say at once that I fail to see any connexion between copyhold tenure and any express agreements between lord and villain.

[2] Bracton, 192 b: 'Si autem dominus ita dederit sine manumissione, servo et heredibus suis tenendum libere, presumi poterit de hoc quod servum voluit esse liberum, cum aliter servus heredes habere non possit nisi cum libertate et ita contra dominum excipientem de villenagio competit ei replicatio.' Cf. 23 b and Britton, i. 247; Fleta, 238; Littleton, secs. 205, 207.

[3] Bracton, 24 b: 'Si autem in charta hoc tantum contineatur, habendum et tenendum tali (cum sit servus) per liberum servitium huiusmodi verba non faciunt servum liberum nec dant ei liberum tenementum... Quia tenementum nichil confert nec detrahit personae, nisi praecedat, ut dictum est, homagium vel manumissio, vel quod tantundem valet de concessione domini, scilicet quod villanus libere teneat et quiete et per liberum servitium, *sibi et haeredibus suis*. Si autem hoc solum dicatur, quod teneat per liberum servitium [sibi et heredibus suis], si ejectus fuerit a quocunque non recuperet per assisam noue disseisine, ut liberum tenementum, quia domino competit assisa et non villano. Si tamen dominus ipsum ejecerit, quaeritur, an contra dominum agere possit de conventione, cum prima facie non habet personam standi in judicio ad hoc, quod dominus teneat ei conventionem, videtur quod sic, propter factum domini sui, ut si agat de conventione, et dominus excipiat de servitute, replicare poterit de facto domini sui, sicut supra dicitur de feoffamento. Nec debent jura juvare dominum contra voluntatem suam, quia semel voluit conventionem, et quamvis damnum sentiat, non tamen fit ei injuria et ex quo prudenter et scienter contraxit cum servo suo, tacite renunciavit exceptionem villenagii.'

There can be no doubt, that in it Bracton is speaking of a covenant made by the lord not with a free man or a freed man, but with a villain. This comes out strongly when it is said, that the lord, and not the villain, has the assize against intruders, and when the author puts the main question—is the feoffor bound to hold the covenant or not? The whole drift of the quotation can be understood only on the fundamental assumption that we have lord and villain before us. But there are four words which militate against this obvious explanation ; the words '*sibi et heredibus suis.*' We know what their meaning is —they imply enfranchisement and a freehold estate of inheritance. They involve a hopeless contradiction to the doctrine previously stated, a doctrine which might be further supported by references to Britton, Fleta and Bracton himself[1]. In short, if we accept them, we can hardly get out of confusion. Were our text of Bracton much more definitely and satisfactorily settled than it is[2], one would still feel tempted to strike them out ; as it is we have a text studded with interpolations and errors, and it seems quite certain that 'sibi et heredibus suis' has got into it simply because the compositor of Tottell's edition repeated it from the conclusion of the sentence immediately preceding, and so mixed up two cases, which were to be distinguished by this very qualification. The four words are missing in all the MSS. of the British Museum, the Bodleian and the Cambridge University Library[3]. I have no doubt that further verification will only confirm my opinion. On my assumption Bracton clearly distinguishes between two possibilities. In one case the deed simply binds the lord as to a particular person, in the other it binds him in perpetuity; and in this latter case, as there ought not to

---

[1] The freehold would be given and still 'non recuperet per assisam no. diss. quia domino competit assisa et non villano.'

[2] See my article, 'The Text of Bracton,' in the Law Quarterly Review, i. 189, et sqq. ; and Maitland, Introduction to the Note-book of Bracton, 26 sqq.

[3] The Cambridge MSS. have been inspected for me by Mr. Maitland.

be any heirs of a bondman but the lord, bondage is annihilated by the deed. It is not annihilated when one person is granted a certain privilege as to a particular piece of land, and in every other respect the grantee and all his descendants remain unfree[1]:—he has no freehold, but he has a special covenant to fall back upon. This seems to lie at the root of what Bracton calls privileged villainage by covenant as distinguished from villain socage[2].

Legal practice as to conventions.

The reader may well ask whether there are any traces of such an institution in practice, as it is not likely that Bracton would have indulged in mere theoretical disquisi-

[1] Comp. Bracton, f. 194 b : 'Quia ex quo mentionem fecit de heredibus praesumitur vehementer, quod dominus voluit servum esse liberum *quod quidem non esset, si de heredibus mentionem non fecerit.*'

[2] Bracton, f. 208 b : 'Est etiam villenagium non ita purum, sive concedatur libero homini *vel villano* ex conventione tenendum pro certis servitiis et consuetudinibus nominatis et expressis, quamvis servitia et consuetudines sunt villanae. Et unde si liber ejectus fuerit vel villanus *manumissus vel alienatus* (*corr. alienus* best MSS.) recuperare non poterunt ut liberum tenementum, cum sit villenagium et cadit assisa, vertitur tamen in juratam ad inquirendum de conventione propter voluntatem dimittentis et consensum, quia si quaerentes in tali casu recuperarint villenagium, non erit propter hoc domino injuriatum propter ipsius voluntatem et consensum, et contra voluntatem suam jura ei non subveniunt, quia si dominus potest *villanum manumittere et feoffare* multo fortius poterit *ei quandam conventionem facere,* et quia si potest id quod plus est, potest multo fortius id quod minus est.' We have here another difficulty with the text. The wording is so closely allied to the passage on 24 b. just quoted, and the last sentences seem to indicate so clearly that the case of a privileged villain is here opposed to manumission and feoffment, that the 'villanus manumissus vel alienus' looks quite out of place. Is it a later gloss? Even if it is retained, however, the passage points to a very material limitation of the lord's power. The holding in question can certainly not be described as being held 'at will.' To me the words in question look like a gloss or an addition, although very probably they were inserted early, perhaps by Bracton himself, who found it difficult to maintain consistently a villain's contractual rights against the lord. Another solution of the difficulty is suggested to me by Sir Frederick Pollock. He thinks '*villanus manumissus vel alienus*' correct, and lays stress on the fact, that personal condition does not matter in this case : that even though the tenant be free or *quoad* that lord as good as free, the assize lies not and there shall only be an action on the covenant. If we accept this explanation which saves the words under suspicion, we shall have to face another difficulty : the text would turn from *villanus* (*suus*) to *villanus alienus* and back to *villanus* (*suus*) without any intimation that the subject under discussion had been altered.

tions on such an important point. Now it would be difficult to find very many instances in point; the line between covenant and enfranchisement was so easily passed, and an incautious step would have such unpleasant consequences for landlords, that they kept as clear as possible of any deeds which might indirectly destroy their claims as to the persons of their villains[1]. On the other hand, even privileged serfs would have a great difficulty in vindicating their rights on the basis of covenant if they remained at the same time under the sway of the lord in general. The difficulties on both sides explain why Fleta and Britton endorse only the chief point of Bracton's doctrine, namely, the implied manumission, and do not put the alternative as to a covenant when heirs are not mentioned. Still I have come across some traces in legal practice[2] of contracts in the shape of the one discussed. A very interesting case occurred in Norfolk in 1227, before Martin Pateshull himself. A certain Roger of Sufford gave a piece of land to one of his villains, William Tailor, to hold freely by free services, and when Roger died, his son and heir William of Sufford confirmed the lease. When it pleased the lord afterwards to eject the tenant, this latter actually brought an assize of novel disseisin and recovered possession. Bracton's marginal note to the case runs thus: 'Note, that

---

[1] The later practice is well known. Any agreement with a bondman led to a forfeiture of the lord's rights. It may be seen at a glance that such could not have been the original doctrine. Otherwise why should the old books lay such stress on the mention of heirs?

[2] Besides the case from the Note-book which I discuss in the text, Bracton, f. 199, is in point: 'Item esto quod villanus teneat per liberum servitium sibi tantum, nulla facta mentione de heredibus, si cum ejectus fuerit proferat assisam, et cum objecta fuerit exceptio villenagii, replicet quod libere teneat et petat assisam, non valebit replicatio, ex quo nulla mentio facta est de heredibus, *quia liberum tenementum in hoc casu non mutat statum*, si fuerit sub potestate domini constitutus. Ut in eodem itinere (in ultimo itinere Martini de Pateshull) in comitatu Essex, assisa noue disseisine, si Radulphus de Goggenhal.' The villain fails in his assize and there has been no manumission, still it seems admitted that in this case the villain has acquired *liberum tenementum* by the lord's act. How can this be except on the supposition that there is a covenant enforceable by the villain against the lord?

the son of a villain recovered by an assize of novel disseisin a piece of land which his father had held in villainage, because the lord of the villain by his charter gave it to the son [i.e. to the plaintiff], even without manumission[1].' The court went in this case even further than Bracton's treatise would have warranted : the villain was considered as having the freehold, and an assize of novel disseisin was granted ; but although such a treatment of the case was perhaps not altogether sound, the chief point on which the contention rested is brought out clearly enough. There was a covenant, and in consequence an action, although there was no manumission; and it is to this point that the marginal note draws special attention[2].

Waynage. Again, we find in the beginning of Bracton's treatise a remark[3] which is quite out of keeping with the doctrine that the villain had no property to vindicate against his lord ; it is contradicted by other passages in the same book, and deserves to be considered the more carefully on that account. Our author is enumerating the cases in which the serf has an action against his lord. He follows Azo closely, and mentions injury to life or to limb as one cause. Azo goes on to say that a plaint may be originated by *intollerabilis injuria*, in the sense of corporeal injury. Bracton takes the expression in a very different sense ; he thinks that economic ruin is meant, and adds, ' Should the lord go so far as to take away the villain's very *waynage*, i.e. plough and plough-team, the villain has an action.' It is true that

[1] Bract. Note-book, pl. 1814: ' Nota quod filius villani recuperat per assisam noue disseisine terram quam pater suus tenuit in villenagio quia dominus villani illam dedit filio suo per cartam suam eciam sine manumissione.'

[2] F. W. Maitland tells me, that Concanen's Report of *Rowe* v. *Brenton* describes *bond conventioners* in Cornwall.

[3] Bracton, f. 6: ' Et in hoc legem habent contra dominos, quod stare possunt in judicio contra eos de vita et membris propter saevitiam dominorum, vel propter intollerabilem injuriam, ut si eos destruant, quod salvum non possit eis esse waynagium suum. [Hoc autem verum est de illis servis, qui tenent de antiquo dominico coronae, sed de aliis secus est, quia quandocunque placuerit domino, auferre poterit a villano suo waynagium suum et omnia bona sua.] Expedit enim reipublicae ne quis re sua male utatur.'

Bracton's text, as printed in existing editions, contains a
qualification of this remark; it is said that only serfs on
ancient demesne land are possessed of such a right.   But
the qualification is meaningless; the right of ancient
demesne tenants was quite different, as we shall see by-and-
by. The qualifying clause turns out to be inserted only in
later MSS. of the treatise, is wanting in the better MSS.,
and altogether presents all the characters of a bad gloss[1].
When the gloss is removed, we come in sight of the fact that
Bracton in the beginning of his treatise admits a distinct
case of civil action on the part of a villain against his lord.
The remark is in contradiction with the Roman as well as
with the established English doctrine, it is not supported
by legal practice in the thirteenth century, it is omitted by
Bracton when he comes to speak again of the 'persona
standi in judicio contra dominum[2].'   But there it is, and it
cannot be explained otherwise than as a survival of a time
when some part of the peasantry at least had not been
surrendered to the lord's discretion, but was possessed of
civil rights and of the power to vindicate them.   The
notion that the peasant ought to be specially protected in
the possession of instruments of agricultural labour comes
out, singularly enough, in the passage commented upon, but
it is not a singular notion in itself.   It occurs, as every one
knows, in the clause of the Great Charter, which says that
the villain who falls into the king's mercy is to be amerced
'saving his waynage.' We come across it often enough
in Plea Rolls in cases against guardians accused of having
wasted their ward's property.   One of the special points
in such cases often is, that a guardian or his steward has
been ruining the villains in the ward's manors by destroying their waynage[3]. Of course, the protection of the
peasant's prosperity, guaranteed by the courts in such

---

[1] See my article in the L. Q. R., i. 195.

[2] Bracton, f. 196-202.

[3] Coram Rege, 15 Edw. I, m. 18: '... licet habeant alia averia per que
distringi possent distringit eos per averia de carucis suis quod est contra
statutum domini Regis.' (Record Office.)

trials, is wholly due to a consideration of the interests of the ward; and the care taken of villains is exactly parallel to the attention bestowed upon oaks and elms. Still, the notion of waynage is in itself a peculiar and an important one, and whatever its ultimate origin may be, it points to a civil condition which does not quite fall within the lines of feudal law.

Villains not to be devised.

Another anomaly is supplied by Britton. After putting the case as strongly as possible against serfs, after treating them as mere chattels to be given and sold, he adds, 'But as bondmen are annexed to the freehold of the lord, they are not devisable by testament, and therefore Holy Church can take no cognisance of them in Court Christian, although devised in testament.' (I. 197.) The exclusion of villains is not peculiar to them; they share it with the greater part of landed possessions. 'As all the courts of civil jurisdiction had been prohibited from holding jurisdiction as to testamentary matters, and the Ecclesiastical Courts were not permitted to exercise jurisdiction as to any question relating to freehold, there was no court which could properly take cognisance of a testamentary gift of land as such [1].' The point to be noted is, that villains are held to be annexed to the freehold, although in theory they ought to be treated as chattels. The contradiction gives us another instance of the peculiar modification of personal servitude by the territorial element. The serf is not a colonus, he is not bound up with any particular homestead or plot of land, but he is considered primarily as a cultivator under manorial organisation, and for this reason there is a limitation on the lord's power of alienating him. Let it be understood, however, that the limitation in this case does not come before us as a remnant of independent rights of the peasant. It is imposed by those interests of the feudal suzerain and of the kin which precluded the possibility of alienating land by devise [2].

---

[1] Spence, Equitable Jurisdiction, i. 136.
[2] The Mirror of Justices, p. 110, follows Britton in this matter. This

An inquiry into the condition of villains would be Villain tenure and villain service. altogether incomplete, if it did not touch on the questions of villain tenure and villain services. Both are intimately connected with personal status, as may be seen from the very names, and both have to be very carefully distinguished from it. I have had to speak of prescription as a source of villainage. Opinions were very uncertain in this respect, and yet, from the mere legal point of view, there ought not to have been any difficulty about the matter. Bracton takes his stand firmly on the fundamental difference between status and tenure in order to distinguish clearly between serfs and free men in a servile position[1]. The villain is a man belonging to his lord personally; a villain holding (*villenagium*) is land held at the will of the lord, without any certainty as to title or term of enjoyment, as to kind or amount of services[2]. Serfs are mostly, though not necessarily, found on villain land; it does not follow that all those seated on villain land are serfs. Free men are constantly seen taking up a *villenagium*; they do not lose by it in personal condition; they have no protection against the lord, if he choose to alter their services or oust them from the holding, but, on the other hand, they are free to go when they please. There is still less reason to treat as serfs such free peasants as are subjected to base services, i.e. to the same kind of services and payments as the villains, but on certain conditions, not more and not less. Whatever the customs may be, if they are certain, not only the person holding by them but the

curious book is altogether very interesting on the subject of villeinage, but as its information is of a very peculiar stamp, I have not attempted to use it currently on the same level with other authorities. I prefer discussing it by itself in App. III.

[1] Bracton, f. 26 b, 200. Cf. Bract. Note-book, pl. 141 : 'Dicit quod tunc temporis scilicet in itinere iusticiariorum tenuit ipse quamdam terram in uillenagium quam emerat, et tunc cognouit quod terra illa fuit uillenagium, et precise defendit quod nunquam cognouit se esse uillanum.'

[2] Britton, ii. 13; Y. B. 20/21 Edw. I, p. 41 : 'Kar nent plus neit a dire, jeo tenk les tenements en vileynage de le Deen etc. ke neit a dire ke jeo tenk les tenements . . . . . a la volunte le Deen etc.'

plot he is using are free, and the tenure may be defended at law[1].

Such are the fundamental positions in Bracton's treatise, and there can be no doubt that they are borne out in a general way by legal practice. But if from the general we turn to the particular, if we analyse the thirteenth-century decisions which are at the bottom of Bracton's teaching, we shall find in many cases notions cropping up, which do not at all coincide with the received views on the subject. In fact we come across many apparent contradictions which can be attributed only to a state of fermentation and transition in the law of the thirteenth century.

Martin of Besten-over's case.

Martin of Bestenover's case is used by Bracton in his treatise as illustrating the view that tenure has no influence on status[2]. It was a long litigation, or rather a series of litigations. Already in the first year of King John's reign we hear of a final concord between John of Montacute and Martin of Bestenover as to a hundred acres held by the latter[3]. The tenant is ejected however, and brings an assize of mort d'ancestor against Beatrice of Montacute, who, as holding in dower, vouches her son John to warranty. The latter excepts against Martin as a villain. A jury by consent of the parties is called in, and we have their verdict reported three times in different records[4]. They say that Martin's father Ailfric held of John Montacute's father a hundred acres of land and fifty sheep besides, for which he had to pay 20s. a year, to be tallaged reasonably, when the lord tallaged his subjects, and that he was not allowed to give his daughter away in marriage before making a fine to the lord according to agreement. We do not know the decision of the judges in John's time, but both from the tenor of the verdict and from what followed, we may conclude that Martin succeeded in vindicating his right to the land.

[1] Bracton, f. 168.
[2] Ibid., f. 199 b.
[3] Palgrave, Rotuli Curiae Regis, ii. 192.
[4] Placitorum Abbrev. 25, 29; Note-book, pl. 88. (The father is called Ailfricus in the Plea Roll Divers terms 2 John, 2 d., at the Record Office.)

Proceedings break out again at the beginning of Henry III's reign.

In 1219 John of Montacute is again maintaining that Martin is his villain, in answer as it seems to an action *de libertate probanda* which Martin has brought against him. The court goes back to the verdict of the jury in John's time, and finds that by this verdict the land is proved to be of base tenure, and the person to be free. The whole is repeated again[1] on a roll of 1220; whether we have two decisions, one of 1219 and the other of 1220, or merely two records of the same decision, is not very clear, nor is it very important. But there are several interesting points about this case. The decision in 1220 is undoubtedly very strong on the distinction between status and tenure: ' nullum erat placitum in curia domini Regis de villenagio corporis ipsius Martini nisi tantum de villenagio et consuetudinibus terre,' etc. As to tenure, the court delivers an opinion which is entitled to special consideration, and has been specially noticed by Bracton both in his Note-book and in his treatise. ' If Martin,' say the judges on the roll of 1219, ' wishes to hold the land, let him perform the services which his father has been performing; if not, the lord may take the land into his hands[2].' The same thing is repeated almost literally on the roll of 1220. Bracton draws two inferences from these decisions. One is suggested by the beginning of the sentence ; ' If Martin wishes to hold the land.' Both in the Note-book and in the treatise Bracton deduces from it, that holding and remaining on the land depended on the wish of Martin, who as a free man was entitled to go away when he pleased[3].

---

[1] Bract. Note-book, pl. 88.

[2] Case 70 : ' Consideratum est quod terra illa est uilenagium ipsius Hugonis (corr. Johannis), et quod si Martinus uoluerit terram tenere faciat consuetudines quas pater suus fecit, sin autem capiat terram suam in manum suam.'

[3] Marginal remark in the Note-book to pl. 70 : ' Nota quod liber homo potest facere uillanas consuetudines racione tenementi uillani set propter hoc non erit uillanus, quia potest relinquere tenementum.' Comp. Mr. Maitland's note to the case.

The judgment does not exactly say this, but as to the right of a free person to leave the land there can be no doubt.

Tenant right of free man holding in villainage.

The second conclusion is, that if a free man hold in villainage by villain services he cannot be ejected by the lord against his will, provided he is performing the services due from the holding. What Bracton says here is distinctly implied by the decisions of 1219 and 1220, which subject the lord's power of dealing with the land to a condition—non-performance of services[1]. There can be no question as to the importance of such a view; it contains, as it were, the germ of copyhold tenure[2]. It places villainage substantially on the same footing as freehold, which may also be forfeited by discontinuance of the services, although the procedure for establishing a forfeiture in that case would be a far more elaborate one. And it must be understood that Bracton's deduction by no means rests on the single case before us. He appeals also to a decision of William Raleigh, who granted an assize of mort d'ancestor to a free man holding in villainage[3]. Unfortunately the original record of this case has been lost. The decision in a case of 1225 goes even further. It is an assize of novel disseisin brought by a certain William the son of Henry against his lord Bartholomew the son of Eustace. The defendant excepts against the plaintiff as his villain; the court finds, on the strength of a verdict, that he is a villain, and still they decide that William may hold the land in dispute, if he consents to perform the services; if not, he forfeits his land[4]. Undoubtedly the decision before

---

[1] Bracton, f. 199 b: 'Unde videtur per hoc, quod licet liber homo teneat villenagium per villanas consuetudines, contra voluntatem suam ejici non debet, dum tamen facere voluerit consuetudines quae pertinent ad villenagium, et quae praestantur ratione villenagii, et non ratione personae.'

[2] Cf. Blackstone's characteristic of copyholds: 'But it is the very condition of the tenure in question that the lands be holden only so long as the stipulated service is performed, quamdiu velint et possint facere debitum servitium et solvere debitas pensiones.' (Law Tracts, ii. 153.)

[3] Bract. f. 200.

[4] Bract. Note-book, pl. 1103: 'Et ideo consideratum est quod Willelmus conuictus est de uilenagio et si facere uoluerit predictas consuetudines teneat illam

us is quite isolated, and it goes against the rules of procedure in such cases. Once the exception proved, nothing ought to have been said as to the conditions of the tenure. Still the mistake is characteristic of a state of things which had not quite been brought under the well-known hard and fast rule. And the best way to explain it is to suppose that the judges had in their mind the more familiar case of free men holding in villainage, and gave decision in accordance with Martin of Bestenover *v.* Montacute, and the case decided by Raleigh[1]. All these instances go clean against the usually accepted doctrine, that holding in villainage is the same as holding at the will of the lord : the celebrated addition ' according to the custom of the manor ' would quite fit them. They bring home forcibly one main consideration, that although in the thirteenth century the feudal doctrine of non-interference of the state between lord and servile tenantry was possessed of the field, its victory was by no means complete. Everywhere we come across remnants of a state of things in which one portion at least of the servile class had civil rights as well as duties in regard to the lord.

Matters were even more unsettled as to customs and services in their relation to status and tenure. What services, what customs are incompatible with free status, with free tenure? Is the test to be the kind of services or merely their certainty? Bracton remarks that the

The test of services.

bouatam terre per easdem consuetudines, sin autem faciat Bartholomeus de terra et de ipso Willelmo uoluntatem suam ut de uillano suo et ei liberatur Cf. Mr. Maitland's note.

[1] I should like to draw attention to one more case which completes the picture from another side. Bract. Note-book, pl. 784 : ' Symon de T. petit versus Adam de H. et Thomam P. quod faciant ei consuetudines et recta seruicia que ei facere debent de tenemento quod de eo tenent in uillenagio in T. Et ipsi ueniunt et cognoscunt quod uillani sunt. Et Symon concedit eis quod teneant tenementa sua faciendo inde seruicia quae pertinent ad uillenagium, ita tamen quod non dent plus in auxilium ad festum St. Mich. nec per annum quam duodecim denarios scilicet quilibet ipsorum et hoc nomine tallagii.'—The writ of customs and services was out of place between lord and villain. The usual course was distraint. The case is clearly one of privileged villainage, but it is well to note that although the services are in one respect certain, the persons remain unfree.

G

payment of merchet, i.e. of a fine for giving away one's daughter to be married, is not in keeping with personal freedom. But he immediately puts in a kind of retractation[1], and indeed in the case of Martin of Bestenover it was held that the peasant was free although paying merchet. To tenure, merchet, being a personal payment, should have no relation whatever. In case of doubt as to the character of the tenure, the inquiry ought to have been entirely limited to the question whether rents and services were certain or not[2], because it was established that even a free tenement could be encumbered with base services. In reality the earlier practice of the courts was to inquire of what special kind the services and customs were, whether merchet and fine for selling horses and oxen had been paid, whether a man was liable to be tallaged at will or bound to serve as reeve, whether he succeeded to his tenancy by 'junior right' (the so-called Borough English rule), and the like.

All this was held to be servile and characteristic of villainage[3]. I shall have to discuss the question of services and customs again, when I come to the information supplied by manorial documents. It is sufficient for my present purpose to point out that two contradictory views were taken of it during the thirteenth century; 'certain or uncertain?' was the catchword in one case; 'of what kind?' in the other. A good illustration of the unsettled condition of the law is afforded by the case Prior

---

[1] Bracton, f. 208 b.

[2] Ibid., f. 200.

[3] Bract. Note-book, pl. 63: 'Dicunt quod idem W. nullum habuit liberum tenementum quia ipse uillanus fuit et fecit omnimoda uilenagia quia non potuit filiam suam maritare nec bouem suum uendere. 1819: R. de M. posuit se in magnam assisam Dom. Reg. in comitatu de consuetudinibus et seruiciis que Th. B. petit uersus eum, unde idem Th. exigebat ab eodem R. quod redderet ei de uillenagio per annum 19 den. et aruram trium dierum et messuram trium dierum . . . et gersumam pro filia sua maritanda et unam gallinam ad Natale et tot oua ad Pascha et tallagium et quod sit prepositus suus. Set quia illa sunt seruilia et ad uillenagium spectancia et non ad liberum tenementum, consideratum est quod magna assisa non iacet inter eos, set fiat inquisicio per xii,' etc. Cf. 794, 1005, 1225, 1661.

of Ripley *v.* Thomas Fitz-Adam. According to the Prior, the jurors called to testify as to services and tenures had, while admitting the payment of tallage and merchet, asked leave to take the advice of Robert Lexington, a great authority on the bench, whether a holding encumbered by such customs could be free[1].

The subject is important, not only because its treatment shows to what extent the whole law of social distinctions was still in a state of fermentation, but also because the classification of tenures according to the nature of customs may afford valuable clues to the origin of legal disabilities in economic and political facts. The plain and formal rule of later law, which is undoubtedly quite fitted to test the main issue as to the power of the lord, is represented in earlier times by a congeries of opinions, each of which had its foundation in some matter of fact. We see here a state of things which on the one hand is very likely to invite an artificial simplification, by an application of some one-sided legal conception of serfdom, while on the other hand it seems to have originated in a mixture and confusion of divers classes of serfs and free men, which shaded off into each other by insensible degrees.

The procedure in trials touching the question of status was decidedly favourable to liberty. To begin with, only one proof was accepted as conclusive against it—absolute proof that the kinsfolk of the person claimed were villains by descent[2]. The verdict of a jury was not sufficient to settle the question[3], and a man who had been refused an assize in consequence of the defendant pleading

The procedure in questions of status.

---

[1] Bract. Note-book, 281 : ' Et Prior dicit quod in parte bene recordantur set in parte parum dicunt quia iuratores dixerunt quod debuit dare xii. den. pro filia sua maritanda, et debuit plures alias consuetudines et petierunt respectum ut assensum habere possent a domino Roberto de Lexintona utrum hoc esset liberum tenementum ex quo sciunt quid debuit facere et quid non et nullum respectum habere potuerunt.'

[2] Example—Bract. Note-book, pl. 1887. Fitzherbert, Abr. Villen. 38 (13 Ed. I) : ' Quia predictus J. nullam probacionem producit neque sectam et cognoscit quod ille est in seisina ... de patre predicti W. quem potuit produxisse ad probacionem, consideratum est quod predicti W. et R. liberi maneant.'

[3] Bracton, f. 199. The jury came in only by consent of the parties.

villainage in bar had the right notwithstanding such decision to sue for his liberty. When the proof by kinship came on, two limitations were imposed on the party maintaining servitude: women were not admitted to stand as links in the proof because of their frailty and of the greater dignity of a man, and one man was not deemed sufficient to establish the servile condition of the person claimed[1]. If the defendant in a plea of niefty, or a plaintiff in an action of liberty, could convincingly show that his father or any not too remote ancestor had come to settle on the lord's land as a stranger, his liberty as a descendant was sufficiently proved[2]. In this way to prove personal villainage one had to prove villainage by birth. Recognition of servile status in a court of record and reference to a deed are quite exceptional.

The coincidence in all these points against the party maintaining servitude is by no means casual; the courts proclaimed their leaning 'in favour of liberty' quite openly, and followed it in many instances besides those just quoted. It was held, for instance, that in defending liberty every means ought to be admitted. The counsel pleading for it sometimes set up two or three pleas against his adversary and declined to narrow his contention, thus transgressing the rules against duplicity of plea 'in favour of liberty[3].' In the case of a stranger settling on the land, his liberty was always assumed, and the court declined to construe any uncertainty of condition against him[4]. When villainage was pleaded in bar against a person out of the power of the lord, the special question was very

Britton, i. 207; Fitzherbert, Abr. Villen. 37.

[2] Court Rolls of Havering atte Bower, Essex, Augment. Off. Rolls, xiv. 38. (Curia—die Jovis proxima ante festum St. Bartholomaei Apostoli anno r. r. Ricardi II, 21mo.) 'Inquisicio ... dicit ... quod non est aliquis homo natiuus de sanguine ingressus feodum domini, set dicunt quod est quidam Johannes Shillyng qui Sepius dictus fuerat natiuus. Et dicunt ultra quod quidam Johannes Shillyng pater predicti Johannis fuit alienigena et quod predictus Johannes Shillyng quod ad eorum cognitionem est liber et libere condicionis et non natiuus.'

[3] Fitzherbert, Abr. Villen. 32 (H. 19 Edw. II).

[4] Ibid. 5 (13 Edw. I).

often examined by a jury from the place where the person excepted to had been lately resident, and not by a jury from the country where he had been born[1]. This told against the lord, of course, because the jurors might often have very vague notions as to the previous condition of their new fellow-countryman[2].

It would be impossible to say in what particular cases this partiality of the law is to be taken as a consequence of enlightened and humanitarian views making towards the liberation of the servile class, and in what cases it may be traced to the fact that an original element of freedom had been attracted into the constitution of villainage and was influencing its legal development despite any general theory of a servile character. There is this to be noticed in any case, that most of the limitations we have been speaking of are found in full work at the very time when villainage was treated as slavery in the books. One feature, perhaps the most important of all, is certainly not dependent on any progress of ideas: however complete the lord's power over the serf may have been, it was entirely bound up with the manorial organisation. As soon as the villain had got out of its boundaries he was regularly treated as a free man and protected in the enjoyment of liberty so long as his servile status had not been proved[3]. Such protection was a legal necessity, a necessary complement to the warranty offered by the state to its real free men. There could be no question of allowing the lord to seize on any person whom he thought fit to claim as his serf. And, again, if the political power inherent in the manor gave the lord *A* great privileges and immunities as to the people living under his sway, this same manorial power began to tell against him as soon as such people had got under the sway of lord *B* or within the privileged

---

[1] Fitzherbert, l. c. : ' E ce issu fuit trie par gents de paiis ou le maner est e nemi ou il nasquist par touts les justices.'

[2] Rotuli Parliam. ii. 192. Hargrave's argument in the Negro Somerset's case is very good on all these points. Howell, State Trials, xx. 38, 39.

[3] Bracton, 201 ; Britton, i. 202 sq.

town *C.* The dependant could be effectually coerced only if he got back to his unfree nest again or through the means of such kinsfolk as he had left in the unfree nest[1]. And so the settlement of disputed rights connected with status brings home forcibly two important positions : first the theory of personal subjection is modified in its legal application by influence in favour of liberty; and next this influence is not to be traced exclusively to moral and intellectual progress, but must be accounted for to a great extent by peculiarities in the political structure of feudalism.

Enfran-
chisement.
One point remains to be investigated in the institution of villainage, namely modes in which a villain might become free. I have had occasion to notice the implied manumission which followed from a donation of land to a bondman and his heirs, which in process of time was extended to all contracts and concords between a lord and his serf. A villain was freed also, as is well known, by remaining for a year and a day on the privileged soil of a crown manor or a chartered town[2]. As to direct manumission, its usual mode was the grant of a charter by which the lord renounced all rights as to the person of his villain. Traces of other and more archaic customs may have survived in certain localities, but, if so, they were quite exceptional. Manumission is one of the few subjects touched by Glanville in the doctrine of villainage, and he is very particular as to its conditions and effects. He says that a serf cannot buy his freedom, because he has no money or goods of his own. His liberty may be bought by a third person however, and his lord may liberate him as to himself, but not as regards third persons. There seems to be a want of clearness in, if not some contradiction between these two last statements,

---

[1] Bracton, f. 6, and on many other occasions.

[2] Co. Lit. 137, b. Cf. King Henry I's writ in favour of the Monastery of Abingdon. Bigelow, Placita Anglo-Normannica, 96: 'Facias habere F. abbati omnes homines suos qui de terra sua exierunt propter herberiam curie mee.' Henry II puts it the other way, p. 220 : 'Nisi sunt in dominio meo.'

because one does not see how manumission by a stranger could possibly be wider than that effected by the lord. Again, the whole position of a freed man who remains a serf as regards everybody but his lord is very difficult to realize, even if one does not take the later view into account, which is exactly the reverse, namely that a villain is free against everybody but his lord. I may be allowed to start a conjecture which will find some support in a later chapter, when we come to speak about the treatment of freedom and serfdom in manorial documents. It seems to me that Glanville has in mind liberation *de facto* from certain duties and customs, such as agricultural work for instance, or the payment of merchet. Such liberation would not amount to raising the status of a villain, although it would put him on a very different footing as to his lord[1]. However this may be, if from Glanville's times we come down to Bracton and to his authorities, we shall find all requirements changed, but distinct traces of the former view still lingering in occasional decisions and practices. There are frequent cases of villains buying their freedom with their own money[2], but the practice of selling them for manumission to a stranger is mentioned both in Bracton's Treatise[3] and in his Note-

---

[1] A most curious pleading based on the conceptions of Glanville occurs in a Cor. Rege case of 10 Henry III, which was pointed out to me by F. Maitland. See App. IV. Mr. York Powell suggests that the limitation may have originated in the fact, that in early times a man could no more give away a slave from his family estate without the consent of the family than he could give away the estate itself or part of it. There was no reason for such limitation in the case of a slave that had been bought with one's private money. Hence the necessity of selling a slave in order to emancipate him. The conjecture seems a very probable one, but the question remains, how such ancient practice could have left a trace in the feudal period. The explanation in the text may possibly account for the tenacity of the notion.

[2] Note-book, pl. 31, 343.

[3] Bracton, f. 194, 195. Bracton's text has been rendered almost unintelligible here by the careless punctuation of his editors, and Sir Travers Twiss' translation is as wrong and misleading as usual. I will just give the passage in accordance with the reading of Digby, 222 (Bodleian Libr.), which is the best of all the MSS. I have seen : ' Quia esto quod seruus uelit manumitti et cum nichil habeat proprium eligat fidem alicuius qui eum emat quasi pro

book. A decision of 1226 distinctly repeats Glanville's
teaching that a man may liberate his serf as to himself
and not as to others. The marginal note in the Note-
book very appropriately protests against such a view, which
is certainly quite inconsistent with later practice[1]. Such
flagrant contradictions between authorities which are separated barely by some sixty or seventy years, and on points
of primary importance too, can only tend to strengthen
the inference previously drawn from other facts—that the
law on the subject was by no means square and settled
even by the time of Bracton, but was in every respect in a
state of transition.

denariis suis, per talem emptionem non consequitur emptus aliquam libertatem
nisi tantum quod mutat dominum. In re empta in primis solui debet pretium,
postea sequitur traditio rei: soluitur hic pretium pro natiuo, set nulla subse-
quitur traditio, sed semper manet in uillenagio quo prius. Si tenementum
adquirat tenendum libere et heres manumissoris uel alius successor eum
eiciat, si petat per assisam et heres opponat uillenagium, et villanus replicet
de manumissione et emptione, heres triplicare poterit, quod imperfecta fuit
emptio siue manumissio eo quod nunquam in uita uenditoris subsecuta fuit
traditio, et ita talis semper remanebit sub potestate heredis.'

[1] Note-book, pl. 1749: 'Iudicatum est quod liber sit quantum ad heredem
manumittentis et non quantum ad alios, quod iudicium non est uerum.'

CHAPTER III.

ANCIENT DEMESNE.

THE old law books mention one kind of villainage which Definition. stands out in marked contrast with the other species of servile tenure. The peasants belonging to manors which were vested in the crown at the time of the Conquest follow a law of their own. Barring certain exceptions, of which more will be said presently, they enjoy a certainty of condition protected by law. They are personally free, and although holding in villainage, nobody has the right to deprive them of their lands, or to alter the condition of the tenure, by increasing or changing the services. Bracton calls their condition one of privileged villainage, because their services are base but certain, and because they are protected not by the usual remedies supplied at common law to free tenants, but by peculiar writs which enforce the custom of the manor[1]. It seems well worth the while to carefully investigate this curious case with a view to get at the reasons of a notable deviation from the general course, for such investigation may throw some reflected light on the treatment of villainage in the common law.

Legal practice is very explicit as to the limitation of ancient demesne in time and space. It is composed of the manors which belonged to the crown at the time of the Conquest[2]. This includes manors which had been given away subsequently, and excludes such as had lapsed to the

---

[1] Bracton, 209; cf. 7 and 200. Britton, ii. 13.

[2] Bracton, 209: 'Villenagium privilegiatum . . . tenetur de Rege a Conquestu Angliae.' Cf. Blackstone, Law Tracts, ii. 128.

king after the Conquest by escheat or forfeiture[1]. Possessions granted away by Saxon kings before the Conquest
are equally excluded[2]. In order to ascertain what these
manors were the courts reverted to the Domesday description of *Terra Regis.* As a rule these lands were entered as
crown lands, T. R. E. and T. R. W., that is, were considered
to have been in the hand of King Edward in 1066, and
in the hand of King William in 1086. But strictly and
legally they were crown lands at the moment when King
William's claim inured, or to use the contemporary phrase,
'on the day when King Edward was alive and dead.' The
important point evidently was that the Norman king's
right in this case bridged over the Conquest, and for this
reason such possessions are often simply said to have been
royal demesne in the time of Edward the Confessor. This
legal view is well illustrated by a decision of the King's
Council, quoted by Belknap, Chief Justice of the Common
Pleas, in 1375. It was held that the manor of Tottenham,
although granted by William the Conqueror to the Earl of
Chester before the compilation of Domesday, was ancient
demesne, as having been in the hands both of St. Edward
and of the Conqueror[3]. And so 1066 and not 1086 is the
decisive year for the legal formation of this class of manors[4].

---

[1] Madox, History of the Exchequer, i. 704: 'Tallagium dominiorum et
escaetarum et custodiarum.'

[2] Bract. Note-book, 1237 (the prior of St. Swithin denies a manor to be
ancient demesne): '. . . per cc annos ante conquestum Anglie [terre] date
fuerunt priori et conventui et ab aliis quam regibus.'

[3] Y. B. Trin. 49 Edw. III, pl. 8 (Fitzherbert, Abr. Monstraver. 4): '. . . touts
les demesnes qui fuerent en la maine Seint E. sont aunciens demesne, mesque
ils fuerent aliens a estraunge mains quant le liver de Domesday se fist, come
il avient del manor de Totenham qui fut en autre maine a temps de Domesday fait, come en le dit livers fait mencion, que il fuit adonques al Counte
de Cestre.'

[4] Very curious pleadings occurred in 1323. Y. B. 15 Edw. II, p. 455:
'*Ber(wick)* Ils dient en l'Exchequer que serra (*corr.* terra) R. serra ecrit sur le
margin en cas ou cest ancien demene en Domesday, mes ceo fust escript sur
le dyme foille apres sur un title terra R., mesine (*corr.* mes une *or* mesqe?)
R. fuit escript sur le margin de chescun foille apres, e tout ceo la est anciene
demene a ceo quil nient (*corr.* dient), mes ascunes gens entendent que les
terres qui furent les demenes le Roy St. Edward sont auncien demene, e

In many respects the position of the peasantry in ancient Tenure in
ancient demesne is nearly allied to that of men holding in villain-demesne a age at common law.   They perform all kinds of agri-kind of cultural services and are subject to duties quite analogousvillainage. to those which prevail in other places; we may find on these ancient manors almost all the incidents of servile custom. Sometimes very harsh forms of distress are used against the tenants[1]; forfeiture for non-performance of services and non-payments of rents was always impending, in marked contrast with the considerate treatment of free tenantry in such cases[2].   We often come across such base customs as the payment of merchet in connexion with the 'villain socmen' of ancient demesne[3].   And such instances would afford ample proof of the fact that their status has branched off from the same stem as villainage, if such proof were otherwise needed.

The side of privilege is not less conspicuous.   The indica-Privileges
of ancient tions given by the law books must be largely supplementeddemesne.

autres dient fors les terres que le Conquerour conquist, que furent en la seissin St. Edward le jour quil mourust sont anciene demene.' Although a difference of opinion is mentioned it is not material, for this reason, that the entry as *Terra Regis*, at least T. R. E., is absolutely required to prove a manor ancient demesne.   I give the entry on the Plea Roll in App. V.

[1] I think only distress can be implied by the remark of Bereford J. Y. B. 30/31 Edw. I, p. 19: 'Quant vous vendrez a loustel, fetes de vostre archevileyn ceo qe vous vodrez.'   The words are strange and possibly corrupt.

[2] Blackstone, Law Tracts, ii. 153: 'They cannot alienate tenements otherwise than by surrender into the lord's hand.'   Bracton, 209.

[3] In a most curious description of the customs of villain sokemen of Stoneleigh, Warwick, in the Register of Stoneleigh Abbey, I find the following entries: 'Item sokemanni predicti filias suas non possunt maritare sine licencia domini prout patet anno viij Regis E. filii Regis E. per rotulum curie in quo continetur quod Matildis de Canle in plena curia fecit finem cum domino pro ij sol. quia maritauit filiam suam Thome de Horwelle sine licencia domini. . . . Item anno Regis H. lvj continetur in rotulo curie quod Willelmus Michel fuit in misericordia quia maritauit filiam suam sine licencia domini et similiter decenarii fuerunt in misericordia quia hoc concelauerunt.' As to the Stoneleigh Register, see App. VI.   Another instance of merchet in an ancient demesne manor is afforded by the Ledecumbe (Letcombe) Regis Court Rolls of 1272.   Chapter House, County Bags, Berks. No. 3, m. 12: 'Johannes le Jeune se redemit ad maritandum et fecit finem xij sol. . . . Johannes Atwel redemit filiam suam anno predicto' (Record Office).

from plea rolls and charters. The special favour shown to the population on soil of ancient demesne extends much further than a regulation of manorial duties would imply, it resolves itself to a large extent into an exemption from public burdens. The king's manor is treated as a franchise isolated from the surrounding hundred and shire, its tenants are not bound to attend the county court or the hundred moot[1], they are not assessed with the rest for danegeld or common amercements or the murder fine[2], they are exempted from the jurisdiction of the sheriff[3], and do not serve on juries and assizes before the king's justices[4]; they are free from toll in all markets and custom-houses[5]. Last, but not least, they do not get taxed with the country at large, and for this reason they have originally no representatives in parliament when parliament forms itself. On the other hand, they are liable to be tallaged by the king without consent of parliament, by virtue of his private right as opposed to his political right[6]. This last privilege gave rise to a very abnormal state of things, when ancient demesne land had passed from the crown to a subject. The rule was, that the

---

[1] Henry II's charter to Stoneleigh Abbey : ' Quieta de schiris et hundredis, et murdro et danegeldo, et placitis et querelis, et geldis et auxiliis, et omni consuetudine et exactione' (Dugdale, Monasticon, v. 447).

[2] Close Roll, 12 Henry III, m. 11, d : 'Monstrauerunt domino Regi homines de Esindene et de Beyford, quod occasione misericordiae c. librarum, in quam totus Comitatus Hertfordie incidit coram iusticiariis ultimo itinerantibus . . . hidagium quoddam assedit vicecomes super eos ad auxilium faciendum ceteris de comitatu ad misericordiam illam acquietandam et inde eos distringit. Quia vero predicti homines nec alii de dominicis domini Regis sectam faciunt ad comitatum et ea racione non tenentur ad misericordiam ceterorum de comitatu illo acquietandam auxilium facere aut inde participes esse, mandatum est vicecomiti Hertfordie quod homines predictos in hidagio et demanda pacem habere permittat' (Record Office). Placita de Quo Warranto, 777, 778: ' Non quieti de communi amerciamento nisi tantum in Stonle.'

[3] Viner, Abr. v. Anc. Dem. C[2], 1 ; cf. E, 20. Madox, Hist. of Exch., i. 418, note *l*: 'Quieti de auxilio vicecomitis et baillivorum suorum.'

[4] Cor. Rege, Mich. 5 E. II, m. 77: '(Juratores dicunt quod homines de Wycle) in itinere respondent per quatuor et prepositum sicut cetere ville de corpore comitatus.' This against their claim to hold in ancient demesne.

[5] Viner, Abr. Anc. Dem. B. 1, 4, 6.

[6] Madox, Exch., i. 412, 698.

new lord could not tallage his tenants unless in consequence
of a royal writ, and then only at the same time and in the
same proportion as the king tallaged the demesnes remaining in his hand[1]. This was an important limitation of
the lord's power, and a consequence of the wish to guard
against encroachments and arbitrary acts. But it was at
the same time a curious perversion of sovereignty:—the
person living on land of this description could not be taxed
with the county[2], and if he was taxed with the demesnes,
his lord received the tax, and not the sovereign. I need
not say that all this got righted in time, but the anomalous
condition described did exist originally. There are traces
of a different view by which the power of imposing tallage
would have been vested exclusively in the king, even
when the manor to be taxed was one that had passed
out of his hand[3]. But the general rule up to the fourteenth century was undoubtedly to relinquish the proceeds to the holder of the manor. Such treatment is
eminently characteristic of the conception which lies at
the bottom of the whole institution of ancient demesne. It
is undoubtedly based on the private privilege of royalty.
All the numerous exceptions and exemptions from public
liabilities and duties flow from one source: the king does

---

[1] Stubbs, ii. 566, 567 (Libr. ed.); Madox, Exch., i. 751.

[2] Cor. R. M. 5 E. II, m. 77: 'Quando communitas comitatus talliatur . . .
predicti homines taxantur sicut ceteri villani ejusdem comitatus' (against the
ancient demesne claim).

[3] Fitzherbert, Abr. Monstauerunt, 6 (H. 32 E. III): '. . . quant le roi taile
les burghs a taunt come ils paia a taile pur tant il nous distreint.' *Th.*: 'Entend qe les feoffes le roy auront taile?' quasi diceret non, 'car cest un regalte
qui proprement attient al roy et a nul auter.' *Clam.*: 'Tout aura il tail il
serra leue en due maner sil auront breve hors del chauncerie al viconte, sc.
quod habere facias racionable taile.' The men of King's Ripton, Hunts.,
who were constantly wrangling about their rights with the Abbot of Ramsey,
the lord of the manor, maintained that they had never been tallaged nisi
tantummodo ad opus Regis, and their claim was corroborated by an inspection of the Exchequer Rolls (Madox, Exch., i. 757, n). Before granting a
writ of tallage to the Abbot of Stoneleigh in 1253, Henry III had an inquisition
made as to the precedents. It was found that 'Nunquam predictum manerium de Stonle talliatum fuit postquam Johannes Rex predictum manerium
dedit predicti Abbati et Conventui' (Stoneleigh Reg., f. 25).

not want his land and his men to be subjected to any vexatious burdens which would lessen their power of yielding income[1]. Once fenced in by royal privilege, the ancient demesne manor keeps up its private immunity, even though it ceases to be royal. And this is the second fact, with which one has to reckon. If the privileged villainage of ancient demesne is founded on the same causes as villainage pure and simple, the distinguishing element of 'privilege' is supplied to it by the private interest of the king. This seems obvious enough, but it must be insisted upon, because it guards against any construction which would pick out one particular set of rights, or one particular kind of relations as characteristic of the institution. Legal practice and later theory concerned themselves mostly with peculiarities of procedure, and with the eventuality of a subject owning the manor. But the peculiar modes of litigation appropriate to the ancient demesne must not be disconnected from other immunities, and the ownership of a private lord is to be considered only as engrafted on the original right of the king. With this preliminary caution, we may proceed to an examination of those features which are undoubtedly entitled to attract most attention, namely, the special procedure which is put in action when questions arise in any way connected with the soil of ancient demesne.

Parvum breve de recto. Bracton says, that in such cases the usual assizes and actions do not lie, and the 'little writ of right close' must be used 'according to the custom of the manor.' The writ is a 'little and a close' one, because it is directed by the king to the bailiffs of the manor and not to the justices or to the sheriff[2].

It does not concern freehold estate, but only land of base though privileged tenure. An action for freehold also may

---

[1] The Law-books say so distinctly. Britton, ii. 13: 'Et pur ceo qe teus sokemans sount nos gaynours de nos terres, ne voloms mie qe teles gentz seint a nule part somouns de travailer en jurez ne en enquestes, for qe en maners a queus il appendent.' Cf. Fleta, p. 4.

[2] Natura Brevium, f. 3 b (ed. Pynson).

be begun in a manorial court, but in that case the writ will be 'the writ of right patent' and not 'the little writ of right close[1].'

The exclusion of the tenants from the public courts is a self-evident consequence of their base condition; in fact, pleading ancient demesne in bar of an action is, in legal substance, the same thing as pleading villainage[2]. Of course, an outlet was provided by the manorial writ in this case, and there was no such outlet for villains outside the ancient demesne; but as to the original jurisdiction in common law courts, jurisdiction that is in the first instance, the position was identical. Though legally self-evident, this matter is often specially noticed, and sometimes stress is laid on peculiarities of procedure, such as the inapplicability of the duel and the grand assize[3] in land to ancient demesne, peculiarities which, however, are not universally found[4], and which, even if they were universally found, would stand as consequence and not as cause. This may be accounted for by the observation that the legal protection bestowed on this particular class of holdings, notwithstanding its limitations, actually imparted to them something of

---

[1] Y. B. H. 49 E. III, pl. 12 (Fitzherbert, Abr. Aunc. Dem. 42, quotes pl. 7 instead of 12 by mistake): *Belk(nap)*, 'Verite est qe le terre est demandable par le briefe de droit patent en le court le seigniour apres la confirmacion (*sc.* par chartre) par ce qe le brief de droit serra commence en le court le seignior, mes apres la confirmacion il ne serra demande en auncien demesne par brief de droit close secundum consuetudinem,' etc.

[2] Bracton actually calls the plea of ancient demesne an exception of villainage, f. 200: 'Si autem in sokagio villano, sicut de dominico domini Regis, licet servitia certa sunt, obstabit ei exceptio villenagii, quia talis sokmannus liberum tenementum non habet quia tenet nomine alieno.' Cf. Fitzherbert, Abr. Aunc. Dem. 32.

[3] Bract. Note-book, pl. 652: 'Non debent extra manerium illud placitare quia non possunt [ponere] se in magnam assisam nec defendunt se per duellum.' On the cases when an assize could be taken as to tenements in ancient demesne, see the opinion printed in Horwood's Introduction to Y. B. 21/22 Edw. I, p. xviii.

[4] Stoneleigh Reg., f. 76 sqq: 'Item in placito terre possunt partes si voluerint ponere jus terre sue in duello campionum vel per magnam assisam, prout patet in recordo rotuli de anno xlv Regis Henrici inter Walterum H. et Johannem del Hul etc. et inter Galfridum Crulefeld et Willelmum Elisaundre anno xx Regis Edwardi filii Regis Henrici,' etc.

the nature of freehold, and led to a great confusion of attributes and principles. Indeed, the difficulty of keeping within the lines of privileged 'villainage' is clearly illustrated by the fact that the 'little writ,' with all its restrictions, and quite apart from any contention with the lord, recognises the tenant in ancient demesne as capable of independent action.

Villains, or men holding in villainage, have no writ, either manorial or extra-manorial, for the protection or recovery of their holdings, and the existence of such an action for villain socmen is in itself a limitation of the power of lord and steward, even when they are no parties to the case. And so the distinction between freehold and ancient demesne villainage is narrowed to a distinction of jurisdiction and procedure. This is so much the case that if, by a mere slip as it were, a tenement in ancient demesne has been once recovered by an assize of novel disseisin, the exclusive use of the 'little writ' is broken, and assizes will ever lie hereafter, that is, the tenement can be sued for as 'freehold' in common law courts[1]. Surely this could happen only because the tenure in ancient demesne, although a kind of villainage, closely resembled freehold.

The 'little writ' in manors alienated from the Crown.   One has primarily to look for an explanation of these great privileges to manors, which had been granted by the king to private lords. On such lands the 'little writ' lay both when 'villain socmen' were pleading against each other[2], and when a socman was opposed to his lord as a plaintiff[3]. This last eventuality is, of course, the most striking and important one. There were some disputes and some mistakes in practice as to the operation of the rule. The judges were much exercised over the question whether an action was to be allowed against

---

[1] Bract. Note-book, 1973 : ' Nota quod si manerium quod solet esse de dominico domini Regis datum fuerit alicui et postea semel capta fuerit assisa noue uel mortis de consuetudine, iterum capiantur assise propter consuetudinem.'

[2] Britton, ii, 142.

[3] If the lord brings an action against the tenant, ancient demesne is no plea, Viner, Abr., Anc. Dem. G. 4. This was not quite clear however, because ancient demesne is a good plea whenever recovery in the action would make the land frank fee.

the lord in the king's court.   The difficulty was, that the
contending parties had different estates in the land, the
one being possessed of the customary tenancy in ancient
demesne, and the other of the frank fee.   There are
authoritative fourteenth-century decisions to the effect
that, in such an action, the tenant had the option between
going to the court at Westminster or to the ancient
demesne jurisdiction[1].

The main fact remains, that a privileged villain had
'personam standi in judicio' against his lord, and actually
could be a plaintiff against him.   Court rolls of ancient
demesne manors frequently exhibit the curious case of a
manorial lord who is summoned to appear, distrained,
admitted to plead, and subjected to judgment by his own
court[2].   And as I said, one looks naturally to such instances
of egregious independence, in order to explain the affinity
between privileged villainage and freehold.   The explanation would be insufficient, however, and this for two simple
reasons.   The passage of the manor into the hands of a
subject only modifies the institution of ancient demesne,
but does not constitute it ; the 'little writ of right' is by no
means framed to suit the exceptional case of a contention
between lord and tenant ; its object is also to protect the
tenants against each other in a way which is out of the
question where ordinary villainage is concerned.   The two
reasons converge, as it were, in the fact that the 'little writ
of right' is suable in all ancient demesne manors without

---

[1] Y. B., M. 41 Edw. III, 22 : ' *Chold*: Si le seigniour disseisie son tenaunt
il est en eleccion del tenant de user accion en le court le seigniour ou en le
court le roy' (Fitzherbert, Abr. Aunc. Dem. 9).   Liber assis. 41 Edw. III,
pl. 7, f. 253 : ' *Wichingham*: Si le tenant en auncien demesne fuit disseisi
par le seignior en auncien demesne il est a volunte le tenant de porter
lassise al comen ley ou en auncien demesne mes e contra si le seignior soit
disseisi par le tenant, il ne puit aillours aver son recoverie que en le court
le roy.'

[2] Stoneleigh Register : ' Item anno regni Regis Eduardi filii Regis
Henrici vij Ricardus Peyto tulit breue de recto versus abbatem de
Stonle et alios de tenementis in Fynham in curia de Stonle.'   There
are several instances in the Court Rolls of King's Ripton, Hunts.   See
App. V.

exception, that it applies quite as much to those which remain in the crown as to those which have been alienated
from it[1]. And this leads us to a very important deduction.
If the affinity of privileged villainage and freehold is connected with the 'little writ of right' as such, and not merely
with a particular application of it, if the little writ of right
is framed for all the manors of ancient demesne alike, the
affinity of privileged villainage and freehold is to be
traced to the general condition of the king's manors in
ancient demesne[2].

Although the tenants in ancient demesne are admitted
to use the 'little writ of right' only, their court made it go
a long way; and in fact, all or almost all the real actions of
the common law had their parallel in its jurisdiction. The
demandant, when appearing in court, made a protestation
to sue in the nature of a writ of mort d'ancestor or of
dower[3] or the like, and the procedure varied accordingly,
sometimes following very closely the lines of the procedure
in the high courts, and sometimes exhibiting tenacious
local usage or archaic arrangements[4].

Procedure
of revision.   Actions as to personal estate could be pleaded without

[1] Bract. Note-book, 834 : 'Preceptum est vicecomiti quod preciperet ballivis manerii Dom. Regis de Haueringes quod recordari facerent in Curia
Dom. Regis de H. loquelam que fuit in eadem curia per breue Dom. Regis
inter,' etc.: 652 is to the same point. I must say, however, that I do not
agree with Mr. Maitland's explanation, vol. ii. p. 501, n. 4 : 'John Fitz Geoffrey
(the defendant pleading ancient demesne) cannot answer without the King.
Tenet nomine alieno. Bract. f. 200. The privileges of tenants in ancient
demesne are the King's privileges.' John Fitz Geoffrey is the King's
firmarius, and the other defendants vouch him to warranty. After having
pleaded to the jurisdiction of the Court he puts in a second plea, 'salvo
predicto responso,' namely, that the tenement claimed is encumbered by
other and greater services than paying 15s. to hold freely. This is clearly
the farmer's point of view, and as such, he cannot answer without the king.
I lay stress on the point because a person pleading ancient demesne, although
not holding *nomine proprio* in strict law, is compelled to answer without the
King in the manorial court and by the manorial writ.
[2] I need not say that the 'little writ' did not lie against the King himself.
No writs did. Cp. Fleta, p. 4.
[3] Y. B., 11/12 Edw. III, 325 (Rolls Ser.).
[4] I shall have to speak of the constitution and usages of the court in
another chapter.

writ, and as for the crown pleas they were reserved to the high courts[1]. But even in actions regarding the soil a removal to these latter was not excluded[2]. Evocation to a higher court followed naturally if the manorial court refused justice and such removal made the land frank fee[3]. The proceedings in ancient demesne could be challenged, and thereupon a writ of false judgment brought the case under the cognizance of the courts of common law. If on examination an error was found, the sentence of the lower tribunal was quashed and the case had to proceed in the higher[4]. Instances of examination and revision are frequent in our records[5]. The examination of the proceedings by the justices was by no means an easy matter, because they were constantly confronted by appeals to the custom of the manor and counter appeals to the principles of the common law of England. It was very difficult to adjust these conflicting elements with nicety. As to the point of fact, whether an alleged custom was really in usage or not, the justices had a good standing ground for decision. They asked, as a rule, whether precedents could be adduced and proved as to the usage[6]; they allowed a great latitude for the peculiarities of customary

[1] Actions on statutes could not be pleaded in ancient demesne because, it was explained, the tenantry not being represented in parliament, were no parties in framing the statute; Viner, Abr. Anc. Dem. E. 19. Another explanation is given in Y. B., H. 8 Edw. II, p. 265.

[2] As a matter of course, any question as to whether a manor was ancient demesne, and whether a particular tenement was within the jurisdiction of it, could be decided only in the high courts.

[3] Viner, Abr., I. 21.

[4] Y. B., H. 3 Edw. III, 29: ' *Caunt*: Si le jugement soit une foitz revers, la court auncien demesne ad perdu conusance de ce ple a touts jours.'

[5] Stoneleigh Reg.: ' Item si contingat quod error sit in iudiciis eorum et pars ex eorum errore gravetur contra consuetudines, pars gravata habebit breve Regis, ad faciendum venire recordum et processum inter partes factos coram justiciariis domini Regis de Banco; qui justiciarii inspecto recordo et processu quod erratum est in processu iusto iudicio emendabunt et ipsos sokemannos propter errorem et falsum iudicium secundum quantitatem delicti ad multam condempnabunt.'

[6] Bract. Note-book, 834: ' Et illi de curia qui veniunt quesiti, si unquam tale factum fuit judicium in prefata curia, et quod ostendant exemplum, et nichil inde ostendere possunt, nec exemplum nec aliud.'

law ; but the difficulty was that a line had to be drawn some-
where [1]. This procedure of revision on the whole is quite
as important a manifestation of the freehold qualities of privileged villainage as pleading by writ. Men holding in pure
villainage also had a manorial court to go to and to plead
in, but its judicial organisation proceeded entirely from
the will and power of the lord, and it ended where his will
and power ended ; there was no higher court and no revision for such men. The writ of false judgment in respect
of tenements in ancient demesne shows conclusively that
the peculiar procedure provided for the privileged villains
was only an instance and a variation of the general law
of the land, maintaining actionable rights of free persons.
And be it again noted, that there was no sort of difference
as to revision between those manors which were in the
actual possession of the crown and those which were out
of it [2]. Revision and reversal were provided not as a
complement to the legal protection of the tenant against
the lord, but as a consequence of that independent position
of the tenant as a person who has rights against all men
which is manifested in the *parvum breve* [3]. It is not
without interest to notice in this connexion that the *parvum
breve* is sometimes introduced in the law books, not as a
restriction put upon the tenant, nor as the outcome of villainage, but as a boon which provides the tenant with
a plain form of procedure close at hand instead of the
costly and intricate process before the justices [4].

---

[1] Y. B., 11/12 Edw. III, p. 325 (Rolls Ser.) : '*Stonore*: Dit qe toutz les
excepcions poent estre salve par usage del manoir forspris un, cest a dire
qe la ou il egarde seisine de terre par defalte apres defalte la ou le tenant
avait attourne en court qe respoundi pur lui.' Cf. Y. B., H. 3 Edw. III, 29,
and T. 3 Edw. III, 29.

[2] Bract. Note-book, pl. 834 and 1122 concern the royal manors of Havering
and Kingston.

[3] I say against all men, because in the case of a stranger's interfering
with the privileged villain's rights, it was for him to prove any exemption,
e. g. conveyance by charter, which would take the matter out of the range
of the manorial court.

[4] Britton, ii. 13 : ' Et pur ceo qe nous voloms qe ils eyent tele quiete,
est ordeyne le bref de droit clos pledable par baillif del maner de tort fet del

If protection against the lord had been the only object of the procedure in cases of ancient demesne, one does not see why there should be a 'little writ' at all, as there was a remedy against the lord's encroachments in the writ of 'Monstraverunt,'[1] pleaded before the king's justices. As it is, the case of disseisin by the lord, to whom the manor had come from the crown, was treated simply as an instance of disseisin, and brought under the operation of the writ of right, while the 'Monstraverunt' was restricted to exaction of increased services and change of customs[2]. The latter writ was a very peculiar one, in fact quite unlike any other writ. The common-law rule that each tenant in severalty has to plead for himself did not apply to it; all join for saving of charges, albeit they be several tenants[3]. What is more, one tenant could sue for the rest and his recovery profited them all; on the other hand, if many had joined in the writ and some died or withdrew, the writ did not abate for this reason, and even if but one remained able and willing to sue he could proceed with the writ[4]. These exceptional features were evidently meant to facilitate the action of humble people against a powerful magnate[5]. But it seems to me that the deviation from the rules governing

un sokeman al autre, qe il tiegne les plaintifs a droit selom les usages del maner par simples enquestes.'

[1] Natura brevium, f. 4 b (ed. Pynson).

[2] Stoneleigh Reg.: 'Si dominus a sokemanis tenentibus suis exigat alias consuetudines quam facere consueuerunt quum manerium fuit in manibus progenitorum Regis eos super hoc fatigando et distringendo, prefati tenentes habent recuperare versus dominum et balliuos suos per breve Regis quod vocatur Monstraverunt nobis homines de soka de Stonle,' etc.

[3] Viner, Abr. Anc. Dem. C², 3.

[4] Fitzherbert, Abr. Monstraverunt, 5 (P. 19, Edw. III): '*Seton*: Cest un cas a par luy en cest breue de Monstrauerunt qe un purra sue pur luy e tous les autres del ville tout ne soient pas nosmes en le breve e par la suite de un tous les autres auront auantage et cesty qe vient purra estre resceu e respondra par attourne pur touts les auters coment qe unque ne resceu lour attournement; issint qe cest suit ne breue nest semblable a auter.'

[5] As it was the peasants had the greatest difficulty in conducting these cases. In 1294 some Norfolk men tried to get justice against Roger Bigod, the celebrated defender of English liberties. They say that they have been pleading against him for twenty years, and give very definite references. The jury summoned declares in their favour. The earl opposes them by the

writs at common law is to be explained not only by the general aim of the writ, but also by its origin.

In form it was simply an injunction on a plaint. When for some reason right could not be obtained by the means afforded by the common law, the injured party had to apply to the king by petition. One of the most common cases was when redress was sought for some act of the king himself or of his officers, when the consequent injunction to the common law courts or to the Exchequer to examine the case invariably began with the identical formula which gave its name to the writ by which privileged villains complained of an increase of services; *monstravit* or *monstraverunt N.N.; ex parte N.N. ostensum est:*—these are the opening words of the king's injunctions consequent upon the humble remonstrations of his aggrieved subjects[1]. Again, we find that the application for the writ by privileged villains is actually described as a plaint[2]. In some cases it would be difficult to tell on the face of the initiatory document, whether we have to do with a '*breve de monstraverunt*' to coerce the manorial lord, or with an extraordinary measure taken by the king with a view to settling his own interests[3].

And this brings me to the main point. Although the writ under discussion seems at first sight to meet the

astonishing answer that they are not his tenants at all. It all ends by the collapse of the plaintiffs for no apparent reason; they do not come into court ultimately, and the jurors plead guilty of having given a false verdict; see App. VII. In the case of the men of Wycle against Mauger le Vavasseur, to which I have referred several times, the trial dragged on for five years; the court adjourned the case over and over again; the defendant did not pay the slightest attention to prohibitions, but went on ill-treating the tenantry. At last he carried off a verdict in his favour; but the management of the trial certainly casts much suspicion on it. Cf. Placitorum Abbreviatio, 303.

[1] Madox, History of the Exch., i. 723, c, d; 724, e; 725, f.

[2] Bract. Note-book, pl. 1237: 'Homines prioris S[ti] Swithini . . . questi fuerunt Dom. Regi.'

[3] Madox, Exch., i. 725, u; the 'Monstraverunt' of the men of King's Ripton quoted above on the question of tallage. This matter of tallage could certainly be treated as an alteration of services, and sent for trial to the Common Bench.

requirement of the special case of manors alienated from
the crown, on closer inspection it turns out to be a variation
of the peculiar process employed to insist upon a right
against the crown. Parallel to the 'Monstraverunt' against
a lord in the Common Pleas we have the ' Monstraverunt '
against the king's bailiff in the Exchequer. The following
mandate for instance is enrolled in the eventful year 1265 :
'Monstraverunt Regi homines castri sui de Brambur et
Schotone quod Henricus Spring constabularius castri de
Brambur injuste distringit eos ad faciendum alia servicia
et alias consuetudines quam facere consueverunt temporibus
predecessorum Regis et tempore suo. Ideo mandatum est
vicecomiti quod venire etc. predictum Henricum a die
Pasche in xv dies ad respondendum Regi et predictis
hominibus de predicta terra et breve etc.'[1] There is not
much to choose between this and the enrolment of a 'breve
de monstraverunt ' in the usual sense beyond the fact that
it is entered on a Roll of Exchequer Memoranda. In
1292 a mandate of King Edward I to the Barons of the
Exchequer is entered in behalf of the men of Costeseye in
Norfolk who complained of divers grievances against Athelwald of Crea, the bailiff of the manor. The petition itself
is enrolled also, and it sets forth, that whereas the poor men
of the king of the base tenure in the manor of Costeseye
held by certain usages, from a time of which memory runs
no higher, as well under the counts of Brittany as under the
kings to whom the manor was forfeited, now bailiff Athelwald distrains them to do other services which ought to be
performed by pure villains. They could sell and lease their
lands in the fields at pleasure, and he seizes lands which
have been sold in this way and amerces them for selling ;
besides this he makes them serve as reeves and collectors,
and the bailiff of the late Queen Eleanor tallaged them
from year to year to pay twenty marks, which they were
not bound to do, because they are no villains to be tallaged

The ' Mon-
straverunt '
on the
king's own
land.

---

[1] Exch. Memoranda, Q. R. 48/49 Henry III, m. 11. The position of the
castle of Bamborough was certainly a peculiar one at the time. Cf. Close
Roll, 49 Henry III, m. 7, d.

high and low[1]. Such is the substance of this remarkable
document, to which I shall have to refer again in other
connexions. What I wish to establish now is, that we
have on the king's own possessions the exact counterpart of the 'breve de monstraverunt.' The instances
adduced are perhaps the more characteristic because the
petitioners had not even the strict privilege of ancient
demesne to lean upon, as one of the cases comes from
Northumberland, which is not mentioned in Domesday,
and the other concerns tenants of the honour of Richmond.

There can be no doubt that the tenantry on the ancient
demesne had even better reasons for appealing to immemorial usage, and certainly they knew how to urge their
grievances. We may take as an instance the notice of a
trial consequent upon a complaint of the men of Bray
against the Constable of Windsor. Bray was ancient
demesne and the king's tenants complained that they were
distrained to do other services than they were used to do.
The judgment was in their favour[2].

The chief point is that the writ of 'Monstraverunt'
appears to be connected with petitions to the king against
the exactions of his officers, and may be said in its origin
to be applicable as much to the actual possessions of the
crown as to those which had been granted away from it.
This explains a very remarkable omission in our best
authorities. Although the writ played such an important
part in the law of ancient demesne, and was so peculiar in
its form and substance, neither Bracton nor his followers
mention it directly. They set down 'the little writ of right
close' as the only writ available for the villain socmen.

---

[1] Exch. Memoranda, Q. R. Trin. 20 Edw. I, m. 21, d. I give the documents
in full in App. VIII. The petitioners are not villains, but they are tenants
of base tenure. They evidently belong to the class of villain socmen outside
the ancient demesne, of which more hereafter.

[2] Placitorum Abbrev. 25 : 'Consideratum est quod constabularius de
Windesore de quo homines de Bray questi fuerunt quod ipse vexabat eos
de serviciis et consuetudinibus indebitis et tallagia insueta ab eis exigebat
accipiat ab eis tallagia consueta et ipsi homines alia servicia et consuetudines quas facere solent faciant.' (Pasch. et Trin., 1 John.)

As the protection in point of services is nevertheless distinctly affirmed by those writers, and as the Monstraverunt appears in full working order in the time of Henry III and even of John[1], the obvious explanation seems to be that Bracton regarded the case as one not of writ but of petition, a matter, we might say, rather for royal equity than for strict law. Thus both the two modes of procedure which are distinctive of the ancient demesne, namely the 'parvum breve' and the 'Monstraverunt,' though they attain their full development on the manors that have been alienated, seem really to originate on manors which are in the actual possession of the crown.

If we now examine the conditions under which the manors of the ancient demesne were alienated by the crown, we shall at once see that no very definite line could be drawn between those which had been given away and those which remained in the king's hand. The one class gradually shades off into the other. A very good example is afforded by the history of Stoneleigh Abbey. In 1154 King Henry II gave the Cistercian monks of Radmore in Staffordshire his manor of Stoneleigh in exchange for their possessions in Radmore. The charter as given in the Register of the Abbey seems to amount to a complete grant of the land and of the jurisdiction. Nevertheless, we find Henry II drawing all kinds of perquisites from the place all through his reign, and it is specially noticed that his writs were directed not to the Abbot or the Abbot's bailiffs, but to his own bailiffs in Stoneleigh[2]. In order to

Alienation of Royal Manors.

---

[1] Madox, Exch. i. 411, u: 'Homines de Branton reddunt compotum de x libris, ut Robertus de Sachoill eis non distringat ad faciendum ei alias consuetudines quam Regi facere consueverunt dum fuerunt in manu sua.' (Pipe Roll 13 Jo., 7, 10 b, Devenesc).

[2] Dugdale, Monasticon, v. 443; Stoneleigh Reg. f. 14 b. Cf. Court Rolls of Ledecumbe Regis (Chapter House, County Bags, Berks, A. 3): 'Anno domini MCCLXVIII, solverunt homines de Ledecumbe Regis C. sol. ad scaccarium domini Regis, pro redditu domini Regis et predicti homines habent residuum in custodia sua excepta porcione prioris Montis Acuti de tempore suo et porcione prioris de Bermundseye de tempore suo.' The manor had been let in fee farm to the monks of Cluny, who demised it to the Prior of Montacute, who in his turn let it to the Prior of Bermondsey.

get rid of the inconveniences consequent upon such mixed ownership, Abbot William of Tyso bought a charter from King John, granting to the Abbey all the soke of Stoneleigh[1]. But all the same the royal rights did not yet disappear. There were tenants connected with the place who were immediately dependent on the king[2], and his bailiff continued to exercise functions by the side of, and in conjunction with, the officers of the Abbot[3]. In the 50th year of Henry III a remarkable case occurred :— a certain Alexander of Canle was tried for usurping the rights of the Abbot as to the tenantry in the hamlet of Canle, and it came out that one of his ancestors had succeeded in improving his position of collector of the revenue into the position of an owner of the rents. Although the rights which were vindicated against him were the rights of the Abbot, still the king entered into possession and afterwards transferred the possession to the Abbot[4]. In one word, the king is always considered as 'the senior lord' of Stoneleigh ; his lordship is something more direct than a mere feudal over-lordship[5].

We find a similar state of things at King's Ripton. The manor had been let in fee farm to the Abbots of Ramsey. In case of a tenement lapsing into the lord's hands, it is seized sometimes by the bailiff of the king, sometimes by

---

[1] Stoneleigh Reg. f. 15 a : 'Totam sokam de Stonleya et omnes redditus et consuetudines et rectitudines quas Henricus rex pater noster ibi habuit salua regali justicia nostra. Uigore quarum chartarum prefatus Abbas et conventus habent et possident totam sokam de Stonle que quondam pertinuit ad le Bury (*sic*) in dicta soka existens edificatum, ubi quidam comes quondam de licencia Regis moram traxit. Qui locus nunc edificiis carens vocatur le Burystede iuxta Crulefeld prout fossatis includitur, et est locus nemorosus.'

[2] Stoneleigh Reg. f. 13 a : 'Isti duo tenent (burgagia in Warrwick) per seruicium sustinendi unum plumbum in manerio de Stonle competens monasterio Regis.'

[3] Placita de Quo Warranto, 778 : 'Item clamat quod Ballivus dom. Regis in manerio de Stonleye nullam faciet districtionem seu attachiamenta sine presencia Ballivi Abbatis.'

[4] See App. VI.

[5] Stoneleigh Reg. 13 a : 'W. W. tenet unum burgagium per seruicium inveniendi domino regi seniori domino de Stonle quartam partem unius tripodis.'

the bailiffs of the Abbot[1]. The royal writs again are directed not to the Abbot, but to his bailiff. The same was the case at Stoneleigh[2], and indeed this seems to have been the regular course on ancient demesne manors[3]. This curious way of ignoring the lord himself and addressing the writ directly to his officers seems an outcome of the fundamental assumption that of these manors there was no real lord but the king, and that the private lord's officers were acting as the king's bailiffs.

According to current notions the demesnes of the crown ought not to have been alienated at all. Although alienated by one king they were considered as liable to be resumed by his successors[4]. And as a matter of fact such resumptions were by no means unusual. Edward I gave an adequate expression to this doctrine when he ordered an inquisition into the state of the tenantry at Stoneleigh:—he did not wish any encroachment made on the old constitution of the manor, for he had always in mind the possibility that his royal rights would be resumed by himself or by one of his successors[5].

---

[1] King's Ripton Court Rolls, Augment. Off. Rolls, xxiii. 94, m. 10: 'Dicta Matildis optulit se versus Margaretam Greylaund de placito dotis, que non venit. Ideo preceptum est capere in manum domini Regis medietatem mesuagii etc.—pro defectu ipsius Margarete. Eadem Matildis optulit se uersus Willelmum vicarium—qui non uenit. Ideo preceptum est capere in manum domini Regis medietatem quinque acrarum terre etc. (Curia de Riptone Regis die Lune in festo sanctorum Protessi et Marciniani anno [r. r. E. xxiv. et J. abb. x]); m. 10, d.—Qui venit et quantum ad aliam acram dicit, quod non est tenens set quod Abbas seysiuit illam in manum suam. (Curia—in festo Assumpcionis—anno supra dicto).' In the first case the seizure corresponds to the 'cape in manum' of a freehold. As there could be no such thing in the case of villainage, and the procedural seizure was resumption by the lord, the point is worth notice and may be explained by the King's private right still lingering about the manor. The last case is one of escheat or forfeiture.

[2] Stoneleigh Reg. 75 v: 'Item si aliquis deforciatur de tenemento suo et tulerit breve Regis clausum balliuis manerii versus deforciantes, dictum breve non debet frangi nisi in curia.'

[3] Natura brevium, 13 : 'Balliuis suis.'

[4] Britton, i. 221: 'Rois aussi ne porrount rien aliener les dreits de lour coroune ne de lour reaute, qe ne soit repellable par lour successours.'

[5] Stoneleigh Reg. 30: 'Nos attendentes, quod huiusmodi alienaciones et

If we turn to the court rolls of a manor which is actually in the king's hand and compare them with those of a manor which he has granted to some convent or some private lord, we see hardly any difference between them. The rolls of the manor of Havering at the Record Office, although comparatively late, afford a good insight into the constitution of a manor retained in the king's own hand. They contain a good many writs of right, and though, naturally enough, the tenants do not bring actions against the king, we find an instance in which the king brings an action against his tenant, and pleads before a court which is held in his own name[1]. This is good proof that the condition of the tenants was by no means dependent on the arbitrary action of the manorial officers. When King Henry II granted Stoneleigh to the Cistercians he displaced a number of 'rustics' from their holdings, and while doing this he recognised their right and enjoined the sheriff of Warwickshire to give them an equivalent for what they had lost in consequence of the grant[2]. The notion from which all inquiry consequent upon a 'Monstraverunt' starts is always this, that the tenants were holding by *certain* (i. e. by fixed) services at the time when the manor was in the king's own hand. The certainty is not created by the fact that the manor passes away from the king to some one else ; it exists when the land is royal land and therefore

consuetudinum mutaciones eciam in nostri et heredum nostrorum preiudicium et exheredacionem cedere possent, si manerium illud in manus nostras aliquo casu deuenerit sustinere nolumus sicut nec debemus manerium illud aut ea que ad illud pertinent aliter immutari quam esse solebant temporibus predictis.'

[1] The writs are directed sometimes to the bailiffs of the Archbishop of Canterbury and of the Duke of Albemarle, who had the manor in custody for King Richard II, but in the twenty-third year they are inscribed to the King's bailiffs. (Augmentation Court Rolls, xiv. 38). As to the trial mentioned in the text see App. IX.

[2] Stoneleigh Reg. 11 a : ' Precipio tibi quod sine dilacione deliberes Abbati de Stonleia omnes terras et tenuras quas ego dedi et carta mea confirmaui. Et de terra quam rustici uersus calumpniantur et quam ego ei dedi et concessi, inquire si rectum in ea habuerunt et si rectum in ea habent, dona eis rusticis alibi in terra mea excambium ad valenciam.'

cannot be destroyed on land that has been alienated. So true is this that Bracton and Britton give their often cited description of privileged villainage without alluding to the question whether or no the manor is still in the king's hand[1]; Britton even applies this description primarily to the king's own possessions by his way of stating the law as the direct utterance of the king's command. The well-known fact that the 'ferm' or rent of royal manors was not always fixed, that we constantly hear of an increased rental (*incrementum*) levied in addition to the old 'ferm' (*assisa; redditus antiquitus assisus*), can be easily reconciled with this doctrine[2]. The prosperity of the country was gradually rising; both in agricultural communities and in towns new tenements and houses, new occupations and revenues were growing, and it was not the interest either of the communities or of the lord to compress this development within an unelastic bond. In principle the increased payments fell on this new growth on the demesne, although this may in some cases have been due to exactions against which the people could remonstrate only in the name of immemorial custom, and only by way of petition since nobody could judge the king. In principle, too, certainty of condition was admitted as to the privileged villains on the king's demesnes[3].

This serves to explain the procedure followed by the court when a question of services was raised by a writ of 'Monstraverunt.' The first thing, of course, was to ascertain whether the manor was ancient demesne or not, and

Trial of services in 'Monstraverunt.'

---

[1] Bracton, f. 209 : 'Ad quemcumque manerium peruenerit.'

[2] Madox, Firma Burgi, 54 ; Pipe Rolls, passim. Cf. Rot. Cur. Regis Ric., p. 15 : 'Homines de Kingestone—c. sol. . . . . pro respectu tenendi villam suam ad eandem firmam quam reddere solebant tempore Henrici Regis.'

[3] Madox, Exch. 1437, z : 'Homines de Lechton x marcas pro habenda inquisicione per proxima halimota et per legales milites et alios homines de visneto, quas consuetudines ipsi fecerunt tempore Henrici Regis Patris.' (Pipe Roll, 4 John.) Cf. 442, a : 'Homines de Stanleya reddunt compotum de uno palefrido, ut inquiratur per sacramentum legalium hominum, quas consuetudines et quae servitia homines de manerio de Stanleia facere consueverunt Regi Henrico patri Ricardi Regis dum essent in manu sua.' (Pipe Roll, 9 John.)

for this purpose nothing short of a direct mention in Domesday was held to be sufficient[1]. When this question had been solved in the affirmative, a jury had to decide what the customs and duties were, by which the ancestors of the plaintiffs held at the time when the crown was possessed of the manor. In principle it was always considered that such had been the services at the time of the Conquest[2], but practically, of course, there could be no attempt to examine into such ancient history. The men of King's Ripton actually pleaded back to the time of King Cnut, and maintained that no prescription was available against their rights as no prescription could avail against the king[3].

[1] Y. B., Trin., 49 E. III, pl. 8 (Fitzherbert, Abr. Monstrav. 4) : ‘ *Han.* mist auant record de Domesday qui parla *ut supra :—Terra sancti Stephani* en le title qui parla de ceo maner que il fuit en sa maine. Et auxi il mist auant chartre le Roy que ore est, par quel le roy reherse quil ave viewe la chartre le roy Henri le primer, et reherce tout le chartre, et ceo chartre voilet que Henri aue viewe par ceo parolle *inspeximus* la chartre le roy William Conquerour qui aue done graunte e confirme mesme le manor a un Henri Butle, a luy, et a ces heirs a ceo iour, quel chartre issint volent *inspeximus cartam domini Edwardi Regis Anglie* issint par le recorde et par les chartres est expressement reherce par le roy qui ore est, que William Conquerour fuit en possession de ceo maner, Seinct Edward auxint, en quel cas ceo serra aiudge auncient demesne tantamont come si la terre ust estre en la main Seint Edward par expresse parolx en le Domesday. *Belknap* : Le comen fesance de chartres est de faire parolle en le chartre *dedimus concessimus et confirmauimus* et uncore le chartre est bon assets al part, mesque le roy nauer riens a ceo temps, issint que riens passe par ceo paroll *dedimus* mes il auer par parole de confermement, issint que il nest my proue par ce chartre que ils auoient la possession, pur ceo que les chartres poient estre effectuels a auter entent, scilicet, en nature de confermement, et auxi ces chartres fait par Seint E. et W. Conquerour ne sont my monstres a ore pur record, issint que mesque il furent monstre, et auxi purroit estre proue que le maner fuit en lour possession, nous ne puissomus pas aiudger la terre auncien demesne, pur ceo que auncien demesne sera aiudge par le liuer de domesday qui est de record, et nemy en autre maner. Et puis les plaintifs fuerent nonsues.’

[2] Fitzherbert, Abr. Cause de remover ple, 18 (Y. B., M., 21 Edw. III) : ‘ *Wilby* : Il conuient que il count en le *monstrauerunt* que il luy distreint pur auters customes que ses auncestres ne fecerunt en temps W. Conquerour, cas le *monstrauerunt* ne gist pas forsque en cas ou plusiours services sont demandez que ces auncestres ne solent faire en cel temps.’

[3] Coram Rege, Tr. 3 Edw. I, m. 14, d : ‘ Et unde predicti homines (de Kyngesripton) queruntur quod temporibus Cnout regis quo manerium illud fuit in manu dicti antecessoris sui tenuerunt tenementa sua per seruicia sub-

The courts naturally declined to go higher than men could remember, but they laid down this limitation entirely as one of practice and not of principle[1]. Metingham demanded that the claimants should make good their contention even for a single day in Richard Cœur de Lion's time[2]. The men of Wycle combine both assertions in their contention against Mauger; they appeal to the age of the first Norman kings, but offer to prove the certainty of their services in the reigns of Richard and John[3].

Now all that has been said hitherto applied to 'the tenants *Nature of tenancy in ancient demesne.*

scripta, videlicet reddendi pro qualibet virgata terre 5 solidos, etc. Et omnes antecessores sui tenuissent tenementa sua per predicta seruicia usque ad conquestum Anglie, et a conquestu usque ad tempus regis Henrici aui regis Johannis aui domini regis nunc, usque ad tempus cuiusdam Abbatis de Rameseye Roberti Dogge nomine qui tempore Henrici Regis distrinxit antecessores suos ad dandum relevium pro voluntate sua, etc. Et Abbas dicit quod non debet eis ad hoc breue respondere, quia desicut in narracione sua non faciunt mencionem quod ipsi extitissent in tali statu in quo fuerunt tempore regis Knout, quem statum ipsi clamant habere, tempore aliorum regum de quo memoria haberi possit nec de quo breue de recto currit nec aliqua verificacio per patriam fieri possit. . . . Et Reginaldus et alii bene cognoscunt quod ipse Abbas et predecessores sui exstiterunt in seysina percipiendi ab ipsis et antecessoribus suis predicta seruicia indebita a tempore predicti Henrici regis. Set desicut istud breue quod conceditur in fauorem dominicorum domini Regis non habet prescriptionem temporis, petunt judicium si [racione?] alicujus longiqui termini debeant ab actione excludi sua.'

[1] Y. B., M., 15 Edw. II, p. 455 : ' *Bereford* : Coment puit cest brief vous servir la ou il (the defendant) dist qe luy et ces predecessors ont este de vous et de vos auncestres (seisi) de tout temps come, etc., et vos ont taille, etc. Devoms nous enguerre (enquerre *corr.*) si vos feistes touz services en temps le Roy S[t]. Edward, ou non de temps que vos avez pris title? *Devon* : Sir navyl (nanyl *corr.*), mais nous disons qe touz les tenants qui tindrent en temps S[t]. Edward tinderent, etc. (par certains services) . . . tanqe a ore xv ans devant le brief purchace etc. e ceo puit home enquere.'

[2] Y. B., 21/22 Edw. I, 499 et sqq.

[3] Coram Rege, Pasch. 1 Edw. II, m. 26 : ' Postquam idem manerium ad manus antecessorum predicti Maugeri deuenit usque ad tempus memorie, videlicet temporibus regum Ricardi, Johannis et statum illum toto tempore predicto pacifice continuaverunt et habuerunt.' Coram Rege, M. 5 Edw. II, m. 77 : ' Unde queruntur quod cum ipsi homines et eorum antecessores tempore Regum Anglie progenitorum domini Regis nunc, videlicet tempore Regis Willelmi Conquestoris et Willelmi Regis filii sui et eciam tempore Regis Henrici primi solebant tenere terras suas per quaedam certa seruicia videlicet,' etc.

in ancient demesne' indiscriminately, without regard to any diversity of classes among them. Hitherto I have not noticed any such diversity, and in so doing I am warranted by the authorities. Those authorities commonly speak of 'men' or 'tenants in ancient demesne' without any further qualification[1]. Sometimes the expression 'condition of ancient demesne' also is used. But closer examination shows a variety of classes on the privileged soil, and leads to a number of difficult and interesting problems.

To begin with, the nature of the tenancy in general has been much contested. As to the law of later times Mr. Elton puts the case in this way: 'There is great confusion in the law books respecting this tenure. The copyholders of these manors are sometimes called tenants in ancient demesne, and land held in this tenure is said to pass by surrender and admittance. This appears to be inaccurate. It is only the freeholders who are tenants in ancient demesne, and their land passes by common law conveyances without the instrumentality of the lord. Even Sir W. Blackstone seems to have been misled upon this point. There are however, as a rule, in manors of ancient demesne, customary freeholders and sometimes copyholders at the will of the lord, as well as the true tenants in ancient demesne[2].' Now such a description seems strangely out of keeping with the history of the tenure. Blackstone speaks of privileged copyhold as descended from privileged villainage[3]; and as to the condition in the thirteenth century of those 'men' or 'tenants in ancient demesne' of whom we have been speaking, there can be no doubt. Bracton and his followers lay down quite distinctly that their tenure is villainage though privileged villainage. The men of ancient demesne are men of free blood holding in villainage[4]. And

---

[1] I will here cite Bract. Note-book, pl. 1237, as an instance, although there is hardly any call for quotation on this point.

[2] Law of Copyhold, 8. Cf. the same author's Tenures in Kent, 182.

[3] Blackstone, Law Tracts, ii., especially pp. 128, 129.

[4] Bracton: 'liberi de condicione . . . tenentes villenagium.' Britton: 'hommes de franc saunc.'

to take up the special point mentioned by Mr. Elton—
conveyance by surrender and admittance is a quite necessary feature of the tenure[1] : conveyance by charter makes
the land freehold and destroys its ancient demesne condition[2]. But although this is so clear in the authorities of
the thirteenth century, there is undoubtedly a great deal of
confusion in later law books, and reasons are not wanting
which may account for this fact and for the doctrine propounded by Mr. Elton in conformity with certain modern
treatises and decisions.

We may start with the observation, that privileged
villains or villain socmen are not the only people to be
found on the soil of the ancient demesne. There are free
tenants there and pure villains too[3]. Free socage is often
mentioned in these manors, and it is frequently pleaded in
order to get a trial transferred to the Common Law Courts.
When the question is raised whether a tenement is free or
villain socage, the fact that it has been conveyed by feoffment and charter is treated, as has just been pointed out,
as establishing its freehold character and subjecting it to
the ordinary common law procedure[4]. On the other hand,

Classes of tenantry.

---

[1] Stoneleigh Reg., 75 : ‘Item si quis de voluntate et assensu domini facto
fine cum domino voluerit dare tenementum suum ad opus alicuius, ueniet in
curia cum virga et sursum reddet huiusmodi tenementum ad manum domini
sine carta ad opus ementis vel cui datur et ballivus domini habitis prius
herietis et aliis de iure domino debitis dictum tenementum emptori seu cui
dabitur et heredibus suis secundum consuetudinem manerii habendum et
tenendum liberabit in (cum *corr.* ?) virga. Et dictus recipiens tunc faciet
finem cum domino prout possunt conuenire. . . . Item extraneus non debet
vocari ad warantum in placito terre in curia de Stonle quia sokemanni non
possunt feoffare alios per cartas cum ipsi nullas habeant de rege. Set si
quos feoffauerint de licencia domini sine carta, ipsos feoffant secundum
consuetudinem manerii prout continetur in rotulo curie de anno xx Regis
Edwardi filii Regis Edwardi in placito terre inter,’ etc.

[2] Placitorum Abbrev. 233, Berks. Cf. Britton, i. 287, note c.

[3] Bracton, f. 7.

[4] Jurate et Assise, 45 Henry III, Placitorum Abbr., p. 150 : ‘Et Galfridus
de Praule bene cognoscit quod predictum manerium est antiquum dominicum
Dom. Regis set dicit quod predictum tenementum est liberum tenementum
ita quod assisa debet inde fieri. . . . Dicit enim quod ipse feofatus est de
predicto tenemento de quodam Willelmo Harold per cartam suam quam
profert. . . . Et juratores quesiti si antecessores ejusdem Willelmi feofati

registers and extents of ancient demesne manors sometimes
treat separately of 'nativi' or 'villani' as distinguished from
the regular customary tenants, and describe their services
as being particularly base[1]. In trials it is quite a common
thing for a lord, when accused of having altered the services,
to plead that the plaintiffs were his villains to be treated at
will. Attempts were made in such cases to take advantage
of the general term 'men of ancient demesne,' and to argue
that all the population on the crown manors must be of
the same condition, the difference of rank applying only to
the amount and the kind of services, but not to their certainty, which ought to be taken for granted[2]. But strictly
and legally the lord's plea was undoubtedly good : the
courts admitted it, and when it was put forward proceeded
to examine the question of fact whether the lord had been
actually seised of certain or of uncertain services[3]. It is of

fuerunt per cartam vel si aliquis de tenura illa unquam placitaverunt per
diversa brevia vel non, dicunt quod non recolunt.'

[1] Stoneleigh Reg., 12 : 'Fuerunt eciam tunc quatuor natiui siue serui in le
lone quorum quilibet nouum mesuagium et unum quartronum terre cum
pertinenciis per seruicia subscripta videlicet leuando furcas, etc. . . . et debebant . . . redimere sanguinem suum et dare auxilium domino ad festum
S^{ti}. Michaelis scilicet ayde et facere braseum Domini et alia seruicia seruilia.'
As to some details, see Dugdale, Antiquities of Warwickshire, i. 176.

[2] Coram Rege, Pasch. 1 Edw. II, m. 26 : '(Maugerus) defendit vim et injuriam quando, etc. Et dicit quod qualitercunque iidem homines asserant
se et antecessores suos tenentes, etc. certa seruicia dominis de Wycle antecessoribus ipsius Maugeri et sibi fecisse et facere debere, quod omnes antecessores sui domini de eodem manerio extiterunt seisiti de predictis hominibus et eorum antecessoribus tenentibus tenementa quae ipsi modo tenent
ibidem ut de uillanis suis taillabilibus alto et basso ad voluntatem ipsorum
dominorum et redempcionem sanguinis et alia villana seruicia et incerta et
villanas consuetudines faciendo a tempore quo non extat memoria. . . . Et
predicti homines dicunt quod ipsi sunt tenentes de antiquo dominico, etc.,
prout curie satis liquet et quod omnes tenentes in dominico Regis per certa
seruicia et certas consuetudines tenent et tenere debent, quidam per maiora
et quidam per minora secundum consuetudinem, set semper per certa,' etc.
Coram Rege, Mich. 5 Edw. II, m. 77, v : ' Nec dedici potest quia tenentes de
antiquo dominico certa seruicia et certas consuetudines tenentur facere et
non ad voluntatem dominorum.'

[3] Y. B., M., 15 Edw. II, p. 455 : ' Bouser : Auxint bien sont tenans en
auncien demesne ascuns vileins et ascuns autres come ailleurs et les sokemans plederent par le petit brief de droit et les vileyns nient. Herle : Il
semble que assets est il traverse de votre brief, car vous dites que vous tenez

considerable importance to note that the difference between villains pure and villains privileged was sometimes connected with the distinction between the lord's demesne and the tenant's land in the manor[1]. The demesne proper was frank fee in the hands of the lord, and could be used by him at his pleasure. If he chose to grant it away to villains in pure villainage, the holdings thus formed could have no claim to rank as privileged land. It was assumed that some such holdings had been formed at the very beginning, as it were, that is at a time beyond memory of man, but tenements at will could be created at a later time on approved waste or on soil that had escheated to the lord and in this way passed through his demesne[2]. One of the reasons of later confusion must be looked for in the fact that the pure villain holdings gradually got to be recognised at law as copyhold or base customary tenures. They were thus brought dangerously near to ancient demesne socage, which was originally nothing but base customary tenure. The very fact of copyhold thus gaining on villain socage may have pushed this last on towards freehold. Already the Old Natura Brevium does not know exactly how to

par certeyn service . . . et il dit que vous estes son vilein et que il et ses predecessors ont este seisiz de tailler vous et vos auncestres haut et bas, etc. Et stetit verificare.' Cf. Bract. Note-book, pl. 1230.

[1] Bracton, 209 : ' Item est manerium domini regis et dominicum in manerio, et sic plura genera hominum in manerio, vel quia ab initio vel quia mutato villenagio.' The meaning of this badly worded passage is made clearer by a comparison with f. 7 : ' In dominico domini regis plura sunt genera hominum ; sunt enim ibi servi sive nativi ante conquestum, in conquestu, et post, et tenent villenagia et per villana servitia et incerta qui usque in hodiernum diem villanas faciunt consuetudines et incertas et quicquid eis preceptum fuerit (dum tamen licitum et honestum). . . . Est etiam aliud genus hominum in maneriis domini regis, et tenent de dominico et per easdem consuetudines et servitia villana, per quae supradicti (villani socmanni) et non in villenagio, nec sunt servi nec fuerunt in conquestu, ut primi, sed per quandam conventionem quam cum dominis fecerunt.' Cf. Elton, Tenures of Kent, 180.

[2] Fitzherbert, Abr. Monstrav. 3 (Pasch. 41 Edw. III). ' *Kirt*: Les tenements queux ils teignent fuerent en auncien temps entre les maines les villeins queux deuirrent sans heire perque les tenements fuerent seisies en maine le seigneur et puis le senescal le seigneur lessa mesme ceux terres par rolle a mesme ceux ore tenants a tener a volunte del seigneur fesaunt certain services ; issint ne sont ils forsque tenants a volunte le seigneur.'

make distinctions. It speaks of three species of socage—free, ancient demesne, and base. The line is soon drawn between the first two, but the third kind is said to be held by uncertain services, and sued by writ of 'Monstraverunt' instead of having the writs of right and 'Monstraverunt' of ancient demesne socage[1]. Probably what is meant is a species of copyhold which is not socage, and the writ of 'Monstraverunt' attributed to it may perhaps be the plaint or petition which is the initial move in a suit for the protection of copyhold in the manorial court.

Villain socage.

In the time of Henry III and of the Edwards the nature of ancient demesne tenure was better understood. At the close of the thirteenth century the lawyers distinguish three kinds of men—free, villains, and socmen[2]. In order to be quite accurate people spoke of *villain socmen* or *little socage*[3] in opposition to free. But even at that time there were several confusing features about the case. The certainty of condition made the tenure of the villain socmen so like a freehold that it was often treated as such in the manorial documents. In the Stoneleigh Register the peculiar nature of socage in ancient demesne is described fully and clearly. It is distinguished in so many words from tenancy at will, and a detailed description of conveyance by surrender in contrast with conveyance by charter seems to give the necessary material for the distinction between it and freehold[4]. But still the fundamental notion of free men holding

---

[1] Natura Brevium, f. 105. Cf. 16.

[2] Y. B., 21/22 Edw. I, p. 499: 'Treis maners de gents.'

[3] Bracton, f. 209; Fitzherbert, Monstrav. 3 (Pasch. 41 Edw. III): '*Belknap*: Mesmes les tenementz en auncien temps fuerent en mains le petit sokmans, et eux fierent teux services comme gents de petits sokemans fierent en auncien temps et eux les teignent comme gents de petit sokmans.'

[4] Stoneleigh Reg., 32: 'Et quod in eodem manerio sunt diuerse tenure secundum consuetudinem manerii illius totis temporibus retroactis usitatam, videlicet quidam tenentes eiusdem manerii tenent terras et tenementa sua in sokemanria de feodo et hereditate de qua quidem tenura talis habetur et omni tempore habebatur consuetudo, videlicet quod quando aliquis tenens eiusdem tenure terram suam alicui alienare uoluerit, veniet in curiam coram ipso Abbate vel eius senescallo et per uirgam sursum reddat in manum domini terram sic alienandam. . . . Et si aliquis terram aliquam huiusmodi tenure infra manerium predictum per cartam uel sine carta absque licentia

in villainage gets lost sight of. Only some of the cottiers are said to hold in villainage. The more important tenants, the socmen holding virgates and half-virgates, are not only currently described as freeholders in the Register, but they are entered as such on the Warwickshire Hundred Roll[1]. The term 'parva sokemanria' is applied in the Stoneleigh Register only to a few subordinate holdings which are undoubtedly above the level of pure villainage, but cannot be definitely distinguished from the other kinds of socage in the Register. This may serve as an indication of the tendency of manorial communities to consider privileged villainage as a free tenure, but legal pleadings and decisions were also creating confusion for another reason, because they tended, as has been said, to consider the whole body of men on the ancient demesne in one lump as it were. The courts very often applied as the one test of tenure and service the question whether a person was a descendant by blood of men of ancient demesne or a stranger[2]. In connexion with this the court rolls testify to the particular care taken to control any intrusion of strangers into the boundaries of a privileged manor[3]. This was done primarily in the interests of the lord, but the tenantry also seem to have

dicti Abbatis alienauerit aliter quam per sursum reddicionem in curia in forma predicta, quod terra sic extra curiam alienata domino dicti manerii erit forisfacta in perpetuum. Dicunt eciam quod quidam sunt tenentes eiusdem manerii ad voluntatem eiusdem Abbatis. Et si quis eorundem tenencium terram sic ad voluntatem tentam alienauerit in feodo, quod liceat dicto Abbati terram illam intrare et illam tanquam sibi forisfactam sibi in perpetuum retinere.'

[1] A comparison of the data in the Stoneleigh Register and in the Roll is given in App. VI. Cf. Bract. Note-book, pl. 834 : ' Legales homines de manerio de Havering.'

[2] Coram Rege, Mich. 5 Edw. I, m. 77 : '(Juratores) quesiti si predicti Margeria et alii et omnes antecessores a tempore quo non extat memoria terras suas successiue de heredibus in heredes tenuerint uel ipsi aut aliquis antecessorum suorum sunt vel fuerint aduenticii, dicunt quod ignorant.'

[3] Court Rolls of King's Ripton, Augment. Off. xxiii. 94, m. 7 : ' Memorandum quod concessum est Rogero de Kenlowe habendum introitum ad Caterinam filiam Thome prepositi cum uno quarterio terre in villa de Ryptone Regis pro duabus solidis in gersuma, ita tamen quod mortua dicta Katerina ille qui propinquior est heres de sanguine predicte Katerine gersumabit dictum quarterium terre secundum consuetudinem manerii et ville.' A. r. r. Edw.

sometimes been jealous of their prerogatives[1], and it is only in the course of the fourteenth century that they begin to open their gates to strangers, 'adventicii[2].' However this may be, the practice of drawing the line between native stock and strangers undoubtedly countenanced the idea that all the tenants of native stock were alike, and in this way tended to confuse the distinction between freeholders, pure villains, and villain socmen.

The courts made several attempts to insist on a firm classification, but some of these were conceived in such an unhappy spirit that they actually embroiled matters. The conduct of the king's judges was especially misdirected in one famous case which came up several times before the

xxiii, m. 8, v: 'Nicholaus de Aula reddit sursum unam dimidiam acram terre ad opus Willelmi ad portam de Broucton . . . . Et preceptum preposito respondere de exitibus eiusdem terre quia est extraneus . . . Johannes Arnold reddit sursum duas rodas terre ad opus Hugonis Palmeri . . . Et preceptum est quod ponatur in seysinam, quia est de sanguine de Riptone Regis.'

[1] Court Rolls of King's Ripton, Augment. Off. xxiii. 94, m. 15 : ' Curia de Kingsripton tenta die Jovis proxima post translacionem S[ti]. Benedicti anno r. r. E. xxix[n] et dom. Joh. [abb. xv. Venit] Willelmus fil. Thome Unfroy de Kingesripton et reddidit sursum in manibus senescalli totum jus quod [habuit] in illis tribus acris terre in campis de Kingesriptone quondam Willelmi capellani de eadem [villa ad opus filiorum] Rogeri de Kellawe *extranei* legitime procreatorum de Katerina filia Thome prepositi que est de con[di-cione sokemannorum ?] *bondorum* de Kingesripton. . . . Rogerus de Kellawe extraneus qui se maritauit cuidam Katerine filie Thome prepositi de Kinges-ripton que est de nacione et condicione eiusdem ville venit et petiit in curia nomine filiorum suorum ex legitimo matrimonio exeuntium de corpore pre-fate Katerine illas vi acras terre. . . . (Juratores dicunt) quod nichil inde sciunt nec aliquid super isto articulo presentare volunt ad presens. Et sic infecto negocio maximo contemptu domini et balliuorum suorum extra curiam recesserunt. Et ideo preceptum est balliuis quod die in . . . faciant de eisdem juratis xl solidos ad opus domini.'

[2] Stoneleigh Reg., 30 (Edward II injunction) : ' Et quidam forinseci qui sokemanni non sunt auctoritate sua propria et per negligenciam dicti Abbatis et conuentus, ut dicitur, a quibusdam sokemannorum illorum quasdam terras et tenementa alienauerunt. Nos igitur super premissis plenius certiorari uolentes assignauimus vos una cum his, quos vobis associaueritis, ad inqui-rendum qui sokemanni huiusmodi terras et tenementa ibidem alienauerunt huiusmodi forinsecis aut extrinsecis et quibus,' etc. Cf. the Statute of I Richard II, Stat. I. cap. 6. It was altogether a dangerous transaction for the socmen, because they were risking their privileges thereby. It must have been lucrative.

courts during the thirteenth century. The tenants of
Tavistock in Devonshire were seeking protection against
their lords, and appealing to the right of ancient demesne.
The case was debated two or three times during Henry III's
reign, and in 1279 judgment was given against the plaintiffs by an imposing quorum, as many as eight judges with
the Chief Justice Ralph Hengham at their head. It was
conceded that Tavistock was ancient demesne, but the
claimants were held to be villains and not villain socmen,
and this on the ground that the Domesday description did
not mention socmen, but only villains [1]. It seems strange
to dispute a decision given with such solemnity by men
who were much better placed to know about these things
than we are, but there does not seem to be any possible
doubt that Hengham and his companions were entirely
wrong. Their decision is in contradiction with almost all
the recorded cases ; it was always assumed that the stiff
Domesday terminology was quite insufficient to show
whether a man was a pure villain or a free man holding in
villainage, which last would be the villain socman in ancient
demesne. If Hengham's doctrine had been taken as a
basis for decision in these cases, no ancient demesne
tenancy would have been recognised at all out of the
Danelaw counties, that is in far the greater part of England,
as Domesday never mentions socmen there at all. In the
Danelaw counties, on the other hand, the privilege would
have been of no use, as those who were called socmen there
were freeholders protected without any reference to ancient
demesne. Altogether the attempt to make Domesday
serve the purpose of establishing the mode of tenure for

---

[1] Placitorum Abbrev., p. 270 (Coram Rege, Mich. 7/8 Edw. I) : ' Et eciam
comperto in libro de Domesday quod non fit aliqua mencio de sokemannis set
tantummodo de villanis et servis et eciam comperto per inquisicionem quod
multi eorum sunt adventicii quibus tenementa sua tradita fuerunt ad voluntatem
dominorum suorum ... consideraverunt quod predictus Galfridus eat inde sine
die et quod predicti homines teneant tenementa predicta in predicto manerio
per servilia servicia si voluerint, salvo statu corporum suorum, et quod de
cetero non possunt clamare aliquod certum statum et sint in misericordia pro
falso clameo.'

the thirteenth century must be called a misdirected one.
It was quite singular, as the courts generally went back
upon Domesday only with the object of finding out whether
a particular manor had been vested in the crown at the time
of the Conquest or not.   It should be noted that Bracton
considered the case from a very different point of view, as
one may judge by the note he jotted down on the margin
of his Note-book against a trial of 1237–8.   He says: 'Nota
de villanis Henrici de Tracy de Tawystoke qui nunquam
fuerunt in manu Domini Regis nec antecessorum suorum
et loquebantur de tempore Regis Edwardi coram W. de
Wiltona[1].'   Wilton's decision must have been grounded on
the assumption that the ancestors of the claimants were
strangers to the manor, or else that the manor had never
formed part of the ancient demesne.   This would, of
course, be in direct contradiction to the opinion that the
Tavistock tenants were descended from the king's born
villains.

   I cannot help thinking that Hengham's decision may
have been prompted either by partiality towards the lord
of the manor or by an ill-considered wish to compress the
right of ancient demesne within the narrowest bounds
possible.   In any case this trial deserves attention by
reason of the eminent authorities engaged in drawing up
the · judgment, and as illustrating the difficulties which
surround the points at issue and lead to confusion both in
the decisions and in the treatment of them by law writers.
In order to gain firm ground we must certainly go back
again to the fundamental propositions laid down with great
clearness by Bracton.   It was not all the tenants on ancient
demesne soil that had a right to appeal to its peculiar
privileges—some had protection at Common Law and
some had no protection at all.   But the great majority of
the tenants enjoyed special rights, and these men of ancient
demesne were considered to be free by blood and holding
in villainage.   If the books had not noticed their personal
freedom in so many words, it would have been proved by

---

[1] Bract. Note-book, pl. 1237.

the fact that they were always capable of leaving their tenements and going away at pleasure.

Bracton does not restrict himself to this statement of the
case ; he adds a few lines to give a historical explanation
of it. ‘ At the time of the Conquest,’ says he, ‘ there were
free men holding their lands freely, and by free services or
free customs. When they were ejected by stronger people,
they came back and received the same lands to be held in
villainage and by villain services, which were specified and
certain [1].’

The passage is a most interesting one, but it calls for
some comment. How is it that the special case of ancient
demesne gets widened into a general description of the
perturbations consequent upon the Conquest ? For a
general description it is ; by the ‘ stronger folk,’ the ‘ poten-
tiores,’ are certainly not meant the king and his officers
only. On the other hand, how can it be said of any but
the ancient demesne tenants that they resumed their
holdings by certain though base services ? The wording is
undoubtedly and unfortunately rather careless in this most
important passage, still the main positions which Bracton
intended to convey are not affected by his rather clumsy
way of stating them. Ancient demesne tenure, notwithstanding its peculiarities, is one species of a mode of holding which was largely represented everywhere, namely
of the status of free men holding in villainage ; this
condition had been strongly affected if not actually produced by the Conquest. It is interesting to compare the
description of the Conquest, as given at greater length but
in a looser way, in the Dialogus de Scaccario. It is stated
there that those who had actually fought against the
Conqueror were deprived of their lands for ever after.
Those who for some reason had not actually joined in
the contest were suffered to hold their lands under
Norman lords, but with no claim to hereditary succession.
Their occupation being uncertain, their lords very often
deprived them of their lands and they had no means to

Bracton's historical explana- tion.

---

[1] Bracton, f. 7.

procure restitution. Their complaints gave rise to a discussion of the matter before the king, and it was held that
nothing could be claimed by these people by way of succession from the time preceding the Conquest, and that
actionable rights could originate only in deeds granted by
the Norman lords[1]. The Dialogus as compared with
Bracton lays most stress on the opposite side of the
picture ; the disabilities of persons holding at will are set
forth not only as a consequence of the state of things
following conquest *de facto*, but as the result of a legal
reconsideration of the facts. As a classification of tenures
the passage would not be complete, of course, since neither
the important species of free socage recognised by Domesday nor the ancient demesne tenure appears. It is only
the contrast between villainage and holding by charter that
comes out strongly. But in one way the Dialogus rein-
forces Bracton, if I may be allowed to use the expression:
for it traces back the formation of a very important kind of
villainage to the Conquest, and connects the attempts of
persons entangled into it to obtain protection with their
original rights before the Conquest.

Saxon
origin
of ancient
demesne
tenure.

Reverting now to the question of ancient demesne, we
shall have to consider what light these statements throw on
the origin of the tenure. I have noticed several times that

---

[1] Dialogus de Scaccario, i. 10: ' Post regni conquisitionem, post justam
rebellium subversionem, cum rex ipse regisque proceres loca nova perlustra-
rent, facta est inquisitio diligens, qui fuerint qui contra regem in bello dimi-
cantes per fugam se salvaverint. His omnibus et item haeredibus eorum qui
in bello occubuerunt, spes omnis terrarum et fundorum atque redituum, quos
ante possederant, praeclusa est ; magnum namque reputabant frui vitae
beneficio sub inimicis. Verum qui vocati ad bellum nec dum convenerant,
vel familiaribus vel quibuslibet necessariis occupati negotiis non interfuerant,
cum tractu temporis devotis obsequiis gratiam dominorum possedissent, sine
spe successionis, sibi tantum pro voluptate (voluntate ?) tamen dominorum
possidere coeperunt. Succedente vero .tempore cum dominis suis odiosi
passim a possessionibus pellerentur, nec esset qui ablata restitueret, communis
indigenarum ad regem pervenit querimonia, quasi sic omnibus exosi et rebus
spoliati ad alienigenas transire cogerentur. Communicato tandem super his
consilio, decretum est, ut quod a dominis suis exigentibus meritis interveniente pactione legitima poterant obtinere, illis inviolabili jure concederentur ;
ceterum autem nomine successionis a temporibus subactae gentis nihil sibi
vendicarent.'

ancient demesne socage was connected in principle with the
condition of things in Saxon times, immediately before the
Conquest. The courts had to impose limitations in order
to control evidence ; the whole institution was in a way
created by limitation, because it restricted itself to the
T. R. E. of Domesday as the only acceptable test of Saxon
condition. But, notwithstanding all these features imposed
by the requirements of procedure, ancient demesne drew its
origin distinctly from pre-Conquest conditions. The manors
forming it are taken as the manors of St. Edward[1] ; the
tenants, whenever they want to make a solemn claim, set
forth their rights from the time of St. Edward[2], or even
Cnut[3]. But does this mean that the actual privileges of
the tenure were extant in Saxon times ? Surely not. Such
things as freedom from common taxation, exemption from
toll, separate jurisdiction, certainly existed in behalf of the
king's demesnes before the Conquest, but there is no
intimation whatever that the king's tenants enjoyed any
peculiar right or protection as to their holdings and services.
The 'little writ of right' and the 'Monstraverunt' are as
Norman, in a wide sense of the word, as the freedom
from serving on assizes or sending representatives to parliament. But although there is no doubt that this tenure
grew up and developed several of its peculiarities after
the Conquest, it had to fall back on Saxon times for its
substance[4], which may be described in few words—legal
protection of the peasantry. The influence of Norman
lawyers was exercised in shaping out certain actionable
rights, the effect of conquest was to narrow to a particular

---

[1] Stoneleigh Reg., 4 a : ' Que quidem maneria existencia in possessione et manu domini regis Edwardi per universum regnum vocantur
antiquum dominicum corone regis Anglie prout in libro de Domesday
continetur.'

[2] ' Loquebantur de tempore S[ti] Edwardi Regis coram W. de Wilton.'

[3] The men of King's Ripton.

[4] I do not think there is any ground for the suggestion thrown out by
M. Kovalevsky in the Law Quarterly, iv. p. 271, namely, that the law of ancient
demesne was imported from Normandy. Whatever the position of the
villains was in the Duchy, Norman influence in England made for subjection,
because it was the influence of conquest. It must be remembered that in a

class a protection originally conferred broadly, and the action of Saxon tradition was to supply a general stock of freedom and independent right, from which the privileged condition of Norman times could draw its nourishment, if I may put it in that way. It would be idle now to discuss in what proportion the Saxon influence on the side of freedom has to be explained by the influx of men who had been originally owners of their lands, and what may be assigned to the contractual character of Saxon tenant-right. This subject must be left till we come to examine the evidence supplied by Saxon sources of information. My present point is that the ancient demesne tenure of the Conquest is a remnant of the condition of things before the Conquest[1].

It may well be asked why the destructive effects of Norman victory were arrested on ancient demesne soil? Was not the king as likely to exercise his discretion in respect of the peasantry as any feudal lord, and is it likely that he would have let himself be fettered by considerations and obligations which did not bind his subjects? In view of such questions one is tempted to treat the protection of the tenants on the ancient demesne merely as a peculiar boon granted to the people whom the king had to give away. I need not say that such an interpretation would be entirely wrong. I hope I have been able to make out convincingly that legal protection given against private lords on manors which had been alienated was only an outgrowth from that certainty of condition which was allowed on the king's own lands. I will just add now that one very striking fact ought to be noticed in this connexion; certainty of tenure and service is limited to one particular class in the

sense the feudal law of England was the hardest of all in Western Europe, and this on account of the invasion.

[1] Stubbs, Const. Hist. i. 454: 'In those estates, which, when they had been held by the crown since the reign of Edward the Confessor, bore the title of manors in ancient demesne, very much of the ancient popular process had been preserved without any change, and to the present day some customs are maintained in them which recall the most primitive institutions.' I shall have to speak about the mode of holding the courts in another chapter.

manor, although that class is the most numerous one.
If this privilege came into being merely by the fixation of
status at the time when a manor passed from the crown,
the state of the villain pure would have got fixed in the
same way as that of the villain socman.   But it did not,
and so one cannot shirk the difficult question, What gave
rise to the peculiar protection against the lord when the
lord happened to be king ?

I think that three considerations open the way out of the
difficulty.   To begin with, the king was decidedly considered as the one great safeguard of Saxon tradition
and the one defender against Norman encroachments.
He had constantly to hear the cry about 'the laws of
Edward the Confessor,' and although the claim may be
considered as a very vague one in general matters, it
became substantiated in this case of tenure and services by
the Domesday record.   Then again, the proportion of free
owners who had lapsed into territorial dependence must
have been much greater on the king's land than anywhere
else ; it was quite usual to describe an allodial owner from
the feudal point of view as holding under the king in a particular way, and villain socage was only one of several kinds
of socage after all.   Last, but not least, the protection
against exactions was in reality directed not against the
king personally but against his officers, and the king personally was quite likely to benefit by it almost as much as
his men.   It amounted after all only to a recognition of
definite customs in general, to a special judicial organisation of the manor which made it less dependent upon the
steward, and to the facilities afforded for complaint and
revision of judgments.   As to this last it must be noted that
the king's men were naturally enough in a better position
than the rest of the English peasantry; the curse of villainage was that manorial courts were independent of superior
organisation as far as the lower tenants were concerned.
But courts in royal manors were the king's courts after all,
and as such they could hardly be severed from the higher
tribunals held in the king's name.

I may be allowed to sum up the conclusions of this chapter under the following heads :—

1. The law of ancient demesne is primarily developed in regard to the manors in the king's own hand.

2. The special protection granted to villain socmen in ancient demesne is a consequence of a certainty of condition as much recognised in manors which the king still holds as in those which he has alienated.

3. This certainty of condition is derived from the Conquest as the connecting link between the Norman and the Saxon periods.

CHAPTER IV.

LEGAL ASPECT OF VILLAINAGE. CONCLUSIONS.

I HAVE been trying to make out what the theories of the lawyers were with regard to villainage in its divers ramifications. Were we to consider this legal part of the subject merely as a sort of crust superposed artificially over the reality of social facts, we should have to break through the crust in order to get at the reality. But, of course, the law regulating social conditions is not merely an external superstructure, but as to social facts is both an influence and a consequence. In one sense it is a most valuable product of the forces at play in the history of society, most valuable just by reason of the requirements of its formalism and of those theoretical tendencies which give a very definite even if a somewhat distorted shape to the social processes which come within its sphere of action.

The formal character of legal theory is not only important because it puts things into order and shape; it suggests a peculiar and efficient method of treating the historical questions connected with law. The legal intellect is by its calling and nature always engaged in analysing complex cases into constitutive elements, and bringing these elements under the direction of principles. It is constantly struggling with the confusing variety of life, and from the historian's point of view it is most interesting when it succumbs in the struggle. There is no law, however subtle and comprehensive, which does not exhibit on its logical surface seams and scars, testifying to the incomplete fusing together of doctrines that cannot be brought under the cover of one principle. And so a dialectic examination of legal forms which makes manifest the contradictions and confused notions they contain actually helps us to an insight into the historical stratification of ideas and facts, a stratification which cannot be abolished however much lawyers may crave for unity and logic.

Uncertainty and contradictions of legal theory.

In the particular case under discussion medieval law is especially rich in such historical clues. The law writers are trying hard to give a construction of villainage on the basis of the Roman doctrine of slavery, but their fabric gives way at every point. It would be hardly a fair description to say that we find many survivals of an older state of things and many indications of a new development. Everything seems in a state of vacillation and fermentation during the thirteenth century. As to the origin of the servile status the law of bastards gets inverted ; in the case of matrimony the father-rule is driving the mother-rule from the ground ; the influence of prescription is admitted by some lawyers and rejected by others. As to the means whereby persons may issue out of that condition, the views of Glanville and Bracton are diametrically opposed, and there are still traces in practice of the notion that a villain cannot buy his freedom and that he cannot be manumitted by the lord himself in regard to third persons. In their treatment of services in their reference to status the courts apply the two different tests of certainty and of kind. In their treatment of tenure they still hesitate between a complete denial of protection to villainage and the recognition of it as a mode of holding which is protected by legal remedies. And even when the chief lines are definitely drawn they only disclose fundamental contradictions in all their crudeness.

In civil law, villains are disabled against their lords but evenly matched against strangers ; even against a lord legal protection is lingering in the form of an action upon covenant and in the notion that the villain's wainage should be secure. In criminal and in police law villains are treated substantially as free persons: they have even a share, although a subordinate one, in the organisation of justice. The procedure in questions of status is characterised by outrageous privileges given to the lord against a man in 'a villain nest,' and by distinct favour shown to those out of the immediate range of action of the lord. The law is quite as much against giving facilities to prove a man's servitude as it is against granting that man any rights when once his servitude has been established. The reconciliation of all these contradictions and anomalies cannot be attempted on dogmatic grounds. The law of villainage must not be constructed either on the assumption of slavery, or on that of liberty, or on that of *colonatus* or ascription. It contains elements from each of these three conditions, and it must be explained historically.

The material hitherto collected and discussed enables us to distinguish different layers in its formation. To begin with, the influence of lawyers must be taken into account. This is at once to be seen in the treatment of distinctions and divisions. The Common Law, as it was forming itself in the King's Court, certainly went far to smoothe down the peculiarities of local custom. Even when such peculiarities were legally recognised, as in the case of ancient demesne, the control and still more the example of the Common Law Courts was making for simplification and reducing them more or less to a generally accepted standard. The influence of the lawyers was exactly similar in regard to subdivisions on the vertical plane (if I may use the expression): for these varieties of dependence get fused into general servitude, and in this way classes widely different in their historical development are brought together under the same name. The other side of this process of simplification is shown where legal theory hardens and deepens the divisions it acknowledges. In this way the chasm between liberty and servitude increases as the notion of servitude gets broader. In order to get sharp boundaries and clear definitions to go by, the lawyers are actually driven

Influence of lawyers.

to drop such traits of legal relations as are difficult to manage with precision, however great their material importance, and to give their whole attention to facts capable of being treated clearly. This tendency may account for the ultimate victory of the quantitative test of servitude over the qualitative one, or to put it more plainly, of the test of certainty of services over the discussion of kind of services. Altogether the tendency towards an artificial crystallisation of the law cannot be overlooked.

Roman law, Norman law, and royal jurisdiction.

In the work of simplifying conditions artificially the lawyers had several strong reagents at their disposal. The mighty influence of Roman law has been often noticed, and there can be no doubt that it was brought to bear on our subject to the prejudice of the peasantry and to the extinction of their independent rights. It would not have been so strong if many features of the vernacular law had not been brought half way to meet it. Norman rules, it is well known, exercised a very potent action on the forms of procedure [1] ; but the substantive law of status was treated very differently in Normandy and in England, and it is not the influx of Norman notions which is important in our case, but the impetus given by them to the development of the King's Courts. This development, though connected with the practice of the Duchy, cannot be described simply or primarily as Norman. Once the leaven had been communicated, English lawyers did their own work with great independence as well as ingenuity of thought, and the decision of the King's Court was certainly a great force. I need not point out again to what extent the law was fashioned by the writ procedure, but I would here recall to attention the main fact, that the opposition between 'free' and 'unfree' rested chiefly on the point of being protected or not being protected by the jurisdiction of the King's Court.

Social bias of legal theories.

If we examine the action of lawyers as a whole, in order to trace out, as it were, its social bias, we must come to the con-

[1] Brunner, Entstehung der Schwurgerichte, has made an epoch in the discussion of this phenomenon.

clusion that it was exercised first in one direction and then in the opposite one. The refusal of jurisdiction may stand as the central fact in the movement in favour of servitude, although that movement may be illustrated almost in every department, even if one omits to take into account what may be mere instances of bad temper or gross partiality. But the wave begins to rise high in favour of liberty even in the thirteenth century. It does not need great perspicuity to notice that, apart from any progress in morals or ideas, apart from any growth of humanitarian notions, the law was carried in this direction by that development of the State which lays a claim to and upon its citizens, and by that development of social intercourse which substitutes agreement for bondage. Is it strange that the social evolution, as observed in this particular curve, does not appear as a continuous *crescendo*, but as a wavy motion? I do not think it can be strange, if one reflects that the period under discussion embraces both the growth and the decay of feudalism, embraces, that is, the growth of the principle of territorial power on the ruins of the tribal system and also the disappearance of that principle before the growing influence of the State.

Indirectly we have had to consider the influence of feudalism, as it was transmitted through the action of its lawyers. But it may be viewed in its direct consequences, which are as manifest as they are important. In England, feudalism in its definite shape is bound up with conquest[1], and it is well known that, though very much hampered on the political side by the royal power, it was exceptionally complete on the side of private law by reason of its sudden, artificial, and enforced introduction. One of the most important results of conquest from this point of view was certainly the systematic way in which the subjection of the peasantry was worked out. If we look for comparison to France as the next neighbour of England and a country which has influenced England, we shall find the same elements at work, but they combine in a variety of

Influence of conquest.

---

[1] I shall treat at length of the Norman Conquest in my third essay.

modes according to provincial and local peculiarities. Although the political power of the French baron is so much greater than that of an English lord, the *roturier* often keeps his distance from the serf better than was the case in England. In France everything depends upon the changing equilibrium of local forces and circumstances. In England the Norman Conquest produced a compact estate of aristocracy instead of the magnates of the continent, each of whom was strong or weak according to the circumstances of his own particular case; it produced Common Law and the King's Courts of Common Law; and it reduced the peasantry to something like uniform condition by surrounding the *liberi et legales homines* with every kind of privilege. The national colouring given by the *Dialogus de Scaccario* to the social question of the time is not without meaning in this light:—the peasants may be regarded as the remnant of a conquered race, or as the issue of rebels who have forfeited their rights.

English feudalism.

The feudal system once established produced certain effects quite apart from the Conquest, effects which flowed from its own inherent properties. The Conquest had east free and unfree peasantry together into the one mould of villainage; feudalism prevented villainage from lapsing into slavery. I have shown in detail how the manor gives a peculiar turn to personal subjection. Its action is perceivable in the treatment of the origin of the servile status. The villain, however near being a chattel, cannot be devised by will because he is considered as an annex to the free tenement of the lord. The connexion with a manor becomes the chief means of establishing and proving seisin of the villain. On the other hand, in the trial of *status*, manorial organisation led to the sharp distinction between persons in the power of the lord and out of it. This fact touches the very essence of the case. The more powerful the manor became, the less possible was it to work out subjection on the lines of personal slavery. Without entering into the economic part of the question for the present, merely from the legal point of view it was a necessary consequence of the rise of a local and territorial power that the working people under its sway were subjected by means of its territorial organisation and within its limited sphere of local action. Of course, the State upheld some of the lord's rights even outside the limits of the manor, but these were only a pale reflection of what took place within the manor, and they were more difficult to enforce in proportion as the barriers between the manors rose higher; it became very difficult for one lord to reclaim runaways who were lying within the manor of another lord.

If we remove those strata of the law of villainage which owe their origin to the action of the feudal system and to the action of the State, which rises on the ruins of the feudal system, we come upon remnants of the pre-feudal condition. They are by no means few or unimportant, and it is rather a wonder that so much should be preserved notwithstanding the systematic work of conquest, feudalism, and State. When I speak of pre-feudal condition I do not mean to say, of course, that feudalism had not been in the course of formation before the Norman Conquest. I merely wish to oppose a social order grounded on feudalism to a social order which was only preparing for it and developing on a different basis. The Conquest brought together the free and unfree. Our survivals of the state of things before the Conquest group themselves naturally in one direction, they are manifestations of the free element which went into the constitution of villainage. It is not strange that it should be so, because the servile element predominated in those parts of the law which had got the upper hand and the official recognition. A trait which goes further than the accepted law in the direction of slavery is the difficulties which are put by Glanville in the way of manumission. His statement practically amounts to a denial of the possibility of manumission, and such a denial we cannot accept. His way of treating the question may possibly be explained by old notions as to the in-

Survivals of pre-feudal condition.

ability of a master to put a slave by a mere act of his will
on the same level with free men.

Elements
of freedom.

However this may be, our survivals arrange themselves
with this single possible exception in the direction of freedom. Perhaps such facts as the villain's capacity to take
legal action against third persons, and his position in the
criminal and police law, ought not to be called survivals.
They are certain sides of the subject. They are indissolubly allied to such features of the civil law as the
occasional recognition of villainage as a protected tenure,
and the villain's admitted standing against the lord when
the lord had bound himself by covenant. In the light of
these facts villainage assumes an entirely different aspect
from that which legal theory tries to give it. Procedural
disability comes to the fore instead of personal debasement.
A villain is to a great extent in the power of his lord,
not because he is his chattel, but because the courts
refuse him an action against the lord. He may have
rights recognised by morality and by custom, but he has
no means to enforce them; and he has no means to
enforce them because feudalism disables the State and
prevents it from interfering. The political root of the
whole growth becomes apparent, and it is quite clear, on
the one hand, that liberation will depend to a great extent
on the strengthening of the State; and, on the other hand,
that one must look for the origins of enslavement to the
political conditions before and after the Conquest.

One undoubtedly encounters difficulties in tracing and
grouping facts with regard to those elements of freedom
which appear in the law of villainage. Sometimes it may
not be easy to ascertain whether a particular trait must be
connected with legal progress making towards modern
times, or with the remnants of archaic institutions. As a
matter of fact, however, it will be found that, save in very
few cases, we possess indications to show us which way we
ought to look.

Another difficulty arises from the fact that the law of
this period was fashioned by kings of French origin and

lawyers of Norman training. What share is to be assigned
to their formal influence? and what share comes from that
old stock of ideas and facts which they could not or would
not destroy? We may hesitate as to details in this respect.
It is possible that the famous paragraph of the so-called
Laws of William the Conqueror, prescribing in general terms
that peasants ought not to be taken from the land or
subjected to exactions[1], is an insertion of the Norman period,
although the great majority of these Laws are Saxon glean-
ings. It is likely that the notion of *wainage* was worked
out under the influence of Norman ideas; the name seems
to show it, and perhaps yet more the fact that the plough
was specially privileged in the duchy. It is to be assumed
that the king, not because he was a Norman but because
he was a king, was interested in the welfare of subjects on
whose back the whole structure of his realm was resting.
But the influence of the strangers went broadly against the
peasantry, and it has been repeatedly shown that Norman
lawyers were prompted by anything but a mild spirit towards them. The *Dialogus de Scaccario* is very instructive
on this point, because it was written by a royal officer who
was likely to be more impartial than the feudatories or
any one who wrote in their interest would be, and yet it
makes out that villains are mere chattels of their lord,
and treats them throughout with the greatest contempt.
And so, speaking generally, it is to the times before the
Conquest that the stock of liberty and legal independence
inherent in villainage must be traced, even if we draw
inferences merely on the strength of the material found on
this side of the Conquest. And when we come to Saxon
evidence, we shall see how intimately the condition of the
ceorl connects itself with the state of the villain along the
main lines and in detail.

　　The case of ancient demesne is especially interesting in Ancient
this light. It presents, as it were, an earlier and less demesne.
perfect crystallisation of society on a feudal basis than the
manorial system of Common Law. It steps in between the

---

[1] Leg. Will. Conq. i. 29 (Schmid, p. 340).

Saxon *soc* and *tun* on the one hand, and the manor on the other. It owes to the king's privilege its existence as an exception. The procedure of its court is organised entirely on the old pattern and quite out of keeping with feudal ideas, as will be shown by-and-by. Treating of it only in so far as it illustrates the law of status, it presents in separate existence the two classes which were fused in the system of the Common Law; villain socmen are carefully distinguished from the villains, and the two groups are treated differently in every way. A most interesting fact, and one to be taken up hereafter, is the way of treating the privileged group as the normal one. Villain socmen are *the* men of ancient demesne; villains are the exception, they appear only on the lord's demesne, and seem very few, so far as we can make a calculation of numbers. Villain socmen enjoy a certainty of condition which becomes actual tenant-right when the manor passes from the crown into a private lord's hand. As to its origin there can be no doubt—ancient demesne is traced back to Saxon times in as many words and by all our authorities.

Clues as to the condition of Saxon peasantry.
A careful analysis of the law of ancient demesne may even give us valuable clues to the condition of the Saxon peasantry. The point just noticed, namely, that the number of villain socmen is exceedingly large and quite out of proportion to that of other tenants, gives indirect testimony that the legal protection of the tenure was not due merely to an influx of free owners deprived of their lands by conquest. This is the explanation given by Bracton, but it is not sufficient to account for the privileged position of almost all the tenants within the manor. A considerable part of them surely held before the Conquest not as owners and not freely, but as tenants by base services, and their fixity of tenure is as important in the constitution of ancient demesne as is the influx of free owners. If this latter cause contributed to keep up the standard of this status, the former cause supplied that tradition of certainty to which ancient demesne right constantly appeals.

Another point to be kept firmly in view is that the careful distinction kept up on the ancient demesne between villain socmen and villains, proves the law on this subject to have originated in the general distribution of classes and rights during the Saxon period, and not in the exceptional royal privilege which preserved it in later days; I mean, that if certainty of condition had been granted to the tenantry merely because it was royal tenantry, which is unlikely enough in itself, the certainty would have extended to tenants of all sorts and kinds. It did not, because it was derived from a general right of one class of peasants to be protected at law, a right which did not in the least preclude the lord from using his slaves as mere chattels.

And so I may conclude : an investigation into the legal aspect of villainage discloses three elements in its complex structure. Legal theory and political disabilities would fain make it all but slavery; the manorial system ensures it something of the character of the Roman *colonatus*; there is a stock of freedom in it which speaks of Saxon tradition.

CHAPTER V.

THE SERVILE PEASANTRY OF MANORIAL RECORDS.

Manorial documents. IT would be as wrong to restrict the study of villainage to legal documents as to disregard them. The jurisprudence and practice of the king's courts present a one-sided, though a very important view of the subject, but it must be supplemented and verified by an investigation of manorial records. With one class of such documents we have had already to deal, namely with the rolls of manorial courts, which form as it were the stepping-stone between local arrangements and the general theories of Common Law. So-called manorial 'extents' and royal inquisitions based on them lead us one step further; they were intended to describe the matter-of-fact conditions of actual life, the distribution of holdings, the amount and nature of services, the personal divisions of the peasantry; their evidence is not open to the objection of having been artificially treated for legal purposes. Treatises on farming and instructions to manorial officers reflect the economic side of the system, and an enormous number of accounts of expenditure and receipts would enable the modern searcher, if so minded, to enter even into the detail of agricultural management[1]. We need not undertake this last inquiry, but some comparison between the views of lawyers and the actual facts of manorial administration must be attempted. Writers on Common Law invite one to the task by recognising a great variety of local customs;

[1] Thorold Rogers has made great use of this last class of manorial documents in his well-known books.

Bracton, for instance, mentioning two notable deviations from general rules in the department of law under discussion. In Cornwall the children of a villain and of a free woman were not all unfree, but some followed the father and others the mother[1]. In Herefordshire the master was not bound to produce his serfs to answer criminal charges[2]. If such customs were sufficiently strong to counteract the influence of general rules of Common Law, the vitality of local distinctions was even more felt in those cases where they had no rules to break through. It may be even asked at the very outset of the inquiry whether there is not a danger of our being distracted by endless details. I hope that the following pages will show how the varieties naturally fall into certain classes and converge towards a few definite positions, which appear the more important as they were not produced by artificial arrangement from above. We must be careful however, and distinguish between isolated facts and widely-spread conditions. Another possible objection to the method of our study may be also noticed here, as it is connected with the same difficulty. Suppose we get in one case the explanation of a custom or institution which recurs in many other cases; are we entitled to generalise our explanation? This seems methodically sound as long as the contrary cannot be established, for the plain reason that the variety of local facts is a variety of combinations and of effects, not of constitutive elements and of causes. The agents of development are not many, though their joint work shades off into a great number of variations. We may be pretty sure that a result repeated several times has been effected by the same factors in the same way; and if in some instances these factors appear manifestly, there is every reason to suppose them to have existed in all the cases. Such reflections are never convincing by themselves, however, and the best thing to test them will be to proceed from these broad statements to an inquiry into the particulars of the case.

[1] Bracton, 271 b.   [2] Bracton, 124.

Termino-logical classifica-tion.   The study of manorial evidence must start from a discussion as to terminology. The names of the peasantry will show the natural subdivisions of the class. If we look only to the unfree villagers, we shall notice that all the varieties of denomination can easily be arranged into four classes : one of these classes has in view social standing, another economic condition, a third starts from a difference of services, and a fourth from a difference of holdings. The line may not be drawn sharply between the several divisions, but the general contrast cannot be mistaken.

Terms to indicate social standing.   The term of most common occurrence is, of course, *villanus*. Although its etymology points primarily to the place of dwelling, and indirectly to specific occupations, it is chiefly used during the feudal period to denote servitude. It takes in both the man who is personally unfree and stands in complete subjection to the lord, and the free person settled on servile land. Both classes mentioned and distinguished by Bracton are covered by it. The common opposition is between *villanus* and *libere tenens*, not between *villanus* and *liber homo*. It is not difficult to explain such a phraseology in books compiled either in the immediate interest of the lords or under their indirect influence, but it must have necessarily led to encroachments and disputes: it has even become a snare for later investigators, who have sometimes been led to consider as one compact mass a population consisting of two different classes, each with a separate history of its own. The Latin 'rusticus' is applied in the same general way. It is less technical however, and occurs chiefly in annals and other literary productions, for which it was better suited by its classical derivation. But when it is used in opposition to other terms, it stands exactly as *villanus*, that is to say, it is contrasted with *libere tenens* [1].

---

[1] Cartulary of Malmesbury (Rolls Series), ii. 186 : ' Videlicet quod prefatus Ricardus concessit praedictis abbati et conventui et eorum tenentibus, tam rusticis, quam liberis—quod ipsi terras suas libere pro voluntate sua excolant.'

The fundamental distinction of personal status has left Villains some traces in terminology. The Hundred Rolls, personally especially the Warwickshire one [1], mention *servi* very often. Sometimes the word is used exactly as *villanus* would be [2]. *Tenere in servitute* and *tenere in villenagio* are equivalent [3]. But other instances show that *servus* has also a special meaning. Cases where it occurs in an 'extent' immediately after *villanus*, and possibly in opposition to it, are not decisive [4]. They may be explained by the fact that the persons engaged in drawing up a custumal, jotted down denominations of the peasantry without comparing them carefully with what preceded. A marginal note *servi* would not be necessarily opposed to a *villani* following it ; it may only be a different name for the same thing. And it may be noted that in the Hundred Rolls these names very often stand in the margin, and not in the text. But such an explanation would be out of place when both expressions are used in the same sentence. The description of Ipsden in Oxfordshire has the following passage : *item dictus R. de N. habet de proparte sua septem servos villanos.* (Rot. Hundr. ii. 781, b: cf. 775, b, *Servi Custumarii.*) It is clear that it was intended, not only to describe the general condition of the peasantry, but to define more particularly their status. This observation and the general meaning of the word will lead us to believe that in many cases when it is used by itself, it implies personal subjection.

[1] As to the Warwickshire Hundred Roll in the Record Office, see my letter in the Athenæum, 1883, December 22.

[2] Rot. Hundred. ii. 471, a : '*Libere tenentes* prioris de Swaveseia. . . . Henricus Palmer—1 mesuagium et 3 rodas terre reddens 12 d. et 2 precarias. *Servi* Adam scot tenet 10 acras reddens 4s. et 6 precarias . . . . *Cotarii* . . . .'

[3] Rot. Hundred. ii. 715, a : 'In *servitute* tenentes. Assunt et ibidem 10 tenentes qui tenent 10 virgatas terre in *villenagio* et operantur ad voluntatem domini et reddunt per annum 25 s.'

[4] Rot. Hundred. ii. 690, 691 : 'Villani—servi—custumarii. Et tenent ut villani, ut servi, ut libere tenentes.' Rot. Hundred. ii. 544, b : 'De custumariis Johannes Samar tenet 1 mesuagium et 1 croft . . . . per servicium 3 sol. 2 d. et secabit 2 acras et dim., falcabit per 1 diem. De servis. Nicholaus Dilkes tenet 15 acras—et faciet per annum 144 opera et metet 2 acras. De aliis servis . . . . De cotariis . . . . De aliis cotariis.'

The term *nativus* has a similar sense. But the relation
between it and *villanus* is not constant; sometimes this
latter marks the genus, while the former applies to a
species; but sometimes they are used interchangeably[1],
and the feminine for villain is *nieve* (*nativa*). But while
villanus is made to appear both in a wide and in a restricted sense, and for this reason cannot be used as a
special qualification, *nativus* has only the restricted sense
suggesting status[2]. In connection with other denominations *nativus* is used for the personally unfree[3]. When
we find *nativus domini*, the personal relation to the
lord is especially noticed[4]. The sense being such, no
wonder that the nature of the tenure is sometimes described in addition[5]. Of course, the primary meaning
is, that a person has been born in the power of the
lord, and in this sense it is opposed to the stranger—
forinsecus, extraneus[6]. In this sense again the Domesday

[1] Rot. Hundred. ii. 528, a : ' Henr. de Walpol habet latinos (*corr. nativos*),
qui tenent 180 acras terre et redd. 10 libr. et 8 sol. et 4 d. et ob. Nomina
eorum qui tenent de Henrico de Walpol in *villenagio*.' Chapter House,
County Boxes, Salop. 14, c : ' Libere tenentes . . . . Coterelli . . . . Nativi.'

[2] Hale, in his Introduction to the Domesday of St. Paul's, xxiv, speaks
of the ' nativi a principio ' of Navestock, and distinguishes them from the
villains. ' The ordinary praedial services due from the tenentes or villani
were not required to be performed in person, and whether in the manor
or out of it the villanus was not in legal language " sub potestate domini."
Not so the nativus.' Hale's explanation is not correct, but the twofold
division is noticed by him.

[3] Domesday of St. Paul's, 157 (Articuli visitationis) : ' An villani sive custumarii vendant terras. Item, an *nativi custumarii* maritaverunt filias—vel
vendiderint vitulum—vel arbores—succidant.' A Suffolk case is even more
clear. Registrum cellararii of Bury St. Edmunds, Cambridge University
Gg. iv. 4, f. 30, b : ' Gersumarius vel custumarius qui *nativus* est . . . . Antecessor recognovit se nativum domini abbatis in curia domini regis.'

[4] Cartulary of Eynsham in Oxfordshire, MS. of the Chapter of Christ Church
in Oxford, N. 27, p. 25, a : ' In primis Willelmus le Brewester *nativus domini*
tenet de dictis prato et terris. . .'

[5] Eynsham Cartulary, 49, b : ' Johannes Kolyns nativus domini tenet 1 virgatam terre cum pertinenciis in bondagio.'

[6] Cartulary of St. Mary of Worcester (Camden Series), 15. a : ' Nativi, cum
ad aetatem pervenerint nisi immediate serviant patri—faciant 4 benripas et
forinsici similiter.' Survey of Okeburn, Q. R. Anc. Miscell. Alien Priories,
$\frac{2}{7}$: ' Aliquis nativus non potest recedere sine licencia neque catalla amo-

of St. Paul's speaks of 'nativi a principio' in Navestock[1].
But the fact of being born to the condition supposes personal subjection, and this explains why *nativi* are sometimes
mentioned in contrast with freemen[2], without any regard
being paid to the question of tenure. Natives, or villains
born, had their pedigrees as well as the most noble among
the peers. Such pedigrees were drawn up to prevent any
fraudulent assertion as to freedom, and to guide the lord
in case he wanted to use the native's kin in prosecution
of an action *de nativo habendo*. One such pedigree preserved in the Record Office is especially interesting, because it starts from some stranger, *extraneus*[3], who came
into the manor as a freeman, and whose progeny lapses
into personal villainage; apparently it is a case of vi lainage by prescription.

The other subdivision of the class—freemen holding Free men
unfree land[4]—has no special denomination. This deprives villain
us of a very important clue as to the composition of the land.
peasantry, but we may gather from the fact how very
near both divisions must have stood to each other in
actual life. The free man holding in villainage had the
right to go away, while the native was legally bound
to the lord; but it was difficult for the one to leave land
and homestead, and it was not impossible for the other
to fly from them, if he were ill-treated by his lord or the
steward. Even the fundamental distinction could not be
drawn very sharply in the practice of daily life, and in

vere nec extraneus libertatem dominorum ad commorandum ingrediat sine
licentia.'

[1] Domesday of St. Paul's, 80: 'Nativi a principio. Isti tenent terras
operarias.'

[2] Queen's Remembrancer's Miscellanies, 902-62: 'Rotuli de libertate de
Tynemouth, de liberis hominibus, non de nativis.'

[3] Queen's Remembrancer's Miscellanies, 902-77: 'Nativi de Sebrighte-
worth (Proavus extraneus).' See App. X.

[4] Warwickshire Hundr. Roll, Queen's Remembrancer's Miscellaneous
Books, 29, 19, b: 'Johannes le Clerc tenet 1 virg. terre pro eodcm sed est
libere condicionis.' Augment. Off., Duchy of Lancaster, Court Rolls, Bundle
32, 283: 'Unum mesuagium et 19 acre terre in Holand que sunt in manu
domini per mortem W. qui eas tenuit in bondagio. Ipse fuit liber, quia natus
fuit extra libertatem domini.'

every other respect, as to services, mode of holding, etc.,
there was no distinction. No wonder that the common
term *villanus* is used quite broadly, and aims at the tenure
more than at personal status.

Terms to
indicate
economic
condition.
　　　　Terms which have in view the general economic condition of the peasant, vary a good deal according to localities. Even in private documents they are on the whole
less frequent than the terms of the first class, and the
Hundred Rolls use them but very rarely. It would be very
wrong to imply that they were not widely spread in
practice. On the contrary, their vernacular forms vouch
for their vitality and their use in common speech. But
being vernacular and popular in origin, these terms cannot obtain the uniformity and currency of literary names
employed and recognised by official authority. The vernacular equivalent for *villanus* seems to have been *niet* or
neat[1]. It points to the regular cultivators of the arable,
possessed of holdings of normal size and performing the
typical services of the manor[2]. The peasant's condition
is here regarded from the economical side, in the mutual
relation of tenure and work, not in the strictly legal sense,
and men of this category form the main stock of the
manorial population. The Rochester Custumal says[3] that
neats are more free than cottagers, and that they hold

[1] Glastonbury Inquisitions of 1189 (Roxburghe Series), 48 : 'Radulfus
niet tenet dimidiam virgatam.'

[2] Glastonbury Inquis. (Roxburghe Series), 26 : ' Rogerus P. tenet virg. terre:
pro una medietate dat. xxx d. et pro alia medietate operatur sicut neth et
seminat dimidiam acram pro churset et dat hueortselver.' Ibid. 22 : 'Osbertus
tenet 1 virgatam terre medietatem pro ii sol. et dono et pro alia medietate
operatur quecumque jussus fuerit sicut neth.' Cartulary of Abingdon (Rolls
Series), ii. 304 : ' Illi sunt neti de villa. Aldredus de Brueria 5 sol. pro
dimidia hida et arat et varectat et seminat acram suo semine et trahit foenum
et bladum.' Ibid. ii. 302 : 'Bernerius et filius suus tenent unam cotsetland
unde reddunt cellario monachorum 6 sestaria mellis et camerae 31 d.'—'*De
netis*. Robertus tenet dimidiam hidam unde reddit 5 sol. et 3 den. et arabit
acram et seminabit semine suo et trahet foenum et bladum. Hoc de netis.'

[3] Black Book of Rochester Cathedral (ed. Thorpe), 10, a : 'Consuetudines
de Hedenham et de Cudintone. Dominus potest ponere ad opera quemcumque voluerit de netis suis in die St. Martini. Et sciendum quod neti idem
sunt quod Neiatmen qui aliquantulum liberiores sunt quam cotmen, qui
omnes habent virgatas ad minus.'

virgates. The superior degree of freedom thus ascribed to them is certainly not to be taken in the legal sense, but is merely a superiority in material condition. The contrast with cottagers is a standing one [1], and, being the main population of the village, *neats* are treated sometimes as if they were the only people there [2]. The name may be explained etymologically by the Anglo-Saxon *geneat*, which in documents of the tenth and eleventh century means a man using another person's land. The differences in application may be discussed when we come to examine the Saxon evidence.

Another Saxon term—*gebúr*—has left its trace in the *burus* and *buriman* of Norman records. The word does not occur very often, and seems to have been applied in two different ways—to the chief villains of the township in some places, and to the smaller tenantry, apparently in confusion with the Norman *bordarius*, in some other [3]. The very possibility of such a confusion shows that it was going out of common use. On the other hand, the Danish equivalent *bondus* is widely spread. It is to be found constantly in the Danish counties [4]. The original meaning is that of cultivator or ' husband '—the same in fact as that

[1] Cartulary of Shaftesbury, Harl. MSS. 61, f. 60 : ' Et habebit unum animal quietum in pastura, si est net, et de aliis herbagium. Et si idem fuerit cotsetle debet operari 2 diebus.' Ibid. 59 : ' Tempore Henrici Regis fuerunt in T. 18 Neti sed modo non sunt nisi 11 et ex 7 qui [non] sunt Nicholaus tenet terram [trium] et 4 sunt in dominico ; et 7 cotmanni fuerunt tempore Henrici Regis qui non sunt modo, quorum trium tenet terram Nicholaus et 4 sunt in dominico.' Ibid. 65 : '.Cotsetle . . . debet metere quantum unus nieth . . . et debet collocare messem vel . . . aliud facere . . . dum Neth messem attrahat . . . pannagium sicut Neth.' Ibid. 89 : ' Si moriatur cotsetle pro diviso dabit 12 d. et vidua tenebit pro illo id divisum tota vita sua. Si moriatur neatus dabit melius catellum et pro hoc tenebit quietus.'

[2] Glastonbury Inquis. 51 : ' Et nieti tenent 9 acras unde reddunt 3 s.' Ibid. 47 : ' Nieti habent unum pratum pro 5 s.'

[3] Glastonbury Inquis. 105 : ' Ernaldus buriman dimidiam virgatam, Iohannes burimannus dimidiam virgatam.' Cf. Custumal of Bleadon, p. 189 ; Cartulary of Shaftesbury, Harl. MSS. 61, f. 45.

[4] It is to be found sometimes out of the Danish shires, e. g. in Oxfordshire. Rot. Hundred. ii. 842, b : ' Bondagium : Johannes Bonefaunt tenet unam virgatam terre de eodem Roberto . . . reddit . . . 11 sol. pro omni servicio et scutagium quando currit 20 d.' Of course there were isolated Danish settlements outside the Denelaw.

of *gebúr* and boor. Feudal records give curious testimony of the way in which the word slid down into the 'bondage' of the present day. We see it wavering, as it were, sometimes exchanging with *servus* and *villanus*, and sometimes opposed to them[1]. Another word of kindred meaning, chiefly found in eastern districts, is *landsettus*, with the corresponding term for the tenure[2]; this of course according to its etymology simply means an occupier, a man sitting on land.

Terms to indicate the nature of services.

Several terms are found which have regard to the nature of services. Agricultural work was the most common and burdensome expression of economical subjection. Peasants who have to perform such services in kind instead of paying rents for them are called *operarii*[3]. Another designation which may be found everywhere is *consuetudinarii* or *custumarii*[4]. It points to customary services, which the people were bound to perform. When such tenants are opposed to the villains, they are probably free men holding in villainage by customary work[5]. As the name does not give any indication as to the importance of the holding

---

[1] Rot. Hundred. ii. 486, a: 'Tenentes Alicie la Blunde. *Bondi*, A. habet in eadem villa 2 villanos, quorum quilibet tenet mesuagium cum 30 a. Id. Al. hab. 1 bondum qui ten. 20 a. *Custumarii*, Id. Al. habet 1 villanum, qui tenet 1 mes. cum 44 a.' Rot. Hundred. ii. 486, a: 'De W. le Blunde. *Villani*, R. de Badburnham. *Bondi cotarii*.' Cf. Ibid. 422, b; 423, a: 'Libere tenentes . . . . Custumarii . . . . Bondi.'

[2] Ramsey Inquisitions, Galba, E. x. 34: 'W. L. tenet in landsetagio 12 a. pro 9 den. et ob. R. 24 a. de landsetagio et 12 a. de novo.' Cartulary of Ramsey (Rolls Series), i. 426: 'G. C. dat dim. marcam ut K. filius suus fiat heusebonde de 6 a. terrae de lancetagio.' Registr. Cellararii of Bury St. Edmund's, Cambridge University, Gg. iv. 4, f. 400, b: '9 acre unde 4 a. fuerunt libere et 5 lancettagii.' Cartulary of Ramsey (Rolls Series), i. 425: 'S. Cl. recognovit, quod 24 a., quas tenet, sunt in lanceagio dom. Abbatis *salvo corpore suo* et quod faciet omnes consuetudines serviles . . . . *lancectus nacione*.'

[3] Domesday of St. Paul's, 17: 'Item omnes operarii dimidiae virgatae debent invenire vasa et utensilia ter in anno ad braciandum.' Cf. 28.

[4] Rot. Hundred. ii. 422, 423. Cf. 507, a: 'Libere tenentes . . . Nicholaus Trumpe 3 a. terre cum mesuagio et red. per ann. 20 d. Custumarii . . . Nicholaus Trumpe ten. 1 a. terre et redd. 2 sol.'

[5] Exch. Q. R. Misc. Alien Priories, ⅔. (Chilteham): '. . . . Redditus villanorum de 126 villanis 41 libre, 14 s. 11 d. Item sunt 70 custumarii qui debent arare bis per annum cum 17 carucis . . . . Item sunt 25 villani qui debent herciare quilibet eorum per 2 dies,' etc.

a qualification is sometimes added to it, which determines the size of the tenement [1].

In many manors we find a group of tenants, possessed of small plots of land for the service of following the demesne ploughs. These are called *akermanni* or *carucarii* [2], are mostly selected among the customary holders, and enjoy an immunity from ordinary work as long as they have to perform their special duty [3]. On some occasions the records mention *gersumarii*, that is peasants who pay a *gersuma*, a fine for marrying their daughters [4]. This payment being considered as the badge of personal serfdom, the class must have consisted of men personally unfree.

Those names remain to be noticed which reflect the size of the holding. In one of the manors belonging to St. Paul's Cathedral in London we find *hidarii* [5]. This does not mean that every tenant held a whole hide. On the

Terms to indicate the size of the holding.

---

[1] Cartulary of St. Peter of Gloucester (Rolls Series), iii. 203 : 'Omnes consuetudinarii majores habebunt tempore falcationis prati unum multonem, farinam, et salem ad potagium. Et minores consuetudinarii habebunt quilibet eorum 1 panem et omnes 1 caseum in communi, unam acr. frumenti pejoris campi de dominico et unum carcasium multonis, et unum panem ad Natale.'

[2] Cartulary of Malmesbury (Rolls Series), i. 154, 155. Cf. i. 186, 187. Cartulary of St. Mary of Worcester (Camden Society), 43, b; Rot. Hundred. ii. 775, b.

[3] Rot. Hundred. ii. 602, a. Cf. Exch. Q. R. Alien Priories, $\frac{2}{3}$: 'Item sunt in eadem villata de Wardeboys 6 dimidias virgatas—que vocantur Akermannelondes, quorum W. L. tenet $\frac{1}{2}$ virgatam pro qua ibit ad carucam Abbatis si placeat abbati vel dabit sicut illi qui tenent 6 Maltlondes preter 15 d.' Rot. Hundred. i. 208 : 'Utrum akermanni debent servicium suum vel servicii redempcionem.'

[4] Registr. Cellararii of Bury St. Edmund's, Cambridge University, Gg. iv. 4, f. 26 : 'Gersumarii (Custumarii) . . . . Gersuma pro filia sua maritanda.' Ibid. 108, b : 'Tenentes 15 acrarum custumarii—omnes sunt gersumarii ad voluntatem domini.' Cartulary of Bury St. Edmund's, Harl. MSS. 3977, f. 87, d : 'Nichol. G. gersumarius tenet 30 a. pro 8 sol. que solent esse custumarie.' I may add on the authority of Mr. F. York Powell that *landsettus* (land-seti), as well as *akermannus* (aker-maðr) and *gersuma* (görsemi), are certainly Danish loan-words, which accounts for their occurrence in Danish districts.

[5] Hale, Introduction to the Domesday of St. Paul's, xxv : 'If we compare the services due from the Hidarii with those of the libere tenentes on other manors, it will be evident, that the Hidarii of Adulvesnasa belonged to the ordinary class of villani, their distinction being probably only this, that they were jointly, as well as severally, bound to perform the services due from the hide of which they held part.'

L 2

contrary, they have each only a part of the hide, but their plots are reckoned up into hides, and the services due from the whole hide are stated. *Virgatarius*[1] is of very common occurrence, because the virgate was considered as the normal holding of a peasant. It is curious that in consequence the virgate is sometimes called simply *terra*, and holders of virgates—*yerdlings*[2]. Peasants possessed of half virgates are *halfyerdlings* accordingly. The expressions 'a full villain[3]' and 'half a villain' must be understood in the same sense. They have nothing to do with rank, but aim merely at the size of the farm and the quantity of services and rents. *Ferlingseti* are to be met with now and then in connexion with the *ferling* or *ferdel*, the fourth part of a virgate[4].

The constant denomination for those who have no part in the common arable fields, but hold only crofts or small plots with their homesteads, is 'cotters' (*cotsetle, cottagiarii, cottarii*[5], etc.). They get opposed to villains as to owners of normal holdings[6]. Exceptionally the term is used for those who have very small holdings in the open

[1] Eynsham Inquest, 49, a : 'Summa (prati) xvi a. et iv perticas que dimidebantur xi virgatariis et rectori ut uni eorum et quia jam supersunt tantummodo 4 virgatarii et rector, dominus habet in manu sua 7 porciones dicti prati.'

[2] Cartulary of Battle, Augmentation Office, Miscell. Books, 57, f. 35, s : 'Yherdlinges . . . . custumarii.' Ibid. 42, b : 'Majores Erdlinges scil. virgarii. Halferdlinges (majores cottarii) Minores cottarii.'

[3] Black Book of Peterborough, 164 : 'In Scotere et in Scaletorp—24 plenarii villani et 2 dimidii villani—Plenarii villani operantur 2 diebus in ebdomada.'

[4] Glastonbury Inqu. (Roxburghe Series), 23 : 'Operatur ut alii ferlingseti.'

[5] Glastonbury Inqu. (Roxburghe Series), 137 : 'Cotsetle debent faldiare ab Hoccade usque ad festum S. Michaelis.' Cartulary of St. Peter of Gloucester (Rolls Series), iii. 71 : 'Burgenses Gloucestriae reddunt una cum aliis tenentibus ad manerium Berthonae praedictae per annum de coteriis cum curtillagiis in suburbio Gloucestriae quorum nomina non recolunt 29 solidos 7 d. de redditu assiso.' Ibid. iii. 116 : 'Cotlandarii : Johannes le Waleys tenet unum mesuagium cum curtillagio et faciet 8 bederipas et 3 dies ad fenum levandum, et valent 13½d.'

[6] Norfolk Feodary, Additional MSS. 2, a : 'Et idem Thomas tenet de predicto Roberto de supradicto feodo per predictum servicium sexaginta mesuagia ; 21 villani de eodem Thoma tenent. Item idem Thomas tenet de predicto Roberto 9 cotarios, qui de eo tenent in villenagio.' Cf. Rot. Hundred. ii. 440, a.

fields. In this case the authorities distinguish between greater and lesser cotters[1], between the owners of a 'full cote' and of 'half a cote[2].' The *bordarii*, so conspicuous in Domesday, and evidently representing small tenants of the same kind as the cottagers, disappear almost entirely in later times[3].

We may start from this last observation in our general estimate of the terminology. One might expect to find traces of very strong French influence in this respect, if in any. Even if the tradition of facts had not been interrupted by the Conquest, names were likely to be altered for the convenience of the new upper class. And the Domesday Survey really begins a new epoch in terminology by its use of *villani* and *bordarii*. But, curiously enough, only the first of these terms takes root on English soil. Now it is not a word transplanted by the Conquest; it was in use before the Conquest as the Latin equivalent of *ceorl*, *geneat*, and probably *gebúr*. Its success in the thirteenth and fourteenth centuries is a success of Latin, and not of French, of the half-literary record language over conversational idioms, and not of foreign over vernacular notions. The peculiarly French '*bordier*,' on the other hand, gets misunderstood and eliminated. Looking to Saxon and Danish terms, we find that they hold their ground tenaciously enough ; but still the one most prevalent before the Conquest—*ceorl*—disappears entirely, and all the others taken together cannot balance the diffusion of the 'villains.' The disappearance of *ceorl* may be accounted for by the important fact that it was primarily the designation of a free man, and had not

Results as to terminology.

---

[1] Cartulary of Battle, Augment. Office, Misc. Books, 57, f. 37, b : 'Virgarii .... Cotarii, qui tenent dimid. virgatam.' Ibid. 36, b : 'Cottarii majores et minores.'

[2] Glastonbury Inquis. (Roxburghe Series), 114 : 'Rad. Forest. ½ cotsetland pro 18 d. et operatur sicut dimidius cotarius sed non falcat.'

[3] Glastonbury Inquis. (Roxburghe Series), 14 : 'Predictus W. habet tres bordarios in auxilium officii sui. Illi tres bord. habent corredium suum in aula abbatis, in qua laborant.' Terrae Templariorum, Queen's Rem. Misc. Books, 16, f 27 : 'Unusquisque bordarius debet operari una die in ebdomada.' Cf. 27, b.

quite lost this sense even in the time immediately before the Conquest. The spread of the Latin term is characteristic enough in any case. It is well in keeping with a historical development which, though it cannot be reduced to an importation of foreign manners, was by no means a mere sequel to Saxon history[1]. A new turn had been given towards centralisation and organisation from above, and *villanus*, the Latin record term, illustrates very aptly the remodelling of the lower stratum of society by the influence of the curiously centralised English feudalism.

The position of the peasantry gets considered chiefly from the point of view of the lord's interests, and the classification on the basis of services comes naturally to the fore. The distribution of holdings is also noticed, because services and rents are arranged according to them. But the most important fact remains, that the whole system, though admitting theoretically the difference between personal freedom and personal subjection, works itself out into uniformity on the ground of unfree tenure. Freemen holding in villainage and born villains get mixed up under the same names. The fact has its two sides. On the one hand it detracts from the original rights of free origin, on the other it strengthens the element of order and legality in the relations between lord and peasant. The peasants are *custumarii* at the worst—they work by custom, even if custom is regulated by the lord's power. In any case, even a mere analysis of terminological distinctions leads to the conclusion that the simplicity and rigidity of legal contrasts was largely modified by the influence of historical tradition and practical life.

Rights of the lord. Classification.

Our next object must be to see in what shape the rights of the lord are presented by manorial documents. All expressions of his power may be considered under three different heads, as connected with one of the three funda-

---

[1] The history of the terms in Saxon times and the terminology of the Domesday Survey will be discussed in the second volume. My present object is to establish the connexion between feudal facts and such precedents as are generally accepted by the students of Saxon and early Norman evidence.

mental aspects of the manorial relation. There were customs and services clearly derived from the *personal subjection of the villain*, which had its historical root in slavery. Some burdens again lay on the *land*, and not on the *person*. And finally, manorial exactions could grow from the *political sway* conferred by feudal lordship. It may be difficult to distinguish in the concrete between these several relations, and the constant tendency in practice must have been undoubtedly directed towards mixing up the separate threads of subjection. Still, a general survey of manorial rights has undoubtedly to start from these fundamental distinctions.

There has been some debate on the question whether Sale of the lord could sell his villains. It has been urged that villains. we have no traces of such transactions during the feudal period, and that therefore personal serfdom did not exist even in law[1]. It can be pointed out, on the other side, that deeds of sale conveying villains apart from their tenements, although rare, actually exist. The usual form of enfranchisement was a deed of sale, and it cannot be argued that this treatment of manumission is a mere relic of former times, because both the Frank and the Saxon manumissions of the preceding period assume a different shape ; they are not effected by sale. The existing evidence entitles one to maintain that a villain could be lawfully sold, with all his family, his *sequela*, but that in practice such transactions were uncommon[2]. The fact is a most important one in itself ; the whole aspect of society and of its work would have been different if the workman had been a saleable commodity passing easily from hand to

[1] Thorold Rogers, History of Agriculture and Prices, i. p. 71.

[2] Glastonbury Cart., Wood MSS., i. f. 225, b (Bodleian Libr.) : 'Noverit universitas vestra me vendidisse domino Ricardo vicario de Domerham Philippum Hardyng nativum meum pro 20 solidis sterling unde ego personam ipsius Philippi ab omni nativitate et servitute liberavi.' Cf. Gloucester Cartulary (Rolls Series), ii. 4. Madox, Formulare Anglicanum, 416, gives several deeds of sale and enfranchisement by sale. Dr. Stubbs had some doubts about the time of these transactions, but deeds of sale of the twelfth and thirteenth centuries occur, and are preserved in the Record Office. See Deputy Keeper's Reports, xxxvi. p. 178.

hand. Nothing of the kind is to be noticed in the medieval system. There is no slave market, and no slave trade, nothing to be compared with what took place in the slave states of North America, or even to the restricted traffic in Russia before the emancipation. The reason is a curious one, and forcibly suggested by a comparison between the cases when such trade comes into being, and those when it does not. The essential condition for commercial transfer is a protected market, and such a market existed more or less in every case when men could be bought and sold. An organised state of some kind, however slightly built, is necessary as a shelter for such transfer. The feudal system proved more deficient in this respect than very raw forms of early society, which make up for deficiencies in State protection by the facilities of acquiring slaves and punishing them. The landowner had enough political independence to prevent the State from exercising an efficient control over the dependent population, and for this very reason he had to rely on his own force and influence to keep those dependents under his sway. Personal dependence was locally limited, and not politically general, if one may use the expression. It was easy for the villain to step out of the precincts of bondage ; it was all but impossible for the lord to treat his man as a transferable chattel. The whole relation got to be regulated more by internal conditions than by external pressure, by a customary *modus vivendi*, and not by commercial and state-protected competition. This explains why in some cases political progress meant a temporary change for the worse, as in some parts of Germany and in Russia : the State brought its extended influence to bear in favour of dependence, and rendered commercial transactions possible by its protection. In most cases, however, the influence of moral, economical, and political conceptions made itself felt in the direction of freedom, and we have seen already that in England legal doctrine created a powerful check on the development of servitude by protecting the actual possession of liberty, and throwing the burden of

proof in questions of status on the side contending against
such liberty.

But not all the consequences of personal servitude could   Merchet.
be removed in the same way by the conditions of actual life.
Of all manorial exactions the most odious was incontest-
ably the *merchetum*, a fine paid by the villain for marrying
his daughter[1]. It was considered as a note of servile
descent, and the man free by blood was supposed to be
always exempted from it, however debased his position
in every other respect. Our authorities often allude to
this payment by the energetic expression 'buying one's
blood' (servus de sanguine suo emendo). It seems at first
sight that one may safely take hold of this distinction in
order to trace the difference between the two component
parts of the villain class. In the status of the socman,
developed from the law of Saxon free-men, there was
usually nothing of the kind. The *maritagium* of military tenure of course has nothing in common with it,
being paid only by the heiress of a fee, and resulting from
the control of the military lord over the land of his retainer. The *merchetum* must be paid for every one of the
daughters, and even the granddaughters of a villain ; it
had nothing to do with succession, and sprang from personal subjection.

When the bride married out of the power of the lord
a new element was brought to bear on the case : the lord
was entitled to a special compensation for the loss of a
subject and of her progeny[2]. When the case is mentioned

---

[1] Glastonbury Inquis., tempore abb. Michaelis, Addit. MSS. 17,450, f. 7 :
' Petrus filius Margarete tenet virgatam terre .. nec potest filiam suam maritare
sine licentia domini vel ballivorum.' Cf. Cartulary of Newent, Add MSS. 15,
668, f. 46 : 'emit filiam suam.' Cartulary of St. Peter of Gloucester (Rolls
Series), iv. 219 : 'Item, quod quilibet praepositus habeat potestatem concedendi cuicunque nativae, ut possit se maritare tam extra terram domini quam
infra, acceptis tamen salvis plegiis pro ea de fine faciendo ad proximam
curiam ; cum si forte praesentiam ballivi expectasset in partibus remotioribus
agentis casu interveniente forte nunquam gauderet promotione maritali.'

[2] Cartulary of Christ Church, Canterbury, Harl. MSS. 1006, f. 55 : 'Tenens
de monday land, si filiam infra villam maritaverit 16 d. et si extra homagium
2 sol.' Black Book of Coventry, Ashmol. MSS. 864, f. 5 : 'Radulfus Bedellus

in manorial documents, the fine gets heightened accordingly, and sometimes it is even expressly stated that an arbitrary payment will be exacted. The fine for incontinence naturally connects itself with the merchet, and a Glastonbury manorial instruction enjoins the Courts to present such cases to the bailiffs ; the lord loses his merchet from women who go wrong and do not get married [1].

Origin and modifications of merchet.

Such is the merchet of our extents and Court rolls. As I said, it has great importance from the point of view of social history. Still it would be wrong to consider it as an unfailing test of *status*. Although it is often treated expressly as a note of serfdom [2], some facts point to the conclusion that its history is a complex one. In the first place this merchet fine occurs in the extents sporadically as it were. The Hundred Rolls, for instance, mention it almost always in Buckinghamshire, and in some hundreds of Cambridgeshire. In other hundreds of this last county it is not mentioned. However much we lay to the account of casual omissions of the compilers, they are not sufficient to explain the general contrast. It would be preposterous to infer that in the localities first mentioned the peasants were one and all descended from slaves, and that in those other localities they were one and all personally free. And so we are driven to the inference, that different customs prevailed in this respect in places immediately adjoining each other, and that not all the feudal serfs descended from Saxon slaves paid merchet.

If, on the one hand, not all the serfs paid merchet, on

de 10 hidis tenet 1 virgatam terre et prati. Et dabit merchettam pro filia sua maritanda, si eam maritaverit extra villenagium Episcopi.'

[1] Cartulary of Glastonbury, Wood MSS. i. (Bodleian), f. 111. s : ' Si nul de neffes folement se porte de son corps parque le seignour perd la vente de eux.'

[2] Warwickshire Hundred Roll, Queen's Rem. Misc. Books, No. 26, f. 26, a : ' Redempcio carnis et sanguinis et alia servicia ad voluntatem domini.' Rot. Hundred. ii. 335, b : ' In villenagio 8 virgate terre quarum quelibet debet ei per annum 6 s. vel opera ad valorem, tenentes etiam illarum sunt servi de sanguine suo emendo ad voluntatem dicti Abbatis et ad alia facienda, que ad servilem condicionem pertinent. In cottariis cotagia 6 de eadem servitute et condicione.'

the other there is sufficient evidence to show that it was paid in some cases by free people. A payment of this kind was exacted sometimes from free men in villainage, and even from socage tenants. I shall have to speak of this when treating of the free peasantry; I advert to the fact now in order to show that the most characteristic test of personal servitude does not cover the whole ground occupied by the class, and at the same time spreads outside of its boundary.

This observation leads us to several others which are not devoid of importance. As soon as the notion arose that personal servitude was implied by the payment of merchet,—as soon as such a notion got sanctioned by legal theory, the fine was extended in practice to cases where it did not apply originally. We have direct testimony to the effect that feudal lords introduced it on their lands in places where it had never been paid [1], and one cannot help thinking that such administrative acts as the survey of 1279–1280, the survey represented by the Hundred Rolls, materially helped such encroachments. The juries made their presentments in respect of large masses of peasantry, under the preponderating influence of the gentry and without much chance for the verification of particular instances. The description was not false as a whole, but it was apt to throw different things into the same mould, and to do it in the interest of landed proprietors. Again, the variety of conditions in which we come across the merchet, leads us to suppose that this term was extended through the medium of legal theory to payments which differed from each other in their very essence : the commutation of the 'jus primae noctis,' the compensation paid to the lord for the loss of his bondwoman leaving the

[1] How very difficult it was sometimes to decide the question, whether merchet had been paid or not, may be seen from the following instances :—Coram Rege, 27 Henry III, m. 3 : 'Et non possunt inquirere nec scire quod tempore Johannis Regis dederunt merchettum vel heryettum sed bene credunt quod hoc fuit ex permissione ipsius Regis et non per aliquam convencionem, quam fecerat eis pro predictis 50 libris.' Cartulary of Ramsey (Rolls Series), i. 441 : 'De merchetto nesciunt sine majori consilio.'

manor, and the fine for marriage to be levied by the township or the hundred, were all thrown together. Last, but
not least, the vague application of this most definite of
social tests corroborates what has been already inferred
from terminology, namely, that the chief stress was laid
in all these relations, not on legal, but on economic distinctions. The stratification of the class and the determination of the lord's rights both show traits of legal status,
but these traits lose in importance in comparison with
other features that have no legal meaning, or else they
spread over groups and relations which come from different
quarters and get bound up together only through economic
conditions.

Servile
customs.
      The same observations hold good in regard to other
customs which come to be considered as implying personal
servitude[1]. Merchet was the most striking consequence
of unfreedom, but manorial documents are wont to connect
it with several others. It is a common thing to say that a
villain by birth cannot marry his daughter without paying
a fine, or permit his son to take holy orders, or sell his calf
or horse, that he is bound to serve as a reeve, and that his
youngest son succeeds to the holding after his death[2].
This would be a more or less complete enumeration, and I
need not say that in particular cases sometimes one and
sometimes another item gets omitted. The various pieces
do not fit well together: the prohibition against selling
animals is connected with disabilities as to property, and not
derived directly from the personal tie[3] ; as for the rule of

---

[1] Y. B. 21/22 Edw. I, p. 107.

[2] Note-book of Bracton, pl. 1230.

[3] Gloucester Cartulary (Rolls Series), iii. 218 : ' Item quod non permittitur,
quod aliquis vendat equum masculum vel bovem sibi vitulatum sine licentia,
nisi consuetudo se habeat in contrarium.' Rot. Hundred. ii. 628, a : ' Si habeat
equum pullanum, bovem vel vaccam ad vendendum, dominus propinquior erit
omnibus aliis et vendere non debent sine licentia domini.' Rochester Cartulary
(ed. Thorpe), 2, a : ' Si quis habuerit pullum de proprio jumento aut vitulum
de propria vacca et pervenerit ad perfectam etatem, non poterit illos vendere,
nisi prius ostendat domino suo et sciat utrum illos velit emere sicut alios.'
Rot. Hundred. ii. 463, a : ' Item si ipse habeat pullum vel boviculum et laboraverit cum illo non potest vendere sine licentia domini, sed si non laboraverit
licitum.'

succession, it testifies merely to the fact that the so-called
custom of Borough English was most widely spread among
the unfree class. The obligation of serving as a reeve or in
any other capacity is certainly derived from the power of
a lord over the person of his subject; he had it always at
his discretion to take his man away from the field, and
to employ him at pleasure in his service. Lastly, the
provision that the villain may not allow his son to receive
holy orders stands on the same level as the provision that
he may not give his daughter in marriage outside the
manor: either of these prohibited transactions would have
involved the loss of a subject.

We must place in the same category all measures intended to prevent directly or indirectly the passage of the
peasantry from one place to the other. The instructions
issued for the management of the Abbot of Gloucester's
estates absolutely forbid the practice of leaving the lord's
land without leave[1]. Still, emigration from the manor
could not be entirely stopped; from time to time the
inhabitants wandered away in order to look out for field-
work elsewhere, or to take up some craft or trade. In
this case they had to pay a kind of poll-tax (chevagium),
which was, strictly speaking, not rent: very often it was
very insignificant in amount, and was replaced by a trifling
payment in kind, for instance, by the obligation to bring
a capon once a year[2]. The object was not so much to
get money as to retain some hold over the villain after he
had succeeded in escaping from the lord's immediate sway.
There are no traces of a systematic attempt to tax and
ransom the work of dependents who have left the lord's

Control over the movements of the peasantry.

---

[1] Cartulary of St. Mary of Beaulieu, Nero, A. xii. f. 93, b : ' Pro filio coronando et pro licencia recedendi faciet sicut illi.' Cartulary of St. Peter of
Gloucester (Rolls Series), iii. 218 : ' Item quod nullo masculo tribuatur licentia
recedendi a terra domini sine licentia superioris hoc proviso, quod consuetudines a servis dominus debitas ad plenum recipiat, contradicentes atta-
chiando ut inde respondeant ad curiam.'

[2] Duchy of Lancaster Court Rolls, Bundle 85, No. 1157 (Record Office) :
' Et quia non sunt residentes dant chevagium.' Lancaster Court Rolls, Bundle
62, No. 750, m. 1 : ' Johannes le Grust dat comiti ii solidos et ii capones ut
possit manere ubi sibi placuerit.'

territory—nothing to match the thorough subjection in which they were held while in the manor. And thus the lord was forced in his own interest to accept nominal payments, to concentrate his whole attention on the subjects under his direct control, and to prevent them as far as possible from moving and leaving the land. In regulations for the management of estates we often find several paragraphs which have this object in view. Sometimes the younger men get leave to work outside the lord's possessions, but only while their father remains at home and occupies a holding. Sometimes, again, the licence is granted under the condition that the villain will remain in one of his lord's tithings[1], an obligation which could be fulfilled only if the peasant remained within easy reach of his birth-place. Special care is taken not to allow the villains to buy free land in order to claim their freedom on the strength of such free possession[2]. Every kind of personal commendation to influential people is also forbidden[3].

Notwithstanding all these rules and precepts, every page of the documents testifies to frequent migrations from the manors in opposition to the express will of the land-owners. The surveys tell of serfs who settle on strange land even in the vicinity of their former home[4]. It is by no means exceptional to find mention of enterprising landlords drawing away the population from their neighbours' manors[5]. The fugitive villain and the settler who

[1] Lancaster Court Rolls, Bundle 62, No. 750, m. 3 : 'Capones de reditu ut custumarii possint manere super terram Radulfi de Wernore sed dictus Will. erit in visu franciplegii dom. comitis.'

[2] Suffolk Court Rolls (Bodleian), 3 : 'Preceptum inquirere nomina eorum qui terram servilem vendiderunt per cartam et quibus, et qui sunt qui terram liberam adquisierunt et ibi resident et prolem suscitant et ob hoc libertatem sibi vindicant.' Cartulary of St. Alban's, 454 : 'Ubi villani emunt terras liberorum de catallis nostris.'

[3] Cart. Glouc. (Rolls Ser.), iii. 217: 'Item, inhibeatur nativis domini manerii ne aliquid alicui dent per annum in recognitione, ut aliquo gaudeant patrocinio.'

[4] Lancaster Court Rolls, Bundle 62, No. 756, m. 1 : 'Nativus receptatus apud Latfeld sine licentia domini.'

[5] Cartulary of Shaftesbury, Harl. MSS. 61, f. 59 : 'Fugitivi domine, R. fil. Al. manet in Br. sub Willelmo.' Ramsey Inqu., Galba E. x. f. 27, b : 'Isti

comes from afar are a well-marked feature of this feudal society[1].

The limitations of rights of property have left as distinct traces in the cartularies as the direct consequences of personal unfreedom. These two matters are connected by the principle that everything acquired by the slave is acquired by his master; and this principle finds both expression and application in our documents. On the strength of it the Abbot of Eynsham takes from his peasant land which had been bought by the latter's father[2]. The case dates from the second half of the fourteenth century, from a time when the social conflict had become particularly acute in consequence of the Black Death, and of the consequent attempts on the part of landlords to stretch their rights to the utmost. But we have a case from the thirteenth century: the Prior of Barnwell quotes the abovementioned rule in support of a confiscation of his villain's land[3]. In both instances the principle is laid down expressly, but in other cases peasants were deprived of their property without any formal explanation.

Limitations as to property.

Of course, one must look upon such treatment as exceptional. But an important and constant result of the general conception is to be found in some of the regular feudal exactions. The villain has no property of his own, and consequently he cannot transmit property. Strictly speaking, there is no inheritance in villainage. As a matter of fact the peasant's property did not get confiscated after his death, but the heirs had to surrender a part

Heriot.

sunt nativi abbatis : E. et O. manent apud Gomcestre.' Ibid. 51 : 'A. est nativus domini abbatis, sed dicit se esse hominem episcopi.' Cartulary of Shaftesbury, Harl. MSS. 61, f. 59 : ' Nicholaus habet 4 nativos domine, partim terram tenentes in calumpnia domine partim super terram Nicholai.'

[1] Coram Rege, Pasch. 7 Edw. I, m. 7 : 'Villanus fugitivus an in villenagio tenens et adventicius.'

[2] Eynsham Inqu. (Chapter of Christ Church, Oxford), 25, a : 'Quas Adam pater ipsius adquisivit et quia *quicquid servis adquiritur domino adquiritur* faciat inde dominus quod sibi videatur expediens.'

[3] Register of St. Mary of Barnwell, Harl. MSS. 3601, f. 60 : 'Quidam villanus de Bertone tenuit unum mesuagium de duobus dominis . . . . . . *quicquid servus acquirit acquiritur domino suo.*'

of it, sometimes a very considerable one. A difference is made between chattels and land. As to the first, which are supposed to be supplied by the lord, the duty of the heir is especially onerous. On the land of the Bishopric of Lichfield, for instance, he has to give up as *heriot* the best head of horned cattle, all horses, the cart, the caldron, all woollen cloth, all the bacon, all the swine except one, and all the swarms of bees[1]. The villains of St. Alban's have to give the best head of cattle, and all house furniture[2]. But in most cases only the best beast is taken, and if there be no cattle on the tenement, then money has to be paid instead[3]. The Cartulary of Battle is exceptionally lenient as to one of the Abbey's manors[4]: it liberates from all duty of the kind those who do not own any oxen. It sometimes happens, on the other hand, that the payment is doubled ; one beast is taken from the late occupier by way of heriot, and the other from his widow for the life interest which is conceded to her after the death of her husband[5]. Such 'free bench' is regulated very differently by different customs. The most common re-

[1] Black Book of Coventry, Ashmol. MSS. 864, f. 6 : ' Et cum obierit, dominus habebit suum melius animal et nihilominus habebit omnes equos masculos, carrectam ferratam, ollum eneum, pannum laneum integrum, bacones integros, omnes porcos excepta una sue, et omnes ruscos apium, si qua hujusmodi habuerit.'

[2] Formulary of St. Alban's, Camb. Univ., Ee. iv. 20.

[3] Lancaster Court Rolls, Bundle 32, No. 283 : ' Petrus filius Gerardi nativus domini defunctus est et habuit in bonis domino pertinentibus unam vaccam que appreciatur ad 5 sol. et venditur W. instauratori.' Cartulary of Christ Church, Canterbury, Addit. MSS. 6157, f. 25, b : ' Et sciendum, quod si quis custumarius domini in ipso manerio obierit, dominus habebit de herietto meliorem bestiam. Et si bestiam non habuerit, dabit domino pro herietto 2 sol. 6 d.'

[4] Cartulary of Battle, Augment. Off. Misc. Books, No. 57, f. 21, a : ' Et post mortem cujuslibet predictorum nativorum dominus habebit pro herieto melius animal, si quod habuerit, si vero nullam vivam bestiam habeant, dominus nullum herietum habebit ut dicunt. Filii vel filiae predictorum nativorum dabunt pro ingressu tenementi post mortem antecessorum suorum tantum sicut dant de redditu per annum.

[5] Gloucester Cartulary, iii. 193 : ' Et post decessum suum dominus habebit melius auerium ejus nomine herieti, et de relicta similiter. Et post mortem ejus haeres faciet voluntatem domini, antequam terram ingrediatur.'

quirement is, that the widow may not marry again and must remain chaste. In Kent the widow has a right to half the tenement for life, even in case of a second marriage ; in Oxfordshire, if she marries without the lord's leave, she is left in possession only during a year and a day [1].

In all these instances, when a second payment arises alongside of the heriot, such a payment receives also the name of heriot because of this resemblance, although the two dues are grounded on different claims. The true heriot is akin in name and in character to the Saxon ' here-geat ' —to the surrender of the military outfit supplied by the chief to his follower. In feudal times and among peasants it is not the war-horse and the armour that are meant, ox and harness take their place, but the difference is not in the principle, and one may even catch sometimes a glimpse of the process by which one custom shades off into the other. On the possessions of St. Mary of Worcester, for instance, we find the following enactment [2] : Each virgate has to give three heriots, that is a horse, harness, and two oxen ; the half-virgate two heriots, that is a harnessed horse and one ox ; other holdings give either a

[1] Gloucester Cartulary (Rolls Series), iii. 208 : ' Dicunt etiam quod relicta sua non potest in dicta terra maritari sine licentia domini.' Cartulary of Christ Church, Canterbury, Add. MSS. 6159, f. 25, b : ' Si autem per licenciam domini se maritaverit, heredes predicti defuncti predictum tenementum per licenciam domini intrabunt et uxorem relictam dicti defuncti de medietate dicti tenementi dotabunt.' Rot. Hundred. ii. 768, b : ' Item si obierit, dominus habebit melius auerium nomine herietti et per illum heriettum sedebit uxor ejus vidua per annum et unum diem et si ulterius vidua esse voluerit faciet voluntatem domini.'—The custom in some of the manors of St. Peter of Gloucester was peculiar. Gloucester Cartulary (Rolls Series), iii. 88 : ' Matilda relicta Praepositi tenet dim. virg. contin. 24 a. (8 sol.)—Et tenet ad terminum vitae abbatis ... Et debet redimere filium et filiam ad voluntatem domini ... Et si obierit, dominus habebit melius auerium nomine domini, et aliud melius auerium nomine rectoris, et de marito cum obierit similiter.' When the lord was an ecclesiastical corporation he not unfrequently got two beasts, one as a heriot and the other as a mortuary due to him as rector of the parish.

[2] Worcester Cartulary (Camden Series), 102 : ' De antiquis consuetudinibus villanorum, quaelibet etiam virgata dabit iii heriet, sc. equum cum hernesio et duos boves, et dimidia virgata duos heriet, sc. equum cum hernesio et bovem. Alii autem dabunt equum vel bovem.'

horse or an ox. In such connexion the payment has nothing servile about it, and simply appears as a consequence of the fact or assumption that the landlord has provided his peasant with the necessary outfit for agricultural work. And still the heriot is constantly mentioned along with the merchet as a particularly base payment, and though it might fall on the succession of a free man holding in villainage, it is not commonly found on free land. The fact that this old Saxon incident of dependence becomes in the feudal period a mark of servile tenure, is a fact not without significance.

Relief.

It is otherwise with the *relief* (relevium), the duty levied for the resumption of the holding by the heir: it extends equally to military tenure and to villainage. Although the heriot and relief get mixed up now and then, their fundamental difference is realised by the great majority of our documents and well grounded on principle. In one case the chattels are concerned, in the other the tenement; one is primarily a payment in kind, the other a money-fine. As to the amount of the relief the same fluctuations may be traced as in the case of the heriot. The most common thing is to give a year's rent; but in some instances the heir must settle with the lord at the latter's will, or ransom the land as a stranger, that is by a separate agreement in each single case[1]. Fixed sums occur also, and they vary according to the size and quality of the holding[2].

Political rights.

On the boundary between personal subjection and political subordination we find the liability of the peasantry to pay *tallage*. It could be equally deduced from the

[1] Glastonbury Inqu. (Roxburghe Series), 89, a: 'Item non vendet bovem vel equum de sua nutritura sine licencia domini, nec coronare faciet filium nec maritabit filiam sine licencia domini, dabit heriettum melius animal, faciet finem cum domino pro ingressu habendo ad voluntatem domini communiter per 40 solidos et omnia alia faciet que nativo incumbunt.' The relief ought to be discussed in connexion with the obligations of the holding. I speak of it here because the documents mention it almost always with the heriot.

[2] Cartulary of St. Mary of Beaulieu, Nero, A. xx. f. 84, b: 'Pro filio coronando, filia maritanda, fine terre ... secundum qualitatem personarum et quantitatem substancie et terre.'

principle that a villain has nothing of his own and may be exploited at will by his master or from the political grant of the power of taxation to the representative of feudal privilege. The payment of arbitrary tallage is held during the thirteenth century to imply a servile status[1]. Such tallage at will is not found very often in the documents, although the lord sometimes retained his prerogative in this respect even when sanctioning the customary forms of renders and services. Now and then it is mentioned that the tallage is to be levied once a year[2], although the amount remains uncertain.

As a holder of political power the lord has a right to inflict fines and amercements on transgressors[3]. The Court-rolls are full of entries about such payments, and it seems that one of the reasons why very great stress was laid on attendance at the manorial Courts was connected with the liability to all sorts of impositions that was enforced by means of these gatherings. Tenants had to attend and to make presentments, to elect officers, and to serve on juries; and in every case where there was a default or an irregularity of any kind, fines flowed into the lord's exchequer.

Lastly, we may classify under the head of political exactions, monopolies and privileges such as those which were called *banalités* in France: they were imposed on the peasantry by the strong hand, although there was no direct connexion between them and the exercise of any particular function of the State. English medieval documents often refer to the privileged mill, to which all the villains and sometimes the freemen of the Soke were bound to bring

---

[1] Rot. Hundred. ii. 747, a: 'Debet talliari ad voluntatem domini quolibet anno.'

[2] Ibid. ii. 528, b: 'Et debet talliari ad voluntatem domini semel in anno et debet gersummare filiam et fieri prepositus ad voluntatem domini.'

[3] Cartulary of Battle, Augment. Off. Misc. Books, No. 57, f. 93, a: 'Amerciamenta tenentium, qui redditum tempore statuto non persoluerunt.' Reg. Cellararii of Bury St. Edmund's, Cambridge Univ., Gg. iv. 4. 52, b; cf. Eynsham Inqu. ii. a: (Inquisitio de statu villani): 'Subtraxerunt sectam curie a longo tempore dicendo se esse liberos.'

their corn [1]; there is also the manorial fold in which all the
sheep of the township had to be enclosed [2]. In the latter
case the landlord profited by the dung for manuring his
land. Special attention was bestowed on supervising the
making of beer: Court-rolls constanly speak of persons
fined for brewing without licence. Every now and then
we come across the wondrous habit of collecting all the
villagers on fixed days and making them drink *Scotale* [3],
that is ale supplied by the lord—for a good price, of
course.

Villain
tenure.

Let us pass now to those aspects of manorial usage
which are directly connected with the mode of holding
land. I may repeat what I said before, that it would be
out of the question to draw anything like a hard and fast
line between these different sides of one subject. How
intimately the personal relation may be bound up with the
land may be gathered, among other things, from the fact
that there existed an oath of fealty which in many places
was obligatory on villains when entering into possession
of a holding. This oath, though connected with tenure,
bears also on the personal relation to the lord [4]. The oath
of fealty taken by the tenant in villainage differed from
that taken by the freeholder in that it contained the words,
' I will be justified by you in body and goods'; and again
the tenant in villainage, though he swore fealty, did no
homage; the relationship between him and his lord was
not a merely feudal relationship; the words, ' I become
your man,' would have been out of place, and there could
be no thought of the lord kissing his villain. But however
intimate the connexion between both aspects of the

---

[1] Formulary of St. Alban's, Cambridge Univ., Ee. iv. 20, f. 165, a: ' Servilia—videlicet secta curie de tribus septimanis in tres et secta molendini.'
We find it denied in the king's court that a free man can be bound to do
suit to the lord's mill; Bracton's Note-book, p. 161 : ' Nota quod liber homo
non tenetur sequi molendinum domini sui nisi gratis velit.'

[2] Bury St. Edmund's, Registrum album, Cambridge Univ., Ee. iii. 60, f.
155, b : ' Liberi excepti a falda domini.'

[3] As to Scotale, see Stubbs, Const. Hist. § 165.

[4] Reg. Cellararii of Bury St. Edmund's, Cambridge Univ., Gg. iv. 4. 30, b :
' Per fidelitatem custumarii . . . et per alias consuetudines serviles.'

question, in principle the tenure was quite distinct from the status, and could influence the condition of people who were personally free from any taint of servility.

The legal definition of villainage as unfree tenure does not take into account the services or economic quality of the tenure, and lays stress barely on the precarious character of the holding[1]. The owner may take it away when he pleases, and alter its condition at will. The Abingdon Chronicle tells us[2] that before the time of Abbot Faritius it was held lawful on the manors of the Abbey to drive the peasants away from their tenements. The stewards and bailiffs often made use of this right, if anybody gave them a fee out of greed, or out of spite against the holder. Nor was there any settled mode of succession, and when a man died, his wife and children were pitilessly thrown out of their home in order to make place for perfect strangers. An end was put to such a lawless condition of things by Faritius' reforms: he was very much in want of money, and found it more expedient to substitute a settled custom for the disorderly rule of the stewards. But he did not renounce thereby any of his manorial rights: he only regulated their application. The legal feature of base tenure — its insecurity — was not abolished on the Abingdon estates. Our documents sometimes go the length of explaining that particular plots are held without any sort of security against dispossession. We find such remarks in the Warwickshire Hundred Rolls for instance[3]. Sometimes the right is actually enforced: in the Cartulary of Dunstable Priory we have the record of an exchange between two landlords, in consequence of which the peasants

---

[1] Y. B. 20/21 Edward I, p. 41: 'Kar nent plus neit a dire, Jeo tenk les tenements en vileynage, ke neit a dire ke, Jeo tenk les tenements demendez ver moy a la volunte le Deen,' etc.　See above, Chapter II.

[2] Chron. Mon. de Abingdon, ii. 25 (Rolls Series).

[3] Exch. Q. R., Misc. Books, No. 29, f. 8, a: 'Habet 22 servos tenentes 35 acras terre ad voluntatem domini in servagio.' f. 10, b: 'Habet ibidem 25 servos tenentes 12 virgatas terre et dimidiam in servagio ... et possunt omnes removeri pro voluntate domini.'

were removed from eight hides of land by one of the contracting parties[1].

Control of the lord over the villain's land.

The villain is in no way to be considered as the owner of the plot of land he occupies; his power of disposing of it is stinted accordingly, and he is subjected to constant control from the real owner. He cannot fell timber; oaks and elms are reserved to the lord[2]. He cannot change the cultivation of the land of his own accord; it would be out of the question, for instance, to turn a garden-close into arable without asking for a licence[3]. He is bound to keep hedges and ditches in good order, and is generally responsible for any deterioration of his holding. When he enters into possession of it, he has to find a pledge that he will perform his duties in a satisfactory manner[4]. There can be no thought of a person so situated alienating the land by an act of his own will; he must surrender it into the hand of the lord, and the latter grants it to the new holder after the payment of a fine. The same kind of procedure is followed when a tenement is passed to the right heir in the lifetime of the former possessor[5]. A

---

[1] Harl. MSS. 1885, f. 7: 'Volens autem dominus de Wahell retinere ad opus suum totum parcum de Segheho . . . abegit omnes rusticos qui in predicto loco iuxta predictum boscum manebant.' Cf. Cor. Rege, Pasch. 14 Edw. I, Oxon. 9.

[2] Battle Abbey, Augment. Off. Misc. Books, 57, f. 21, a : 'Et memorandum quod omnes supradicti nativi non possunt . . . prostrare maremium crescens in tenementis que tenent sine licencia et visu ballivi vel servientis domini et hoc ad edificandum et non aliter.' Add. Charters, 5290 ' (transgressiones Stephani Chenore) . . . fecit vastum . . . in boscis quos idem Stephanus tenuit de domino in bondagio cum de quercis fraxinis pomariis et aliis arboribus vastos (ramos?) asportavit.'

[3] Suffolk Court Rolls (Bodleian), 2, a : 'Rob. Gl. assertavit pomaria sua et fecit wastum super vilenagium Comitis.'

[4] Suffolk Court Rolls (Bodleian): 'Quia Henricus bercarius plegios non potuit invenire ad heredificandum mesuagium quod fuit W. C. et ibi attractum suum facere.'

[5] Duchy of Lancaster Court Rolls (Record Off.), Bundle 32, No. 285 : 'Emma . . . venit et sursum reddit 1 cotagium et 5 acras et dimidiam terre quas tenuit de domino in bondagio. Et venit Thomas filius ejus et capit dictam terram et dat ad ingressum 10 solidos.' B. 62, No. 750 : 'Galfridus percarius venit et tradidit terram suam . . . domino comiti pro paupertate. Robertus filius eius postea venit et finem fecit pro habenda seisina dicte terre.'

default in paying rents or in the performance of services, and any other transgression against the interests of the lord, may lead to forfeiture[1]. The lord takes also tenements into his hand in the way of escheat, in the absence of heirs. Court-rolls constantly mention plots which have been resumed in this way by the lord[2]. The homage has to report to the steward as to all changes of occupation, and as to the measures which are thought necessary to promote the interests of the landowner and of the tenantry[3].

As to the treatment of tenure in manorial documents, it is to be noticed that a distinction which has no juridical meaning at all becomes all important in practice. At common law, as has been said repeatedly, the contrast between free land and servile land resolves itself into a contrast between precarious occupation and proprietary right. This contrast is noticed occasionally and as a matter of legal principle by manorial documents[4] quite apart from the consequences which flow from it, and of which I have been speaking just now. But in actual life this fundamental feature is not very prominent; all stress is laid on the distinction between land held by rent and land held by labour. In the common phraseology of surveys and manorial rolls, the tenements on which the rent prevails over labour are called 'free tenements,' and those on the contrary which have to render labour services, bear the names of 'servile holdings.' This

Tenure by rent considered free; tenure by agricultural work, servile.

---

[1] Duchy of Lancaster Court Rolls, B. 43, No. 484: 'Dicit etiam quod dicta terra capta est in manu domini Edmundi pro redditibus et serviciis inde a retro existentibus.' Essex Court Rolls, 3 (Bodleian): 'Preceptum est capere in manu prioris totam residuam terram custumariam quam Matildis le Someters predicta tenet de feodo prioris quia vendidit de terra sua custumaria . . . libere per cartam contra consuetudinem manerii.'

[2] Glastonbury Inqu. (Roxburghe Series), 65; Gloucester Cartulary (Rolls Series), iii. 196.

[3] Capitula halimoti, Bodleian MSS., Wood, i. f. 111, b: 'Si nul soit en un graunt tenement e ne puisse les droitures de son tenement sustener e un aultre homme en un petit tenement que meutz tendroit le graunt tenement al prow le seigneur e le tenement.'

[4] Rot. Hundred. ii. 321, a: In villenagio tres virgatae et dimidia. . . . Et sunt tenentes illarum servi de sanguine suo emendo. . . . In libere tenentibus *pro certis serviciis* per annum,' etc.

fact is certainly not to be treated lightly as a mere result of deficient classification or terminology. It is a very important one and deserves to be investigated carefully.

In the ancient survey of Glastonbury Abbey, compiled in 1189, the questions to be answered by the jury are enumerated in the following way: 'Who holds freely, and how much, and by what services, and by whose warrant, and from what time? Has land which ought to perform work been turned into free land in the time of Bishop Henry, or afterwards? By whose warrant was this change made, and to what extent is the land free? Is the demesne land in cultivation, or is it given away in free tenure or villain tenure; is such management profitable, or would it be better if this land was taken back by the lord[1]?' The contrast is between land which provides labour and land which does not; the former is unfree, and villain tenure is the tenure of land held by such services; portions of the demesne given away freely may eventually be reclaimed. The scheme of the survey made in answer to these questions is entirely in keeping with this mode of classification. All holdings are considered exclusively from the economic point of view; the test of security and precarious occupation is never applied. It is constantly noticed, on the other hand, whether a plot pays rent or provides labour, whether it can be transferred from one category into the other, on what conditions demesne land has been given to peasants, and whether it is expedient to alter them. Let us take the following case as an instance: John Clerk had in the time of Bishop Henry one virgate in Domerham and holds it now, and another virgate in Stapelham for ten shillings. When he farmed the Domerham manor he left on his own authority the virgate in Stapelham and took

---

[1] Glastonbury Inquis. (Roxburghe Series), 21: 'Quantum quisque teneat, omne ejus servitium; quis tenet libere et quantum et quo servitio et quo guaranto et quo tempore; si aliqua terra fuerit facta libera in tempore Henrici episcopi, vel postea, que debuit operari; quo guaranto hoc fuit, et in quantum sit libera; si dominicum sit occupatum vel foras positum in libertate vel vilenagio, et si ita fuerit domino utilius sicut est vel revocatum.'

half a virgate in Domerham, as it was nearer. This half
virgate ought to work and is now free. And the virgate in
Stapelham, though it was free formerly, has to work now,
after the exchange [1]. The opposition is quite clear, and
entirely suited to the list of questions addressed to the jury.
The meaning of the terms *free* and *freedom* is also brought
out by the following example. Anderd Budde holds half
a virgate of demesne land, from the time of Bishop Henry,
by the same services as all who hold so much. The village
has to render as gift twenty-nine shillings and six pence.
Six pence are wanting (to complete the thirty shillings?)
because Anderd holds more freely than his ancestors
used to [2].

Such phraseology is by no means restricted to one
document or one locality. In a Ramsey Cartulary we find
the following entry in regard to a Huntingdonshire manor :
' Of seven hides one is free ; of the remaining six two virgates pay rent. The holder pays with the villains ; he
pays merchet and joins in the boon-work as the villains.
The remaining five hides and three virgates are in pure
villainage [3].' The gradation is somewhat more complex
here than in the Somersetshire instance : besides free land
and working land we have a separate division for mixed
cases. But the foundation is the same in both documents.
Earlier surveys of Ramsey Abbey show the same classification of holding into free and working virgates (*liberae, ad
opus* [4]).

---

[1] Ibid. 130 : ' J. clericus tenuit in tempore Henrici episcopi apud Domerham unam virgatam quam adhuc tenet et aliam virgatam apud Stapelham pro
10 solidis. Recepta villa de Domerham ad firmam, ipse propria auctoritate
dimisit virgatam de Stapelham et dimidiam virgatam in Domerham in excambium cepit quia propinquior fuit. Hec dimidia virgata operari solet, nunc
autem est libera. Virgata vero de Stapelham post illud excambium operari
solet que ante hoc libera fuit.'

[2] Ibid. 121 : ' De dono xxix solidi et vi denarii. Et de Anderdo deficiunt
vj den. quia tenet liberius quam predecessores sui solebant tenere.'

[3] Ramsey Cartulary (Rolls Series), i. 364 : ' De his septem hydis est
una *hyda libera*. De sex hydis, quae restant, tenet Marsilia filia A. de R.
duas virgatas ad censum. Quinque hydae et tres virgatae, quae restant,
tenentur *in puro villenagio*.'

[4] Galba, E. x. f. 38.

Terra ad
furcam et
flagellum.

In opposition to free service, that is rent, we find both the *villenagium* [1] and the *terra consuetudinaria* or *customaria* [2], burdened with the usual rural work. Sometimes the document points out that land has been freed or exempted from the common duties of the village [3]; in regard to manorial work the village formed a compact body. The notion which I have been explaining lies at the bottom of a curious designation sometimes applied to base tenure in the earlier documents of our period—*terra ad furcam et flagellum* [4], fleyland. The Latin expression has been construed to mean land held by a person under the lord's jurisdiction, under his gallows and his whip, but this explanation is entirely false. The meaning is, that a base holding is occupied by people who have to work with pitchfork and flail, and may be other instruments of agriculture [5], instead of simply paying rent. In view of such a phraseology the same

---

[1] Extensio de terris Roberti de Sto. Georgio (Lincoln) Inquis. p. mort. 30 Henry III, No. 36: ' Idem habuit in *villenagio* 13 bovatas terre et 3 partes unius bovate que 9 rustici tenent et quelibet bovata valet per annum 5 sol. pro omni servicio . . . habuit in *liberis serviciis* unam bovatam quam Radulfus filius G. de eo tenuit per cartam pro 2 solidis per annum pro omni servicio.'

[2] Bury St. Edmund's, Reg. Cellararii, Cambr. Univ., Gg. iv. 4, f. 32, a : ' W. de Bruare tenet i rodam custumarie et per alias consuetudines serviles . . . alteram libere et per servicium 2 denariorum.' Cf. Gloucester Cartulary (Rolls Series), iii. 65.

[3] Battle Abbey, Reg. Augment. Off. Misc. Books, No. 57, f. 72, b : ' Isti prenominati (liberi tenentes) sunt quieti per redditum suum de communibus servitiis, debent tamen herietum et relevium.' Glastonbury Cart., Wood MSS., i. p. iii. : ' Si nul soit enfraunchi de ces ouveraignes dont la uile le est le plus charge.'

[4] Ramsey Inqu., Galba, E. x. 39, d : ' Walterus abbas fecit R. francum de terra patris sui que fuerat ad furcam et flagellum. . . . Multos de servicio rusticorum francos fecit.' Ramsey Cartulary (Rolls Series), i. 487: ' . . . quaelibet virgata de fleyland.' The same land appears as ' quaelibet virgata operaria quae non fuerit posita ad censum.'

[5] Spalding Priory, Reg., Cole MSS., vol. 43, f. 272: ' De tenentibus terram operariam de priore in Spalding : W. de A. tenet 40 acras terre pro quibus debet operari qualibet die per annum ad voluntatem Domini ad quocumque opus Dominus voluerit, cum Carecta, Cortina, Vanga, Flagello, Tribulo, Furca, Falce.' Coram Rege, Mich., 51/52 Henry III, m. b : ' Et similiter predictus Petrus distringit eos pro consuetudinibus et servitiis que nec antecessores eorum nec ipsi facere consueverunt ut cum furcis et flagellis.'

tenement could alternately be considered as a free or a
servile one, according to its changing obligations[1].   Some
surveys insert two parallel descriptions of duties which are
meant to fit both eventualities; when the land is *ad opus*,
it owes such and such services; when it is *ad censum*,
it pays so much rent.   It must be added, that in a vast
majority of cases rent-paying land retains some remnants
of services, and, *vice versâ*, land subjected to village-work
pays small rents[2]; the general quality of the holding is
made to depend on the prevailing character of the duties.

The double sense in which the terms 'free tenure' and
'servile tenure' are used should be specially noticed, because
it lays bare the intimate connexion between the formal
divisions of feudal law and the conditions of economic reality.
I have laid stress on the contrast between the two phraseo-
logies, but, of course, they could not be in use at the same
time without depending more or less on each other.   And
it is not difficult to see, that the legal is a modification of
the economic use of terms, that it reduces to one-sided
simplicity those general facts which the evidence of every
day life puts before us in a loose and complex manner;
that land is really free which is not placed in a constant
working submission to the manor, in constant co-operation
with other plots, similarly arranged to help and to serve in
the manor.   However heavy the rent, the land that pays
it has become independent in point of husbandry, its dependence appears as a matter of agreement, and not an
economic tie.   When a tenement is for economic purposes
subordinated to the general management of the manor,
there is almost of necessity a degree of uncertainty in
its tenure; it is a satellite whose motions are controlled

---

[1] Eynsham Cartulary, Christ Church MSS., No. 97, f. 6, a : 'Willelmus F.
tenet unum cotagium et quartam partem unius virgate terre qui facere consuevit pro rata porcione sicut virgatarius.   Modo ponitur ad firmam dum
domina placet ad 6 solidos, 8 d.,' etc.   Cf. Domesday of St. Paul's (Camden
Series), 81.   This is in substance the difference between ' bondagium et
husbandland,' Inquis. p. mort. 46 Henry III, No. 25; Hexham Priory Cartulary (Surtees Series), p. xx.

[2] Domesday of St. Paul's (Camden Series), 49.

by the body round which it revolves. On the other hand, mere payments in money look like the outcome of some sort of agreement, and are naturally thought of as the result of contract.

Custom in the exercise of manorial rights.

Everything is subject to the will and pleasure of the lord ; but this will and pleasure does not find expression in any capricious interference which would have wantonly destroyed order and rule in village life. Under cover of this will, customs are forming themselves which regulate the constantly recurring events of marriage, succession, alienation, and the like. Curious combinations arise, which reflect faithfully the complex elements of village life. An instruction for stewards provides, for instance, that one person ought not to hold several tenements ; where such agglomerations exist already they ought to be destroyed, *if it can be done conveniently and honestly*[1]. In one of the manors of St. Paul of London the plots held by the ploughmen are said to be resumable by the lord without any injury to hereditary succession[2]. 'The rule of hereditary succession' is affirmed in regard to normal holdings by this very exception. We find already the phrase of which the royal courts availed themselves, when in later days they extended their protection to this base tenure : the tenants hold 'by the custom of the manor[3].' On the strength of such custom the life of the unfree peasantry takes a shape closely resembling that of the free population ; transactions and rights spring into being which find their exact parallel in the common law of the 'free and lawful' portion of the community. Walter, a villain of St. Alban's, surrenders into the hand of the monastery two curtilages,

[1] St. Alban's Formulary, Cambridge Univ., Ee. iv. 20 : 'Ne uno homini plures terre tradantur, et si modo unus plures tenet, dividantur, si commode et honeste fieri poterit.'

[2] Domesday of St. Paul's (Camden Series), 52 ; Duchy of Lancaster Court Rolls, B. 62, No. 750 : 'Et quia huiusmodi tenementum nullus potest vendicare hereditarie ut de aliis villenagiis successive.'

[3] Hereford Rolls, 8 (Bodleian) : ' Et concessum est ei tenere dictum mesuagium et unam acram terre sibi et heredibus suis secundum consuetudinem manerii per servicia inde debita et consueta.' Essex Rolls, 8 (Bodleian): ' Amicia de R. que tenet ex consuetudine manerii.'

which are thereupon granted to his daughter and her husband for life, upon condition that after their death the land is to revert to Walter or to his heirs[1]. An Essex villain claims succession by hereditary right, for himself and his heirs[2]. I have already spoken of the 'free bench' to be found equally on free and unfree land. In the same way there exists a parallel to the so-called 'Curtesy of England' in the practice of manorial courts ; if the son inherits land from his mother during his father's life, the latter enjoys possession during his life, or, it may be, only until his son comes of age. In view of all this manorial documents have to draw a distinction between tenements in villainage and land held at the will of the lord, not in the general, but in the special and literal sense of the term[3]. From a formal point of view, villain tenure by custom obtained its specific character and its name from a symbolical act performed in open Court by the steward ; a rod was handed over to the new holder by the lord's representative, and a corresponding entry made in the roll of the Court. Hence the expression *tenere per virgam aut per rotulum Curie*[4].

I ought perhaps to treat here of the different and interesting forms assumed by services and rents as consequences Customary duties of the lord

---

[1] Extractus Rotulorum de Halimotis, Cambridge Univ., Dd. vii. 22, f. 1, a.

[2] Essex Rolls, 8 (Bodleian), m. 6: 'Johannes filius W. B. venit et clamavit unum mesuagium et quatuor acras terre cum pertinenciis ut jus et hereditatem suam post mortem dicti W. patris sui faciendo inde dominis predictis servicia debita et consueta nomine villenagii et dat domino ad inquirendum de jure suo et si sit plene etatis et heres dicti W. nec ne,' etc.

[3] Eynsham Cartulary, Christ Church MSS., No. 27, f. 11, b: 'Matildis B. tenet de domino unum cotagium cum curtilagio in voluntate domini.' Cf. Glastonbury Inqu. (Roxburghe Series), 66 ; Gloucester Cartulary (Rolls Series), iii. 134 ; Domesday of St. Paul's (Camden Series), 23.

[4] Reg. Cellararii Mon. Bury St. Edmund's, Cambridge Univ., Gg. iv. 4, f. 52, b: '(Curia 7 Edw. II) ... dicunt quod quidam Robertus Heth pater dictorum R. W. et J. tenuit de conventu per virgam in villa de Berton magna ... Et quia dedixerunt cepisse dictam terram per virgam ideo potest seisiri dicta terra in manum domini.' Registr. album vestiarii abbatiae S. Edmundi, Cambridge Univ., Ee. iii. 60, f. 188, b: 'Tenentes de mollond ... tenent per virgam in curia.' Eynsham Cartulary, Christ Church MSS., No. 97: 'Ricardus W. tenet unum cotagium et duas acras terrae campestres per rotulum curie pro 3 sol.' Cf. 12, a.

in regard to the peasantry.

of manorial organisation. But I think that this subject will be understood better in another connexion, namely as part of the agrarian system. One side only of it has to be discussed here. Everywhere customs arise which defend the villains from capricious extortions on the part of the lord and steward. These customs mostly get 'inbreviated[1],' described in surveys and cartularies, and although they have no legally binding power, they certainly represent a great moral authority and are followed in most cases.

A very characteristic expression of their influence may be found in the fact that the manorial rolls very often describe in detail, not only what the peasants are bound to do for the lord, but what the lord must do for the peasants ; especially when and how he is to feed them. Of course, the origin of such usage cannot be traced to anything like a right on the part of the villain ; it comes from the landlord's concessions and good-will, but grace loses its exceptional aspect in this case and leads to a morally binding obligation [2]. When the villain brings his yearly rent to his lord, the latter often invites him to his table [3]. Very common is the practice of providing a meal for the labourers on the *boon-days*, the days on which the whole population of the village had to work for the lord in the most busy time of the summer and autumn. Such boon-work was considered as a kind of surplus demand ; it exceeded the normal distribution of work. It is often mentioned accordingly that such service is performed out of affection for the lord, and sometimes it gets the eloquent name of ' love-bene.' In proportion as the manorial administration gets more work done in this exceptional manner, it becomes more and more gracious in regard to the people. ' Dry requests ' (siccae precariae) are followed by ' requests with beer ' (precariae cerevisiae). But it was not beer

---

[1] Note-book of Bracton, pl. 1237.

[2] Ely Register, Cotton, Claudius, C. xi. f. iii. b : ' Habebit duas pugillatas avene ex gratia, ut juratores dicunt, per longum tempus usitata.'

[3] Warwickshire Roll. Exch. Q. R. No. 29, f. 94, b : ' Servus .... cum fecerit exennium .... comedet cum domino.'

alone that could be got on such days. Here is a description of the customs of Borle, a manor belonging to Christ Church, Canterbury, in Essex. 'And let it be known that when he, the villain, with other customers shall have done cutting the hay on the meadow in Raneholm, they will receive by custom three quarters of wheat for baking bread, and one ram of the price of eighteen pence, and one pat of butter, and one piece of cheese of the second sort from the lord's dairy, and salt, and oatmeal for cooking a stew, and all the morning milk from all the cows in the dairy, and for every day a load of hay. He may also take as much grass as he is able to lift on the point of his scythe. And when the mown grass is carried away, he has a right to one cart. And he is bound to carry sheaves, and for each service of this kind he will receive one sheaf, called "mene-schef." And whenever he is sent to carry anything with his cart, he shall have oats, as usual, so much, namely, as he can thrice take with his hand [1].'

All such customs seem very strange and capricious at first sight. But it is to be noticed that they occur in different forms everywhere, and that they were by no means mere oddities; they became a real and sometimes a heavy burden for the landlord. The authorities, the so-called 'Inquisitiones post mortem' especially, often strike a kind of balance between the expense incurred and the value of the work performed. By the end of the thirteenth century it is generally found that both ends are just made to meet in cases of extra work attended by extra feeding, and in some instances it is found that the lord has to lay out more than he gets back [2]. The rise in the prices of commodities had rendered the service unprofitable. No wonder that such 'boon-work' has to be given up or to be commuted for money.

[1] Christ Church, Canterbury, Cartulary, Add. MSS. 6159, f. 22, b. Cf. Gloucester Cartulary (Rolls Series), iii. 203.

[2] Custumal of Battle Abbey (Camden Ser.), 30 : 'Et debet herciare per duos dies .... pretium operis iiij. d. Et recipiet de domino utroque die repastus pretii iij. d. Et sic erit dominus perdens j. d. Et sic nichil valet illa herciatio ad opus domini.'

Customs in the arrangement of agricultural work.

These regularly recurring *liberationes* or *liberaturae* as they are called, that is, meals and provender delivered to the labourers, have their counterpart in the customary arrangement of the amount and kind of services. I shall have to speak of their varieties and usual forms in another connexion, but it must be noticed now, that these peasants unprotected at law were under the rule of orderly custom. We have seen already that the payments and duties which followed from the subjection of the villains were for the most part fixed according to constant rules in each particular case. The same may be said of the economical pressure exercised in the shape of service and rent. It did not depend on the caprice of the lord, although it depended theoretically on his will. The villains of a manor in Leicestershire are not bound to work at weeding the demesne fields unless by their own consent, that is by agreement[1]. A baker belonging to Glastonbury Abbey is not bound to carry loads unless a cart is provided him[2]. A survey of Ely mentions that some peasants are made to keep a hedge in order as extra work and without being fed. But it is added that the jurors of the village protest against such an obligation, as heretofore unheard of[3]. All these customs and limitations may, of course, be broken and slighted by the lord, but such violent action on his part will be considered as gross injustice, and may lead to consequences unpleasant for him—to riots and desertion.

It is curious that the influence of custom makes itself felt slowly but surely among the most debased of the villains. The Oxfordshire Hundred Roll treats for instance of the *servi* of Swincombe. They pay merchet ; if any of them dies without making his will the whole of his moveable property falls to the lord. They are indeed degraded.

[1] Coram Rege, Pasch., 14 Edw. I, Lege, 18 : 'Villani circulare (sic) non consueverunt nisi ex voluntate.'
[2] Glastonbury Inqu. (Roxburghe Series), 82 : 'Sed non debet carriare nisi dominus prestaverit suum plaustrum.'
[3] Cotton MSS., Claudius, C. xi, f. 30, b : 'Sed juratores dicunt quod nunquam hoc fecerunt nec de iure facere debent.'

And still the lord does not tallage them at pleasure, they are secure in the possession of their waynage (*salvo con-tenemento*)[1].

We may sum up the results already obtained by our analysis of manorial documents in the following propositions :—

1. The terminology of the feudal period and the treatment of tenure in actual life testify to the fact that the chief stress lay more on tenure than on status, more on economical condition than on legal distinctions.

2. The subdivisions of the servile class and the varieties of service and custom show that villainage was a complex mould into which several heterogeneous elements had been fused.

3. The life of the villain is chiefly dependent on custom, which is the great characteristic of medieval relations, and which stands in sharp contrast with slavery on the one hand and with freedom on the other.

---

[1] Rot. Hundred. ii. 758, a : ' Servi . . . nec potest filiam maritare nec uxorem ducere sine licencia domini; debet et salvo contenemento suo talliari et ad omnia auxilia communia scottare et lottare secundum facultatem suam,' etc.

CHAPTER VI.

FREE PEASANTRY.

I HOPE the heading of this chapter may not be mis-understood. It would be difficult to speak of free peasantry in the modern sense at the time with which we are now dealing. Some kind or form of dependence often clings even to those who occupy the best place among villagers as recognised free tenants, and in most cases we have a very strong infusion of subjection in the life of otherwise privileged peasants. But if we keep to the main distinctions, and to the contrast which the authorities themselves draw between the component elements of the peasant class, its great bulk will arrange itself into two groups: the larger one will consist of those ordinarily designated as *villains*; a smaller, but by no means an insignificant or scanty one, will present itself as *free*, more or less protected by law, and more or less independent of the bidding of the lord and his steward. There is no break between the two groups; one status runs continuously into the other, and it may be difficult to distinguish between the intermediate shades; but the fundamental difference of conception is clearly noticeable as soon as we come to look at the whole, and it is not only noticeable to us but was noticed by the con-temporary documents.

General condition of England.

In very many cases we are actually enabled to see how freedom and legal security gradually emerge from subjec-tion. One of the great movements in the social life of the thirteenth and fourteenth centuries is the movement towards the commutation of services for money rents. In every survey we find a certain number of persons who now pay money, whereas they used to do work, and who have thus emancipated themselves from the most onerous form of subjection[1]. In the older documents it is commonly specified that the lord may revert to the old system, give up the rents, and enforce the services[2]. In later documents this provision disappears, having become obsolete, and there is only a mention of certain sums of money. The whole process, which has left such distinct traces in the authorities, is easily explained by England's economic condition at that time. Two important factors co-operated to give the country an exceptionally privileged position. England was the only country in Europe with a firmly constituted government. The Norman Conquest had powerfully worked in the sense of social feudalism, but it had arrested the disruptive tendencies of political feudalism. The opposition between the two races, the necessity for both to keep together, the complexity of political questions which arose from conquest and settlement on the one hand, from the intercourse with Normandy and France on the other,—all these agencies working together account for a remarkable intensity of action on the part of the centripetal forces of society, if I may use the expression: there was in England a constant tendency towards the concentration and organisation of political power in sharp contrast with the rest of Europe where the state had fallen a prey to local and private interests. One of the external results of such a condition was the growth of a royal power supported by the sympathy of the lower English-born classes, but arranging society by the help of Norman principles of fiscal administration. Not less momentous was the formation of an aristocracy which was compelled to act as a class instead of acting as a mere collection of individuals

---

[1] Rot. Hundred. ii. 528, b : ' Et modo omnia illa arrentata sunt et dant per annum 14 sol. 8 d.'

[2] Exch. Q. R. Min. Acc., Bundle 510, No. 13 : ' Et solebant facere servicia consueta, sed per voluntatem et ad placitum domini extenta sunt in denariis.' Cf. Abingdon Cartulary, ii. 303. Rot. Hundred. ii. 453, a : ' Omnes isti prenominati nomine villenagii sunt ad voluntatem domini de operibus eorun-dem.' Cf. Ibid. 407, b.

each striving for his own particular advantage ; as a class it had to reckon with, and sometimes represent, the interests and requirements of other classes. In all these respects England was much ahead of Germany, where tribal divisions were more powerful than national unity, and the state had to form itself on feudal foundations in opposition to a cosmopolitan Imperial power ; it was not less in advance of France, where the work of unification, egotistically undertaken by the king, had hardly begun to get the upper hand in its conflict with local dynasties ; not less in advance of Italy, so well situated for economic progress, but politically wrecked by its unhappy connexion with Germany, the anti-national influence of the Papacy, and the one-sided development of municipal institutions. By reason of its political advantages England had the start of other European countries by a whole century and even by two centuries. The 'silver streak' acted already as a protection against foreign inroads, the existence of a central power insured civil order, intercourse between the different parts of the island opened outlets to trade, and reacted favourably on the exchange of commodities and the circulation of money.

Another set of causes operated in close alliance with these political influences. The position of England in relation to the European market was from the first an advantageous one. Besides the natural development of seafaring pursuits which lead to international trade, and always tend to quicken the economic progress, there were two special reasons to account for a speedy movement in the new direction : the woollen trade with Flanders begins to rise in the twelfth century, and this is the most important commercial feature in the life of North-Western Europe ; then again, the possession of Normandy and the occupation of Aquitaine and other provinces of France by the English opened markets and roads for a very brisk commercial intercourse with the Continent. As an outcome of all these political and economical conditions we find the England of the thirteenth century undoubtedly moving from *natural husbandry* to the *money-system.*

The consequences are to be seen on every side in the arrangements of state and society. The means of govern- ment were modified by the economic change. Hired troops took the place of feudal levies ; kings easily renounced the military service of their tenants and took scutages which give them the means of keeping submissive and well-drilled soldiers. The same process took place all through the country on the land of secular and ecclesiastical lords. They all preferred taking money which is so readily spent and so easy to keep, which may transform itself equally well into gorgeous pageants and into capital for carrying on work, instead of exacting old-fashioned un- wieldly ploughings and reapings or equally clumsy rents in kind.

On the other hand, the peasants were equally anxious to get out of the customary system : through its organisa- tion of labour it involved necessarily many annoyances, petty exactions and coercion ; it involved a great waste of time and energy. The landlord gained by the change, because he received an economic instrument of greater efficiency ; the peasant gained because he got rid of per- sonal subjection to control ; both gained ; for a whole system of administration, a whole class of administrators, stewards, bailiffs, reeves, a whole mass of cumbrous accounts and archaic procedure became unnecessary.

In reality the peasantry gained much more than the lord. Just because money rents displaced the plough- ings and reapings very gradually, they assumed the most important characteristic of these latter—their customary uniformity ; tradition kept them at a certain level which it was very difficult to disturb, even when the interests of the lord and the conditions of the time had altered a great deal. Prices fluctuate and rise gradually, the buying strength of money gets lowered little by little, but customary rents remain much the same as they were before. Thus in process of time the balance gets altered for the benefit of the rent payer. I do not mean to say that such views and such facts were in full operation from the very beginning : one of the chief reasons for holding the Glastonbury inquest of 1189 was the wish to ascertain whether the rents actually corresponded to the value of the plots, and to make the necessary modifications. But such fresh assessments were very rare, it was difficult to carry them into practice, and the general tendency was distinctly towards a stability of customary rents.

Social results of commutation.

The whole process has a social and not merely an economical meaning. Commutation, even when it was restricted to agricultural services, certainly tended to weaken the hold of the lord on his men. Personal interference was excluded by it, the manorial relation resolved itself into a practice of paying certain dues once or several times a year ; the peasant ceased to be a tool in the husbandry arrangements of his master. The change made itself especially felt when the commutation took place in regard to entire villages [1] : the new arrangement developed into the custom of a locality, and gathered strength by the number of individuals concerned in it, and the cohesion of the group. In order not to lose all power in such a township, the lords usually reserved some cases for special interference and stipulated that some services should still be rendered in kind [2].

Again, the conversion of services into rents did not always present itself merely in the form just described : it was not always effected by the mere will of the lord, without any legally binding acts. Commutation gave rise to actual agreements which came more or less under the notice of the law. We constantly find in the Hundred Rolls and in the Cartularies that villains are holding land by written covenant. In this case they always pay rent. Sometimes a villain, or a whole township, gets emancipated

---

[1] Worcester Cartulary (Camden Series), 54, b : 'Haec villa tradita est ab antiquo villanis ad firmam, ad placitum cum omnibus ad nos pertinentibus.' Cf. Gloucester Cartulary, iii. 37.

[2] Worcester Cartulary (Camden Series), l. c. : 'Praeterea percipimus medietatem proventuum et herietum, praeterea debent metere, ligare et compostare bladum de antiquo dominico de Hordewell . . . . et gersummabunt filias.'

from certain duties by charter[1], and the infringement of
such an instrument would have given the villains a standing
ground for pleading against the lord. It happened from time
to time that bondmen took advantage of such deeds to
claim their liberty, and to prove that the lord had entered
into agreement with them as with free people[2]. To prevent
such misconstruction the lord very often guards expressly
against it, and inserts a provision to say that the agreement is not to be construed against his rights and in favour
of personal freedom[3].

The influence of commutation makes itself felt in the Molmen.
growth of a number of social groups which arrange themselves between the free and the servile tenantry without
fitting exactly into either class. Our manorial authorities
often mention mol-land and mol-men[4]. The description
of their obligations always points one way: they are rent-
paying tenants who may be bound to some extra work,
but who are very definitely distinguished from the ' custumarii,' the great mass of peasants who render labour
services[5]. Kentish documents use ' mala' or ' mal' for a

---

[1] Glastonbury Cartulary, Bodleian MSS., Wood, i., f. 241, a : ' Jocelynus dei
gratia Bathoniensis episcopus. .... Noveritis nos quietos clamasse omnes
homines abbatie Glastonie de Winterburne in perpetuam de arruris et aliis
operacionibus quas facere debebant castro Marleberghe de terra de Winterburne, quos homines nostros Henricus illustris rex Anglie nobis concessit.'

[2] Wartrey Priory Cartulary, Fairfax MSS. f. 19, a : ' Et Adam dicit quod
predictus Prior villenagium in persona ipsius Ade allegare non potest quia
dicit quod dudum convenit inter quemdam Johannem dudum priorem de
Wartre. . . . et quendam Henricum de W. . . patrem ipsius Ade videlicet quod
isdem Prior. . . . per quoddam scriptum indenturam concesserunt Henrico. . . .
quoddam toftum simul cum duabus bovatis terre.'

[3] Malmesbury Cartulary (Rolls Series), ii. 199 : ' Nos tradidisse . . .
Roberto le H. de K. et Helenae uxori suae, et Agneti filiae eorum primo-
genitae nativis nostris, omnibus diebus vitae eorum, unam domum. Ita
quod non licet praedicto Roberto alicui vendere nec occasione istius tradi-
tionis aliquam libertatem ipsis vendicare.'

[4] As to molmen, I shall follow in substance my article in the English
Historical Review, 1886, IV. p. 734. We already find the class in Cartularies
of the twelfth century, in the Burton Cartulary, and in the Boldon Book.
See Round in the English Historical Review, 1886, V. 103, and Stevenson,
ibidem, VI. 332.

[5] Any number of examples might be given. I referred in my article to
a Record Office document, Exch. Treas. of Rec. Min. Acc. 32/8 : ' Rogerus

particular species of rent, and explain the term as a payment in commutation of servile customs[1]. In this sense
it is sometimes opposed to *gafol* or *gable*—the old Saxon
rent in money or in kind, this last being considered as
having been laid on the holding from all time, and not as
the result of a commutation[2]. Etymologically there is
reason to believe that the term *mal* is of Danish origin[3],
and the meaning has been kept in practice by the Scotch
dialect[4]. What immediately concerns our present purpose
is, that the word mal-men or mol-men is commonly used in
the feudal period for villains who have been released from
most of their services by the lord on condition of paying

Improve-
ment of
condition.

certain rents. Legally they ought to remain in their former
condition, because no formal emancipation has taken place ;
but the economical change reacts on their status, and the
manorial documents show clearly how the whole class
gradually gathers importance and obtains a firmer footing
than was strictly consistent with its servile origin[5].

prepositus tenet 28 acras pro 13 solidis solvendis ad 4 terminos principales.
Et dat 2 gallinas at Natale domini de precio 3 den., et 18 ova ad Pascham,
et debet 2 homines ad 2 precarias ad cibum domini et non extenduntur eo
quod nihil dabunt in argento si servicium illud dominus habere noluerit.
Item idem adiuvabit leuare fenum ad precariam domini quod nihil valet ut
supra. Item idem faciet 2 averagia Londinium que valent 2d... *Custumarii.*
Johannes Cowe tenet 13 acras et dimidiam pro 27d... Et debet 3 opera
qualibet septimana, scilicet per 44 septimanas videlicet a festo Natali beate
Marie usque ad gulam Augusti que continet in operibus per predictum
tempus vi^{xx}xii (i. e. 132) et valet in denariis 5 sol.' etc.

[1] Black Book of St. Augustine, Canterbury, Cotton MSS. Faustina, A. i.
31 : ' De quolibet sullung (*ploughland*) 20 solidos de mala ad quatuor terminos quos antecessores nostri dederunt pro omnibus iniustis et incausa-
cionibus (*sic*) quas uobis ore plenius exponemus.'

[2] Rochester Costumal (ed. Thorpe), 2, b : ' F. habet 21 jugum terre te
Gavelland unius servicii et unius redditus. Unumquodque jugum reddit
10 solidos ad 4 terminos—hoc est *Mal.* In media quadragesima 40d. Hoc
est *Gable.*' The Cartulary of Christ Church, Canterbury, in the British
Museum (Add. MSS. 6159) always gives the rents under the two different
headings of *Gafol* and *Mal.*

[3] The etymology of the word is traced by Stevenson, l. c.

[4] Ashley, Economic History, i. pp. 56, 57.

[5] Registrum Album Abbatiae Sancti Edmundi de Burgo, Cambridge University, Ee. iii. 60 f. ; 188, b : ' Memorandum quod anno regni Regis Edwardi
filii Regis Henrici 18—dominus Johannes de Norwold abbas Sti. Edmundi
ad ulteriores portas manerii sui de Herlawe, ad instanciam Cecilie le Grete

In the Bury St. Edmund's case just quoted in a foot-
note the fundamental principle of servility is stated emphatically, but the statement was occasioned by gradual encroachments on the part of the molmen, who were evidently
becoming hardly distinguishable from freeholders [1]. And in
many Cartularies we find these molmen actually enumerated
with the freeholders, a very striking fact, because the clear
interest of the lord was to keep the two classes asunder, and
the process of making a manorial 'extent' and classifying
the tenants must have been under his control. As a matter
of fact, the village juries were independent enough to make
their presentments more in accordance with custom than in
accordance with the lord's interests. In a transcript of a
register of the priory of Eye in Suffolk, which seems to
have been compiled at the time of Edward I, the molmen
are distinguished from villains in a very remarkable manner
as regards the rule of inheritance, Borough English being
considered as the servile mode, while primogeniture is restricted to those holding mol-land [2]. Borough English was
very widely held in medieval England to imply servile
occupation of land [3], and the privilege enjoyed by molmen

de Herlawe hereditatem suam de mollond infra campum dicte ville jacentem
post mortem viri sui a pluribus tenentibus Abbatis petentis coram eodem
Abbate, eo pretextu quod vir suus adventicius dictam hereditatem suam ipsa
invita vendidit et alienauit, per subscriptos inquisivit, utrum ipse seu alii
quicumque infra villam predictam mollond tenentes libere tenuerunt seu
tenent, et per cartas aut alio modo. . . Qui omnes et singuli jurati dixerunt
per sacramentum suum quod omnes *tenentes de molland solebant esse custumarii*
et fuerunt, sed Abbas Hugo primus et Abbas Sampson posterum et alii
Abbates relaxarunt eis seruicia maiora et consuetudines pro certa pecunia ; modo
arentati in aliquibus operibus ceteris, sed nihil habent inde nec tenent per
cartas, sed per virgam in curia. Et sunt geldabiles in omnibus inter custu-
marios et quod omnes sunt custumarie et servilis condicionis sicut et alii.'

[1] Exch. Treas. of Rec. 59/66. The classes follow each other in this way :
' Liberi tenentes, Molmen, Custumarii.' Cf. Rot. Hundred. ii. 425, a.

[2] Harl. MSS. 639, f. 69, b : ' Inquisicio facta per totam socam de Badefeud
dicit quod si aliquis servus domini moritur et plures habuerit filios, si tota
terra fuerit mollond primogenitus de iure et consuetudine debet eam retinere ;
si tota fuerit villana iunior ; si maior pars fuerit mollond primogenitus, is
maior pars fuerit villana iunior eam optinebit.'

[3] I cannot surrender this point (cf. Stevenson, l. c.). That Borough
English existed in many free boroughs and among free sokemen is true, of
course, and there it had nothing to do with servile status. It would have been

in this case shows that they were actually rising above the general condition of villainage, the economical peculiarities of their position affording a stepping-stone, as it were, towards the improvement of their legal status. It is especially to be noticed, that in this instance we have to reckon with a material difference of custom, and not merely with a vacillating terminology or a general and indefinite improvement in position. An interesting attempt at an accurate classification of this and other kinds of tenantry is displayed by an inquisition of 19 Edward I preserved at the Record Office. The following subdivisions are enumerated therein :—

Liberi tenentes per cartam.
Liberi tenentes qui vocantur fresokemen.
Sokemanni qui vocantur molmen.
Custumarii qui vocantur werkmen.
Consuetudinarii tenentes 4 acras terre.
Consuetudinarii tenentes 2 acras terre[1].

The difference between molmen and workmen lies, of course, in the fact that the first pay rent and the second perform week-work. But what is more, the molmen are ranged among the sokemen, and this supposes a certainty of tenure and service not enjoyed by the villains. In this way the intermediate class, though of servile origin, connects itself with the free tenantry.

Censuarii and gavelmen.

The same group appears in manorial documents under the name of *censuarii*[2]. Both terms interchange, and we find the same fluctuation between free and servile condition in regard to the *censuarii* as in regard to *molmen*. The thirteenth-

---

wrong to treat the custom of inheritance as a sure test from a general point of view. But as a matter of fact it was treated as such a test from a local point of view by many, if not most, manorial arrangements. I refer again to the case from the Note-book of Bracton, pl. 1062. The lord is adducing as proof of a plea of villainage : 'Hoc bene patet, quia postnatus filius semper habuit terram patris sui sicut alii villani de patria.' I have said already that the succession of the youngest son appears with merchet, reeveship, etc., as a servile custom.

[1] Q. R. Min. Acc. Box 587.

[2] Ramsey Cartulary (Rolls Series), i. 267: 'Decem hidae, ex quibus persona, liberi et censuarii tenent tres hidas et dimidiam, et villani tenent sex hidas.'

century extent of the manor of Broughton, belonging to the Abbey of Ramsey in Huntingdonshire, when compared with Domesday, shows clearly the origin of the group and the progress which the peasantry had made in two hundred years. The Domesday description mentions ten sokemen and twenty villains; the thirteenth-century Cartulary speaks in one place of *liberi* and *villani*, sets out the services due from the latter, but says that the Abbot can 'ponere omnia opera ad censum;' while in another place it speaks as though the whole were held by *liberi et censuarii*[1].

A similar condition is indicated by the term *gavelmanni*, which occurs sometimes, although not so often as either of the designations just mentioned[2]. It comes evidently from *gafol* or *gafel*, and applies to rent-paying people. It ought to be noticed, however, that if we follow the distinction suggested by the Kentish documents, there would be an important difference in the meaning. Rent need not always appear as a result of commutation; it may be an original incident of the tenure, and there are facts enough to show that lands were held by rent in opposition to service even in early Saxon time. Should *mal* be taken as a commutation rent, and *gafol* strictly in the sense of original rent, the gavelmen would present an interesting variation of social grouping as the progeny of ancient rent-holding peasantry. I do not think, however, that we are entitled to press terminological distinctions so closely in the feudal period, and I should never enter a protest against the assumption that most gavelmen were distinguished from molmen only by name, and in fact originated in the same process of commutation. But, granting this, we have to grant something else. *Vice versa*, it is very probable indeed that the groups of *censuarii* and *molmen* are not to be taken exclusively as the outcome of commutation. If *gafol* gets to be rather indistinct in its meaning, so does *mal*, and as to *census*, there is nothing to show whether it arises in consequence of commutation or of original agree-

[1] Domesday Book, i. 204; Ramsey Cartulary, i. 270, 330-40.
[2] Rochester Cartulary (Thorpe), 2, a : ' Gavelmanni de Suthflete.'

ment.   And so the Kentish distinction, even if not carried out systematically, opens a prospect which may modify considerably the characteristic of the status on which I have been insisting till now.   Commutation was undoubtedly a most powerful agency in the process of emancipation ; our authorities are very ready to supply us with material in regard to its working, and I do not think that anybody will dispute the intimate connexion between the social divisions under discussion and the transition from labour services to rent.   Yet a money rent need not be in every case the result of a commutation of labour services, although such may be its origin in most cases.   We have at least to admit the possibility and probability of another pedigree of rent-paying peasants.   They may come from an old stock of people whose immemorial custom has been to pay rent in money or in kind, and who have always remained more or less *free* from base labour.   This we should have to consider as at all events a theoretic possibility, even if we restricted our study to the terminology connected with rent ; though it would hardly give sufficient footing for definite conclusions.   But there are groups among the peasantry whose history is less doubtful.

Hun-
dredarii.

There are at the British Museum two most curious Surveys of the possessions of Ely Minster, one drawn up in 1222 and the other in 1277[1].   In some of the manors described we find tenants called ' hundredarii.'   Their duties vary a good deal, but the peculiarity which groups them into a special division and gives them their name is the suit of court they owe to the hundred[2].   And although the name does not occur often even in the Ely Surveys, and is very rare indeed elsewhere[3], the thing is quite

---

[1] Cotton MSS. Tiberius B. ii, and Claudius C. xi.

[2] Cotton MSS. Claudius C. xi, f. 49, a : ' De hundredariis et libere tenen-tibus.   Philippus de insula tenet 16 acras de wara et debet sectas ad curiam Elyensem et ad curiam de Wilburtone et in quolibet hundredo per totum annum,' etc.   For a more detailed discussion of the position of hundredors, see Appendix.

[3] In the description of Aston and Cote, a submanor of Bampton, Oxford-shire, *hundredarii* are mentioned in Rot. Hundr. ii. 689.

common. The village has to be represented in the hundred
court either by the lord of the manor, or by the steward,
or by the reeve, the priest, and four men[1]. The same
people have to attend the County Court and to meet the
King's justices when they are holding an eyre[2]. It is not
a necessary consequence, of course, that certain particular
holdings should be burdened with the special duty of
sending representatives to these meetings, but it is quite
in keeping with the general tendency of the time that it
should be so ; and indeed one finds everywhere that some
of the tenants, even if not called ' hundredarii,' are singled
out from the rest to 'defend' the township at hundred and
shire moots[3]. They are exempted from other services in
regard to this ' external,' this ' forinsec' duty, which was
considered as by no means a light one[4].

And now as to their status. The obligation to send
the reeve and four men is enforced all through England,
and for this reason it is *prima facie* impossible that it
should be performed everywhere by freeholders in *the
usual sense of the word*. There can be no doubt that in
many, if not in most, places the feudal organisation of
society afforded little room for a considerable class of free-

Hundred
ors as
villains.

---

[1] Leg. Henrici I, c. 7. The point has been lately elucidated by Maitland,
Suitors of the County Court, Eng. Hist. Rev., July 1888, and Round, Archaeological Review, iv.

[2] Gloucester Cart. iii. 193 : ' Et dicunt quod predictus Thomas et socii sui
subscripti debent aquietare villam de quolibet hundredo Cyrencestriae et de
Respethate praeterquam ad visum franciplegii bis in anno.' Ramsey Inqu.,
Cotton MSS. Galba E. x, 35 : ' Sequebatur comitatum et hundredum pro
dominico abbatis.' Madox, Hist. of the Exchequer, i. 74 : ' Serviet eis nomi-
natim in omnibus placitis ad quae convenienter summonitus erit et ad defensionem totius villae Estone aderit in hundredis et scyris in quibus erit
quantum poterit.' Warwickshire Hundr. Roll, Q. R. Misc. Books, No. 29,
f. 73, a : ' Seriancia ad comitatum et hundredum.'

[3] Ramsey Cart. i. 438 : ' J. R. tenet dimidiam hydam de veteri feoffamento
et non reddit per annum aliquem censum abbati, quia est una de quattuor
virgatis quae defendunt totam villatam de secta comitatus et hundredi per
annum.'

[4] Gloucester Cart. iii. 77 : ' Henricus de Marwent tenet unam virgatam
continentem 48 acras . . . et facit forinseca [servitia], scil. sectas comitatus et
hundredi, et alia forinseca.' Cf. Cart. of Shaftesbury, 65 : ' . . . defendebat
terram suam de omnibus forinsecis avencionibus.'

holding peasants or yeomen[1]. If every township in the realm had to attend particular judicial meetings, to perform service for the king, by means of five representatives, these could not but be selected largely from among the villain class. The part played by these representatives in the Courts was entirely in keeping with their subordinate position. They were not reckoned among the 'free and lawful' men acting as judges or assessors and deciding the questions at issue. They had only to make presentments and to give testimony on oath when required to do so. The opposition is a very marked one, and speaks of itself against the assumption that the five men from the township were on an equal standing with the freeholders[2]. Again, four of these five were in many cases especially bound by their tenure to attend the meetings, and the reeve came by virtue of his office, but he is named first, and it does not seem likely that the leader should be considered as of lower degree than the followers. Now the obligation to. serve as reeve was taken as a mark of villainage. All these facts lead one forcibly to the conclusion that the hundredors of our documents represent the village people at large, and the villains first of all, because this class was most numerous in the village. This does not mean, of course, that they were all personally unfree: we know already, that the law of tenure was of more importance in such questions than personal status[3]. It does not even mean that the hundredors were necessarily holding in villainage: small freeholders may have appeared among them. But the institution could not rest on the basis of legal freehold if it was to represent the great bulk of the peasantry in the townships.

Hundred-ors as free tenants.

    This seems obvious and definite enough, but our inquiry would be incomplete and misleading if it were to stop here. We have in this instance one of those curious contradic-

---

[1] Seebohm, Village Community, 37, 38; Scrutton, Common Fields, 39.

[2] See the instances collected by Maitland, Introduction to Rolls of Manorial Courts, Selden Soc., Ser. II, p. xxix, note 2.

[3] Maitland, op. c.

tions between two well-established sets of facts which are especially precious to the investigator because they lead him while seeking their solution to inferences far beyond the material under immediate examination. In one sense the reeve and the four men, the hundredors, seem villains and not freeholders. In another they seem freeholders and not villains. Their tenure by the 'sergeanty' of attending hundreds and shires ranks again and again with freehold and in opposition to base tenure [1]. Originally the four men were made to go not only with the reeve but with the priest; and if the reeve was considered in feudal times as unfree, the priest, the 'mass-thane,' was always considered as free [2]. It is to be noticed that the attendance of the priest fell into abeyance in process of time, but that it was not less necessary for the representation of the township according to the ancient constitution of the hundred than the attendance of the reeve. This last fact is of great importance because it excludes an explanation which would otherwise look plausible enough. Does it not seem at first sight that the case of the hundredors is simply a case of exemption and exactly on a parallel with the commutation of servile obligations for money? We have seen that villains discharged from the

---

[1] A few instances among many: Gloucester Cart. iii. 49 : 'Radulfus de E. tenet unam virgatam terrae continentem 48 acras et reddit inde per annum non reditum aliquem, sed sequetur comitatum Warwici et hundredum de Kingtone pro domino, et curiam de Clifforde pro omni servitio.' There are four other 'virgatarii liberi' besides this one. Domesday of St. Paul's (Camden Soc.), 30 : 'Thomas arkarius (tenet) iv virgatas pro 28 solidis et debet facere sectam sire et hundredi.' He is a freeholder. Worcester Cart. (Camden Soc.), 64, C : 'De liberis Ricardus de Salford tenet dimidiam hidam de priore, quam Thomas de Ruppe tenuit de eo, et facit regale servitium tantum, et debet esse coram justiciariis itinerantibus pro defensione villae ad custum suum.' The Ely 'hundredarii' are distinguished from the villains, and form by themselves a group which ranks next to the 'libere tenentes' or with them.

[2] Ramsey, Inqu. Cotton MSS. Galba, E. x, f. 52 : 'Ecclesia ipsius ville possidet dimidiam hidam liberam et presbiter debet esse quartus eorum qui sequuntur comitatum et hundredum cum custamento suo.' Cf. 40, 54. Instead of attending separately the priest comes to be included among the four hundredors.

most onerous and opprobrious duties of their class rise at once in social standing, and mix up with the smaller free-holders. Hundredors are relieved from these same base services in order that they may perform their special work, and this may possibly be taken as the origin of their free-dom. Should we look at the facts in this way, the classi-fication of this class of tenants as free would proceed from a lax use of the term and their privileges would have to be regarded as an innovation. The presence of the priest warns us that we have to reckon in the case with a survival, with an element of tradition and not of mere innovation. And it is not only the presence of the priest that points this way.

The Hundred Courts.

At first sight the line seems drawn very sharply between the reeve and the four men on the one hand, and the freehold suitors of the hundred court on the other : while these last have to judge and to decide, the first only make present-ments. But the distinction, though very clear in later times, is by no means to be relied upon even in the thir-teenth century. In Britton's account of the sheriff's tourn the two bodies, though provided with different functions, are taken as constituted from the same class : 'the free landowners of the hundred are summoned and the first step is to cause twelve *of them* to swear that they will make presentment according to the articles. Afterwards the *rest* shall be sworn by dozens and by townships, that they will make lawful presentment to the *first twelve jurors*[1].' The wording of the passage certainly leads one to suppose that both sets of jurors are taken from the freeholder class, and the difference only lies in the fact that some are selected to act as individuals, and the rest to do so by representation. The Assize of Clarendon, which Mr. Maitland has shown to be at the origin of the sheriff's tourn[2], will only strengthen the inference that the two bodies were intended to belong to the same free class : the inquiry, says the Assize, shall be made by twelve of the

---

[1] Britton, i. 177 sqq. See Maitland's Introd. to Manorial Rolls, p. xxvii.
[2] Maitland, op. c. pp. xxix, xxx.

most lawful men of the county, and by four of the most lawful men of every township. What is there in these words to show that the two sets were to be taken from different classes? And does not the expression 'lawful,' extending to both sets, point to people who are 'worthy of their law,' that is to free men? The Assize of Clarendon and the constitution of the tourn are especially interesting because they give a new bearing to an old institution: both divisions of the population which they have in view appear in the ordinary hundred and county court, and in the 'law day' of the 'great' hundred instituted for the view of frankpledge. In the ordinary court the lord, his steward, and the reeve, priest, and four men, interchange, according to the clear statement of Leg. Henrici I. c. 7, that is to say, the vill is to be represented either by the lord, or by his steward, or again by the six men just mentioned. They are not called out as representing different classes and interests, but as representing the same territorial unity. If the landlord does not attend personally or by his personal representative, the steward, then six men from the township attend in his place. The question arises naturally, where is one to look for the small freeholders in the enactment? However much we may restrict their probable number, their existence cannot be simply denied or disregarded. It does not seem likely that they were treated as landlords (terrarum domini), and one can hardly escape the inference that they are included in the population of the township, which appears through the medium of the six hundredors: another hint that the class division underlying the whole structure did not coincide with the feudal opposition between freeholder and villain. Again, in the great hundred for the view of frankpledge, which is distinguished from the ordinary hundred by fuller attendance, and not by any fundamental difference in constitution, all men are to appear who are 'free and worthy of their wer and their wite[1]:' this expression seems an equivalent to the 'free

---

[1] Leg. Henrici I. c. 8. Cf. Ely Register, Cotton MSS., Claudius, C. xi, 52, a: 'et libere tenentes sui qui tenent per socagium debent unam sectam

and lawful' men of other cases, and at the same time it includes distinctly the great bulk of the villain population as personally free.

Results as to hundredors.

I have not been able, in the present instance, to keep clear of the evidence belonging to the intermediate period between the Saxon and the feudal arrangements of society; this deviation from the general rule, according to which such evidence is to be discussed separately and in connexion with the Conquest, was unavoidable in our case, because it is only in the light of the laws of Henry I that some important feudal facts can be understood. In a trial as to suit of court between the Abbot of Glastonbury and two lay lords, the defendants plead that they are bound to appear at the Abbot's hundred court personally or by attorney only on the two law-days, whereas for the judgment of thieves their freemen, their reeves and ministers have to attend in order to take part in the judgment[1]. It is clearly a case of substitution, like the one mentioned in Leg. Henrici, c. 7, and the point is, that the representatives of the fee are designated as reeves and freemen. Altogether the two contradictory aspects in which the hundredors are made to appear can hardly be explained otherwise than on the assumption of a fluctuation between the conception of the hundred as of an assembly of freemen, and its treatment under the influence of feudal

ad frendlese hundred, scil. ad diem Sabbati proximum post festum St. Michaelis. The expression 'friendless' is peculiar. It appears in other instances in the Ely Surveys. May it not mean, that all the free tenants, even the small ones, had to attend and could not be represented by their fellows or 'friends'?

[1] Glastonbury Cart., Wood MSS., i. f. 233, a : 'et N. et G. veniunt et defendunt vim et iniuriam et talem sectam qualem ab eis exigit et bene cognoscunt quod per attornatos suos debent ipsi facere duas sectas per annum ad duos lagedaios ... sed si aliquis latro fuerit ibi iudicandus tunc debent liberi homines sui et prepositi uel seruientes sui debent interesse ad predictum hundredum ad faciendum iudicium et non ipsi in propria persona sua.' Cf. Malmesbury Cart. (Rolls Ser.), ii. 178: 'Item recognouit sectam ad hundredum de Malmesburia per se vel per sufficientem attornatum suum. Item recognouit et concessit quod omnes liberi homines sui de Estleye sequantur de hundredo in hundredum apud Malmesburiam sicut aliquo tempore predecessorum suorum facere consueuerunt.'

notions as to social divisions. In one sense the hundredors
are villains: they come from the vill, represent the bulk
of its population, which consists of villains, and are
gradually put on a different footing from the greater
people present. In another sense they are free men, and
even treated as freeholders, because they form part of
a communal institution intended to include the free class
and to exclude the servile class[1]. If society had been
arranged consistently on the feudal basis, there would have
been no room for the representation of the vill instead
of the manor, for the representation of the vill now by the
lord and now by a deputation of peasants, for a terminology which appears to confuse or else to neglect the distinction between free and servile holding. As it is, the
intricate constitution of the hundred, although largely
modified and differentiated by later law, although cut up
as it were by the feudal principle of territorial service,
looks still in the main as an organisation based on the
freedom of the mass of the people[2]. The free people
had to attend virtually, if not actually, and a series of contradictions sprang up from the attempt to apply this
principle to a legal state which had almost eliminated
the notion of freedom in its treatment of peasantry on
villain land. As in these feudal relations all stress lay
on tenure and not on status, the manorial documents seem
to raise the hundredors almost or quite to the rank of freeholders, although in strict law they may have been villains.
The net results seem to be: (1) that the administrative

[1] This may possibly account for the curious fact, that in every manor there
are some tenants called ' Freeman,' ' Frankleyn,' and the like. They seem
to be there to keep up the necessary tradition of the free element. For instance: Eynsham Cart. MSS. of the Chapter of Christ Church, Oxford, xxix.
f. 4, a : ' Iohannes Freman de Shyfford tenet unam virgatam per cartam . . .
facit sectam ad comitatum et hundredum et hac de causa tenet tenementum
suum.' Cf. Coram Rege 27 Henry III, m. 3 : ' Dicunt quod non est aliquis
liber homo in eodem manerio nisi Willelmus filius Radulfi qui respondet infra
corpus comitatus.' The fact is well known to all those who have had anything to do with manorial records.
[2] Cf. Maitland, Suitors of the County Court, Eng. Hist. Review, July,
1888.

constitution of hundred and county is derived from a social system which did not recognise the feudal opposition between freeholder and villain ; (2) that we must look upon feudal villainage as representing to a large extent a population originally free ; (3) that this original freedom was not simply one of personal status, but actually influenced the conception of tenure even in later days[1].

Socmen.

If in manorial documents these 'hundredors' occupy as it were an ambiguous position, the same may be said of another and a very important class—the *socmen*. The socage tenure has had a very curious terminological history. Everybody knows that it appears in Domesday as a local peculiarity of Danish districts ; in modern law it came to be a general name for any freehold that was neither knight service, frankalmoign, nor grand sergeanty. It became in fact the normal and typical free tenure, and as such it was treated by the Act of Charles II abolishing military tenure. Long before this—even in the thirteenth century —'free socage' was the name of a freehold tenure fully protected by the King's Courts. Very great men occasionally held land in free socage (per liberum socagium) ; they even held of the King in chief by free socage, and the tenure had many advantages, since it was free from the burdensome incidents of wardship and marriage. But no one would have called these men socmen (sokemanni, socomanni). On the other hand, the socmen, free socmen, were to be found all over England and not in the Danish country only. It is of the tenure of these socmen that we have to speak now. In a trial of Edward the First's time the counsel distinguish three manners of persons —free men, villains, and socmen. These last are said

---

[1] Is it not possible to explain by the 'hundredor' the following difficult passage in Domesday, ii. 100 ? 'Hugo de Montfort invasit tres liberos homines . . . unus ex his jacet ad feudum Sancti Petri de Westmonasterio testimonio hundredi, sed fuit liberatus Hugoni in numero suorum hundredorum (*corr.* hundredariorum ?) ut dicunt sui homines.' It is true that the term does not occur elsewhere in Domesday, but the reading as it stands appears very clumsy, and the emendation proposed would seem the easiest way to get out of the difficulty.

to occupy an intermediate position, because they are as *statu liberi* in regard to their lords[1]. The passage occurs in a case relating to ancient demesne, but the statement is made quite broadly, and the term 'socmen' is used without any qualification. As there were many socmen outside the King's possessions on the land of lay and spiritual lords, such usage may be taken as proof that the position of all these people was more or less identical. And so in our inquiry as to the characteristic traits of socage generally we may start from the ancient demesne. Further, we see that the socman's tenure is distinguished from free tenure, socmen from freeholders. In the law books of the time the free but non-military tenure has to be characterised not merely as socage, but as *free* socage : this fact will give us a second clue in analysing the condition.

There are two leading features in ancient demesne socage : it is certain in tenure and service, and it is held by the custom of the manor and not by feoffment. The certainty of the tenure severs the class of socmen from the villains, and is to be found as well in the case of socmen outside the crown demesne as in the case of socmen on the crown demesne. What is to be said of the second trait? It seems especially worthy of notice, because it cannot be said to belong to freehold generally. As to its existence on ancient demesne land I have already had occasion to speak, and it can hardly be doubted. I will just recall to the reader's mind the fundamental facts : that the 'little writ of right' was to insure justice according to the custom of the manor, and that our documents distinguish in as many words between the customary admittance of the socman and the feoffment of the freeholder. This means, that in case of litigation the one had warranty and charter to lean upon, while the other had to appeal to the communal testimony of his fellow-suitors in the court of the manor, and in later days to an entry on the court-roll. Freehold appeared as chartered land (book-

Charter and communal testimony.

---

[1] Y. B. 21/22 Edw. I. (ed. Horwood), pp. xix, 499.

land), while socage was in truth copyhold secured by communal custom[1]. The necessary surrender and admittance
was performed in open court, and the presence of fellow-
tenants was as much a requisite of it as the action of the
lord or his steward.

If we look now to the socmen outside the ancient
demesne, we shall find their condition so closely similar,
that the documents constantly confuse them with the tenants
of the ancient demesne. The free men under soke in the
east of England have best kept the tradition, but even their
right is often treated as a mere variation of ancient
demesne[2]. For this reason we should be fairly entitled,
I think, to extend to them the notion of customary freehold. There is direct evidence in this respect. In extents
of manors socmen are often distinguished from freeholders[3].
True, as already said, that in the king's courts 'free socage'
came to be regarded as one of the freehold tenures, and
as such (when not on the ancient demesne) was protected
by the same actions which protected knight-service and
frankalmoign; but we have only here another proof of

[1] I may be excused for again referring to the Stoneleigh Reg. f. 32, d :
'Quidam tenentes eiusdem manerii tenent terras et tenementa sua in *Soke-
mannia in feodo et hereditate* de qua quidem tenura talis habetur et omne tempore habebatur consuetudo videlicet quod quando aliquis tenens eiusdem
tenure terram suam alicui alienare voluerit veniat *in curiam* coram ipso Abbate
vel eius senescallo et per vergam sursum reddat in manum domini terram
sic alienandam ad opus illius qui terram illam optinebit ... Et si aliquis terram
aliquam huiusmodi tenure infra manerium predictum per cartam vel sine carta
absque licentia dicti Abbatis alienaverit aliter quam per sursum reddicionem
in curia in forma predicta, quod terra *sic extra curia* alienata domino dicti
manerii erit forisfacta in perpetuum.'

[2] Madox, Exch. i. 724, e : ' Monstraverunt Regi homines et tenentes de soca
de Oswald Kirke in Com. Nottinghamiae, quod cum soka illa dudum fuisset
antiquum dominicum coronae Angliae et dominus Henricus quondam Rex
Angliae progenitor Regis socam illam cum pertinenciis dedisset et concessisset
Henrico de Hastyngges habendam et tenendam ad communem legem . . .
Ac licet homines et tenentes predicti et antecessores sui homines et tenentes
de soca illa inter homines communitatis comitatus Nottinghamiae et non cum
tenentibus de antiquis dominicis Coronae Regis a tempore escambii predicti
talliari consueverunt, assessores tamen tallagii Regis in dominicis in Comitatu
Nottinghamiae praedicto . . . (eos) una cum illis de dominicis Regis praedictis talliari fecerunt.' Cf. 428, b, c.

[3] Rot. Hundr. ii. 608, a : ' Liberi tenentes . . . liberi sokemanni.' Cf. 752, a.

the imperfect harmony between legal theory and manorial administration. What serves in the manorial documents to distinguish the 'socman' from the 'freeholder' is the fact that the former holds without charter[1]. We are naturally led to consider him as holding, at least originally, by ancient custom and communal testimony in the same sense as the socmen of ancient demesne. In most cases only the negative side, namely the absence of a charter, is mentioned, but there are entries which disclose the positive side, and speak of tenants or even free tenants holding without charter by ancient tenure[2]. It is to be added, that we find such people in central and western counties, that is outside of the Danelagh. In Domesday their predecessors were entered as villains, but their tenure is nevertheless not only a free but an ancient one.

It must also be added that it is not only free socmen that one finds outside the ancient demesne ; bond socmen are mentioned as well. Now this seems strange at first sight, because the usual and settled terminology treats villain socage as a peculiarity of ancient demesne. My notion is that it is not 'bond' that qualifies the 'socmen,' but *vice versa*. To put it in a different way, the documents had to name a class which held by certain custom, although by base service, and they added the 'socman' to qualify the 'bond' or the 'villain.'

Bond socmen.

Two cases from the Hundred Rolls may serve as an illustration of this not unimportant point. The vill of Soham in Cambridgeshire[3] was owned in 1279 partly by the King, partly by the Earl Marshall, and partly by the Bishop

---

[1] Inquisit. post mortem 53 Henry III, n. 4 (Record Office) : 'Libere tenentes ad voluntatem . . . libere tenentes in socagio . . . libere tenentes per cartam.' Rot. Hundr. ii. 471, a. See Appendix x.

[2] Warwicksh. Hund. Roll. Q. R. Misc. books, xxix. p. 44, b : '(tenens) per antiquam tenuram sine carta.' Gloucester Cart. iii. 67 : 'de liberis tenentibus dicunt quod haeredes O. G. tenent tres virgatas terrae de antiqua tenura.' Cf. iii. 47, 69. Christ Church Cart., Canterbury, Add. MSS. 6159, p. 70 : 'isti tenent antiquo dominico . . . isti tenent antiquum tenementum . . . inferius notati sunt operarii.' Domesday of St. Paul's, 46, 47 : 'de antiqua hereditate.' Cf. Pollock, Land-laws (2nd ed.), p. 209.

[3] Rot. Hundr. ii. 501, b.

of Ely. There are two socmen holding from the King thirty acres each, fourteen socmen holding fifteen acres each, and twenty-six 'toftarii' possessed of small plots. No villains are mentioned, but the socmen are designated on the margin in a more definite way as bond socmen. The manor had been in the possession of the Crown at the time of the Conquest, and it is to be noticed, to begin with, that the chief population of the part which remained with the King appears as socmen—a good illustration of the principle that the special status did not originate when the manor was granted out by the Crown. The sixteen peasants first mentioned are holders of virgates and half-virgates, and form as it were the original stock of the tenantry—it would be impossible to regard them as a later adjunct to the village. Their status is not a result of commutation— they are still performing agricultural work, and therefore *bond* socmen. The Domesday Survey speaks only of villains and 'bordarii,' and it is quite clear that it calls villains the predecessors of the 'bond socmen' of the Hundred Rolls. And now let us examine the portion of the manor which had got into the hands of the Earl Marshall. We find there several *free socmen* whose holdings are quite irregular in size : they pay rent, and are exempted from agricultural work. Then come five *bond socmen,* holding thirty acres each, and nine *bonds* holding fifteen acres each : all these perform the same services as the corresponding people of the King's portion. And lastly come twenty-two tofters. Two facts are especially worth notice : the free socman appears by the side of the bond socman, and the opposition between them reduces itself to a difference between rentpaying people and labourers ; the holdings of the rentpayers are broken up into irregular plots, while the labourers still remain bound up by the system of equalised portions. The second significant fact is, that the term 'socman,' which has evidently to be applied to the whole population except the tofters, has dropped out in regard to the half-virgate tenants of the Earl Marshall. If we had only the fragment relating to his nine bondmen, we might conclude perhaps that there was no certain tenure in the manor. The inference would have been false, but a good many inferences as to the social standing of the peasantry are based on no better foundation. In any case the most important part of the population of Soham, as far as it belonged to the king and to the earl, consisted of socmen who at the same time are called bondmen, and were called villains in Domesday.

Soham is ancient demesne. Let us now take Crowmarsh in Oxfordshire[1]. Two-thirds of it belonged to the Earl of Oxford in 1279, and one-third to the Lord de Valence. At the time of the Domesday Survey it was in the hands of Walter Giffard, and therefore not ancient demesne. On the land of the Earl of Oxford we find in 1279 nine *servi socomanni* holding six virgates, there are a few cotters and a few free tenants besides ; the remaining third is occupied by two 'tenentes per servicium socomannorum,' and by a certain number of cotters and free tenants. It can hardly be doubted that the opposition between *servi* and *liberi* is not based on the certainty of the tenure; the socmen hold as securely as the free tenants, but they are labourers, while these latter are exempted from the agricultural work of the village. The terms are used in the same way as the 'terra libera' and the 'terra operabilis' of the Glastonbury inquest.

I need not say that the socmen of ancient demesne, privileged villains as Bracton calls them, are sometimes subjected to very burdensome services and duties. Merchet is very common among them ; it even happens that they have to fine for it at the will of the lord[2]. But all the incidents of base tenure are to be found also outside the ancient demesne in connexion with the class under discussion. If we take the merchet we shall find that at Magna Tywa, Oxon[3], it is customary to give the steward a sword and four pence for licence to give away one's daughter within twenty miles in the neighbourhood ; in Haneberg,

Servile duties of socmen and freeholders.

[1] Rot. Hundr. ii. 774.
[2] Coram Rege, Hill. 30 Edw. I, m. 17 '(servicia sokemannorum) . . . merchet ad voluntatem.' [3] Rot. Hundr. ii. 846, a.

Oxon[1], a spear and four pence are given in payment. The socmen of Peterborough Abbey[2] have to pay five shillings and four pence under the name of merchet as a fine for incontinence (the legerwite properly so-called), and there is besides a marriage payment (redempcio sanguinis) equal for socmen and villains. The same payment occurs in the land of Spalding Priory, Lincoln[3]. The same fact strikes us in regard to tallage and aids, i.e. the taxes which the lord had a right to raise from his subjects. In Stoke Basset, Oxon[4], the socmen are placed in this respect on the same footing with the villains. The Spalding Cartulary adds that their wainage is safe in any case[5]. On the lands of this priory the classes of the peasantry are generally very near to each other, so that incidents and terms often get confused[6].

And not only socmen have to bear such impositions: we find them constantly in all shapes and gradations in connection with free tenantry. The small freeholder often takes part in rural work[7], sometimes he has to act as a kind of overseer[8], and in any case this base labour would not degrade him from his position[9]. Already in Bracton's day the learned thought that the term 'socage' was etymologically connected with the duty of ploughing:—a curious proof both of the rapidity with which past history had become unintelligible, and of the perfect compatibility

[1] Rot. Hundr. ii. 781, b.

[2] Peterborough Cart., Cotton MSS., Faustina, B. iii. f. 97, 98.

[3] Spalding Priory Cart., Cole MSS., xliii. p. 296.

[4] Rot. Hundr. ii. 780 b.

[5] Spalding Cart. p. 295.

[6] Ibid. p. 283: '*bondus* dat auxilium . . . scil. omnes *sokemanni* unam marcam.' Cf. 292.

[7] Ely Inqu., Cotton MS., Claudius, C. xi. 50, b: 'Tota villata tam liberi, quam alii debent facere 40 perticatas super Calcetum de *Alderhe* [Aldreth's Causeway] sine cibo et opere.' Cf. Domesday of St. Paul's, 75.

[8] Domesday of St. Paul's, 76, 77; Rot. Hundr. ii. 764, b.

[9] Domesday of St. Paul's, 32: 'Omnes isti libere tenentes metunt et arant ad precarias domini et ad cibum eius sine forisfacto.' The general rule is, that freeholders join only in the boon-works (precariae) and not in the regular week-work. But socmen are found engaged in this latter also.

of socage with labour services. Merchet, heriot, and tallage occur even more often[1]. All such exactions testify to the fact that the conceptions of feudal law as to the servile character of particular services and payments were in a great measure artificial. Tallage, even arbitrary tallage, was but a tax after all, and did not detract from personal freedom or free tenure in this sense. Then heriot often occurs among free people in the old Saxon form of a surrender of horse and arms as well as in that of the best ox[2]. Merchet is especially interesting as illustrating the fusion of different duties into one. It is the base payment *par excellence*, and often used in manorial documents as a means to draw the line between free and unfree men[3]. Nevertheless free tenants are very often found to pay it[4]. In most cases they have only to fine in the case when their daughters leave the manor, and this, of course, has nothing degrading in it : the payment is made because the lord loses all claim as to the progeny of the woman who has left his dominion. But there is evidence besides to show that free tenants had often to pay in such a case to the hundred, and the lords had not always succeeded in dispossessing the hundred[5]. Such a fine probably developed out of a payment to the tribe or to a territorial community in the case when a woman severed herself from it. It had nothing servile in its origin. And still, if the documents had not casually mentioned these instances,

---

[1] Ely Inqu., Cotton MSS., Claudius, C. xi. f. 266 : ' De feodis militum et libere tenentibus . . . heriet . . . relevium . . . sed non dabit tallagium et gersumam.' 167 b : ' herietum . . . relevium . . . pannagium . . . tallagium.' Ramsey Cart. i. 297.

[2] Gloucester Cart. iii. 49 and 46 ; Battle Cart., Augm. Off. Misc. Books, N. 57, f. 10, b.

[3] Ely Inqu., Cotton MSS., Claudius, C. xi. f. 186, b : ' Omnes custumarii preter liberos qui non dant gersumam pro filiis et filiabus . . .'

[4] E. g. ibid. 44, a.

[5] Bury St. Edmund's Registrum Album, Cambr. Univ., Ee. iii. 60, f. 154, b : ' Et nota quod si prepositus hundredi capiat gersumam de aliquo libero, dominus habebit medietatem.' Suffolk Court Rolls, 3 (Bodleian) : ' gersuma si evenerit filii vel filie, finem faciet in hundredo, sed celerarius habebit medietatem finis.'

we should have been left without direct evidence as to a difference of origin in regard to merchet or gersum. Is it not fair to ask, whether the merchet of the villains themselves may not in some instances have come from a customary recompense paid originally to the community of the township into the rights of which the lord has entered? However this may be, one fact can certainly not be disputed: men entirely free in status and tenure were sometimes subjected to an exaction which both public opinion and legal theory considered as a badge of servitude.

Feudal oppression in the direction of servitude.
The passage from one great class of society to the other was rendered easy in this way by the variety of combinations in which the distinguishing features of both classes appear. No wonder that we hear constantly of oppression which tended to substitute one form of subjection for another, and thus to lower the social standing of intermediate groups. The free socmen of Swaffham Prior, in Cambridgeshire [1], complain that they are made to bind sheaves while they did not do it before; they used to pay thirty-two pence for licence to marry a daughter, and to give a twofold rent on entering an inheritance, and now the lord fines them at will. One of the tenants of the Bishop of Lincoln [2] declares to the Hundred Roll Commissioners that his ancestors were free socmen and did service to the king for forty days at their own cost, whereas now the Bishop has appropriated the royal rights. The same grievances come from ancient demesne people. In Weston, Bedfordshire [3], the tenantry complain of new exactions on the part of the lord; in King's Ripton [4], Hunts, merchet is introduced which was never paid before; in Collecot, Berks [5], the lord has simply dispossessed the socmen. In some instances the claims of the peasantry may have been exaggerated, but I think that in all probability the chances were rather against the subjected people

[1] Rot. Hundr. ii. 484, b; 485, a.   [2] Ibid. ii 749, b.   [3] Ibid. i. 6.
[4] Coram Rege, Trin., 3 Edw. I, m. 14, d.   [5] Rot. Hundr. i. 19.

than for them, and their grievances are represented in our
documents rather less than fairly [1].

In speaking of those classes of peasants who were by Law of
no means treated as serfs to be exploited at will, I must Kent.
not omit to mention one group which appears, not as a
horizontal layer spread over England, but in the vertical
cut, as it were. I mean the Kentish gavelkind tenantry.
The Domesday Survey speaks of the population of this
county quite in the same way as of the people of neighbouring shires; villains form the great bulk of it, socmen
are not even mentioned, and to judge by such indications,
we have here plain serfdom occupying the whole territory
of the county. On the other hand the law of the thirteenth
century puts the social standing of Kentish men in the
most decided opposition to that of the surrounding people.
The 'Consuetudines Kanciae,' the well-known list of
special Kentish customs [2], is reported to have been drawn
up during an eyre of John of Berwick in the twenty-
first year of Edward I. Be its origin what it may, we
come across several of its rules at much earlier times [3],
and they are always considered of immemorial custom.
The basis of Kentish social law is the assumption that
every man born in the county is entitled to be considered
as personally free, and the Common Law Courts recognised the notion to the extent of admitting the assertion
that a person was born in Kent as a reply against the
'exceptio villenagii.' The contrast with other counties
did not stop there. The law of tenure was as different
as the law of status. It would be needless to enumerate
all the points set forth as Kentish custom. They show
conclusively that the lord was anything but omnipotent
in this county. Interference with the proprietary right
of the peasantry is not even thought of; the tenants
may even alienate their plots freely; the lord can only

---

[1] Cf. a very definite case of oppression, Placit. Abbrev., 150.

[2] Statutes of the Realm, i. 224.

[3] Notebook of Bracton, pl. 1334 and 1644.

claim the accustomed rents and services; if the tenants are negligent in performing work or making payments, distress and forfeiture are awarded by the manorial court according to carefully graduated forms; wardship in case of minority goes to the kin and not to the lord, and heiresses cannot be forced to marry against their wish. As a case of independence the Kentish custom is quite complete, and manorial documents show on every page that it was anything but a dead letter. The Rochester Custumal, the Black Book of St. Augustine, the customs of the Kentish possessions of Battle Abbey, the registers of Christ Church, Canterbury, all agree in showing the Kentish tenantry as a privileged one, both as to the quantity and as to the quality of their services[1]. And so the great bulk of the Kentish peasantry actually appears in the same general position as the free socmen of other counties, and sometimes they are even called by this name[2].

What is more, the law of Kent thus favourable to the peasantry connects itself distinctly with the ancient customs of Saxon ceorls: the quaint old English proverbs enrolled in it look like sayings which have kept it in the memory of generations before it was transmitted to writing. The peculiarities in the treatment of wardship, of dower, of inheritance, appear not only in opposition to the feudal treatment of all these subjects, but in close connexion with old Saxon usage. It would be very wrong, however,

---

[1] Rochester Cart. (Thorpe), 19 a: 'Dominus non debet aliquem operarium injuste et sine judicio a terra sua ejicere.' Ibid. 10, a: 'in crastino Sancti Martini non ponet eos (dominus) ad opera sine consensu eorundem.' Black Book of St. Augustine, Cotton MSS., Faustina, A. i. f. 185, d: '(Consuetudines villanorum de Plumsted) Villani de P. tenent quatuor juga et debent inde arare quatuor acras et seminare . . . et debent metere in autumpno 8 acras de ivernagio vel 4 acras de alio blado. . . . Et debent falcare 2 acras prati. . . . Item debent duo averagia per annum a Plumsted ad Newenton et nihil debent averare ad tunc nisi res que sunt ad opus conventus et que poni debent super ripam.'

[2] Notebook of Bracton, pl. 1334: '. . . et consuetudo est quod uxores maritorum defunctorum habeant francum bancum suum de terris sokemannorum.' Rot. Hundr. i. 201, 202: 'habent et vendunt maritagia sokemannorum aliter quam deberent, quia in Kancia non est warda.'

to consider the whole population of Kent as living under one law. As in the case of ancient demesne, there were different classes on Kentish soil: tenants by knight-service and sergeanty on one side, villains on the other[1]. The custom of Kent holds good only for the tenantry which would have been called gavelmen in other places. It is a custom of gavelkind, of the rent-paying peasantry, the peasantry which pays *gafol*, and as such stands in opposition to the usages of those who hold their land by fork and flail[2]. The important point is that we may lay down as certain in this case what was only put forward hypothetically in the case of molmen and gavelmen in the rest of England: the freehold quality of rent-paying land is not due to commutation and innovation alone—it proceeds from a pre-feudal classification of holdings which started from the contrast between rent and labour, and not from that between certain and uncertain tenure. Again, the law of gavelkind, although not extending over the whole of Kent, belongs to so important and numerous a portion of the population, that, as in the case of ancient demesne, it comes to be considered as the typical custom of the county, and attracts all other variations of local usage into its sphere of influence. The Custumal published among the Statutes speaks of the personal freedom of all Kentish-men, although it has to concern itself specially with the gavelkind tenantry. The notion of villainage gets gradually eliminated from the soil of the province, although it was by no means absent from it in the beginning.

Thirteenth-century law evidently makes the contrast between Kent and adjoining shires more sharp than it ought to have been, if all the varieties within the county were taken into account. But, if it was possible from the legal standpoint to draw a hard and fast line between

[1] Cf. Elton, Tenures of Kent.

[2] Notebook of Bracton, pl. 1419 : 'et ipsi veniunt et dicunt quid nunquam cartam illam fecit nec facere potuit quia uillanus fuit et terram suam defendidit per furcam et flagellum.'

Kent on one side, Sussex or Essex on the other, it is quite impossible, from the historian's point of view, to grant that social condition has developed in adjoining places out of entirely different elements, without gradations and intermediate shades. Is there the slightest doubt that the generalising jurisprudence of the thirteenth century went much too far in one direction, the generalising scribes of the eleventh century having gone too far in the other? Domesday does not recognise any substantial difference between the state of Kent and that of Sussex; the courts of the thirteenth century admitted a complete diversity of custom, and neither one nor the other extreme can be taken as a true description of reality. The importance of the *custom of Kent* can hardly be overrated: it shows conclusively what a mistake it would be to accept without criticism the usual generalising statement as to the different currents of social life in mediaeval England. It will hardly be doubted moreover, that the Kentish case proves that elements of freedom bequeathed by history but ignored by the Domesday Survey come to the fore in consequence of certain facts which remain more or less hidden from view and get recognised and protected in spite of feudalism. If so, can the silence of Domesday or the absence of legal protection in the thirteenth century stand as sufficient proof against the admission of freedom as an important constitutive element in the historical process leading to feudalism? Is it not more natural to infer that outside Kent there were kindred elements of freedom, kindred remnants of a free social order which never got adequate recognition in the Domesday terminology or left definite traces in the practice of the Royal courts?

Peasant free-holders.

One more subject remains to be touched upon, and it may be approached safely now that we have reviewed the several social groups on the border between freeholders and villains. It is this—to what extent can the existence of a class of freeholders among the peasantry of feudal England be maintained? It has been made a test

question in the controversy between the supporters of the
free and those of the servile community, and it would seem,
at first sight, on good ground. Stress has been laid on
the fact, that such communities as are mentioned in
Domesday and described in later documents are (if we
set aside the Danish counties) almost entirely peopled
by villains, that free tenants increase in number through
the agency of commutation and grants of demesne land,
whereas they are extremely few immediately after Domesday, and that in this way there can be no talk of free
village communities this side of the Conquest[1]. This
view of the case may be considered as holding the field
at the present moment: its chief argument has been
briefly summarised by the sentence—the villains of Domesday are not the predecessors in title of later freeholders[2]. I cannot help thinking that a good deal has
to be modified in this estimate of the evidence. Without touching the subject in all its bearings, I may say
at once that I do not see sufficient reason to follow the
testimony of Domesday very closely as to names of classes.
If we find in a place many free tenants mentioned in
the Hundred Roll, and none but villains in Domesday,
it would be wrong to infer that there were none but
villains in the later sense at the time of the Survey, or
that all the free tenements of the Hundred Rolls were
of later creation than the Conquest. It would be especially
dangerous to draw such an inference in a case where the
freeholders of the thirteenth century are possessed of
virgates, half-virgates, etc., and not of irregular plots of
land. Such cases may possibly be explained by sweeping
commutation, which emancipated the entire village at
one stroke, instead of making way for the freehold by
the gradual enfranchisement of plot after plot. But it is
not likely that all the many instances can be referred to
such sweeping emancipation. In the light of Kentish

---

[1] Seebohm, Village Community, 103; followed by Scrutton, Commons and
Common Fields, 38; and Ashley, Economic History, i. 18.

[2] Maitland, Introduction to Manorial Rolls, lxix.

evidence, of free and villain socage, it is at least probable that the thirteenth-century freeholders were originally customary freeholders entered as villains in Domesday, and rising to freedom again in spite of the influence of feudalism. Such an assumption, even if only possible and hypothetical, would open the way for further proof and investigation on the lines of a decline of free village communities, instead of imposing a peremptory termination of the whole inquiry for the period after the Conquest. If the Domesday villains are in no case predecessors in title of freeholders, this fact would go a long way to establish the serfdom of the village community for all the period after the Conquest, and we should have to rely only on earlier evidence to show anything else. Our case would be a hard one, because the earlier evidence is scanty, scattered, obscure, and one-sided. But if the villains of Domesday may be taken to include customary freeholders, then we may try to illustrate our conceptions of the early free village by traits drawn from the life of the later period.

CHAPTER VII.

THE PEASANTRY OF THE FEUDAL AGE. CONCLUSIONS.

I HAVE divided my analysis of the condition of the Legal and feudal peasantry into two parts according to a principle manorial records. forcibly suggested, as I think, by the material at hand. The records of trials in the King's Court, and the doctrines of lawyers based on them, cannot be treated in the same way as the surveys compiled for the use of manorial administration. There is a marked difference between the two sets of documents as to method and point of view. In the case of legal records a method of dialectic examination could be followed. Legal rules are always more or less connected between themselves, and the investigator has to find out, first, from the application of what principles they flow, and to find out, secondly, whether fundamental contradictions disclose a fusion of heterogeneous elements. The study of manorial documents had to proceed by way of classification, to establish in what broad classes the local variations of terms and notions arrange themselves, and what variations of daily life these groups or classes represent.

It is not strange, of course, that things should assume a somewhat different aspect according to the point of view from which they are described. Legal classification need not go into details which may be very important for purposes of manorial administration ; neither the size of the holdings nor the complex variations of services have to be looked to in cases where the law of status is concerned. Still it may be taken for granted that the distinctions and rules followed by the courts had to conform in a general way with matter-of-fact conditions. Lawyers naturally disregarded minute subdivisions, but their broad classes were not invented at fancy; they took them from life as they did the few traits they chose from among many as tests for the purpose of laying down clear and convenient rules. A general conformity is apparent in every point. At the same time there is undoubtedly an opposition between the *curial* (if I may use that term) and the *manorial* treatment of status and tenure, which does not resolve itself into a difference between broad principle and details. Just because the lawyer has to keep to distinct rules, he will often be behind his age and sometimes in advance of it. His doctrine, once established, is slow to follow the fluctuations of husbandry and politics: while in both departments new facts are ever cropping up and gathering strength, which have to fight their way against the rigidity of jurisprudence before they are accepted by it. On the other hand, notions of old standing and tenacious tradition cannot be put away at once, so soon as some new departure has been taken by jurists; and even when they die out at common law such notions persist in local habits and practical life. For these reasons, which hold good more or less everywhere, and are especially conspicuous in mediaeval history, the general relation between legal and manorial documents becomes especially important. It will widen and strengthen conclusions drawn from the analysis of legal theory. We may be sure to find in thirteenth-century documents of practical administration the foundations of a system which prevailed at law in the fifteenth. And what is much more interesting, we may be sure to find in local customaries the traces of a system which had its day long before the thirteenth century, but was still lingering in broken remains.

The will of the lord and the custom of the manor. Bracton defines villainage as a condition of men who do not know in the evening what work and how much they will have to perform next morning. The corresponding tenure is entirely precarious and uncertain at law. But these fundamental positions of legal doctrine we find opposed in daily life to the all-controlling rule of custom. The peasant knows exactly on what days he has to appear personally or by representative at ploughings and reapings, how many loads he is bound to carry, and how many eggs he is expected to bring at Easter[1]; in most cases he knows also what will be required from him when he inherits from his father or marries his daughter. This customary arrangement of duties does not find any expression in common law, and *vice versa* the rule of common law dwindles down in daily life to a definition of power which may be exercised in exceptional cases. The opposition between our two sets of records is evidently connected in this case with their different way of treating facts.

Manorial extents and inquests give in themselves only a one-sided picture of mediaeval village life, because they describe it only from the point of view of the holding: people who do not own land are very seldom noticed, and among the population settled on the land only those persons are named who 'defend' the tenement in regard to the lord. Only the chief of the household appears; this is a matter of course. He may have many or few children, many or few women engaged on his plot: the extent will not make any difference in the description of the tenement and of its services. But although very incomplete in this important respect, manorial records allow us many a glimpse at the process which was preparing a great change in the law. Hired labourers are frequently mentioned in stewards' accounts, and the 'undersette' and 'levingmen' and 'anelipemen[2]' of the extents correspond evidently to this fluctuating

Movement towards free contract and money rents.

---

[1] Chandler, Court Rolls of Great Cressingham, p. 14: '20 solidi de toto Homagio quia recusaverunt preparare fenum domini. Debitum ponatur in respectum usque proximam curiam et interea scrutatur le Domesday.' A manorial extent is evidently meant. Comp. Domesday of St. Paul's.

[2] Ely Inq., Cotton MSS., Claudius, C. xi. 60, a: 'Anelipemen, Anelipewyman et coterellus manens super terram episcopi vel terram alicuius custumariorum suorum metet unam sellionem in autumpno ex consuetudine que vocatur luuebene.' Cp. 42, a, 'quilibet anlepiman et anlepiwyman et quilibet undersetle metet dimidiam acram bladi,' etc., and Ramsey, Cart. i. 50.—I have not been able to find a satisfactory etymological explanation of 'anelipeman'; but he seems a small tenant, and sometimes settled on the land of a villain.

population of rural workmen and squatters gathering behind the screen of recognised peasant holders.

The very foundation of the mediaeval system, its organisation of work according to equalised holdings and around a manorial centre, is in course of time undermined by the process of commutation. Villains are released from ploughings and reapings, from carriage-duties and boon work by paying certain rents; they bargain with the lord for a surrender of his right of arbitrary taxation and arbitrary amercement; they take leases of houses, arable and meadows. This important movement is directly noticed by the law in so far as it takes the shape of an increase in the number of freeholders and of freehold tenements; charters and instruments of conveyance may be concerned with it. But the process is chiefly apparent in a standing contradiction with the law. Legally an arrangement with a villain either ought not to bind the lord or else ought to destroy his power. Even in law books, however, the intermediate form of a binding covenant with the villain emerges, as we have seen, in opposition to the consistent theory. In practice the villains are constantly found possessed of 'soclands,' 'forlands,' and freeholds. The passage from obligatory labour to proprietary rights is effected in this way without any sudden emancipation, by the gradual accumulation of facts which are not strictly legal and at the same time tend to become legal.

Emancipation.

Again, the Royal courts do not know anything about 'molmen,' 'gavelmen,' or 'censuarii.' They keep to the plain distinction between free and bond. Nevertheless, all these groups exist in practice, and are constantly growing in consequence of commutation. The whole law of status gets transformed by their growth as the law of tenure gets transformed by the growth of leases. Molmen, though treated as villains by Royal courts, are already recognised as more 'free' than the villains by manorial juries. The existence of such groups testifies to something more than a precarious passage from service to rent, namely to a change from servile subjection to a status closely resembling that of peasant freeholders, and actually leading up to it. In one word, our manorial records give ample notice of the growth of a system based on free contract and not on customary labour. But the old forms of tenure and service are still existent in law, and the contradiction involved in this fact is not merely a technical one : it lies at the root of the revolutionary movement at the close of the fourteenth century. In this manner facts were slowly paving the way towards a modification of the law. But now, turning from what is in the future, to what is in the past, let us try to collect those indications which throw light on the condition of things preceding feudal law and organisation.

The one-sided conception of feudal law builds up the entire structure of social divisions on the principle of the lord's will. Custom, however sacred, is not equivalent to actionable right, and a person who has nothing but custom to lean upon is supposed to be at the will and mercy of his lord and of base or servile condition. But we find even in the domain of legal doctrine other notions less convenient for the purpose of classification, and more adapted to the practice of daily life. Servile persons and servile land are known from the nature of the services to which they are subject. This test is applied in two directions : (1) regular rural work, ' with pitch-fork and flail,' is considered servile ; and this would exclude the payment of rents and occasional help in the performance of agricultural labour ; (2) certain duties are singled out as marking servitude because they imply the idea of one person being owned by another, and this would exclude subjection derived from the possession of land, however burdensome and arbitrary such subjection might be.

Turning next to manorial records, we find these abortive features of feudal law resting on a very broad basis. Only that land is considered servile which owes labour, if it renders nothing but rent it is termed free. We have here no mere commutation : the notion is an old one, and rather driven back by later law than emerging from it. It is natural enough that the holder of a plot is

[margin note: Contrast between labour and rent.]

considered free if his relations with the lord are restricted to occasional appearances at court, occasional fines, and the payment of certain rents two or three times a year. It is natural enough that the holder of another plot should be treated as a serf because he is bound to perform work which is fitted as a part into the arrangement of his lord's husbandry, and constantly brought under the control and the coercive power of the steward. This matter-of-fact contrast comes naturally to the fore in documents which are drawn up as descriptions of daily transactions and not as evidence for a lawsuit. But the terms 'free' and 'servile' are not used lightly even in such documents. We may be sure that manorial juries and bailiffs would not have been allowed to displace at their pleasure terminological distinctions which might lead people to alter their legal position. The double sense of these terms cannot be taken as arranging society under the same two categories and yet in two entirely different ways : it must be construed as implying the two sides of one and the same thing, the substance in manorial records and the formal distinction in legal records. That is to say, when the test of legal protection was applied, the people who had to perform labour were deprived of it and designated as holding in villainage, and to the people who paid rent protection was granted and they were considered as holding freely. For this very reason the process of commutation creating mol-land actually led to an increase in the number of free tenancies [1].

---

[1] Of course in later times the test applied in drawing the line between freehold and baser tenure was much rather the mode of conveyance than anything else. The commutation into money rent of labour services due from a tenement 'held by copy of court roll' (a commutation which in some cases was not effected before the fifteenth century), did not convert the tenement into freehold ; had it done so, there would have been no copyhold tenure at the present day. But I am here speaking of the thirteenth century when this 'conveyancing test' could not be readily applied, when the self-same ceremony might be regarded either as the feoffment by subinfeudation of a freehold tenant or the admittance of a customary tenant, there being neither charter on the one hand nor entry on a court roll on the other hand. Thus the nature of the services due from the tenement had to be considered, and, at least in general, a tenement which merely paid a money rent was deemed freehold.

The courts made some attempts to utilise personal sub- Personal
subjection.
jection as a distinctive feature of born villains. If it had
been possible to follow out the principle, we should have
been able to distinguish between villains proper and men
of free blood holding in villainage. The attempt miscarried
in practice, although the King's courts were acting in this
case in conjunction with local custom and local juries.
The reason of the failure is disclosed by manorial documents. Merchet, the most debasing incident of personal
villainage, appears so widely spread in the Hundred Rolls
that there can be no question, at least at the close of
the thirteenth century, of treating it as a sure test of personal subjection. We cannot admit even for one moment
that the whole peasant population of entire counties was
descended from personal slaves, as the diffusion of merchet
would lead us to suppose. The appearance of the distinction is quite as characteristic as its gradual collapse. The
original idea underlying it was to connect villain status
with personal slavery, and it failed because the incidents
of personal slavery were confused with other facts which
were quite independent of it and which were expanded
over a very large area instead of a very restricted one.

And now we have ready the several links of one chain. Three tests
of serfdom.
The three tests of serfdom applied by our documents are
connected with each other by the very terms in which they
are stated, and at the same time they present three consecutive stages of development. The notion of serfdom
is originally confined to forms of personal subjection and
to the possession of land under the bane of personal
subjection : in this sense servitude is a narrow term,
and the condition denoted by it is exceptional. In its
second meaning it connects itself with rural labour and
spreads over the whole class of peasants engaged in
it. In its last and broadest sense it includes all the
people and all the land not protected by the Common
Law. We have no evidence as to the chronological landmarks between these several epochs, and it is clear that the
passage from one to another was very gradual, and by no

means implied the absolute disappearance of ancient terms. But it seems hardly doubtful that the movement was effected in the direction described ; both the intrinsic evidence of the notions under discussion and their appearance in our documents point this way.

History of free peasantry.

This being so, we may expect to find some traces of the gradual spread of serfdom in the subdivisions of that comprehensive class called villainage. And, indeed, there are unmistakable signs of the fact that the flood was rising slowly and swamping the several groups of the peasantry which hitherto had been of very various conditions. The Domesday classification will have to be discussed by itself, but it may be noticed even now that its fundamental features are the distinction between serfs and villains, and the very limited number of these first. Judging by this, the bulk of the peasantry was not considered unfree. The inference is corroborated for the epoch of the early Norman kings by the laws of Henry I, in which the villain is still treated on the same footing as the ceorl of Saxon times, is deemed ' worthy of his were and of his wite,' and is called as a free man to the hundred court, although not a landlord, 'terrarum dominus.' The hundredors of later times kept up the tradition : degraded in many ways, they were still considered as representatives of a free population. Ancient demesne tenure is another proof of the same freedom in villainage ; it is protected though base, and supposes independent rights on the part of the peasantry. The position of the group of socmen outside the ancient demesne points the same way : their tenure is originally nothing more and nothing less than a customary freehold or a free copyhold, if one may say so. The law of Kent is constructed on this very basis : it is the law of free ceorls subjected to a certain manorial authority which has not been able to strike very deep roots in this soil.

But the general current went steadily against the peasantry. The disruption of political unity at the time of the great civil war, and the systematic resumption of royal rights by Henry II, must have led to a settlement which impaired the social standing of the villain in the sense of feudal law. The immediate connexion between the lower class and the royal power could not be kept up during the troubled reign of Stephen, when England all but lapsed into the political dismemberment of the neighbouring continental states. Government and law were restored by Henry II, but he had to set a limit to his sphere of action in order that within that sphere he might act efficiently. The very growth of the great system of royal writs necessitated the drawing a sharp line between the people admitted to use them and those excluded from this benefit. One part of the revolution effected by the development of royal jurisdiction is very noticeable in our documents : the struggle between king and magnates as to the right of judging freeholders has left many traces, of which the history of the 'breve quod vocatur praecipe' is perhaps the most remarkable. But the victorious progress of royal juris- diction in regard to freeholders was counterbalanced by an all but complete surrender of it in regard to villains. The celebrated tit. 29 of William the Conqueror's laws provid- ing that the cultivators of the land are not to be subjected to new exactions, had lost its sense in the reign of Henry II, and so soon as it was settled that one class of tenants was to be protected, while another was to be unprotected in the king's court, the lawyers set themselves thinking over the problem of a definite and plain division of classes. Their work in this direction bears all the marks of a fresh de- parture. They are wavering between the formal and the material test : instead of setting up at once the convenient doctrine that villainage is proved by stock, and that in regard to service and tenure the question is decided by their certainty or uncertainty, they try for a long time to shape conclusive rules as to the kind of services and inci- dents which imply villainage, and for a time distinction between rural labour and rent becomes especially im- portant.

On the whole, I think that an analysis of the legal and

manorial evidence belonging to the feudal age leads forcibly to the conclusion that the general classification of society under the two heads of freeholders and villains is an artificial and a late one. A number of important groups appear between the two, and if we try to reduce them to some unity, we may say that a third class is formed by customary freeholders. Another way of stating the same thing would be to say, that the feudal notion of a freehold from which the modern notion has developed must be supplemented from the point of view of the historian by a more ancient form which is hidden, as it were, inside the class distinction of villainage. By the side of the free-holder recognised by later law there stands the villain as a customary freeholder who has lost legal protection. I do not think that the problems resulting from the ambiguous position of the feudal villain can be solved better than on the supposition of this 'third estate.'

SECOND ESSAY.

THE MANOR
AND THE VILLAGE COMMUNITY.

CHAPTER I.

THE OPEN FIELD SYSTEM AND THE HOLDINGS.

MY first essay has been devoted to the peasantry of feudal England in its social character. We have had to examine its classes or divisions in their relation to freedom, personal slavery, and praedial serfage. The land system was touched upon only so far as it influenced such classification, or was influenced by it.

But no correct estimate of the social standing of the peasantry can stop here, or content itself with legal or administrative definitions. In no degree of society do men stand isolated, and a description of individual status alone would be thoroughly incomplete. Men stand arranged in groups for economical and political co-operation, and these groups are composed according to the laws of the division and hierarchical organisation of labour, composed, that is, of heterogeneous elements, of members who have to fulfil different functions, and to occupy higher and lower positions. The normal group which forms as it were the constitutive cell of English mediaeval society is the *manor*, and we must try to make out in what way it was organised, and how it did its work in the thirteenth century, at the time of fully developed feudalism.

The structure of the ordinary manor is always the same. Under the headship of the lord we find two layers of population—the villains and the freeholders ; and the territory occupied divides itself accordingly into demesne land[1]

---

[1] It should be observed that the word demesne (*dominicum*) is constantly used in two different senses, (*a*) the narrower sense in which it stands for

and 'tributary land' (if I may use that phrase) of two different classes. The cultivation of the demesne depends to a certain extent on the work supplied by the tenants of the tributary land. Rents are collected, labour supervised, and all kinds of administrative business transacted, by a set of manorial officers or servants. The entire population is grouped into a village community which centres round the manorial court or halimote, which is both council and tribunal. My investigation will necessarily conform to this typical arrangement. The *holding of the peasant* is the natural starting-point : it will give us the clue to the whole agrarian system. Next may come that part of the territory which is not occupied *in severalty*, but used *in common*. The *agrarian obligations* with regard to the lord and the *cultivation of the demesne land* may be taken up afterwards. The position of *privileged people*, either servants or free-holders, must be discussed by itself, as an exceptional case. And, lastly, the question will have to be put—to what extent were all these elements welded together in the *village community*, and under the sway of the *manorial court*?

Field systems.

The chief features of the field-system which was in operation in England during the middle ages have been sufficiently cleared up by modern scholars, especially by Nasse, Thorold Rogers, and Seebohm, and there is no need for dwelling at length on the subject. Everybody knows that the arable of an English village was commonly cultivated under a three years' rotation of crops[1] ; a two-

the land directly occupied and cultivated by the lord or for his use, and excludes the land held by his villain tenants, and (*b*) the wider sense in which it includes these villain tenements. The first meaning is that which the word usually bears in manorial documents, in which the *dominicum* is contrasted with the *villenagium* or *bondagium*. But in legal pleadings and documents which state the doctrine of the common law and the king's courts the villain tenements are part of the lord's demesne, he is seised of them in his demesne (*in dominico suo*). This discrepancy between what I may call the manorial and the legal uses of the term deserves notice as an indication of the imperfect adjustment of law to fact. I shall use the term in its narrower sense.

[1] Eynsham Cartulary, MSS. of Christ Church, Oxford, N. 27, f. 1, a : 'Est una cultura nuncupata Shyppelond, et continet in toto septem acras dimidiam acram et dimidiam rodam, et valet acra 4d., et bis successive seminatur.' Inqu.

field system is also found very often[1]; there are some instances of more complex arrangements[2], but they are very rare, and appear late—not earlier than the fourteenth century. Walter of Henley's treatise on farming, which appears to belong to the first half of the thirteenth, mentions only the first two systems, and its estimate of the plough-land is based on them. In the case of a three-field rotation a hundred and eighty acres are reckoned to the plough; a hundred and sixty in a system of two courses[3]. We find the same estimate in the chapters on husbandry and management of an estate which are inserted in the law-book known as Fleta[4]. The strips in the fields belonging to the several tenants were divided by narrow balks of turf, and when the field lay fallow, or after the harvest had been removed, the entire field was turned into a common pasture for the use of the village cattle. The whole area was protected by an inclosure while it was under crop.

p. mortem 20 Henry III, N. 14 (Record Office) : ' Extensio manerii de Remdun (Lincoln). Sunt ibidem 360 acre terre et faciunt duas carucatas. Et seminata sunt per annum 240 acre . . . De waracto per annum 12d.'

[1] Glastonbury Survey of 1189 (Roxburghe Ser.), 99 : ' Idem tenet de dominico tres acras a tempore Henrici episcopi quas colit in uno anno et altero non.'

[2] Eynsham Cart., 1, a : ' Est ibidem prope alia cultura nuncupata Clay-furlong et continet cum capitali inferiore octo acras unam rodam tres perticas cum dimidia, et potest ter seminari successive, videlicet post warectum ordium, anno sequente cum grosso pulstro et anno tercio cum frumento, et valet acra 8d. . . . (Alia cultura) et potest ter seminari ut supra mutato grosso pulstro in pisas.'

[3] Two husbandry treatises were chiefly in use in mediaeval England. The fourteenth-century MS., Merton College 91, contains both, and both mention the two systems. (Modus qualiter balliui et prepositi debent onerari super compotum reddendum et qualiter manerium custodiri), f. 152 : ' E la vu les chaumps sunt semez e parti en deus, le iuernage e le trameys sunt tous semez en un champ.'—(Maior husbonderia, otherwise Walter of Henley's treatise), f. 155 : ' Si les terres seent partiz en iii, la une partie en le yuernage, lautre partie en le quaremel, e la tierce partie a warect, donqes est la charrue de terre de x^{xx} acres' (sic, corr. ix^{xx}). ' E si vos terres seent partez en ii, com sont en plusurs pays, la une partie a yuernage e a quaremel, e lautre partie a waret, donqes serra la charue de terre de viii^{xx} acres.' Cf. Thorold Rogers, Six Centuries, 75.

[4] Fleta, ii. 72.

Inhoke.   A curious deviation is apparent in the following instance, taken from the cartulary of Malmesbury. The
Abbey makes an exchange with a neighbour who has
rights of common on some of the convent's land, and
therefore does not allow of its being cultivated and inclosed
(*inhoc facere*).   In return for certain concessions on the
part of the Abbey, this neighbouring owner agrees that
fallow pasture should be turned into arable on the condition that after the harvest it should return to common
use, as well as the land not actually under seed.   Lastly
comes a provision about the villains of the person entering
into agreement with the Abbey: if they do not want to
conform to the new arrangement of cultivation, they will
be admitted to their strips for the purpose of ploughing
up or using the fallow[1].   The case is interesting in two
respects: it shows the intimate connexion between the
construction of the inclosure (*inhoc*) and the raising of the
crop; the special paragraph about the villains gives us to
understand that something more than the usual rotation
of crops was meant: the 'inhokare' appears in opposition
either to the ordinary ploughing up of the fallow, or in a
general sense to its use for pasture; it seems to indicate
extra-cultivation of such land as ought to have remained
uncultivated.   These considerations are borne out by other
documents.   In a trial of Edward I's time the 'inheche' is
explained in as many words as the ploughing up of fallow

---

[1] Malmesbury Cart. (Rolls Ser.), ii. 186: 'De terris inbladandis et inhoc
faciendis in campis de Brokeneberewe et de Burestone, a ponte de Jule-
brocke usque ad Halbrigge de Bremelham, ubi dictus Ricardus dicebat se
habere communam, ita quod nec abbas et conventus, nec eorum tenentes
possint inhoc facere sine consensu dicti Ricardi, nec pro voluntate sua terras
suas ibidem inbladare . . . Abbas et conventus concesserunt praedicto Ricardo
. . . ut cum terrae prenominatae inbladatae fuerint et blada a terris amota,
liberam et plenam communam in praefatis terris una cum abbate et suis
hominibus (habeat) sicut ipse vel praedecessores sui unquam melius et plenius
habere consueverunt. . . . Ita quod si de campo predicto in quo factum est
inhoc pars quaedam remaneat inculta sine blado, in eadem parte habebunt
predictus Ricardus et heredes sui communam cum abbate et conventu et suis.
Similiter si villani praedicti Ricardi nolint inhokare terras suas infra praedictum inhoc sitas, habebunt liberum ingressum et egressum ad warectandum
eas.'

for a crop of wheat, oats, or barley[1]. The Gloucester
Survey, in describing one of the manors belonging to the
Abbey, arranges its land into four fields (*campi*), each
consisting of several parts: the first field is said to contain
174 acres, the second 63, the third 109, the fourth 69 acres.
Two-thirds of the whole are subjected to the usual modes
of cultivation under a three-course system, and one-third
remains for pasture. But out of this last third, 40 acres
of the first field (of 174 acres) get inclosed and used for
crop in one year, and 20 acres of the second in another[2].
In this way the ordinary three-course alternation becomes somewhat more complicated, and it will be hardly
too bold a guess to suppose that such extra-cultivation
implied some manuring of such patches as were deprived
of their usual rest once in three years. In contradiction
to the customary arrangement which did not require any
special manuring except that which was incident to the
use of arable as pasture for the cattle after the harvest,
we find plots set apart for more intense cultivation[3],

[1] Coram Rege, Hill. 3 Edw. I, m. 17, d : ‘Item quicumque facit inheche
scilicet excolit warectum frumento, ordeo vel auena, dabit pro qualibet acra
unum denarium, excepta una acra quam habere debet quietam.’ See App. xii.

[2] Gloucester Cart. iii. 35, 36 : ‘Omnes dictae particulae jacent pro uno
campo, summa 174 acre arabiles, etc. . . . Et de predicto campo possunt inhokari quolibet secundo anno 40 acre et valet inde commodum eo anno
10 solidos. . . . De dictis 63 acris possunt quolibet secundo anno inhokari
20 acre, et valet inde commodum eo anno 11 sol. 8 d. . . . Et est summa totalis
omnium acrarum arabilium 412. Et est summa dictarum acrarum in valore
denariorum 9 librae 12 solidi. De quibus subtracta tertia parte pro campo
jacente ad warectum, 64 sol. scilicet, remanent ad extentam annuam de puro
6 librae 8 sol. et de commodo terrae quae singulis annis potest inhokari
15 sol. 10 d.’—Cf. Minor husbanderia, Merton Coll. MS. 91, f. 152 : ‘E si li ad
Inhom, i deit veer quele cuture i prent del Inhom, e de quel ble est seme
checune cuture, e tel semail deit il cuiler tut per ly e respondre tut per
ly, hors des autres blees.’

[3] Cart. of Boxgrave, Cotton MSS., Claudius, A. vi. p. 2 : ‘Debet compostare
unam helvam ad frumentum et aliam ad ordeum.’ Essex Court Rolls (Bodleian), 4 : ‘Milencia Tegulatrix posuit fimos in communa ad nocumentum
custumariorum.’ Glastonbury Inquest of 1189 (Roxburghe Ser.), 141 : ‘A. de
N. occupavit quendam mariscum per concessum Roberti abbatis et illum
marliavit et coluit.’ Cf. Domesday of St. Paul’s (Camden Ser.), 8 : ‘Dicunt
eciam quod emendatum est manerium in 50 acris marlatis per Willelmum
Thesaurarium ad summam 10 solidorum.’ Ib. 21.

and it is to be noticed that the reckoning in connexion
with them does not start from the division according to
three parts, but supposes a separate classification in two
sections.

The
'Campus.' Another fact worth noticing in the Gloucester instance
is the irregular distribution of acres in the 'fields,' and the
division of the entire arable into four unequal parts. The
husbandry is conducted on the three-course system, and
still four fields are mentioned, and there is no simple relation
between the number of acres which they respectively contain
(174, 63, 109, 69). It seems obvious that the expression
'field' (*campus*) is used here not in the ordinary sense suggested by such records as spring-field, winter-field, and the
like, but in reference to the topography of the district. The
whole territory under cultivation was divided into a number
of squares or furlongs which lay round the village in four
large groups. The alternation of crops distributed the
same area into three according to a mode not described by
the Survey, and it looks probable at first glance that each
of the 'fields' (*campi*) contained elements of all three
courses. The supposition becomes a certainty, if we reflect
that it gives the only possible explanation of the way in
which the twofold alternation of the 'inhoc' is made to fit
with the threefold rotation of crops : every year some of
the land in each *campus* had to remain in fallow, and could
be inclosed or taken under 'inhoc.' Had the *campus* as a
whole been reserved for one of the three courses, there
would have been room for the 'inhoc' only every three
years.

I have gone into some details in connexion with this
instance because it presents a deviation from ordinary
rules, and even a deviation from the usual phraseology,
and it is probable that the exceptional use of words depended on the exceptional process of farming. A new
species of arable—the manured plot under 'inhoc'—came
into use, and naturally disturbed the plain arrangement of
the old-fashioned three courses ; the lands had to be grouped
anew into four sections which went under the accustomed

designation of 'fields,' although they did not fit in with the 'three fields' of the old system. In most cases, however, our records use the word 'field' (*campus*) in that very sense of land under one of the 'courses,' which is out of the question in the case taken from the Gloucester Cartulary. The common use is especially clear when the documents want to describe the holding of a person, and mention the number of acres in each 'field.' The Abbot of Malmesbury, e. g., enfeoffs one Robert with a virgate formerly held 'in the fields' by A., twenty-one acres in one field and twenty-one in another[1]. The charter does not contain any description of *campi* in the territorial sense, and it is evident that the expression 'in the fields' is meant to indicate a customary and well-known husbandry arrangement. The same meaning must be put on sentences like the following :—R. A. holds a virgate consisting of forty-two acres in both fields[2]. The question may be raised whether we have to look for 'both fields' in the winter and spring-field of the three courses rotation, or in the arable and fallow of the two courses. In the first of these eventualities, the third reserved for pasture and rest would be left out of the reckoning ; it would be treated as an appurtenance of the land that was in cultivation. Cases in which the portions in the several fields are unequal seem to point to the second sense[3]. It was impossible to divide the whole territory under cultivation like a piece of paper : conformation of the soil had, of course, much to do with the shape of the furlongs and their distribution, and the

---

[1] Malmesbury Cart. (Rolls Ser.), ii. 27 : 'Concessimus . . . Roberto filio Roberti . . . illam virgatam terre quam A. de C. tenuit in campis, scilicet in uno campo 21 acras et in alio campo 21 acras.'

[2] Gloucester Cart., iii. 194 : 'Robertus Abovetun tenet unam virgatam terre continentem 44 acras in utroque campo.'

[3] Ramsey Register, Cotton MSS., Galba, E. x. 27, d : 'Radulfus tenet 11 seliones in uno campo et 5 in alio de vilenagio.' Worcester Cart. (Camden Ser.), 62, a : 'Henricus clericus tenet unam virgatam, 16 acras in uno campo et 14 in alio. Item tenet aliam virgatam similiter. T. T. tenet unam virgatam, 15 acras excepto dimidio furtendello in uno campo et 11 in alio. O. le E. tenet unam virgatam 13 a. et ½ in uno campo et 12 et dimidiam in alio. T. le F. tenet unam virgatam, 16 acras in uno campo et 12 in alio.'

courses of the husbandry could not impress themselves
on it without some inequalities and stray remnants. It
may happen for this reason that a man holds sixteen
acres in one field and fourteen in the other. There is
almost always, however, a certain correspondence between
the number of acres in each field ; instances of very
great disparity are rare, and suppose some local and
special reasons which we cannot trace. Such disparities
seem to point, however, to a rotation according to two
courses, because the fallow of the three courses could have
been left out of the reckoning only if all the parts in the
fields were equal [1]. I think that a careful inspection of the
surveys from this point of view may lead to the conclusion
that the two courses rotation was very extensively spread
in England in the thirteenth century.

Compulsory rotation of crops.

A most important feature of the mediaeval system of
tillage was its compulsory character. The several tenants,
even when freeholders, could not manage their plots at
their own choice [2]. The entire soil of the township formed
one whole in this respect, and was subjected to the management of the entire village. The superior right of the community found expression in the fact that the fields were
open to common use as pasture after the harvest, as well
as in the regulation of the modes of farming and order of
tillage by the township. Even the lord himself had to conform to the customs and rules set up by the community,
and attempts to break through them, although they become
frequent enough at the close of the thirteenth century, and
especially in the fourteenth, are met by a resistance which
sometimes actually leads to litigation [3]. The freeholders

[1] As in Gloucester Cart., i. 246 : 'Ecclesiam Omnium Sanctorum ... cum
omnibus pertinenciis suis, videlicet unam virgatam terrae, undecim acras
terrae in campo lucrabili.' Cf. 247.

[2] Dunstable Cart., Harleian MSS. 1885, f. 7, d : 'Postquam buttum habuimus bis seminatio fuerit et non amplius, quia omnes ceteri non excolunt
ibi terram, sed at pascua reservant.'

[3] Eynsham Cart., Christ Church, Oxford, MSS., N. 27, f. 74, b : 'Placitum
de Haneberge in recordo de banco de termino Sti Trinitatis anni xliij
(Edw. III) ... Est quidam hamelettus vocatus Tilgerdesle infra bundos ville

alone have access to the courts, but in practice the entire body of the tenantry is equally concerned. The passage towards more efficient modes of cultivation was very much obstructed by these customary rules as to rotation of crops, which flow not from the will and interest of single owners, but from the decision of communities.

The several plots and holdings do not lie in compact patches, but are formed of strips intermixed with each other. The so-called open-field system has been treated so exhaustively and with such admirable clearness by See-bohm, that I need not detain my readers in order to discuss it at length. I shall merely take from the Eynsham Cartulary the general description of the arable of Shifford, Oxon. It consists of several furlongs or areas, more or less rectangular in shape ; each furlong divided into a certain number of strips (*seliones*), mostly half an acre or a rood (quarter acre) in width ; some of these strips get shortened, however (*seliones curtae*), or sharpened (*gorae*), according to the

Intermixture of strips.

de Eynesham, infra quem hamelettum tam in vastis quam in terris, pratis et pasturis eiusdem hameletti iidem Johannes Smyth et omnes alii habent communam cum omnibus averiis suis tanquam pertinens ad tenementa sua que ipsi separati tenent in Hanberge, scilicet in vasto et pastura quolibet anno per totum annum et in terris arabilibus post blada messa et asportata quousque ... resemenentur et quolibet tercio anno tempore warecti per totum annum eo quod omnes terrae arabiles infra dictum hamelettum per duos annos continuos debent seminari et tercio anno warectari, et in pratis post fenum levatum et asportatum usque ad festum purificacionis beate Marie. ... Et dicunt quod diversis vicibus quibus predictus Abbas nunc queritur etc. diuerse parcelle terrarum arabilium in hameletto predicto que tunc temporis warectare debuissent per predictum abbatem et alios seminate fuerunt per quod ipsi tam in parcellis illis sic seminatis que tunc temporis warectare debuerunt quam in aliis vastis, pratis et pascuis hameletti predicti in communa sua cum aueriis suis prout eis bene licuerit usi fuerunt ... Et predictus abbas non cognoscit quod terre arabiles infra hamelettum predictum quolibet tercio anno debent warectari, immo protestando quod eedem terre per tres annos continuos debent seminari et quarto anno warectari.' The case is a rather complicated one, because the persons claiming common are not tenants of the Abbot but of the King. Still, their pretensions are grounded on the customary order of farming in a hamlet belonging to the manor of Eynsham, and this is the point which concerns us. Cf. Coram Rege, Pascha, 25 Henry III : 'Abbas ... partitus fuit terras suas in tres partes quae antea partitae fuerunt in duas partes.' See also Placit. Abbrev. 153. The case is quoted by Scrutton, Common Fields, 57.

shape of the country. At right angles with the strips in the fields lie the 'headlands' (*capitales*), which admit to other strips when there is no special road for the purpose[1]. When the area under tillage abuts against some obstacles, as against a highway, a river, a neighbouring furlong, the strips are stunted (*buttae*). Every strip is separated from the next by *balks* on even ground, and *linches* on the steep slopes of a hill. The holding of a peasant, free or villain, has been appropriately likened to a bundle of these strips of different shapes, the component parts of which lie intermixed with the elements of other holdings in the different fields of the township. There is e. g. in the Alvingham Cartulary a deed by which John Aysterby grants to the Priory of Alvingham in Lincolnshire his villain Robert and half a bovate of land[2]. The half-bovate is found to consist of twelve strips west of Alvingham and sixteen strips east of the village; the several plots lie among similar plots owned by the priory and by other peasants. The demesne land of the priory is also situated not in compact areas, but in strips intermixed with those of the tenantry, in the 'communal fields' according to the phraseology of our documents.

Such a distribution of the arable seems odd enough. It led undoubtedly to very great inconvenience in many ways: it was difficult for the owner to look after his property in the several fields, and to move constantly from one place to another for the purposes of cultivation. A thrifty husbandman was more or less dependent for the results of his work on his neighbours, who very likely were not thrifty. The strips were not always measured with exactness[3], and our surveys mention curious misunderstandings in this respect: it happens that as much as three

---

[1] Some of these expressions are interesting. *Balk* is the O. N. *bálkr*; *gora* is the spear-head or its long triangular shape, O. E. *gár*, O. N. *geirr*. These linguistic affinities have been pointed out to me by Mr. F. York Powell.

[2] Alvingham Priory Cart., Laud MSS. 642 (Bodleian), f. 12. Cf. Malmesbury Cart. ii. 294; Madox, History of the Exchequer, 258.

[3] Eynsham Cart., 5, a: 'I. I. virgatarius ... Idem tenet unam selionem terre apud Blakelond non mensuratam.'

acres belonging to a particular person get mislaid somehow and cannot be identified [1]. It is needless to say that disputes among the neighbours were rendered especially frequent by the rough way of dividing the strips, and by the cutting up of the holdings into narrow strips involving a very long line of boundary. And still the open-field system, with the intermixed strips, is quite a prevalent feature of mediaeval husbandry all over Europe. It covers the whole area occupied by the village community; it is found in Russia as well as in England.

Before we try to find an explanation for it, I shall call the attention of the reader to the following tale preserved by an ancient survey of Dunstable Priory. I think that the record may suggest the explanation with the more authority as it will proceed from well-established facts and not from suppositions [2]. The story goes back to the original division of the land belonging to the Wahull manor by the lords de Wahull and de la Lege. The former had to receive two-thirds of the manor and the latter one-third : a note explains this to mean, that one had to take twenty knight-fees and the other ten. The lord de Wahull took all the park in Segheho and the entire demesne farm in 'Bechebury.' As a compensation for the surrender of rights on the part of his fellow parcener, he ordered the wood and pasture called Northwood to be measured, as also the neighbouring wood called Churlwood. He removed all the peasants who lived in these places, and had also the arable of Segheho measured, and it was found that there were eight hides of villain land. Of these eight hides one-fourth was taken, and it was reckoned that this fourth was an equivalent to the one-third of the park and of the demesne farm, which ought by right to have gone to the lord de la Lege. On the basis of this estimation an exchange was effected.

Division of the land in Segheho.

---

[1] Domesday of St. Paul's, 11 : 'Laurencius de hospitale dimidiam virgatam pro 40 denariis ; tres acre quas tenuit Laurencius sine servicio inveniri non possunt.'

[2] Dunstable Priory Cart., Harleian MSS. 1885, f. 7, d. See Appendix xiii.

In the time of the war (perhaps the rebellion of 1173) the eight hides and other hides in Segheho were encroached upon and appropriated unrighteously by many, and for this reason a general revision of the holdings was undertaken before Walter de Wahull and Hugh de la Lege in full court by six old men; it was made out to which of the hides the several acres belonged. At that time, when all the tenants in Segheho (knights, freeholders, and others) did not know exactly about the land of the village and the tenements, and when each man was contending that his neighbours held unrighteously and more than they ought, all the people decided by common agreement and in the presence of the lords de Wahull and de la Lege, that everybody should surrender his land to be measured anew with the rood by the old men as if the ground had been occupied afresh : every one had to receive his due part on consideration of his rights. At that time R. F. admitted that he and his predecessors had held the area near the castle unrighteously. The men in charge of the distribution divided that area into sixteen strips (buttos), and these were divided as follows : there are eight hides of villain land in Segheho and to each two strips were apportioned.

Inter-mixture produced by the wish to equalise the shares. The narrative is curious in many respects. It illustrates beautifully the extent to which the intermixture of plots was carried, and the inconveniences consequent upon it. Although the land had been measured and divided at the time when the lord de Wahull took the land, everything got into confusion at the time of the civil war, and the disputes originated not in violence from abroad but in encroachments of the village people among themselves : the owners of conterminous strips were constantly quarrelling. A new division became necessary, and it took place under circumstances of great solemnity, as a result of an agreement effected at a great meeting of the tenantry before both lords. The new distribution may stand for all purposes in lieu of the original parcelling of the land on fresh occupation. The mode of treating one of the areas shows

that the intermixture of the strips was a direct consequence of the attempt to equalise the portions. Instead of
putting the whole of this area into one lot, the old men
divide it into strips and assign to every great holding, to
every hide, two strips of this area. Many inconveniences
follow for some of the owners, e. g. for the church which, it
is complained, cannot put its plot to any use on account of
its lying far away, and in intermixture with other people's
land. But the guiding principle of equal apportionment
has found a suitable expression.

We may turn now from the analysis of this case to
general considerations. The important point in the instance quoted was, that the assignment of scattered strips
to every holding depended on the wish to equalise the
shares of the tenants. I think it may be shown that the
treatment adopted in Segheho was the most natural, and
therefore the most widely-spread one. To begin with,
what other form of allotment appears more natural in a
crude state of society? To employ a simile which I have
used already, the territory of the township is not like a
homogeneous sheet of paper out of which you may cut
lots of every desirable shape and size : the tilth will
present all kinds of accidental features, according to
the elevation of the ground, the direction of the water-
courses and ways, the quality of the soil, the situation of
dwellings, the disposition of wood and pasture-ground, etc.
The whole must needs be dismembered into component
parts, into smaller areas or furlongs, each stretching over
land of one and the same condition, and separated from
land of different quality and situation. Over the irregular
squares of this rough chess-board a more or less entangled
network of rights and interests must be extended. There
seem to be only two ways of doing it: if you want the holding to lie in one compact patch you will have to make a
very complicated reckoning of all the many circumstances
which influence husbandry, will have to find some numerical expression for fertility, accessibility, and the like ; or
else you may simply give every householder a share in

Possible modes of dividing the land.

every one of the component areas, and subject him in this way to all the advantages and drawbacks which bear upon his neighbours. If the ground cannot be made to fit the system of allotment, the system must conform itself to the ground. There can be no question that the second way of escaping from the difficulty is much the easier one, and very suitable to the practice of communities in an early stage of development. This second way leads necessarily to a scattering and an intermixture of strips. The explanation is wide enough to meet the requirements of cases placed in entirely different local surroundings and historical connexions; the tendency towards an equalising of the shares of the tenantry is equally noticeable in England and in Russia, in the far west and in the far east of Europe. In Russia we need not even go into history to find it operating in the way described; the practice is alive even now.

Individual occupation of arable and communal rights. This intermixture of strips in the open fields is also characteristic in another way : it manifests the working of a principle which became obliterated in the course of history, but had to play a very important part originally. It was a system primarily intended for the purpose of equalising shares, and it considered every man's rights and property as interwoven with other people's rights and property : it was therefore a system particularly adapted to bring home the superior right of the community as a whole, and the inferior, derivative character of individual rights. The most complete inference from such a general conception would be to treat individual occupation of the land as a shifting ownership, to redistribute the land among the members of the community from time to time, according to some system of lot or rotation. The western village community does not go so far, as a rule, in regard to the arable, at least in the time to which our records belong. But even in the west, and particularly in England, traces of shifting ownership, 'shifting severalty,' may be found as scattered survivals of a condition which, if not general, was certainly much more widely spread in earlier times[1]. The

---

[1] Elton, English Historical Review, i. 435.

arable is sometimes treated as meadows constantly are :
every householder's lot is only an 'ideal' one, and may be
assigned one year in one place, and next year in another.
The stubborn existence of intermixed ownership, even as
described by feudal and later records, is in itself a strong
testimony to the communal character of early property.
The strips of the several holders were not divided by
hedges or inclosures, and a good part of the time, after
harvest and before seed, individual rights retreated before
common use ; every individualising treatment of the soil
was excluded by the compulsory rotation of crops and the
fact that every share consisted of a number of narrow strips
wedged in among other people's shares.   The husbandry
could not be very energetic and lucrative under such pressure,
and a powerful consideration which kept the system working, against convenience and interest, was its equalising and
as it were communal tendency.   I lay stress on the fact :
if the open-field system with its intermixture had been
merely a reflection of the original allotment, it would have
certainly lost its regularity very soon.   People could not
be blind to its drawbacks from the point of view of individual farming ; and if the single strips had become private
property as soon as they ceased to be shifting, exchanges,
if not sales, would have greatly destroyed the inconvenient
network.   The lord had no interest to prevent such exchanges, which could manifestly lead to an improvement
of husbandry; and in regard to his own strips, he must
have perceived soon enough that it would be better to
have them in one compact mass than scattered about in
all the fields.   And still the open-field intermixture holds
its ground all through the middle ages, and we find its survivals far into modern times.   This can only mean, that
even when the shifting, 'ideal,' share in the land of the
community had given way to the permanent ownership by
each member of certain particular scattered strips, this
permanent ownership did by no means amount to private property in the Roman or in the modern sense.
The communal principle with its equalising tendency

remained still as the efficient force regulating the whole, and strong enough to subject even the lord and the free-holders to its customary influence. By saying this I do not mean to maintain, of course, that private property was not existent, that it was not breaking through the communal system, and acting as a dissolvent of it. I shall have to show by-and-by in what ways this process was effected. But the fact remains, that the system which prevailed upon the whole during the middle ages appears directly connected in its most important features with ideas of communal ownership and equalised individual rights.

Arrange-
ment of
holdings.

These ideas are carried out in a very rough way in the mediaeval arrangement of the holding, which is more compli-cated in England than on the continent. According to a very common mode of reckoning, the hide contains four virgates, every virgate two bovates, and every bovate fifteen acres. The bovate (oxgang) shows by its very name that not only the land is taken into account, but the oxen employed in its tillage, and the records explain the hide or carucate [1] to be the land of the eight-oxen plough, that is so much land as may be cultivated by a plough drawn by eight oxen. The virgate, or yard-land, being the fourth part of a hide, cor-responds to one-fourth part of the plough, that is, to two oxen, contributed by the holder to the full plough-team ; the bovate or oxgang appears as the land of one ox, and the eighth part of the hide [2]. Such proportions are, as I said, very commonly found in the records, but they are by no means prevalent everywhere. On the possessions of Glastonbury Abbey, for instance, we find virgates of forty acres, and a hide of 160 ; and the same reckoning appears in manors of Wetherall Priory, Westmoreland [3], of the Abbey of Eynsham, Oxfordshire [4], and many other places.

[1] The expressions are not identical, but they ought both to correspond to the ploughteam.
[2] As to all this, see Seebohm, Village Community.
[3] Glastonbury Inqu. (Roxburghe Ser.), 144, v. Hide, virgate.
[4] Eynsham Cart., 4, a.

The so-called Domesday of St. Paul's reports[1], that in Runwell eighty acres used to be reckoned to the hide, but in course of time new land was acquired (for tillage) and measured, and so the hide was raised to 120 acres. Altogether the supposition of an uniform acre-measurement of bovates, virgates, hides, and knights' fees all over England would be entirely misleading. The oxen were an important element in the arrangement, but, of course, not the only one. The formation of the holding had to conform also to the quality of the soil, the density of the population, etc. We find in any case the most varying figures. The knight's fee contained mostly four or five full ploughs or carucates, and still in Lincolnshire sixteen carucates went to the knight's fee[2]. The carucate was not identical with the hide, but carucate and hide alike had originally meant a unit corresponding to a plough-team. Four virgates were mostly reckoned to the hide, but sometimes six, eight, seven are taken[3]. The yardlands (virgates) or full lands, as they are sometimes called, because they were considered as the typical peasant holdings, consist of fifteen, sixteen, eighteen, twenty-four, forty, forty-eight, fifty, sixty-two, eighty acres, although thirty is perhaps the figure which appears more often than any other[4]. Bovates of

---

[1] Domesday of St. Paul's: 'Manerium istud secundum dictum juratorum continet octo hidas, et hida continet sexcies viginti acras, set antiqua inquisicio dixit, quod non consuevit continere nisi quater viginti, quia postmodum exquisite sunt terre et mensuratae.'

[2] Inqu. post mort. 30 Henry III, N. 36: 'Extensio de terris Roberti de Sancto Georgio (in com. Lincoln.) . . . tenuit in capite de domino Rege 20 bovatas terre et dimidiam pro servicio sexte partis unius feodi militis. . . . Et Robertus de Drayton tenet 2 bovatas et quartam partem unius bovate terre de dicto Roberto per forinsecum servicium tantum, unde 16 carucate terre faciunt feodum militis.'

[3] Rot. Hundred. ii. 631, b: '. . . et ad dictam villam pertinent sex hide quarum quelibet continet 6 virgatas terre et quelibet virgata continet 30 acras.' Ramsey Survey, Galba, E. x. 41: 'In una hydarum istarum . . . septem virgatae 4 acris minus.' Eynsham Cart., 21, a: 'Et abbas habet in eodem manerio 4 carucatas terre et continent 16 virgatas terre in dominico et in villenagio 16 virgatas terre.'

[4] Ramsey Cart. (Rolls Ser.), i. 55, 284, 295, 309, 333, 373, 380; Ely Inqu., Claudius, xi. 82, 95, 97, 121, 129, 186; Gloucester Cart., iii. 128, 142, 145,

ten, twelve, and sixteen acres are to be found in the same locality [1]. We cannot even seize hold of the acre as the one constant unit among these many variables ; the size of the acre itself varied from place to place. In this way any attempt to establish a normal reckoning of the holdings will not only seem hazardous, but will actually stand in contradiction with patent facts.

The holdings not strictly equal in acreage.

Another circumstance seems of yet greater import : even within the boundaries of one and the same community the equality was an agrarian one and did not amount to a strict correspondence in figures. It was obviously impossible to cut up the land among the holdings in such a way as to make every one contain quite the same number of acres as the rest. In the Cartulary of Ramsey it is stated, that in one of the manors the virgate contains sometimes forty-eight acres and sometimes less [2]. The Huntingdon Hundred Rolls mentions a locality where some of the half-virgates have got houses on their plots and some have not [3]. In the Dorsetshire manor of Newton, belonging to Glastonbury, we find a reduction of the duties of one of the virgates because it is a small one [4]. A curious instance is supplied by the same Glastonbury survey as to the Wiltshire manor of Christian Malford : one of the virgates was formed out of two former virgates, which were found insufficient to support two separate households [5].

This last case makes it especially clear that the object

196; Coram Rege, Hill. 3 Edw. I, 17, b ; Eynsham Cart., 11, a ; 88, a ; Rot. Hundr., ii. 605, b.

[1] Chapter-house Boxes, A. $\frac{4}{22}$, m. 31-33.

[2] Ramsey Cart. (Rolls Ser.), i. 354 : 'Aliquando 48 acre faciunt virgatam et aliquando pauciores.'

[3] Rot. Hundr., ii. 628, b.

[4] Glastonbury Inqu. (Roxburghe Ser.), 134 : '. . . R. de W. unam virgatam pro 4 solidis pro omni servicio quia terra parva est.'

[5] Ibid., 113 : 'Super hanc virgatam terre fuerunt olim 2 domus et pro duabus virgatis computata fuit terra illa, sed quia non potuerant 2 homines ibi vivere, redacte ille 2 virgate ad unam, et sicut audierant dicere 7 solidi reddebantur, sed nunquam hoc viderunt et facit idem servitium quod alii faciunt virgarii.'

was to make the shares on the same pattern in point of quality, and not of mere quantity. It is only to be regretted that manorial surveys, hundred rolls, and other documents of the same kind take too little heed of such variations, and consider the whole arrangement merely in regard to the interests of the landlord. For this purpose a rough quantitative statement was sufficient. They give very sparing indications as to the facts underlying the system of holdings ; their aim is to reduce all relations to artificial uniformity in order to make them a fitter basis for the distribution of rents and labour services. But very little attention is required to notice a very great difference between such figures and reality. In most of the cases, when the virgate is described in its component parts, we come across irregularities. Again, each component part is more or less irregular, because instead of the acres and half-acres the real ground presents strips of a very capricious shape. And so we must come to the conclusion, that the hide, the virgate, the bovate, in short every holding mentioned in the surveys, appears primarily as an artificial, administrative, and fiscal unit which corresponds only in a very rough way to the agrarian reality.

This conclusion coincides with the most important fact, Acre ware. that the reckoning of acres in regard to the plough-team is entirely different in the treatises on husbandry from what it is in the manorial records drawn up for the purpose of an assessment of duties and payments. Walter of Henley and Fleta reckon 180 acres to the plough in a three-field system, and 160 in a two-field system. Now these figures are quite exceptional in surveys, whereas 120 acres is most usual without any distinction as to the course of rotation of crops. The relation between the three-field ploughland of 180 acres and the hide of 120 suggests the inference that the official assessment started from the prevalence of the three-field rotation, and disregarded the fallow. But the inference is hardly sufficient to explain the facts of the case. The way towards a solution of the problem is indicated by the terminology of the Ely surveys in the British Museum. These documents very often mention virgates and full yardlands of twelve acres *de ware*; on the other hand, the Court Rolls from Edward I's time till Elizabeth's, and a survey of the reign of Edward III, show the virgate to consist of twenty-four acres [1]. The virgate *de ware* corresponds usually to one-half of the real virgate; I say usually, because in one case it is reckoned to contain eighteen acres in the place of twenty-four mentioned in the rolls and the later survey [2]. Such 'acre ware' are to be found, though rarely, in other manors besides those of Ely minster [3]. The contradiction between the documents may be taken at first glance to originate in a difference between the number of acres under actual tillage and the number of acres comprised in the holding: perhaps the first reckoning leaves out the fallow. This explanation has been tried by Mr. O. Pell, the present owner of one of the Ely manors: he started it in connexion with an etymology which brought together 'ware' and 'warectum': on this assumption twelve acres appeared instead of twenty-four, because the fallow of the two-field system was left out of the reckoning. But this reading of the evidence does not seem satisfactory; it is one-sided at the least. Why should the holding from which the 'warectum' has been left out get its name from the 'warectum'? How is one to explain either from the two-field or from the three-field system the case when eighteen 'acre ware' correspond to twenty-four common acres, or the even more perplexing case when eighteen acres of 'ware' go to the full land and twelve to half-a-full land [4]? In fact, this last instance does not admit of any explanation from natural conditions, because in the natural course of things twelve will never come to

[1] O. C. Pell in the Transactions of the Cambridge Archaeological Society, vi. 17 sqq., 63 sqq.

[2] Ely Inqu., Claudius, C xi. 30, a.

[3] Duchy of Lancaster Court Rolls, B^le 62, N. 750; 3, b. Burton Cartulary, Transactions of the Staffordshire William Salt Society, pp. 22, 28.

[4] Ely Inqu., 31, b.

be one-half of eighteen. Thus we are driven to assume that the 'ware' reckoning is an artificial one : as such it could, of course, treat the half-holdings in a different way from the full holdings. Now the only possible basis for an artificial distribution seems to be the assessment of rents and labour. Starting from this assumption we shall have to say that the virgate 'de wara' represents a unit of assessment in which twelve really existing acres have been left out of the reckoning. The assessment stretches only over half the area occupied by the real holding.

The conclusion we have come to is corroborated by the meaning of the word 'wara.' The etymological connexion with *warectum* is not sound ; the meaning may be best brought out by a comparison with those instances where the word is used without a direct reference to the number of acres. We often find the expression 'ad in-waram' in Domesday, and it corresponds to the plain·'ad gildam Regis.' If a manor is said to contain seven hides *ad inwaram*, it is meant that it pays to the king for seven hides, although there may have been more than seven ploughteams and ploughlands. Another expression of like import is, 'pro sextem hidis se defendit erga Regem.' The Burton Cartulary, the earliest survey after Domesday, employed the word 'wara' in the same sense[1]. It is not difficult to draw the inference from the above-mentioned facts : the etymological connexion for 'wara' is to be sought in the German word for defence—'wehre.' The manor defends itself or answers to the king for seven hides. The expression could get other special significations besides the one discussed : we find it for the poll-tax, by which a freeman defends himself in regard to the state[2], and for the weir, which prevents the fish from escaping into the river[3].

[1] Burton Cart. (William Salt Ser.), 22, 28. Compare Peoples, Ranks and Laws, cap. 3 (Schmid, p. 388).

[2] Peterborough Cart., Cotton MSS., Faustina, B. iii. 97 : 'Libera wara est unus redditus et est talis condicionis quod si non solvatur . . . dupplicatibur in crastino et sic in dies.'

[3] Beaulieu Cart., 103 : 'Et inveniet hominem ad gurgitem faciendum et waram.'

Hides of
assessment. This origin and use of the term is of considerable
importance, because it shows the artificial character of the
system and its close connexion with the taxation by the
State. This is a disturbing element which ought to be
taken into account by the side of the agrarian influence.
There cannot be the slightest doubt that the assessment
started from actual facts, from existing agrarian conditions
and divisions. The hide, the yardland, the oxgang existed
not only in the geld-rolls, but in fact and on the ground.
But in geld-rolls they appeared with a regularity they
did not possess in real fact; the rolls express all modifications in the modes of farming and all exemptions, not
in the shape of any qualification or lighter assessment
of single plots, but by way of striking off from the number
of these plots, or from the number of acres in them; the
object which in modern times would be effected by the
registration of a 'rateable value' differing from the 'actual
value' was effected in ancient times by the registration of
a 'rateable size' differing from the 'actual size'; lastly,
the surveys and rolls of assessment do not keep time with
the actual facts, and often reflect, by their figures and
statistics, the conditions of bygone periods. The hides of
the geld or of the 'wara' tend to become constant and
rigid: it is difficult for the king's officers to alter their
estimates, and the people subjected to the tax try in every
way to guard against novelties and encroachments. The
real agrarian hide-area is changing at the same time because
the population increases, new tenements are formed, and
new land is reclaimed.

We find at every step in our records that the assessment
and the agrarian conditions do not coincide. If a manor
has been given to a convent in free almoign (in liberam et
perpetuam eleemosynam), that is, free from all taxes and
payments to the State, there is no reason to describe it
in units of assessment, and in fact such property often
appears in manorial records without any 'hidation' or
reckoning of knight-fees[1]. The Ramsey Cartulary tells

---

[1] Rot. Hundr., ii. 323 : 'Tenementum quod non est hidatum nec feodatum.'

us that the land in Hulme was not divided into hides and virgates[1]. There are holdings, of course, and they are equal, but they are estimated in acres. When the hidation has been laid on the land and taxes are paid from it, the smaller subdivisions are sometimes omitted : the artificial system of taxation does not go very deep into details. Even if most part of the land has been brought under the operation of that system, some plots are left which do not participate in the common payments, and therefore are said to be 'out of the hide[2].' Such being the case, there can be no wonder that one of the Ramsey manors answers to the king for ten hides, and to the abbot for eleven and a-half[3].

It is to be noted especially, that although in a few cases a difference is made between the division for royal assessment and for the manorial impositions, in the great majority of cases no such difference exists, and the duties in regard to the king and to the lord are reckoned according to the same system of holdings. On the manors of Ely, for instance, the 12 *acreware*[4] form the basis of all the reckoning of rents and work. And so if the royal assessment appear with the features of an artificial fiscal arrangement, the same observation has to be extended to the manorial assessment; and thus we reach by another way the same conclusion which we drew from an analysis of the single holding and of its component parts. No doubt the whole stands in close relation to the reality of cultivation and land-holding, but the rigidity, regularity, and correctness of the system present a necessary contrast to the facts of actual life. As

---

[1] Ramsey Cart. (Rolls Ser.), i. 401 : 'Terrae de Hulmo non sunt distinctae per hydas vel per virgatas.' 413 : 'Nescitur quot virgatae faciunt hidam, nec quot acrae faciunt virgatam.' Cf. 405. Glastonbury Inqu. (Roxburghe Ser.), 5 : '. . . Nescit quantum amuntat in hida.'

[2] Ramsey Cart. i. 441 : 'Terrae quae sunt extra hydam et quae non dant hydagium.' 355 : 'Virgatam extra hydam firmarius appropriavit.' 324 : 'Ponere extra hydam.'

[3] Ibid. 473 : 'Villata defendit, etc. versus Regem pro 10 hydis et versus abbatem pro 11 hydis et dimidia.'

[4] Ely Inqu., Cotton MSS., Claudius, C. xi. 38, b : 'Plena terra que facit 12 acras de ware.'

the soil could not be made to fit into geometrical squares, even so the population could not remain without change from one age to the other within the same boundaries. Thus in course of time the plough-land of 160 and 180 acres, which is the plough-land of practical farming, appears by the side of the statutory hide of 120 acres; and so again inside every single holding there comes up the contrast between its real conformation and distribution, and the outward form it assumed in regard to the king, the lord, and the steward.

Rules of inherit-ance. The inquiry as to the relation between the holding and the population on it is, of course, of the utmost importance for a general estimate of the arrangement. From a formal point of view the question is soon solved: on the one hand, the holding of the villain remains undivided and entire; it does not admit of partition by sale or descent; on the other, the will of the lord may alter, if necessary, the natural course of inheritance and possession; the socage tenure is often free from the first of these limitations, and always free from the second. The indivisibility of villain tenements is chiefly conspicuous in the law of inheritance: all the land went to one of the sons if there were several; very often the youngest inherited; and this custom, to which mere chance has given the name of Borough English, was considered as one of the proofs of villainage[1]. It is certainly a custom of great importance, and probably it depended on the fact that the elder brothers left the land at the earliest opportunity, and during their father's life. Where did they go? It is easy to guess that they sought work out of the manor, as craftsmen or labourers;

---

[1] St. Alban's Formulary, Cambridge Univ., E. e. iv. 20; f. 165, a: 'Item dicunt quod quando predictus Robertus fuerit mortuus quod dominus habebit melius animal suum pro herieto et carettam suam ferro ligatam, omnes pullos suos, omnes porculos suos, omnes pannos suos laneos, omnia vasa sua argentea, aenea et ferrea. Et quod filius suus postnatus habebit terram quam pater suus tenuit et dabit pro ingressu habendo tantum quantum unus alius extraneus et faciet eadem seruilia (sic) que et pater suus fecit.' Ramsey Cart., i. 372: 'Erit dicta terra post mortem patris vel matris gersummata filio juniori vel propinquiori de sanguine secundum consuetudinem ville.'

that they served the lord as servants, ploughmen, and the like; that they were provided with holdings, which for some reason did not descend to male heirs; that they were endowed with some demesne land, or fitted out to reclaim land from the waste. We may find for all these suppositions some supporting quotation in the records. And still it would be hard to believe that the entire increase of population found an exit by these by-paths. If no exit was found, the brothers had to remain on their father's plot, and the fact that they did so can be proved, if it needs proof, from documents[1]. The unity of the holding was not disturbed in the case; there was no division, and only the right heir, the ἑστιοπάμων as they said in Sparta, had to answer for the services; the lord looked to him and no further; but in point of fact the holding contained more than one family, and perhaps more than one household. However this may be, in regard to the lord the holding remained one and undivided. This circumstance draws a sharp line between the feudal arrangement of most counties and that which prevailed in Kent. The gavelkind or tributary tenure there was subjected to equal partition among the heirs.

Let us take a Kentish survey, the Black Book of St. Augustine's, Canterbury, for instance: it describes the peasant holdings in a way which differs entirely from other surveys. It begins by stating what duties lie on each *sulung*, that is, on the Kentish ploughland corresponding to the hide of feudal England. No regular sub-

Kentish
system.

---

[1] Duchy of Lancaster, B'e 62, N. 750, m. 2 : 'Siwardus cepit unam hidam cum dimidia virgata terre et illam tenuit usque ad obitum uxoris sue; postea venit idem Siwardus et rogauit Hugonem fratrem suum ut auderet remanere in terra patris sui prenominati, quia fuit sine terra. Et idem Hugo sibi concessit, saluo iure suo. Item Siwardus cepit uxorem ... de qua habuit Robertum, Radulfum et Gunnildam. Post obitum dicti Siwardi venit Rogerus qui fuit filius Hugonis et exigebat terram prenominatam et per consideracionem curie fuit seisitus in predicta terra, set quia uxor dicti Siwardi pauper fuit, consideratum sibi fuit ut haberet iv acras de predicta terra, quantum sibi custodiret. Postea maritata fuit et revertebant predicte acre terre dicto Rogero ut de jure suo pertinentes ad dictam virgatam terre.' Cf. Q. R. Misc. 902/77.

divisions corresponding to the virgates and bovates are mentioned, and the reckoning starts not from separate tenements, but from their combination into sulungs[1]. Then follow descriptions of the single sulungs, and it turns out that every one of them consists of a very great number of component parts, because the progeny of the original holders has clustered on them, and parcelled them up in very complicated combinations[2]. The portions are sometimes so small, that an independent cultivation of them would have been quite impossible. In order to understand the description it must be borne in mind that the fact of the tenement being owned by several different persons in definite but undivided shares did not preclude farming in common; while on the other hand, in judging of the usual feudal arrangement of holdings we must remember that the artificial unity and indivisibility of the tenement may be a mere screen behind which there exists a complex mass of rights sanctioned by morality and custom though not by law. The surveys of the Kentish possessions of Battle Abbey are drawn up on the same principle as those of St. Augustine's; the only difference is, that the individual portions are collected not in sulungs, but in yokes (*juga*)[3].

[1] Black Book of St. Augustine's, Cotton MSS., Faustina, A. i. 15, a: 'In Taneto sunt 45 sullung 150 acre reddentes gablum denariorum. In festo S^{ti} Martini videlicet de unoquoque sullung reddunt de Gabulo 2 solidos 2 denarios, summa quorum facit 25 libras 105 solidos 10 denarios obolum. Ipsi qui tenent predictos sullung reddunt in equinoctio autumpnae de unoquoque sullung pro horsarer 16 den. et de 150 acris 12 den. Ipsi idem arant pro anererthe in purificacione de unoquoque sullung unam acram et 150 acris 3 virgatas. Ipsi idem reddunt in festo S^{ti} Johannis de unoquoque sullung 2 agnos separabiles et de 150 acris 1 agnum et valenciam dimidii agni. Ipsi idem reddunt in natali de unoquoque sullung unum ferendel ordei,' etc.

[2] Ibid. 60; Suolinga de Ores: 'Heredes Salomonis de Ores tenent 8 acras ... Heredes Willelmi de Ores tenent 12 acras ... Jacobus tenet 3 acras et dimidiam perchatam ... Thomas filius G. de Hores tenet 2 acras ... Ricardus et Salomon filius Augustini ... et Willelmus filius Ricardi tenent 2 acras et dimidiam,' etc.

[3] Augment. Off. Misc. Books, N. 57, f. 96, a: 'Johannes Bairot heredes Hamoni Daniel, heredes Johannis hugheleyn, heredes Roberti atte mede, heredes Walteri et Willelmi Ram et Gilbertus le Rome tenent unum jugum et dimidium de Cukulycumbe.'

And so we have in England two systems of dividing the land of the peasant, of regulating its descent and its duties. In one case the tenant-right is connected with rigid holdings descending to a single heir ; in another the tenements get broken up, and the heirs club together in order to meet the demands of the manorial administration. The contrast is sharp and curious enough. How is one to explain, that in conditions which were more or less identical, the land was sometimes partitioned and sometimes kept together, the people were dispersed in some instances and kept together in others?

Closer inspection will show that however sharp the opposition in law may have been, in point of husbandry and actual management the contrast was not so uncompromising. Connecting links may be found between the two. The Domesday of St. Paul's, for instance, is compiled in the main in the usual way, but one section of it—the description of the Essex manors of Kirby, Horlock, and Thorpe—does not differ from the Kentish surveys in anything but the terminology[1]. The services are laid on hides, and not on the actual tenements. Each hide includes a great number of plots which do not fall in with any constant subdivisions of the same kind as the virgates and bovates. Some of these plots are very small, all are irregular in their formation. It happens that one and the same person holds in several hides. In one word, the Kentish system has found a way for some unexplained reason into the possessions of St. Paul's, and we find subjected to it some Essex manors which do not differ much in their husbandry arrangements from other properties in Essex, and have no claim to the special privileges of Kentish soil.

Once apprised of the possible existence of such intermediate forms, we shall find in most surveys facts tending to connect the two arrangements. The Gloucester Cartulary, for instance, mentions virgates held by four persons[2]. The

Connecting links between the two systems.

---

[1] Domesday of St. Paul's, 38 sqq. Comp. Ramsey Cart., i. 413.

[2] Gloucester Cart., iii. 213 : ' Robertus Altegreue, Willelmus Godere, Jo-

plots of these four owners are evidently brought together into a virgate for the purpose of assessing the services. Two peasants on the same virgate are found constantly. It happens that one gets the greater part of the land and is called the heir, while his fellow appears as a small cotter who has to co-operate in the work performed by the virgate [1]. Indications are not wanting that sometimes virgates crumbled up into cotlands, bordlands, and crofts. The denomination of some peasants in Northumberland is characteristic enough — they are 'selfoders,' obviously dwelling 'self-other' on their tenements [2]. On the other hand, it is to be noticed that the gavelkind rule of succession, although enacting the partibility of the inheritance, still reserves the hearth to the youngest born, a trace of the same junior right which led to Borough English.

United and partible holdings.

I think that upon the whole we must say that in practice the very marked contrast between the general arrangement of the holdings and the Kentish one is more a difference in the way of reckoning than in actual occupation, in legal forms than in economical substance. The general arrangement admitted a certain subdivision under the cover of an artificial unity which found its expression in the settlement of the services and of the relations with the lord [3]. The English case has its parallel on the Continent in this respect. In Alsace, for instance, the holding

hannes Abraham, Isabella relicta Lucae tenent unam virgatam, scilicet quilibet eorum unum quarterium et faciunt conjunctim in omnibus sicut unus virgatarius.' Comp. 59, 201. Hereford Court Rolls (Bodleian), 3, b: ' T. Hake, Ricardus de Poluchulle et Muriel filius Galfridi pyoner tenent unam dimidiam virgatam terre consuetudinarie.'

[1] Bury St. Edmund's Cart., Cambridge University, G. g. iv. 4. f. 35, a: ' Johannes Knop tenet cotagium et contribuit heredi qui tenet maiorem partem tenementorum.'

[2] Inqu. post mort. 55 Henry III, N. 33 : 'Redditarii qui vocantur selfoders.'

[3] Euch. Q. R. Anc. Misc. Court Rolls, xxi. 513/82: 'Dicunt quod aliquis habens virgatam terre et vendiderit omnes partes excepto capitati domo et loco focarii, tenentes locum focarii erunt sectatores curie et alteri non. Similiter de tenentibus dimidiam virgatam et codsetlestoftes : semper tenentes locum focarii colligent firmam et erunt liberi de pannagio et de aliis tallagiis et alteri tenentes partes erunt geldabiles.' (Curia de Brigstock tenta die veneris proxima ante festum Sancti Andree Apostoli anno [r. r. Edw. xxvi]).

was united under one 'Träger' or bearer of the manorial duties ; but by the side of him other people are found who participate with this official holder in the ownership and in the cultivation[1]. The second system also kept up the artificial existence of the higher units, and obvious interests prevented it from leading to a 'morcellement' of land into very small portions in practice. The economic management of land could not go as far as the legal partition. In practice the subdivision was certainly checked, as in the virgate system, by the necessity of keeping together the cattle necessary for the tillage. Virgates and bovates would arise of themselves : it was not advantageous to split the yoke of two oxen, the smallest possible plough ; and co-heirs had to think even more when they inherited one ox with its ox-gang of land. The animal could not be divided, and this certainly must have stopped in many cases the division of land. When the documents speak of plots containing two or three acres, it must be remembered that such crofts and cotlands occur also in the usual system, and I do not see any reason to suppose that the existence of such subdivided rights always indicated a real dispersion of the economic unit : they may have stood as a landmark of the relative rights of joint occupiers. I do not mean to say, of course, that there was no real basis for the very great difference which is assumed by the two ways of describing the tenements. No doubt the hand of the lord lay heavier on the Essex people than on the Kentish men, their occupation and usage of the land was more under the control of the lord, and assumed therefore an aspect of greater regularity and order. Again, the legal privileges of the Kentish people opened the way towards a greater development of individual freedom and a certain looseness of social relations. Still it would be wrong to infer too much from this formal opposition. In both cases the centripetal and the centrifugal tendency are working against each other in the same

---

[1] See Hanauer, Les paysans de l'Alsace au Moyen Age.

way, although one case presents the stronger influence of disruptive forces, and the other gives predominance to the collective power. In the history of socage and military tenure the system of unity arose gradually, and without any sudden break, out of the system of division. The intimate connexion between both forms is even more natural in peasant ownership, which had to operate with small plots and small agricultural capital, and therefore inclined naturally towards the artificial combination of divided interests. In any case there is no room in practice for the rigid and consequent operation of either rule of ownership, and, if so, there is no actual basis for the inference that the unification of the holding is to be taken as a direct consequence of a servile origin of the tenement and a sure proof of it. Unification appears on closer inspection as a result of economic considerations as well as of legal disabilities, and for this reason the tendency operated in the sphere of free property as well as among the villains; among these last it could not preclude the working of the disruptive elements, but in many cases only hid them from sight by its artificial screen of rigid holdings.

The holding and the team.   We have seen that the size and distribution of the holdings are connected with the number of oxen necessary for the tillage, and its relation to the full plough. The hide appears as the ploughland with eight oxen, the virgate corresponds to one yoke of oxen, and the bovate to the single head. It need not be added that such figures are not absolutely settled, and are to be accepted as approximate terms. The great heavy plough drawn by eight or ten oxen is certainly often mentioned in the records, especially on demesne land [1]. The dependent people, when they have to help in the cultivation of the demesne, club together in order to make up full plough teams [2]. It is also obvious that the peasantry had to asso-

---

[1] Domesday of St. Paul's, xv. 7; Gloucester Cartulary, iii. 55, 61; Cartulary of Christ Church, Canterbury, Add. MSS. 6759, f. 21, b.

[2] Battle Cart. Augm. Off. Books, N. 18, f. 7, a : 'Aratra uertuntur in terram domini.' Ely Inqu., Claudius, C. xi. 38 b, 86 b, etc.

ciate for the tilling of their own land, as it was very rare
for the single shareholder to possess a sufficient number
of beasts to work by himself.   But it must be noticed that
alongside of the unwieldy eight-oxen plough we find much
lighter ones.   Even on the demesne we may find them
drawn by six oxen.   And as for the peasantry, they seem
to have very often contented themselves with forming a
plough team of four heads[1].   It is commonly supposed
by the surveys that the holder of a yardland joins with
one of his fellows to make up the team.   This would mean
on the scale of the hide of 120 acres that the team consists
of four beasts[2].   It happens even that a full plough is
supposed to belong to two or three peasants, of which
every one is possessed only of five acres ; in such cases there
can be no talk of a big plough ; it is difficult to admit even
a four-oxen team, and probably those people only worked
with one yoke or pair of beasts[3].   Altogether it would be
very wrong to assume in practice a strict correspondence
between the size of the holding and the parts of an eight-
oxen plough.   The observation that the usual reckoning
of the hide and of its subdivisions, according to the pattern
of the big team, cannot be made to fit exactly with the
real arrangement of the teams owned by the peasantry—
this firmly established observation leads us once more to
the conclusion that the system of equal holdings had
become very artificial in process of time and was determined rather by the relation between the peasants and
the manorial administration than by the actual conditions
of peasant life.   Unhappily the artificial features of the

[1] Ely Inqu., 72 b ; comp. 24, b ; Gloucester Cart., iii. 183.

[2] Eynsham Reg., 6, b : ' Robertus Tony tenet de domino unam virgatam
terre in bondagium . . . Idem semel arabit cum vicino adiuncto.'   Ramsey
Cart., i. 56.   Comp. Q. R. Min. Acc., B^le 513, N. 97 : ' Estimatur quod communiter tres custumarii possunt facere unam carucam (tenent 20 acras).'

[3] Rot. Hundr., ii. 461, b : ' Robertus de Tony habet in villenagio scil. Regi-
naldum Toni qui tenet 5 acras . . . Item si ipse habeat cum uno vel cum duobus
sociis unam carucam, arabit unam selionem terre domini.'   Comp. 462, a.
Add. MSS. 6159, f. 22, b : ' W. J. tenet de domino in villenagio unum mesuagium et 10 acras terre. . . . Et arabit cum caruca sua sive jungat sive non
4 acras.'

system have been made by modern inquirers the starting-point of very far-reaching theories and suppositions. Seebohm has proposed an explanation of the intermixture of strips as originating in the practice of coaration. He argues that it was natural to divide the land tilled by a mixed plough-team among the owners of the several beasts and implements. Every man got a strip according to a certain settled and ever-recurring succession. I do not pretend to judge of the value of the interesting instances adduced by Seebohm from Celtic practices, but whatever the arrangement in Wales or Ireland may have been, the explanation does not suit the English case. A doubt is cast on it already by the fact that such a universal feature as the intermixture of strips appears connected with the occurrence of such a special instrument as the eight-oxen plough. The intermixture is quite the same in Central Russia, where they till with one horse, and in England where more or less big ploughs were used. The doubt increases when we reflect that if the strips followed each other as parts of the plough-team, the great owners would have been possessed of compact plots. Every holder of an entire hide would have been out of the intermixture, and every virgater would have stood in conjunction with a sequence of three other tenants. Neither the one nor the other inference is supported by the facts. The observation that the peasantry are commonly provided with small ploughs drawn by four beasts ruins Seebohm's hypothesis entirely. One would have to suppose that most fields were divided into two parts, as the majority of the tenements are yardlands with half a team. The only adequate explanation of the open-field intermixture has been given above; it has its roots in the wish to equalise the holdings as to the quantity and quality of the land assigned to them in spite of all differences in the shape, the position, and the value of the soil.

Terms of exceptional occurrence. Before I leave the question as to the holdings of the feudal peasantry, I must mention some terms which occur in different parts of England, although more rarely than

the usual hides and virgates[1]. Of the *sulung* I have
spoken already. It is a full ploughland, and 200 acres are
commonly reckoned to belong to it. The name is sometimes found out of Kent, in Essex for instance. In Tillingham, a manor of St. Paul's of London, we come across six
hides 'trium solandarum[2].' The most probable explanation seems to be that the hide or unit of assessment is
contrasted with the *solanda* or *sulland* (sulung), that is
with the actual ploughland, and two hides are reckoned as
a single solanda.

The yokes (juga) of Battle Abbey[3] are not virgates,
but carucates, full ploughlands. This follows from the
fact that a certain virgate mentioned in the record is
equivalent only to one fourth of the yoke. In the Norfolk
manors of Ely Minster we find *tenmanlands*[4] of 120 acres
in the possession of several copartitioners, *participes*. The
survey does not go into a detailed description of tenements
and rights, and the reckoning of services starts from the
entire combination, as in the Kentish documents. A commonly recurrent term is *wista*[5]; it corresponds to the
virgate: a great wista is as much as half-a-hide, or two
virgates[6].

The terms discussed hitherto are applied to the tenements in the fields of the village; but besides those there
are other names for the plots occupied by a numerous
population which did not find a place in the regular holdings. There were craftsmen and rural labourers working
for the lord and for the tenants; there were people living

---

[1] Black Book of St. Augustine's, 53.

[2] Domesday of St. Paul's, 58.

[3] Augm. Off. Misc. Books, N. 57, f. 65, b. See Cartulary of Battle Abbey
(Camd. Soc.), p. 133.

[4] Ely Inqu., 185, a : '... tenent dimidium tenmanland, scilicet 60 acras
terre ... Al. et M. et eorum participes tenent unum tenmanland, scilicet 120
acras terre.' The expression may be corrupted from *tunmanland*, or else it
may be a mark of a beginning of cultivation in Danish times.

[5] Chapter-house Books, A. 4/22, p. 21 : 'Custumarii tenent 22 virgatas
quas vocant wistas.'

[6] Battle Abbey Cart., Augment. Off. Misc. Books, N. 57, f. 27, a ; comp.
15, b.

by gardening and the raising of vegetables. This class is always contrasted with the tenants in the fields. The usual name for their plots is cote, cotland, or cotsetland. The so-called *ferdel*, or fourth part of a virgate, is usually mentioned among them because there are no plough-beasts on it [1]. Another name for the *ferdel* is *nook* [2]. Next come the crofters, whose gardens sometimes extend to a very fair size—as much as ten acres in one enclosed patch [3]. The cotters proper have generally one, two, and sometimes as much as five acres with their dwellings; they cannot keep themselves on this, as a rule, and have to look out for more on other people's tenements. A very common name for their plots is 'lundinaria [4],' 'Mondaylands,' because the holders are bound to work for the lord only one day in the week, usually on Monday. Although the absence of plough-beasts, of a part in coaration, and of shares in the common fields draws a sharp line between these men and the regular holders, our surveys try sometimes to fit their duties and plots into the arrangement of holdings; the cotland is assumed to represent one sixteenth or even one thirty-second part of the hide [5]. The Glastonbury Survey of 1189 contains a curious hint that two cottages are more valuable than one half-virgate: two cotlands were ruined during the war, and they were thrown together into half a virgate, although it would have been more advantageous to keep two houses on them, that is two households [6]. The *bordae* mentioned by the documents are simply cottages or booths without any land belonging to them [7]. The manorial police keeps a look-

---

[1] Glastonbury Inqu. (Roxburghe Ser.), 66, 90.

[2] Worcester Cart., 41, b.

[3] Glastonbury Inqu., 67, 70; Rot. Hundr., ii. 404, b.

[4] Gloucester Cart., iii. 207.

[5] Abingdon Cart., ii. 304: 'In dominio camerae sunt 4 hidae uno cotsettel minus.'

[6] Glastonbury Inqu., 41: 'Robertus blundus tenet dimidiam virgatam eodem servicio. Hec terra solet esse divisa in duo cotsetlanda, set in tempore werre deciderunt, eo ex his duabus terris facta fuit dimidia virgata. Si esset divisa utilius esset domino.'

[7] Domesday of St. Paul's, 19; Ramsey Cart. (Rolls Ser.), i. 309.

out that such houses may not arise without licence and service [1].

A good many terms are not connected in any way with the general arrangement of the holdings, but depend upon the part played by the land in husbandry or the services imposed upon it. To mention a few among them. A plot which has to provide cheese is called Cheeseland [2]. Those tenements which are singled out for the special duty of carrying the proceeds of the manorial cultivation get the name of *averlands* [3]. The terms *lodland* [4], *serland* [5] or *sharland*, are also connected with compulsory labour. The first is taken from the duty to carry loads or possibly to load waggons ; the second may be employed in reference to work performed with the sithe or reap-hook. A plot reserved for the leader of the plough-team, the akerman, was naturally called *akermanland* [6]. Sometimes, though rarely, the holding gets its name from the money rent it has to pay. We hear of *denerates* [7] and *nummates* [8] of land in this connexion.

All these variations in detail do not avail to modify to any considerable extent the chief lines on which the medieval system of holdings is constructed. I presume that the foregoing exposition has been sufficient to establish the following points :— Conclusions.

1. The principle upon which the original distribution depended was that of equalizing the shares of the members of the community. This led to the scattering and to the intermixture of strips. The principle did not preclude

[1] Gloucester Cart., iii. 61.

[2] Black Book of St. Augustine's, 57.   [3] Ibid.

[4] Domesday of St. Paul's, 49.   [5] Gloucester Cart., ii. 109.

[6] Exch. Q. R. Anc. Misc., xxi. 513/82 (Curia de Brigstock, Friday after Annunciation, 27 Edw. I): 'Ille due dimidie rode prati . . . pertinent ad Hakermannislond, et nemo potest habere seysinam predictarum sine breui Domini Regis.'

[7] Glastonbury Inqu., 2 : 'In marisco 110 acras terrae et quoddam molendinum, et octo deneratas terrae secus molendinum.'

[8] Madox, Exch., i. 155, n. 257 : 'Duodecim tamen nummatas quas Ordurcus tenuit . . . usque ad 10 annos debemus tenere, singulis annis reddentes ei 12 denarios ad festum S^ti Michaelis.'

inequality according to certain degrees, but it aimed at putting all the people of one degree into approximately similar conditions.

2. The growth of population, of capital, of cultivation, of social inequalities led to a considerable difference between the artificial uniformity in which the arrangement of the holdings was kept and the actual practice of farming and ownership.

3. The system was designed and kept working by the influence of communal right, but it got its artificial shape and its legal rigidity from the manorial administration which used it for the purpose of distributing and collecting labour and rent.

4. The holdings were held together as units, not merely by the superior property of the lord, but by economic considerations. They were breaking up under the pressure of population, not merely in the case of free holdings, but also where the holdings were servile.

CHAPTER II.

RIGHTS OF COMMON.

THE influence of the village community is especially Meadows. apparent in respect of that portion of the soil which is used for the support of cattle. The management of meadows is very interesting because it presents a close analogy to the treatment of the arable, and at the same time the communal features are much more clearly brought out by it. We may take as an instance a description in the Eynsham Survey. The meadow in Shifford is divided into twelve strips, and these are distributed among the lord and the tenantry, but they are not apportioned to any one for constant ownership. One year the lord takes all the strips marked by uneven numbers, and the next year he moves to those distinguished by even numbers[1]. The tenants divide the rest according to some settled rotation. Very often lots are drawn to indicate the por-

---

[1] Eynsham Cart. 2, c: 'Est quoddam pratum nuncupatum Clayhurste et continet de prato et pastura 35 acras dimidiam rodam 13 perticas. Est ibidem ex parte australi una pecia prati et pasture et continet 10 acras et 7 perticas et nuncupatur twelueacres que annuatim diuiditur in 12 parcellas per virgam equales, unde dominus habet uno anno i, iii, v, vii, ix et xi, heredes le Freman et Walterus le Reue eodem anno habent parcellas ii, iv, vi, viii, x et xii. Alio anno habet dominus parcellas quas tenentes habuerunt et tenentes parcellas domini. Et sic annuatim habet dominus quinque acras, tres perticas et dimidiam perticam.' Cf. 23, c: 'Memorandum quod in prato de Landemede sunt sex parcelle bundate quarum prima parcella nuncupata Stubbefurlong continet 4 acras et dimidiam rodam et est domini anno incarnacionis Domini impari et tenencium anno incarnacionis Domini pari. Quando vero est tenencium, diuiditur per sortem.'

tions of the several households [1]. It must be added that
the private right of the single occupiers does not extend
over the whole year : as in the case of the arable all inclosures fall after the harvest, so in regard to meadows the
separate use, and the boundaries protecting it, are upheld
only till the mowing of the grass : after the removal of the
hay the soil relapses into the condition of undivided land.
The time of the 'defence' extends commonly to 'Lammas
day :' hence the expression 'Lammas-meadow' to designate such land. It is hardly necessary to insist on the
great resemblance between all these features and the corresponding facts in the arrangement of the arable. The
principle of division is supplied by the tendency to assign
an equal share to every holding, and the system of scattered strips follows as a necessary consequence of the principle. The existence of the community as a higher organising unit is shewn in the recurrence of common use after
the 'defence,' and in the fact that the lord is subjected to
the common rotation, although he is allowed a privileged
position in regard to it. The connexion in which the
whole of these rights arises is made especially clear by the
shifting ownership of the strips : private right appears on
communal ground, but it is reduced to a *minimum* as it
were, has not settled down to constant occupation, and
assumes its definite shape under the influence of the idea
of equal apportionment. Of course, by the side of these
communal meadows we frequently find others that were
owned in severalty.

Allotment
of pasture.   Land for pasture also occurs in private hands and in
severalty, but such cases are much rarer [2]. Sometimes

---

[1] A very good instance is supplied by Williams, Rights of Common, 89,
90. Cf. Birkbeck, Sketch of the Distribution of Land in England, 19.

[2] Gloucester Cart. iii. 67 (Extenta de Berthona Regis) : 'De pastura separabili dicunt quod Rex habet quandam moram quae continet $4\frac{1}{2}$ acras et valet
4 solidos et potest sustinere 12 boves per nouem menses. Item de pastura
inseparabili dicunt quod Abbas Gloucestriae debet invenire pasturam ad 18
boves domini Regis, et ad 2 vaccas, et 2 afros, a vigilia Pentecostes quousque
prata sint falcata, levata et cariata.' Exch. Q. R. Treas. of Rec. $\frac{44}{88}$: 'item
dicunt quod sunt ibi de pastura separabili 50 acrae et valet acra 3 d.'

the pasture gets separated and put under 'defence' for one part of the year, and merges into communal ownership afterwards [1]. But in the vast majority of cases the pasture is used in common, and none of the tenants has a right to fence it in or to appropriate it for his own exclusive benefit. It ought to be noted, that the right to send one's cattle to the pasture on the waste, the moors, or in the woods of a manor appears regularly and intimately connected with the right to depasture one's cattle on the open fields of the village [2]. Both form only different modes of using communal soil. As in the case of arable and meadow the undivided use cannot be maintained and gets replaced by a system of equalised shares or holdings, so in the case of pasture the faculty of sending out any number of beasts retires before the equalisation of shares according to certain modes of 'stinting' the common. We find as an important manorial arrangement the custom to 'apportion' the rights of common to the tenements, that is to decide in the manorial Court, mostly according to verdicts of juries, how many head of cattle, and of what particular kind, may be sent to the divers pasture-grounds of the village by the several holdings. From time to time these regulations are revised. One of the Glastonbury Surveys contains, for instance, the following description from the

---

[1] Eynsham Cart. 3, b : ' Dicunt eciam quod omnia prata pasture domini et omnes culture non seminate et [que] deberent seminari sunt separalia per tempus predictum.' 10, b : ' Et sunt dicte pasture separales quousque blada circumcrescentia asportentur.' A curious case is the following ; ibid., 3, b : ' Dicunt eciam quod dominus tenetur pratum suum de Langenhurst custodire nec potest attachiare malefactores in eodem a solis ortu usque ad occasum, aliis temporibus . . . licet, et est separale a festo annunciacionis beate Marie usque gulam Augusti.'

[2] Domesday of St. Paul's, 69 : ' Non est ibi certa pastura nisi quando terre dominice quiescunt alternatim inculte.' Cf. 59 : ' Non est ibi pastura nisi cum quiescit dominicum per wainnagium . . . possunt ibi esse 4 sues cum uno verre et suis fetibus et 4 vacce cum suis fetibus si quiescunt pasture dominice alternatim.' Rot. Hundr. ii. 768, b : ' Item porci eius et aliorum vicinorum suorum pascent in campis dominicis extra tassum dum bladum domini stat in campis, et post bladum domini cariatum ibunt in campis per totum et omnes alie bestie ejus et aliorum vicinorum suorum pascent per totum in stipulo domini sine imparcamento.'

45th year of Henry III. Each hide may send to the common eighteen oxen, sixteen cows, one bull, the off-spring of the cows of two years, two hundred sheep with four rams, as well as their offspring of one year, four horses and their offspring of one year, twenty swine and their offspring of one year[1]. According to a common rule the only cattle allowed to use the village pasture was that which was constantly kept in the village, *levant e couchant en le maner*. In order to guard against the fraudulent practice of bringing over strange cattle and thus making money at the expense of the township, it was required sometimes that the commonable cattle should have wintered in the manor[2].

Pasture an adjunct to holding.

These last rules seem at first sight difficult of explanation : one does not see in what way the bringing in of strange cattle could damage the peasantry of the village, as nobody could drive more than a certain number of beasts to the common, and as the overburdening of it depended entirely on the excess of this number, and not on the origin of the beasts. And so one has to look to something else besides the apprehension that the common would get overburdened, in order to find a suitable explanation of the rule. An explanation is readily supplied by the notion that the use of the common was closely connected with the holding. Strange cattle had nothing to do with the holding, and were to be kept off from the

---

[1] Glastonbury Cart., Wood MSS. 1 (Bodleian), f. 182, b. Cf. f. 239, 240 : 'Memorandum anni 1243 de amensuratione pasture . . . dicunt precise quod ad quamlibet hidatam terre in eadem villa pertinent 16 boues ad terram excolendam, 4 vacce, 4 averia, 50 bidentes et 6 porci . . . ad unam virgatam terre pertinent 4 boues, et 2 vacce, et 1 auerium, et 3 porci et 12 bidentes ad tantam terram colendam et sustinendam.' Leigerbook of Kirkham Priory, Yorkshire, Fairfax MSS. 7, f. 8 a : 'Amensuratio pasture de Sexendale facta anno regni regis Henrici filii regis Iohannis 36to . . . qui dicunt per sacramentum suum quod quelibet bouata terre in Sexendale potest sustinere duo grossa animalia, 30 oues cum sequela unius anni, duos porcos sine sequela et 3 aucas cum sequela dimidii anni, et non amplius.'

[2] In a case of 1233 (Note-book of Bracton, 749) it is complained,—'Cum idem Robertus non possit aliena aueria in pasturam illam recolligere, scil. hominum alterius religionis,' etc.

land of the community; it is as representatives of a
community whose territory has been invaded that the
individual commoners have cause to complain. In fact,
the common pasture, as well as the meadows, were
thought of merely as a portion of the holding. The
arrangements did not admit of the same certainty or
rather of the same kind of determination as the division
of the arable, but the main idea which regulated the
latter was by no means cut short in its operation, if one
may say so: it was not bound up with the exact measure-
ment of arable acres. The holding was the necessary
agricultural outfit of a peasant family, and of this outfit
the means of feeding the cattle were quite as important
a part as the means of raising crops. It is only inac-
curately that we have been speaking of a virgate of 30
acres, and of a ploughland of 180 or 160. The true expression would be to speak of a virgate of 30 acres of
arable and the corresponding rights to pasture and other
common uses. And the records, when they want to give
something like a full description, do not omit to mention
the 'pertinencia,' the necessary adjuncts of the arable.
The term is rather a vague one, quite in keeping with the
rights which, though tangible enough, cannot be cut to so
certain a pattern as in the case of arable[1]. And for this
reason the laxer right had to conform to the stricter one,
and came to be considered as appendant to it.

We have considered till now the different aspects assumed by common of pasture, when it arises within the
manor, and as a consequence of the arrangement of its
holdings. But this is not the only way in which common
of pasture may arise. It may originate in an express
and special grant by the lord either to a tenant or to a

Common in special cases.

[1] Note-book of Bracton, pl. 174: 'Dicunt eciam quod in manerio de Billingi-
heie, sicut inquirere possunt, sunt 12 carucate terre tam in certa terra quam
in marisco predicto, scilicet sex carucate de certa terra et sex carucate in
marisco, et in Northkime sunt sex carucate terre et quatuor bouate tam in
certa terra quam in marisco predicto, set nesciunt aliquam distinctionem
quantum sit in certa terra et quantum in marisco nec aliquid inquirere potuerunt de metis infra mariscos illos.'

stranger [1]; it may also proceed from continuous use from
time beyond legal memory [2]: it must have been difficult
in many cases to prevent strangers from establishing such
a claim by reason of long occupation in some part of a
widely stretching moor or wood pasture [3].　It was not less
difficult in such cases to draw exact boundaries between
adjoining communities, and we find that large tracts of
country are used as a common pasture-ground by two
villages, and even by more [4].　Neighbours deem it often
advantageous to establish a certain reciprocity in this
respect [5].　By special agreement or by tacit allowance

[1] Note-book of Bracton, pl. 749: ' Robertus de Spraxtona summonitus fuit ad
warantizandum Abbati de Riuallibus 42 acras terre et pasturam ad 30 uaccas
cum uno tauro et 48 boues et 40 oues cum pertinenciis in Sproxtona que tenet
et de eo tenere clamat, et unde cartam Simonis de S. auunculi sui cuius heres
ipse est habet,' etc.

[2] Note-book of Bracton, pl. 818: ' Et Saherus et Matillis per attornatos suos
ueniunt et dicunt quod semper, a conquestu Anglie usque nunc communicauerunt cum eodem Roberto et antecessoribus suis in Locke, et idem Robertus
et antecessores semper communicauerunt in terris ipsorum S. et M. in Gaham
. . . et unde dicunt quod si idem Robertus uelit se retrahere de communa
quam habet in terris ipsorum, ipsi nolunt se retrahere et dicunt quod semper
communicauerunt horn underhorn . . . Et Robertus uenit et dicit quod nec
ipse nec antecessores unquam communam habuerunt in Locke nisi post
gwerram et per vim etc. scil. post gwerram motam inter regem S. et
homines suos.'　Spelman renders the *horn unherhorn* by ' horn with horn,'
but the editor of Bracton's Note-book thinks, and I believe rightly, that the
phrase means a common for all manner of horned beasts. Brunner has trans-
lated it by ' gemeinschaftlich—durcheinander.'

[3] Rot. Hundr. ii. 605, e: ' In dicto manerio 1 magnus boscus qui continet
300 acras in quo quidem bosco homines propinquarum villarum ut Wardeboys,
Wodehirst, Woldhirst, S[tl] Ivonis, Niddingworth et Halliwell communicant
omnes bestias suos pascendo cum sokna de Sumersham.'　Note-book of
Bracton, 1194: ' Iuratores dicunt quod mora illa ampla est et magna et
nesciunt aliquas divisas quantum pertinet ad unam uillam, quantum ad aliam.'
In the case of forest land many villages enjoyed and still enjoy rights of
intercommoning over a wide space.　The case of Epping is the familiar
example.

[4] Eynsham Cart. 3, b: ' Dicunt eciam quod dominus et villata de Shyfford
intercommunicant cum villatis de Stanlake, Brytlamptone et Herdewyk a
gula Augusti usque festum S[tl] Martini, cum villatis vero de Astone Cote
et Elcforde a festo S[tl] Michaelis usque dictum festum S[tl] Martini.'

[5] Note-book of Bracton, pl. 914: ' Et Thomas venit et dicit quod nullam
communam clamat in Oure, set uerum uult dicere.　Certe diuise et mete
continentur inter terram Prioris de Oure et terram ipsius Thome de Merk-

lords and tenants intercommon on each other's lands : this practice extends mostly to the waste only, but in some cases the arable and meadow are included after the removal of the crop and of the hay. The procedure of the writ ' quo jure ' was partly directed to regulate these rights and to prevent people from encroaching wantonly upon their neighbours[1]. When land held in one fee or one manor was broken up for some reason into smaller units, the rights of pasture were commonly kept up according to the old arrangements[2].

These different modes of treating the pasture present rather an incongruous medley, and may be classified in several ways and deduced from divers sources.

The chief distinctions of modern law are well known : 'Common Appendant is the right which every freehold tenant of the manor possesses, to depasture his commonable cattle, levant and couchant on his freehold tenement anciently arable, on the wastes of the manor, and originally on all (common) pasture in the manor. Common appurtenant on the other hand is against common right, becoming appurtenant to land either by long user or by grant express or implied. Thus it covers a right to common with animals that are not commonable, such as pigs, donkeys, goats, and geese ; or a right to common claimed for land not anciently

Modern classification of commons.

wrthe et quamdiu placuit eidem Priori habere aesiam in terra ipsius Thome in Markwrthe habuit ipse Thomas aesiam in terra ipsius Prioris de Oure, et si Prior uult subtrahere se, ipse libenter subtrahet se.'

[1] The relation between this writ and the action ' quod reddat ei tantam pasturam ' is well illustrated by a case of 1230 (Note-book of Bracton, pl. 392) : ' Ricardus de Willeye et Iohanna de Willeye summoniti fuerunt ad respondendum Willelmo de Kamuilla quo iure communam pasture exigunt in terra ipsius W. in Arewe, desicut idem Willelmus nullam communam habet in terris ipsorum Ricardi et Iohanne, nec ipsi Ricardus et Johanna seruicium faciunt quare communam habere debeant,' etc. . . . ' Et quia Willelmus cognoscit quod habet communam quantamcumque licet paruam, consideratum est quod nichil capiat per breue istud et sit in misericordia pro falso clamore et perquirat sibi per aliud breue sicut per breue quod reddat ei tantam pasturam,' etc. One may say that the *Quo Jure* was an ' actio negatoria.'

[2] Note-book of Bracton, pl. 561 : ' Et quia Simon non potest dedicere quin terra illa ubi communa est sit de 1 feodo et una uilla, consideratum est quod ipsa communicet cum eodem Simone in terra ipsius Simonis,' etc.

arable, such as pasture, or land reclaimed from the waste within the time of legal memory, or for land that is not freehold, but copyhold[1].' Common in gross is a personal right to common pasture in opposition to the praedial rights. Mr. Scrutton has shown from the Year Books that these terms and distinctions emerge gradually during the fourteenth century, and appear substantially settled only in Littleton's treatise. Bracton and his followers, Fleta and Britton, do not know them. These are important facts, but they hardly warrant the inferences which have been drawn from them. The subject has been in dispute in connexion with discussions as to the free village community. Joshua Williams, in his Rights of Common[2], had assumed common appendant to originate in ancient customary right bestowed by the village community and not by the lord's grant; Scrutton argues that such a right is not recognised by the documents. He lays stress on the fact, that Bracton speaks only of two modes of acquiring common, namely, express grant by the lord, and long usage understood as constant sufferance on the part of the lord amounting to an express grant. But this is only another way of saying that Bracton's exposition is based on feudal notions, that his land law is constructed on the principle 'nulle terre sans seigneur,' and that every tenement, as well as every right to common, is considered in theory as granted by the lord of the manor. It may be admitted that Bracton does not recognise just that kind of title which later lawyers knew as appendancy, does not recognise that a man can claim common by showing merely that he is a freeholder of the manor. Unless he relies on long continued user, he must rely upon grant or feoffment. But the distinction between saying ' I claim common because I am a freeholder of the manor' and saying ' I claim common because I or my ancestors have been enfeoffed of a freehold tenement of the manor and the right of common passed by the feoffment,' though it may be of juristic

---

[1] Scrutton, Commons and Common Fields, 42.
[2] Page 37.

interest and even of some practical importance as regulating the burden of proof and giving rise to canons for the interpretation of deeds, is still a superficial distinction which does not penetrate deeply into the substance of the law. On the whole we find that the freeholder of Bracton's time and of earlier times does normally enjoy these rights which in after time were described as ' appendant ' to his freehold; and it is well worth while to ask whether behind the general assumptions of feudal theory there do not lie certain data which, on the one hand, prepare and explain later terminology, and are connected, on the other, with the historical antecedents of the feudal system.

A little reflection will show that the divisions of later law did not spring into being merely as results of legal reasoning and casuistry. Indeed, from a lawyer's point of view, nothing can be more imperfect than a classification which starts from three or four principles of division seemingly not connected with each other. Common appendant belongs to a place anciently arable, common appurtenant may belong to land of any kind ; the first is designed for certain beasts, the second for certain others ; one is bound up with freehold, the other may go with copyhold ; in one case the right proceeds from common law, in the other from ' specialty.' One may reasonably ask why a person sending a cow to the open fields or to the waste from a freehold tenement can claim common appendant, and his neighbour sending a cow to the same fields from a copyhold has only common appurtenant. Or again, why does a plot of arable reclaimed from the waste confer common appurtenant, and ancient arable common appendant ? Or again, why are the goats or the swine of a tenement sent to pasture by virtue of common appurtenant, and the cows and horses by virtue of common appendant ? And, above all, what have the several restrictions and definitions to do with each other ? Such a series of contrasted attributes defies any attempt to simplify the rules of the case according to any clearly defined principle : it seems a strange growth in which original and later elements, important and secondary features, are capriciously brought together.

In order to explain these phenomena we have to look to earlier and not to later law. What seems arbitrary and discordant in modern times, appears clear and consistent in the original structure of the manor.

Founda-
tions of
later clas-
sification
in early
law.

The older divisions may not be so definitely drawn and so developed as the later, but they have the advantage of being based on fundamental differences of fact. Even when the names and terms do not appear well settled, the subject-matter arranges itself according to some natural contrasts, and it is perhaps by too exclusive study of names and terms that Mr. Scrutton has been prevented from duly appreciating the difference in substance. He says of the end of the thirteenth century : 'In the reports about this time it seems generally to be assumed that if the commoner cannot show an *especialté* or special grant or title, he must show "fraunc tenement en la ville a ques commune est appendant." Thus we have the question :—" Coment clamez vous commune ? Com appendant, ou par especialté,' while Hengham, J. says : ' prescription de terre est assez bon especialté "' (p. 50). This is really the essence of all the rules regarding common of pasture, and, what is more, the contrast follows directly from arrangements which did not come into use in the fourteenth century, but were in full work at the time of Bracton and long before it. What is called in later law common appendant, appears as the normal adjunct to the holding, that is, to a share in the system of village husbandry. If a bovate is granted to a person, so much of the rights of pasture as belongs to every bovate in the village is presumed to be granted with the arable. 'So much as belongs to every bovate in the village ;' this means, that the common depends in this case on a general arrangement of the pasture in the village. Such an arrangement exists in every place ; it is regulated by custom and by the decisions of the manorial court or halimote, it extends equally over the free and over the unfree land, over the waste, the moor and wood, and over the fallow; it admits a certain number and certain kinds of beasts, and excludes others. Only because such a general arrangement is supposed to exist, is the right to common treated in so vague a manner; the documents present, in truth, only a reference to relations which are substantiated in the husbandry system of the manor. But the right of common may exceed these lines in many ways: it may be joined to a tenement which lies outside the manorial system, or a plot freshly reclaimed from the waste, or to a holding belonging to some other manor. It may admit a greater number and other kinds of beasts than those which were held commonable in the usual course of manorial husbandry. In such cases the right to pasture had to proceed from some special agreement or grant, and, of course, had to be based on something different from the ordinary reference to the existing system of common husbandry. If there was no deed to go by, such a right could only be established by long use.

I think that all this must follow necessarily as soon as the main fact is admitted, that common is normally the right to pasture of a shareholder of the manor. The objection may be raised, that such *a priori* reasoning is not sufficient in the case, because the documents do not countenance it by their classification. Would the objection be fair? Hardly, if one does not insist on finding in Bracton the identical terms used in Coke upon Littleton. It is true that Bracton speaks of common in general, and not of common appendant, appurtenant, and in gross, but the right of common which he treats as normal appears to be very peculiar on a closer examination of his rules. It is praedial and not personal; to begin with, it is always thought of as belonging to a tenement [1]. What is more, it cannot belong to a tenement reclaimed from the

Bracton's doctrine.

---

[1] Bracton, f. 223, a: 'Non debet dici communia quod quis habuerit in alieno . . . cum tenementum non habeat ad quod possit communia pertinere, sed potius herbagium dici debet quam communia, cum hoc posset esse personale quid.'

waste [1], and in this way the requirement of 'ancient arable'
is established, that is, the pasture is considered as one of
the rights conceded to the original shares of a manorial
community.   The use of the open field outside the time of
reasonable defence [2] is primarily meant, and the common
pasture appears from this point of view as one of the stages
in the process of common farming. To make up the whole,
the right to common is defined by a 'quantum pertinet [3],'
which has a sense only in connexion with the admeasurement of claims effected by the internal organisation of the
manor. Such is evidently the normal arrangement presup-
posed by Bracton's description, and his only fault is, that
he does not distinguish with clearness between the consequences of the normal arrangement, and of grants or
usurpations which supplement and modify it. It must be
remembered that he only gives the substantive law about
common rights in the course of a discussion of the pleadings in actions 'quo jure' and assizes of pasture. If we
compare with Bracton's text the rules and decisions laid
down in the legal practice of the thirteenth century, we
shall find that the same facts are implied by them. They
all suppose a contrast between 'intrinsec' and 'forinsec'
claims to common, that is between the rights of those who
are members of the manorial group, and the rights, if any,
of those who are outside it, and again a contrast between
the normal rights of commoners and any more extensive

[1] Bracton, f. 226, b: 'Item dicere potest quod nulla communia pertinet ad
tale tenementum, quia illud fuit aliquando foresta, boscus, et locus vastae solitu-
dinis et communia, et iam inde efficitur assartum, vel redactum est in culturam,
et non debet communia pertinere ad communiam, et ubi omnes de patria
solebant communicare.'

[2] Bracton, f. 229, a: 'Hoc non erit intelligendum quod omni tempore, nisi
tantum temporibus competentibus, scilicet post blada asportata et fena levata,
vel quando tenementum iacet incultum et ad waractum.'

[3] Bracton, f. 228, b: 'Item eodem modo si ita feoffatus fuerit quis, sine
expressione numeri vel generis, sed ita, cum pastura quantum pertinet ad
tantum tenementum in eadem villa, talem ligat constitutio sicut prius cum
expressione: quia cum constet de quantitate tenementi, de facili perpendi
poterit de numero aueriorum, et etiam de genere, *secundum consuetudinem
locorum.*'

rights acquired by special grant or agreement. Only the
freeholders are protected in the enjoyment of their commons ; only the freeholders are protected in the enjoyment
of their tenements ; but their claims are based on arrangements in which the unfree land participates in everything
with the free. It may be added that litigation mostly arises
from the adjustment of 'forinsec' claims under the writ
' Quo jure.'   The intercommoning between neighbours gives
rise to a good many disputes, and is much too frequent
to be considered, as it was by later law, a mere ' excuse for
trespassing [1].'   This common ' pur cause de vicinage ' may
be a relic of a time when adjoining villages formed a part
of a higher unit of some kind, of the Mark, of a hundred, for
example. It may be explained also by the difficulty of
setting definite boundaries in wide tracts of moor and forest.
However this may be, its constant occurrence forms another
germ of a necessary contrast between the two classes which
afterwards developed into common appendant and common
appurtenant.   It could not be brought under the same
rules as those which flowed from the internal arrangement
of the manor.   A special difficulty attended it as to
admeasurement : the customary treatment of other holdings
could not in this case serve as a standard.   The very laxity
of the principle naturally gave occasion to very different
interpretations and deductions.   And so we are justified in
saying, that the chief distinctions of later law are to be
found in their substance in the thirteenth century, and
that although a good deal of confusion occurs in details, the earlier documents give even better clues than the
later to the reasons which led to the well-known classification.

Common appendant, if we may use the modern term for *Restric-*
the sake of brevity, is indissolubly connected with the *tions on the lord*
system of husbandry followed by the village community. *as to com-*
A very noticeable feature of it is, that, in one sense, it *mon pas-ture.*
towers over the lord of the manor as well as over the
tenants.   Of course, legally the lord is considered as the

---

[1] Scrutton, 55.

owner of the waste[1], but even from the point of view of
pure law his ownership is restricted by his own grants. In
so much as he has conceded freehold tenements to certain
persons, he is bound by his own deed not to withhold from
these persons the necessary adjuncts of such tenements, and
especially the rights of pasture bound up with them. The
free tenants share with the lord, if he wants to turn his
common pasture to some special and lucrative use; if, for
instance, strangers are admitted to it for money, one part
of the proceeds goes to the tenantry[2]. Again, the lord
may not overburden the common, and sometimes freeholders try their hand at litigation against the lord on the
ground that he sends his cattle to some place where they
ought not to go[3]. The point cannot be overlooked, that
the lord of the manor appears subjected to certain rules set
up by custom and common decision in the meetings of his
tenantry. The number and kind of beasts which may
come to the common from his land is fixed, as well as the
number that may come from the land of a cottager[4]. The
freeholders alone can enforce the rule against him, but it
is set up not by the freeholders, but by the entire community
of the manor, and practically by the serfs more than by the
freeholders, because they are so much more numerous.

Approve-
ment.
    As the common of pasture appears as an outcome of a
system of husbandry set up by the village community, so
every change in the use of the pasture ought in the natural

---

[1] Cartulary of Christ Church, Harl. MSS. 1006, p. 3: 'Prior et conventus
est capitalis dominus commune pasture de B.'

[2] Ely Cart., Cotton MSS. Claudius, xi, f. iii, a: 'In L. debet villata communicare cum suis averiis propriis cum domino Episcopo. Et si dominus
voluerit, ibidem possunt habere extranei bestias pro denariis. Set inde habebunt liberi homines de W. quemlibet septimum denarium preter decimum.'

[3] Registrum cellararii of Bury St. Edmunds, Cambr. Univ., Gg. iv. 4, f. 31,
b: 'Et notandum quod inquisitio super calumpnia Egidii de Neketona
clamantis quod abbas non haberet communam infra precinctum villate de
Bertone scribitur in forma (tali),' etc.

[4] Cart. of Christ Church, Canterbury, Add. MSS. 6159, f. 21, b: 'Sciendum quod dominus potest habere in communia pasture de bosco cum aisia-
mento friscorum et dominicorum domini tempore apto c bidentes per maius
centum.'

course to proceed from a decision of this community. Such a change may be effected in one of two manners : the customary rotation of crops may be altered, or else a part of the waste may be reclaimed for tillage. In the first case, a portion of the open arable and meadow, which ought to have been commonable at a certain time, ceases to be so ; in the second, the right to send cattle to the waste is stinted in so much as the arable is put under defence, or the land is used for the construction of dwellings. By the common law the free tenants alone could obtain a remedy for any transgression in this respect. I have mentioned already that suits frequently arose when the old-fashioned rotation of crops was modified in accordance with the progress of cultivation. As to the right of approving from the waste, the relative position of lord and tenants was for a long time debateable, and, as everybody knows, the lord was empowered to approve by the Statute of Merton of 20 Henry III, with the condition that he should leave sufficient pasture to his free tenants according to the requirements of their tenements. The same power was guaranteed by the Statute of Westminster II against the claims of neighbours. It has been asked whether, before the Statute of Merton, the lord had power to enclose against commoners, if he left sufficient common to satisfy their rights. Bracton's text in the passage where he treats of the Statute is distinctly in favour of the view that this legislative enactment did actually alter the common law, and that previously it was held that a lord could not approve without the consent of his free-tenants[1]. Turning to the practice of the thirteenth-century courts, we find that the lawyers were rather doubtful as to this point. In a case of 1221 the jurors declare, that although the defendant has approved about two acres of land from the waste where

---

[1] Bracton, f. 228, b : 'Inprimis videndum est qualiter constitutio illa sit intelligenda, ne male intellecta trahat utentes ad abusum . . . non omnes nec in omnibus per constitutionem restringuntur, et ideo videndum erit utrum feoffati fuerint large, scilicet per totum, et ubique, et in omnibus locis, et ad omnia averia et sine numero . . . tales non ligat constitutio memorata, quia feoffamentum non tollit licet tollat abusum.'

the plaintiff had common, this latter has still sufficient pasture left to him. And thereupon the plaintiff with-draws[1]. In 1226 a lord who has granted pasture every-where, 'ubique,' and has inclosed part of it, succumbs in a suit against his tenant, and we are led to suppose that if the qualification 'ubique' had been absent, his right of approvement would have been maintained. It must be noticed, however, that the marginal note in Bracton's Note-book does not lay stress on the 'ubique,' and regards the decision as contrary to the law subsequently laid down by the Constitution of Merton[2]. In a case of 1292 one of the counsel for the defendant took it for granted that the Statute of Merton altered the previously existing common law[3]. The language of the Statutes themselves is certainly in favour of such a construction : in the Merton Consti-tution it is stated as a fact that the English magnates were prevented from making use of their manors[4], and the Westminster Statute is as positive as to neighbours ; 'multi domini hucusque ... impediti extiterunt,' etc. It seems hardly possible to doubt that the enactments really repre-sent a new departure, although the way towards it had been prepared by the collision of interests in open Court. The condition negatively indicated by the documents in regard to the time before these enactments cannot be dis-missed by the consideration that the lord would derogate from his grant by approving. Although a single trial may bear directly on the relation between the lord and only one

---

[1] Note-book of Bracton, 1975.

[2] Note-book of Bracton, 1881. The marginal note runs : 'Nota quod nichil includi poterit de forestis et moris licet minimum quid et quamuis quaerens extra clausum habere possit ad sufficientiam.' And a little higher the decision is marked as 'contra constitutionem de Merton.'

[3] See Scrutton, 63, 64.

[4] Bracton, f. 227, b : 'Quia multi sunt magnates qui feoffauerunt milites et libere tenentes suos in maneriis suis de paruis tenementis, et qui impediti sunt per eosdem quod commodum suum facere non possunt de residuo maneriorum suorum.' Reference may also be made to a note on a Plea Roll of 1221 (printed in L. Q. R. iv. 230), which shows that some years before the statute the magnates complained that they were prevented from assarting their pasture land by the claims of virgaters.

of the tenants or a few of them, every change in the occupation of the land touches all those who are members of the manorial community. The removal of difficulties as to approvement was, before the Statute of Merton, not a question of agreement between two persons, but a question as to the relative position of the lord and of the whole body of the tenantry. The lord might possibly settle with every tenant singly, but it seems much more probable that he brought the matter, when it arose, before the whole body with which the management of the village husbandry rested, that is, before the halimote, with its free and unfree tenants. In any case, the influence of the free tenants as recognised by the common law was decisive, and hardly to be reconciled with the usual feudal notions as to the place occupied by the lord in the community. It must be noted that even that order of things which came into being in consequence of the Statute contains an indirect testimony as to the power of the village community. The Act requires the pasture left to the free tenants to be sufficient, and it may be asked at once, what criterion was there of such a sufficiency, if the number of beasts was not mentioned in the instrument by which the common was held. Of course, in case of dispute, a jury had to give a verdict about it, but what had the jury to go by? It was not the actual number of heads of cattle on a tenement that could be made the starting-point of calculation. Evidently the size of the holding, and its relation to other holdings, had to be taken into account. But if so, then the legal admeasurement had to conform to the customary admeasurement defined by the community [1]. And so again the openly recognised law of the kingdom had to be set in action according to local customs, which in themselves had no legally binding force.

Besides the land regularly used for pasture, the cattle of the village were sent grazing along the roads [2] and in the

Rights of common in woods, etc.

---

[1] This is directly stated by Bracton, f. 228, b; vide supra.

[2] Cartulary of Christ Church, Canterbury, Addit. MSS. 6159, f. 52, b: 'Pastura. . . de herbagiis cuiusdam vie inter curiam et ecclesiam de Pritel-

woods [1]. These last were mostly used for feeding swine. In other respects, also, the wood was subjected to a treatment analogous to that of the pasture land. The right of hunting was, of course, subjected to special regulations, which have to be discussed from the point of view of forest law. But, apart from that right, the wood was managed by the village community according to certain customary rules. Every tenant had a right to fell as many young trees as he wanted to keep his house and his hedges in order [2]. It sometimes happens, that the lord and the homage enter into agreement as to the bigger trees, and for every trunk taken by the lord the tenantry are entitled to take its equivalent [3]. Whenever the right had to be apportioned more or less strictly, the size of the holdings was always the main consideration [4].

It would be strange to my purpose to discuss the details of common of estovers, of turbary [5], or of fishery. The chief points which touch upon the problems of social origins are sufficiently apparent in the subject of pasture. The results of our investigation may, I think, be summed up under the following heads :—

1. Rights of common are either a consequence of the

welle.' Domesday of St. Paul's, 1 : ' Nulla est ibi pastura nisi in boscis et viis.'

[1] Rot. Hundr. 613, b : ' Et omnes libere tenentes . . . communicant in bosco de A. cum omnibus bestiis suis libere per totum annum.'

[2] Eynsham Cart. 10, b : ' Est ibidem unus boscus . . . cuius valor non appreciatur pro eo quod minister regis non permittit includi si fiat copicium, sufficiens tamen est pro housebote et heybote.' Gloucester Cart. iii. 67 : ' De boscis dicunt quod rex habet quandam costeram bosci de fago juvene quae continet ad aestimationem 30 acras, unde rex poterit approbare per annum dimidiam marcam, scilicet in subbosco et virgis ad clausturam, et meremium ad carucas et alia facienda sine destructione, et ille boscus est communis omnibus vicinis in herbagio.'

[3] Cart. of Christ Church, Canterbury, Add. MSS. 6159, f. 28, b : ' Boscus ibi est cuius medietas est ecclesie et medietatem clamant tenentes illius denne, ut si dominus arborem unam accipiat, ipsi aliam accipient.'

[4] Worcester Cart. (Camden Ser.), 62, b : ' Quaelibet virgata tenet 3 feorthendels de Bruera, et dimidia virgata 1 feorthendel et dimidium.'

[5] For instance, Madox, Exch. 1, 27, n. 47 : ' Habebunt turbas sufficientes in predicta mora ad focalium fratrum . . . secundum quantitatem terrarum suarum in eadem villa.'

communal husbandry of the manor, or else they proceed from special agreement or long use.

2. The legal arrangement of commons depends on a customary arrangement, in which free and unfree tenants take equal part [1].

3. The feudal theory of the lord's grant is insufficient to explain the different aspects assumed by rights of common, and especially the opposition between lord and free commoners.

---

[1] A very remarkable instance of the way in which rights of common were divided and arranged between lords and villains is afforded by the Court Rolls of Brightwaltham. Maitland, Manorial Rolls, Selden Soc. ii. 172. I shall have to discuss the case in the Fifth Chapter of this Essay.

CHAPTER III.

RURAL WORK AND RENTS.

Arrange-
ment of
work and
rent. OUR best means of judging of the daily work in an English village of the thirteenth century is to study the detailed accounts of operations and payments imposed on the tenants for the benefit of a manorial lord. Surveys, extents, or inquisitions were drawn up chiefly for the purpose of settling these duties, and the wealth of material they afford enables us to form a judgment as to several interesting questions. It tells directly of the burden which rural workmen had to bear in the aristocratic structure of society; it gives indirectly an insight into all the ramifications of labour and production since the dues received by the lord were a kind of natural percentage upon all the work of the tenants; the combination of its details into one whole affords many a clue to the social standing and history of the peasant classes of which we have been treating.

Opera-
tions: Let us begin by a survey of the different kinds of labour duties performed by the dependent holdings which Ploughing. clustered round the manorial centre. Foremost stands ploughing and the operations connected with it. The cultivation of the demesne soil of a manor depended largely on the help of the peasantry. By the side of the ploughs and plough-teams owned by the lord himself, the plough-teams of his villains are made to till his land, and manorial extents commonly mention that the demesne portion has to be cultivated by the help of village customs, 'cum consuetudinibus villae[1].' The duties

---

[1] Domesday of St. Paul's, 93: 'Potest wainnagium fieri cum 12 bobus et quatuor stottis cum consuetudinibus ville.' 75: 'Item (juratores) dicunt

Ploughing. 279

different ways. Sometimes every dependent plough has
its number of acres assigned to it, and the joint owners of
its team are left to settle between themselves the proportions in which they will have to co-operate for the performance of the duty[1]. In most cases the 'extent' fixes
the amount due from each individual holder. For instance,
every virgater is to plough one acre in every week. This
can only mean that one acre of the lord's land is reckoned
on every single virgate in one week, without any reference
to the fact that only one part of the team is owned by the
peasant. If, for example, there were four virgaters to
share in the ownership of the plough, the expression under
our notice would mean that every team has to plough four
acres in the week[2]. But the ploughs may be small, or the
virgaters exceptionally wealthy, and their compound plough
team may have to cultivate only three acres or even less.
The lord in this case reckons with labour-weeks and acres,
not with teams and days-work. A third possibility would be
to base the reckoning on the number of days which a team
or a holder has to give to the lord[3]. A fourth, to lay on
the imposition in one lump by requiring a certain number
of acres to be tilled, or a certain number of days of
ploughing[4]. It must be added, that the peasants have
often to supplement their ploughing work by harrowing,
according to one of these various systems of apportionment[5].

---

quod potest fieri wainnagium totius dominici cum 2 carucis bonis habentibus
20 capita in jugo et 2 herciatoribus cum consuetudinibus operariorum.'

[1] Add. MSS. 6159, f. 44, a : '(Leyesdon) . . . debet quelibet caruca con-
iuncta arrare unam acram et habebunt 3 denarios pro acra et quadrantem.'

[2] Glastonbury Inqu. of 1189 (Roxburghe Ser.), 64 : '(Virgatarius) a festo
S[t] Michaelis qualibet ebdomada arat unam acram donec tota terra domini
sit culta.'

[3] Ely Inqu., Cotton MSS. Claudius, c. xi. f. 185 : 'Unusquisque arabit per
tres dies, si habeat sex boves ; per duos, si habeat quatuor boves ; per unum,
si habeat duos boves ; per dimidium, si habeat unum bovem.'

[4] Add. MSS. 6159, f. 53, a : 'Item debent predicte 22 virgate terre arrare
ad frumentum, ad auenam et ad warectum 113 acras et valent 56 solidos
6 denarios.'

[5] Gloucester Cart. iii. 92 : 'Et quicquid araverit debet herciare tempore

The duties here described present only a variation of the common 'week-work' of the peasant, its application to a certain kind of labour. They could on occasion be replaced by some other work[1], or the lord might lose them if the time assigned for them was quite unsuitable for work[2]. There is another form of ploughing called *gafol-earth*, which has no reference to any particular time-limits. A patch of the lord's land is assigned to the homage for cultivation, and every tenant gets his share in the work according to the size of his holding. Gafol-earth is not only ploughed but mostly sown by the peasantry[3].

A third species of ploughing-duty is the so-called *aver-earth* or *grass-earth*. This obligation arises when the peasants want more pasture than they are entitled to use by their customary rights of common. The lord may grant the permission to use the pasture reserved for him, and exacts ploughings in return according to the number of heads of cattle sent to the pasturage[4]. Sometimes the

seminis. Et faciet unam hersuram que vocatur landegginge et valet 1 den.' iii. 194: 'Et debet herciare quotidie si necesse fuerit quousque semen domini seminetur, et allocabitur ei pro operacione manuali, et valet ultra obolum. Et quia non est numerus certus de diebus herciandis, aestimant juratores 40 dies.'

[1] Ramsey Cart. i. 345: 'Qualibet autem septimana, a festo S^{ti} Michaelis usque ad tempus sarclationis tribus diebus operatur, quodcunque opus sibi fuerit injunctum; et quarto die arabit unum sellionem, sive jungatur cum alio, sive non.'

[2] Glastonbury Inqu. of 1189, p. 64: 'A die circumcisionis similiter, excepta ebdomada Pasche, si possit per gelu, et si gelu durat per 12 dies, quietus debet esse. Si amplius durat, restituet araturam.'

[3] Add. MSS. 6159, f. 49, b: 'Idem tenentes de predictis 22 et dimidia (terris) debent arrare ad seysonam frumenti 45 acras de gable et de qualibet terra 2 acras.' 35, b: '*Gauilherth*: Willelmus de Bergate debet arrare dimidiam acram; Nicholaus de Jonebrigge et socii ejus unam virgam; heredes Johannis 8 pedes; Ricardus Cutte 8 pedes . . . Summa acrarum 25 acre 1 pes. Hec debent arrare et seminare.'

[4] Rot. Hundred. ii. 768, b: 'Item si habeat carucam integram vel cum sociis conjunctam, illa caruca arabit domino 2 acras terre ad yvernagium et herciabit quantum illa caruca araverit in die, et istud servicium appellatur Greserthe, pro quo servicio ipse W. et omnes alii consuetudinarii habebunt pasturas dominicas ad diem (*sic. corr.* a die) ad Vincula S^{ti} Petri usque ad festum beate Marie in Marcio et prata dominica postquam fenum fuerit cariatum.'

same imposition is levied when more cattle are sent to the commons than a holding has a right to drive on them[1]. It is not impossible that in some cases the very use of rights of common was made dependent on the perform-ance of such duties[2]. A kindred exaction was imposed for the use of the meadows[3]. Local variations have, of course, to be taken largely into account in all such matters : the distinction between gafol-earth and grass-earth, for instance, though drawn very sharply in most cases, gets somewhat confused in others.

Manorial records mention a fourth variety of ploughing-work under the name of *ben-earth, precariae carucarum*. This is extra work in opposition to the common plough-ings described before[4]. It is assumed that the subject population is ready to help the lord for the tillage of his land, even beyond the customary duties imposed on it. It sends its ploughs three or four times a year ' out of love,' and ' for the asking.' It may be conjectured how agreeable this duty must have been in reality, and indeed by the side of its common denominations, as boon-work

[1] Glastonbury Cart., Wood MSS. 1, f. 44, b : ' Tenens dimidiam hidam habet 4 animalia in pascius quieta, et si plus habuerit—arabit et herciabit pro unoquoque dimidiam acram.'

[2] Add. MSS. 6159, f. 26, b : ' De qualibet caruca arant unam acram de averherde ; et si per negligenciam alicujus remanserit acra non arata, tunc mittet dominus semen quod sufficiat ad unam acram ad domum illius et oportebit illum reddere bladum ad mensuram propinque acre et habebit tum herbagium de acra assignata.' Cart. of Beaulieu, Cotton MSS. Nero, A. xii, f. 102, b : ' Et si habeat bovem vel vaccam iunctam, arabit pro quolibet virgo dimidiam acram ad festum S[ti] Martini sine cibo.' Glastonbury Inqu. of 1189, f. 116 : ' De qualibet carruca debent arare ad seminandum 7 acras, et ad warectum 7 acras, ut boves possint ire cum bobus domini in pastura.'

[3] Exch. Q. R. Min. Acc. Bk. 514; T. G. 41, 173 : '(Extenta manerii de Burgo) medwelond . . . debent arare tantam terram quantum habent de prato.'

[4] Exch. Q. R. Min. Acc. Bk. 513, 97 : ' Beinerth : 12 custumarii arabunt 6 acras terre ad semen yemale. Grasherthe : 12 arabunt cum quanto iungunt per unum diem ad semen yemale.' Ely Inqu., Cotton MSS. Claudius, C. xi. f. 30, a : ' Arabit de beneerthe si habeat carucam integram 3 rodas, et si iungat cum aliis ipse et ille cum quo iungit assidue arabunt 3 rodas.' Domesday of St. Paul's, 26 : ' Et ad precariam carucarum arabit unam rodam scil. quartam partem acre sine cibo.' Glastonbury Inqu. of 1189, p. 98 : ' R. de Wttone tenet dimidiam hidam pro una marca et debet habere ad preces per annum 12 homines et bis arare ad preces.'

and asked-work, we find much rougher terms in the speech
of some districts—it is deemed *unlawenearth* and *godlese-*
bene[1]. It must be said, however, that the lord generally
provided food on these occasions, and even went so far
as to pay for such extra work.

Other expressions occur in certain localities, which are
sometimes difficult of explanation. *Lentenearth*[2], in the
manors of Ely Minster, means evidently an extra ploughing in Lent. The same Ely records exhibit a ploughing
called *Filstnerthe* or *Filsingerthe*[3], which may be identical
with the Lentenearth just mentioned : a *fastnyngseed*[4]
occurs at any rate which seems connected with the ploughing under discussion. The same extra work in Lent is
called *Tywe*[5] in the Custumal of Bleadon, Somersetshire.
When the ploughing-work is paid for it may receive the
name of *penyearth*[6]. The Gloucester survey speaks of the
extra cultivation of an acre called Radacre, and the Ely
surveys of an extra rood 'de Rytnesse[7].' I do not ven-
ture to suggest an explanation for these last terms ; and

---

[1] Gloucester Cart. iii. 115 : 'Johannes Barefoth tenet dimidiam virgatam
terre continentem 24 acras . . . et debet arare qualibet secunda septimana
a festo S[ti] Michaelis usque ad festum Beati Petri ad Vincula uno die . . . Et
praeterea debet quater arare in terra domini, et vocantur ille arurae un-
lawenherþe.' Black Book of St Augustine's, Cotton MSS. Faustina, A. i.
f. 44 : ' . . . arare 18 acras ad frumentum de godlesebene.'

[2] Ely Inqu., Cotton MSS. Claudius, C. xi, f. 45, a : 'Preterea idem arabit
de Lentenerþe dimidiam acram.'

[3] Ibid., 30, b : 'Item iste cum quanto iungit arabit de filstnerthe eodem
tempore (ante Natale) per unum diem . . . Item arabit in quadragesima tres
acras et 3 rodas et araturam de filsingerhe (*sic*). Item arabit in estate
3 acras et de beneerthe 3 rodas ut in hyeme, set nihil arabit de filsingerþe.'

[4] Ibid., 35, a : 'Item per idem tempus arabit (ante Natale) dimidiam
acram pro fastningsede sine cibo et opere si habeat carucam integram. Et
si iungat cum aliis, tunc iste et socenarii sui cum quibus iunget arabunt
tantum et non amplius.'

[5] Custumal of Bleadon, 189.

[6] Gloucester Cart. ii. 134 : 'Et facit unam aruram que vocatur peniherþe
et valet tres denarii, quia recipiet de bursa domini quartum denarium.' Cf.
ii. 162 : 'Et praeterea faciet unam aruram que vocatur yove (yoke ?), scil.
arabit dimidiam acram, et recipiet de bursa domini unum denarium obolum,
et valet ultra unum denarium obolum.'

[7] Gloucester Cart. iii. 80 : '(Dimidius virgatarius) debet unam aruram que
vocatur radaker, scil. arare unam acram ad semen yemale, et triturare semen

I need not say that it would be easy to collect a much greater number of such terms in local use from the manorial records. It is sufficient for my purpose to mark the chief distinctions.

All the other labour-services are performed more or less Reaping. on the same system as the ploughings, with the fundamental difference that the number of men engaged in them has to be reckoned with more than the number of beasts. The extents are especially full of details in their descriptions of reaping or mowing corn and grass ; the process of thrashing is also mentioned, though more rarely. In the case of meadows (*mederipe*) sometimes their dimensions are made the basis of calculation, sometimes the number of work-days which have to be employed in order to cut the grass [1]. As to the corn-harvest, every holding has its number of acres assigned to it [2], or else it is enacted that every house has to send so many workmen during a certain number of days [3]. If it is said that such and such a tenant is bound to work on the lord's field at harvest-time with twenty-eight men, it does not mean that he has to send out such a number every time, but that he has to furnish an amount of work equivalent to that performed by twenty-eight grown-up labourers in one day; it may be divided into fourteen days' work of two labourers, or into seven days' of four, and so forth.

Harvest-time is the most pressing time in the year for rural work ; it is especially important not to lose the

---

ad eamdem acram, scil. duos bussellos frumenti.' On iii. 79 we have another reading for the same thing : ' Et arabit unam acram quae vocatur Eadacre et [debet] triturare semen ad eamdem acram, et valet arura cum trituracione seminis 4 denarios.' What is the right term?—Ely Inqu., Cotton MSS. Claudius, C. xi. f. 133, a : ' Et arabit qualibet die a festo S^{ti} Michaelis usque ad gulam Augusti dimidiam rodam, que faciunt per totum quinque acras . . . Et praeterea arabit unam rodam de Rytnesse.'

[1] Add. MSS. 6159, f. 53, b : ' Item tota villata de Bocayng debet falcare 12 acras prati et dimidiam, et valet 4 solidos.'

[2] Domesday of St. Paul's, 47 : ' Et preter hec unaquaque domus hide debet metere 3 dimidias acras avene et colligere unum sellionem fabarum.'

[3] Gloucester Cart. iii. 84, 85 : ' Ricardus Bissop tenet unum messuagium et 10 acras terre . . . (operabitur) in messe domini cum 24 hominibus.'

opportunity presented by fine weather to mow and garner in the crop before rain, and there may be only a few days of such weather at command. For this reason extra labour is chiefly required during this season, and the village people are frequently asked to give extra help in connexion with it. The system of *precariae* is even more developed on these occasions than in the case of ploughing[1]. All the forces of the village are strained to go through the task; all the houses which open on the street send their labourers[2], and in most cases the entire population has to join in the work, with the exception of the housewives and perhaps of the marriageable daughters[3]. The landlord treats the harvesters to food in order to make these exertions somewhat more palatable to them[4]. These 'love-meals' are graduated according to a set system. If the men are called out only once, they get their food and no drink : these are 'dry requests.' If they are made to go a second time, ale is served to them (*precariae cerevisiae*). The mutual obligations of lords and tenantry are settled very minutely[5]; the latter may have to mow

---

[1] Eynsham Cart. 88, b : 'Idem metet dimidiam acram bladi domini sine cibo domini et valet opus 4 denarios et vocatur la bene. Idem faciet cum uno homine beripam sine cibo domini et vocatur mederipe, et valet opus 4 den. . . . Idem veniet ad magnam bederipam domini ad cibum domini cum omnibus famulis suis et ipse supervidebit operari in propria persona sua. Quod si famulos non habuerit, tunc operabitur in propria (persona).'

[2] Ramsey Cart. i. 488 : 'Quaelibet domus habens ostium apertum versus vicum tam de malmannis quam de cotmannis et operariis inveniet unum hominem ad louebone.'

[3] Ely Inqu., Cotton MSS. Claudius, C. xi. f. 38, b : 'Ad precariam ceruisie inveniet omnem familiam preter uxorem domus et filiam maritabilem . . . Quod si voluerint metere propria blada metent in suis croftis et non alibi.'

[4] Domesday of St. Paul's, 75, 76 : 'Et falcare dimidiam acram sumptibus suis et postmodum falcare cum tota villata pratum domini ita quod totum sit falcatum, et qualibet falx habebit unum panem . . . et ad siccas precarias in autumpno inveniet unum hominem, et ad precarios ceruisie veniet cum quot hominibus habuerit ad cibum domini.' Cf. 61.

[5] Cart. of Battle, Augment. Off. Misc. Books, N. 57, f. 36, a : 'Quilibet virgarius . . . debet invenire ad quemlibet precarium autumpnalem ad metendum 2 homines et habebunt singuli singulos panes ponderis 18 librarum cere et duo unum ferchulum carnis precii unius denarii, si sit dies carnis et potagium ad primum precarium. Ad secundum uero erit panis medietas de frumento et medietas ordei et cetera alia ut supra. Ad terciam precariam erit panis

a particular acre with the object of saying 'thanks' for some concession on the part of the lord[1]. The same kind of 'requests' are in use for mowing the meadows. The duties of the peasants differ a great deal according to size of their holdings and their social position. The greater number have of course to work with scythe and sickle, but the more wealthy are called upon to supervise the rest, to ride about with rods in their hands[2]. On the other hand, a poor woman holds a messuage, and need do no more than carry water to the mowers[3].

A very important item in the work necessary for medieval husbandry was the business of carrying produce from one part of the country to the other. The manors of a great lord were usually dispersed in several counties, and even in the case of small landowners it was not very easy to arrange a regular communication with the market. The obligation to provide horses and carts gains in importance accordingly[4]. These *averagia* are laid out for short and

Carriage duties.

totus de frumento et cetera ut prenotatur. Ad quartam precariam quod vocatur hungerbedrip quilibet de tenentibus domini preter Henricum de Chaus inveniet unum hominem ad metendum et habebunt semel in die cibum, scil. panem et potum et unum ferculum secundum quod serviens illius loci providere placuerit, et caseum.'

[1] Ely Inqu., Cotton MSS. Claudius, C. xi. 166, b : 'Metet dimidiam acram que vocatur þanc alfaker.' The name may possibly mean, that the peasant earned the gratitude of the lord by ploughing the half-acre. This construction would be supported by other instances of 'sentimental' terminology. Cf. Warwickshire Hundr. Roll, Q. R. Misc. Books, N. 18, f. 94, b : 'Lovebene.' Cartul. of Okeburn, Al. Prior. 2/2, 17 : 'Post precarias consuetudinarias debet de gratia, ut dicitur, quocienscumque precatus fuerit, (operare) per unum hominem.' Roch. Custum., ed. Thorp, 10, b : 'Et pro prato de Dodecote falcando, pro amore, non pro debito, habebunt unum multonem et unum caseum de 4 d.'

[2] Gloucester Cart. i. 110 : 'Idem Thomas cum virga sua debet interesse operationibus quo ad metebederipas.'

[3] Glastonbury Inqu. of 1189, p. 91 : 'Editha tenet unam mesuagium et unam croftam pro 6 d. et fert aquam falcatoribus.'

[4] Add. MSS. 6159, f. 53, a : 'Item sunt in dicto manerio 22 virgate et debent invenire in proxima septimana post festum Sti Michaeli, per unum diem a mane usque ad horam meridianam 44 carecta, ad fima domini cariandum.' Domesday of St. Paul's, 62 : 'Quod si boves non habuerit vel alia animalia ad arandum faciet aliud opus quod jussum fuerit et educet 10 plaustra de fimo post Pascha et habebit dignerium de domino et infra hundredum portabit unum plaustrum vel duas carectatas.'

long distances, and the peasants have to take their turn
at them one after the other[1]. They were bound to carry
corn to London or Bristol according to the size of their
holdings[2]. Special importance was attached to the carriage of the 'farm,' that is of the products designed for
the consumption of the lord[3]. In some surveys we find
the qualification that the peasants are not obliged to carry ·
anything but such material as may be put on the fire, i.e.
used in the kitchen[4]. In the manor itself there are many
carriage duties to be performed : carts are required for the
grain, or for spreading the dung. The work of loading
and of following the carts is imposed on those who are
not able to provide the implements[5]. And alongside of
the duties of carriage by horses or oxen we find the corresponding manual duty. The 'averagium super dorsum
suum' falls on the small tenant who does not own either
horses or oxen[6]. Such small people are also made to
drive the swine or geese to the market[7]. The lord and
his chief stewards must look sharp after the distribution

[1] Ely Inqu., Cotton MSS. Claudius C. xi. 38, b : 'Averagium secundum
turnum vicinorum suorum curtum et longum.'

[2] Domesday of St. Paul's, 55 : 'Rogerus dives . . . cum villata ad firmam
portandam Londinium facit quantum requiritur de 20 acris.' Glastonbury Inqu. of 1189, f. 97 : 'Quater faciet summagium apud Bristolliam.'
Domesday of St. Paul's, 47 : 'Preterea debet hida portare 4 summagia
et dimidiam per totum ab horreo domini usque ad navem ter in anno
divisim.'

[3] Add. MSS. 6159, f. 28, a : ' Item de predictis cotariis unusquisque habet
unum horsacram et de ista acra debet unusquisque invenire unum equum
ad ducendum cum aliis frumentum de firma ad Cantuariam, et pisas, et sal,
et presencia portare.'

[4] Black Book of St. Augustine's, Cotton MSS. Faustina, A. 1, f. 186 : ' Nihil
debent averare ad tunc, nisi res que sunt ad opus conventus et que poni
debent super ignem.'

[5] Glastonbury Inqu. of 1189, f. 65 : 'W. Sp. tenet unum fordil pro 15 den.
et operatur quolibet die lune per totum annum et (debet) ladiare cum alio
ferdilario sicut dimidii virgatarii.' Domesday of St. Paul's, 19 : ' Omnes isti
(cotarii) debent operari semel . . . Debent eciam portare et chariare.'

[6] Rot. Hundr. ii. 605, b : ' Et faciet averagium super dorsum suum ad
voluntatem domini.'

[7] Glastonbury Inqu. of 1189, f. 71 : ' Portat et fugat aucas, et gallinas, et
porcos Glastonie.' Domesday of St. Paul's, 27 : ' (Cotarii) isti debent singulis
diebus Lune unam operacionem et portare et fugare porcos Londoniam.'

of these duties in order to prevent wealthy tenants from being put to light duties through the protection of the bailiffs, who may be bribed for the purpose [1].

It would be hard to imagine any kind of agricultural work which is not imposed on the peasantry in these manorial surveys. The tenants mind the lord's ploughs, construct houses and booths for him, repair hedges and dykes, work in vineyards, wash and shear the sheep [2], etc. In some cases the labour has to be undertaken by them, not in the regular run of their services, but by special agreement, as it were, in consideration of some particular right or permission granted to them [3]. Also it happens from time to time that the people of one manor have to perform some services in another, for instance, because they use pasture in that other manor [4]. Such 'forinsec' labour may be due even from tenants of a strange lord. By the side of purely agricultural duties we find such as are required by the political or judicial organisation of the manor. Peasants are bound to guard and hang thieves, to carry summonses and orders, to serve at the courts of the superior lord and of the king [5].

In consequence of the great variety of these labour-services they had to be reduced to some chief and plain subdivisions for purposes of a general oversight. Three main classes are very noticeable notwithstanding all variety: the *araturae, averagia,* and *manuoperationes.* These last

Classification of labour-services.

[1] Gloucester Cart. iii. 218 : ' Item, quod nullus prepositus aliquid ab aliquo recipiat, ut ipsum ad firmam esse permittat vel ad levem ponat operationem mutando cariagia summagia debita in operibus manualibus.'

[2] See, for instance, Glastonbury Inqu. of 1189, pp. 22, 29 ; Gloucester Cart. iii. 17 ; Domesday of St. Paul's, 54.

[3] Cart. of Bury St. Edmunds, Harl. MSS. 3977, f. 82 : ' (Debet) metere pro porcis quilibet dimidiam acram siliginis.'

[4] Black Book of St. Augustine's, Cotton MSS. Faustina, A. 1, f. 44 : 'Aratum hominum de N.' Cartul. of Battle, Augm. Off. Miscell. Books, N. 18, f. 2, a : ' Forinseca servicia . . . arant . . . seminant.'

[5] Domesday of St. Paul's, 38 : ' . . . et furem captum in curia custodiet et iudicatum suspendet et sparget fimum ad cibum domini.' Ibid. 62 : ' G. G. tenet 5 acras . . . (debet) qualibet septimana 2 opera et sequitur precarias in autumpno . . . R. H. 5 acras per idem servicium et preterea defendit eas versus regem.'

are also called *hand-dainae* or *daywerke*[1]; and the records give sometimes the exact valuation of the work to be performed during a day in every kind of labour. Sometimes all the different classes are added up under one head for a general reckoning, and without any distinction as to work performed by hand or with the help of horse or ox. Among the manors of Christ Church, Canterbury[2], for instance, we find at Borle ' 1480 work-days divided into 44 weeks of labour from the virgaters, 88 from the cotters, 320 from the tofters holding small tenements in the fields.' In Bockyng the work-days of 52 weeks are reckoned to be 3222. It must be added, that when such a general summing up appears, it is mostly to be taken as an indication that the old system based on labour in kind is more or less shaken. The aim of throwing together the different classes of work is to get a general valuation of its worth, and such a valuation in money is commonly placed by the side of the reckoning. The single day-work yields sometimes only one penny or a little more, and the landlord is glad to exchange this cumbrous and cheap commodity for money-rents, even for small ones.

Payments in kind.

We must now proceed to examine the different forms assumed by payments in kind and money: they present a close parallel to the many varieties of labour-service. Thirteenth-century documents are full of allusions to payments in kind—that most archaic form of arranging the relations between a lord and his subjects. The peasants give corn under different names, and for various reasons: as *gavelseed*, in addition to the money-rent paid for their land[3]; as *foddercorn*, of oats for the feeding of

[1] Gloucester Cart. iii. 54 : ' Debet a festo S[ti] Michaelis usque ad festum S[ti] Petri ad Vincula qualibet septimana per 4 dies operari opus manuale cum uno homine, et valet quolibet dieta obolum.' Glastonbury Inqu. 28 : ' Si est ad opus a festo S[ti] Petri ad Vincula usque ad festum S[ti] Michaelis nisi festum intercurrat qualibet die faciet unam dainam.'

[2] Add. MSS. 6159, f. 25, a ; 53, b.

[3] Domesday of St. Paul's, 33 : ' Singule virgate debent per annum . . . de gavelsed 3 mensuras quarum 7 faciunt mensuram de Colcester.' Black Book of St. Augustine's, Cotton MSS., Faustina, A. i, 31, d : ' Sunt praeterea 5 sullungi et 50 acre in eadem hamiletto qui debent bladum de gabulo.'

horses[1] ; as *gathercorn*, which a manorial servant has to
collect or gather from the several homesteads[2] ; as *corn-
bole*, a best sheaf levied at harvest-time[3]. Of other provender supplied to the lord's household honey is the most
common, both in combs and in a liquid form[4]. Ale is
sometimes brewed for the same purpose, and sometimes
malt and *braseum* furnished as material to be used in the
manorial farm[5]. Animals are also given in rent, mostly
sheep, lambs, and sucking-pigs. The mode of selection
is peculiar in some cases. In the Christ Church (Canterbury) manor of Monckton each sulung has to render two
lambs, and the lord's servant has the right to take those
which he pleases, whereupon the owner gets a receipt, evidently in view of subsequent compensation from the other
co-owners of the sulung[6]. If no suitable lamb is to be
found, eight pence are paid instead of it as mail (*mala*).
On one of the estates of Gloucester Abbey a freeman has
to come on St. Peter's and Paul's day with a lamb of the
value of 12*d.*, and besides, 12 pence in money are to be
hung in a purse on the animal's neck[7]. Poultry is brought

---

[1] Domesday of St. Paul's, 6 : 'Et unum quarterium de auena ad foddercorn.'

[2] Add. MSS. 6159, 26, b : 'Et de gadercorn reddunt de quolibet swlinge
4 coppas de puro ordeo et de presenti gallum, et gallinam de qualibet domo
. . . quas serviens curie debet circumeundo querere.'

[3] Ely Inqu., Cotton MSS., Claudius, C. xi. 185, b ; Bury St. Edmunds
Cart., Harl. MSS. 3977, f. 84, b.

[4] Glastonbury Inqu. of 1189, p. 67 (cf. 145) : 'Henricus Wlde tenet 25
acras de prato pro stacha mellis. Utilius quod esset in manu domini.'
Gloucester Cart. ii. 128 : 'Honilond T. T. tenet 6 acras terre pro 8 lagenis
mellis vel pretio.'

[5] Ramsey Cart. i. 300 : 'Faciet etiam unam mutam (leg. mittam) et dimidiam braesii, quam recipiet in curia pro voluntate sua bene mundatam, et
per se ipsum, et illam carriabit apud Rameseiam. Quae si refutetur, de-
fectum ejus propriis sumptibus in omnibus supplebit, nisi mensura sibi tradita
sit minor.'

[6] Add. MSS. 6159, f. 26, b : 'De quolibet Swlinge duos agnos reddunt in
estate. Ita quidem quod serviens curie, si invenerit agnum in sulungis illis
qui ei placuerit, accipiat eum cuiuscumque sit, et ille ad quem pertinebit
adquietacionem. Quod si agnus inventus non fuerit 8 den. dabit quando
mala persolvat.'

[7] Gloucester Cart. iii. 77 : 'Walterus Fremon tenet 6 acras terrae cum

almost everywhere, but these prestations are very different
in their origin. The most common reason for giving capons
is the necessity for getting the warranty of the lord[1] : in
this sense the receipt and payment of the rent constitute
an acknowledgment on the part of the lord that he is
bound to protect his men, and on the part of the peasant
that he is the lord's villain. 'Wood hens' are given for
licence to take a load of wood in a forest ; similar prestations occur in connexion with pasture and with the use
of a moor for turbary[2]. At Easter the peasantry greet
their protectors by bringing eggs : in Walton, a manor of
St. Paul's, London, the custom is said to exist in honour
of the lord, and at the free discretion of the tenants[3].
Besides all those things which may be 'put on the fire
and eaten,' rents in kind sometimes take the shape of some
object for permanent use, especially of some implement
necessary for the construction of the plough[4]. Trifling
rents, consisting of flowers or roots of ginger, are sometimes imposed with the object of testifying to the lord's
seignory; but the payers of such rents are generally freeholders[5]. I need not dwell long on the enumeration of
all the strange prestations which existed during the Middle
Ages, and partly came down to our own time : any reader
curious about them will find an enormous mass of inter-

mesuagio et reddit inde per annum die Apostolorum Petri et Pauli unum
multonem pretii 12 den. vel ultra, cum 12 den. circa collum suum ligatis.'
    [1] Exch. Q. R. Treas. of Rec. 59/69: 'Capones . . . pro warentia.'
    [2] Gloucester Cart. iii. 71: 'Propter illam gallinam conquererunt habere de
bosco domini regis unam summam bosci, quae vocatur dayesen.' Exch.
Q. R. Min. Acc. Bk. 513, N. 97: 'Wodehennus... ad Natale.' Suffolk Rolls
(Bodleian), 3: 'Dicet curia quod R. debet facere domino sicut alii custumarii, scil. oues et gallinas, quia fodit etsi non pascat.' Ely Inqu., Cotton
MSS., Claudius, C. xi, f. 52, a: 'Redditus caponum per annum pro aueriis
termino pasche.'
    [3] Domesday of St. Paul's, 51: 'Et ad pascha ova ad libitum tenencium et
ad honorem domini.'
    [4] Glastonbury Inqu. of 1189, p. 35: 'Hoc est accrementum redditus tem-
pore Roberti; Ordricus pro 4 retiis terre altero anno 1 soccum.' Gloucester
Cart. iii. 79: 'Walterus de Hale tenet unam acram terre et reddit inde per
annum unum vomerem ad festum S[u] Michaelis pretii 8 den. pro omni servitio.'
    [5] Warwickshire Hundr. Roll, Exch. Q. R. Misc. Books, N. 18, f. 2, a: 'Per
servicium unius radicis gyngibrii . . . unius rose.'

esting material in Hazlitt's 'Tenures of Land and Customs of Manors.'

In opposition to labour and rents in kind we find a great many payments in money. Some of these are said in as many words to have stept into the place of labour services ; of mowing, carrying, making hedges[1], etc. The same may be the case in regard to produce : *barlick-silver* is paid instead of barley, *fish-silver* evidently instead of fish, *malt-silver* instead of malt ; a certain payment instead of salt, and so on[2]. But sometimes the origin of the money rent is more difficult to ascertain. We find, for instance, a duty on sheep, which is almost certainly an original imposition when it appears as *fald-silver*. Even so the *scythe-penny* from every scythe, the *bosing-silver* from every horse and cart, the *wood-penny*, probably for the use of wood as fuel, must be regarded as original taxes and not quit-rents or commutation-rents[3]. *Pannage* is paid in the same way for the swine grazing in the woods[4]. *Ward-penny* appears also in connexion with cattle, but with some special shade of meaning which it is difficult to bring out definitely; the name seems to point to protection, and also occurs in connexion with police arrangements[5].

I must acknowledge that in a good many cases I have been unable to find a satisfactory explanation for various

Money-payments.

Classification of money payments.

[1] Gloucester Cart. iii. 55 : 'Omnes praedicti consuetudinarii . . . debent cariare molas, scil. petras molares ad molendinum domini, vel dabunt in communi 13 den. quadrantem.' Rot. Hundr. ii. 750, b : 'Et modo eorum servicia convertuntur in denariis.'

[2] Add. MSS. 6159, f. 53, a : 'Barlicksilver. Item debet Willelmus de B. per annum 6 quarteria ordei et 6 quarteria auene,' etc.

[3] Roch. Custum. 4, a : 'Dabunt eciam denarium pro falce quod anglice dicunt sithpeni.' Glastonbury Inqu. of 1189, p. 59 : 'Et dabit 4 stacas et dimidiam frumenti ad consuetudinem et eadem die 1 denarium illi qui colligit fualia.' Ely Reg., Cotton MSS., Claudius, C. xi. f. 82, b : 'De bosingsiluer 1 denarium ad festum S^{ti} Martini si habeat equum et carectam.'

[4] Add. Charters, 5, 629 : '(Stephanus) retraxit et abduxit porcos suos tempore pannagii.'

[5] Rot. Hundr. ii. 453, a : 'Memorandum quod omnes isti prenominati tam liberi quam villani qui habent bestias precii 30 den. dant domino predicto per annum 1 den. pro quadam consuetudine que vocatur Wartpenny.'

U 2

terms which occur in the records for the divers payments.
An attentive study of local usages will probably lead to definite conclusions as to most of them[1]. From a general point
of view it is interesting to notice, that we find already in our
records some attempts to bring all the perplexing variety
of payments to a few main designations. Annual rents
are, of course, reckoned out under the one head of 'census.'
Very obvious reasons suggested the advisability of computing the entire money-proceed yielded by the estate[2].
It sometimes happens that the general sum made up in this
way, fixed as it is at a constant amount, is used almost as a
name for a complex of land[3]. A division of rents into old
and new ones does not require any particular explanation[4].
But several other subdivisions are worth notice. The rent
paid from the land often appears separately as *landgafol* or
landchere. It is naturally opposed to payments that fall
on the person as poll taxes[5]. These last are considered
as a return for the personal protection guaranteed by the
lord to his subjects. Of the contrast between *gafol* as a
customary rent and *mál* as a payment in commutation I
have spoken already, and I have only to add now, that *gild*

[1] What may be, for instance, the explanation of the *huntenegild*, which
not unfrequently appears in the records. E.g. Gloucester Cart. iii. 22:
'Johannes Carpentarius et relicta Kammock tenent dimidiam virgatam terrae
et faciunt idem quod praescripti, exceptis huntenesilver et gallina.' Add.
MSS. 6159, f. 23, a: 'Ricardus atte mere tenet de domino in villenagio 20
acras terre; reddit inde per annum de unthield ad festum purificacionis
4 sol. 5 den. ob. et ad pascham 6 d. Et ad festum S[tl] Michaelis 17 denarios.' The payment is a very important one and hardly connected with
hunting.

[2] Domesday of St. Paul's, 140 (Inqu. of 1181): 'Keneswetha... summa
denariorum 10 libre et 7 sol. et obolus.' Cf. xx.

[3] Battle Cart., Augment. Off. Misc. Books, N. 18, f. 5, a: 'Juga que sunt
in sex libris in Wy.'

[4] Christ Church Reg., Harl. MSS. 1006, f. 56: 'Newerentes.'

[5] Domesday of St. Paul's, 83: 'Inferius notati tenentes terras dant land-
gablum. Et si habent uxores 2 denarios de havedsot quia capiunt super
dominium boscum et aquam et habent exitum, et si non habent uxorem vel
uxor virum, dabit unum denarium. Galfridus filius Ailwardi pro terra quondam Theodori cui non attinet 5 denarios landgabuli.' Ramsey Inqu., Cotton
MSS., Galba E. x. f. 46, b: 'S. de W. dat pro terra sua 16 denarios et 12
denarios pro se et uxore sua.' Exch. Q. R. Min. Acc. Bk. 587, T. P. R.
8109: 'Denarii... ad existendum in warentia.'

is sometimes used in the same sense as *mál*[1]. Another term in direct opposition to *gafol* is the Latin *donum*[2]. It seems to indicate a special payment imposed as a kind of voluntary contribution on the entire village. To be sure, there was not much free will to be exercised in the matter ; all the dependent people of the township had to pay according to their means[3]. But the tax must have been considered as a supplementary one in the same sense as supplementary boon-work. It may have been originally intended in some cases as an equivalent for some rights surrendered by the lord, as a *mál* or *gild*, in fact[4]. In close connexion with the *donum* we find the *auxilium*[5], also an extraordinary tax paid once a year, and distinguished from the ordinary rent. It appears as a direct consequence of the political subjection of the tenantry[6] : it is, in fact, merely an expression of the right to tallage. Our records mention it sometimes as apportioned according to the number of cattle owned by the peasant, but this concerns only the mode of imposition of the duty and hardly its origin[7]. As I have said already, the *auxilium* is

---

[1] Archaeologia, xlvii. 127 : '(Soke of Rothley) Gildi hoc est quietum de consuetudinibus servilibus quae quondam dare consueverint sicuti Hornchild et hiis similibus.'

[2] Glastonbury Inqu. of 1189, p. 4 : '... unam virgatam et dimidiam et 5 acras pro 5 solidis de gabulo et 7 denariis de dono.'

[3] Glastonbury Inqu. of 1189, p. 39 : 'Omnes simul dant de dono 40 solidos secundum terras quas tenent.' Ibid. 5 : 'Debet dare de dono quantum pertinet de quinque libris.' Ramsey Cart. i. 46 : 'De denariis qui vocantur 20 solidi dat dimidius virgatarius 6 denarios.'

[4] Ramsey Cart. i. 440 : 'Villa dat 20 solidos, qui dantur quod cum aliquis in misericordia domini, det ante judicium sex denarios, et post, si expectet judicium, duodecim denarios, nisi sit pro furto, vel aliqua maxima transgressione.'

[5] Gloucester Cart. iii. 78 : 'Dicta terra consuevit dare de auxilio 14 denarios et obolum qui modo allocantur consuetudinario in solutione octo marcarum.'

[6] Exch. Q. R. Treas. Rec. 20/68 : 'Item debent domino ad festum S^{ti} Michaelis auxilium ad placitum suum et ad forinsecum servitium.'

[7] Gloucester Cart. iii. 180 : 'Et dabit pro terra 6 denarios ad auxilium. Dabit etiam auxilium pro averiis suis secundum numerum eorundem.' iii. 50 : 'Et dabit auxilium secundum numerum animalium.' iii. 208 : 'Et si impositum fuerit eidem quod in taxatione auxilii aliquod animal concelaverit, potest cogi ad sacramentum praestandum et se super hoc purgan-

in every respect like the *donum.* One very characteristic trait of both taxes is, that they are laid primarily on the whole village, which is made to pay a certain round sum as a body[1]. The burden is divided afterwards between the several householders, and the number of cattle, and more particularly of the beasts of plough kept on the holding, has of course to be taken into account more than anything else. But the manorial administration does not much concern itself with these details: the township is answerable for the whole sum.

Payments
to State
and
Church.

It is to be added that the payment is sometimes actually mentioned as a political one in direct connexion with 'forinsec' duties towards the king. The burdens which lay on the land in consequence of the requirements of State and Church appear not unfrequently in the documents. Among those the *scutage* and *hidage* are the most important. The first of these taxes is so well known that I need not stop to discuss it. It may be noticed however that in relation to the dependent people scutage is not commonly spoken of ; the tax was levied under this name from the barons and the armed gentry, and was mostly transmitted by these to the lower strata of society under some other name, as an aid or a tallage. Hidage is historically connected with the old English Danegeld system, and in some cases its amount is set out separately from other payments, and the tenants of a manor have to pay it to the bailiff of the hundred and not to the steward. A smaller payment called *ward-penny* is bound up with it, probably as a substitute for the duty of keeping watch and ward[2]. In the north the hidage is replaced

dum. Et si per vicinos suos convictus fuerit super hoc, puniendus est pro voluntate domini.'

[1] Gloucester Cart. iii. 203: '... omnes isti consuetudinarii de Colne dant in communi ad auxilium 46 solidos 8 denarios.' Rochester Custumal, 4, a : ' De omnibus decem jugis debent scotare ad donum domini ville et ad servicium domini Regis.'

[2] Domesday of St. Paul's, 64 : ' Dicunt quod manerium de Berlinge defendit se versus regem pro duabus hidis et dimidia ... Reddunt ... pro hidagio baillivo hundredi de Reilee 31 denarios et 13 denarios de Wardpeni, de quibus dominicum reddit de 20 acris 2 den. et obolem pro hidagio et 2 denarios pro Wardpeni.'

by *cornage*[1], a tax which has given rise to learned controversy and doubt; it looks like an assessment according to
the number of horns of cattle, *pro numero averiorum*, as
our Latin extents would say. The Church has also an
ancient claim on the help of the faithful; the *church-
scot* of Saxon times often occurs in the feudal age under
the name of *churiset* or *cheriset*[2]. It is mostly paid in
kind, but may be found occasionally as a money-rent.

A survey of the chief aspects assumed by the work and the Questions
payments of the dependent people was absolutely necessary, suggested by a survey
in order to enable us to understand the descriptions of rural of work
arrangements which form the most instructive part of the and rents.
so-called extents. But every survey of terms and distinctions (even if it were much more detailed than the one I
am able to present), will give only a very imperfect idea of
the obligations actually laid on the peasantry. It must
needs take up the different species one by one and consider them separately, whereas in reality they were meant
to fit together into a whole. On the other hand it may
create a false impression by enumerating in systematic order
facts which belonged to different localities and perhaps to
different epochs. To keep clear of these dangers we have
to consider the deviations of practical arrangements from
the rules laid down in the books and the usual combinations of the elements described.

When one reads the careful notices in the cartularies as Cases
to the number of days and the particular occasions when where the usual order
work has to be performed for the lord, a simple question is was not
suggested by the minuteness of detail. What happened adhered to.
when this very definite arrangement came into collision
with some other equally exacting order? One of the three
days of week-work might, for instance, fall on a great feast;
or else the weather might be too bad for out-of-doors
work. Who was to suffer or to gain by such casualties?
The question is not a useless one. The manorial records

---

[1] Exch. Esch. Ultra Trentam, 1/49: 'Pro cornagio de feodis militum 17
sol. 8 den.'

[2] Glastonbury Inqu. of 1189, p. 65: 'In die S^{ti} Martini debet dimidiam
dainam frumenti de cheriset.'

raise it occasionally, and their ways of settling it are not always the same. We find that in some cases the lord tried to get rid of the inconveniences occasioned by such events, or at least to throw one part of the burden back on the dependent population; in Barling, for instance, a manor of St. Paul's, London[1], of two feasts occurring in one week and even in two consecutive weeks, one profits to the villains and the other to the lord; that is to say, the labourer escapes one day's work altogether. But the general course seems to have been to liberate the peasants from work both on occasion of a festival and if the weather was exceptionally inclement[2]. Both facts are not without importance: it must be remembered that the number of Church festivals was a very considerable one in those days. Again, although the stewards were not likely to be very sentimental as to bad weather, the usual test of cold in case of ploughing seems to have been the hardness of the soil—a certain percentage of free days must have occurred during the winter at least. And what is even more to be considered—when the men were very strictly kept to their week-work under unfavourable circumstances, the landlord must have gained very little although the working people suffered much. The reader may easily fancy the effects of what must have been a very common occurrence, when the village householders sent out their ploughs on heavy clay in torrents of rain. The system of customary work on certain days was especially clumsy in such respects, and it is worth notice that

[1] Domesday of St. Paul's, 66: 'Beatrix relicta Osberti Casse tenet 15 acras et a festo S[ti] Michaelis usque ad Vincula qualibet septimana debet 3 operaciones nisi festum impedierit; quod si festum feriabile evenerit in septimana die lune et aliud die mercurii, unum festum erit ei utile, aliud domino. Quod si festum evenerit eadem septimana die veneris, addito alio festo in alia septimana veniente, dividentur illi duo dies inter dominum et operarium ut supradictum est.'

[2] Glastonbury Inqu. of 1189, p. 64: 'A festo S[ti] Petri ad Vincula debent qualibet ebdomada metere uel aliud opus facere usque ad festum S[ti] Michaelis nisi festum intercurrat, die lune, die martis et die mercurii.' Ibid. 62: 'Ab Hoccadei usque ad festum S[ti] Johannis qualibet ebdomada arabit dimidiam acram, si possit propter duritiem.'

in harvest-time the landlords rely chiefly on boon-days. These were not irrevocably fixed, and could be shifted according to the state of the weather. Still the week-work was so important an item in the general arrangement of labour-services that the inconveniences described must have acted powerfully in favour of commutation.

Of course, the passage from one system to the other, however desirable for the parties concerned, was not to be effected easily and at once: a considerable amount of capital in the hands of the peasantry was required to make it possible, and another necessary requirement was a sufficient circulation of money. While these were wanting the people had to abide by the old labour system. The facts we have been discussing give indirect proof that there was not much room for arbitrary changes in this system. Everything seems ruled and settled for ever. It may happen, of course, that notwithstanding the supposed equality between the economic strength of the different holdings, some tenants are unable to fulfil the duties which their companions perform [1]. As it was noticed before, the shares could not be made to correspond absolutely to each other, and the distribution of work and payments according to a definite pattern was often only approximate [2]. Again, the lord had some latitude in selecting one or the other kind of service to be performed by his men [3]. But, speaking generally, the settlement of duties was a very constant one, and manorial documents testify that every attempt by the lord to dictate a change was met by emphatic protests on the part of the peasantry [4]. The tenacity of

Relation between the customary system and the arbitrary authority of the lord.

---

[1] Glastonbury Inqu. of 1189, p. 59: 'Willelmus filius Osanore (tenet) unam virgatam eodem servitio, sed non potest perficere servitium.'

[2] Domesday of St. Paul's, 51: 'Et omnes alii similiter operabuntur sive plus teneant sive minus, pro racione 5 acrarum.' Glastonbury Inqu. of 1189, p. 104: 'W. de H. tenet unam virgatam pro dimidia virgata . . . pro alia virgata facit sicut pro quarta parte dimidie hide.'

[3] Gloucester Cart. iii. 199: 'Et sciendum quod dominus potest eligere utrum voluerit habere servitium predictum de Johanne Spere, uel quod duplicet servitium R. de A. inferius inter akermannos scripti.'

[4] Rot. Hundr. ii. 757, a: 'Set isti tenentes memorati ut asserunt ad alias consuetudines et servitia antiquitus esse consueverunt.'

custom may be gathered from the fact that when we chance to possess two sets of extents following each other after a very considerable lapse of time, the renders in kind and the labour-services remain unmodified in the main [1]. One has to guard especially against the assumption that such expressions as 'to do whatever he is bid' or 'whatever the lord commands' imply a complete servility of the tenant and unrestricted power on the part of the lord to exploit his subordinate according to his pleasure. Such expressions have been used as a test of the degree of subjection of the villains at different epochs; it has been contended, that the earlier our evidence is, the more complete the lord's sway appears to be [2]. The expressions quoted above may seem at first glance to countenance the idea, but an attentive and extended study of the documents will easily show that, save in exceptional cases, the earlier records are by no means harder in their treatment of the peasantry than the later. The eleventh century is, if anything, more favourable to the subjected class as regards the imposition of labour-services than the thirteenth, and we shall see by-and-by that the observation applies even more to Saxon times. In the light of such a general comparison, we have to explain the above-mentioned phrases in a different way. 'Whatever he is bid' applies to the quality and not to the quantity of the work [3].

---

[1] E.g. a comparison of the inquests contained in the Ramsey Cartulary published in the Rolls Series with the earlier extents contained in Cotton MS., Galba, E. x, and with the Hundred Rolls of Huntingdonshire and Cambridgeshire, will support the opinion expressed in the text.

[2] Seebohm, Village Community.

[3] The meaning of the expression may be gathered from the following extracts from the Ramsey Cartulary, i. 358: 'Die autem Jovis proxima ante Pascha et die Jovis contra festum S[ti] Benedicti quodcunque opus sibi fuerit injunctum operabitur.' Cf. 357: 'Et si opus fuerit, faciet hayam in campis, habentem longitudinem duarum perticarum, et allocabitur ei pro opere unius diei. Et die quo carriare fenum debet, ducet unam carrectatam domi de alio feno Abbatis, uel aliud carriagium cum carrecta faciet, si sibi fuerit injunctum.' 361: 'A gula autem Augusti usque ad festum Sancti Michaelis qualibet septimana operabitur per unum diem integrum, qualecunque opus sibi praecipiatur.' 365: 'Et operatur quaelibet virgata a festo Sancti Michaelis

It does not mean that the steward has a right to order the peasant about like a slave, to tear him at pleasure from his own work, and to increase his burden whenever he likes. It means simply that such and such a virgater or cotter has to appear in person or by proxy to perform his week-work of three days, or two days, or four days, according to the case, and that it is not settled beforehand what kind of work he is to perform. He may have to plough, or to carry, or to dig trenches, or to do anything else, according to the bidding of the steward. A similar instance of uncertainty may be found in the expression 'without measure[1]' which sometimes occurs in extents. It would be preposterous to construe it as an indication of work to be imposed at pleasure. It is merely a phrase used to suit the case when the work had to be done by the day and not by a set quantity; if, for instance, a man had to plough so many times and the number of acres to be ploughed was not specified. It is true that such vague descriptions are mostly found in older surveys, but the inference to be drawn from the fact is simply that manorial customs were developing gradually from rather indefinite rules to a minute settlement of details. There is no difference in the main principle, that the dependent

---

usque ad festum Translationis Sancti Benedicti qualibet septimana tribus diebus ... *quodcumque opus praeceptum fuerit;* videlicet, si flagellare oportet, flagellabit infra villam viginti quatuor garbas de frumento et siligini, de hordeo triginta garbas, de avena triginta garbas. Extra villam flagellabit de frumento viginti garbas, de avena viginti quatuor garbas. Nec exibit extra hundredum ad flagellandum *nisi ex gratia.* Quodcunque *aliud genus operis facere* debeat, operabitur tota die si ballivus voluerit; praeterquam in bosco, ubi si secare debeat, operabitur usque ad nonam; et si pascere eum dominus voluerit, operabitur usque ad vesperam. Si debeat spinas vel virgas colligere, colliget unum fesciculum, et portabit usque ad curiam pro opere unius diei. In quadragesima autem nullum genus operis faciet ad cibum proprium usque nonam nisi quod herciabit tota die.' It seems quite clear that the lord has in some cases the choice between different kinds of work, but the amount to be required is settled once for all. When we find in the Glastonbury Inquisition of 1189 the sentence, 'operabitur quodcumque ei praeceptum fuerit sicut neth,' it means evident, that the peasant's work, whatever it is, is settled according to the standard of the neat's holding.

[1] Glastonbury Inqu. of 1189, p. 41: 'Et herciat semel sine mensura aliqua ei assignata cum hoc quod habet in carruca.'

householder was not to be treated as a slave and had a customary right to devote part of his time to the management of his own affairs.

The holdings and the population.
Another point is to be kept well in view. The whole arrangement of a manorial survey is constructed with the holding as its basis. The names of virgaters and cotters are certainly mentioned for the sake of clearness, but it would be wrong to consider the duties ascribed to them as aiming at the person. John Newman may be said to hold a virgate, to join with his plough-oxen in the tillage of twenty acres, to attend at three boon-days in harvest time, and so forth. It would be misleading to take these statements very literally and to infer that John Newman was alone to use the virgate and to work for it. He was most probably married, and possibly had grown-up sons to help him ; very likely a brother was there also, and even servants, poor houseless men from the same village or from abroad. Every householder has a more or less considerable following (*sequela*)[1], and it was by no means necessary for the head of the family to perform all manorial work in his own person. He had to appear or to send one workman on most occasions and to come with all his people on a few days—the boon-days namely. The description of the *precariae* is generally the only occasion when the extents take this into account, namely, that there was a considerable population in the village besides those tenants who were mentioned by name[2]. I need not point out, that the fact has an important meaning. The medieval system, in so far as it rested on the distribution of holdings, was in many respects more

---

[1] Placitorum Abbreviatio, p. 212 : 'Alia carta eiusdem eidem Elie facta et heredibus suis de dicta bovata terre una cum dicto Rogero villano suo et secta et sequela sua.' Ramsey Cart. i. 355 : 'Prior de Sancto Ivone habet ingressum in una virgata terrae per Henricum de Kylevile, in qua tres sunt mansiones, et unus pro caeteris facit servitium debitum manerio.'

[2] Ramsey Inqu., Cotton MSS., Galba, E. x. f. 49 : 'Quicumque acceperit pro mercede sua 18 denarios debet operari cum domino suo tribus diebus vel dare unum denarium.' Cf. *Servi* : Rot. Hundr. ii. 781, b : 'Servi : Dabit ad exennium contra Natale 6 panes . . . et venit ad prandium domini pro predicto exennio sexta manu si voluerit.'

advantageous to the tenantry than to the lord. It was
superficial in a sense, and from the point of view of the
lord did not lead to a satisfactory result; he did not get
the utmost that was possible from his subordinates. The
factor of population was almost disregarded by it, households very differently constituted in this respect were
assumed to be equal, and the tenacity of custom prevented an increase of rents and labour-services in proportion to the growth of resource and wealth among the
peasants. Some attempts to get round these difficulties
are noticeable in the surveys: they are mostly connected
with the regulation of boon-works. But these exceptional
measures give indirect proof of the very insufficient manner
in which the question was generally settled.

The liabilities of the peasantry take the shape of pro- Stages
duce, labour, and money-rents. Almost in every manor in the
arrange-
all three kinds of impositions are to be found split up into ment of
a confusing variety of customary obligations. It is out of duties.
the question to trace at the present time, with the help of
fragmentary and later material, what the original ideas
were which underlie these complicated arrangements. But
although a reduction to simple guiding principles account-
ing for every detail cannot be attempted, it is easy to perceive that chance and fancy were not everything in these
matters. The several duties are brought together so as to
form a certain whole, and some of the aims pursued in
the grouping may be perceived even now.

The older surveys often show the operation of a system Farm-
which is adapted by its very essence to a very primitive system.
state of society; it may be called the farm-system, the
word *farm* being used in the original sense of the Saxon
feorm, food, and not in the later meaning of fixed rent,
although these two meanings appear intimately connected
in history. The *farm* is a quantity of produce necessary
for the maintenance of the lord's household during a
certain period: it may be one night's or week's or one fort-
night's farm accordingly. A very good instance of the
system may be found in an ancient cartulary of Ramsey,

now at the British Museum, which though compiled in the
early thirteenth century, constantly refers to the order of
Henry II's time. The estates of the abbey were taxed
in such a way as to yield thirteen full farms of a fort-
night, and each of these was to be used for the maintenance of the monks through a whole month. The extension
of the period is odd enough, and we do not see its reason
clearly; it followed probably on great losses in property
and income at the time of Abbot Walter. However this
may be, the thirteen fortnights' farms were made to serve
all the year round, and to cover fifty-two weeks instead
of twenty-six. A very minute description of the single
farm is given as it was paid by the manor of Ayllington
(i. e. Elton). Every kind of produce is mentioned : flour
and bread, beer and honey, bacon, cheese, lambs, geese,
chicken, eggs, butter, &c. The price of each article
is mentioned in pence, and it is added, that four pounds
have to be paid in money. By the side of the usual
farm there appears a 'lent' farm with this distinction,
that only half as much bacon and cheese has to be
given as usual, and the deficiency is to be made up by
a money payment. Some of the manors of the abbey
have to send a whole farm, some others only one half,
that is one week's farm, but all are assessed to pay sixteen
pence for every acre to be used as alms for the poor[1].
This description may be taken as a standard one, and it
would be easy to supplement it in many particulars from
the records of other monastic institutions. The records of
St. Paul's, London, supply information as to a distribution
of the farms at the close of the eleventh century, which
covered fifty-two weeks, six days, and five-sixths of a day[2].
The firmae of St. Alban's were reckoned to provide for
the fifty-two weeks of the year, and one in advance[3].
The practice of arranging the produce-rents according to
farms was by no means restricted to ecclesiastical manage-

[1] Cotton MSS., Galba, E. x. f. 19. See Appendix xiv.
[2] Domesday of St. Paul's, Hale's Introduction, pp. xxxviii, xxxix.
[3] Gesta Abbatum (Rolls Ser.), 74. Cf. Glastonbury Inqu. of 1189, p. 145.

ment ; it occurs also on the estates of the Crown, and was probably in use on those of lay lords generally. Every person a little conversant with Domesday knows the *firmae unius noctis*, at which some of the royal manors were assessed [1]. In the period properly called feudal, that is in the twelfth and thirteenth centuries, the food-revenue had very often become only the starting-point for a reckoning of money-rents. The St. Alban's farms, for example, are no longer delivered in kind ; their equivalent in money has taken their place. But the previous state of things has left a clear trace in the division by weeks. Altogether it seems impossible to doubt that the original idea was to provide really the food necessary for consumption. One cannot help thinking that such practice must have come from the very earliest times when a Saxon or a Celtic chieftain got his income from the territory under his sway by moving from one place to another with his retinue and feeding on the people for a certain period. This very primitive mode of raising income and consuming it at the same time may occasionally strike our eye even in the middle of the thirteenth century. The tenants of the Abbot of Osulveston in Donington and Byker are bound to receive their lord during one night and one day when he comes to hold his court in their place. They find the necessary food and beverage for him and for his men, provender for his horses, and so forth. If the abbot does not come in person, the homage may settle about a commutation of the duties with the steward or the sergeant sent for the purpose. If he refuses to take money, they must bring everything in kind [2].

---

[1] See, for instance, the beginning of the description of Dorsetshire.

[2] Exch. Q. R. Min. Acc. Bk. 587, T. P. R. 8109 : 'Sciendum quod tenentes Abbatis de Osoluestone in Donington et Byker cum pertinentiis fuerunt semel in anno pro voluntate Abbatis ad curiam suam tenendum ibidem et invenient eidem Abbati et toti familie sue quam secum duxerit omnia necessaria sufficientia in adventu suo per unum diem integrum et noctem sequentem, vel noctem precedentem et diem sequentem in esculentis et poculentis tam vino quam cervisia, feno et prebenda pro equis eorum et equis carucariorum salem querencium, una cum candela et ceteris costis omnimodis inter necessaria computandis. Et si abbas non venerit facient finem cum celerario

This is an exceptional instance : generally the farm has to be sent to the lord's residence, probably after a deduction for the requirements of the manor in which it was gathered. When it had reached this stage the system is already in decay. It is not only difficult to provide for the carriage, but actually impossible to keep some of the articles from being spoilt. Bread sent to Westminster from some Worcestershire possession of the minster would not have been very good when it reached its destination. The step towards money-payments is natural and necessary.

Before leaving the food-rents we must take notice of one or two more peculiarities of this system. It is obvious that it was arranged from above, if one may use the expression. The assessment does not proceed in this case by way of an estimate of the paying or producing strength of each unit subjected to it, *i. e.* of each peasant household. The result is not made up by multiplying the revenue from every holding by the number of such holdings. The whole reckoning starts from the other end, from the wants of the manorial administration. The requirements of a night or of a week are used as the standard to which the taxation has to conform. This being the case, the correspondence between the amount of the taxes and the actual condition of the tax-payer was only a very loose one. Manors of very different size were brought into the same class in point of assessment, and the rough distinctions between a whole farm and half-a-farm could not follow at all closely the variety of facts in real life, even when they were supplemented by the addition of round sums of money.

si voluerit vel cum alii quem Abbas nomine suo miserit ad minus 20 solidis. Et si is qui nomine Abbatis missus ibidem fuit et finem recusauit, procurabitur ut premittitur. Et si aliquid de necessariis in administrando defuerit, omnes tenentes qui comestum contribuere debent die crastino in plena curia super necessariorum defectu per senescallum calumpniabuntur et graviter amerciabuntur. Et talis fuit consuetudo ab antiquo et habetur quolibet anno pro certo redditu, et de quo Petrus de Thedingworth quondam Abbas de Osoluestone et predecessores sui a tempore quo non extat memoria sub forma predicta fuerunt seisiti.'

These observations lead at once to important questions ; Assessment under the farm- system.
how was the farm-assessment distributed in every single
manor, and what was its influence on the duties of the
single householder?   It seems hardly doubtful, to begin
with, that the food-rent changed very much in this respect.
Originally, when the condition of things was more or less
like the Osulvestone example, the farm must have been
the result of co-operation on the part of all the householders
of a township, who had to contribute according to their
means to furnish the necessary articles.   But the farm of
St. Paul's, London, even when it is paid in produce, is a
very different thing : it is the result of a convention with
the firmarius, or may be with the township itself in the
place of a firmarius[1].   It depends only indirectly on the
services and payments of the peasantry.   Part of the flour,
bread, beer, etc., may come from the cultivation of the
demesne lands ; another portion will appear as the proceed
of week-work and boon-work performed by the villains,
and only one portion, perhaps a very insignificant one, will
be levied directly as produce.   In this way there is no
break between the food-rent system and the labour-system.
One may still exist for purposes of a general assessment
when the other has already taken hold of the internal
arrangement of the manor.

Most of our documents present the labour arrange- Labour-service system.
ment in full operation.   Each manor may be regarded
as an organised group of households in which the central
body represented by the lord's farm has succeeded in
subordinating several smaller bodies to its directing influence.   Every satellite has a movement of its own, is
revolving round its own centre, and at the same time it is
attracted to turn round the chief planet, and is carried
away in its path.   The constellation is a very peculiar one
and most significant for the course of medieval history.
Regarded from the economic standpoint it is neither a
system of great farming nor one of small farming, but

[1] See about this point, Hale's Introduction.   It is generally very good on
the subject of the farm.

a compound of both. The estate of the lord is in a sense managed on a great scale, but the management is bound up with a supply and a distribution of labour which depend on the conditions of the small tributary households. It would be impossible now-a-days to say for certain how much of the customary order of week-work and boon-work was derived from a calculation of the requirements of the manorial administration, and how much of it is to be regarded as a percentage taken from the profits of each individual tenant[1]. Both elements probably co-operated to produce the result: the operations performed for the benefit of the lord were ordered in a certain way partly because so many acres had to be tilled, so much hay and corn had to be reaped on the lord's estate; and partly because the peasant virgaters or cotters were known to work for themselves in a certain manner and considered capable of yielding so much as a percentage of their working power. But although we have a compromise before us in this respect, it must be noted that the relation between the parts and the whole is obviously different under the system of labour services from what it was under the farm-system. It has been pointed out that the food-rent arrangement was imposed from above without much trouble being taken to ascertain the exact value and character of the tributary units subjected to it. This later element is certainly very prominent in the customary labour-system, which on the whole appears to be constructed from below. Is it necessary to add that this second form of subjection was by no means the lighter one? The very differentiation of the burden means that the aristocratical power of the landlord has penetrated deep enough to attempt an exact evaluation of details.

Money-rents system.

I have had occasion so many times already to speak of the process of commutation, that there is no call now to explain the reasons which induced both landlords and peasants to exchange labour for money-rents. I have only

---

[1] Domesday of St. Paul's, 21 : ' Potest wainagium fieri cum tribus caruciis octo capitum cum consuetudinibus villate.'

to say now that the same remark which applied to the
passage from produce 'farms' to labour holds good as to the
passage from labour to money payments. There is no
break between the arrangements. In a general way the
money assessment follows, of course, as the third mode of
settling the relation between lord and tenant, and we may
say that *rentals* are as much the rule from the fourteenth
century downwards as *custumals* are the rule in the
thirteenth and earlier centuries. But if we take up the
Domesday of St. Paul's of 1222, or the Glastonbury Inquest
of 1189, or even the Burton Cartulary of the early twelfth
century, in every one of these documents we shall find a
great number of rent-paying tenants[1], and even a greater
number of people fluctuating, as it were, between labour
and rent. In some cases peasants passed directly from the
obligation of supplying produce to the payment of corresponding rents in money. The gradual exemption from
labour is even more apparent in the records. It is
characteristic that the first move is generally a substitution
of the money arrangement with the tacit or even the expressed provision that the assessment is not to be considered as permanent and binding[2]. It remains at the
pleasure of the lord to go back to the duties in kind. But
although such a retrogressive movement actually takes
place in some few cases, the general spread of money
payments is hardly arrested by these exceptional instances[3].

One more subject remains to be discussed. Is there

---

[1] The Templar's Book of 1185 at the Record Office (Q. R. Misc. Books,
N. 16) is already a rental in substance.

[2] Glastonbury Inqu. of 1189, p. 117: 'Nigellus capellanus tenet unam virgatam, sed illa virgata non solet ad operacionem redigi.   Cum dominus voluerit operabitur sicut alie.'   Rot. Hundr. ii. 815, a: '. . . dabit 8 solidos per
annum pro operibus suis qui solidi poterunt mutari in aliud servicium ad
valorem pro voluntate domini.'

[3] Glastonbury Inqu. of 1189, p. 29: 'G. de P. (tenet) unum mesuagium et
tres acras et dimidiam pro 2 solidis et facit sicut homines de Mera quando
sunt ad gabulum. Hoc tenementum non solet esse ad opus.' 116: 'Leviva
vidua tenet dimidiam hidam; unam virgatam tenet eodem servitio; aliam tenet
pro gabulo et non potest ad operationem poni sicut alia.'

Influence of social distinction on the distribution of duties. in the surveys any marked difference between different classes of the peasantry in point of rural duties?

An examination of the surveys will show at once that the free and the servile holdings differ very materially as to services, quite apart from their contrast, in point of legal protection and of casual exactions such as marriage fines, heriots, and the like. The difference may be either in the kind of duties or in their quantity. Both may be traced in the records. If we take first the diversities in point of quality we shall notice that on many occasions the free tenants are subjected to an imposition on the same occasion as the unfree, but their mode of acquitting themselves of it is slightly different—they have, for instance, to bring eggs when the villains bring hens. The object cannot be to make the burden lighter; it amounts to much the same, and so the aim must have been to keep up the distinctions between the two classes. It is very common to require the free tenants to act as overseers of work to be performed by the rest of the peasantry. They have to go about or ride about with rods and to keep the villains in order. Such an obligation is especially frequent on the boon-days (*precariae*), when almost all the population of the village is driven to work on the field of the lord. Sometimes free householders, who have dependent people resident under them, are liberated from certain payments; and it may be conjectured that the reason is to be found in the fact that they have to superintend work performed by their labourers or inferior tenants [1]. All such points are of small importance, however, when compared with the general opposition of which I have been speaking several times. The free and the servile holdings are

---

[1] Bury St. Edmund's Reg., Harl. MSS. 3977, f. 82, d: 'Omnes liberi et non liberi dabunt festivales exceptis illis liberis qui habent residentes sub illos.' Glastonbury Cart., Wood MSS. i. f. 176, b: 'Abbas et conventus remiserunt R. de W. . . . omnia carriagia . . . nec non et illas custodias quae predictus R. et antecessores sui personaliter facere consueverunt cum virga sua super bederipas ipsorum . . . et super arruras precarias que ei fieri debent in manerio de Pultone.'

chiefly distinguished by the fact that the first pay rent and the last perform labour.

Whenever we come to examine closely the reason under-lying the cases when the classification into servile and free is adopted, we find that it generally resolves itself into a contrast between those who have to serve, in the original sense of the term, and those who are exempted from actual labour-service. Being dependent nevertheless, these last have to pay rent. I need not repeat that I am speaking of main distinctions and not of the various details bound up with them. In order to understand thoroughly the nature of such diversities, let us take up a very elaborate description of duties to be performed by the peasants in the manor of Wye, Kent, belonging to the Abbey of Battle[1]. Of the sixty-one yokes it contains thirty are servile, twenty-nine are free, and two occupy an inter-mediate position. The duties of the two chief classes of tenants differ in many respects. The servile people have to pay rent and so have the free, but while the first con-tribute to make up a general payment of six pounds, each yoke being assessed at seven shillings and five-pence, the free people have to pay as much as twenty-three shillings and seven-pence per yoke. Both sets have to perform ploughings, reapings, and carriage duties, but the burden of the servile portion is so much greater in regard to the carriage-work, that the corresponding yokes sometimes get their very name from it, they are *juga averagiantia*, while the free households are merely bound to help a few times during the summer. Every servile holding has a certain number of acres of wood assigned to it, or else corresponding rights in the common wood, while the free tenants have to settle separately with the lord of the manor. And lastly, the relief for every unfree yoke is fixed at forty pence, and for every free one is equal to the annual rent. This comparison of duties shows that the peasants called free were by no means subjected to very light burdens : in fact it looks almost as if they were

Free and servile duties as rent and labour.

[1] Custumals of Battle Abbey (Camd. Soc.), p. 122.

more heavily taxed than the rest. Still they were exempted from the most unpopular and inconvenient labour-
services.

Altogether, the study of rural work and rents leads to the
same conclusion as the analysis of the legal characteristics
of villainage. The period from the Conquest onwards
may be divided into two stages. In later times, that is
from the close of the thirteenth century downwards, the
division between the two great classes of tenants and
tenements, a contrast strictly legal, is regulated by the
material test of the certainty or uncertainty of the service
due, and the formal test of the mode of conveyance. In
earlier times the classification depends primarily on the
economic relation between the manorial centre and the
tributary household, labour is deemed servile, rent held to
be free. It is only by keeping these two periods clearly
distinct, that one is enabled to combine the seemingly
conflicting facts in our surveys. If we look at the most
ancient of these documents, we shall have to admit that
a rent-paying holding is free, nevertheless it would be
wrong to infer that when commutation became more or
less general, classification was settled in the same way.
A servile tenement no longer became free because rent
was taken instead of labour; it was still held 'at the will
of the lord,' and conveyed by surrender and admittance.
When all holdings were fast exchanging labour for rent,
the old notions had been surrendered and a new basis for
classification found in those legal incidents just mentioned.
The development of copyhold belongs to the later period,
copyhold being mostly a rent-paying servile tenure.
Again, if we turn to the earlier epoch we shall have to
remember that the contrast between labour and rent is
not to be taken merely as a result of commutation. Local
distinctions are fitted on to it in a way which cannot be
explained by the mere assumption that every settlement
of a rent appeared in the place of an original labour obligation. The contrast is primordial, as one may say, and
based on the fact that the labour of a subject appears

directly subservient to the wants and arrangements of the superior household, while the payment of rent severs the connexion for a time and leaves each body to move in its own direction till the day when the tributary has to pay again.

There can be no doubt also that the more ancient surveys disclose a difference in point of quantity between free and servile holdings, and this again is a strong argument for the belief that free socage must not be considered merely as an emancipated servile tenancy. Where there has been commutation we must suppose that the labour services cannot have been more valuable than the money rent into which they were changed. The free rent into which labour becomes converted is nothing but the price paid for the services surrendered by the lord. It must have stood higher, if anything, than the real value of the labour exchanged, because the exchange entailed a diminution of power besides the giving up of an economic commodity. No matter that ultimately the quit-rents turned out to the disadvantage of the lord, inasmuch as the buying strength of money grew less and less. This was the result of a very long process, and could not be foreseen at the time when the commutation equivalents were settled. And so we may safely lay down the general rule, that when there is a conspicuous difference between the burdens of assessment of free and unfree tenants, such a difference excludes the idea that one class is only an emancipated portion of the other, and supposes that it was from the first a socially privileged one. The Peterborough Black Book, which, along with the Burton Cartulary, presents the most curious instance of an early survey, describes the services of socmen on the manors of the abbey as those of a clearly privileged tenantry[1]. The

[margin note:] Difference in quantity between the impositions of free and unfree population.

---

[1] Black Book of Peterborough (Camden Ser.), 164: 'In Scotere et Scaletoys sunt undecim carrucatae ad geldum Regis et 24 plenarii villani . . . Plenarii villani operantur duobus diebus in ebdomada . . . Et ibi sunt 29 sochemanni et operantur uno die in ebdomada per totum annum et in Augusto duobus diebus. Et isti villani et omnes sochemanni habent 21 carrucas et omnes arant una vice ad hyvernage et una ad tremeis.'

interesting point is, that these socmen are even subjected to week-work and not distinguishable from villains so far as concerns the quality of their services. Nevertheless the contrast with the villains appears throughout the Cartulary and is substantiated by a marked difference in point of assessment : a socman has to work one or two days in the week when the villain is made to work three or four.

Three main points seem established by the survey of rural work and rents.

1. Notwithstanding many vexatious details, the impositions to which the peasantry had to submit left a considerable margin for their material progress. This system of customary rules was effectively provided against general oppression.

2. The development from food-farms to labour organisation, and lastly to money-rents, was a result not of one-sided pressure on the part of the landlords, but of a series of agreements between lord and tenants.

3. The settlement of the burdens to which peasants were subjected depended to a great extent on distinctions as to the social standing of tenants which had nothing to do with economic facts.

CHAPTER IV.

THE LORD, HIS SERVANTS AND FREE TENANTS.

DESCRIPTIONS of English rural arrangements in the age Medieval rural system. we are studying always suppose the country to be divided into manors, and each of these manors to consist of a central portion called the demesne, and of a cluster of holdings in different tributary relations to this central portion. Whether we take the Domesday Survey, or the Hundred Rolls, or the Custumal of some monastic institution, or the extent of lands belonging to some deceased lay lord, we shall again and again meet the same typical arrangement. I do not say that there are no instances swerving from this beaten track, and that other arrangements never appear in our records. Still the general system is found to be such as I have just mentioned, and a very peculiar system it is, equally different from the ancient *latifundia* or modern plantations cultivated by gangs of labourers working on a large scale and for distant markets, from peasant ownership scattered into small and self-dependent households, and even from the conjunction between great property and farms taken on lease and managed as separate units of cultivation.

The characteristic feature of the medieval system is the close connexion between the central and dominant part and the dependent bodies arranged around it. We have had occasion to speak in some detail of these tributary bodies—it is time to see how the lord's demesne which acted as their centre was constituted.

Bracton mentions as the distinguishing trait of the The home-farm. demesne, that it is set aside for the lord's own use, and ministers to the wants of his household[1]. Therefore it is sometimes called in English 'Board Lands.' The definition is not complete, however, because all land occupied by the owner himself must be included under the name of demesne, although its produce may be destined not for his personal use, but for the market. 'Board lands' are only one species of domanial land, so also are the 'Husfelds' mentioned in a charter quoted by Madox[2]. This last term only points to its relation to the house, that is the manorial house. And both denominations are noteworthy for their very incompleteness, which testifies indirectly to the restricted area and to the modest aims of domanial cultivation. Usually it lies in immediate connexion with the manorial house, and produces almost exclusively for home consumption.

This is especially true as to the arable, which generally forms the most important part of the whole demesne land. There is no exit for a corn trade, and therefore everybody raises corn for his own use, and possibly for a very restricted local market. Even great monastic houses hold only 300 or 400 acres in the home farm; very rarely the number rises to 600, and a thousand acres of arable in one manor is a thing almost unheard of[3]. Husbandry on a large scale appears only now and then in places where sheep-farming prevails, in Wiltshire for instance. Exceptional value is set on the demesne when fisheries are connected with it or salt found on it[4].

---

[1] Bracton, iv. 9. 5, f. 263 : 'Est autem dominicum quod quis habet ad mensam suam et proprie, sicut sunt Bordlands Anglice.'

[2] Madox, History of the Exchequer, i. 407 : 'Concessisse unam virgatam terrae in Husfelds, scilicet 20 acras uno anno et 20 acras alio.'

[3] In Beauchamp, a manor of St. Paul's, London, the home farm is one of the largest. Domesday of St. Paul's, 28 : 'In dominico tam de wainagio veteri quam de novo essarto 676 acre terre arabilis et de prato 18 acre et de pastura 8 acras [sic] et in magno bosco bene vestito quinquies 20 acre et in duabus granis Dorile et Langele 16 acras.'

[4] As to the economic aspects of the subject, see Thorold Rogers, History of Agriculture and Prices; Ashley, Introduction to the Study of Economic History; and Cunningham, Growth of Industry and Commerce (2nd ed.).

The following description of Bockyng in Essex [1], a Bockyng, Essex. manor belonging to the Chapter of Christ Church, Canterbury, may serve as an example of the distribution and relative value of demesne soil. The cartulary from which it is drawn was compiled in 1309.

The manorial house and close cover five acres. The grass within its precincts which may serve as food for cattle is valued at 8*d.* a year. Corn is also sold there to the value of 12*d.* a year, sometimes more and sometimes less, according to the quantity sown. The orchard provides fruit and vegetables worth 13*s.* 4*d.* a year ; the duty levied from the swine gives 6*d.*

The pigeon-house is worth 4*d.*

Two mills, 7*l.* 1*s.* 8*d.*

A fishery, 12*d.*

A wood called Brekyng Park, containing 480 acres, and the brushwood there is worth 40*s.*

Grass in the wood 12*d.*, because it grows only in a few places.

Pannage duty from the swine, 10*s.*

Another wood called Le Flox contains 10 acres, and the brushwood is worth 6*d.*

Pannage from the swine, 6*d.*

Grass, 6*d.*

Arable, in all fields, 510 acres, the acre being assessed at 6*d.* all round.

Each plough may easily till one acre a day, if four horses and two oxen are put to it.

Two meadows, one containing eight acres, of which every single acre yields 4*s.* a year ; the other meadow contains seven acres of similar value.

Pasture in severalty—30 acres, at 12*d.* an acre.

Of these, 16 acres are set apart for oxen and horses, and 14 for cows.

Some small particles of pasture leased out to the tenants, 4*s.*

The prior and the convent are lords of the common

[1] Harl. MSS. 1006, f. 2.

pasture in Bockyng, and may send 100 sheep to these commons, and to the fields when not under crop. Value 20s.

As important an item in the cultivation of the home farm as the soil itself is afforded by the plough-teams. The treatises on husbandry give very minute observations on their composition and management. And almost always we find the manorial teams supplemented by the *consuetudines villae,* that is by the customary work performed on different days by the peasantry[1]. As to this point the close connexion between demesne and tributary land is especially clear ; but after all that has been said in the preceding chapter it is hardly necessary to add that it was not only the ploughing-work that was carried on by the lord with the help of his subjects.

The demesne and the village.

As a matter of fact, villages without a manorial demesne or without some dependence from it are found only exceptionally and in those parts of England where the free population had best kept its hold on the land, and where the power of the lord was more a political than an economical one (Norfolk and Suffolk, Lincoln, Northumberland, Westmoreland, etc.[2]). And there are hardly any cases at all of the contrary, that is of demesne land spreading over the whole of a manor. Tillingham, a manor of St. Paul's, London, comes very near it[3]: it contains 300 acres as home farm, and only 30 acres of villain land. But as a set-off, a considerable part of the demesne is distributed to small leaseholders.

---

[1] Ramsey Cart. (Rolls Series), i. 282 : ' Quae culturae coli possunt sufficienter cum tribus carucis propriis et consuetudine carrucarum ville et duabus precariis carucis (corr. carucarum?), quae consuetudo ad valentiam trium carucarum aestimatur.' Domesday of St. Paul's, 13, 14 : ' Potest ibidem fieri wainagium cum 5 carucis quarum tres habent 4 boves et 4 equos et due singule 6 equos cum consuetudinibus villate propter (corr. praeter?) dominicum de Luffehale et alia quae remota sunt, que tamen sunt in dispositione firmarii.' Cf. Glastonbury Inqu. of 1189, pp. 28, 107.

[2] As an instance, Bury St. Edmund's Register, Harl. MSS. 743, f. 194 : ' (Bucham) abbas S[ti] Edmundi capitalis dominus . . . tenet in eadem villa preter homagium liberorum nihil.'

[3] Domesday of St. Paul's, 58.

It must be noted that, as a general rule, the demesne arable of the manor did not lie in one patch apart from the rest, but consisted of strips intermixed with those of the community[1]. This fact would show by itself that the original system, according to which property and husbandry were arranged in manorial groups, was based on a close connexion between the domanial and the tributary land. We might even go further and point out that the mere facilities of intercourse and joint work are not sufficient to account for this intermixture of the strips of the lord and of the homage. The demesne land appears in fact as a share in the association of the village, a large share but still one commensurate with the other holdings. In two respects this subjection to a higher unit must necessarily follow from the intermixture of strips: inasmuch as the demesne consists of plots scattered in the furlongs of the township, it does not appropriate the best soil or the best situation, but has to gather its component parts in all the varied combinations in which the common holdings have to take theirs. And besides this, the demesne strips were evidently meant to follow the same course of husbandry as the land immediately adjoining them, and to lapse into undivided use with such land when the 'defence' season was over. Separate or private patches exempted from the general arrangement are to be found on many occasions, but the usual treatment of demesne land in the thirteenth century is certainly more in conformity with the notion that the lord's land is only one of the shares in the higher group of the village community.

The management of the estate, the collection of revenue, the supervision of work, the police duties incumbent on the manor, etc., required a considerable number of foremen and workmen of different kinds[2]. Great lords usually confided

'Ministeriality.'

---

[1] Eynsham Inqu., Chapter of Christ Church, Oxford, N. 27, f. 5, a : 'Robertus Clement ... tenet de dominicis superius mensuratis dum domino placet unam selionem apud Weylond atte Wyche, unam selionem apud Blechemanfurlong, tres seliones in Wellefurlong, et unam selionem apud Groueacres pro 11 solidis per annum.'

[2] It is well known that the second book of Fleta contains a sketch of the

the general supervision of their estates to a *seneschal*, steward or head manager, who had to represent the lord for all purposes, to preside at the manorial courts, to audit accounts, to conduct sworn inquests and extents, and to decide as to the general husbandry arrangements. In every single manor we find two persons of authority. The bailiff or beadle was an outsider appointed by the lord, and had to look to the interests of his employer, to collect rents and enforce duties, to manage the home farm, to take care of the domanial cattle, of the buildings, agricultural implements, etc. These functions were often conferred by agreement in consideration of a fixed rent, and in this case the steward or beadle took the name of *firmarius* [1]. By his side appears the reeve, or *praepositus*, nominated from among the peasants of a particular township, and mostly chosen by them [2]. Manorial instructions add sometimes that no villain has a right to hold aloof from such an appointment, if it is conferred on him [3]. The reeve acts as the representative of the village community, as well in regard to the lord as on public occasions. He must, of course, render help to the steward in all the various duties of the latter. The reeve has more especially to superintend the performance of labour imposed on the

functions of manorial officers. In thirteenth-century MSS. we find also a special tract on the matter entitled de Senescalcia. See Cunningham, Growth of Industry and Commerce (2nd ed.), p. 222. Let it be understood that I do not attempt an exhaustive survey of the subject, but only a general indication of its bearings.

[1] Domesday of St. Paul's, 122; forms of agreement by which the manors were let to farm in the twelfth century: 'Haec est conventio inter capitulum Lundoniensis ecclesiae beati Pauli et Robertum filium Alwini sacerdotis. Capitulum concedit ei Wicham manerium suum ad firmam quamdiu vixerit et inde bene servierit. Primo quidem anno pro 58 solidis et 4d. et pro una parva firma panis et cervisiae cum denariis elemosine. Deinceps vero singulis annis pro duabus firmis brevibus panis et cervisiae.'

[2] Exch. Q. R. Miscell.: 'Consuetudines de Aysle: memorandum quod homagium debet eligere prepositum et dominus manerii potest eum retinere. ... Et memorandum quod homines debent habere pastorem ovilis per electionem curie.'

[3] The duty of serving as reeve is therefore often treated as one of the characteristic marks of serfdom; e. g. Cambr. Univ., Gg. iv. 4, f. 26.

peasantry. Manorial ploughings, reapings, and the other like operations are conducted by him, sometimes with the help of the free tenants in the place. Of the public duties of the reeve we have had occasion to speak. Four men, acting as representatives of the village, accompany him.

Next after the reeve comes, on large estates, the *messor*, who takes charge of the harvest, and sometimes acts as collector of fines imposed for the benefit of the lord[1]. The *akermanni* or *carucarii* are the leaders of the unwieldy ploughs of the time[2], and they are helped by a set of drivers and boys who have to attend to the oxen or horses[3]. Shepherds for every kind of cattle are also mentioned[4], as well as keepers and warders of the woods and fences[5]. In the Suffolk manors of Bury St. Edmund's we find the curious term *lurard* to designate a person superintending the hay harvest[6].

By the side of a numerous staff busy with the economic management of the estate, several petty officers are found to be concerned with the political machinery of the manor. The duty to collect the suitors of the hundred and of the county court is sometimes fulfilled by a special 'turn-bedellus[7].' A 'vagiator' (vadiator?) serves writs and dis-trains goods for rents[8]. The carrying of letters and orders is very often treated as a service imposed on particular tenements. It must be noted that sometimes all these duties are intimately connected with those of the husbandry

[1] Harl. MSS. 1006, f. 18: 'Debet esse messor ad frumentum et amercia-menta domini colligendum.'

[2] Shaftesbury Inqu., Harl. MSS. 61, f. 60: 'Arator . . . debet invenire omnia instrumenta aratri ante rotas.'

[3] Ibid., f. 54: 'Bubulci et gadince.' Glastonbury Inqu. of 1189: 'Petras bovarius . . . custodit boves domini et vadit ad aratrum.'

[4] 'Hereward,' Glastonbury Inqu., 24, 105, etc.; Domesday of St. Paul's, 53.

[5] Cartul. of Battle (Camden Ser.), f. 39, b: 'wodeward.'

[6] Bury St. Edmund's Reg., Cambr. Univ., Gg. iv. 4, f. 322, a: 'Ad istud pertinet tenementum falcacio claustri sed cum falce lurardi.'

[7] Glastonbury Inqu. of 1189, p. 36: 'Reginaldus thernebedellus tenet dimidiam virgatam terre et summonet homines ad comitatum et hundre-dum.'

[8] Ibid., 7; cf. 156.

system and imposed on all the officers of the demesne who own horses [1].

A third category is formed by the house-servants, who divide among themselves the divers duties of keeping accounts, waiting on the lord personally, taking charge of the wardrobe, of the kitchen, etc. The military system and the lack of safety called forth a numerous retinue of armed followers and guards. All-in-all a mighty staff of *ministeriales*, as they were called in Germany, came into being. In England they are termed sergeants and servants, *servientes*. In Glastonbury Abbey there were sixty-six servants besides the workmen and foremen employed on the farm [2]. Such a number was rendered necessary by the grand hospitality of the monastery, which received and entertained daily throngs of pilgrims. In Bury St. Edmund's the whole staff was divided into five departments, and in each department the employments were arranged according to a strict order of precedence [3].

Formation of the class. The material for the formation of this vast and important class was supplied by the subject population of the estates. The Gloucester manorial instruction enjoins the stewards to collect on certain days the entire grown-up population and to select the necessary servants for the different callings. It is also enacted that the men should not be left without definite work, that in case of necessity they should be moved from one post to the other [4], etc.

---

[1] Ely Cart., Cotton MSS., Claudius, C. xi, f. 15, d : ' Debet namiare cum bedello et ceteris avermannis' (men provided with horses). Glastonbury Inqu. of 1189, p. 31 : ' Robertus de Eadwic sequitur hundredum et comitatum ad suum costum . . . Custodit preces arature et messis et debet adjuvare ad namia capienda infra hundredum et est quietus de pannagio.'

[2] Glastonbury Cart., Wood MSS., i. f. 92, 93; Compoti of Nicholas de Wedergrave, who had charge of the monastery from the 21st of November, 16 Edward II, till the 12th of March, 16 Edw. II, as to the liberaciones et conredia servientium : ' Et quod retinuit et necessarie oportuit retinere in eadem abbathia 60 ministros et servientes pro hospitalitate et aliis obsequiis faciendis in eadem abbathia.'

[3] Bury St. Edmund's Register, Harl. MSS., 743, f. 260: ' Scriptum Johannis Northwold abbatis de quinque servanciis' (A. D. 1294); f. 260, d : ' . . . de minutis officiis.'

[4] Gloucester Cart. (Rolls Ser.), iii. 213, 214 : ' Hoc intellecto quod quando-

The requirements of the manorial administration and of the lord's household opened an important outlet for the village people. Part of the growing population thus found employment outside the narrow channel of rural arrangements. The elder or younger brothers, as it might be, took service at the lord's court. The husbandry treatises of the thirteenth century go further and mention hired labourers as an element commonly found on the estate. We find, for instance, an elaborate reckoning of the work performed by gangs of such labourers hired for the harvest[1]. In documents styled 'Minister's Accounts' we may also find proof, that from the thirteenth century downwards the requirements of the lord's estate are sometimes met by hiring outsiders to perform some necessary kind of work. These phenomena have to be considered as exceptional, however, and in fact as a new departure.

The officers and servants were remunerated in various ways. Sometimes they were allowed to share in the profits connected with their charges. The swine-herd of Glastonbury Abbey, for instance, received one sucking-pig a year, the interior parts of the best pig, and the tails of all the others which were slaughtered in the abbey[2].

Remuneration of the class.

cumque placuerit loci ballivo amoveantur ab uno loco usque ad alium ad commodum domini infra terminum, salvis eisdem liberationibus et stipendiis prius provisis. Nec aliquis admittatur ad servitium domini sine saluis plegiis de fideliter serviendo et de omittenda satisfaciendo. Et moraturi tunc praemuniantur quod sibi provideant ad morandum . . . Item quod nullus famulus sit in curia cui plenum non deputetur officium. Ita quod si unum officium suo statui sit insufficiens in alio suppleatur defectus.'

[1] Merton College MSS., 91, f. 153 : 'Coment hom deyt alower oueraygnes en feyneson e en aust. Vous purrez bien auer sarcler 3 acres pur un dener e auer fauche lacre de pre pur 4 deners. . . . E vous devez sauer qe 5 hommes poent bien lyer et syer 2 acres le iour checune manere de ble qe luns plus e lautre mens. . . E la ou les 4 prenent 7 d. ob. le iour e le quint pur ceo qil est lyour le iour 2 d., donqe devez donner pur lacre 4 den. E pur ceo qen mouz de pays i ne sevent nient sier par lacre si poet hom sauer par siours e par les jurnees ceo qil fount. Mesqe vous reteignez les siours par les eez ceo est a sauer qe 5 hommes ou 5 femmes le quel qe vous voudrez que home apele 5 home font un eez, e 25 hommes font 5 eez, e poent 25 hommes shyer e lier 10 acres le iour entiers ouerables. . . . E si il accunte plus de jurnees qe ne fiert solon ceste acounte, si ne lor deuez pas alower.'

[2] Glastonbury Inqu. of 1189, 16, 17.

The chief scullion (*scutellarius*) had a right to all remnants of viands,—but not of game,—to the feathers and the bowels of geese [1]. Again, all the household and workmen constantly employed had certain quantities of food, drink, and clothing assigned to them [2]. Of one of the Glastonbury clerks we hear that he received one portion (*liberacio*) as a monk and a second as a servant, and that by reason of this last he was bound to provide the monastery with a goldsmith [3].

Those of the foremen and labourers of estates who did not belong to the immediate following of the lord and did not live in his central court received a gratification of another kind. They were liberated from the labour and payments which they would have otherwise rendered from their tenements [4]. The performance of the specific duties

[1] Glastonbury Inqu. of 1189, 14, 15. Cf. 13 : 'Ernaldus C. tempore episcopi Henrici habuit de quolibet preposito et quolibet firmario unum denarium ad natale pro taliis quas inveniet eis et morsuras candelarum.'

[2] Bury St. Edmund's Registrum Album, Cambr. Univ., Ee. iii. 60, f. 169, a : 'Isti habent biscum panem . . . grangiator, bedellus, lurard.' Glastonbury Cart., Wood MSS., 1, f. 126 : 'Et quod habeat . . . quolibet anno de tota vita sua unam robam de secta armigerorum nostrorum et unam robam competentem vel duas marcas pro uxore sua.' f. 142 : 'Concessisse Thome de Panis redditum unius robe annuatim recipiendi apud Glastoniam de secta armigerorum nostrorum videlicet quartam partem panni cum furrura agnina precii 2 solidorum uel duos solidos et si aliquo anno armigeris nostris robas non dederimus, volumus et concedimus . . . capiat illo anno . . . 20 solidos.' f. 146, d : '. . . tres panes, videlicet unum panem uocatum priestlof et alterum panem uocatum bastardlof et tercium panem uocatum seriauntlof de panetria predicti abbatis. . . . Et redditum unius robe . . . videlicet quartam partem unius panni de lecta officiariorum cum furrura agnina. Et pro predicta Aluecia uxore sua unam robam videlicet et octo virgas panni de secta secundorum clericorum cum furrura de scurellis.'

[3] Glastonbury Inqu. of 1189, p. 3. Cf. 16 : 'Vinitor habet talem liberacionem sicut prepositus grangie.'

[4] Cellarer's Register of Bury St. Edmund's, Cambr. Univ., Gg. iv. 4, f. 49, b : 'Inquisitio generalis dicit quod omnes gersumarii debent esse prepositi vel heywardi ad voluntatem domini nec se excusare possint racione alicuius tenementi ut patet in curia ibidem tenta anno regis Henrici 54to. Et notandum quod quicumque est prepositus aule de Bertone magna habebit infra manerium unum equum sumptibus domini cum una stotte et dimidiam acram ordei de meliore post terram compostatam et habebit stipulam pisei vel fabarum sine diminucione. Et si tenet duas terras custumarias plenas erit quietus pro operibus suis pro una terra et habebit ad natale

of administration took the place of the ordinary rural work
or rent, and in this way the service of the lord was feudal-
ised on the same principle as the king's service—it was
indissolubly connected with land-holding.

In manorial extents we come constantly across such
exempted tenements conceded without any rural obligations or with the reservation of a very small rent. It is
important to notice, that such exemptions, though temporary and casual at first, were ultimately consolidated by
custom and even confirmed by charters. A whole species
of free tenements, and a numerous one, goes back to such
privileges and exemptions granted to servants[1]. And so
this class of people, in the formation of which unfree elements are so clearly apparent, became one of the sources
in the development of free society. Such importance and
success are to be explained, of course, by the influence of
this class in the administration and economic management
of the estates belonging to the secular and ecclesiastical
aristocracy. It is very difficult at the present time to
realise the responsibility and strength of this element.
We live in a time of free contract, credit, highly mobilised
currency, easy means of communication, and powerful
political organisation. There is no necessity for creating
a standing class of society for the purpose of mediating
between lord and subject, between the military order
and the industrial order. Every feature of the medieval
system which tended to disconnect adjoining localities,
to cut up the country into a series of isolated units,

*Import-
ance of the
'minis-
teriality.'*

domini 1 den. ad oblacionem, die purificacionis unam candelam precii quarterii et ad carnipriuium debet participari una perna baconis inter omnes
famulos curie et ad pascham habebit 1 d. pro oblacione sua.'   Eynsham
Inqu. 6: 'Et quis eorum fuerit prepositus manerii, liber erit et quietus de
omnibus servitiis et consuetudinibus quas facit Johannes Mareys predictus,
auxiliis, pannagiis et denario Sᵗⁱ Petri exceptis.'

[1] Suffolk Court Rolls (Bodleian), 3: 'Terra debuit custodiam clauium
conuentus.' Ely Inqu., Cotton MSS., Claudius, C. xi. f. 26, a : 'Ad idem
tenementum pertinet esse coronarium et replegiare homines episcopi . . . et
facere capciones et disseisinas infra insulam et extra.' Shaftesbury Cart.,
Harl. MSS., 61, f. 60: 'Iacobus tenet 5 acras et servabit boves excepta
pestilencia et violencia.'

contributed at the same time to raise a class which acted
as a kind of nervous system, connecting the different
parts with a common centre and establishing rational
intercourse and hierarchical relations. The *libertini* had
to fulfil kindred functions in the ancient world, but
their importance was hardly so great as that of medieval
sergeants or *ministeriales*. We may get some notion of
what that position was by looking at the personal influence
and endowments of the chief servants in a great household
of the thirteenth century. The first cook and the gatekeeper of a celebrated abbey were real magnates who held
their offices by hereditary succession, and were enfeoffed
with considerable estates[1]. In Glastonbury five cooks
shared in the kitchen-fee[2]. The head of the cellar, the
gatekeeper, and the chief shepherd enter into agreements
in regard to extensive plots of land[3]. They appear as
entirely free to dispose of such property, and at every step
we find in the cartularies of Glastonbury Abbey proofs of
the existence of a numerous and powerful ' sergeant' class.
John of Norwood, Abbot of Bury St. Edmund's, had to

---

[1] Glastonbury Cart., Wood MSS., 1, f. 126 : ' Carta abbatis Galfridi facta
Willelmo Pasturel (pistori) de terris et tenementis in Glastonia : . . . reddendo inde per annum nobis et successoribus nostris unam rosam ad festum
nativitatis beati Johannis baptiste pro omni seruicio saluo seruicio regali
quantum pertinet ad tantam terram et salvo nobis et successoribus nostris
sectis curiarum nostrarum Glastonie sicut alii liberi eiusdem uille nobis
faciunt.' Glastonbury Inqu. of 1189, p. 10 : ' Galterus portarius tenet tenementum suum scilicet portam hereditarie cum his pertinentiis.' Shaftesbury
Cart., Harl. MSS., 61, f. 90 : ' Maria Dei gratia Abbatissa ecclesie Sti Ead-
wardi . . . Cum dilectus noster Thurstanus portarius portam nostram cum
omnibus ad eam pertinentibus toto tempore vite sue libere et quiete et iure
hereditario possedisset et Robertus filius et heres eius, dum post eum con-
tigit Thomam heredem eiusdem Roberti post decessum patris eius eo quod
minoris esset etatis in custodiam nostram deuenire . . . cumque ipsum diucius
tenuissemus in custodia pensatis predecessorum suorum obsequiis qui nobis
fideliter et laudabiliter ministrauerunt . . . iura ad ipsum et ad heredes eius
racione custodie dicte porte pertinencia . . . presenti pagina duximus ex-
primenda.'

[2] Glastonbury Inqu. of 1189, p. 13.

[3] Glastonbury Cart., Wood MSS., 1, f. 125 : ' Carta Murielle Pasturel facta
Galfrido Abbati Glastoniensi de tenementis et redditibus pertinentibus (ad)
servanciam de la lauandrie.'

resort to a regular *coup d'état* in order to displace the privileged families which had got hold of the offices and treated them as hereditary property[1]. In fact the great 'sergeants' ended by hampering their lords more than serving them. And the same fact of the rise of a 'ministerial' class may be noticed on every single estate, although it is not so prominent there as in the great centres of feudal life. The whole arrangement was broken by the substitution of the 'cash nexus' for more ancient kinds of economic relationship, and by the spread of free agreements: it is not difficult to see that both these facts acted strongly in favour of driving out hereditary and customary obligations.

We have considered the relative position of the unfree holdings, of the domanial land around which they were grouped, and of the class which had to put the whole machinery of the manor into action. But incidentally we had several times to notice a set of men and tenements which stood in a peculiar relation to the arrangement we have been describing: there were in almost every manor some free tenants and some free tenements that could not be considered as belonging to the regular fabric of the whole. They had to pay rents or even to perform labour services, but their obligations were subsidiary to the work of the customary tenants on which the husbandry of the manorial demesne leaned for support. From the economic point of view we can see no inherent necessity for the connexion of these particular free tenements with that particular manorial unit. The rent, large or small, could have been sent directly to the lord's household, or paid in some other manor without any perceptible alteration in favour of either party; the work, if there was such to

Free tenants in the manor.

---

[1] Bury St. Edmund's Reg., Harl. MSS., 743, f. 270 sqq. : '.... ita tamen quod nullus obedienciariorum predictorum potestatem habeat seu auctoritatem conferendi aliquod officium seu servanciam alicui ad terminum vite nec statum liberi tenementi alicui in premissis de cetero concedendi, set huiusmodi seruientes officia predicta necessaria ex collacione predictorum obedienciariorum habentes ad voluntatem obedienciariorum predictorum removeantur quociens necesse fuerit (A.D. 1294).'

perform, was without exception of a rather trifling kind, and could have been easily dispensed with and commuted for money. Several reasons may be thought of to explain the fact that free tenements are thus grouped along with the villain holdings and worked into that single unit, the manor. It may be urged that the division into manors is not merely and perhaps not chiefly an economic one, but that it reflects a certain political organisation, which had to deal with and to class free tenants as well as servile people. It may be conjectured that even from the economic point of view, although the case of free tenants would hardly have called the manorial unit into existence, it was convenient to use that class when once created for the grouping of villain land and work: why should the free tenants not join the divisions formed for another purpose but locally within easy reach and therefore conveniently situated for such intercourse with the lord as was rendered necessary by the character of the tenement? Again, the grouping of free tenants may have originated in a time when the connexion with the whole was felt more strongly than in the feudal period; it may possibly go back to a community which had nothing or little to do with subjection, and in which the free landowners joined for mutual support and organisation. It is not impossible to assume, on the other hand, that in many cases the free tenant was left in the manorial group because he had begun by being an unfree and therefore a necessary member of it. All such suppositions seem *prima facie* admissible and reasonable enough, and at the same time it is clear, that by deciding in favour of one of them or by the relative importance assigned to each we shall very materially influence the solution of interesting historical problems.

In order to appreciate rightly the position of the free tenements in the manor we have to examine whether these tenements are all of one and the same kind or not, and this must be done not from the legal standpoint whence it has already been reviewed, but in connexion with the practical

management of the estate. I think that a survey of the
different meanings which the term bears in our documents
must lead us to recognise three chief distinctions: first
there is free land which once formed part of the demesne
but has been separated from it; then there is the land
held by villagers outside the regular arrangements of the
rural community, and lastly there are ancient free holdings
of the same shape as the servile tenements, though differing from the latter in legal character. Each class will
naturally fall into subdivisions [1].

Under the first head it is to be observed that domanial
land very often lost its direct connexion with the lord's
household, and was given away to dependent people on
certain conditions. One of the questions addressed to the
juries by the Glastonbury Inquest of 1189 was prompted
by this practice: it was asked what demesne land had been
given out under free agreement or servile conditions, and
whether it was advantageous to keep to the arrangement
or not. One of the reasons which lay at the root of the
process has been already touched upon. Grants of domanial land occur commonly in return for services rendered
in the administration of the manor: reeves, ploughmen,
herdsmen, woodwards are sometimes recompensed in this
manner instead of being liberated from the duties incumbent on their holding. A small rent was usually affixed
to the plot severed from the demesne, and the whole
arrangement may be regarded as very like an ordinary
lease. An attenuated form of the same thing may be
noticed when some officer or servant was permitted to use
certain plots of domanial land during the tenure of his
office. It happened, for instance, that a cotter was entrusted to take care of a team of oxen belonging to the
lord or obliged to drive his plough. He might be repaid

Free tenements carved out of the demesne.

[1] A fourth class would be composed of tenements belonging to people
personally strange to the manor. Such 'forinsec' tenants were often
high and mighty persons who had nothing to do with the agrarian arrangements of the place. I do not speak of this class, because its position is
evidently an artificial one and of no importance for the internal organisation
of the manor, though interesting from the legal point of view.

either by leave to use the manorial plough on his own land
on specified occasions, or else by an assignment to him of
the crop on certain acres of the home farm [1].   Such
privileges are sometimes granted to villagers who do not
seem to be personally employed in the manorial administration, but such cases are rare, and must be due to special
reasons which escape our notice.

It is quite common, on the other hand, to find deficiencies in the normal holdings made up from the
demesne, e.g. a group of peasants hold five acres apiece
in the fields, and one of the set cannot receive his
full share : the failing acres are supplied by the demesne.   Even an entire virgate or half-virgate may be
formed in this way [2].   Sometimes a plot of the lord's land
is given to compensate the bad quality of the peasant's
land [3].   Of course, such surrenders of the demesne soil
were by no means prompted by disinterested philanthropy.
They were made to enable the peasantry to bear its burdens, and may-be to get rid of patches of bad soil or
ground that was inconveniently situated [4].   In a number
of cases these grants of demesne are actual leases, and
probably the result of hard bargains.

Inland.

However this might be, we find alongside of the estate
farmed for the lord's own account a great portion of the
demesne conceded to the villagers.   The term 'inland,'
which ought properly to designate all the land belonging
directly to the lord, is sometimes applied to plots which
have been surrendered to the peasantry, and so dis-

[1] Shaftesbury Inqu., Harl. MSS., 61, f. 45, d : 'Bubulci et Gadinci habent
sabbatum per ordinem carucarum donec eorum aretur terra.'   Glastonbury
Inqu. of 1189, p. 14 : 'Habebit etiam unam acram in autumpno uno anno apud
Strete et alio anno aliam acram apud Waltonam.'

[2] Glastonbury Inqu. of 1180, p. 46 : 'Stephanus fil. B. . . . de dominico
2 acras ad implementum terre sue.'   Cf. 39 : '3 acras ad perficiendum
suas 5 acras.'   Ibid. 81 : 'Norman de Pola dimidiam virgatam. Totum tenementum suum est de dominico.'

[3] Ibid. 39 : 'unam acram pro 4d. ad emendacionem terre sue.'

[4] Ibid. 27 : 'Robertus prepositus unam acram pro quodam soc quam
magister Alured tenuit, et dicunt juratores sic esse utilius quam esset in
cultura, quia longe est a dominico.'

tinguishes them from the regular customary holdings [1]. Such concessions of demesne land were not meant to create freehold tenements. Their tenure was precarious, the right of resumption was more expressly recognised in the case of such plots than in that of any other form of rural occupation, but the rights thus acquired tended to become perpetual, like everything else in this feudal world ; and as they were founded on agreement and paid for with money rents, their transformation into permanent tenures led to an increase of free tenements and not of villainage. We catch a glimpse of the process in the Domesday of St. Paul's. In 1240 a covenant was made between the Chapter of the Cathedral and its villagers of the manor of Beauchamp in Essex : in consequence of the agreement all the concessions of demesne land which had been made by the farmers were confirmed by the Chapter. The inquests show that those who farmed the estates had extensive rights as to the use of domanial land, but their dealings with the customary tenants were always open to a revision by the landlords. A confirmation like this Beauchamp one transferred the plot of demesne land into the class of free tenements, and created a tenure defensible at law [2]. All such facts increase in number and importance with the increase of population : under its pressure the area of direct cultivation for the lord is gradually lessened, and in many surveys we find a sort of belt formed around the home farm by the intrusion of the dependent people into the limits of the demesne [3]. The Domesday of St. Paul's is

---

[1] Domesday of St. Paul's, p. 118 : 'Anno domini 1240 Hugone de S[to] Eadmundo existente custode manerii de bello campo homines infrascripti tenentes terras de dominico quas vocant inlandes sine auctoritate capituli augmentaverunt redditum assizum, ut auctoritas capituli interveniret.'

[2] Ibid., p. 121 : 'Ricardus A. non feffatus nisi per firmarium consuevit dare annuatim 4 solidos ; de cetero dabit 4 sol. 7 den. et ob.' Cf. 52 : 'Subscripti sunt feffati de pasturis et frutectis usque ad titulum in proximum.' Add. MSS. 6159, f. 70 : 'Robertus Cob tenet 5 acras pro 25 d. per capitulum ut sit perpetuum.' Domesday of St. Paul's, 60 : 'Ricardus Wor 13 acras de terra arabili et unum mariscum 10 acrarum pro 4 sol. et 10 d. et per cartam capituli.'

[3] Ramsay Inqu., Cotton MSS., Galba E. x. fol. 49 : 'De nova purprestura

especially instructive on this point. Every estate shows one part of the lord's land in the possession of the peasants; sometimes the 'dominicum antiquitus assisum' is followed by 'terrae de novo traditae [1].'

Leases. A second group of free tenements consists of plots which did not belong either to the demesne or to the regular holdings in the fields, but lay by the side of these holdings and were parcelled out in varying quantity and under various conditions. We may begin by noticing the growth of leases. There is no doubt that the lease-system was growing in the thirteenth century, and that it is not adequately reflected in our documents. An indirect proof of this is given by the fact, that legal practice was labouring to discover means of protection for possession based on temporary agreement. The writ 'Quare ejecit infra terminum' invented by William Raleigh between 1236 and 1240 protected the possession of the 'tenant for term of years' who formerly had been regarded as having no more than a personal right enforceable by an action of covenant [2].

Manorial extents are sparing in their notices of leases because their object is to picture the distribution of ownership, and temporary agreements are beyond their range. But it is not uncommon to find a man holding a small piece of land for his life at a substantial rent. In this case his tenure is reckoned freehold, but still he holds under what we should now call a lease for life; the rent is a substantial return for the land that he has hired. That English law should regard these tenants under leases for life as freeholders, should, that is, throw them into one

50 acras . . . . quas 4 homines de dominico tenent.' Cf. Domesday of St. Paul's, 7. 20.

[1] Glastonbury Inqu. of 1189, 111 : ' Homines tenent septem virgatas terre de dominico de terra superius nominata, in parte erat liberata in tempore Henrici episcopi et in parte postea cum 7 acris quas Johannes clericus tenet.' Domesday of St. Paul's, 51: 'Tenentes de dominico antiquitus assiso.' 53 : ' Dicunt ecram quod terre de dominico de novo tradite satis utiliter tradite sunt.'

[2] Bracton, f. 220. See F. W. Maitland in the Harvard Law Review, iii. 173.

great class with tenants who have heritable rights, who do but military service or nominal service, who are in fact if not in name the owners of the land, is very remarkable ; hirers are mingled with owners, because according to the great generalisation of English feudalism every owner is after all but a hirer. Still we can mark off for economic purposes a class of tenants whom we may call 'life-lease-holders,' and we can see also a smaller class of leaseholders who hold for terms of years[1]. They often seem to owe their existence to the action of the manorial bailiffs or the farmers to whom the demesne has been let. We are told that such and such a person has 'entered' the tenement by the leave of such and such a farmer or bailiff, or that the tenement does not belong to the occupier by hereditary right, but by the bailiff's precept[2]. Remarks of that kind seem to mean that these rent-paying plots, liberated from servile duties, were especially liable to the interference of manorial officers. Limits of time are rarely mentioned, and leases for life seem to be the general rule[3].

---

[1] Rot. Hundr. ii. 336, a : 'In firmariis Johannes clericus tenet unam dimidiam virgatam terre ad terminum vitae suae pro 6 solidis per annum pro omni servicio.' Cf. 344, 346. Add. MSS. 6159, p. 70 : 'Hanc terram tenuit postmodum Thomas de Retendon et cum esset conventus a capitulo super ingressu in illa eo quod aliquando dixisset quod tenuit eam in feodo et non posset illud monstrare et recognovit se non habere ius in illa et reddidit eam quietam decano et capitulo qui postmodum concesserunt eandem terram cum manso ipsi Thomae tenendum de ipsis ad vitam suam tantum pro 2 sol. et 6 d. per annum.' Glastonbury Cart., Wood MSS., 1, 240, a : 'Magister Nicholaus de Malmesburi rector ecclesie de Cristemalforde . . . quod cum ego recepissem terram Ricardi de Leyweye in manerio de Cristemalforde . . . ad terminum 15 annorum et uiri religiosi Glastonie se opposuissent dicentes (dicenti?) me esse infeodatum de terra predicta, presenti scriptura confiteor me post predictos 18 annos in dicta terra non posse vendicare feodum nec liberum tenementum.'

[2] Glastonbury Inqu. of 1189, p. 79 : 'Johannes clericus . . . idem tenet unum cotsetle pro 16 d. pro omni servitio ex presto firmariorum Reginaldi scilicet de Waltona.' Domesday of St. Paul's, 94 : 'Gilbertus filius N. tenet tres virgatas in quas Gilbertus avus suus habuit ingressum per Theodoricum firmarium et modo reddit pro illis 36 solidos,' etc. Ibid. 40 : 'Thomas filius Godrici 22 acras pro 22 d. cuius medietas quondam Stephani, set habet eam per Ricardum firmarium.' Ibid. 25 : 'Walterus de mora 14 acras pro 4 solidis et 8 d. quondam Elvine, cui non attinet, cuius ingressus ignoratur.'

[3] Warwickshire Hundred Roll, Q. R. Misc. Books, 429, f. 13, b : 'Unde

The tenure is only in the course of formation, and by no means clearly defined. One does not even see, for instance, how the question of implements and stock was settled— whether they were provided by the landlord or by the tenant.

Forlands.   We feel our way with much greater security in another direction. The fields of the village contain many a nook or odd bit which cannot be squeezed into the virgate arrangement and into the system of work and duties connected with it. These '*subsecivae*,' as the Romans would have said, were always distributed for small rents in kind or in money[1]. The manorial administration may also exclude from the common arrangement entire areas of land which it is thought advantageous to give out for rent. Those who take it are mostly the same villagers who possess the regular holdings, but their title is different; in one case it is based on agreement, in the other on custom[2]. Plots of this kind are called *forlands*[3]. In close connexion with them we find the *essarts* or *assarts*—land newly reclaimed from the waste, and therefore not mapped out according to the original plan of possession and service. The Surveys often mark the different epochs of cultivation —the old and the new essarts[4]. The documents show

Willelmus de Wexton tenet unum cotagium libere ad terminum vite sue pro 4 solidis metens in autumpno per 1 diem.' A peculiar case is found in Glastonbury Inqu. of 1189, p. 69: 'Godwin palmer ... dimidiam virgatam ... ex tempore Roberti Abbatis per Thomam Cameriarum in cujus custodia fuit tunc manerium.' (Later hand): 'Iste Godwin dedit Henrico abbati dimidiam marcam et acrevit gabulum de 12 d. Hec convencio durabit dum dominus Abbas erit.'

[1] Domesday of St. Paul's, 25: 'Robertus filius Roger filii mercatoris unam acram et dimidiam pro 6 d. Item paruum augmentum pro 1 d.'

[2] Rot. Hundr. i. 451: 'Item Andreas prepositus tenet tantum terre sicut dictus Goscelinus villanus in omnibus. Et preter hoc tenet 3 acras pro libra cimini. Item Rogerus Doning facit sicut dictus Goscelinus in omnibus et debet domino suo pro uno seillione terre 6 d. per annum. Willelmus Mathew tenet eodem modo et preter hoc dat domino suo pro una acra 4 capones precii 6 den.'

[3] Worcester Cart., 27, a: 'de forlandis. De Thoma de G. pro 5 acris ... De acra quam Symon Carpenter tenuit. De Alicia vidua pro dimidia acra. De Johanne Roberti pro 4 buttis in crofta,' etc.

[4] Domesday of St. Paul's, p. 7 sqq.: '(Kenesworthe) isti tenent de domi-

also that the spread of the area under cultivation was effected in different ways; sometimes by a single settler with help from the lord [1], and sometimes by the entire village, or at any rate by a large group of peasants who club together for the purpose [2]. In the first case there was no reason for bringing the reclaimed space under the sway of the compulsory rotation of crops or the other regulations of communal agriculture. In the second, the distribution of the acres and strips among the various tenants was proportioned to their holdings in the ancient lands of the village. The rents on essart land seem very low, and no wonder: everywhere in the world the advance of cultivation has been made the starting-point of privileged occupation and light taxation. The Roman Empire introduced the *emphyteusis* as a contract in favour of the pioneers of cultivation, the French feudal law endowed the *hôtes* (*hospites*) on newly reclaimed land with all kinds of advantages. English practice is not so explicit on this point, but it is not difficult to gather from the Surveys that it was not blind to the necessity of patronising agricultural progress and encouraging it by favourable terms.

Of *mol-land* I have already spoken in another chapter. I will only point out now that this class of tenements appears to have been a very common one. Thirteenth-century surveys often describe certain holdings in two different ways—on the supposition of their paying rent, and also on that of their rendering labour-services; when they pay rent they pay so much, when they supply labour they supply so much. By the side of such holdings, which are wavering, as it were, between the two systems, we find the *terra assisa* or *ad censum*. This class,

nico et de essarto.' 21 sqq.: '(Erdelege) isti tenent de essarto veteri.' 75: '(Nastox) nova essarta.'

[1] Worc. Cart., 13: 'Idem tenet assartum pro medietate fructus et Prior invenit medietatem seminis.'

[2] The essarts of St. Paul, London, are divided into small portions among the peasantry, and the same men own them who are possessed of the regular holdings—all indications that the clearing was made according to a general plan and by the whole village.

to which molland evidently belongs, is distinguished from free tenure by the fact that its rent is regarded as a manorial arrangement; there is no formal agreement and no charter, and therefore no action before the king's courts to guard against disseisin or increase of services. In practice the difference is not felt very keenly, and these tenements gradually came to be regarded as 'free' in every sense. A characteristic feature of the movement may be noticed in the terms '*Socagium ad placitum*' and '*Socagium villani*[1].' These expressions occur in the documents, although they are not very common. It would be hard to explain them otherwise than from the point of view indicated just now. The tenement is paying a fixed and certain rent and therefore *socage*, but it is not defended by feoffment and charter; it is not recognised by law, and therefore it remains *at the will* of the lord and unfree[2]. The grant of a charter would raise it to the legal standing of free land.

Ancient freeholds.

Every student of manorial documents will certainly be struck by one well-marked difference between villain tenements and free tenements as described in the extents and surveys. The tenants in villainage generally appear arranged into large groups, in which every man holds, works, and pays exactly as his fellows; so that when the tenement and services of some one tenant have been described we then read that the other tenants hold similar tenements and owe similar services. On the other hand, the freeholds seem scattered at random without any definite plan of

---

[1] Worcester Cart., 47, 48: 'de soccagiis et forlandis villanorum.' Cf. 49.

[2] A curious species of land tenure is the so-called *rofliesland* (rough lease?). Glastonbury Inqu. of 1189, 29: 'W. de W. tenet unum Rofliesland eodem servicio; tota terra est in voluntate domini.' 65: 'W. tenet 5 acras et filius suus 5 acras; unus eorum tenet carucam domini, alter fugat boves. Terra quam filius eius tenet est Rofles.' 66: 'R. fil. A. tenet unum ferdel de Rofliesland pro 2 solidis pro omni servicio per camerarium.' 90: 'Idem tenet dimidiam virgatam de rofliesland pro duobus solidis, quod utilius esset edificari.' Cf. 164, sub voce Roflesland. The name is found often in old leases in Wilts and Somerset as a 'Rough lease' or 'Rowlease.' I think the term must indicate one of those informal agreements of which I speak in the text. See also Reg. Malmesbur. ii. 9, 10.

arrangement, parcelled up into unequal portions, and subjected to entirely different duties. One man holds ten
acres and pays three shillings for them ; another has eight
and a half acres and gives a pound of pepper to his lord ;
a third is possessed of twenty-three acres, pays 4s. 6d.,
and sends his dependants to three boonworks ; a fourth
brings one penny and some poultry in return for his one
acre. The regularity of the villain system seems entirely
opposed to the capricious and disorderly phenomena of
free tenure.

And this fact seems naturally connected with some
remarkable features of social organisation. No wonder
that free land is cut up into irregular plots : we know that
it may be divided and accumulated by inheritance and
alienation, whereas villain land is held together in rigid
unity by the fact that it is, properly speaking, the lord's
and not the villain's land. Besides, all the variations of
free tenure which we have discussed hitherto have one
thing in common, they are produced by express agreement
between lord and tenant as to the nature and amount of
services required from the tenant. Whether we take the
case of a villain receiving a few acres in addition to his
holding, or that of a servant recompensed by the grant of
a privileged plot, or that of a peasant confirmed in the
possession of soil newly reclaimed from the waste, or that
of a bondman who has succeeded in liberating his holding
from the burdensome labour service of villainage, in all
these instances we come across the same fundamental
notion of a definite agreement between lord and tenant.
And again, the capricious aspect of free tenements seems
well in keeping with the fact that they are produced by
separate and private agreements, by consecutive grants
and feoffments, while the villain system of every manor is
mapped out at one stroke, and managed as a whole by the
lord and his steward. This contrast between the two
arrangements may even seem to widen itself into a difference between a communal organisation which is servile,
and a system of freeholding which is not communal. All

these inferences are natural enough, and all have been actually drawn.

A close inspection of the Surveys will, however, considerably modify our first impressions, and suggest conclusions widely different from those which I have just now stated. The importance of the subject requires a detailed discussion, even at the risk of tediousness. I shall take my instances from the Hundred Rolls, as from a survey which reflects the state of things in central counties and gives an insight into the organisation of secular as well as ecclesiastical estates.

We need not dwell much on the observation that the servile tenements sometimes display no perfect regularity. Sometimes the burdens incumbent on them are not quite equal. Sometimes again the holdings themselves are not quite equal. In Fulborne, Cambridgeshire, e. g., the villains of Alan de la Zuche are assessed very irregularly [1], although their tenements are described as virgates and half-virgates. Of course, the general character of the virgate system remains unaltered by these exceptional deviations, which may be easily explained by the consideration that the social order was undergoing a process of change. The disruption of some of the villain holdings and the modification of certain duties are perhaps less strange than the fact that such alterations should be so decidedly exceptional. Still, the occurrence of irregularities even within the range of villainage warns us not to be too hasty in our inferences about free tenements ; it shows, at any rate, that irregularities may well arise even where there has once been a definite plan, and that it is worth while to enquire whether some traces of such an original plan may not still be discovered amidst the apparent disorder of free tenements.

Free virgates.

And a little attention will show us many cases in which

[1] Rot. Hundr. ii. 437: 'Symon et Petrus . . . tenent de eodem Alano unam virgatam terre et solvunt per annum 8 s. et debent arare tres dimidias acras terre . . . Adam Swetcoc tantum tenet de predicto Alano et solvit 9 sol. 3 d. et facit per omnia sicut predicti Simon et Petrus et tantum plus quod debet metere . . . Thomas Alwyne tantum tenet de predicto Alano et solvit 8 s. et debet arare 3 acras avene et metere duas acras,' etc. Cf. 446, 473.

free tenements are arranged on the virgate system. There is hardly any need for quotations on this point: the Hundred Rolls of all the six counties of which we possess surveys, supply an unlimited number of instances. True, fundamental divisions of land and service may often be obscured and confused by the existence of plots which do not fit into the system; but as in the case of servile tenements we occasionally find irregularities, so in the case of free tenements we often see that below the superficial irregularities there lie traces of an ancient plan. The manor of Ayllington (Elton), Huntingdonshire, belonging to the Abbey of Ramsey, presents a good example in point[1]. It is reckoned to contain thirteen hides and a half, each hide comprising six virgates, and each virgate twenty-four acres. The actual distribution of the holdings squares to a fraction with this computation, if we take into the reckoning the demesne, the free and the villain tenements. Three hides are in the lord's hand, one is held by a large tenant, John of Ayllington, eleven virgates and a half by other freeholders, forty-two virgates and a half by the villains; the grand total being exactly thirteen hides. The numerous cotters are not taken into account, and evidently left 'outside the hides' (extra hidam); this is a very common thing in the Surveys. If we neglect them, and turn to the holdings in the 'hidated' portion of the manor, we shall notice that the greater part of the free tenements are arranged on the same system as the servile tenements. We find six free tenants with a virgate apiece, one with half a virgate, three with a virgate and a half, and three jointly possessed of two virgates. In contrast with this principal body of tenants stand several small freeholders endowed with irregular plots reckoned in acres and so much varying in size that it is quite impossible to arrange them according to any plan, not to speak of the virgate system. But these small tenants are all sub-tenants enfeoffed by the principal freeholders whose own tenements are distributed into regular agrarian unity. It is easy to see that

[1] Rot. Hundr. ii. 656.

even when the stock of free tenancies stood arranged according to a definite plan, deviations from this plan would easily arise owing to new feoffments made by the lord out of the demesne land or out of the waste [1]. What I am concerned to say is, not that the Hundred Rolls show a distribution of free holdings quite as regular as that of the servile tenements, but that amidst all the irregularities of the freehold plots we frequently come across unmistakable traces of a system similar to that which prevailed on villain soil. These traces are not always of the same kind, and present various gradations. In a comparatively small number of instances the duties imposed on the shareholders are equal, or nearly so ; much more often the rent and labour rendered by them to the lord vary a great deal, although their tenements are equal. The Ayllington instance, quoted above, belongs to the former class, but the proportionate distribution of duties is somewhat obscured by the fact that part of them is reckoned in labour. The normal rent is computed at six shillings per virgate [2], though there are a few noticeable exceptions, but the duty of ploughing is imposed according to two different standards, and it is not easy to reduce these to unity. The freeholders of one group have to plough eight acres per virgate for the lord, while for the members of the other group the ploughing work is reckoned in the same way as in the case of the villains, each placing his team at the disposal of the lord one day

---

[1] In Sawtrey le Moyne and Sawtrey Beaumeys (659, 660) the free tenants are partly virgaters and half-virgaters, partly holders of small plots. I need not say that all my quotations are of cases which might be multiplied to any extent.

[2] The undated Survey of the Ramsey Cartulary (ii. 487) has a different reckoning : 'Item omnes positi ad censum qui tenent virgatam, vel dimidiam virgatam, dabunt per annum pro virgata octo solidos, vel pro dimidia virgata quatuor solidos.' There are several other small discrepancies with the Hundred Roll description. The document endorsed in the Cartulary seems the earlier one, and the differences have to be explained in all probability by some attempt on the part of the Monastery to set up a higher rent at the time of its compilation. One does not see the slightest ground for any reduction of the rent in process of time. Generally speaking, the conditions described in the Hundred Roll are more irregular than those mentioned in the Cartulary.

of every week from Michaelmas to the 1st of August, four
weeks being excepted in honour of Christmas, Easter, and
Trinity[1]. Ravenston, in Buckinghamshire, is a much
clearer example. Twelve villains hold of the Prior of
Ravenston twelve acres each, and their service is worth
eighteen shillings per holding ; four villains hold six acres
each, and their service is valued at nine shillings. One
free tenant has twelve acres and pays sixteen shillings ;
six have six acres each, and pay seven shillings. There
are three other tenants whose duties cannot be brought
within the system[2]. The portion of Fulborne, in Cambridgeshire, belonging to Baldwin de Maneriis, may also serve
as an illustration of an almost regular distribution of land
and service among the freeholders[3]. Instances in which
the duties, although not exactly, are still very nearly equal,
are very frequent. In Radewelle, Bedfordshire, the mean
rent of the six is two shillings per half-virgate, although
the villains perform service to the amount of eight shillings
per virgate[4]. Bidenham, Bedfordshire, also presents an assessment of four shillings per free virgate[5]. In that part of
Fulborne which is owned by Alan de la Zuche the virgates
and half-virgates of the free holders are variously rented ;
but twelve shillings per half-virgate is of common occurrence[6], while in the fee of Maud Passelewe we find only four
and five shillings as the rent for the half-virgate[7]. Pap-
worth Anneys exhibits a ferdel of seven and a half acres, for
which ten to twelve shillings are paid[8]. As to the cases in
which the service varies a great deal, although the land is
held in shares, I need not give quotations because they are
to be found on every page of the printed Hundred Rolls.
We may say, in conclusion, that the process of disruption

---

[1] The Ramsey Cartulary has simply: 'Et virgatarius arabit et herciabit
qualibet septimana per unum diem sicut operarius.'

[2] Rot. Hundr. ii. 348.

[3] Ib. 443, 444. Isabel, the daughter of William le Frend, is taken as a
typical half-virgater.

[4] Rot. Hundr. ii. 326.   [5] Ib. ii. 327.

[6] Ib. ii. 436.   [7] Ib. ii. 438.

[8] Ib. ii. 473.

acts much more potently in the sphere of free holding than it does in regard to villainage ; but that it has by no means succeeded in destroying all regularity even there.

Free share-holders.

Thus, even among the freeholders, landholding is often what I shall take leave to call 'shareholding.' Now, whatever ultimate explanation we may give of this fact, it has one obvious meaning. That part of the free population which holds in regular shares is not governed entirely by the rules of private ownership, but is somehow implicated in the village community. Bovates and virgates exist only as parts of carucates or hides, and the several carucates or hides themselves fit together, inasmuch as they suppose a constant apportionment of some kind. Two sets of important questions arise from this proposition, both intimately connected with each other, although they suggest different lines of enquiry. We may start from an examination of the single holding, and ask whether its regular shape can be explained by the requirements of its condition or by survivals of a former condition. Or again, we may start from the whole and inquire whether the equality the elements of which we detect is equality in ownership or equality in service. Let us take up the first thread of the inquiry.

Origins of free share-holding.

How can we account for the occurrence of regular ' shareholding ' among the freeholders ? Two possibilities have to be considered : the free character of the tenements may be newly acquired and the 'shareholding' may be a relic of a servile past ; or, on the other hand, the freehold character of the tenements may be coeval with the 'shareholding,' and in this latter case we shall have to admit the existence of freeholds which from of old have formed an element in the village community. In the first of these cases again we shall have to distinguish between two suppositions :—Servile tenements have become free ; this may be due either to some general measure of enfranchisement, a lord having preferred to take money rents in lieu of the old labour services, and these money rents being the modern equivalent for those old services, or else to par-

ticular and occasional feoffments made in favour of those
who, for one reason or another, have earned some benefit
at the lord's hand.　To put it shortly, we may explain the
phenomenon either by a process of commutation such as
that which turned 'workland' into 'molland,' or by special
privileges which have exempted certain shares in the land
from a general scheme of villainage ; or, lastly, by the
existence of freeholds as normal factors in the ancient
village community.

Let us test these various suppositions by the facts recorded in our surveys.　At first sight it may seem possible
to account for the freehold virgates by reference to the
process which converted 'workland' into 'molland.'　We
have seen above that if a lord began to demand money
instead of work, the result might, in some cases, be the
evolution of new tenures which gradually lost their villain
character and became recognised as genuine freeholds.
And no doubt one considerable class of cases can be explained by this process.　But a great many instances seem
to call for some other explanation.　To begin with, the mere
acceptance of rent in lieu of labour did not make the tenement a freehold ; servile tenements were frequently put
ad censum [1], and it seems difficult to believe that many lords
allowed a commutation of labour for rent to have the
effect of turning villainage into freehold.　Another difficulty
is found on the opposite side.　What force kept the shares
together when they had become free?　Why did they
not accumulate and disperse according to the chances of
free development?　It may be thought that custom, and
express conditions of feoffment, must have acted against
disruption.　I do not deny the possibility, but I say
that it is not easy to explain the very widely diffused

---

[1] Rot. Hundr. 470 : '(villani) quilibet istorum tenet dimidiam virgatam
terre de predicta Elena de quibus xxx et i operantur in uno anno et alii
xxxij operantur in alio anno et in eodem anno quo operantur dant domine per
annum 8 d. et alii qui non operantur dant per annum quilibet dimidius virgatarius 2 s. 10 d. et auxilium Vicecomitis 1 d. obolum et quilibet dat obolum,
quadrantem ad festum St. Michaelis.'

phenomenon of free shareholding by a commutation which tended to break up the shares and to make them useless for the purposes of assessment. Still I grant that these considerations, though they should have some weight, are not decisive, and I insist chiefly on the following argument.

The peculiar trait which distinguishes ' molland ' is the transition from labour service to money rent, and the rent is undoubtedly considered as an equivalent for the right to labour services which the lord abandons. It must be admitted that in some cases the lord may have taken less than the real equivalent in order to get such a convenient commodity as money, or because for some reason or another he was in need of current coin. Still I am not afraid to say that, in a general way, commutation supposes an exchange against an equivalent. Indeed the demand for money rents was considered rather as increasing than as decreasing the burden incumbent on the peasantry[1]. Now, although it would be preposterous to try and make out in every single case whether the rent of the free virgate is an adequate equivalent for villain services or not, there is a very sufficient number of instances in which a rough reckoning may be made without fear of going much astray[2]. And if we attempt such a reckoning we shall be struck by the number of cases in which the rent of the free virgate falls considerably short of what it yielded by the virgate of the villain. We have seen that in Ravenston, Bedfordshire, the villain service is valued at eight shillings per virgate, and that the free assessment amounts only to four shillings. In Thriplow, Cambridge-

---

[1] Maitland, Select Pleas in Manorial Courts, vol. i. 95 : A reeve complains that Richer Jocelin's son and Richard Reeve and his wife have insulted him, by saying among other things '. . . quod cepisse debuit munera de divitibus ne essent censuarii et pauperes ad censum posuisse debuit.'

[2] It might perhaps be objected that the difference in favour of the free people ought to be explained by a depreciation of money which in process of time lowered the value of quit rents. But the explanation would hardly suit the age in which the Hundred Rolls were compiled. The phenomenon mentioned in the text may be observed in all the Cartularies, and there is no reason to think that the free rents which occur in them are already antiquated survivals of agreements which had lost their economic sense.

shire, the villains perform labour duties valued at 9*s*. 4*d*.
per bovate, the freeholders are assessed variously; but
there is a certain number among them which forms, as it
were, the stock of that class, and their average rent is 5*s*. 6*d*.
per bovate[1]. In Tyringham, Buckinghamshire, the villain
holding is computed at six acres and one rood, and its
service at five shillings; the free virgates have a like number of acres and pay various rents, but almost without
exception less than the villains[2]. In Croxton, Cambridgeshire, there are customers with twenty acres, and others
with ten acres; the first have to pay ten shillings and to
assist at four boonworks. The free holders are possessed
of plots of irregular size, and their rent is also irregular; but on the average much lower than that of the
customers[3]. Let it be noted that the customary tenants
have commuted their labour services into money payments,
and, in fact, they are to be considered as molmen in the
first stage of development. Still, their payments are computed on a different scale from those of the free.

In Brandone, Warwickshire, the typical villain, William
Bateman, pays for his virgate 5*s*. 3*d*., and sends one man
to work twice a week from the 29th of June until the 1st of
August, and thence onward his man has to work two
days one week and three days the next. The free half-
virgate merely pays five shillings, and does suit to the
manorial court. This last point makes no difference, because
the villain had to attend the manorial court quite as
regularly as the freeholder, and indeed more regularly,
because he was obliged to serve on inquests[4]. In Bathekynton, Warwickshire, the difference in favour of the free
is also noticeable, but not so great[5]. And these are by no

---

[1] Rot. Hundr. ii. 542.   [2] Ib. 348.   [3] Ib. 508.

[4] Exch. Q. R. Misc. Books, N 29, f. 11 a.

[5] Exch. Q. R. Misc. Books, N 29, f. 12 : ‘Idem Thomas habet ibidem 12
villanos tenentes 4 virgatas terre et dimidiam in villenagio, unde Johannes
Aylind tenet dimidiam virgatam terre pro 5 s. 8 d. faciens fenum domini per
unum diem cum uno homine, metens blada eiusdem domini per 1 diem eum
uno homine, etc. Idem Thomas habet ibidem 11 liberos tenentes 11 virgatas
terre et dimidiam. Unde Willelmus en la Nurne tenet dimidiam virgatam

means exceptional cases. Nothing is more common than to find free tenements held by trifling services, and whatever we may think of single cases, it would be absurd to explain such arrangements in the aggregate as the results of a bargain between lord and serfs. It is evident, therefore, that a reference to 'molland,' to a commutation of labour into rent, does not suit these cases [1].

Can we explain these cases of 'free shareholding' by feoffments made to favoured persons? We have seen that the lord used to recompense his servants by grants of land and that he favoured the spread of cultivation by exacting but a light rent from newly reclaimed land. Such transactions would undoubtedly produce free tenements held on very advantageous terms, but still they seem incapable of solving our problem. Tenements created by way of beneficial feoffment are in general easily recognised. The holdings of servants and other people endowed by favour are always few and interspersed among the plots of the regular occupiers of the land, be they free or serfs. The 'essarted' fields are sometimes numerous, but usually cut up into small strips and as it were engrafted on the original stock of tenements. Altogether privileged land mostly appears divided into irregular plots and reckoned by acres and not by shares. And what we have to account for is a vast number of instances in which what seem to be some of the principal and original shares in the land are held freely and by comparatively light services. I do not think that we can get rid of a very considerable residue of cases without resorting to the last of the suppositions mentioned above. We must admit that some of the freeholders in the Hundred Rolls are possessed of shares in the fields not because they have emerged from serfdom,

et 4 acras terre pro 4 solidis faciens sectam ad curiam de Bathekynton bis per annum pro omni demanda.'

[1] Bodekesham, Cambs. (R. H. ii. 487), is probably a case of molland. The often-quoted instance of Ayllington is doubtful, although the Ramsey Cartulary speaks of the *liber tenentes* as *malmanni*. The expression was probably in use for all rent-paying people, although properly a designation of those who had commuted their services. See *Appendix XV*.

but because they were from the first members of a village
community over which the lord's power spread. It would
be very hard to draw absolute distinctions in special cases,
because the terminology of our records does not take
into account the history of tenure and only indicates net
results. But a comparison of facts *en bloc* points to at
least three distinct sources of the freehold virgates. Some
may be due to commutation, others to beneficial feoffments, but there are yet others which seem to be ancient
and primitive. The traits which mark these last are
'shareholding' and light rents. The light rents do not
look like the result of commutation, the 'shareholding'
points to some other cause than favours bestowed by the
lord.

We shall come to the same conclusion if we follow the
other line of our inquiry. It may be asked, whether the
community into which the share is made to fit should be
thought of primarily as a community in ownership or a
community in assessment, whether the shares are constructed for the purpose of satisfying equal claims or for
the purpose of imposing equal duties? The question is
a wide one, much wider than the subject immediately in
hand, but it is connected with that subject and some
of the material for its solution must be taken up in the
course of our present inquiry.

I have been constantly mentioning the assessment of
free tenements, their rents and their labour services. The
question of their weight as compared with villain services
has been discussed, but I have not hitherto taken heed
of the varying and irregular character of these rents and
services. But the variety and irregularity are worthy of
special notice. One of the most fundamental differences
between the free and servile systems is to be found in this
quarter. The villains are equalised not only as regards
their shares in the fields, but also as regards their duties
towards the lord ; indeed, both facts appear as the two
sides of one thing. The virgate of the villain is quite as
much, if not more, a unit of assessment as it is a share

of the soil. Matters look more complex in the case of free land. As I have said before, there are instances in which the free people are not only possessed of equal shares but also are rented in proportion to those shares. In much the greater number of instances, however, there is no such proportion. All may hold virgates, but one will pay more and the other less; one will perform labour duties, and the other not; one will pay in money, and the other bring a chicken, or a pound of pepper, or a flower. Whatever we may think of the gradual changes which have distorted conditions that were originally meant to be equal, it is impossible to get rid of the fact that, in regard to free tenements, equal shares do not imply equal duties or even duties of one and the same kind.

One of two things, either the shares exist only as a survival of the servile arrangement out of which the free tenements may have grown, or else they exist primarily for the purpose not of assessing duties but of apportioning claims. In stating these possibilities I must repeat what I said before, that it would be quite wrong to bring all the observed phenomena under one head. I do not intend in the least to deny that the freer play of economic and legal forces within the range of free ownership must have produced combinations infinitely more varying, irregular and complicated than those which are to be found in villainage. A large margin must be allowed for such modifications which dispersed and altered the duties that were originally proportioned to shares. But a few simple questions will serve to show that other elements must be brought into the reckoning. Why should the disruptive tendency operate so much more against proportionate assessment than against the distribution into shares itself; in other words, why are equal tenements so much commoner than equal rents? If shareholding and equal rents were indissolubly connected as the two sides of one thing, or even as cause and effect, why should one hold its ground when the other had disappeared, and how could the dependent element remain widely active when the principal

one had lost its meaning? If the discrepancies between rent
and shares had been casual, we might try to explain them
entirely by later modifications. But these discrepancies are
a standing feature of the surveys, and it seems to me that
we can hardly escape the inference that shareholding has
its *raison d'être* quite apart from the duties owed to the
lord, and in this case we have to look to the communal
arrangement of proprietary rights for its explanation; it
was a means of giving to every man his due. If this
principle is granted, all the observable facts fall into
their right places. One can easily imagine how free holdings came to exist within the village community in spite
of their loose connexion with the manor. In regard
to duties, they were practically outside the community;
not so as to proprietary rights and the agricultural
arrangements proceeding from them, for example such
arrangements as affected the rotation of crops, the use of
commons and fallow pasture, the setting up of hedges,
the repair of dykes, etc. There is no real contradiction
between the facts, that in relation to the lord every free
shareholder was, as it were, bound by a separate and
private agreement, while in relation to the village he had
to conform to communal rule.

This last remark may require some further development.
The striking differences between the duties of the several
freeholders of one manor seem to show that these people
were not enfeoffed by the lord at the same time and under
the same conditions. If A is in every respect a fellow
of B, and still has to pay twice as much as B, it is clear
that his relation to the lord has been settled under different
circumstances from those which governed the settlement
of B's position. Now, from the point of view of later law
this meant that the two freeholds were created each by a
special feoffment. But this would be a very formal and
inadequate way of considering the case. Very often the
differences might be produced by subsequent arrangements
which, though not giving rise to new title, destroyed the
original uniformity of condition. Often again we may

suspect that the relation between lord and tenant had its
origin not really in a gift of land made by the former
to the latter but in a submission made by the latter to
the former. I make bold to prefer this view, chiefly on
account of those trifling and indeed fictitious duties which
are constantly found in the Surveys[1]. They can only
have one meaning—that of 'recognitions[2].' Trifling in
themselves, they establish the subordinate relation of one
owner to the other; and although their imposition must
be considered from the formal standpoint of feudal law
as the result of a feoffment, it is clear that their real
foundation must often have been a submission to patronage.
The subject is a wide one and includes all kinds of free
tenure, communal as well as other. When a knight was
enfeoffed by a monastery in consideration of some infini-
tesimal payment, there might be several reasons for such
a transaction. The abbot may have thought it good policy
to acquire the support of a considerable person, he may
have been forced to give the land and only glad to obtain
some recognition, however trifling, of the gift; or again, he
may have made a beneficial feoffment in return for a sum
of ready money paid by way of gersuma or fine, but he
may also have extended his supremacy over a piece of
land which did not belong to him originally at all. Even
in feudal times this could be done by means of a fictitious lawsuit ending in 'a final concord'; or even simply
by an instrument of quit claim and feoffment without any

[1] R. H. ii. 349, 350 : 'In Weston, Bucks, the service of the villain virgater
is estimated at 5 s. 2 d. . . . Elyas Clericus tenet dim. virgatam et reddit
Johanni de Patishull 1 d. Willelmus fil. Willelmi de Ravenestone tenet dim.
virgatam de eodem feodo et reddit per annum 1 d. Thomas Acpelard tenet
dimidiam virgatam terre et reddit dicto Willelmo de Nodaris 3 d. Stephanus
Elys tenet dimidiam virgatam et solvit eodem Willelmo 2 d. Thomas Thebaud
tenet dimidiam virgatam et reddit eidem Willelmo 1 d. . . . Item Robertus le
Cobeler tenet dimidiam virgatam terre et solvit eodem 1 libram cimini.
Omnes isti prescripti dant per annum forinsecum et scutagium domino
Willelmo de Nodaris quando currit.' Cf. Torrington, Bucks, R. H. ii. 352.
[2] R. H. ii. 713 (Stanton, Oxon.) : 'ad alternacionem cujuslibet domini de
Stanton debet recognoscere eundem dominum de uno spervario et dabit
dimidiam marcam eidem domino.'

suit[1]. At the time when feudalism was only settling itself, in the twelfth and thirteenth centuries, this must have been a common thing, even if we do not take into account the Saxon practice of 'commendation.'

However this may be, the trifling duties imposed on freeholds lead to the inference that the agreement between lord and tenant had been made on the basis of the latter's independent right, and not on that of the lord's will and power. They testify to a subjection of free people and not to the liberation of serfs. And as they are found constantly allied with shareholding, we have to say that they imply manorial relations superimposed on a community which, if not entirely free, contained free elements within it. The manorial duties are more varied and capricious than are the shares just because they are a later growth.

I should not like to leave this intricate inquiry without testing its results by yet another standard. I have been trying to prove two things : that some of the feudal freeholds are ancient freeholds, not liberated from servitude but originally based on the recognised right of the holders ; that such ancient freeholds were included in the communal arrangement of ownership, although the assessment of their duties was not communal. To what extent are these propositions supported by an analysis of that admittedly ancient tenure, the tenure of the socmen? We must look chiefly to the 'free' socmen ; but I may be allowed, on the strength of the chapter on Ancient Demesne, to take the bond socmen also into account.

Let us take the manor of Chesterton, in Cambridgeshire[2]. It is royal, but let out in feefarm to the Prior of Barnwell, and its men make use of the *parvum breve de recto*. There is one free tenant of eighty-eight acres holding *de antiquitate* and the Scholars of Merton hold forty-four acres freely. They have clearly taken the place of some freeman, whether by purchase or by gift I do not know ; they are bound to perform ploughings and to carry corn. Both tenements are worthy

---

[1] See e. g. Ramsey Cartul. i. 138, 142.   [2] R. H. ii. 402, 403.

of notice because charters are not mentioned and still the holdings are set apart from the rest. In the one case the tenure is expressly stated to be an ancient one, and presumably the title of the other tenement is of the same kind. The number of acres is peculiar and points to some agrarian division of which eighty-eight and forty-four were fractions or multiples. The bulk of the population are described as customers. They used to hold half-virgates, it is said, but some of them have sold part of their land according to the custom of the manor. And so their tenements have lost their original regularity of construction, although it seems possible to fix the average holdings at twelve or fifteen acres. Anyhow, it is impossible to reduce them to fractions of eighty-eight; for some reason or another, the reckoning is made on a different basis. The duties vary a good deal, and it would be even more difficult to conjecture what the original services may have been than to make out the size of the virgate.

The example is instructive in many ways. It is a stepping-stone from villainage to socage, or rather to socman's tenure. There can be no question of differences of feoffment. The manorial power is fully recognised, and on the other hand the character of ancient demesne is also conspicuous with its protection of the peasantry. And still the whole fabric is giving way—the holdings get dispersed and the service loses its uniformity. All these traits are a fair warning to those who argue from the irregularity of free tenements and the inequality of their rents against the possibility of their development out of communal ownership. Here is a well-attested village community; its members hold by custom and have not changed their condition either for the better or for the worse in point of title. Later agencies are at work to distort the original arrangement—a few steps more in that direction and it would be impossible to make out even the chief lines of the system. Stanton, in Cambridgeshire, is a similar case[1]. I would especially direct the attention of

---

[1] R. H. ii. 466. Cf. 609.

the reader to the capricious way in which the services are
assessed. And still the titles of the tenants are the result
not of various grants but of manorial custom applied to the
whole community. I repeat, that irregularity in the size
of holdings and in the services that they owe is no proof
that these holdings have not formed part of a communal
arrangement or that their free character (if they have a
free character) must be the result of emancipation; these
irregularities are found on the ancient demesne where
there has been no enfranchisement or emancipation,
and where on the other hand the tenants have all along
been sufficiently 'free' to enjoy legal protection in their
holdings.

If we have to say so much with regard to ancient demesne
and bond socmen, we must not wonder that free socmen
are very often placed in conditions which it would be
impossible to reduce to a definite plan. On the fee of
Robert le Noreys, in Fordham[1], we find some scattered
free tenants burdened with entirely irregular rents, four
villains holding eighteen acres each and subjected to heavy
ploughing work, three socmen of twenty acres each paying
a rent of 4s. 2d. per holding, and obliged to assist at reaping and to bring chicken, one socman of nine acres paying
10d., one of seven acres also assessed at 10d., two of eleven
acres paying 15d., etc.

It is no cause for wonder that such instances occur at the
end of the thirteenth century. It is much more wonderful
that, in a good many cases, we are still well able to perceive
a great deal of the original regularity. Swaffham Prior,
in Cambridgeshire, is a grand example of an absolutely
regular arrangement in a community of free socmen[2].
The Prior of Ely holds it for three hides and has 220 acres
on his home-farm. The rest is divided among sixteen free
socmen paying 5s. each and performing various labour services. These services have been considerably increased by
the Prior. Mixed cases are much more usual—I mean
cases in which the original regularity has suffered some

---

[1] R. H. ii. 502.   [2] R. H. ii. 484, 485.

modifications, though a little attention will discover traces of the ancient communal arrangement[1].

On the whole, I think that the notices of socmen's tenure in the Hundred Rolls are especially precious, because they prove that the observations that we have made as regards freehold generally are not merely ingenious suggestions about what may conceivably have happened. There is undoubtedly one weak point in those observations, which is due to the method which we are compelled to adopt. It is difficult, if not impossible, to classify the actual cases which come before us, to say—in this case freehold is the result of commutation, in that case the lord has enfeoffed a retainer or a kinsman, while in this third case, the freehold virgate has always been freehold. The edge of the inquiry is blunted, if I may so say, by the vagueness of terminological distinctions, and we must rely upon general impressions. The socman's tenure, on the contrary, stands out as a clear case, and a careful analysis of it abundantly verifies the conclusions to which we have previously come by a more circuitous route.

It seems to me that the general questions with which we started in our inquiry may now be approached with some confidence. The relation of free tenancies to the manorial system turns out to be a complex one. The great majority of such tenements appears as a later growth engrafted on the system when it was already in decay. Commutation of services, the spread of cultivation over the waste, and the surrender of portions of the demesne to the increasing dependent population, must largely account for the contrast between Domesday and the Hundred Rolls. But an important residue remains, which must be explained on the assumption that in many cases the shares of the community were originally distributed among free people who had nothing or little to do with manorial work.

Three conclusions have been arrived at in this chapter.

1. The home-farm, though the necessary central unit of

[1] R. H. 469, 470, 475.

the manorial group, did not, as a rule, occupy a large area, and the break-up of feudalism tended to lessen its extension in favour of the dependent population.

2. The peculiar feature of medieval husbandry—the grouping of small households round an aristocratic centre —entailed the existence of a large class engaged in collecting revenue, superintending work, and generally conducting the machinery by which the tributary parts were joined with their centre.

3. The position of free tenements within the manor may be ascribed to one of three causes: (*a*) they have been the tenements of serfs, but, in consequence either of some general commutation or of special feoffments, they have become free; or (*b*) their connexion with the manor has all along been rather a matter of jurisdiction than a matter of proprietary right, that is to say, they form part of the manor chiefly because they are within the scope of the manorial court; or (*c*) they represent free shares in a village community upon which the manorial structure has been superimposed.

CHAPTER V.

THE MANORIAL COURTS.

The village community.
THE communal organisation of the village is made to subserve the needs of manorial administration. We feel naturally inclined to think and to speak of the village community in opposition to the lord and to notice all points which show its self-dependent character. But in practice the institution would hardly have lived such a long life and played such a prominent part if it had acted only or even chiefly as a bulwark against the feudal owner. Its development has to be accounted for to a great extent by the fact that lord and village had many interests in common. They were natural allies in regard to the higher manorial officers. The lord had to manage his estates by the help of a powerful ministerial class, but there was not much love lost between employers and administrators, and often the latent antagonism between them broke out into open feuds. If it is always difficult to organise a serviceable administration, the task becomes especially arduous in a time of undeveloped means of communication and of weak state control. It was exceedingly difficult to audit accounts and to remove bad stewards. The strength and self-government of the village group appeared, from this point of view, as a most welcome help on the side of the owner[1]. He had practically to

[1] A good specimen of the accusations which might be made against a manorial agent is afforded by the Court-rolls of the Abbey of Ramsey. Seld. Soc. ii. p. 95.

surrender his arbitrary power over the peasant population and their land, he had to conform to fixed rules as to civil usage, manorial claims and distribution of territory; but the common standards established by custom did not only hamper his freedom of disposition, they created a basis on which he could take his stand above and against his stewards. He had precise arrangements to go by in his supervision of his ministers, and there was something more than his own interest and energy to keep guard over the maintenance of these forms: the village communities were sure to fight for them from beneath. The facilities for joint action and accumulation of strength derived from communal self-government vouched indirectly for the preservation of the chief capital invested by the lord in the land: it was difficult for the steward to destroy the economic stays of the villainage.

There are many occasions when the help rendered by the village communities to the lord may be perceived directly. I need hardly mention the fact that the surveys, which form the chief material of our study, were compiled in substance by sworn inquests, the members of which were considered as the chief representatives of the community, and had to give witness to its lore. The great monastic and exchequer surveys do not give any insight into the mode of selection of the jurors: it may be guessed with some probability that they were appointed for the special purpose, and chosen by the whole court of the manor. In some cases the ordinary jurors of the court, or chief pledges, may have been called upon to serve on the inquest. There is another point which it is impossible to decide quite conclusively, namely, whether questions about which there was some doubt or the jurors disagreed were referred to the whole body of the court. But, although we do not hear of such instances in our great surveys, it is surely an important indication that the extant court-rolls constantly speak of the whole court deciding questions when the verdict of ordinary jurors seemed insufficient. And such reserved cases were by no means restricted

The village and the manorial officers.

to points of law ; very often they concerned facts of the same nature as those enrolled in the surveys[1].

Village officers. On a parallel with the stewards and servants appointed by the lord, although in subordination to them, appear officers elected by the village. As we have seen, the manorial beadle was matched by the communal reeve, and a like contrast is sometimes found on the lower degrees[2]. In exceptional cases the lord nominates the reeve, although he still remains the chief representative of village interests and the chief collector of services. But in the normal course the office was elective, and curious intermediate forms may be found. For instance, the village selects the messarius (hayward), and the lord may appoint him reeve[3]. This is a point, again, which shows most clearly the intimate connexion between the interests of the lord and those of the village. The peasants become guarantors for the reeve whom they chose. A formula which comes from Gloucester Abbey requires, that only such persons be chosen as have proved their capacity to serve by a good conduct of their own affairs : all shortcomings and defects are to be made good ultimately by the rural community that elected the officer, and no excuses are to be accepted unless in cases of exceptional hardship[4]. The economic tracts of the thirteenth century state the same principle in even a more explicit manner.

Communal liability. From the manorial point of view the whole village is responsible for the collection of duties. There are pay-

---

[1] Seld. Soc. ii. 22: ' Et dicit curia quod tenementum et una acra servilis condicionis sunt et una acra libere.'

[2] Coram Rege, Pascha 9 Edw. I, 34, 6 : ' Messarius abbatis et messarius villate.'

[3] Okeburn Inqu. 56 (Add. MSS. 24316) : ' Eligere debent unum messarium de se ipsis et domini de ipso electo poterunt facere prepositum.'

[4] Gloucester Cart. iii. 221 : ' Prepositus eligetur per communitatem halimoti qui talem eligant qui ad suam terram propriam excolendum et cetera bona sua discrete et circumspecte tractanda idoneus merite notatur et habeatur, pro cuius defectibus et abmittendis totum halimotum respondeat, nisi ubi urgens necessitas aut causa probabilis illud halimotum coram loci ballivo rationabilem praetendere poterit excusationem.' Cf. Walter of Henley, ed. Lamond, pp. 10, 64, 66.

ments expressly imposed on the whole. Such is the case with the yearly auxilium or donum. The partition of these between the householders is naturally effected in a meeting of the villagers[1]. Most services are laid on the virgaters separately. But they are all held answerable for the regularity and completeness with which every single member of the community performs his duties. As to free holdings, it is sometimes noticed especially to what extent they are subjected to the general arrangement: whether they participate with the rest in payments, and whether the tenants have to work in the same way as the villains[2]. Very often the documents point out that such and such a person ought to take part in certain obligations but has been exempted or fraudulently exempts himself, and that the village community has to bear a relative increase of its burdens[3]. A Glastonbury formula orders the steward to make inquiries about people who have been freed from the performance of their services in such a way that their responsibility has been thrown on the village[4].

But it would be very wrong to assume that the rural community could act only in the interest of the lord. Its solidarity is recognised in matters which do not concern him, or even which call forth an opposition between him and the peasantry.

I have already spoken of the curious fact that the village is legally recognised as a unit, separated from the manor

Village and manor.

---

[1] Seld. Soc. ii. 12: 'Nicholaus filius sacerdotis . . . et Robertus de Magedone . . . in misericordia quia contradixerunt tallagium quod positum fuit super eos per vicinos suos.' Glastonb. Inqu. of 1189, p. 33: 'Totum manerium reddit de dono 73 solidos et 4 den. sicut homines ville illud statuunt.'

[2] Ramsey Cart. i. 401: 'Sunt in scot et in lot et in omnibus cum villata.' Spalding Priory Reg., Cole MSS. xliii. p. 283: 'Libere tenens facit fossatum maris et omnes communas ville secundum quantitatem bouatae.'

[3] Ramsey Cart. i. 398: 'Henricus le Freman solebat esse in communa villatae, ut in tallagio et similibus. Nulla inde facit.' p. 394 (a villager does not pay his part of the tallage), 'quod quidem tallagium tota villata et ad magnum ipsorum gravamen hucusque persolvit.'

[4] Glastonbury Cart., Wood MSS. i. f. 111: 'Si nul soit enfraunchi de ses ouvrages dont la ville est le plus charge.'

although existing within it. When the reeve and the four men attend the sheriff's tourn or the eyre, they do not represent the lord only, but also the village community. Part of their expenses are borne by the lord and part by their fellow villagers[1]. The documents tell us of craftsmen who have to work for the village as well as for the lord[2]. On a parallel with services due to the landowner, we find sometimes kindred services reserved for the village community[3]. If a person has been guilty of misdemeanours and is subjected to a special supervision, this supervision applies to his conduct in regard both to the lord and to the fellow villagers[4]. No doubt the relations of the village to its lord are much more fully described in the documents than the internal arrangement of the community, but this could not be otherwise in surveys compiled for the use of lords and stewards. Even the chance indications we gather as to these internal arrangements are sufficient to give an insight into the powerful ties of the village community.

The village as a juristic person.

Indeed, the rural settlement appears in our records as a 'juridical person.' The Court Rolls of Brightwaltham, edited for the Selden Society by Mr. Maitland, give a most beautiful example of this. The village of Brightwaltham enters into a formal agreement with the lord of the manor as to some commons. It surrenders its rights to the lord in regard to the wood of Hemele, and gets rid in return of the rights claimed by the lord in Est-

---

[1] Add. MSS. 6159, f. 25, b : ' Dominus debet invenire duos homines sumptibus suis coram eisdem justiciariis et villata de Rode sumptibus suis tres homines invenient. Et hoc per consuetudinem a tempore quo non extat memoria ut dicitur.' Cf. Domesday of St. Paul's, 15 : ' Alanus filius Alexandri de Cassingburne tres virgatas pro 20 solidis et preter haec 10 acras de villata et 10 de dominico propter sectam sire et hundredi quam modo non facit.'

[2] Custumal of Bleadon, 257 : ' Invenit fabrum pro ferdello domino et toti villae.'

[3] Shaftesbury Cart., Harl. MSS. 61, f. 63 : ' Ibit ad scotaliam domine sicut ad scotaliam vicinorum.'

[4] Ramsey Cart. i. 425 : ' Ponitur in respectu quousque videatur quomodo se gerat versus dominum abbatem et suos vicinos.'

field and in a wood called Trendale[1]. Nothing can be more explicit: the village acts as an organised community; it evidently has free disposition as to rights connected with the soil; it disposes of these rights not only independently of the lord, but in an exchange to which he appears as a party. We see no traces of the rightless condition of villains which is supposed to be their legal lot, and a powerful community is recognised by the lord in a form which bears all the traits of legal definition. In the same way the annals of Dunstable speak of the seisin of the township of Toddington[2], and of a feoffment made by them on behalf of the lord.

I have only to say in addition to this summing up of the subject, that the quasilegal standing of the villains in regard to the lord appears with special clearness when they stand arrayed against him as a group and not as single individuals. We could guess as much on general grounds, but the self-dependent position assumed by the 'communitas villanorum' of Brightwaltham is the more interesting, that it finds expression in a formal and recorded agreement.

[1] Seld. Soc. ii. 172: 'Ad istam curiam venit tota communitas villanorum de Bristwalton et de sua mera et spontanea voluntate sursum reddidit domino totum jus et clamium quod idem villani habere clamabant racione commune in bosco domini qui vocatur Hemele et landis circumadjacentibus, ita quod nec aliquid juris vel clamii racione commune in bosco predicto et landis circumadjacentibus exigere, vendicare vel habere poterint in perpetuum. Et pro hac sursum reddicione remisit eis dominus de sua gracia speciali communam quam habuit in campo qui vocatur Estfeld,' etc.

[2] Annals of Dunstable (Annales Monast.) iii. 379, 380: 'Et prior dicit, quod praedicta tenementa aliquo tempore fuerunt in seisina hominum villate de Thodingdone, qui quidem homines, unanimi voluntate et assensu, feofaverunt praedictum Simonem, praedecessorem praedicti prioris, de praedictis tenementis, tenendum eidem Simoni et successoribus suis in perpetuum. Jurati dicunt . . . quod praedicta tenementa aliquo tempore fuerunt in seisina praedictorum hominum villatae de Thodingdone et quod omnes illi, qui aliquid habuerunt in praedictis duabus placiis terrae, congregati in uno loco ad quandam curiam apud Thodingdone tentam, unanimi assensu concesserunt praedicto Symoni, quondam priori de Dunstaple, praedecessori prioris nunc, praedictas placeas terrae, cum pertinentiis, tenendum eidem et successoribus suis in perpetuum, reddendo inde eisdem hominibus et eorum haeredibus per annum sex denarios temporibus falcacionis prati.'

The village
as a farmer.   We catch a glimpse of the same phenomenon from
yet another point of view. It is quite common to
find entire estates let to farm to the rural community
settled upon them[1]. In such cases the mediation of the
bailiff might be dispensed with; the village entered into
a direct agreement with the lord or his chief steward and
undertook a certain set of services and payments, or
promised to give a round sum. Such an arrangement was
profitable to both parties. The villains were willing to
pay dearly in order to free themselves from the bailiff's
interference with their affairs; the landowner got rid of a
numerous and inconvenient staff of stewards and servants;
the rural life was organised on the basis of self-government
with a very slight control on the part of the lord. Such
agreements concern the general management of manors as
well as the letting of domain land or of particular plots
and rights[2]. Of course there was this great disadvantage
for the lord, that the tie between him and his subjects was
very much loosened by such arrangements, and sometimes
he had to complain that the conditions under which the
land was held were materially disturbed under the farmer-
ship of the village. It is certain, that in a general way
this mode of administration led to a gradual improvement
in the social status of the peasantry.

One great drawback of investigations into the history

---

[1] Madox, Firma Burgi, 54, f. : '... statim visis litteris capiat in manum
Regis maneria de Cochame et Bray, quae sunt in manibus hominum praedictorum maneriorum, et salvo custodiat, ita quod deinceps Regi possit respondere de firma praedictorum maneriorum ad scaccarium.'   54, g :
'Miramur quamplurimum quod 30s. quos monachi de Lyra de elemosyna
nostra constituta singulis annis per manus ballivorum villae vestrae, antequam predictam villam caperitis ad firmam recipere.' Cf. Exch. i. 407, a,
412, b; Rot. Hundr. ii. 134 : 'Benmore juxta Langport fuit de dominico
domini Regis pertinens ad Sumerton ubi omnes homines domini Regis de
Sumerton, Sutton, Puttem et Merne solebant communicare cum omnimodis
averiis suis, set per negligenciam villanorum de Sumertone qui manerium
tunc temporis ad firmam tenuerunt et Henricus de Urtiaco vetus eandem
moram sibi appropriavit.'
[2] Gloucester Cart. iii. 181 : 'Omnes isti villani tenent de dominio quoddam pratum quod vocatur Hay continens 23 acras et reddunt inde per annum
23 solidos 3 denarios.'

of medieval institutions consists in the very incomplete The village and agricultural arrangements. manner in which the subject is usually reflected in the documents. We have to pick up bits of evidence as to very important questions in the midst of a vast mass of uninteresting material, and sometimes whole sides of the subject are left in the shade, not by the fault of the inquirer, but in consequence of disappointing gaps in the contemporary records. Even conveyancing entries, surrenders, admittances, are of rare occurrence on some of the more ancient rolls, and the probable reason is, that they were not thought worthy of enrolment[1]. As for particulars of husbandry they are almost entirely absent from the medieval documents, and it is only on the records of the sixteenth and yet later centuries that we have to rely when we look for some direct evidence of the fact that the manorial communities had to deal with such questions[2]. And so our knowledge of these institutions must be based largely on inference. But even granting all these imperfections of the material, it must be allowed that the one side of manorial life which is well reflected in the documents—the juridical organisation of the manor—affords very interesting clues towards an understanding of the system and of its origins.

Let us repeat again, that the management of the manor Collegiate decisions and seignorial power. is by no means dependent on capricious and onesided expressions of the lord's will. On the contrary, every known act of its life is connected with collegiate decisions. Notwithstanding the absolute character of the lord with regard to his villains taken separately, he is in truth but the centre of a community represented by meetings or courts. Not only the free, but also the servile tenantry are ruled in accordance with the views and customs of a congregation of the tenants in their divers classes. There

---

[1] Cf. Prof. Maitland's Introduction to the rolls of the Abbey of Ramsey. Seld. Soc. ii. 87.

[2] See the record of proceedings in the Court of the manor of Hitchin, printed by Mr. Seebohm at the end of his volume on the 'Village Community.'

can be no doubt that the discretion of the lord was often stretched in exceptional cases, that relations based on moral sense and a true comprehension of interests often suffered from violence and encroachment. But as a general rule, and with unimportant exceptions, the feudal system is quite as much characterised by the collegiate organisation of its parts as by their monarchical exterior. The manorial courts were really meetings of the village community under the presidency of the lord or of his steward.

Village Courts.
It is well known that later law recognises three kinds of seignorial courts: the Leet, the Court Baron, and the Customary Court. The first has to keep the peace of the King, the others are concerned with purely manorial affairs. The Leet appears in possession of a police and criminal jurisdiction in so far as that has not been appropriated by the King's own tribunals—its parallel being the sheriff's tourn in the hundred. The Court Baron is a court of free tenants entrusted with some of the conveyancing and the petty litigation between them, and also with the exercise of minor franchises. The Customary Court has in its charge the unfree population of the manor. In keeping with this division the Court Baron consists according to later theory of a body of free suitors which is merely placed under the presidency of the steward, while in the Customary Court the steward is the true and only judge, and the copyholders, customary tenants or villains, around him are merely called up as presenters.

Court Leet.
The masterly investigations of Mr. Maitland, from which any review of the subject must start, have shown conclusively, that this latter doctrine, as embodied in Coke, for instance, draws distinctions and establishes definitions which were unknown to earlier practice. The Leet became a separate institution early enough, although its name is restricted to one province—Norfolk—even at the time of the Hundred Rolls[1]. The foundation of the court was laid by the frank-pledge system and the necessity of

---

[1] Introduction to Seld. Soc. ii. p. xvi.

keeping it in working order. We find the Leet Court
sometimes under the names 'Curia Visus franci plegii,' or
'Visus de borchtruning[1],' and it appears then as a more
solemn form of the general meeting. It is held usually
twice a year to register all the male population from twelve
years upwards, to present those who have not joined the
tithings, and sometimes to elect the heads or representatives
of these divisions—the 'Capitales plegii[2].' Sometimes the
tithing coincides with the township, is formed on a territorial basis, as it were, so that we may find a village called
a tithing[3]. This leads to the inference, that the grouping
into tens was but an approximate one, and this view is
further supported by the fact that we hear of bodies of
twelve along with those of ten[4].

As to attending the meeting, a general rule was enforced   View of
to that effect, that the peasantry must attend in person   Frank-
and not by reason of their tenure[5]. But as it was out of   pledge.
the question to drive all the men of a district to the
manorial centres on such days, exceptions of different
kinds are frequent[6]. Besides the women and children, the
personal attendants of the lord get exempted, and also shepherds, ploughboys, and men engaged in driving waggons
laden with corn. Servants and aliens were considered as

---

[1] Add. MSS. 6159, f. 54, a : 'Visus de borchtruning.'

[2] Gloucester Cart. iii. 221 ; Malmesbury Cart. ii. 17. Cf. Kovalevsky,
'History of police administration in England' (Russian), 137.

[3] Glastonbury Inqu. of 1189, p. 101 : 'De tidinga Estone 5 solidos vel
placita que orientur.' Cf. Maitland, Introduction to Seld. Soc. ii. pp. xxx,
xxxiii.

[4] Rot. Hundr. ii. 461, b : 'Et predicti Radulfus et Robertus habent suas
duodenas.'

[5] Y. B. 21-22 Edw. I, 399: 'Presence a vewe de franc pledge demande
par la reson de la persone, non de la tenure.'

[6] Glastonbury Cart., Wood MSS. i. f. 100, b : 'Predictus Abbas consensit
quod omnes homines eorum de predictis villis qui fuerint duodecim annorum
et amplius faciant sectam ad predictum hundredum bis in annis perpetuum
. . . exceptis omnibus bercariis, carrucariis predictarum villarum et carrectariis
cuiuscumque hominis fuerint et omnibus aliis hominibus tam de predictis
villis quam aliunde qui sunt de manupastis ipsius abbatis qui nullam sectam
facient ad predictum hundredum nisi ibidem fuerint implacitati vel alios im-
placitent.'

under the pledge of the person with whom they were staying.

Communal accusation. The aim of its whole arrangement was to ensure the maintenance of peace, and therefore everybody was bound on entering the tithing to swear, not only that he would keep the peace, but that he would conceal nothing which might concern the peace[1]. It is natural that such a meeting as that held for the view of frank-pledge should begin to assume police duties and a certain criminal jurisdiction. Mr. Maitland has shown how, by its intimate connexion with the sheriff's tourn, the institution of frank-pledge was made to serve the purpose of communal accusation in the time of Henry II. The Assize of Clarendon (1166) gave the impulse in regard to the Sheriff's Court, and private lords followed speedily on the same line, although they could not copy the pattern in all its details, and the system of double presentment described by Britton and Fleta proved too cumbersome for their small courts with only a few freeholders on them. In any case the jurisdiction of the Court Leet is practically formed in the twelfth century, and the Quo Warranto inquiries of the thirteenth only bring out its distinctions more clearly[2].

Court baron and customary court. The questions as to the opposition between Court Baron and Customary Court are more intricate and more important. Mr. Maitland has collected a good deal of evidence to prove that the division did not exist originally, and that we have before us in the thirteenth century only one strictly manorial court, the 'halimotum.' I may say, that I came to the same conclusion myself in the Russian edition of the present work quite independently of his argument. Indeed a somewhat intimate acquaintance with the early Court Rolls must necessarily lead to this doctrine. If some distinctions are made, they touch upon a difference between ordinary meetings and those which

[1] Glastonbury Cart., Wood MSS. i. f. 112 : '. . . ne soit a la peis le roi come tere tenaunt en diseine ou en fraunche pleivine.' f. 111 : 'Serment de ceux qui entrent en diseine . . . ne celeras chose qe apent a la pei le roi de engleterre.'
[2] Introduction to Seld. Soc. ii. p. xviii.

were held under exceptional circumstances and attended
by a greater number of suitors than usual. The expression
'libera curia' which meets us sometimes in the documents
is an exact parallel with that of 'free gallows,' and means
a court held freely by the lord and not a court of free
men. Mr. Maitland adds, that he has found mention of
a court of villains and one of knights, but that he never
came across a court of barons in the sense given in later
jurisprudence to the term 'Court Baron.' Here I must
put in a trifling qualification which does not affect his
main position in the least. The Introduction to the Selden
Society's second volume, which is our greatest authority
on this subject, mentions a case when the halimot was
actually divided on the principle laid down by Coke and
later lawyers generally. I mean the case of Steyning,
where the Abbot holds a separate court for free tenants
and another for his villains. The instance belongs to the
time of the Edwards, but it is marked as an innovation
and a bad one[1]. It shows, however, that the separation
of the courts was beginning to set in. The Steyning case
is not quite an isolated one. I have found in the Hundred
Rolls the expression *Sockemanemot* to designate a court
attended by free sokemen[2], and it may be suggested that
the formation of the so-called Court Baron may have
been facilitated by the peculiar constitution and customs of
those courts where the unfree element was almost entirely
absent. The Danish shires and Kent could not but exercise a certain influence on the adjoining counties. However this might be, the general rule is, undoubtedly, that
no division is admitted, and that all the suitors and affairs
are concentrated in the one manorial court—the *halimot*.

It met generally once every three weeks, but it happens

The halimot.

---

[1] Seld. Soc. ii. p. lxx.

[2] Rot. Hundr. ii. 143: 'Ermoldus de Boys dominus de Asynton solebat
facere sectam ad Boxford ad Sockomanemot pro terra Ricardi Serle in
Cornerche, nunc illa secta subtracta per 4 annos.' The expression 'frank-
halimote' occurs often, but it is evidently an equivalent to 'libera curia,'
and interchanges with 'liberum manerium.' See Rot. Hundr. ii. 69, 74,
127.

sometimes that it is called together without a definite
limit of time at the pleasure of the lord[1]. Cases like that
of the manors of the Abbey of Ramsey, in which the courts
are summoned only twice a year, are quite exceptional,
and in the instance cited the fact has to be explained by
the existence of an upper court for these estates, the court
of the honour of Broughton[2]. The common suitors are
the peasants living within the manor—the owners of holdings in the fields of the manor. In important trials, when
free men are concerned, or when a thief has to be hanged,
suitors are called in from abroad — mostly small free
tenants who have entered into an agreement about a
certain number of suits to the court[3]. These foreign
suitors appear once every six weeks, twice a year, for
special trials upon a royal writ, for the hanging of
thieves[4], etc. The duty of attending the court is constantly mentioned in the documents. It involved undoubtedly great hardships, expense, and loss of time : no
wonder that people tried to exempt themselves from it as
much as possible[5]. Charters relating to land provide
for all manner of cases relating to suit of court. We
find it said, for instance, that a tenant must make his
appearance on the next day after getting his summons,
even if it was brought to him at midnight[6]. When a
holding was divided into several parts, the most common
thing was that one suit remained due from the whole[7].

[1] Eynsham Inqu., Christ Church MSS. 15, a : ' Curia debet ibi teneri si
dominus voluerit.'

[2] Seld. Soc. ii. 49, etc.

[3] Beaulieu Cart., Harl. MSS. 748, f. 113 : ' De sectatoribus intrinsecis . . .
et qui habent terram in campis . . . et ad forciamentum curie omnes predicti
tam liberi quam alii cum 12 burgensibus vel pluribus venient ad curiam per
racionabilem summonicionem.' Glastonb. Cart., Wood MSS. i. 101, d :
' Ipse et heredes et homines sui de Acforde facient bis in anno sectam ad
hundredum abbatis de Nywentone et ad afforciamentum curie.'

[4] Rot. Hundr. ii. 710, a ; Ramsey Cart. i. 491.

[5] Warwick Hundred Roll, Exch. Q. R. Misc. Books, 29, p. 10 : ' Quidam
de tenentibus dicunt quod nunquam fecerunt sectam.'

[6] Gloucester Cart. iii. 208.

[7] Chapterhouse Box 152, No. 14 : ' Hereditas de qua una secta de-
betur.'

All these details are by no means without importance, because they show that fiscal reasons had as much to do with the arrangement of these meetings as real interests : every court gave rise to a number of fines from suitors who had made default.

The procedure of the halimot was ruled by ancient custom. All foreign elements in the shape of advocates or professional pleaders were excluded. Such people, we are told by the manorial instructions, breed litigation and dead-letter formalism, whereas trials ought to be conducted and judged according to their substance[1]. Another ceremonial peculiarity of some interest concerns the place where manorial courts are held. It is certain that the ancient gemóts were held in the open air, as Mr. Gomme shows in his book on early folk-mots. And we see a survival of the custom in the meeting which used to be held by the socmen of Stoneleigh on Motstowehill[2]. But in the feudal period the right place to hold the court was the manorial hall. We find indeed that the four walls of this room are considered as the formal limit of the court, so that a man who has stept within them and has then gone off without sufficient reason is charged with contempt of court[3]. Indeed, the very name of 'halimot' can hardly be explained otherwise than as the moot held in the hall[4]. The point is of some interest, because the hall is not regarded as a purely material contrivance for keeping people protected against the cold

Procedure of the halimot.

---

[1] Ramsey Cart. i. 412 : 'Prohibitum est in plena curia, ne quis ducat placitatores in curiam abbatis ad impediendum vel prorogandum judicium domini Abbatis.' Gesta Abbatum (St. Alban's), 455 : 'Non permittatur quod in halimotis adventicii placitatores partes cum sollemnitate sustineant sed communiter per bundos (i. e. bondos) de curia veritas inquiratur, sine callumnia verborum.'

[2] Stoneleigh Reg. f. 75 : 'Curia de Stonle ad quam sokemanni faciebant sectam solebat ab antiquo teneri super montem iuxta villam de Stonle vocatam Motstowehull, ideo sic dictum quia ibi placitabant sed postquam abbates de Stonle habuerunt dictam curiam et libertatem pro aysiamento tenencium et sectatorum fecerunt domum curie in medio ville de Stonle.'

[3] Selden Soc. ii. p. 67.

[4] Introduction to Seld. Soc. vol. ii. p. 76.

and the rain, but appears in close connexion with the manor, and as its centre and symbol.

The halimot and agriculture.

We hear very little of husbandry arrangements made by the courts [1], and even of the repartition of duties and taxes [2]. Entries relating to the election of officers are more frequent [3], but the largest part of the rolls is taken up by legal business of all sorts.

Presentments.

The entire court, and sometimes a body of twelve jurors, present those who are guilty of any offence or misdemeanour. Ploughmen who have performed their ploughing on the lord's land badly, villains who have fled from the fee and live on strange soil, a man who has not fulfilled some injunction of the lord, a woman who has picked a lock appended to the door of her cottage by a manorial bailiff, an inveterate adulterer who loses the lord's chattels by being fined in the ecclesiastical courts— all these delinquents of very different kinds are presented to be punished, and get amerced or put into the stocks, according to the nature of their offences. It ought to be noticed that an action committed against the interests of the lord is not punished by any onesided act of his will, or by the command of his steward, but treated as a matter of legal presentment. The negligent ploughman is not taken to task directly by the bailiff or any other overseer, but is presented as an offender by his fellow-peasants, and according to strict legal formality. On the other hand, the entries are worded in such a way that the part played by the court is quite clear only as to the presenting of misdeeds, while the amercement or punishment is decreed in some manner which is not specified exactly. We read, for instance, in a roll of the Abbey of Bec how 'the court has presented that Simon Combe has set up a fence on the lord's land. Therefore let it be abated. . . . The court presented that the following had encroached

---

[1] The Durham halimot books (Surtees Society) supply some instances.

[2] Glastonbury Inqu. of 1189, p. 33: 'De dono 73 solidos sicut homines ville illud statuunt.'

[3] Selden Soc. ii. 36, 168.

ont he lord's land, to wit, William Cobbler, Maud Robins, widow (fined 12*d.*), John Shepherd (fined 12*d.*) ... Therefore they are in mercy[1].' Who has ordered the fence to be thrown down, and who has imposed the fines on the delinquents? The most natural inference seems to be that the penalties were imposed by the lord or the presiding officer who represented him in the court. But it is by no means impossible that the court itself had to decide on the penalty or the amount of the amercement after first making the presentment as to the fact. Its action would merely divide itself into two independent decisions. Such a procedure would be a necessity in the case of a free tenant who could not be fined at will ; and there is nothing to show that it was entirely different in regard to the servile tenantry. When the lord interferes at pleasure this is noted as an exceptional feature[2]. It is quite possible, again, that the amercement was imposed on the advice or by a decision of certain suitors singled out from the rest as persons of special credit, as in a case from the same manorial rolls of Bec[3]. It is hardly necessary to draw very precise conclusions, as the functions of the suitors do not appear to have been sharply defined. But for this very reason it would be wrong to speak of the onesided right of the lord or of his representative to impose the penalty.

The characteristic mixture of different elements which we notice in the criminal jurisdiction of the manorial court may be seen also if we examine its civil jurisdiction. We find the halimot treating in its humble region all the questions of law which may be debated in the courts of common law. Seisin, inheritance, dower, leases, and the like are discussed, and the pleading, though

Civil jurisdiction.

---

[1] Selden Society, vol. ii. 6, 7, 8.

[2] Ibid. 31: 'Johannes Smert ... Henricus Coterel maritavit se sine licencia domini, ideo distringantur ad faciendum voluntatem domini.'

[3] Ibid. p. 44: ' Postea taxata fuit dicta misericordia per Rogerum de Suhtcote, Willelmum de Scaccario, Hugonem de Cumbe liberos sectatores curie usque ad duas marcas.'

subject to the custom of the manor, takes very much the shape of the contentions before the royal judges. Now this civil litigation is interesting from two points of view : it involves statements of law and decisions as to the relative value of claims. In both respects the parties have to refer to the body of the court, to its assessors or suitors. The influence of the ' country' on the judgment goes further here than in the Common Law Courts, because there is no independent common law to go by, and the custom of the manor has generally to be made out by the manorial tenants themselves. And so a party 'puts himself on his country,' not only in order to decide some issue of fact, but also in regard to points of customary law. Inquisitions are made and juries formed quite as much to establish the jurisprudence of the court as to decide who has the better claim under the said jurisprudence. Theoretically it is the full court which is appealed to, but in ordinary cases the decision rests with a jury of twelve, or even of six. The authority of such a verdict goes back however to the supposed juridical sense or juridical knowledge of the court as a body. Now it cannot be contested that such an organisation of justice places all the weight of the decision with the body of the suitors as assessors. The presiding officer and the lord whom he represents have not much to do in the course of the deliberation. If we may take up the comparison which Mr. Maitland has drawn with German procedure[1], we shall say that the ' Urtheilfinder' have all the best of it in the trial as against the ' Richter.' This ' Richter ' is seemingly left with the duties of a chairman, and the formal right to draw up and pronounce a decision which is materially dependent on the ruling of the court. But a special reserve of equity is left with the lord, and in consequence of its operation we find some decisions and sentences altered, or their execution postponed[2]. I have to endorse one more

---

[1] Introduction to Seld. Soc. ii. p. lxv.
[2] Ibid. pp. 163, 166.

point of Mr. Maitland's exposition, namely, his view of the presentment system as of a gradual modification of the original standing of the manorial suitors as true assessors of the court. Through the influence of the procedure of royal courts, on the one hand, of the stringent classifications of the tenantry in regard to status on the other, the presenters were gradually debased, and legal learning came to maintain that the only judge of a customary court was its steward. But a presentment of the kind described in the manorial rolls vouches for a very independent position of the suitors, and indeed for their prevalent authority in the constitution of the tribunal.

The conveyancing entries, although barren and mono- Surrender tonous at first sight, are very important, in so far as they and show, better perhaps than anything else, the part played admittance. by the community and by its testimony in the transmission of rights. It has become a common-place to argue that the practice of surrender and admittance characterises the absolute ownership that the lord has in the land held in villainage, and proceeds from the fact that every holder of servile land is in truth merely an occupier of the plot by precarious tenure. Every change of occupation has to be performed through the medium of the lord who 're-enters' the tenement, and concedes it again as if there had been no previous occupation at all and the new tenant entered on a holding freshly created for his use. None the less, a theory which lays all the stress in the case on the surrender into the hand of the lord, and explains this act from the point of view of absolute ownership, is wrong in many respects.

To begin with the legal transmission of a free holding, Meaning of although the element of surrender has as it were evaporated surrender. from it, it is quite as much bound up with the fiction of the absolute ownership of the lord as is the surrender and admittance of villains and copyholders. The ceremony of investiture had no other meaning but that of showing that the true owner re-entered into the exercise of his right, and every act of homage for land was connected

with an act of feoffment which, though obligatory, first
by custom and then by law, was nevertheless no mere
pageant, because it gave rise to very serious claims of service and casual rights in the shape of wardship, marriage,
and the like.   The king who wanted to be everybody's
heir was much too consequent an exponent of the feudal
doctrine, and his successors were forced into a gentler
practice.   But the fiction of higher ownership was lurking
behind all these contentions of the upper class quite as
much as behind the conveyancing ceremonies of the
manorial court.   And in both cases the fiction stretched
its standard of uniformity over very different elements:
allodial ownership was modified by a subjection to the
'dominium directum,' on the one hand; leases and precarious occupation were crystalised into tenure, on the other.
It is not my object to trace the parallel of free and peasant
holding in its details, but I lay stress on the principle
that the privileged tenure involved the notion of a personal concession quite as much as did the base tenure, and
that this fundamental notion made itself felt both in conveyancing formalities and in practical claims.

The rod
and the
festuca.

I am even inclined to go further: it seems to me that
the manorial ceremony of surrender and admittance, as
considered from the point of view of legal archæology,
may have gone back to a practice which has nothing to
do with the lord's ownership, although it was ultimately
construed to imply this notion.   The tenant enfeoffed of
his holding on the conditions of base tenure was techni-
cally termed tenant by copy of court roll or tenant by the
rod—*par la verge*.   This second denomination is connected
with the fact that, in cases of succession as well as in those
of alienation, the holding passed by the ceremonial action
of the steward handing a rod to the person who was to have
the land.   Now, this formality looks characteristic enough;
it is exactly the same as the action of the 'salman' in Frankish law where the transmission of property is effected
by the handing of a rod called 'festuca.'   The important
point is, that the 'salman' was by no means a representa-

tive of lordship or ownership, but the necessary middleman
prescribed by customary law, in order to give the transaction its consecration against all claims of third persons.
The Salic law, in its title 'de affatomire,' presents the ceremony in a still earlier stage : when a man wants to give his
property to another, he has to call in a middleman and
witnesses ; into the hands of this middleman he throws a rod
to show that he relinquishes all claim to the property in
question. The middleman then behaves as owner and
host, and treats the witnesses to a meal in the house and on
the land which has been entrusted to him. The third and
last act is, that this intermediate person passes on the
property to the donee designated by the original owner,
and this by the same formal act of throwing the rod [1].
The English practice has swerved from the original, because the office of the middleman has lapsed into the
hands of the steward. But the characteristic handing of
the rod has well preserved the features of the ancient
'laisuwerpitio' ('the throwing on to the bosom'), and,
indeed, it can hardly be explained on any other supposition but that of a survival of the practice. I beg the
reader to notice two points which look decisive to me :
the steward when admitting a tenant does not use the
rod as a symbol of his authority, because he does not
keep it—he gives it to the person admitted. Still more,
in the surrender the rod goes from the peasant-holder to
the steward. Can there be a doubt that it symbolises
the plot of land, or rather the right over the plot, and
that in its passage from hand to hand there is nothing
to show that the steward as middleman represents absolute ownership, while the peasants at both ends are restricted to mere occupation on sufferance [2]? Is it necessary

[1] Comp. Heussler, Institutionen des deutschen Privatrechts, i. 215 ; ii.
622 ; but I cannot agree with him as the ceremony being employed only
where there was to be a 'donatio mortis causa.' In connexion with this
the part played by the Salman is misunderstood, as it seems to me.

[2] The court rolls of Common Law manors do not think it necessary to
give the particulars about the transmission of the rod. But the description
of the practice at Stoneleigh, which, though ancient demesne, presents

to explain that these ceremonial details are not trifles from a historical point of view? Their arrangement is not a matter of chance but of tradition, and if later generations use their symbols mechanically, they do not invent them at haphazard. Symbols and ceremonies are but outward expressions of ideas, and therefore their combinations are ruled by a certain logic and are instinct with meaning. In a sense their meaning is deeper and more to be studied than that supplied by theories expressed in so many words: they give an insight into a more ancient order of things. It may be asked, in conclusion, why a Frankish form should be found prevalent in the customary arrangement of the English manorial system? The fact will hardly appear strange when we consider, firstly, that the symbolical acts of investiture and conveyancing were very similar in Old English and Old Frankish law[1], and that many practices of procedure were imported into England from France, through the medium of Normandy. It is impossible at the present date to trace conclusively the ceremonies of surrender and admittance in all their varieties and stages of development, but the most probable course of progress seems to have been a passage from symbolical investiture in the folk-law of free English ceorls through the Frankish practice of 'affatomire,' to the feudal ceremony of surrender and admittance by the steward.

The court roll.

And now let us take up the second thread of our inquiry into the manorial forms of conveyancing. A tenant by the verge is also a tenant by copy of court roll. The steward who presided at the court had to keep a record of its proceedings, and this record had a primary importance for the servile portion of the community. While the free people could enter into agreements and perform legal acts in their own name and by charter, the villains had to

manorial customs of the same character as those followed on ordinary estates, leaves no doubt as to the course of the proceedings. See above the passage quoted on pp. 113-6. Comp. a parallel ceremony as to freehold, Madox, Formulare, p. 54. The instance has been pointed out to me by Prof. Maitland.

[1] See Pollock, Land-laws, 199, 208 (2nd ed.).

content themselves with ceremonial actions before the court. They were faithful in this respect to old German tradition, while the privileged people followed precedents which may be ultimately traced to a Roman origin. The court roll or record of manorial courts enabled the base tenant to show, for instance, that some piece of land was his although he had no charter to produce in proof of his contention. And we find the rolls appealed to constantly in the course of manorial litigation[1]. But the rolls were nothing else than records of actions in the court and before the court. They could actually guide the decision, but their authority was not independent; it was merely derived from the authority of the court. For this reason the evidence of the rolls, although very valuable, was by no means indispensable. A claimant could go past them to the original fount, that is, to the testimony of the court. And here we must keep clear of a misconception suggested by a first-sight analysis of the facts at hand. It would seem that the verdict of neighbours, to which debateable claims are referred to in the manorial courts, stands exactly on a par with the verdicts of jurymen taken by the judges of the Royal Courts. This is not so, however. It is true that the striving of manorial officers to make the procedure of halimotes as much like the common law procedure as possible, went far to produce similarity between forms of actions, presentments, verdicts and juries, in both sets of tribunals. But nevertheless, characteristic distinctions remained to show that the import of some institutions brought near each other in this way was widely different. I have said already that the peasant suitors of the halimote are appealed to on

---

[1] Seld. Soc. ii. 33; insertion of a lease in the roll; p. 35: 'Lis conquievit inter ipsos ita quod concordati fuerunt in hac forma de voluntate domini et in plena curia ita videlicet quod predictus Willelmus de Baggemere concessit, remisit et quietum clamavit pro se et heredibus suis ... et hoc paratus est verificare per recordum rotulorum seu 12 juratores ejusdem curie per voluntatem domini et senescalli.' p. 166: 'Et sciatis quod si haberem ad manus rotulos curie tempore Willelmi de Lewes ego vobis certificarem et vobis monstrarem multa mirabilia non opportune facta.'

questions of law as well as on questions of fact. But the most important point for our present purpose is this : the jurors called to substantiate the claim of a party in a trial are mere representatives of the whole court. The testimony of the court is taken indirectly through their means, and very often resort is had to that testimony without the intermediate stage of a jury. Now this is by no means a trifle from the point of view of legal analysis. The grand and petty juries of the common law are means of information, and nothing more. They form no part of the tribunal, strictly speaking ; the court is constituted by the judges, the lawyers commissioned by the king, who adopt this method in investigating the facts before them, because a knowledge of the facts at issue, and an understanding of local conditions surrounding them, is supposed to reside naturally in the country where the facts have taken place [1]. Historically the institution is evolved from examinations of witnesses and experts, and has branched off in France into the close formalism of inquisitorial process. The manorial jury, on the other hand, represents the court, and interchanges with it [2]. For this reason, we may speak directly of the court instead of treating of its delegates. And if the verdict of the court is taken, it is not on account of the chance knowledge, the presumable acquaintance of the suitors with facts and conditions, but as a living remembrance of what took place before this same court, or as a re-assertion of its power of regulating the legal standing of the community. The verdict of the suitors is only another form of the entry on the rolls, and both are means of securing the continuity of an institution and not merely of providing information to outsiders. Of

---

[1] These points have been conclusively settled by the masterly investigations of Brunner, Zeugen- und Inquisitions-beweis (Abhandlungen der Wiener Akademie) and Entstehung der Schwurgerichte.

[2] Seld. Soc. ii. 41 : 'Quod talis sit consuetudo manerii et quod dicta Augnes sic venit in plena curia cum marito suo et totum jus et clamium quod haberet vel aliquo modo habere poterit in toto vel in parte hujus burgagii in manus domini ad opus ejusdem R. reddidit ponit super curiam ... Et 12 juratores curie,' etc.

course, claims may not be always reduced to such elementary forms that they can be decided by a mere reference to memory, the memory of the constituted body of the court. A certain amount of reasoning and inference may be involved in their settlement, a set of juridical doctrines is necessary to provide the general principles of such reasoning. And in both respects the manorial court is called upon to act. It is considered as the repositary of legal lore, and the exponent of its applications. This means that the court is, what its name implies, a tribunal and not a set of private persons called upon to assist a judge by their knowledge of legal details or material facts [1].

The whole exposition brings us back to a point of primary importance. The title by which land is held according to manorial custom is derived from communal authority quite as much as from the lord's grant. Without stepping out of the feudal evidence into historical inquiry, we find that civil arrangements of the peasantry are based on acts performed through the agency of the steward, and before the manorial court, which has a voice in the matter and vouches for its validity and remembrance. The 'full court' is noticed in the records as quite as necessary an element in the conveyancing business as the lord and his steward, although the legal theory of modern times has affected to take into account only these latter [2]. Indeed,

Communal testimony.

---

[1] I do not mean to say that the analytical distinctions which we make between fact and law, between presenters to a tribunal and assessors of a tribunal, were clearly perceived or consequently carried out in the twelfth or thirteenth centuries. On the contrary there was a good deal of confusion in details, and the instinctive logic of facts had more to do in dividing and settling institutions than conscious reasoning. Juries and assizes of the Royal Courts might be called upon incidentally to decide legal questions, but, in the aggregate, there can be hardly a doubt that the sworn inquests before the Royal judges were working to provide the Courts with a knowledge of local facts and perhaps conditions, while the manorial court gave legal decisions.

[2] Seld. Soc. ii. 41 : ' Et 12 juratores curie . . . dicunt super sacramentum suum quod predicta Agnes venit in *plena curia* et totum jus et clamium quod aliquo modo habere potuit in dicto burgagio in manus domini reddidit.' 42: ' Et juratores . . . dicunt super sacramentum suum quod Juliana per quam

it is the part assumed by the court which appears as the distinctive, if not the more important factor. A feoffment of land made on the basis of free tenure proceeds from the grantor in the same way as a grant on the conditions of base tenure ; freehold comes from the lord, as well as copyhold. But copyhold is necessarily transferred in court, while freehold is not. And if we speak of the presentment of offences through the representatives of townships, as of the practice of communal accusation, even so we have to call the title by which copyhold tenure is created a claim based on communal testimony.

Courts on the ancient demesne. All the points noticed in the rolls of manors held at common law are to be found on the soil of ancient demesne, but they are stated more definitely there, and the rights of the peasant population are asserted with greater energy. Our previous analysis of the condition of ancient demesne has led us to the conclusion, that it presents a crystallisation of the manorial community in an earlier stage of development than in the ordinary manor, but that the constitutive elements in both cases are exactly the same. For this reason, every question arising in regard to the usual arrangements ought to be examined in the light of the evidence that comes from the ancient demesne.

We have seen that it would be impossible to maintain that originally the steward was the only judge of the manorial tribunal ; the whole court with its free and unfree suitors participates materially in the administration of justice, and its office is extended to questions of law as well as to issues of fact. On the other hand, it was clear that the steward and the lord were already preparing the position which they ultimately assumed in legal theory,

dicta Matildis petit hujusmodi messuagium nunquam fuit seisita de ipso mesuagio, set Willelmus Ponfrayt maritus ipsius Juliane, unde secundum consuetudinem manerii Juliana post mortem W. mariti sui nichil poterit clamare nisi dotem in huiusmodi mesuagium *nisi fuerit in plena curia* una cum marito suo de huiusmodi *perquisito conjunctim seisita.*' Cf. p. 40: ' Unde Willelmus pro *premissis in plena curia recordatis et inrotulatis* dat domino 10 solidos.'

that in the exercise of their functions they were beginning to monopolise the power of ultimate decision and to restrict the court to the duty of preliminary presentment. The same parties are in presence in the court of ancient demesne, but the right of the suitors has been summed up by legal theory in quite the opposite direction. The suitors are said to be the judges there; legal dogmatism has set up its hard and fast definitions, and drawn its uncompromising conclusions as if all the historical facts had always been arrayed against each other without the possibility of common origins and gradual development. Is it necessary to say that the historical reality was very far from presenting that neat opposition? The ancient demesne suitors are villains in the main, though privileged in many respects, and the lord and steward are not always playing such a subordinate part that one may not notice the transition to the state of things that exists in common law manors. It is curious, anyhow, that later jurisprudence was driven to set up as to the ancient demesne court a rule which runs exactly parallel to the celebrated theory that there must be a plurality of free tenants to constitute a manor. Coke expresses it in the following way: 'There cannot be ancient demesne unless there is a court and suitors. So if there be but one suitor, for that the suitors are the judges, and therefore the demandant must sue at common law, there being a failure of justice within the manor[1].' We shall have to speak of this rule again when treating of classes in regard to manorial organisation. But let us notice, even now, that in this view of the ancient demesne court the suitors are considered as the cardinal element of its constitution. The same notion may be found already in trials of the fourteenth and even of the thirteenth century. A curious case is reported in the Year Books of 11/12 Edw. III[2]. Herbert of St. Quentyn brought a writ of false

---

[1] 4 Inst. 270, cap. 58.

[2] Y. B. 11/12 Edw. III (Rolls Ser.), p. 325, sqq.: '. . . les suters de Cokam firent venir plein record . . . les suiters agarderent seisine de terre

judgment against John of Batteley and his wife, the judgment having been given in the court of Cookham, an
ancient demesne manor. The suitors, or suit-holders as
they were called there, sent up their record to the King's
Bench, and many things were brought forward against the
conduct of the case by the counsel for the plaintiff, the
defendant trying to shield himself by pleading the custom
of the manor to account for all unusual practices. The
judges find, however, that one point at least cannot be
defended on that ground. The suitors awarded default
against the plaintiff because he had not appeared in
person before them, and had sent an attorney, who had
been admitted by the steward alone and not in full court.
Stonor, C. J., remarks, 'that it is against law that the
person who holds the court is not suffered to record an
attorney for a plea which will be discussed before him.'
The counsel for the plaintiff offer to prove that the
custom of the manor did not exclude an attorney appointed before the steward, on condition that the steward
should tell it to the suitors in the next court after receiving him. The case is interesting, not merely because
it exhibits the suit-holders in the undisputed position of
judges, but also because it shows the difficulties created by
the presence of the second element of the manorial system,
the seignorial element, which would neither fit exactly into
an entirely communal organisation nor be ousted from it[1].

... il firent faux judgement... *Stonore*: Cest usage est molt encontre
la ley, qe cesti qe doit tenir les plees ne poet pas recorder un attourne en
ple qe serra plede devant lui mesme. *Trew*: Nous voloms averer qe les
usages sont tiels, qe le seneschal de la court poet resceivir un attourne, issint
qil dei entre les suiters coment il ad resceu un tiel attourne en tiel ple a la
proschein court apres la resceite, et vous dions qe cesti Adam qe respondi
par attourne fut resceu attourne en la manere.' Cf. Lysons, Magna Brit. i.
266. Y. B. 3 Edw. III. 29 : ' Rob. le W. porta son brief de faux judgement
devers un home et sa feme, et apres le record avowe par les suters de la
court de Bloxham ... les suters agarderent qe Robert et ses plegis fuerent
in le mercie, et quod narratio sua fuit iniqua, et recordarent un nonsuit la
ou la partie fust en court, per qe nous prioms qe cel record soit revers.'
Viner, Abr. ii. A. 5, O. 6.

[1] Y. B. 11/12 Edw. III (Rolls Ser.), p. 517 : ' *Trew*. Le brief suppose qe
le defendant tint le ple et qil fut baillif, ou seuters tenent le ple qe ont

The difficulty stands quite on the same line with that which meets us in the common law manor, where the element of the communal assessors has been ultimately suppressed and conjured away, as it were, by legal theory. The results are contradictory, but on the same line, as I say. And the more we go back in time, the more we find that both elements, the lord and the community, are equally necessary to the constitution of the court. In the thirteenth century we find already that the manorial bailiffs are made responsible for the judgment along with the suitors and even before them [1].

The rolls of ancient demesne manors present a considerable variety of types, shading off from an almost complete independence of the suitors to forms which are not very different from those of common law manors. Stoneleigh may be taken as a good specimen of the first class.

The manor was divided into six hamlets, and every one of these consisted of eight virgates of land which were originally held by single socmen; although the regularity of the arrangement seems to have been broken up very soon

The court at Stoneleigh.

record; jugement de bref. Et non allocetur, quia ipse tenet curiam et ei dirigitur breve.'

[1] Note Book of Bracton, pl. 1122: 'Preceptum fuit ballivis de Kingestona quod in plena curia sua de Kingestona recordari facerent loquelam ... et recordum venire facerent per quatuor qui recordo illi interfuerunt, etc. ... Ideo balliui inde sine die et Radulfus in misericordia.' 834: 'Preceptum fuit vicecomiti quod preciperet balliuis manerii Domini Regis de Haueringes quod recordari facerent in curia domini Regis de Haueringes loquelam que fuit in eadem curia per breve domini Regis ... unde predicte Agnes et Dyonisia queste fuerunt falsum sibi factum fuisse iudicium in eadem curia et quod diligenter inquirerent qui fuerunt illi de maneriis Domini Regis de Writele, Neuport et Hatfeuld qui interfuerunt predicto iudicio faciendo simul cum hominibus Domini Regis de Haueringes et illos venire facerent aput Aueringe ad diem quem predicti homines et balliui Haueringe predicti loquelam recordari facerent, ita quod tam predicti ballivi et homines de Haueringe quam predicti homines de predictis maneriis recordum illud haberent coram justiciariis aput Westmonasterium per 4 legales homines de manerio de Aueringes et 6 de maneriis de Writele, de Neuport et de Hatfeuldia ex illis qui recordo illi interfuerunt. ... Consideratum est quod illi de predictis maneriis falsum fecerunt iudicium et ideo omnes de manerio in misericordia preter Willelmum Dun ... qui *noluerunt consentire judicio*.'

in consequence of increase of population, extension of the cultivated area, and the sale of small parcels of the holdings. The socmen met anciently to hold courts in a place called Motstowehill, and afterwards in a house which was built for the purpose by the Abbot. The way in which the Register speaks of the admission of a socman to his holding is very characteristic : ' Every heir succeeding to his father ought to be admitted to the succession in his fifteenth year, and let him pay relief to the lord, that is, pay twice his rent. And he will give judgments with his peers the socmen ; and become reeve for the collection of the lord's revenue, and answer to writs and do everything else as if he was of full age at common law.' The duty and right to give judgment in the Court of Stoneleigh is emphatically stated on several occasions, and altogether the jurisdictional independence of the court and of its suitors is set before us in the smallest but always significant details. If somebody is bringing a royal close writ of right directed to the bailiffs of the manor it cannot be opened unless in full court. When the bailiff has to summon anybody by order of the court he takes two socmen to witness the summons. Whenever a trial is terminated either by some one's default in making his law or by non-defence the costs are to be taxed by the court. The alienation of land and admittance of strangers are allowed only upon the express consent of the court [1]. In one word, every page of the Stoneleigh Register shows a closely and powerfully organised community, of which the lord is merely a president.

---

[1] Stoneleigh Reg., f. 75 : 'Item si aliquis deforciatur de tenemento suo et tulerit breve Regis clausum ballivis manerii versus deforciantes, dictum breve non debet frangi nisi in curia ... Item quando ballivus aliquem summoneat ex precepto curie, tunc assumet secum duos sokemannos quos voluerit pro testanda summonicione predicta ... Item qualitercumque placitum terminetur in curia sive in deficiendo in lege vadiata sive per non defensionem dampna sunt semper taxanda per curiam ... Item debent sokemanni respondere per 12 coram justiciariis et coronatore domini Regis. Et ipsi dabunt iudicia curie de Stonle ... Item nullus adiudicabitur tenens terre nisi qui a curia tenens acceptatur per fidelitatem et alias consuetudines licet tenens extra curiam aliquem feoffaverit per cartam vel sine carta.'

The rolls of King's Ripton are not less explicit in this respect. People are fined for selling land without the licence of the court, for selling it 'outside the court[1].' The judgment depends entirely on the verdict given by the community of suitors or its representatives the jurors. When the parties rely on some former decision, arrangement, or statement of law, they appeal to the rolls of the court, which, as has been said already, present nothing else but the recorded jurisprudence of the body of suitors[2]. The extent of the legal self-government of this little community may be well seen in the record of a trial in which the Abbot of Ramsey, the lord of the manor, is impleaded upon a little writ of right by one of his tenants[3]. But it is hardly necessary to dwell on so normal an event. I should like to take up for once the opposite standpoint, and to show that in these very communities on the ancient demesne elements are apparent which have thrived and developed in ordinary manors to such an extent as to obscure their self-government. In the Rolls of King's Ripton we might easily notice a number of instances in which the influence of the lord makes itself felt directly or indirectly through the means of his steward. We come, for instance, on the following forms of pleading : An action of dower is brought, and the defendants ask that the laws and customs hitherto used

Rolls of King's Ripton.

---

[1] Selden Soc. ii. 122 : 'Capiatur in manum domini quarta pars unius rode prati jacens in Smalemade quam Rogerus Greylong vendidit Nicholao le Neuman sine licencia curie.' Cf. 112 : 'Praesentatum est quod Hugo Graeleng solvit sursum extra curiam ad opus Thome Aspelon de Broucton liberi unam portionem cuiusdam mesuagii . . . Ideo preceptum quod capiatur in manum domini.'

[2] We hear constantly such phrases as the following : 'Quod iuncta est secum vocat rotulos ad warrantum ; ponit se super rotulos.' But we have also : ' Et partes pecierunt quod inquiratur per villatam que dixit quod sufficientem duxit sectam. Postea testificatum fuit per totam villatam quod dictus Nicolaus tenebatur dicto Bartholomeo in predictis 5d.' (Seld. Soc. ii. 118). In one case the party relies on the evidence of the Register of Ramsey (p. 111), which was compiled, of course, on the basis of sworn inquests held in the different manors.

[3] Seld. Soc. ii. 112.

in the court should be observed in regard to them—they
have a right to three summonses, three distraints, and three
essoins, and if they make default after that, the land ought
to be taken into the lord's hand, when, but only if it is
not replevied in the course of fifteen days, it will be lost for
good and all. All these demands are granted by the steward,
with whom the decision, at least formally, rests[1]. Again,
when we hear that the whole court craves leave to defer
its judgment till the next meeting, it is clear that it rests
with the steward to grant this request[2]. We may find
now and then a consideration for the interests of the lord
which transcends the limits of mere formal right, as in a
case where a certain Margery asks the court, without any
writ of right or formal action, that an inquest may be held
as to a part of her messuage which is detained in the hands
of the Abbot, although she performs the service due for it.
The inquest is held, and apparently ends in her favour, but
she is directed at the same time to go and speak with the
lord about the matter. Ultimately she gets what she wants
after this private interview[3]. The proceedings are irregular and interesting: the usual forms of action are disregarded; a verdict is given, but the material decision
is left with the lord, and is to be sought for by private
intercession. Quite close to this entry we find an instance
which is in flagrant contradiction with such a considerate
treatment of all parties. The jurors of the court are called
upon to decide a question of testament and succession.

---

[1] Augment. Court Rolls, Portf. xxiii. No. 94, m. 3: 'Quod quidem per
senescallum concessum est eisdem' (the entry is omitted in Mr. Maitland's
publication).

[2] Seld. Soc. ii. 111.

[3] Augment. Court Rolls, Portf. xxiii. No. 94, m. 25 v. (the entry is not in the
Selden volume): 'Margeria que fuit uxor Nicholai de Aula de Kingesripton
venit et petit unum parvum mesuagium existens in manu domini quod quondam fuit de mesuagio suo proprio et quod ipsa Margeria singulis annis defendit versus dominum Abbatem, unde petit quod ius suum super hoc inquiratur per bonam inquisicionem. Que venit et dicit . . . Et ideo preceptum
eidem quod inde habeat colloquium cum domino. Et postea colloquio habito
cum domino concessum est ei quod pacifice habeat faciendo seruicia inde
debita et consueta.'

They say that none of them was present when the testament was made, and that they know nothing about it, and will say nothing about it. 'And so leaving their business undone, and in great contempt of the lord and of his bailiffs, they leave the court. And therefore it is ordered that the bailiffs do cause to be levied a sum of 40s. to the use of the lord from the property of the said jurors by distress continued from day to day[1].' This case may stand as a good example both of the sturdy self-will which the peasantry occasionally asserted in their dealings with the lord, and of the opportunities that the lord had of asserting his superiority in a very high-handed manner.

But we need not even turn to any egregious instances in which the lord's power is thus displayed. The usual forms of surrender are there to show that, as regards origins, we have the same thing here as in ordinary manors, although the peculiarities of the ancient demesne have brought forward the features of communal organisation in a very marked way, and have held the element of lordship in check.

We have seen that there was only one halimot in the thirteenth and the preceding centuries, and that the division into customary court and court baron developed at a later time. We have seen, secondly, that this halimot was a meeting of the community under the presidency of the steward, and that the relative functions of community and steward became very distinct only in later days. It remains to be seen how far the fundamental class division between free tenants and villains affected the management of the court. As there was but one halimot and not two, both classes had to meet and to act concurrently in it. The free people now and then assert separate claims: a chaplain wages his law on the manor of Brightwaltham that he did not defame the lord's butler, but when he gets convicted by a good inquest of jurors of having broken the lord's hedges and carried away the lord's fowls, he will not justify himself of these trespasses and departs in contempt,

Free suitors in the halimot.

[1] Selden Soc. ii. 127.

doubtless because he will not submit to the judgment of people who are not on a par with him [1]. Freeholders object to being placed on ordinary juries of the manor [2], although they will serve as jurors on special occasions, and as a sort of controlling body over the common presenters [3]. Amercements are sometimes taxed by free suitors [4]. But although some division is apparent in this way, and the elements for a separation into two distinct courts are gathering, the normal condition is one which does not admit of any distinction between the two classes. We come here across the same peculiarity that we have seen in police and criminal law, namely, that the fundamental line of civil condition seems disregarded. Even when a court is mainly composed of villains, and in fact called curia villanorum, some of its suitors may be freeholders [5]. Even in a court composed of free people, like that of Broughton, there may be villains among them [6]. The parson, undoubtedly a free man, may appear as a villain in some rolls [7]. Altogether, the fact has to be noticed as a very important one, that whatever business the freeholders may have had in connexion with the manorial system, this business was transacted by courts which consisted chiefly of servile tenants [8]. In fact the pre-

[1] Selden Soc. ii. 173.

[2] Ibid. 94 : ' Reginaldus fil. Benedicti injuste dedicit esse unus de 12 juratoribus allegando libertatem . . . Dicunt eciam quod Willelmus de Bernewell injuste allegat libertatem propter quam contradicit esse unus de juratis.' Cf. Cor. Rege incerti anni Johann. 5 : ' Predecessores sui et ipse tenuerunt liberum tenementum et quod quidam ex juratis sunt consuetudinarii monialium.' Cor. Rege Pascha, 9 Edw. I, 34, b : ' (Amerciamentum sochemanni) per pares vel per liberos de curia et vicinos ad curiam venientes.'

[3] Hereford Rolls (Bodleian), 12: ' Compertum per libere tenentes quod custumarii falso presentant . . . ideo custumarii in misericordia.' Rot. Hundr. ii. 469 : ' Quatuor homines et prepositus presentabant defaltas predictis liberis hominibus et ipsi liberi presentabant ballivis.'

[4] Seld. Soc. ii. 44.

[5] Introduction to Seld. Soc. ii. p. lxx.

[6] Seld. Soc. ii. 67.

[7] Ibid. 164.

[8] See as to all this Mr. Maitland's Introduction to the Selden volume (ii), pp. lxix, lxx.

senting inquests, on which the free tenants refused to serve,
would not be prevented by their composition from attaint-
ing these free tenants.

This seems strange and indeed anomalous. One point Require-
remains to be observed which completes the picture: free suit-
although the great majority of the thirteenth century ors.
peasantry are mere villains, although on some manors we
hardly distinguish freeholders, there is a legal requirement
that there should be at least a few freeholders on every
manor. Later theory does not recognise as a manor an
estate composed only of demesne land and copyhold. Freeholds are declared to be a necessary element, and should
they all escheat, the manor would be only a reputed one[1].
We have no right to treat this notion as a mere invention
of later times. It comes forward again and again in the
shape of a rule, that there can be no court unless there are
some free tenants to form it. The number required varies.
In Henry VIII's reign royal judges were contented with
two. In John's time as many as twelve were demanded, if
a free outsider was to be judged. The normal number
seems to have been four, and when the record of the proceedings was sent up to the King's tribunal four suitors had
to carry it. The difference between the statement of Coke
and the earlier doctrine lies in the substitution of the manor
for the court. Coke and his authorities, the judges of Henry
VIII's reign, speak of the manor where the older jurisprudence spoke of the court. Their rule involves the more
ancient one and something in addition, namely, the inference
that if there be no court baron there is no manor. Now
this part of the doctrine, though interesting by itself, must
stand over for the present. Let us simply take the assertion that free suitors are necessary to constitute a court,
and apply it to a state of things when there was but one
strictly manorial court, the halimot. In 1294 it is noted

---

[1] Introd. to Selden Soc. ii. p. lxi, and following. Comp. Coram Rege, 27
Henry III, 2: 'Dicunt quod non est aliquis liber homo in eodem manerio
nisi Willelmus filius Radulfi qui respondet infra corpus comitatus.'

in the report of a trial that, 'in order that one may have a court he must have at least four free tenants, without borrowing the fourth tenant [1].' Now a number of easy explanations seem at hand: four free tenants at least were necessary, because four such tenants were required to take the record up to the king's court and to answer for any false judgment; a free tenant could protest against being impleaded before unfree people; some of the franchises could not be exercised unless there were free suitors to form a tribunal. But all these explanations do not go deep enough: they would do very well for the later court baron, but not for the halimot. It is not asserted that free suitors are necessary only in those cases where free tenants are concerned—it is the court as such which depends on the existence of such free suitors, the court which has largely, if not mostly, to deal with customary business, and consists to a great extent of customary tenants. And, curiously enough, when the court baron disengages itself from the halimot, the rule as to suitors, instead of applying in a special way to this court baron, for which it seems particularly fitted, extends to the notion of the manor itself, so that we are driven to ask why the manor is assumed to contain a certain number of free tenants and a court for them. Why is its existence denied where these elements are wanting? Reverting to the thirteenth century, we have to state similar puzzling questions: thus if one turns to the manorial surveys of the time, the freehold element seems to be relatively insignificant and more or less severed from the community; if one takes up the manorial rolls, the halimot is there with the emphatically expressed features and even the name of a court of villains; but when the common law is concerned, this same tribunal appears as a court of freeholders. The manors of the Abbey of Bec on English soil contained hardly any freeholders at all. Had the Abbey no courts? Had it no manors from the standpoint of Coke's theory? What were the halimots

---

[1] Y. B. 21-22 Edw. I, 526 (Rolls Series).

whose proceedings are recorded in the usual way on its manorial rolls? In presence of these flagrant contradictions I cannot help thinking that we here come across one of those interesting points where the two lines of feudal doctrine do not meet, and where different layers of theory may be distinguished.

Without denying in the least the practical importance of such notions as that which required that one's judges should be one's peers, or of such institutions as the bringing up of the manorial record to the King's Court, I submit that they must have exercised their influence chiefly by calling forth occasions when the main principle had to be asserted. Of course they could not create this principle: the idea that the halimot was a communal court constituted by free suitors meeting under the presidency of the steward, must have existed to support them. That idea is fully embodied in the constitution of the ancient demesne tribunal, where the suitors were admitted to be the judges, although they were villains, privileged villains and nothing else. Might we not start from the original similarity between ancient demesne and ordinary manors, and thus explain how the rule as to the necessary constitution of the manorial court was formed? It seems to me a mere application of the higher rule that a court over free people must contain free people, to a state of things where the distinction between free and unfree was not drawn at the same level as in the feudal epoch, but was drawn at a lower point. We have seen that a villain was in many respects a free man; that he was accepted as such in criminal and police business; that he was free against everybody but his lord in civil dealings; that the frank-pledge system to which he belonged was actually taken to imply personal freedom, although the freeholders ultimately escaped from it. I cannot help thinking that a like transformation of meaning as in the case of frank-pledge did take place in regard to the free suitors of the manorial court. The original requirement cannot have concerned freeholders in the usual legal sense, but free and lawful men, 'worthy of were and wite'—a

Free suitors and freeholders.

description which would cover the great bulk of the villains and exclude slaves and their progeny. When the definitions of free holding and villainage got to be very stringent and marked, the *libere tenentes* assumed a more and more overbearing attitude and got a separate tribunal, while the common people fell into the same condition as the progeny of slaves. In a word, I think that the general movement of social development which obliterated the middle class of Saxon ceorls or customary free tenants (leaving only a few scattered indications of its existence) made itself felt in the history of the manorial court by the substitution of exceptional freeholders for the free suitors of the halimot. Such a substitution had several results: the diverging history of the ancient demesne from that of the ordinary manorial courts, the elevation of the court baron, the growth of the notion that in the customary court the only judge was the steward. One significant little trait remains to be observed in this context. It has been noticed [1] that care seems to be taken that there should be certain Freemen or Franklains in every manor. The feature has been mentioned in connexion with the doctrine of free suitors necessary to a court. But these people are by no means free tenants ; in the usual legal sense they are mostly holding in villainage, and their freedom must be traced not to the dual division of feudal times, but to survivals of the threefold division which preceded feudalism, and contrasted slave, free ceorl, and military landowner.

Honorial Courts.

Before concluding this chapter I have to say a few words upon those forms of the manorial court which appear as a modification of the normal institution. Of the ancient demesne tribunal I have already spoken, but there are several other peculiar formations which help to bring out the main ideas of manorial organisation, just because they swerve from it in one sense or another. Mr. Maitland has spoken so well of one of these variations, that I need not do anything more than refer the reader to his pages

[1] Comp. Mr. Maitland in his often-quoted Introduction, p. lxxi.

about the Honour and its Court[1]. He has proved that it
is no mere aggregate of manors, but a higher court, constructed on the feudal principle, that every lord who had
free tenants under him could summon them to form a
court for their common dealings. It ought to be observed,
however, that the instance of Broughton, though its main
basis is undoubtedly this feudal doctrine, still appears
complicated by manorial business, which is brought in
by way of appeal and evocation, as well as by a mixture
between the court of the great fief and the halimot of
Broughton.

A second phenomenon well worth consideration is the The soke.
existence in some parts of the country of a unit of jurisdiction and management which does not fall in with the
manor,—it is called the *soke*, and comprises free tenantry
dispersed sometimes over a very wide area. A good example of this institution is given by Mr. Clark's publication on the Soke of Rothley in Lincolnshire[2]. We need
not go into the details of the personal status of the tenants,
they clearly come under the description of free sokemen.
Our present concern is that they are not simply arranged
into the manor of Rothley as usual, but are distinguished
as forming the soke of this manor. They are rather
numerous—twenty-three—and come to the lord's court,
but their services are trifling as compared with those of
the customers, and their possessions are so scattered, that
there could be no talk of their joining the agrarian unit
of the central estate. What unites them to the manor is
evidently merely jurisdiction, although in feudal theory
they are assumed to hold of the lord of Rothley. But they
are set apart as forming the soke, and this shows them
clearly to be subjected to jurisdiction rather than anything
else. It is interesting to note such survivals in the thirteenth century, and within the realm of feudal law the
case of Rothley is of course by no means the only one[3].

[1] Introduction to Seld. Soc. ii. p. lxvi.
[2] Archaeologia, vol. 47, p. 27, and following.
[3] Rot. Hundr., Cartulary of Ramsey, i.

If we contrast this exceptional appearance of the soke outside the manor with the normal arrangement by which all the free tenants are fitted into the manor, we shall come to the conclusion that originally the element of jurisdiction over freeholders might exist separately from the management of the estate, but that in the general course of events it was merged into the estate and formed one of the component elements of the manorial court. The case of Rothley is especially interesting because the men of the soke or under the soke do not go to a court of their own, but simply join the manorial meetings. If they are still kept apart, it is evident that their relation to the court, and indeed to the manor, was what made them distinct from everybody else. In short, to state the difference in a pointed form, the other people were tenants and they were subjects.

The Aston case.
One more point remains to be noticed. In order to make it clear we must by way of exception start from the arrangements of a later epoch than that which we have been discussing. The manor of Aston and Cote, which may have been carved out with several others from the manor of Bampton, presents a very good instance of a village meeting which does not coincide with the manorial divisions, and appears constructed on the lines of a village community which has preserved its unity, although several manors have grown out of it. It was stated by the lord of the manor of Aston and Cote in 1657, that 'there hath been a custom time out of mind that a certain number of persons called the *Sixteen*, or the greater part of them, have used to make orders, set penalties, choose officers, and lot meadows, and do all such things as are usually performed or done in the courts baron of other manors.' All the details of this case are interesting, but we need not go into them, because they have been set out with sufficient care in the existing literature, and summed up by Mr. Gomme in his book on the Village Community[1]. It is the main point which

---

[1] Gomme, Village Community, 162, etc.

we must consider. Here is an assembly meeting to transact legal and economic business, which acts on the pattern of manorial courts. And if not a manorial court, what is it? I think it is difficult to escape the conclusion that it is a meeting of the village community outside the lines of manorial division. The supposition that it represents the old manor of Bampton, to which Aston, Cote, Bampton Pogeys, Bampton Priory are subordinated, is entirely insufficient to explain the case, because then we should not have had to recognise new manors in the fractions which were detached from Bampton, and there would have been no call to speak of a peculiar assembly assuming the competence of a court baron—we should have had the manorial court and the lord of Bampton, and not the Sixteen to speak of. The fact is patent and significant. It shows by itself that there may have been cases where the village community and the manor did not coincide, and the village community had the best of it.

The first proposition does not admit of doubt. It was of quite common occurrence that the land of one village should be broken up between several manors, although its open field system and all its husbandry arrangements remained undivided. The question arises, how was that system to work? There could be express agreement between the owners[1]; ancient custom and the interference of manorial officers chosen from the different parts could help on many occasions. But it is impossible to suppose, in the light of the Bampton instance, that meetings might not sometimes exist in such divided villages which took into their hands the management of the many economic questions arising out of common husbandry: questions about hedges, rotation of crops, commonable animals, usage as to wood, moor, pasture, and so forth. A diligent search in the customs of manors at a later period, say in the sixteenth and seventeenth centuries, must certainly disclose a number of similar instances. Our own material

Manor and Township.

---

[1] Cart. of Malmesbury (Rolls Ser.), ii. 221.

does not help us, because it passes over questions of husbandry, and touches merely jurisdiction, ownership, and tenant-right. And so we must restrict ourself to notice the opening for an inquiry in that direction.

Township and Manor.

Such an inquiry must also deal with the converse possibility, namely, the cases in which the manor is so large that several village units fit into it. We may find very frequently in some parts of the country large manors which are composed of several independent villages and hamlets[1]. On large tracts of land these villages would form separate open field groups. Although the economic evidence is not within our reach in early times, we have indications of separate village meetings under the manorial court even from the legal point of view taken by the court-rolls. In several instances the entries printed in the second volume of the Selden Society publications point to the action of townships as distinct from the manorial court, and placed under it. In Broughton a man distrained for default puts himself on the verdict of the whole court and of the township of Hurst, both villains and freemen, that he owes no suit to the court of Broughton, save twice a year and to afforce the court. Be it noted that the court of Hurst is distinguished

---

[1] A very good case in point is presented by Hitchin, because the boundaries and the jurisdiction of the manor comprise a great number of villages and hamlets which managed their open fields quite independently of the central township of Hitchin, and could not but do so, as they lay quite apart and a good way from it, as may be seen on the Ordnance Map. And still the manor comprises 'the township of Hitchin and the hamlet of Walsworth, the lesser manors of the Rectory of Hitchin, of Moremead, otherwise Charlton, and of the Priory of the Biggin, being comprehended within the boundaries of the said manor of Hitchin, which also extends into the hamlets of Langley and Preston in the said parish of Hitchin, and into the parishes of Ickleford, Ipolitts, Kimpton, Kingswalden, and Offley.' (See-bohm, Village Community, 443, 444.) As Mr. Seebohm tells me, the contrast between the central portion, that of the township, managed in one open field system, and the outlying parts, is probably reflected in the curious denominations of the manor as Portman and Foreign. It is well known how frequently our surveys mention hamlets; in many cases these annexes of townships are so widely scattered, that it would be impossible to suppose one open field system for them.

from the township, which appears subordinated to it, probably because there were other townships in the manor of Hurst. At the same time the township is called upon to act as an independent unit in the matter. Even so in the rolls of Hemingford, the township which forms the centre of the manor and gives its name to it, is sometimes singled out from the rest of the court as an organised corporation [1]. When township and tithing coincided, as in the case of Brightwaltham, the tithing gets opposed to the general court in the same way [2]. Altogether the corporate unity of townships is well perceivable behind the feudal covering of the manor. Mr. Maitland says with perfect right, 'the manor was not a unit in the governmental system; the county was such a unit, so was the hundred. So again was the vill, for the township had many police duties to perform; it was an amerciable, punishable unit; not so the manor, unless it coincided with the vill [3].' And then he proceeds to suggest that the true explanation of the manor is that it represents an estate which could be and was administered as a single economic and agrarian whole. I am unable to follow him entirely as to this last point, because it seems pretty clear that the open field arrangements followed the division into townships, and not those into manors. From the point of view of the services, of the concentration of duties of the tenantry in regard to the lord, the manor was a whole, and for this very reason it was a whole as regards geldability, but this is only one side of the economic structure of society, the upper side, if one may be allowed to say so. The arrangement of actual cultivation is the other side, and it is represented by the township with its communal open fields. Now in a great many cases the estate and the community fitted into each other; and of these instances there is no need to speak any further. But if both did not fit, the agrarian unity is the township and not the manor.

[1] Seld. Soc. ii. 68, 90.
[2] Ibid. 162, 166.
[3] Introd. to Seld. Soc. ii. p. xxxix.

The open field system appears in this connexion as outside the manor, and proceeding from the rural community by itself.

Let us sum up the results obtained in this chapter.

1. The village communities contained in the manorial system are organised on a system of self-government which affords great help to the lord in many ways, but certainly limits his power materially, and reduces him to the position of a constitutional ruler.

2. The original court of the manor was one and the body of its suitors was one. The distinction between courts for free tenants and customary courts grows up very gradually in the fourteenth century, and later.

3. The steward was not the only judge of the halimot. The judgment came from the whole court, and its suitors, without distinction of class, were necessary judicial assessors.

4. The court of ancient demesne presents the same elements as the ordinary halimot, although it lays greater stress on the communal side of the organisation.

5. The conveyancing entries on the rolls do not prove the want of right on the part of the peasant holders. On the contrary, they go back to very early communal practice.

6. The rule which makes the existence of the manor dependent on the existence of free suitors is derived from the conception of the court as a court of free and lawful men, taking in villains and excluding slaves.

7. The manor by itself is the estate; the rural community and the jurisdiction of the soke are generally fused with it into one whole; but in some cases the two latter elements are seen emerging as independent growths from behind the manorial organisation.

CHAPTER VI.

THE MANOR AND THE VILLAGE COMMUNITY.

Conclusions.

IF we look at the village life of mediaeval England, not
for the purpose of dissecting it into its constitutive elements,
but in order that we may detect the principles that hold it
together and organise it as a whole, we shall be struck by
several features which make it quite unlike the present
arrangement of rural society. Even a casual observer will
not fail to perceive the contrast which it presents to that
free play of individual interests and that undisputed supremacy of the state in political matters, which are so
characteristic of the present time. And on the other hand
there is just as sharp a contrast between the manorial
system and a system of tribal relationships based on blood
relationship and its artificial outgrowths; and yet again
it may be contrasted with a village community built upon
the basis of equal partnership among free members. It is
evident, at the same time, that such differences, deep
though they are, cannot be treated as primordial and
absolute divisions. All these systems are but stages of
development, after all, and the most important problem
concerning them is the problem of their origins and mutual
relations. The main road towards its solution lies undoubtedly through the demesne of strictly historical in-

vestigation. Should we succeed in tracing with clearness the consecutive stages of the process and the intermediate links between them, the most important part of the work will have been done. This is simple enough, and seems hardly worth mentioning. But things are not so plain as they look.

To begin with, even a complete knowledge of the sequence of events would not be sufficient since it would merely present a series of arrangements following upon each other in time and not a chain of causes and effects. We cannot exempt ourselves from the duty of following up the investigation by speculations as to the agencies and motives which produced the changes. But even apart from the necessity of taking up ultimately what one may call the dynamic thread of the inquiry, there is considerable difficulty in obtaining a tolerably settled sequence of general facts to start with. Any one who has had to do with such studies knows how scanty the information about the earlier phenomena is apt to be, how difficult it is to distinguish between the main forms and the variations which mediate and lead from one to another. The task of settling a definite theory of development would not have been so arduous, and the conflicting views of scholars would not have suggested such directly opposite results, if the early data had not been so scattered and so ambiguous. The state of the existing material requires a method of treatment which may to some extent supplement the defects in the evidence. The later and well-recorded period ought to be made to supply additional information as to the earlier and imperfectly described ones. It is from this point of view that we must once more survey the ground that we have been exploring in the foregoing pages.

The first general feature that meets our eye is the cultivation of arable on the open-field system : the land tilled is not parcelled up by enclosures, but lies open through the whole or the greater part of the year ; the plot held and tilled by a single cultivator is not a compact piece, but is composed of strips strewn about in all parts of the village fields and intermixed with patches or strips possessed by fellow villagers. Now, both facts are remarkable. They do not square at all with the rules and tendencies of private ownership and individualistic husbandry. The individual proprietor will naturally try to fence in his plot against strangers, to set up hedges and walls that would render trespassing over his ground difficult, if not impossible. And he could not but consider intermixture as a downright nuisance, and strive by all means in his power to get rid of it. Why should he put up with the inconvenience of holding a bundle of strips lying far apart from each other, more or less dependent because of their narrowness on the dealings of neighbours, who may be untidy and unthrifty? Instead of having one block of soil to look to and a comparatively short boundary to maintain, every occupier has a number of scattered pieces to care for, and neighbours, who not only surround, but actually cut up, dismember, invade his tenement. The open-field system stands in glaring contradiction with the present state of private rights in Western Europe, and no wonder that it has been abolished everywhere, except on some few tracts of land kept back by geographical conditions from joining the movement of modern civilisation. And even in mediaeval history we perceive that the arrangement does not keep its hold on those occasions when the rights of individuals are strongly felt: it gives way on the demesne farm and on newly reclaimed land.

At the same time, the absence of perpetual enclosures and the intermixture of strips are in a general way quite prevalent at the present time in the East of Europe. What conditions do they correspond to? Why have nations living in very different climates and on very different soils adopted the open-field system again and again in spite of all inconveniences and without having borrowed it from each other?

There is absolutely nothing in the manorial arrangement to occasion this curious system. It is not the fact that peasant holdings are made subservient to the wants of the lord's estate, that can explain why early agriculture is in the main a culture of open fields and involves a marvellous intermixture of rights. The absence of any logical connexion between these two things settles the question as to historical influence. The open-field arrangement is, I repeat it, no lax or indifferent system, but stringent and highly peculiar. And so it cannot but proceed from some pressing necessity.

It is evidently communal in its very essence. Every trait that makes it strange and inconvenient from the point of view of individualistic interests, renders it highly appropriate to a state of things ruled by communal conceptions. It is difficult to prevent trespasses upon an open plot, but the plot must be open, if many people besides the tiller have rights over it, pasture rights, for instance. It involves great loss of time and difficulty of supervision to work a property that lies in thirty separate pieces all over the territory of a village, but such a disposition is remarkably well adapted for the purpose of assigning to fellow villagers equal shares in the arable. It is grievous to depend on your neighbours for the proceeds and results of your own work, but the tangled web of rights and boundaries becomes simple if one considers it as the management of land by an agricultural community which has allotted the places where its members have to work. Rights of common usage, communal apportionment of shares in the arable, communal arrangement of ways and times of cultivation— these are the chief features of open-field husbandry, and all point to one source—the village community. It is not a manorial arrangement, though it may be adapted to the manor. If more proof were needed we have only to notice the fact, that open-field cultivation is in full work in countries where the manor has not been established, and in times when it has not as yet been formed. We may take India or tribal Italy as instances.

The system as exhibited in England is linked to a division into holdings which gives it additional significance. The holding of the English peasant is distinguished by two

characteristic features : it is a unit which as a rule does
not admit of division ; it is equal to other units in the
same village. There is no need to point out at length
to what extent these features are repugnant to an individualistic order of things. They belong to a rural
community. But even in a community the arrangement
adopted seems peculiar. We must not disregard some
important contradictions. The holdings are not all equal,
but are grouped on a scale of three, four, five divisions—
virgates, bovates, and cotlands for instance. And the question may be put : why should an artificial arrangement
contrived for the sake of equality start from a flagrant
inequality which looks the more unjust, because instead of
those intermediate quantities which shade off into each
other in our modern society we meet with abrupt transitions ?
A second difficulty may be found in the unchangeable nature
of the holding. The equal virgates are in fact an obstacle
to a proportionate repartition of the land among the
population, because there is nothing to insure that the
differences of growth and requirements arising between
different families will keep square with the relations of the
holdings. In one case the family plot may become too
large, in another too scanty an allowance for the peasant
household working and feeding on that plot. And ultimately, as we have seen, the indivisible nature of the
holding looks to some extent like an artificial one, and
one that is more apparent than real. Not to speak of that
provincial variation, the Kentish system of gavelkind, we
notice that even in the rest of England large units are
breaking into fractions, and that very often the supposed
unity is only a thin covering for material division. Why
should it be kept up then ?

Such serious contradictions and incongruities lead us
forcibly to the conclusion that we have a state of transition
before us, an institution that is in some degree distorted
and warped from its original shape. In this respect the
manorial element comes strongly to the fore. The rough
scale of holdings would be grossly against justice for purely

communal purposes, but it is not only the occupation of
land, but also the incidence of services that is regulated
by it. People would not so much complain of holding five
acres instead of thirty, if they had to work and to pay six
times less in the first case. Again, a division of tenements
fixed once and for all in spite of changes in the numbers
and wants of the population, looks anything but convenient.
At the same time the fixed scheme of the division offers
a ready basis for computing rents and assessing labour
services. And for the sake of the lord it was advisable to
preserve outward unity even when the system was actually
breaking up : for dealings with the manorial administration
virgates remained undivided, even when they were no
longer occupied as integral units.

Although the holdings are undoubtedly made subservient
to the wants of the manor, it would be going a great deal
too far to suppose that they were formed with the primary
object of meeting those wants. If we look closer into the
structure we find that it is based on the relation between
the plough-team and the arable, a relation which is more or
less constant and explains the gradations and the mode of
apportionment. The division of the land is no indefinite
or capricious one, because the land has to be used in
certain quantities, and smaller quantities or fractions would
disarrange the natural connexion between the soil and the
forces that make it productive. The society of those days
appears as an agricultural mass consisting not of individual
persons or natural families, but of groups possessed of the
implements for tilling the land. Its unit of reckoning is
not the man, but the plough-beast. As the model plough-
team happens to be a very large one, the large unit of the
hide is adopted. Lesser quantities may be formed also,
but still they correspond to aliquot parts of the full team of
eight oxen. Thus the possible gradations are not so many
or so gentle as in our own time, but are in the main the
half plough-land, the virgate, and the oxgang. What else
there is can be only regarded as subsidiary to the main
arrangement: the cotters and crofters are not tenants in the

fields, but gardeners, labourers, craftsmen, herdsmen, and the like. If the country had not been mainly cultivated as ploughland, but had borne vines or olives or crops that required no cumbersome implements, but intense and individualistic labour, one may readily believe that the holdings would have been more compact, and also more irregular.

The principles of coaration give an insight into the nature of these English village communities. They did not aim at absolute equality; they subordinated the personal element to the agricultural one, if we may use that expression. Not so much an apportionment of individual claims was effected as an apportionment of the land to the forces at work upon it. This observation helps us to get rid of the anomalies with which we started: the holding was united because an ox could not be divided; the plots might be smaller or larger, but everywhere they were connected with a scheme of which the plough-team was the unit. An increasing population had to take care of itself, and to try to fit itself into the existing divisions by family arrangements, marriage, adoption, reclaiming of new land, employment for hire, by-professions, and emigration. The manorial factor comes in to make everything artificially regular and rigid.

If we examine the open-field system and its relation to the holdings of individual peasants, we see, as it were, the framework of a peasant community that has swerved from the path of its original development. The gathering of scattered and intermixed strips into holdings points to practices of division or allotment: these practices are the very essence of the whole, and they alone can explain the glaring inconveniencies of scattered ownership coupled with artificial concentration. But redivision of the arable is not seen in the documents of our period. There is no shifting of strips, no changes in the quantities allotted to each family. Everything goes by heredity and settled rules of family property, as if the husbandry was not arranged for communal ownership and re-allotment. I should like to compare the whole to the icebound surface of a northern sea : it is not smooth, although hard and immoveable, and the hills and hollows of the uneven plain remind one of the billows that rolled when it was yet unfrozen.

The treatment of the arable gives the clue to all other sides of the subject. The rights of common usage of meadow and pasture carry us back to practices which must have been originally applied to arable also. When one reads of a meadow being cut up into strips and partitioned for a year among the members of the community by regular rotation or by lot, one does not see why only the grass land should be thus treated while there is no re-allotment of the arable plots. As for the waste, it does not even admit of set boundaries, and the only possible means of apportioning its use is to prescribe what and how many heads of cattle each holding may send out upon it. The close affinity between the different parts of the village soil is especially illustrated by the fact, that the open-field arable is treated as common through the greater part of the year. Such facts are more than survivals, more than stray relics of a bygone time. The communal element of English mediaeval husbandry becomes conspicuous in the individualistic elements that grow out of it.

The question has been asked whether we ought not to regard these communal arrangements as derived from the exclusive right of ownership, and the power of coercion vested in the lord of the soil. I think that many features in the constitution of the thirteenth century manor show its gradual growth and comparatively recent origin. The so-called manorial system consists, in truth, in the peculiar connexion between two agrarian bodies, the settlement of villagers cultivating their own fields, and the home-estate of the lord tacked on to this settlement and dependent on the work supplied by it. I take only the agrarian side, of course, and do not mention the political protection which stands more or less as an equivalent for the profits received by the lord from the peasantry. And as for the agrarian arrangement, we ought to keep it quite distinct from forms which are sometimes confused with it through loose terminology.

A community paying taxes, farmers leasing land for rent, labourers without independent husbandry of their own, may be all subjected to some lord, but their subjection is not manorial. Two elements are necessary to constitute the manorial arrangement, the peasant village and the home farm worked by its help.

If we turn now to the evidence of the feudal period, we shall see that the labour-service relation, although very marked and prevalent in most cases, is by no means the only one that should be taken into account. In a large number of cases the relation between lord and peasants resolves itself into money payments, and this is only another way of saying that the manorial group disaggregates itself. The peasant holding gets free from the obligation of labouring under the supervision of the bailiff, and the home estate may be either thrown over or managed by the help of hired servants and labourers.

But alongside of these facts, testifying to a progress towards modern times, we find survivals of a more ancient order of things, quite as incompatible with manorial husbandry. Instead of performing work on the demesne, the peasantry are sometimes made to collect and furnish produce for the lord's table and his other wants. They send bread, ale, sheep, chicken, cheese, etc., sometimes to a neighbouring castle and sometimes a good way off. When we hear of the *firma unius noctis*, paid to the king's household by a borough or a village, we have to imagine a community standing entirely by itself and taxed to a certain tribute, without any superior land estate necessarily engrafted upon it ; a home farm may or may not be close by, but its management is not dependent on the customary work of the vill (*consuetudines villae*), and the connexion between the two is casual. The facts of which I am speaking are certainly of rare occurrence and dying out, but they are very interesting from a historical point of view, they throw light on a condition of things preceding the manorial system, and characterised by a large over-lordship exacting tribute, and not cultivating land by help of the peasantry.

We come precisely to the same conclusion by another way. The feudal landlord is represented in the village by his demesne land, and by the servants acting as his helpers in administration. Now, the demesne land is often found intermixed with the strips of the peasantry. This seems particularly fitted for a time when the peasantry did not collect to work on a separate home farm, but simply devoted one part of the labour on their own ground to the use of the lord. What I mean is, that if a demesne consisted of, say, every fifth acre in the village fields, the teams of four virgaters composing the plough would traverse this additional acre after going over four of their own instead of being called up under the supervision of the bailiff, to do work on an independent estate. The work performed by the peasants when the demesne is still in intermixture with the village land, appears as an intermediate stage between the tribute paid by a practically self-dependent community, and the double husbandry of a manorial estate linked to a village.

Another feature of transition is perceivable in the history of the class of servants or ministers who collect and supervise the dues and services of the peasants. The feudal arrangement is quite as much characterised by the existence of these middlemen as modern life by the agreements and money dealings which have rendered it useless. In the period preceding the manorial age we see fewer officers, and their interference in the life of the community is but occasional. The gathering of tribute, the supervision of a few labour duties in addition, did not require a large staff of ministers. It was in the interest of the lord to dispense as much as possible with their costly help, and to throw what obligations there were to be performed on the community itself. It seems to me that the feudal age has preserved several traces of institutions belonging to that period of transition. The older surveys, especially the Kentish ones, show a very remarkable development of carriage duties which must have been called forth by the necessity of sending produce to the lord's central halls or courts, while the home farms were still few and small. The riding bailiffs appear in ancient documents in a position which is gradually modified as time goes on. They begin by forming a very conspicuous class among the tenants, in fact the foremost rank of the peasantry. These radmen, radulfs, rodknights, riders, are privileged people, and mostly rank with the free tenants, but they are selected from among the villagers, and very closely resemble the hundredors, whose special duties have kept up their status among the general decay. In later times, in the second half of the thirteenth century and in the fourteenth, it would be impossible to distinguish such a class of riding tenants. They exist here and there, but in most cases their place has been taken by direct dependents of the lord. Besides, as the home-farm has developed on every manor, their office has lost some of the importance it had at a time when there was a good deal of business to transact in the way of communicating between the villages and the few central courts to which rents had to be carried. And, lastly, I may remind the reader of the importance attached in some surveys to the supervision of the best tenants over the rest at the boon works. The socmen, or free tenants, or holders of full lands, as the case may be, have to ride out with rods in their hands to inspect the people cutting the corn or making hay. These customs are mostly to be found in manors with a particularly archaic constitution. They occur very often on ancient demesne. And I need hardly say that they point to a still imperfect development of the ministerial class. The village is already set to work for the lord, but it manages this work as much as possible by itself, with hardly any interference from foreign overseers.

One part of the village population is altogether outside the manorial labour intercourse between village and de-mesne. The freeholders may perform some labour-services, but the home-farm could never depend on them, and when such services are mentioned, they are merely considered as a supplement to the regular duties of the servile holders

At the same time, the free tenants are members of the village community, engrained in it by their participation in all the eventualities of open field life, by their holdings in the arable, by their use of the commons. This shows, again, that the manorial element is superimposed on the communal, and not the foundation of it. I shall not revert to my positive arguments in favour of the existence of ancient freehold by the side of tenements that have become freehold by exemption from servile duties. But I may be allowed to point out in this place, that negatively the appearance of free elements among the peasantry presents a most powerful check to the theory of a servile origin of the community : it throws the burden of proof on those who contend for such an origin as against the theory of a free village feudalized in process of time.

In a sense the partizans of the servile community are in the same awkward position in respect to the manorial court. Its body of suitors may have consisted to a great extent of serfs, but surely it must have contained a powerful free admixture also, because out of serfdom could hardly have arisen all the privileges and rights which make it a constitutional establishment by the side of the lord. The suitors are the judges in litigation, the conveyancing practice proceeds from the principle of communal testimony, and in matters of husbandry, custom and self-government prevail against any capricious change or unprecedented exaction. And it has to be noticed that the will and influence of the lord is much more distinct and overbearing in the documents of the later thirteenth and of the fourteenth century, than in the earlier records ; one more hint, that the feudal conception of society took some time to push back older notions, which implied a greater liberty of the folk in regard to their rulers.

Whichever way we may look, one and the same observation is forced upon us : the communal organisation of the peasantry is more ancient and more deeply laid than the manorial order. Even the feudal period that has formed the immediate subject of our study shows everywhere traces of a peasant class living and working in economically self-dependent communities under the loose authority of a lord, whose claims may proceed from political sources and affect the semblance of ownership, but do not give rise to the manorial connexion between estate and village.

APPENDIX.

—٠٠—

I.

See p. 52, n. 2.

[Y. B. Pasch. 1 Edw. II, pl. 4. f. 4.]

Symon de Paris porta breve de transgression vers *H*. bailliffe sire Trans.
Robert Tonny et plusours autres, et se pleint, qe *W*. et *H*. certein
jour luy pristrent et emprisonerent etc. a tort encountre la pees
etc. *Pass* respond pur toutz, forspris le bailliffe, qe riens nount
fait encountre la pees, et pour le bailliff yl avowea le restreinement
par la resoun qe lavantdit *S.* si est villeine lavandit *R.* qi bailliffe yl
est, et fuist trove a *N.* en soun mes, le quel vint a lui tendist office
de Provoist et il la refusa et ne se voilleit justicier etc.   *Tond.*
rehercea le avowery, et dit qe a cele avowery ne doit il estre
resceve pur ceo qe *S.* est Fraunc Citizene de Londre, et ad este
touz ceux diz anz, et ad este Vicounte le Roy en mesme la Citee,
et rend accounts al Eschequer, et ceo voloms averrer par Record,
et uncore huy ceo jour est Alderman et de la Ville de Londre, et
demande jugement, sils puissent villenage en sa persone allegger.
Herle.   A ceo qil dient qil est citezen de Londre nous navoms qe
faire, mes nous vous dioms, qil est villein *R.* de Eve et de Treve,
et les Auncestres Ael et Besayel et toux ces Auncestres ses *terres
tennantz deinz le manoire de N.* et ces Auncestres seisitz des villeins
services des Auncestres *S.* come affaire Rechat de Char et de Sank
et de fille marier, et de euz tailler haut et bas, *etc.*, et uncore est
seisi de ces freres de mesme le piere et de mesme la mere et
demande Jugement si sour luy, come sour soun villein en soun
mese trove, ne puisse avowere faire.   *Tond.* Fraunc homme et de
fraunc estat et eux nient seisi de luy, come de lour villein prest etc.
Ber. Jeo ai oi dire qe un homme fuist prist en la bordel, et fuist

prist et pendu, et sil eust demorre a lostiel, il neust en nul mal *etc.* auxient de ceste parte, sil eust este fraunc Citezen pur qe neust il demorre en la Citee? *Ad alium diem ; Tond.* se tient qil ne fuist seisi de lui come de soun villein ne de ses villeins services etc. *Pass.* la ou il dit qe nous ne sumes pas seisis de lui come de nostre villein, il nasquit en nostre villeinage, ou commence nostre seisine, et nous lui trova mese en soun mes, et la nostre seisine continue, Jugement. *Ber.* Vous pledietz sour la seisine, et il pleident sour le droit issint naverrez james bon issue de plee. *Herle.* Seisi en la fourme qe nous avoms dit. *Ber.* La Court ne restreinera tiel travers sanz ceo qe vous dietz, que vous estez seisitz de lui *come de vostre villein et de ses villeinz services,* et sic fecit. *Et alii e contra.*

II.

See p. 54, n. 1.

[Y. B. Trin. 29 Edw. III, f. 41. I do not give a translation of this document because it has been explained with some detail in my text.]

Sur l'es-
tatut de
labourer.

LE servant suit par attorney, et le Master in propre persone. Que dit qe le servant fuit soun villein regardant al Manoire de *C.* et dit qil avoit mestre de ses services et de luy, pur qe nous luy prisoms come nostre vilieìn, come list a nous. Jugement si *etc.* tort in nostre party par tiel reteignement puit assigner. *Et nota,* qil fist protestacion, qil ne conust pas qil fuit in le service le plaintiffe etc. *Et nota,* qe le servant dit auxi, qil fuit le villein le Master qi plede, et dit qil fuit distreint, et auxi les amis pur luy tanqe qil convensist par cohercion venir a ses Seigneours. *Burt.* Le servant est par attorney, qe ne puit par soun ple faire sans Master villein. Purqe ceo ple ne gist in soun bouche. *Et non allocatur* par *Wilb.* qi dit qe le ple nest pas al breve : car mesqe il fuit icy in propre persone, et voillet conustre qil fuit villein ce nabat pas vostre breve (le quel qil fuit frank ou villein) si vous poies maintenir qil fuit in vostre service, si ce ne fuit par autiel mattier (come il ad plede) ou autre semblable. Et puis le servant weyva, et dit qil ne fist pas covenant etc. *Et alii e contra. Et nota,* qe l'opinion fuit, qe si villein fuit chace et distreint de venir a son Seignour propre, qe ce luy excusera del' penance del l'estatut. *Sed Burt. negavit,* eo qe ce vient de sa folie qil voilleit faire covenant dautre servir, qant il fuit appris qil fuit autry villein. *Et ideo quere.*

Qant al' plea le Master *Burt.* challange ceo qil navoit pas alleger qil fuit seisi de luy come de soun villein. *Et non allocatur* par *Wilb.* Qui dit, sil soit soun villein, soun plee est assez fort : car seisi et nient seisi ne fera pas issue. *Et sic nota.* Puis *Burt.* dit Op. Curiae. que l'on allege est quil est soun villein regardant a soun manoire de *C.* nous dioms qe mesme le manoire fuit in le seisin un *A.* que infeffa le defendant de mesme le manoire ; et dioms qe tout le temps que il fuit allant et walkant a large a sa frank volunte come frankhome, sans ce qil fuit unque seisi de luy in son temps, et cety qe ad l'estat *A.* ne fuit unques seisi de luy, tanques ore qil de soun tort demesne luy pris hors de nostre service. Purque nous nentendons pas que par tiel cause il nous puit ouster de nostre accord. *Finch.* Et nous Jugement, depuis qil ne dedit pas qil nest nostre villein de nostre manoire de *C.* et le quel nous fuit seisis de luy devant, ou non, ou nostre feffor seisi, *etc.* ou ce ne puit my estre a purpose : car il alast alarge, purtant ne fuit il enfranchy. Purque *etc.* *Th.* Si vostre feffor ne fuit unques seisi de luy, coment qil vous dona le manoire, jeo di que ce de que il navoit pas le possession ne puit pas vestir in vous. Purque *etc.* *Jer.* Villeins regardants al' manoires sont de droit al' Seignour de prendre les a sa volunte, et sil face don le manoire a un autre, a quel heur que l'autre les happa, il est asses bon. *Th.* Sir, uncre mesque il soit issint entre luy et le grantor ou le villein, nous qe sums estrange ne serrons pas ly purtant : car si home qi soit estrange veigne in pais, et demurges par *xx* ou *xxx* ans, et nul home met debat sur luy, ne luy claime come seruant, il list a moy de prendre soun service, et de luy recevoir in mon service pur le terme solonque nostre covenaunt : et il nest pas reason qe jeo soy perdant, depuis qe in moy default ne puit etre ajuge, *causa ut supra.* *Gr.* Per mesme le reason qe vous luy purrets retenir tanque al' fine de terme, si poit un autre : *et sic de singulis, et sic in infinitum* : issint le Seignour ouste de soun villein a toujours, et ce ne seroit pas reason. Puis *Th.* n'osa pas demurrer ; mes dit qil ne fuit pas soun villein de soun manoire de *C.* Prest etc. *Fiff.* Ceo n'est pas respons : *car coment qil n'est pas soun villein del' manoire, etc. sil fuit soun villein in gros, asses suffist.* *Et non* Op. Curiae. *allocatur* pur ce quel avoit traverse soun respons in le manere come ce fuit livere, etc.

Common Pleas Roll (Record Office).

[Trin. 29 E. III, r. 203, v. Oxon.]

Thomas Barentyn et Radulfus Crips Shephird attachiati fuerunt
ad respondendum tam domino Regi quam Priori hospitalis Sancti
Iohannis Ierusalem in Anglia quare, cum per ipsum dominum
Regem et consilium suum pro communi utilitate regni Regis
Anglie ordinatum sit, quod si aliquis seruiens in seruicio alicuius
retentus ante finem termini concordati a dicto seruicio sine causa
racionabili vel licencia recesserit, penam imprisonamenti subeat
et nullus sub eadem pena talem in seruicio suo recipere vel retinere presumat, et predictus Thomas predictum Radulfum nuper
seruientem predicti Prioris in seruicio suo apud Werpesgrave
retentum qui ab eodem seruicio ante finem termini inter eos
concordati sine causa racionabili et licencia predicti Prioris recessit, in seruicium predicti Thome quamquam memoratus
Thomas de prefato Radulfo eidem Priori restituendo requisitus
fuerit admisit et retinuit in Regis contemptum et predicti Prioris
grave dampnum ac contra ordinacionem predictam Et unde predictus Prior per Ricardum de Fifhide attornatum suum queritur
quod cum per ipsum Regem et consilium suum etc. ordinatum
sit quod si aliquis serviens in servicium alicuius retentus ante
finem etc. a dicto seruicio sine causa etc. recesserit penam imprisonamenti subeat et nullus sub eadem pena talem in seruicio
suo recipere vel retinere presumat, predictus Thomas predictum
Radulfum nuper seruientem predicti Prioris in seruicio suo apud
Werpesgrove retentum scilicet die Lune proxima post festum
Sancti Laurentii anno regni domini Regis nunc Anglie vicesimo
octavo ad deseruiendum ei in officio pastoris etc. scilicet die
Lune in septimana Pentecostes a festo Sancti Michaelis Archangeli
tunc proximo sequenti per unum annum proximum sequentem
qui ab eodem seruicio ante finem termini . . . recessit, in seruicium
predicti Thome quamquam idem Thomas de prefato Radulfo
eidem Priori restituendo requisitus fuerit admisit et retinuit in
Regis contemptum et predicti Prioris grave dampnum ac contra
ordinacionem etc. et predictus Radulfus a seruicio predicti
Prioris ante finem sine causa etc. videlicet predicto die Lune in
septimana Pentecostes recessit in Regis contemptum ad predicti

Prioris grave dampnum ac contra ordinacionem etc. unde dicit quod deterioratus est et dampnum habet ad valenciam viginti librorum. Et inde producit sectam.

Et predicti Thomas et Radulfus per Stephanum Mebourum attornatum suum veniunt. Et defendunt vim et iniuriam quando etc. et quicquid etc. Et protestantur quod ipsi non cognoscunt quod predictus Radulfus fuit seruiens predicti Prioris nec retentus cum eodem Priore prout Prior superius versus eos narravit et predictus Thomas dicit quod predictus Radulfus est *villanus suus ut de manerio suo de Chalgrave* per quod ipse seisivit eundem Radulfum tanquam villanum suum prout ei bene licuit. Et hoc paratus est verificare unde petit iudicium si predictus Prior injuriam in persona sua assignare possit. Et predictus Radulfus dicit quod ipse est villanus predicti Thome ut de manerio predicto et quia idem Radulfus extra dominium predicti Thome morabatur parentes ipsius Radulfi districti fuerunt ad venire faciendum predictum Radulfum ad predictum Thomam dominum suum et ad eorum sectam et excitacionem idem Radulfus venit ad predictum Thomam absque hoc quod ipse retentus fuit cum predicto Priore ad deseruiendum ei per tempus predictum prout idem Prior superius versus eum narravit. Et de hoc ponit se super patriam. Et predictus Prior similiter. Et idem Prior quo ad placitum predicti Thome *dicit quod predictus Radulfus non est villanus ipsius Thome ut de manerio suo predicto* prout idem Thomas superius allegat. Et hoc petit quod inquiratur per patriam. Et predictus Thomas similiter. Preceptum etc.

III.

See p. 66, n. 2, and p. 76, n. 2.

The so-called Mirror of Justice is still in many respects an unsolved riddle, and a very interesting one, as it seems to me. The French edition of 1642 from which quotations are so frequently made presents a text perverted to such an extent, that the gentleman from Gray's Inn to whom we owe the English translation of 1648 took it upon himself to deal with his original very freely, and in fact composed a version of his own which turned out even less trustworthy than the French. Ancient MSS. of the work are very scarce indeed; the fourteenth century MS. at Corpus

College, Cambridge, is the only one known to me; although there are also some transcripts of the seventeenth century. This means that the work had no circulation in its time. It is very unlike Bracton, or Britton in this respect, and indeed in every other. Instead of giving a more or less learned or practical exposition of the principles of Common Law it appears as a commentary written by a partisan, acrimonious in form, almost revolutionary in character, full of stray bits of information, but fanciful in its way of selecting and displaying this information. 'Wahrheit und Dichtung' would have been a proper title for this production, and no wonder that it has excited suspicion. It has commanded the attention of the present generation of scholars notwithstanding the odd way in which the author, Andrew Horne, or whoever he may be, cites as authority fictitious decisions given by King Alfred and by a number of legal worthies of Saxon times who never gave judgment save in his own fruitful imagination. This may be accounted for by peculiar medieval notions as to the manner in which legal discussion may be most efficiently conducted, but altogether the Mirror, as it stands, appears quite unique, quite unlike any other legal book of the feudal period. It must be examined carefully by itself before the information supplied by it can be produced as evidence on any point of English medieval history. Such an examination should lead to interesting results, but I must reserve it for another occasion. What I have said now may be taken simply as a reason for the omission in my text of those passages of the Mirror which bear on the question of villainage. I may be allowed to discuss these passages in the present Appendix without anticipating a general judgment on the character of the book and on its value.

The author of the Mirror shows in many places, that he is hostile not only to monarchical pretensions, but also to the encroachments of the aristocracy. He is a champion of the lower orders and gladly endorses every rule set up by the Courts 'in favour of liberty.' In this light he considers the action 'de nativitate' as conferring an advantage upon the defendant, the person claimed as a villain, but considered as free until the contrary has been proved[1]. Another boon consists in the

---

[1] 'Cest action est mixte en favour de franchise car rarement se sustreit nul del fief de son seiniur, s'il ne soy claime frank' (p. 165).

fact, that the trial must be reserved for the decision of the Royal Courts and cannot be entertained in the County[1]. So far the Mirror falls in with the usual exposition of our Authorities—it takes notice of two facts which are generally recognised as important features in trying a question of status. But the Mirror does not stop there, but further formulates an assertion which cannot be considered as generally accepted in practice, though it may have emerged now and then in pleadings and even in decisions.

It is well known, that the main argument in a trial of villainage turned on the question of kinship. As Britton (pp. 205, 206, ed. Nichols) states the matter, we are led to suppose that the plaintiff had to produce the villain kinsmen of the person claimed, and the defendant could except against them. Glanville (v. 4) says, that both parties had the right to produce the kindred and in case of doubt or collision a jury had to decide. If the fact of relationship were established on both sides, it was necessary to see on which side the nearer relatives stood. Legal practice, so far as we can judge from the extant plea rolls, followed Glanville, although questions arising from these suits were much more varied and complicated than his statement implied. (See, for instance, Bracton's Note Book, 1041, 1167.) But in the Mirror we find the distinct assertion, that if the defendant in a case of 'nativity' succeeded in proving a free stem in any generation of his ascendants, this was sufficient to prove him free[2]. This connects itself with the view, that there can be no prescription against free blood, a view which, as we have seen in the text, was in opposition to the usual conception that people may fall into servitude in the course of several generations of debasement. The notion embodied in the Mirror was lingering, as it were, in the background.

---

[1] P. 168.

[2] P. 212: 'Si le defendant puisse monstrer frank cep de ses Anncestres en la conception ou en la nativity ou puis, y' ert le defendant tenable pur frank a touts jours tout y soyent present pere et mere frere et cosins et tout son parenter que soy coynossent estre serfs al actor, et tesmoignent le defendant estre serf. Le autre notability est, que nient pluis ne fait long tenure de villeinage franchome serf que long tenure de frank fieu ne fait home serf frank, car franchise ne soy defait jammes par prescription de temps.' P. 166: 'Servage est un subjection issuant de cy grand antiquite, que nul frank ceppe ne purra estre trouve par human remembrance.' Cf. Britton, i. 196.

In accordance with this liberal treatment of procedure, we find our author all in favour of liberty when treating of the ways by which bondage may be dissolved. He gives a very detailed enumeration of all such modes of enfranchisement, and at least one of his points appears unusual in English law. I mean his doctrine that a serf ejected from his holding by the lord becomes free, if no means of existence are afforded to him [1].

The motive adduced is worthy of notice by itself. 'Servus dicitur a servando,' a serf is a man under guardianship, like a woman in this respect [2], and so, if the guardian forgets his duty of taking care of his subject, he forfeits his rights. The Roman derivation 'a servando' is often met elsewhere, but instead of being applied to the bondman as a captive who has been kept alive instead of being slain, it is here made the starting point of a new conception and one very favourable to the bondman. It is not the only indication that the author of the Mirror had been speculating about the origin of servitude. By the law of nature all men are free, of course, but yet, says he, there exists by human law a class of men to whom nothing belongs, and who are considered as the property of other people : an anomaly which he guesses may possibly come from the time when Noah pronounced his malediction against Canaan, the son of Cham, or else from the defeat of Goliath by David [3].

It is curious too, and at first sight rather inconsistent, that our author sometimes speaks against those very serfs towards whom he seems, as a rule, so favourably disposed. He dwells on their disability, marks as an abuse that they are admitted to act in the courts without the help of their lords, although nothing can be owned by them [4], and, what is more, he insists on the necessity of their being excluded from the system of frank-pledge, which

---

[1] P. 167 : 'ou si son seignior luy eject de son fief, et luy done suste-nance (*corr.* ne luy done sustenance).' 294 : 'Abusion est que home puisse challenger celuy pur son naife a que il ne trova unque sustenance, de sicome serf nest *my serf forsque tant come il est en gard*, et de sicome nul ne poet challenger son serf pur serf tout soit il en sa garde s'il retrouve (*corr.* ne trouve) sustenance a son serf que luy vault mees et terre en son fief, ou il purra gaigner sa sustenance, ou autrement luy retient en son service.' Cf. 169.

[2] Cf. p. 155.

[3] P. 166.

[4] P. 294.

ought to be restricted entirely to free men[1]. All this seems rather strange at first, and certainly not in favour of liberty. It turns out, however, that these very qualifications are prompted by the same liberal spirit which we noticed from the first; they are suggested by a most characteristic attempt to draw a definite line between the serf and the villain.

The villain is no serf, in any sense of the word. He is a free man[2], his tenure is a free tenure[3]. He is enfeoffed of his land, with the obligation to till it, as the knight is enfeoffed of his fee in return for military service; the burgess enfeoffed of his freehold in the borough for a rent[4]. The right of ownership on the part of the villain is clearly recognised in the Great Charter, which prescribes the mode and extent of amercing villains, and thereby supposes their independent right of property, while the serf has nothing of his own, and could not be amerced in his own[5]. The author undoubtedly hits here on a point where the usual feudal theory

[1] Ib. p. 294. 'Abusion est que serfs sont frank pledges ou pledges de frank home.' Cf. 110.

[2] P. 169. 'Nota que villeins ne sont my serfs car serfs sont dits de garder sicom est dit.' 295: 'Abusion est a tenir villeins serfs, et ceste abusion merust grand destruction de poor people, grand poverty, et grand peche.'

[3] P. 291: 'Abusion est que lon dit que villenage neste my frank tene-ment . . . . car villein et serf ne sont my en (corr. un) voice, ne en (corr. un) signification, eins poet chascun frank home tenir villenage a luy et a ses heires fesant le servage et le charge del fiew.'

[4] P. 170: 'Ascuns receverent fiefs assoubs de chescun obligation sicome per service faire ou en pure almoigne, ascuns a tenir par homage, et en service al defense del Realme, et ascuns par villeins customes d'arrer, over charrier, sarclir, franchir, seier, tasser, batre ou tilt autres manners de services, et ascun foits sans reprise de manger; et dont plusors fines sont troves levees en le tresore que font mencion de ceux services et viles customes faire, aussi bien come autres de pluis curtoise services, et dount tout soit que tiels gents *ne eient point de chartres, ne monuments* sils soient nequident engettes ou disturbes de lour possessions a tort, *droit les succort per l'assize de novel disseisine* attenir en le state come devant per cy que ils puissent *averrer que ils scavoient lour certaintie de services et doveraignes per an come ceux que auncestres avant eux furent astrers de pluis longe temps per case que les disseisors nen furent seigniors.'*

[5] 169: 'Villeins sont cultivers de fief demorants en villages uplande, car de Vile est dit Villeins, de Burgh Bourghois, et de Cite Cittizens, et de Villeins est mencion fait en le Chartre de Franchise, ou est dit, que villein ne soit mie cy grivement amercie que sa gaigneur ne soit a luy salve, car de serf ne fait il my mention pur ceo que ils ount rien propre que perdrent. Et de Villeins sont lour gaignures appelle Villenages.'

had been discountenanced by statute : it was certainly difficult to maintain at the same time that the villain, as serf, had nothing but what had been precariously entrusted to him by the lord, and at the same time that he must suffer for misdeeds in the character of an owner. Strained in one sense the article of the Charter could be made to mean that, at the time of the Great Charter, there was no such thing as the civil disability of servitude in England. Strained in another sense suggested by the Mirror, it would lead to a standing distinction between villains, as owners, and serfs, as people devoid of civil rights. We know that legal practice preferred a compromise which was anything but consistent in point of doctrine, but, as I have said in my text, the notion of the civil right of the villain, and especially in his so-called wainage, seems to have been deep-rooted enough to counterbalance in some respects the current feudal doctrine.

It would have been difficult for the author of the Mirror to maintain that practice was in accordance with his theory; and he falls out of his part now and then, as, for instance, when he speaks of the enfranchisement of the serf from whom the lord had received homage in addition to fealty—this is a case clearly applying to villains as well as to those whom he calls serfs, and it is not the only time that he forgets the distinction [1]. But when his attention is not distracted by details he takes his ground on the assumption that the original rights of the villains were gradually falling into disuse through the encroachments of the stronger people. We even find in the Mirror that the villains ought to have the assise of novel disseisin as a remedy in case of dispossession. If they were oppressively made to render other than the accustomed services they had to resort to the writ, ' ne injuste vexes,' and it is a sign of bad times that they are getting deprived of it. Edward the Confessor took good care that the legal rights of the villains should not be curtailed [2]. It is needless again to point

---

[1] 167. On the other hand it is mentioned, that serfs cannot be devised because they are astriers and annexed to the free tenement of the lord.

[2] 171 : ' Et de *ceo soy entremist Seint Edward* en son temps d'enquirer de toutes les .... que luy fesoit a tiel gaignors oustre lour droit et en fist grande vengeance. Et puis pargents que meins doulent pecheir que faire ne duissent sont plusiours ceux villeins *par tortious distresses chasses a faire a lour seignours le service de Rechat de sank,* et plusors autre customes voluntaries pur mener les en servage a lour poiar, dont *lour*

out that this view of villainage is well in keeping with the fundamental notion which I tried to bring out in my text, the notion,
namely, that the law of villainage contained heterogeneous elements,
and had been derived partly from the status of free ceorls.

IV.

See p. 87, n. 1.

[Coram Rege 10 Henry III, N. 26. m. 4. d.]

Assisa venit recognitura si Iohannes Cheltewynd iniuste etc.
disseisiuit Willelmum filium Roberti de libero tenemento suo in
Cheltewynd post ultimum etc. Et Iohannes venit et dicit quod
non disseisiuit eundem Willelmum de aliquo libero tenemento quia
villanus suus est et nullum habet liberum tenementum et quod
Robertus pater suus fuit villanus. Et Willelmus dicit quod tenementum illud liberum est et quod Robertus pater suus libere
tenuit de Ada patre Iohannis de Chetewod et per cartam quam
profert in haec verba quod Adam de Chetwud concessit Roberto
filio Wourami patri Willelmi et heredibus suis dimidiam virgatam
terre cum pertinenciis in Chetwud in feodum et hereditatem
tenendam de eodem Roberto et heredibus suis libere quiete cum
omnibus consuetudinibus et libertatibus quas ceteri franci homines
habent pro 26 denariis per annum reddendo pro omni servicio et
pro omnibus rebus ad eum et heredes suos pertinentibus.
Et Iohannes bene cognoscit cartam illam et dicit quod idem
Robertus fuit villanus patris sui et per pecuniam domini sui
redemptus fuit a seruitute et quod antequam esset liberatus a
servitute fuit idem Willelmus nativus, et petit judicium si per
cartam quam pater suus ei fecerat debeat esse liber tempore
Iohannis cum redemptus esset per pecuniam patris Iohannis et
Robertus nichil proprium habuit cum esset villanus. Et dicit quod
idem Willelmus non fuit nisi custos patris sui de eadem terra dum
pater suus fuit alibi manens.

remedie per le ne injuste vexes per les negligence des Royes' (the end of the
sentence is evidently omitted or 'is falling into disuse' must have been
meant).—p. 305: '*abusion est que le briefe de ne injuste vexes va issint en
decline.*'

Post uenit Willelmus et retraxit se et ideo in misericordia
Pauper est. Et Iohannes dat ei III marcas et Willelmus remanet
etc. Ita quod idem Willelmus ibit quocumque uoluerit. Et
Iohannes quietum clamauit Willelmum de omni seruitute.

V.

See p. 90, n. 4.

[De Banco Roll, Michaelmas, 15 Edw. II, m. 271.]

Abbas de Sancto Edmundo attachiatus fuit ad respondendum
Rogero filio Willelmi Henri homini praedicti Abbatis de manerio de Mildenhale quod est de antiquo dominico corone Anglie
etc. de placito quare exigit ab eo alias consuetudines et alia
servicia quam facere debent et antecessores sui tenentes de eodem
manerio facere consueverunt temporibus quibus manerium illud
fuit in manibus progenitorum Regis quondam Regum Anglie contra
prohibicionem Regis etc. Et unde idem Rogerus per Petrum de
Elyngham attornatum suum dicit quod ipse et antecessores sui
et quilibet tenens unum messuagium et quindecim acras terre
cum pertinenciis in eodem Manerio sicut idem Rogerus tenet
tempore quo Manerium illud fuit in manibus Sancti Edwardi
Regis quondam Regis Anglie progenitoris Domini Regis nunc
tenuit tenementa sua per fidelitatem et servicium inveniendi
unum hominem ad tenendum vel fugandum carucam Domini
singulis diebus anni quando caruce arare consueverunt tantum
pro omni servicio et habere consuevit carucam Domini qualibet
altera septimana singulis annis per diem Sabbati ad terram suam
propriam arandam vel carucam illam aliis locandam et similiter
sextam partem vesture unius acre ordei et medietatem vesture
unius rode frumenti de melioribus tempore messis et prandium
suum ad nonam singulis annis per sex dies in anno in aula
Domini sumptibus ejusdem Domini scilicet in diebus Sancti
Michaelis, Omnium Sanctorum, Natalis Domini, Purificacionis
Beate Marie, Pasche et Pentecostes et oblacionem suam singulis
annis per quatuor dies in anno scilicet in diebus Natalis Domini,
Purificacionis Beate Marie, Pasche et Assumpcionis Beate Marie
Virginis scilicet quolibet die unum denarium et per hujusmodi

certas consuetudines et servicia ipse et omnes antecessores sui tenementa quae ipse modo tenet tenuerunt a tempore quo non exstat memoria usque ad tempus istius Abbatis quod idem Abbas praeter praedicta servicia exigit ab eo singulis vicibus quibus aliquis Abbas est de novo creatus finem ei praestandum pro capa sua ad voluntatem suam et pro filiis et filiabus suis maritandis et pro terris suis dimmittendis et pro ingressu habendo in heredita- tem suam post obitum antecessoris sui finem similiter ad volun- tatem suam ac idem Rogerus die Jovis proxima ante festum Apostolorum Simonis et Jude anno regni Domini Regis nunc quartodecimo apud Sanctum Edmundum in praesencia Thome de Wridervill Roberti Tillote Philippi de Wangeford Roberti de Lyvermere et aliorum liberasset praedicto Abbati breve Regis de prohibicione et ei inhibuisset ex parte Domini Regis ne idem Abbas exigeret ab eo alias consuetudines et alia servicia quam ipse et antecessores sui tenentes de eodem Manerio facere con- sueverunt temporibus quibus Manerium illud fuit in manibus pro- genitorum Regis quondam Regum Anglie. Idem Abbas spreta regia prohibicione praedicta nihilominus postmodum exigit ab eo praedicta superonerosas consuetudines et ad ea sibi facienda per graves et intollerabiles districciones distringit quominus terram suam excolere potest unde dicit quod deterioratus est et damp- num habet ad valenciam centum librarum. Et inde producit sectam etc.

Et Abbas per Willelmum de Bakeham attornatum suum venit Et dicit quod non debet praedicto Rogero ad hoc breve nec ad aliquod aliud breve respondere. Quia dicit quod idem Rogerus est villanus ipsius Abbatis et villanus ecclesie sue Sancti Edmundi. Et quod ipse seisitus est de ipso tanquam de villano suo unde petit judicium etc. Et Rogerus dicit quod ipse est homo ipsius Abbatis de Manerio de Mildenhale quod est de antiquo dominico corone Anglie Et quod Mildenhale sit de antiquo dominico Corone Anglie paratus est verificare per librum Domesday Et super hoc inspecto libro praedicto comperta sunt in eodem verba subscripta.—Suffolk—Inter terras Stigandi quas Willelmus Den- vers servat in manu Regis.—Lacforde Hundred. Mildenehalla dedit Rex Edwardus Sancto Edmundo et post tenuit Stigandus sub Sancto Edmundo in vita Regis Edwardi pro manerio xij carucate terre tunc et post xxx uillani modo xxxiij. Tunc viij. Bordarii post et modo xv. semper xvj. servi semper vj caruce in dominio et viij caruce hominum et xx acre prati ecclesia xl acrarum et j molendinum et iij piscaciones et dimidiam xxxj eque silvatice xxxvij averia et lx porci et Mille oves et viij socemanni xxx acrarum semper dimidia caruca. Huic iacet i bervita—Et quia ex verbis praedictis videtur Curie quod Mildenhale est de antiquo dominico corone etc. dictum est praedicto Abbati quod respondeat quod sibi viderit expedire etc.

Et Abbas dicit sicut prius quod praedictus Rogerus est villanus suus et ecclesie sue praedicte et quod ipse seisitus est de ipso ut de villano suo et quod ipse et omnes Abbates de Sancto Edmundo praedecessores ipsius Abbatis ex tempore quo non extat memoria seisiti fuerunt de ipso Rogero et antecessoribus suis ut de villanis suis talliando ipsos alto et basso pro voluntate sua et faciendo de ipsis praepositos et messores suos et capiendo ab eis merchetum pro filiis et filiabus suis maritandis et finem pro terris suis dimittendis et pro ingressu habendo in terris et tenementis post mortem antecessorum suorum ad voluntatem ipsorum Abbatum. Et hoc paratus est verificare etc.

Et Rogerus dicit sicut prius quod ipse est homo de antiquo dominico corone Anglie de praedicto Manerio de Mildenhale et quod ipse et omnes antecessores sui a tempore quo non exstat memoria tenuerunt tenementa sua praedicta de praedecessoribus praedicti Abbatis et de progenitoribus Domini Regis Regum Anglie quondam Dominis ejusdem Manerii per praedicta certa servicia et consuetudines in narracione sua superius contenta absque hoc quod praedecessores praedicti Abbatis fuissent seisiti de ipso Rogero aut antecessoribus suis ut de villanis suis talliando ipsos alto et basso vel faciendo de ipsis praepositos et messores aut capiendo de ipsis incertas consuetudines et servicia sicut praedictus Abbas dicit. Et hoc petit quod inquiratur per patriam Et praedictus Abbas similiter Ideo praeceptum est Vicecomiti quod venire faciat hic a die Pasche in tres septimanas xij etc. per quos etc. et qui nec etc. ad recognicionem etc. Quia tam etc.

See p. 97, n. 2.

The Mildenhall trial just quoted may serve as an instance of litigation between lord and tenant of a manor in ancient demesne, when it took place before the Royal Courts. The Rolls of King's Ripton, Hunts, now published by Prof. F. W. Maitland, for the

Selden Society, give an insight into the working of the Manorial Court itself when it had to decide between lord and tenant in a question of right (pp. 118 *et sqq*). Jane the daughter of William of Alconbury claims eight acres of land against the Abbot of Ramsey, lord of the manor. He does not choose to answer at once and takes advantage of all the procrastinations usual in such matters. Three times he gets summoned and does not appear; the Court proceeds to distrain him and after three distraints he essoins himself three times before making up his mind to answer by attorney and to ask a view of the land. Pleadings follow in the usual course, and ultimately a sworn inquest has to decide on the question whether the plaintiff was of full age at the time of a transaction through which the land claimed came into the hands of the Abbot. The point is, that the lord of the Manor is placed entirely on the same footing in regard to the action of his tenant as any other suitor.

In 1296 an action of dower occurs between a certain Maud Grayling and a number of persons holding land within the manor. It is opened by a *writ of right* which is bound up with the roll, but has not been printed by Mr. Maitland as it does not contain anything of special interest. The beginning of this writ is typical— it does not mention the abbot, but only the bailiffs of the abbot: [Edwardus Dei gratia Rex Angliae] Dux Aquitaniae, Ballivis Abbatis de Rameseye de Riptone Regis Salutem. Precipimus vobis quod sine dilacione et secundum con[suetudinem manerii de Riptone Regis ple]num rectum teneatis Matildi que fuit uxor Hugonis Grayling de medietate sex messuagiorum sexaginta et qua[tuor acrarum] et unius rode [terre dimidia acra prati] cum pertinenciis in Riptone Regis, unde etc. (Court of Augmentation, Portf. XXIII, N. 94, r. 9). On pp. 100–104 Mr. Maitland gives the translation of two most valuable records of *Monstraverunt* in the Court of King's Bench between the men of King's Ripton and the Abbot. The suit is very similar to that of the men of Mildenhall; and indeed all these ancient demesne trials turn on the same points.

VI.

See p. 91, n. 3.

The Stoneleigh Register, in the possession of Lord Leigh, is certainly one of the most interesting surveys of a medieval manor extant, and gives a better insight into the condition of ancient demesne than any other document I know of. Its publication would be particularly desirable in the interests of social history. This compilation is indeed a late one, but it has been made with great care and evident accuracy from the original records which go back even to Henry II's time. One part is especially important, because it gives selections from the Court Rolls of the Manorial Court. An extract from the compiler's Introduction will show the nature and grouping of his material.

F. 2, a: In quorum primo libro agitur de generacione nobilium regum Anglie incipiendo modicum ante conquestum usque ad presens sumarie concepta. Et de possessionibus et graciis per eos nobis factis et collatis, tam in monasterio de Rademora quam in monasterio de Stonleya. Ac eciam de diversis memorandis consuetudinibus, placitis, feuffamentis, diuisionibus tenementorum in villa et hamelettis de Stonle. Et de bundis et peranbulacionibus dicti manerii de Stonle. Ac subsequenter de actis abbatum de Stonle a tempore fundacionis quod infra intitulabitur *usque ad presens videlicet usque ad feriam quartam in festo Sancti Gregorii pape anno domini millesimo trecentesimo nonagesimo secundo*, anno vero domini Regis Anglie Ricardi secundi post conquestum sexto decimo. In secundo libro continentur memoranda de villis de Hartone, Cobsitone. . . . Erdyngtone . . . In tertio libro continentur diversa memoranda tam nos quam alios tangencia et alia informatiua abbatum iuniorum consilia racionabilia secundum antiquas consuetudines, extentas, computaciones per quas poterit a nociuis abstineri, videlicet in diuisionibus possessionum et aliis faciendis pro bono et conseruacione juris monasterii. In quarto libro summarie scribuntur copie diuersorum priuilegiorum et diuersarum composicionum decimarum et placitorum. Et de diuersis casibus et defensionibus super eisdem. Item in casu quo facta esset commissio alicui abbati a curia Romana et a generali capitulo.

The following passage is characteristic of the conception of ancient demesne: (4, a) Prefatus dominus Edwardus rex habuit in dominico suo iure hereditario manerium de Stonle cum membris, videlicet Kenilworth, Bakyngtone, Ruytone et Stratone, una cum aliis terris et maneriis. Que quidem maneria existencia in possessione et manu domini Regis Edwardi per universum regnum vocantur antiquum dominicum corone Regis Anglie prout in libro de Domusday continetur.

See p. 116, n. 4.

F. 21, a: Henricus Dei gracia Rex . . . venire facias coram nobis Alexandrum de Canle . . . et Hugonem le Seynsterer, ita quod sint apud Kenilworth in octabis Sti Edwardi ostensuri quo warranto subtraxerunt prefatis Abbati et Conventui quasdam consuetudines, libertates et jura ad Sokam de Stonle spectantes . . . anno regis nostri quinquagesimo . . . Et unde predictus Abbas pro se et Rogero Loueday *qui sequitur pro Rege* dicunt quod, cum manerium de Stonle fuit antiquum dominicum domini Regis . . . quilibet tenens ipsius manerii unam virgatam terre *consuevit reddere ipsi domino Regi per annum* 30 denarios et facere sectam ad curiam suam de Stonle de tribus septimanis in tres . . . predictus Alexander qui unam virgatam terre de antiquo et tres rodas de assarto tenet, de quibus reddit Roberto de Canle predictum redditum et 18 denarios pro predicta secta subtrahenda et pro predicto assarto denarium et obolum . . . Predictus Robertus de Canle tenet duas virgatas terre pro 5 solidis et omnes tenentes predicti secundum tenuras suas detinent predicto Abbati predictas sectas pro quibus dictus Robertus de Canle capit a predictis tenentibus secundum tenuras [*folio 22*] suas, scilicet pro una uirgata 30 denarios et de maiori tenura plus et de minori minus. Et de totis assartis capit totum seruicium. . . .

Et predictus Alexander Hugo et alii veniunt et defendunt vim et injuriam etc. . . . et bene cognoscunt, quod antecessores eorum tenuerunt tenementa sua in dicto hameletto de progenitoribus domini Regis per seruicium 30 denariorum pro virgata terre . . . et bene cognoscunt quod ipsi reddunt predicto Roberto de Canle redditus suos, sed qualiter ipse uel antecessores sui huiusmodi seruicia perquisierint, ignorant. . . . Jurati . . . per sacramentum suum dicunt, quod tempore Henrici Regis avi domini Regis nunc tenuerunt omnes. . . . faciendo inde domino Regi seruicia et consuetudines ad tenementa sua pertinentes. Quo tempore quidam Ketelburnus antecessor Roberti predicti et vicinus ipsorum tenencium qui tenuit de Rege sicut alii vicini sui, et quia predicti tenentes domini Regis fuerunt exiles in bonis et predictus Ketelburnus fuit maior et discrecior eis, locuti fuerunt cum ipso quod ipse colligeret redditum eorum et illum deferret pro eis ad curiam regis, tanquam per manum ipsorum. Et post mortem ipsius Ketelburni quidam heres ipsius Ketelburni accreuit et duxit in uxorem quandam sororem cuiusdam constabularii de castro de Kenilworth. Qui quidam heres ex permissione dicti constabularii atraxit ad se omnia servicia vicinorum suorum et reddidit antecessoribus domini Regis pro qualibet virgata dicte ville 30 denarios et fecit sectam pro eis ad curiam domini Regis. Et cepit pro secta predicta certum redditum et pro assartis predictis et ipsum redditum penes se retinuit . . . [*folio* 23] Dicunt eciam quod idem Robertus de Canle coram iusticiariis domini Regis ultimo itinerantibus in comitatu isto tulit *breve de natiuitate versus predictum Alexandrum Hugonem et alios et petiit eos, ut natiuos suos, et tunc ibidem declaratum fuit quod liberi fuerunt et ipse Ricardus remansit in misericordia. Unde dicunt, quod ipsi sunt adeo liberi penes se, sicut predictus Robertus penes se et tenere debent tenementa sua de domino Rege in capite.* . . . Et ideo consideratum est, quod dominus Rex recuperet seysinam suam . . . et predictus Alexander Hugo et alii sint *intendentes domino Regi et balliuis suis uel illis quibus dominus Rex eos dare voluerit* . . . Item coram eisdem justiciariis inquisicio facta fuit per preceptum domini Regis quod . . . tempore quo rex Henricus avus domini regis Henrici filii regis Johannis contulit abbati manerium de Stonle cum soka . . . fuit idem Rex in seysina de toto manerio integro de Stonle . . . et idem Abbas similiter in seysina . . . quousque Petrus de Canle qui fuit collector redditus de Canle ad instanciam vicinorum suorum ad redditus illos deferendum domino Regi et pro eis soluendum, subtraxit a se per diuturnam colleccionem suam et per remissionem et negligenciam dominorum sine impedimento et calumpnia sectas, relevia, escaetas octo tenencium qui tenebant *octo virgatas terre de domino Rege et postea de Abbate de Stonle* [*folio* 23d] Anno regni Regis Henrici . . . quinquagesimo primo . . . *Dominus Rex habuit seysinam dicti hameletti per duas ebdomadas et deinde dominus Rex per vicecomitem suum posuit prefatum*

Abbatem in plenam seysinam dicti hameletti de Stonle die Sti Clementis eodem anno ad magnam crucem ville de Stonle.

See p. 117, n. 1.

The Stoneleigh Register has the following entry on f. 12 : Memorandum quod tempore fundacionis fuerunt in manerio de Stonle lx et xiij *villani* quatuor *bordarii* cum duobus presbyteris tenentes *xxx carucatas* terre prout continetur in libro de Domesday, fuerunt eciam tunc quatuor *natiui siue serui* in le lone (*sic*) quorum quilibet unum mesuagium et unum quartronem terre tenebat per servicia subscripta, videlicet leuando furcas . . . et debebant . . . redimere sanguinem suum et dare auxilium domino ad festum Sti Michaelis scilicet Ayde, et facere braseum et alia seruicia seruilia, quorum nomina fuerunt Henricus Croud, cuius heres Iohannes Shukeburghe ; secundus vocabatur Robertus Bedul, cuius heredes extincti sunt in prima pestilencia. Tercius fuit Galfridus Dore cuius eciam heredes extincti sunt in eadem pestilencia. Quartus fuit Robertus Stot qui eciam mortuus est sine herede. Fuerunt eciam *quatuor liberi tenentes* in villa de Stonle qui tenuerunt hereditarie quinque mesuagia et quinque virgatas terre cum pertinenciis de Rege in capite per seruicia sokemanrie, videlicet Paganus de Stonle qui tenuit duas virgatas terre, qui Paganus abauus fuit Iohannis de Stonle, patris Roberti le Eyr. Qui Iohannes de Stonle dedit unum quartronem terre Iuliane filie sue et Roberto Carteri marito dicte Iuliane, cuius heres est Iohannes Iulian. Dedit eciam prefatus Iohannes de Stonle cum alia filia sua Alicia nomine unum mesuagium et unum quartronem terre Roberto filio Reginaldi Baugy, marito ipsius Alicie et ipsorum heredibus. Qui Robertus et Alicia dederunt dictum tenementum Willelmo filio Roberti Staleworthe de Flechamstede et heredibus suis prout inferius pleniter continetur. Quorum heres est linealiter Willelmus Staleworthe qui modo ea tenet. Predictus vero Robertus le Eyr dedit omnia residua tenementi sui cum redditibus et seruiciis Ioanni Sparry et Iohanni Hockele approwatoribus Abbatis de Stonle. Et ipsi approwatores de licencia Domini Regis per breue ad quod dampnum predicta tenementa Roberti le Heyr dederunt Roberto de Hockele Abbati de Stonle et successoribus suis in perpetuum anno regni Regis Edwardi tercii post conquestum vicesimo . . .

Fuerunt eciam duo liberi tenentes in parva Sokemanria, qui tenuerunt hereditarie duo mesuagia et medietatem unius virgate terre cum pratio et pertinenciis de Rege in capite. Quorum heredes ea dederunt in feudo de licencia domini Abbatis Alexandro Lynburgh, Henrico Rachel, Ricardo Sheperde et Simoni Malyn. Et ipsi ea dederunt Iohanni Hockele approwatori Thome Pype Abbatis de Stonle. Qui abbas ipsa tenementa una cum aliis tenementis amortizauit per breue ad quod dampnum, prout in carta regia inferius contenta plenius apparet. Item fuerunt tenentes cottarii in predicta villa de Stonle tempore fundacionis Abbatii xxiv tenentes xxiv cotagia in villa de Stonle pro certis redditibus.

In the description just quoted the greater bulk of the tenants is described as villains according to the terminology of Domesday and only a few (six in all) are said to be free socmen and little socmen. But a remarkable passage on the constitution of the Court and the rights and duties of its suitors describes these very villains as socmen.

F. 73. Curia de Stonle ad quam Sokemanni faciebant sectam solebat ab antiquo teneri super montem iuxta uillam de Stonle vocatam Motstowehull. Ideo sic dicta quia ibi placitabant. Sed postquam Abbates de Stonle habuerunt dictam Curiam et libertatem pro aysiamento tenencium et sectatorum fecerunt domum Curie in medio Ville de Stonle. Ad quam curiam veniunt et sectam faciunt omnes sokemanni manerii de Stonle de tribus septimanis in tres. Et quilibet eorum tenens unam virgatam terre solvet domino annuatim 30 denarios, scilicet unum denarium per acram quia quelibet virgata continet 30 acras et non plus. Et in quolibet hameletto manerii sunt 8 virgate terre. Et si quod amplius habent, hoc utique habent de approvacione et assartacione vastorum. Item quodlibet hamelletum dabit domino sextam porcionem ad communem finem bis per annum ad curiam visus franciplegii. Ad quem finem prefati socemanni sectatores curiae nihil solvent sed inferiores tenentes, nisi in casu quod deficiant tenentes inferiores. Item prefati sokemanni in obitibus suis dabunt herietum integrum, scilicet unum equum et hernesium et arma si habuerint. Sin autem melius averium integrum quod habuerint. Et quilibet heres patri succedens debet admitti ad hereditatem suam anno etatis sue quintodecimo et solvet domino releuium, scilicet dupplicabit redditum suum. Et dabit iudicia cum aliis paribus suis sokemannis. Et erit prepositus colligendo redditum domini quando eligetur per pares suos. Et debet respondere brevibus et omnia alia facere ac si plene esset etatis per legem communem. Item Sokemanni habebunt in forinsecsis boscis manerii per visum forestariorum estoverium, scilicet. . . . Et omnes tenentes Sokemannorum simul cum tenentibus domini venient cum faucillis ad bederipam domini ad metendum blada domini. Et ipsi etiam Sokemanni venient ad ipsam bederipam equitantes cum virgis suis ad videndum quod bene operantur, et ad praesentandum et ad amerciandum deficientes et male operantes. Et si non venerint ad dictam bederipam in forma predicta, debent graviter amerciari.

In the Warwickshire roll (Queen's Remembrancer's Miscellaneous Books, N. 29) villains are mentioned, but only exceptionally and in very small number. It looks as if they represented that class of the tenantry which in the Register is described as *servi vel nativi*. It would be out of the question to print here the detailed account of the distribution and character of the holdings given in the Hundred Roll—this must be left to the future editor of that document. But I may say here, that the holdings are much scattered, and that it would be difficult to trace the original plan mentioned in the Register. Still the division into principal tenants, mesne tenants, and cotters is clearly discernible, and the principal tenants are called free in the manor itself as well as in the hamlets. In two cases they are also spoken of as socmen.

VII.

See p. 101, n. 5.

[County Placita, Norfolk, No. 5, 21 Ed. III.]

Edwardus Dei gracia Rex Anglie et Francie et Dominus Hibernie Thesaurariis et Camerariis suis salutem. Volentes certis de causis cerciorari super tenore recordi et processus loquele que fuit inter Willelmum de Narwegate et quosdam alios homines Rogeri Bygod nuper Comitis Norfolk de Manerio de Haluergate quod est de antiquo dominico corone Anglie ut dicitur, et ipsum comitem coram Domino E. nuper Rege Anglie auo nostro anno regni sui vicesimo primo per breve ejusdem aui

nostri de eo quod idem Comes ostenderet quare a praefatis hominibus exigebat alias consuetudines et alia seruicia quam facere
deberent et ipsi et antecessores sui tenentes de eodem Manerio
facere consueverunt temporibus quibus Manerium illud fuit in
manibus progenitorum nostrorum quondam Regum Anglie, vobis
mandamus quod scrutatis rotulis praefati aui nostri de tempore
praedicto qui sunt in thesauraria nostra sub custodia vestra (ut
dicitur) tenorem recordi et processus praedictorum nobis in Cancellaria nostra sub sigillo scaccarii nostri sine dilacione mittatis
et hoc breve.   Teste Leonello filio nostro carissimo Custode
Anglie apud Redyng vi die Julii anno regni nostri Anglie vicesimo primo regni vero nostri Francie octavo.

Placita coram Domino Rege de termino Sancti Michaelis.   Anno
  regni Regis Edwardi filii Regis Henrici xxj finiente incipiente
  xxij°.

Rogerus Bygod Comes Norfolk et Marescallus Anglie attachiatus fuit ad respondendum Willelmo de Narwegate, Henrico filio
Simonis de Culyng, Thome filio Henrici de Haluergate, Ricardo
atte Howe, Roberto Sewyne et Ricardo filio Henrici Margerie
hominibus praedicti Rogeri le Bygod de Manerio de Haluergate
quod est de antiquo dominico corone Anglie de placito quare
exigit a praefatis Willelmo de Narwegate et aliis alias consuetudines
et alia seruicia quam facere debent et antecessores sui tenentes de
eodem Manerio facere consueverunt temporibus quibus Manerium
illud fuit in manibus praedecessorum Regis Regum Anglie.   Et
unde queruntur cum antecessores sui tenentes de eodem Manerio
tempore Domini Willelmi Regis Conquestoris quando praedictum
Manerium fuit in manum suam tenuerunt tenementa sua per
certa seruicia videlicet pro qualibet acra terre quam in eodem
Manerio tenuerunt duos denarios per annum et qui plus tenuerunt
plus dederunt et sectam ad Curiam Regis in eodem Manerio de
tribus septimanis in tres septimanas et quando aliquis eorum in
Curia praedicta pro aliqua transgressione esset amerciandus per
sex denarios tantum amerciatus esse debet, et similiter per dup-
plicacionem firme sue minoris vel majoris post mortem antecesso-
sorum suorum et solent talliari quando Dominus Rex talliare fecit
dominia sua Anglie pro omni seruicio et per praedicta certa
seruicia terras et tenementa sua tenuerunt a tempore Regis
Willelmi praedicti usque ad tempus Domini Henrici Regis

patris Domini Regis nunc, quod Rogerus Bygod antecessor
praedicti Rogeri qui nunc est ab eis et antecessoribus suis alias
consuetudines et alia seruicia exigebat et ad ea facienda distrinxit
videlicet pro qualibet acra quam in praedicto Manerio tenuerunt
quatuor denarios per annum et tallagium alto et basso cariagium
aueragium et merchettum pro filiis et filiabus suis maritandis et
de eisdem propositum faciendum iniuste et pro voluntate sua
distrinxit. Et praedictus Rogerus Bygod qui nunc est illam
iniuriam continuando a praefatis Willelmo et aliis praedicta
seruicia villana et incerta exigit et eos ad ea facienda distringit
et inde producunt sectam etc.

Et praedictus Rogerus Bigod venit et defendit vim et iniuriam
quando etc. Dicit quod praedicti Willelmi et alii non debent
ad breve suum respondere. Dicit enim quod ipsi in brevi suo
dicunt se esse homines ipsius Rogeri de Manerio praedicto et
tenentes de eodem Manerio qui quidem Willelmus et alii non sunt
homines ipsius Rogeri de Manerio praedicto nec fuerunt die
inpetracionis brevis sui videlicet xij die Maij Anno regni Regis
nunc xxj⁰ nec eciam aliqua tenementa tenent in praedicto Manerio
nec tenuerunt die praedicto nec antea per magnum tempus unde
petit iudicium etc.

Et praedictus Willelmus de Narwegate dicit quod ipse est homo
praedicti Comitis de Manerio praedicto et tenet in eodem Manerio
unum Messuagium unum croftum et dimidiam acram Marisci et
tenuit die impetracionis brevis praedicti. Et Thomas filius Henrici
dicit quod ipse est homo praedicti Comitis et tenet in praedicto
Manerio unum messuagium et octo acras marisci et tenuit die
praedicto etc. Et de hoc ponunt se super patriam. Et praedictus
Comes similiter. Ideo veniant inde Jurati coram Rege a die
Sancti Hillarii in xv dies ubicumque etc. Quia tam etc. Et
praedicti Henricus Ricardus atte Howe Robertus et Ricardus
filius Henrici dicunt quod reuera ipsi iam viginti annis elapsis
inpetrauerunt quoddam breve consimile etc. tempore quo ipsi
fuerunt homines ipsius Comitis et tenentes de Manerio praedicto
coram Domino Rege versus praedictum Comitem et ab illo
tempore usque nunc illud placitum sine interrupcione sunt
prosecuti ita quod si aliquod breve amiserunt medio tempore
statim breve consimile resussitauerunt. Unde dicunt quod si
praedictus Comes pendente praedicto placito et diligenter prose-
cuta quod eis pro uno placito et pro uno et eodem brevi debeat

reputari ipsos a tenementis suis in eodem Manerio eiecit homines ipsos nunc ab agendo repellere non debet. Et quod ita sit etc. offerunt verificare etc. tam per placita que secuntur Dominum Regem quam per placita de Banco etc. et eciam per placita ultimi itineris Salomonis de Roffa in comitatu Norffolk etc. Et praedictus Rogerus Comes etc. dicit quod praedicti Henricus Ricardus, Robertus et Ricardus non continuauerunt placitum suum praedictum sine interruptione in forma praedicta etc. et hoc offert etc. Ideo mandatum est Thesaurariis et Camerariis etc. quod scrutatis brevibus et rotulis de placitis que sequuntur Dominum Regem a die praedicto usque ad festum Sancti Michaelis anno regni Regis nunc xijᵒ et eciam brevibus et rotulis de itinere praedicti Salomonis Et similiter mandatum est Elye de Bekyngham quod scrutatis rotulis et brevibus de tempore Thome de Weylaund etc. que sunt sub custodia sua etc. Et quid inde etc scire faciant Domino Regi a die Pasche in xv dies ubicumque etc. Idem dies datus est partibus etc. Ad quem diem venit praedictus Comes et praedicti Henricus filius Simonis, Ricardus atte Howe, Robertus Sewyne et Ricardus filius Henrici non sunt prosecuti Ideo ipsi et plegii sui de prosequendo in misericordia videlicet Adam atte Gates, Henricus de Blafeld et Eustachius Hose de eadem. Et praedictus Comes inde sine die etc. Postea in octabis Sancti Hillarii Anno regni regis nunc vicesimo quarto venerunt praedicti Willelmus de Narugate et Thomas filius Henrici et praedictus Rogerus Bygod venit et similiter Jurati venerunt qui dicunt super sacramentum suum quod praedicti Willelmus et Thomas praedictis die et anno non fuerunt homines praedicti Comitis neque tenentes de praedicto Manerio. Ideo consideratum est quod praedicti Willelmus et Thomas nichil capiant per breve suum set sint in misericordia pro falso clamio. Et praedictus Rogerus Comes inde sine die etc.

[In dorso:]

Memorandum quod tenor recordi et processus infrascripti exemplificatus fuit sub magno sigillo Domini Regis sub hac forma videlicet. Edwardus Dei gracia Rex Anglie et Francie et Dominus Hibernie Omnibus ad quos etc. salutem Inspeximus tenorem recordi et processus cuiusdam placiti qnod fuit coram Domino E. quondam Rege Anglie auo nostro anno regni sui vicesimo primo inter Willelmum de Norwegate et quosdam alios et Rogerum Bygod nuper Comitem Norfolk quem coram nobis

in Cancellaria nostra venire facimus in hec verba Placita coram
Domino Rege etc. recitando totum tenorem praedictum usque
in finem et tunc sic Nos autem tenorem recordi et processus
praedictorum tenore praesencium duximus exemplificandum In
cuius etc. Teste Leonello filio nostro carissimo Custode Anglie
apud Redyng xx die Julii anno regni nostri Anglie vicesimo
primo regni vero nostri Francie octauo que quidem brevia non
irrotulantur aliter quam hic inseritur.

VIII.

See p. 104, n. I.

[Exch. Memoranda Q. R. 20 Edw. I, Trin, m. 21 d.]

Baronibus pro hominibus de manerio de Costeseye.

Rex mittit Baronibus peticionem hominum manerii de Costeseye
presentibus inclusam mandantes, quod audita intellecta et diligenter examinata peticione predicta de diversis gravaminibus et
iniuriis per preceptum baronum et per Ricardum Athelwald de
Crek ballivum eiusdem manerii eisdem hominibus multipliciter
illatis, predictis hominibus iusticie complementum inde exhiberi
faciatis prout de iure et secundum legem et consuetudinem regni
Anglie fuerit faciendum Ne oporteat ipsos homines ad Regem
iterato habere recursum ex causa praedicta. Teste Rege apud
Enleford VII die Maii XX°.

Peticio hominum de manerio de Costeseye. A nostre Seignur le
Rey e a sun conseil se pleynent les pours genz le Rey de la basse
tenure de le maner de Costeseye ce est a sauer de la foreyn sokne
com de Colton, Eston, Hiningham, Thodeham, Rongelsunde,
Weston, Tauerham, Berford, Wramplingham et Dunholt ke
Richard de Crek bailif le Rey del maner avantdit a tort lur
greve e distreynt e lur met hors de lur usages en dreyt de lur
tenaunce uses del tens memore ne curt. Ce est a sauer par la
ou memes cele genz sa en arere en les tens les cuntes de Bretayne,
e en le tens le Rey Johan e le Rey Henri ke deus asoile e
en le tens nostre Seignur le Rey Edward ke deu gard e de
tuz iceus a queus le maner avant dit a este done ou lesse a la
volunte de Reys avaunt nomes pur ke le Cunte de Bretayne e
le viscunte de Dohay mesnes le maner forfirent, unt vendu, done

e lesse lur terres champestres per aper (?) saunz conge demaunder
en curt, forpris lur mes e lur croftes, la vient mesme celuy
Richard bailif auant nome e lur terres saunz conge venduz per
aper (?) ad seysi a greuuesement les ad amercie pur les tenemenz
issi uendus solonc les usages de lur tenaunce. Estre ce memes
celuy Richard a tort greve e distreint les genz auaunt nomes
pur office de prouosterie e de coylure (collector) ne ils ne
deyuent estre ne soleyent, mes les viles de Costeseye et de Banburg
seruent et deyuent servir de tel office pur lur tenaunce charge
de tel seruise. E priunt la grece lur seignur le Rey ke il voyle
fere enquere par pais si le plest coment ils deyuent tenir e ke la
duresse fete a eus par le bailif auant dit seit redresse. Estre ce
les poure genz auant nomes sunt mut enpoureriz pur un taylage
voluntref ke le bailif Alianor Reyne de Engletere la mere nostre
seignur le Rey ke deus asoile nut pris a tort de an en an ce
est a sauer xx markes de hom apele communage ke auaunt
sun tens ne fut donc mes a la premere venue de nouel signur
une conisaunce de Cs. cum fu done a nostre seignur le Rey
Edward kant le maner li fu done forpris les viles de Costeseye
e de Banburg ke sunt taylables haut e bas a la volunte le Rey
cum costemers del maners. Pur ce est ke les paure genz auaunt
nome priunt la grace nostre seignur le Rey si le plest pur le
regard de pite ke il empreynt pite de eus e lur face suffrir
lur usages del tens dunc memore ne curt e grace del torteuus
taylage pur le quel il sunt mut empoairiz.

IX.

See p. 108, n. 1.

[Augmentation Court Rolls, XIV. 38.]
(Havering atte Bower, Essex.)

Curia ibidem tenta die Iouis proxima ante festum S. Iohannis
ante portam latinam anno r. r. Ricardi Secundi post Conquestum
vicesimo. Ricardus Rex Ballivis Thome Archiepiscopi Ebor et
Edwardi comitis de Hauering atte Boure. Precipio vobis quod sine
dilatione et secundum consuetudinem manerii de Hauering atte
Boure plenum rectum teneatis Roberto Merston de London et
Ricardo Quylter de Hauering etc.

Hec est finalis concordia facta in curia Thome archiepiscopi

Cantuar et Edwardi Comitis Roteland apud Hauering atte Boure—
coram Ricardo Wytl . . . tunc senescallo et Ricardo Wylde tunc
ballivo et aliis domini Regis fidelibus tunc ibi presentibus inter
etc.

Curia Thome Archiepiscopi Cantuarensis et Edwardi Comitis
Roteland tenta ibidem die Iouis proxima ante festum S. Bartholomaei apostoli anno r. r. Ricardi Secundi post conquestum vicesimo
primo.

Inquisicio ex officio coram Ricardo Wythmerssh senescallo de
Haueryng atte Boure per sacramentum Walteri Herstman——--
juratorum qui dicunt supra sacramentum suum quod Alicia Dyere
que de domino Rege tenuit duas acras terre in marisco obiit seisita.
Et quod Thomas de Donne filius predicte Alicie est eius heres
propinquior et plene etatis, ideo preceptum seisire dictam terram in
manus domini et respondere de exitu quali etc. Item dicunt quod
idem Thomas ingressus est feodum domini videlicet unum
mesuagium cum pertinentiis in Romford quod habuit ex dono et feo-
famento Iohannis Cole ideo preceptum ipsum distringere pro
fidelitate et relevio etc. Item predicta Inquisitio onerata super
sacramentum suum si aliquis homo nativus de sanguine ingressus
fuerit feodum domini nec ne et quantum feodum illud valeat per
annum dicit quod non est aliquis homo nativus de sanguine
ingressus feodum domini. Set dicunt quod est quidam Iohannes
Shillyng qui sepius dictus fuerat fore nativus. Et dicunt ultra quod
quidam Iohannes Shillyng pater predicti Iohannis fuit alienigena
et quod predictus Iohannes Shillyng quo ad eorum cognitionem est
liber et libere conditionis et non nativus. Item prefata inquisitio
dicit quod Robertus Clement de London Sadelere ingressus est
feodum domini videlicet unum mesuagium cum pertinenciis in
Romford quod habuit ex dono et concessione Iohannis Cole
Taillor ideo preceptum ipsum distringere pro fidelitate et relevio
etc.

Item dicunt quod quidam homo veniens in comitiva domini
Regis dimisit quemdam equum in hospicio Iohannis atte Heth et
cepit ibidem unum alium equum etc. et dimisit predictum equum
ibidem stare per unum mensem absque aliquid clamando de
predicto equo ideo preceptum dictum equum seisire ad opus domini
Regis et inde Regi respondere.

Curia ibidem tenta die Iouis proxima post festum S. Martini
anno r. r. Ricardi secundi post conquestum vicesimo primo.

Compertum est per inquisicionem ex officio captam per sacramentum Thome Olyuere . . . Qui dicunt super sacramentum suum quod quidam Iohannes Pecok quondam tenuit unam peciam terre in marisco vocatam Wattiscroft pro qua quidem terra reparabat et reparare tenebatur quoddam murum in marisco erga Tamisiam in defensum aque inundantis. Et idem Iohannes Pecok de terra predicta obiit seisitus. Et quod quidam Iohannes filius predicti Iohannis Pecok est eius heres propinquus. Et dicunt quod predictus murus est wastatus pro defectu reparacionis ita quod aque Tamisie inundans superfluit murum predictum et demergit mariscum predictum ad grave dampnum domini Regis et tenencium suorum.

Et predictus Iohannes filius Iohannis Pecok in propria persona sua dicit quod non supponitur per presentacionem predictam quod terra predicta vocata Wattiscroft prefato Iohanni filio predicti Iohannis Pecok descendebat post mortem Iohannis Pecok patris sui nec quod predictus Iohannes filius Iohannis Pecok aliquo tempore fuit tenens terre predicte vocate Wattiscroft. Et si videtur Curie quod protestacio est sufficiens, etc. dicit per protestacionem quod ipse non fuit heres predicti Iohannis Pecok patris sui tempore mortis sue, etc. Et ulterius protestando dicit quod predicta terra vocata Wattiscroft tenetur ad communem legem. Et ulterius dicit pro placito quod ipse numquam habuit poscessionem manualem de terra predicta set dicit quod quidam Iohannes Harwere post decessum predicti Iohannis patris sui et longo tempore ante inquisicionem predictam captam intravit in terram predictam ad usum cujusdam Iohannis Selman . . . *Et dictum est pro domino Rege* quod predictus Iohannes filius predicti Iohannis Pecok fuit tenens terre predicte die quo inquisicio predicta capta fuit. Et petitum est per dominum Regem quod inquiratur per patriam. Et pro predicto Iohanne filio, etc. similiter. [Jurati] dicunt super sacramentum suum quod predictus Iohannes Pecok vivente predicto Iohanne patre suo occupavit predictam terram vocatam Wattiscroft per voluntatem patris sui et cepit inde exitus et proficua. Et postea predictus Iohannes Pecok pater, etc. obiit post cujus mortem predictus Iohannes filius, etc. intrauit ut filius et heres et terram predictam ocupavit et inde cepit exitus proficua, etc. Et dicunt quod est eorum consuetudo quod nullus homo adquireret sibi aliquam terram in marisco que oneratur ex reparacione alicuius muri in marisco erga Tamisiam nisi haberet sufficientem tenuram in eodem dominio extra mariscum que poterit portare omnes reparaciones illius·muri in marisco quum necesse fuerit. Et dicunt esciam quod Iohannes Selman non fuit tenens terre predicte vocate Wattiscroft die quo officium predictum captum fuit set quod predictus Iohannes filius, etc. terram predictam occupavit usque in diem quo predictum officium captum fuit. Et dicunt quod est ad dampnum domini Regis quod murus predictus non fuit reparatus predicto die, etc. de triginta et octo solidis uno obolo.

Curia ibidem tenta die Iouis in festo S. Iohannis Apostoli et Evangeliste anno r. r. Ricardi post Conquestum vicesimo primo.

Dominus Rex mandauit breue suum clausum Ballivis Edwardi Ducis Albemarle de Haueryng atte Boure . . . Precepimus vobis quod sine dilacione et secundum consuetudinem manerii de Haueryng atte Boure plenum rectum teneatis Ricardo filio Iohannis Legati de uno mesuagio viginti et octo acris terre et una acra prati cum pertinenciis, etc. . . . Et predictus Ricardus invenit plegios ad prosequendum breue predictum . . . Et fecit protestacionem ad sequendum breue predictum in natura breuis de convencione. Virtute cuius brevis preceptum Ballivo quod summonere faciat per bonos summonitores secundum consuetudinem manerii de Haueryng atte Boure, etc. . . .

Curia tenta ibidem die Iouis proxima . . . vicesimo tercio.

Dominus Rex mandauit breue suum clausum Ballivis suis de Haueryng atte Boure.

Curia ibidem tenta die Iouis proxima ante festum S. Laurencii martiris anno r. r. Ricardi secundi post conquestum vicesimo tercio. . . .

Ricardus Dei gratia Rex Anglie . . . Ballivis suis de Haueryng, etc.

Hec est finalis concordia facta in curia domini Regis de Haueryng atte Boure die Iouis . . . coram Ricardo Withmerssh tunc senescallo et Iohanne Bokenham tunc Balliuo et aliis domini Regi fidelibus tunc presentibus inter W., etc.

X.

See p. 143, n. 3.

Exchequer Q. R. Ancient Miscellanea.

$$\frac{902}{77}$$ (No date, about 1300.)

Inquisitio:

Will's Frere	Walt's Michel	Joh'es Broket
Rob's Diaconus	Elias de Leyes	Thomas Coker
Rob's Snellyng	Elias Pany	Will's Hardyng
Joh'es Longus	Godefrid' Newman	Will's Walysce
		Joh'es Ordmar

Qui dicunt subscripta per sacramentum suum.

Pater extraneus

Nativus— Nich's ate Neuthon'
- Maur' ate Neuthon' { Estrelda } man' apud Machynge / Agnes
- Joh'es Rotlonde . { Joh'es Rotlonde / Walt's Rotlonde / Thomas Rotlonde } man' London'.
- Will's Pany . . . { Joh'es Pany / Will's Pany / Ric's Pany / Elias Pany—modo tenens / Agnes Pany nullus ab eo.
- Simon ate Neuthon'
- Thomas le Couper . { Ric's le Couper / Simon le Couper / Johes le Couper / Isabella la Couper
- Joh'es Bate . . . Walt's ate Neuthon'—modo tenens
- Cristina . . . . Will's
- Wymarks . . . . nullus ab eo

Pater extraneus ignotus adhuc propter diurnitatem temporis

- Joh'es Woderove . Galfr's Woderove { Will's Woderove / n. / n.
- Will's Vaccarius . nullus ab eo

Nativus— Rog's ate Neuthon'
- Will's Pistor . . . { Steph's Pistor / Will's Pistor / Rog's Pistor / Joh'es Pistor / Cristina Pistor / Isabella
- Cristina ate Neuthon' nullus ab eo (sic)
- Agnes ate Neuthon' { Joh'es Broket / Johe's Broket Junior / Matild' Broket / Isabella Broket / Agnes Broket

Nativus— Alanus ate Hache . nullus ab eo

Editha la Daye

Nativus— Rog's ate Hache . .
- Adam ate Hache . { Ric's ate Hache Junior / Nich's ate Hache / Rog's ate Hache / Will's ate Hache / Will's ate Hache / Will's ate Hache / Joh'es ate Hache / Alic' ate Hache / Matild' ate Hache / Emmot' ate Hache / Marger' ate Hache
- Matild' ate Hache . nullus ab eo
- Orgor' ate Hache .

Nativus— Walts' ate Hache
- Ranulfus ate Broke { Will's ate Broke / Walt's ate Broke / Walt's ate Broke / Ric's ate Broke—London' / Cristin' ate Broke / Matild' ate Broke / Agnes ate Broke
- Matheus ate Broke { Walterus Mathy / Will's Mathy / Agnes Mathy / Emmot' Mathy
- Matild' ate Broke . nullus ab ea.

XI.

See p. 188, n. 2.

The best way to form an opinion as to the position of the hundredors among other classes will be, I think, to start from a closer examination of the Ely Surveys, which give the term several times. They are peculiar in this respect, and only in this. A comparison with other Cartularies will show at once, that the same thing is to be found elsewhere over and over again.

Both Ely Surveys—that of 1222 (Tiberius, B. ii) and that of 1277 (Claudius, C. xi)—are remarkably alike, and may serve as an illustration of the continuity of the fundamental organisation of a feudal village. I shall take the later Cartulary because it is a trifle fuller, and coincides in time with the Hundred Rolls. It would not be sufficient to give only the entries relating to the hundredors, because the reader would not be able to judge of their position in relation to other classes. I may be allowed in consequence to present rather large extracts.

In the manor of Wilburton belonging to the Ely Minster we find the following classification of the tenantry[1] [f. 49 sqq.]

De hundredariis. Et libere tenentibus.

Philippus de insula tenet 16 acras de mara et debet sectas ad curiam Elyensem et ad curiam de Wilbartone, *et in quolibet hundredo per totum annum.* Et dat ad sixþepany et wardpany, et arabit cum caruca sua per duos dies in hyeme et habebit quolibet die unum denarium. Et arabit in XL^ma per 2 dies et habebit quolibet die unum denarium . . . Et inveniet omnes tenentes suos ad magnam precariam autumpni ad cibum episcopi. Et dabit pro filia sua.

Ricardus filius Rogeri tenet 12 acras de ware et debet sectas . . . (the same as Philip). Et dabit leirwite pro filia sua et gersumam cum ipsam maritare uoluerit, scilicet 30 et 2 den. Et tallagium cum aliis. Et de herieto meliorem bestiam uel 30 et 2 denarios, si non habeat bestiam. Oues sue non iacebunt in faldo domini . . .

---

[1] It ought to be mentioned that the hundreds to which suit is due belonged to the Church of Ely.

De operariis et plenis terris.

Samson filius Jordani tenet 12 acras terre de Wara que faciunt unam plenam terram . . . Et sciendum quod tota villata, tam liberi quam alii, debent facere 40 perticatas super calcetum de Alderhe sine cibo et opere.

In Lyndon the division of the tenantry is somewhat more complex [f. 52 sqq.].

De militibus.

Philippus de insula tenet tres carucatas in Hinegeton per seruicium unius militis. Et sciendum quod omnes tenentes sui ibidem debent uenire ad precariam carucarum episcopi cum quanto iungant per duos dies in hyeme et per 2 dies in XL^{ma} . . . Et dominus Philippus de Insula debet sectam ad curiam Elyensem. Et ad curiam de Lyndon, in aduentu senescalli.

Nigellus de Cheucker tenet 2 carucatas terre per seruicium unius militis cum terra sua de Harefeud . . . Et liberi tenentes sui *qui tenent per soccagium debent unam sectam ad frendlese hundred,* scilicet ad diem sabbati proximum post festum S^{ti} Michaelis.

De hundredariis.

Robertus de Aula tenet 40 acras terre de wara per *seruicium sequendi curiam Elyensem. Et quodlibet hundredum et curiam de Lyndon.* . . . Et ueniet ad precarias cum caruca sua . . . Et inueniet omnes tenentes suos ad magnam precariam episcopi in autumpno ad cibum domini. Et ipsemet ibit ultra eos eo die. Et habebit cibum suum similiter cum balliuis domini. Et *ueniet coram justiciariis ad custum suum proprium . . . Et sciendum quod iste et quilibet hundredarius* dabit gersumam pro filia sua maritanda, scilicet 32 denarios. Et dominus episcopus habebit meliorem bestiam de domo sua pro herietto siue 32 denarios, si bestiam non habuerit et operabitur super calcetum de Alderhe sine cibo pro se et tenentibus suis.

Galfridus le Sokeman tenet 12 acras et dimidiam de wara . . . .

De consuetudinariis qui vocantur Molmen.

Patrik filius Henrici le frankeleyn tenet 10 acras terre in hylle pro duobus solidis . . . Et ueniet ad precariam carucarum cum caruca sua uel cum quanto iungit . . . Et debet sectas ad curiam de Lyndon . . . Et dabit gersumam pro filia sua maritanda ad voluntatem domini. Et in obitu suo dominus habebit meliorem bestiam domus pro hereto uel triginta duos denarios, si bestiam non habuerit. Et dabit tallagium. Et filius suus et heres dabit releuium.

De operariis qui tenent plenas terras.

Radulfus filius Osbern tenet unam plenam terram que continet 10 acras de wara.

The next survey is that of Dudington (f. 63 sqq.).

De libere tenentibus et hundredariis in Dudlingtone et Wimblingtone.

(The typical hundredor is made to pay merchet, leyrwite, and heriet as above.)

De consuetudinibus censuariorum in Dudingtone.

Radulfus filius Willelmi tenet unum mesuagium quod continet dimidiam acram pro 12 denariis . . . Et dabit gersumam pro filia sua et leyrwite ad voluntatem domini, Et dupplicabit redditum suum pro suo releuio.

De consuetudinibus operariorum in Dudington.

(They hold 'full lands' of 12 acres, and perform all kinds of agricultural work.)

If we turn now to the Survey of Wyvelingham (f. 111 sqq.), we shall not find the heading 'hundredarii,' but it will not be difficult to discern the tenants who correspond to the hundredors of the former Surveys.

De libere tenentibus.

Henricus Torel tenet dimidiam virgatam terre pro decem et octo denariis equaliter. Et ueniet in autumpno ad magnam precariam domini cum omnibus hominibus suis quot habuerit laborantes ad cibum domini. Et dabit tallagium si dominus voluerit. Et gersumam pro filia sua. Et debet sectam curie et molendini. Et ibit cum aliis extra uillam ad districtiones faciendum.

Willelmus Nuncius tenet dimidiam virgatam pro 18 denariis equaliter. Et faciet omnia alia sicuti predictus Henricus Torel.

Thomas filius Oliue tenet unam virgatam terre pro 6 denariis equ. ad festum S^{ti} Andreae. Et arabit tres rodas terre per annum. . . . Et herciabit cum equo suo ante Natale per unum diem integrum sine cibo et per unum diem in quadragesima sine cibo . . . Et falcabit cum uno homine per unum diem integrum sine cibo. Et adiuuabit fenum leuandum et cariandum sine cibo. Et sarclabit per unum diem integrum sine cibo. Et illud quod messuerit cariabit sine cibo. Item portabit breuia domini episcopi uel senescalli usque ad Dudington uel ad locum consimilem. Et dabit tallagium, herietum et leyrwite, et gersumam pro filia sua. Et *debet sectam Comitatus hundredi, et curie,* et molendini. Oues sue iacebunt in faldo domini ut supra . . .

De operariis.

Thomas Wecheharm tenet dimidiam virgatam terre que continet 15 acras terre.

In Shelford (f. 125 sqq. Cf. Rot. Hundr. ii. 544) there are only two main headings : ' de militibus ' and ' de consuetudinariis et censuariis ; ' but I think it is quite evident from the Survey that the first ought to run ' de militibus et libere tenentibus,' or something to the same effect, and that it includes the hundredors.

De militibus.

Johannes de Moyne miles tenet unum mesuagium et unam rodam terre que fuit coteria operabilis in tempore Galfridi de Burgo Elyensis episcopi pro duobus solidis equ. Idem Johannes tenet unum mesuagium quod fuit Michaelis de la Greue pro 14 den. equ. Et inueniet unum hominem ad quamlibet trium precariarum ad cibum domini. Et metet dimidiam acram de louebene sine cibo. Et inueniet unum hominem ad fenum leuandum et tassandum in curia domini episcopi. Et dabit tallagium cum consuetudinariis pro tanta portione.

Johannes filius Nicholai Collogne tenet dimidiam hydam terre *per seruicium sequendi comitatum et hundredum.* Idem tenet quartam partem curie sue pro uno niso (*sic*) uel duobus solidis . . .

In Stratham the Molmen are reckoned with the freeholders and hundredors (f. 44).

De libere tenentibus et censuariis.

Walterus de Ely miles tenet 50 acras de wara unde debet sectam *ad curiam de Ely. Et ad curiam de Stratham. Et in hundredum de Wycheford* . . . Et faciet omnes consuetudines sicut Johannes filius Henrici subscriptus.

Johannes filius Henrici Folke tenet 10 acras de wara. Et debet *sectam hundredi per totum annum, scilicet ad quodlibet hundredum et sectam ad curiam de Ely et de Stratham.* . . . Et dabit gersumam pro filia sua maritanda.

De consuetudinibus operariorum, etc.

The entries quoted are sufficient, it seems, to establish the following facts :—

1. The hundredors of the Ely Minster are people holding tenements burdened with the obligation of representing the manor in the hundred and in the county.

2. The tenure may be quite distinct from the personal condition of the holder. A knight may possess the tenement of a hundredor in one place and a military fee in another (Philip de Insula in Wilburton and in Lyndon.)

3. A free tenant is not *eo ipso* a hundredor. Some holdings are singled out for the duty. (Henry Torel, William ' Nuncius,' and Thomas filius Olive in Wyvelingham. Cf. Lyndon.)

4. In many cases the hundredors are mentioned without being expressly so called, and such cases present the transition between the Ely Surveys and other Cartularies which constantly speak of privileged tenants holding by suit to the hundred and to the county. (See the quotations on p. 189, n. 2, and p. 191, n. 1.)

But there is another side to the picture. In the cases of which we have been speaking till now the obligation to attend the hundred and the county is treated as a service connected with tenure, and has to meet the requirements of the State which enforces the representation of the villages at the Royal Courts. Such a system of representation follows from the conception of the County and of the Hundred as political parts of the kingdom on the one hand, and as composed of Manors and Villages or Vills, on the other. This may be called the *territorial* system. But another conception is lingering behind it—that namely of the County, as a folk, and of the Hundred, as an assembly of the free and lawful population. The great Hundred is derived from it, but even in the ordinary meetings all the freeholders are entitled, if not obliged, to join. The Manor and the Vill have nothing to do with this right, which is not one of representation, but an individual one and extends to a whole class. This may be called the *personal* system of the Hundred. It is embodied in the so-called 'Leges' of Henry I. And therefore we find constantly in the documents, that the suit to the hundred, to the county, and also that to the sheriff's tourn and to meet the justices, are mentioned in connection with two different classes of people. On one hand stand the representatives of the township, on the other the free men, free tenants or socmen bound individually to attend the hundred and to perform other duties which are enforced on the same pattern. The Hundred Rolls give any number of examples.

I. 55 : liberi homines de Witlisford et quatuor homines et prepositus solebant venire ad turnum vicecomitis set post bellum de Evesham per Baldewynum de Aveny subtracta fuit illa secta, set nesciunt quo warranto.

I. 154 : Idem abbas (de Wauthan) subtraxit ad turnum vicecomitum sectam 4 hominum et prepositi de manerio suo de Esthorndone et de liberis hominibus suis in eadem villa et in villa de Stanford.

I. 180 : Omnes liberi tenentes et quatuor homines et prepositus de Morton Valence subtraxerunt sectam ad turnum vicecomitis bis in anno ad idem hundredum.

In Shropshire we find the question put to the jurors of the inquest (II. 69) : Si homines libere tenentes et 4 homines et prepositus de singulis villis venerint ad summonicionem sicut preceptum est.

II. 130 : Dominus Ricardus Comes Gloverniae subtraxit 4 thethingas videlicet Stockgiffard, Estharpete Stuctone et Westone de hundredo de Wintestoke et ipsas sibi appropriavit. Item dicunt quod Thomas de Ban ... et ceteri libere tenentes predictarum 4 thethingarum solebant sequi dictum hundredum et se subtraxerunt a termino predicto.

II. 131 : Dicunt quod una decena de Borewyk et alia decena Chyletone cum liberis hominibus subtrahuntur de hundredo domini Regis de la Hane.

I. 17 : Manerium de Collecote et 8 liberi Sokemanni tenentes in dicto manerio solebant facere sectam ad hundredum de Kenoteburie et subtracti sunt a tempore Alani de Fornham quondam vicecomitis usque nunc.

The last instances quoted do not speak directly of the four men and the reeve, but their meaning is quite clear and very significant. The suit of the tithing and of the manor is contrasted with the personal suit of the free tenants. We find often entries as to the attendance of the manor, the township, or the tithing.

I. 181 : Dicunt quod abbas de Theokesberie pro terra sua in Codrinton . . . Episcopus Wygorniensis pro manerio suo de Clyve per quatuor homines et prepositum solebant facere sectam ad istum hundredum ad turnum vicecomitis bis in anno usque ad provisiones Oxonienses.

I. 105 : Villata de Monston per 2 annos et villata de Stratton per 10 annos subtraxerunt sectam hundredi.

I. 78 : Dicunt quod idem Walterus (de Bathonia) removit villanos de Sepwasse in forinsecum et feofavit liberos de eadem terra in quo terra quidam tuthinmannus (*corr.* quedam tethinga ?) jungi solebat et sequi ad hundredum forinsecum predictum et est secta ejusdem tethinge subtracta de tempore Regis Henrici patris Regis Edwardi anno ejus quarto.

It appears that the feoffment of free tenants was no equivalent for the destruction of the tithing. The entry is remarkable but not very clear. (Cf. I. 87, II. 133, and Maitland, Introduction to the Selden Soc. vol. II, pp. xxxi, xxxiii.) In any case the main facts are not doubtful. The population of the kingdom was bound to attend the assemblies of the hundred and of the county by representatives from the villages or tithings, which sometimes, though not always, coincided with the manors.

There were many exceptions of different kinds, but the Crown was striving to restrict their number and to enforce general attendance at least for the tourn and the eyre. The representation in these last cases, though much wider and more regular than at the ordinary meetings of the hundred and of the shire, was constructed on the same principles, and the difference lay only in the measure in which the royal right was put into practice against the disruptive tendencies of feudalism.

The inquest in the beginning of Edward I's reign gives us a very good insight into the inroads from which the organisation had to suffer, especially in troubled times[1]. This attendance of the township is mentioned in marked contrast with the suit of the free tenants or socmen, which is also falling into disuse on many occasions, and also supposes a general theory, that the free people ought to attend in person.

An important point in the process which modified the representation of the vills in the hundred has to be noticed in the fact, that the suit from a single village was not considered as a unit which did not admit of any partition. When the village itself was divided among several landlords the suit was apportioned according to their parts in the ownership instead of remaining, as it were, outside the partition. We might well fancy that the township of Dudesford, though divided between the Abbots of Buttlesden and of Oseney, would send its deputies as a whole, and would designate them in a meeting of the whole. We find in reality, that the fee of one of the owners has to send three representatives, and the fee of the other two (Rot. Hundr. I. 33; cf. I. 52, 102). This gives rise to a difficulty in the reading of our evidence. The Hundred Rolls speak not only of suit due from the village, the tithing, or the manor, but also of the suit from the tenement. In one sense this may mean that the person holding a free tenement was bound to attend certain meetings of the commons of the realm. In another it was an equivalent to saying that a particular tenement was bound to join in the duty of sending representatives to such meetings. In a third acceptation of the words they might signify, that a particular tenement was charged to represent the village in regard to the suits, and for this reason privileged in other respects. A few extracts from the Hundred Rolls will illustrate the difficulty.

I. 143 : Dicunt quod Johannes de Boneya tenuit quoddam tenementum in Stocke quod solet facere sectam ad comitatum et hun-

---

[1] Rot. Hundr. ii. 82: 'Walterus de Pedecorthin est dominus (de Ingwethin), in qua est una virgata terre et facit sectam ad hundredum bis in anno, set non ad parva hundreda nec ad comitatum, nesciunt quo warranto.' ii. 201: 'Decena de Larncynge solebat facere sectam ad dictum hundredum de Bretford set de consensu W. de Breuse dicta decena divisa fuit in duas partes. Ita quod una pars secta ad curiam domini de Brawatere et alia medietas ad dictum hundredum de Bretford ad dampnum domini dicti hundredi 5 solidorum per annum:' ii. 195: '8 homines de homagio Johannis le Butiler in Stones et Boxham qui debent facere sectam ad predictum hundredum subtraxerunt sectam suam ad duo hundreda generalia per annum et unus predictorum hominum retraxit sectam suam per totum annum debitam.'

dredum, que secta postea subtracta fuit per Regem Alemanniae, etc.

Was John de Boneya a socman bound to attend personally, or a hundredor, a hereditary representative of the village of Stocke?

II. 208 : Prior de Michulham subtraxit sectas et servicia 25 tenencium in manerio suo de Chyntynge qui solebant facere sectam et servicium hundredo de Faxeberewe et sunt subtracti per 6 annos ad dampnum dicti hundredi 5 sol. per annum.

The twenty-five tenants in question may be villains joining to send representatives in scot and in lot with the village (cf. I. 214, 216), or free socmen personally bound to attend.

II. 225: Prior de Kenilworth subtraxit, etc., de una virgata terre in Lillington 15 annis elapsis et de 4 virgatis in Herturburie 18 annis elapsis . . . qui solent sequi ad hundredum de tribus septimanis in tres septimanas.

Here it would be difficult to decide whether the suit is apportioned between the tenements of the village on the principle of their contributing jointly to perform the services, or else bound up with these particular virgates as representing the village (cf. I. 34).

I notice this difficulty because it is my object in this Appendix to treat the evidence as it is given in the documents, and to help those who may wish to study them at first hand. But as we are immediately concerned with the position of the 'hundredor,' I shall also point out that there are cases where a doubt is hardly possible. The tenant who is privileged on account of the duties that he performs in representing his village in the hundred court, may be easily recognised in the following examples.

II. 66 : Dicunt quod Rogerus Hunger de Preston solebat sequi comitatum et hundredum *pro villa de Preston* in tempore Henrici de Audithelege tunc vicecomitis Salop 20 annis elapsis, mortuo vero predicto Roberto Hunger, Abbas de Lilleshul qui intratus fuit in predictam villam per donum Roberti de Budlers de Mungomery extraxit (*corr.* subtraxit) predictam sectam 20^{ti} annis elapsis nesciunt quo warranto, unde dominus Rex dampnificatus est per illam subtraxionem, si idem Abbas warrantum inde non habet de 40 solidis.

I. 21 : Johannes de Grey subtraxit se de secta curie pro villata de Chilton de uno anno et die (*corr.* et dimidio), unde dominus Rex dampnificatus est in 18 denariis.

Though the institution of the hundredors has found expression
in the Hundred Rolls, the name is all but absent from them. The
rare instances when it occurs are especially worthy of consideration. I have three times seen a contraction which probably stands
for it, but in one case it applies distinctly to the hundred-reeve or
to a riding bailiff of the hundred.

I. 197 (Inquest of the hundred of Hirstingstan, Hunts): dicunt
etiam quod homines ejusdem soke rescusserunt aueria que El.
hundredarius ceperat pro debito domini Regis levando et impe-
dierunt eum ad summoniciones faciendum de assisis et juratis et
equum ipsius El. duxerunt ad manerium de Someresham et eum
ibi detinuerunt quousque deliberavit omnia averia per ipsum
capta.

The case is different in regard to the description of Aston and
Cote, Oxfordshire. It is printed on p. 689 of the second volume
of the Hundred Rolls, but printed badly. The decisive headings
are not given accurately, and I shall put it before the reader in the
shape in which it stands in the MS. at the Record Office. The
passage is especially interesting because of the peculiar constitution
of the manor of Bampton, to which Aston and Cote belong. (See
Gomme, Village Community.)

Hundred Rolls, Oxford.

Chancery Series, No. 1, m. 3.

§ Tenentes Abbatis in eadem.
§ Hundr' in Aston'.

§ Robertus le Caus tenet in eadem j. mesuagium et
ij. virgatas terræ de Abbate de Eygn', et reddit per
annum dicto Abbati Eygn' iij.s.

§ Stephanus le Niwe tenet in eadem j. mesuagium
et ij. virgatas terræ de eodem, et reddit per annum
dicto Abbati xv.s. vij.d. ob. q.

§ Robertus de Haddon' tenet in eadem j. mesuagium [et] j. virgatam terræ de Domino W. de Valencia, et reddit per annum dicto W. de Valencia j.d.

§ Henricus Toni tenet in eadem j. mesuagium [et]
j. virgatam terræ de Abbate de Eygn', et reddit eidem
pro redditu iiij.s. pro opere iiij.s. iiij.d. ob. q.

§ Servi.

§ Willelmus Toni tenet in eadem j. mesuagium [et]
j. virgatam terræ de dicto Abbate, et reddit per annum
eidem pro redditu iiij.s., pro opere iiij.s. ix d. ob. q.

§ Nicholaus Toni tenet in eadem consimile tenementum de eodem pro consimili servicio faciendo
eidem.

§ Emma Lovel tenet in eadem j. mesuagium et
dimidiam virgatam terræ cum v. acras de eodem,
et reddit per annum dicto Abbati xj.s. iij.d.

§ Lib[ere] tenentes.

§ Johanna Galard tenet in eadem dimidiam virgatam terræ de dono Willelmi fratris sui, et reddit eidem
per annum vj.*d.* ; et idem Willelmus tenet de hereditate per defensum antecessorum suorum, qui dictam
dimidiam virgatam terræ habuerunt de dono Reg[is],
cujus nomen ignoramus.
   § Thomas Wyteman tenet in eadem j. virgatam
terræ de Philippo de Lenethale, et est de confir-
matione Reg[is], ut dicta dimidia virgata terræ
præscripta ; et tenetur de Willelmo Gallard præ-
dicto, et reddit per annum dicto Philippo xij.*d.*

[The Abbot above mentioned was the Abbot of Eynsham.]

The *Hundr. in Aston* in the margin can hardly admit of
any other extension but *hundredarius* or *hundredarii.* It seems
then, that the term is applied to three tenants named first.
The reason for thinking so is, that all these three are assessed at
certain rents without any mention of labour services, whereas the
three tenants who are next mentioned pay so much as rent
and so much more in commutation of labour service, 'pro
servitio.' The inference would be, that the names in the beginning
apply to people burdened with suit to the hundred and to the
shire, and therefore exempted in other respects. Their rents are
very unequal, but in any case lower than those of the men immediately following. One very important feature admits of no dispute
the hundredors are described as *servi*, that is villains, in opposition to the free tenants of the Abbot of Eynsham. We know
already from the text that the hundredors, if the name be applied
here as in the Ely Surveys, occupied an intermediate position, and
in one sense had certainly to rank with the villains, people of
base tenure belonging to the townships.

Even a more difficult example is contained in the fragment of
the Warwickshire Hundred Roll. The oft-mentioned description
of Stoneleigh in that document begins of course with the demesne
land of the abbot, then mentions two villains and thirty free
cotters holding 'ad terminum vitae.' Then follows a list of five
more free cotters. On the margin between the two sets we read
'de hundred de Stonle.' To whom does this phrase apply?
There is nothing in the tenure which would enable us to make a
positive distinction between the two sets, and it would seem that
the expression has in view some duties assigned in the roll to
the first thirty tenants in conjunction with the villains. It is written
immediately in front of the following passage : 'Omnes supradicti

cotarii ipsius abbatis debent sectam ad curiam suam bis in anno. Et si contingat quod aliquis captus sit in dicto manerio debet imprisonari apud Stanle et tunc omnes villani et cotarii supradicti ipsum servabunt et in custodia eorum erit dum ibi fuerit sumptibus suis et sumptibus tocius manerii.'

The uncertainty of terminology is not without its meaning: the word 'hundredarius' did not get into general use, but it was used in several places for different purposes. It may apply to a bailiff of the hundred, perhaps to the alderman, to the standing representative of a village at the hundred court, and possibly to all the free men who had to do personal suit to this court. It is not in order to impose a uniform sense upon it, that I have treated of it at this length. But in one of its meanings, in that which is given by the Ely Surveys, we find a convenient starting point for discussing the position of an important and interesting class in which the elements of freedom and servitude appear curiously mixed.

XII.

See p. 199, n. 1.

It did not occur to the men of the thirteenth century that it would be important to distinguish between the different modes by which free tenements had been created. To draw the principal distinction was enough for all practical purposes. Stray notices occur however that give some insight into the matter. Very often we find tenements held *per cartam*, probably because this kind of title was rather exceptional and seemed to deserve a special mention, while commonly land was held without charter, on the strength of a ceremonial investiture by the lord. This last mode does not find uniform expression in the documents, but the implied opposition to holding by charter is sometimes stated in express terms which bring out one or the other feature of free land holding.

One of the questions addressed to the jurors—from whose verdicts the Hundred Rolls were made, was—Si aliquis liber sokemannus de antiquo dominico alii sokemanno vendiderit vel alio modo alienaverit aliquid tenendum libere per cartam[1]? The *free* sokeman's tenure is meant, although the inquest is taken

---

[1] R. H. ii. 597. Cf. 469, 470.

on ancient demesne soil, and the point is that none of these persons can alienate by charter, but must use the ceremonial surrender in the court of ancient demesne according to the custom of the manor.   I have already drawn attention to the remarkable opposition between free customary tenure and holding by charter.   It is chiefly important because it discloses a traditional element in the formation of the socman's tenure.

The same traditional element appears in other cases in which the special position of the socman is not concerned.   In Warwickshire a free tenant by sergeanty is said to hold his land without charter by warrant from ancient times, and the peculiar obligations of his sergeanty are described at some length[1].   The charter appears here in contrast with ancient ownership, to the origin of which no date can be assigned.   A similar case is that of Over, Cambs.[2] Robert de Aula holds two virgates of the Abbot of Ramsey *de antiquo conquestu* and seven virgates *de antiquo*.   Further on a certain Robert Mariot is mentioned holding five virgates of Robert de Aula *de antiquo feffamento*.   The weight falls, in all these expressions, on the *de antiquo*, which may even appear without any

---

[1] Exch. Q. R. Misc. Books A. 29, f. 64, b : ' Nota—predictus Ricardus (de Loges) dicit se *non habere Warentum aliquem nisi per antiquam tenuram sine carta* . . . Idem Ricardus habet visum franci plegii unde vocat ad warantum le Domesday (!) . . . Idem Ricardus tenet quicquid tenet in Soume de comite Cestrie, ut idem Ricardus dicit, per seruicium ducendi comitem Cestrie usque curiam Regis per medietatem foreste predicte de Kanoke, obviando ei ad pontem de Rocford ad mandatum comitis et idem comes dabit unam sagittam barbatam dicto Ricardo et capiat in foresta unam feram si voluerit eundo et aliam redeundo si voluerit, et in redeundo obviabit ei ad pontem de Repelwas ad mandatum comitis et dabit ei aliam sagittam.' Cf. Rot. Hundr. ii. 689 : '[Libere tenentes] Johanna Galard tenet in eadem dimidiam virgatam terrae de dono Willelmi fratris sui et reddit eidem per annum 6d. et idem Willelmus tenet *de hereditate per defensum antecessorum suorum qui dictam dimidiam virgatam terrae habuerunt de dono Regis cujus nomen ignoramus.*' Thomas Wyteman tenet in eadem I virgatam terrae de Philippo de Lenettale, *et est de confirmacione Regis, ut dicta dimidia virgata terrae prescripta.* I have already quoted this passage in the note on the hundredors.   I give it as corrected according to the MS. in the Record Office.   In the printed version of the Hundred Rolls it has lost its meaning.

[2] R. H. ii. 477, 478. ' *Libere tenentes.* Robertus de Aula tenet in predicta villa duas virgatas terre de Abbate de Ramesaye de antiquo conquestu et supradictas septem virgatas similiter de antiquo et facit sectam curie bis per annum et si brevis domini Regis ibi sit faciet sectam de tribus septimanis. . . . Robertus Mariot tenet 5 virgatas terre de Roberto de Aula de feodo Episcopi Elyensis de antiquo feffamento.'

further qualification. Of these qualifications one is interesting in itself, I mean 'de conquestu.' In the language of those times it may stand either 1, for conquest in the sense in which that term is now commonly used, or 2, for purchase, or 3, for occupation. The first of these meanings is naturally out of the question in our case. The second does not apply if we take heed how the expressions interchange : it could be replaced by feoffamentum in the third instance, and could not have fallen out after de antiquo in the second. Ancient occupation fits well, and such a construction is supported by other passages. In Ayllington (Elton), Hunts, e.g., we find the chief free tenants all, with one exception, holding *de conquestu* in contrast with the mesne tenants who are said to hold *per cartam*. The opposition is again clearly between traditional occupation and new feoffment settled by written instrument. In Sawtrey Beaumeys, on the other hand, the mode of holding de conquestu seems exceptional[1].

Another terminological opposition which finds expression in the surveys is that between men who hold *per homagium* and those who hold *per fidelitatem*. It seems to be commonly assumed that free tenements owe homage, but without disputing the point in a general way I shall call attention to the description of Kenilworth in the Warwickshire Roll, in which *libere tenentes* are said to hold *per fidelitatem et nullum faciunt homagium*[2]. The deviation must probably be accounted for by the fact that the castle of Kenilworth was Royal demesne and had been given to Edmund, the brother of King Edward I; the peculiar condition described was certainly a species of customary freehold or socman's tenure.

The upshot is, that we find in the Hundred Rolls traces of freeholds possessed by ancient tenure, 'without charter and warrant,' according to customs which came down from the time of the Conquest, or the original occupation of the land, or from a time beyond memory. The examples given are stray instances but important nevertheless, because we may well fancy that in

---

[1] Rot. Hundr. ii. 656, 660. Cf. as to the meaning of antiqua tenura, etc. Rot. Hundr. i. 79, 354.

[2] Exch. Q. R. Misc. Books, No. 29, f. 7: 'Idem Edmundus habet libere tenentes subscriptos. Ricardus de Hulle tenet unum mesuagium et 8 acras terre pro 14 solidis et secta ad curiam suam ibidem de tribus septimanis in tres septimanas (about ten similar holdings) et sciendum quod omnes predicti debent sectam predictam et tenent *per fidelitatem et nullum faciunt homagium*.'

many cases such facts escaped registration. And now how are all these traces of the 'traditional' element to be expressed in legal language? From what source did the right of such people flow? How did they defend it in case it was contested?

The absence of a charter is not by itself a reason to consider this kind of tenure as separated from the usual freehold. A feoffment might well be made without a charter[1]. As long as the form of the investiture by the lord had been kept, it was sufficient to create or to transmit the free tenancy. But the warranty of the lord and the feoffment were necessary as a rule. And here we find cases in which there is no warranty, and the lord is not appealed to as a feoffor. They must be considered as held by surrender and admittance in court and as being in this respect like the tenements of the sokemen. I do not see any other alternative. As to the sokemen we find indeed, that their right is contrasted with feoffment and at the same time considered as a kind of free tenancy, that it is defended by manorial writs, and at the same time well established in custom[2]. But can we say that the warranty of the lord is less prominent in this case than in the *liberum tenementum* created by the usual feudal investiture? Surrender seems to go even further in the direction of a resumption by the lord of a right which he has conferred on the dependent. If surrender stood alone, one would be unable to see in what way this customary procedure could be taken as an expression of 'communal guarantee.' But the surrender is coupled with admittance. The action of the steward called upon to transmit by his rod the possession of a plot of land is indissolubly connected with the action of the court which has to witness and to approve the transaction. The suitors of the court in their collective capacity come very characteristically to the front in the admittance of the socman, and it is on their communal testimony that the whole transaction has to rest. The Rolls of Stoneleigh and of King's Ripton give many a precious hint on this subject[3].

---

[1] Bracton, f. 33 b. Madox, Formulare Anglicanum.

[2] Coram Rege, Pascha 6 Edw. I, f. 6, 6 : 'Et requisitus si aliquid scit dicere quare predictum mesuagium quod est infra predictum manerium esse non debeat de condicione antiqui dominici Regis, utpote per feoffamentum domini Regis vel antecessorum suorum,' etc. Cf. Placit. Abbrev. 150 (quoted p. 113, n. 4).

[3] Besides the extracts from the Stoneleigh Register quoted on p. 113, n. 1, and p. 198, n. 1, I may be allowed to call attention to f. 76 : 'Item nullus

I speak of the socmen in ancient demesne, but there can be no doubt that originally the different classes of this group called soc-men were constantly confused and treated as one and the same condition. The free socmen and the base or bond socmen, the population of manors in the hands of the crown, of those which had passed from the crown to subjects, and, last but not least, a vast number of small proprietors who held in chief from the king with-out belonging to the military class, and without a clearly settled right to a free tenement—all these were treated more or less as variations of one main type. What held them together was the suit owed to some court of a Royal Manor which had 'soke' over them[2]. Ultimately classification became more rigid, and theo-retically more clear; free and socman's tenure were fused into the one 'socage' tenure, well known to later law, but we must not forget that Common Law Socage is derived historically from a very special relation, and that the socman appears even in terminology as distinct from the 'libere tenens.' I must admit, however, that it is only with the help of the documents of Saxon times and of the Conquest period, that it will be possible to establish conclusively the character of the tenure as that of a 'customary freehold.'

---

adiudicabitur tenens terre nisi *quia curia tenens acceptatur* per fidelitatem et alias consuetudines licet tenens extra curiam aliquem feoffaverit per cartam vel sine carta.' Maitland, Manorial Rolls of King's Ripton (Selden Soc. ii\. p. 122: 'Capiatur in manum domini quarta pars unius rode prati jacens in Smalemade quam Rogerus Greyling vendidit Nicholao le Neuman *sine licencia curie.*' Cf. as to the references to the Court-roll in case of doubt and contention Augmentation Off. Court Rolls, Ripton Regis, xxiii, N. 94, f. 10: 'Et quod iuncta est secum vocat *rotulos ad Warantum.* Et predicta Mathildis dicit quod uxor eius non est iuncta et ponit se super rotulos.' Now the im-portance of the Roll is derived from the authority of the Court of which it records the proceedings.

[2] Rot. Hundr. i. p. 104: 'Sokemanni *domini Regis de Soka de* Piclinton tenere solebant 3 carucatas terre et unam bovatam in Brunneby de anteces-soribus Radulfi de Lacely et ipso Radulfo. De quibus hospitalarii habent unam bovatam de dono antecessorum dicti Radulfi. ... Item prior de Elreton 4 bovatas ... que sunt de tenura sokemannorum.' These are free men under Soke, but there is not much to distinguish them from people on ancient demesne soil. Cf. Maddox, Exch. 428, c: 'Liberi sokemanni de Askebi et Tinton reddunt compotum de 20 marcis et 1 palefridi ut Henricus de Nevill eos juste deducat de tenementis quae tenent in eisdem villis, nec ab eis exigat consuetudines vel servitia quae facere non solebant tempore Henrici Regis patris Regis,' etc.

XIII.

See pp. 233, 234.

The passage on which the text of these two pages is based may be found in a Survey of the Dunstaple Priory. The portion immediately concerned is inscribed : ' Notulae de terris in Segheho' (ff. 7, 8). The Walter de Wahull in question is probably the baron of that name (Dugdale, Baron. I. 504), who joined the rebellion of 1173 along with the Earl of Leicester, and was made a prisoner (Rad. de Diceto I. 377, 378 ; Ann. Dunstapl. 21).

Harl. MS. 1885, f. 7.

§ Tempore conquestus terrae, Dominus de Wahull et Dominus de la Leie diviserunt inter se feudum de Walhull', widelicet, Dominus de Walhull' habuit duas partes, et Dominus de la Lee, tertiam, scilicet, unus xx. milites, et alius x. Volens autem Dominus de Wahull' retinere ad opus suum totum parcum de Segheho, et totum dominicum de Broccheburg', fecit metiri tertiam partem in bosco et in plano. Postea, fecit metiri tantumdem terrae, ad mensuram praedictae tertiae partis, in loco qui nunc vocatur Nortwde, et in bosco vicino, qui tunc vocabatur Cherlewde ; et abegit omnes rusticos qui in praedicto loco juxta praedictum boscum manebant. Hiis ita gestis, mensurata est terra de Segheho, et inventae sunt viii. ydae vilenagiae. De hiis viii. ydis conputata est quarta acra ad unam summam, et inventa est quod haec summa valebat tertiam partem parci et dominici. Dedit ergo Dominus de Wahull' Domino de la Leie, scilicet, Stephano, pro tertia parte quam debuit sortiri in bosco et in dominico, culturas praedictorum rusticorum, et boscum qui nunc vocabatur Cherlewd', nunc Nortwd'. Dominus autem de la Leie dedit hanc terram Bald' militi suo, patri Roberti de Nortwd'. Et inter terram praedictorum rusticorum habuimus de dono ecclesiae unam acram. Pro hac acra Robertus pater Gileberti dedit nobis [in] escambium aliam acram quae abutiat ad Fenmed', et jacet ad vest, juxta terram Nigelli de Chaltun'. De ista praedicta acra in Nortwd' quae nostra fuit, jacet roda una ad lomputtes, scilicet, roda capitalis. Alia roda jacet ad uest curiae Roberti praedicti ; quae curia ipsius Roberti primo fuit ad uest, quam post obitum patris mutavit, transferendo horrea sua de uest usque hest. Tres gorae jacent pro dimidia acra, et abutiant ex una parte versus viam quae dicitur via de Nortwd,' et ex alia parte versus Edmundum filium Uctred '. Procedente tempore, tempore guerrae prae-dictae viii. ydae et ceterae de Segheho fuerunt occupatae a multis injuste ; et ob hoc recognitio fuit facta coram Waltero de Wahull', et coram Hugone de Leia, et in plena curia, per vi. senes, et per ipsum Robertum, de hac nostra acra et de omnibus aliis terris, scilicet, quae acrae ad quas hidas pertineant : et per hanc recognitionem, restituit nobis Robertus praedictam acram. Uctre-dus drengus mansit ad uest de via de Nortwde, et grangiae ejus fuerunt ex alia parte viae, scilicet, hest.

Tempore quo omnes tenentes de Segheho, scilicet, Milites, liberi homines, et omnes alii incerti et nescii fuerunt de terris et tenementis ville, et singuli dicebant alios injuste plus aliis possidere, omnes communi consilio, coram Dominis de Wahul' et de la Leie, tradiderunt terras suas per provisum seniorum et per mensuram pertici quasi novus conquestus dividendas, et unicuique rationabili-ter assignandas. Eo tempore recognovit Radulfus Fretetot quod antecessores sui et ipse injuste tenuerant placiam quandam sub castello, que placia per distributores et per perticam mensurata est, et divisa in xvj buttos ; et jacent hii butti ad Fulevell', et abut[tant] sursum ad croftas ville. Hii butti ita partiti sunt. Octo yde sunt in Segheho de vilenagio : singulis ydis assignati sunt ii. butti. Ecclesiae vero dotata fuit de dimidia yda : ad hanc dimidiam ydam assignatus fuit unus buttus : sed postquam illum primum habuimus, bis seminatus fuit, et non amplius, quia ceteri omnes non excol[un]t ibi terram, sed ad pascua reservant : un[de] est, quia locus remotus est, nec pratum habemus nec bladum.

He terre prenominate sunt in campo qui dicitur Hestfeld. Summa, xix acre et tres rode.

XIV.

See p. 302, n. 1.

Cotton MS. Galba E. X. f. 19.

Hec est firma unius cuiusque uille que reddit plenam firmam duarum ebdomadarum.

Duodecim quarteria farine ad panem monachorum suorumque hospitum que singula faciunt quinque treias Ramesie, et unaqueque treia appreciatur duodecim denariis precium uniuscuiusque quarterii fuit quinque sol. Summa precii 12 quarteriorum, 60 sol. et 2 millia

panum uillarum uel 4 quarteria ad usum seruientium. Precium
unius mille dimidiam marcam argenti. Summa precii integra
marca. Ad potum 24 missa de grut quarum singulas faciunt una
treia Ramesii et una ringa. Appreciatur una missa 12 den.
Summa precii de brasio 32 sol. sunt et 2 septaria mellis 32 den. sunt
summa precii 5 sol. et 4 den.

Ad compadium 4 libre in denariis et decem pense lardi. Precium
unius pense 5 sol. sunt. Summa precii 5 obol. Et decem pense
casei. Precium unius pense 3 solidi sunt. Summa precii 30 sol.
Et decem frenscengie peroptime. Precium uniuscuiusque sunt
6 den.—Et 14 agni. Agnus pro denario—Et 120 galline, 6 pro
den.—Et 2000 ovorum. Precium unius mille 2 sol. sunt.—Et 2 tine
butiri. Precium unius tine 40 den.—Et 2 treie fabarum. Prec.
1 treie 8 den. sunt. Et 24 misse prebende. Precium unius misse
8 den.—Summa precii totius supradicte firme 12 libre sunt et 15
sol. et 1 den. exceptis 4 libris supradictis, que solummodo debent
dari in denariis de unaquaque plena firma duarum ebdomadarum.
Et postquam hec omnia reddita fuerunt, firmarius persoluet 5
solidos in denariis, uno denario minus, et sic implebuntur 17
libre plenae in dica cellerarii et unum mille de allic sine dica et
firmarius dabit present cellerario ter in anno sine dica.

Villa que reddit firmam plenam unius ebdomade, dimidium
omnium supradictorum reddet. Excepto quod unaqueque villa
cuiuslibet firme sit, uel duarum ebdomadarum, uel unius plene
firme, uel unius lente firme, dabit equaliter ad mandatum pauperum
16 denarios de acra elemosin.

Villa que reddit lente firmam unius ebdomade, omnino sicut
plena firma unius ebdomade reddet. Exceptis quinque pensis
lardis et 5 pensis casei quas non dat set pro eis 40 solidos in
denariis et alios 40 sol. sicut plena firma.

XV.

See p. 344, n. 1.

Ayllington or Elton, Hunts, is remarkable on account of the
contrast between its free and servile holdings, as described in the
Hundred Rolls. It would be interesting to know whether the
former are to be considered as ancient free tenements, or as the

outcome of modern exemptions. The Hundred Rolls point in the first direction (ii. 656). Some of the tenements under discussion are said to be held de conquestu, and it would be impossible to put any other interpretation on this term than that of 'original occupation.' It means the same as the 'de antiquo conquestu' of other surveys (sup. p. 453).

But when we compare the inquisition published in the Ramsey Cartulary (Rolls Ser. i. 487 sqq.) we come upon a difficulty. There the holdings are constantly arranged under the two headings of *virgatae operariae* and *virgatae positae ad censum*, the population is divided into *operarii* and *censuarii*, and in one case we find even the following passage: 'item quaelibet domus, habens ostium apertum versus vicum, tam de malmannis, quam de cotmannis et operariis, inveniret unum hominem ad lovebone, sine cibo domini, praeter Ricardum Pemdome, Henricum Franceys, Galfridum Blundy, Henricum le Monnier.' And so most of the free people are actually called *molmen*, and this would seem to imply that they were *libere tenentes* only in consequence of commutation.

It seems to me that there is no occasion for such an inference. The *molmen* in the passage quoted are evidently the same as the *censuarii* of other passages, and although, in a general way, the expression *mal* was probably employed of quit-rents, still it was wide enough to interchange with *gafol*, and to designate all kinds of rents, without any regard to their origin. And of course, this is even more the case with *census*. Upon the whole, I do not see sufficient reason to doubt that we have freeholders before us who held their land and paid rent ever since the original occupation of the soil.

INDEX.

—+—

Day-work, 288.
Defence, 260.
Demesne, 223, 313 ; free tenements carved out of it, 327 ; its development, 406.
Denerata, 257.
Dialogus de Scaccario, on villainage, 44 ; on Englishry, 64 ; on the Conquest, 121, 122.
Domesday Survey of Kent, 205 ; on classes, 209.
Donum, 293.

Election of manorial officers, 355.
Elton, C. I., on ancient demesne tenure, 112 ; on shifting ownership of arable, 236.
Ely Surveys, 441.
Emphyteusis, 333.
Enfranchisement, by feoffment, 70 ; modes of manumission, 86 ; by convention, 183 ; as gradual emancipation, 184, 214.
Essartum, 332.
Exemption from labour, 296, 322.
Extraneus, 142.

Fald-silver, 291.
Farm, feorm, 301, 459.
Fastnyng-seed, 282.
Fealty, 164, 454.
Feoffment, 347, 455.
Ferdel, 256.
Ferlingsetus, 148.
Festuca, 372.
Feudalism, Kemble on, 20 ; influence on villainage, 131 ; oppression, 204.
Field systems, 224.
Filstnerthe, Filsingerthe, 282.
Firmarius, 305.
Fish-silver, 291.
Fleta on the hide, 241.
Fleyland, 170.
Foddercorn, 288.
Food-rents, 304.
Forinsecus, 142.
Forland, 332.
Frank pledge, villains in, 66, 418 ; and leet, 363.
Free bench, 160.
Freeman, Edw., 22.
French Revolution, 10.
Fustel de Coulanges, 17, 32.

Gafol, 184, 187.
Gafol-earth, 280.
Gathercorn, 289.
Gavelkind, 207.
Gavelman, 187.

Gavelseed, 288.
Gebur, 145.
Geneat, 145.
Gersumarius, 147.
Gild, 293.
Glanville, on status, 59 ; on manumission, 87.
Gneist, R., 24.
Godlesebene, 282.
Gomme, on early folk-mots, 367.
Gora, 231.
Grass-earth, 280.

Hale, Archdeacon, on the farm system, 305.
Halimote, 364, 370.
Hallam, his work on the Middle Ages, 11 ; on villainage, 48.
Hand-dainae, 288.
Havering atte Bower, Essex, 108, 436.
Headland, 232.
Heriot, 159.
Hidage, 294.
Hide, 239, 241, 244 ; Kemble on, 19.
Hidarius, 147.
Hitchin, Herts, 394.
Holding, 238, 241, 249, 263, 300 ; origin, 401.
Homagium, 455.
Hundred, 67, 192, 445.
Hundredarius, 188, 194, 441, 450.
Hundred Rolls, on merchet, 154 ; on free tenements, 336.
Huntenegeld, 292.
Husfelds, 314.

Inheritance, 246.
Inhoc, 226.
Inland, 328.
Intermixture of strips, 234, 254, 317.

Jugum, 248, 309.
Juratores curiae, 376.

Kemble, 18.
Kentish custom, 205, 248.
King's Ripton, Hunts, 93, 106, 110, 383.

Labourers, hired, 321.
Lammas-meadow, 260.
Landchere, 290.
Landgafol, 292.
Landsettus, 146.
Leases, of demesne land, 329 ; for life and term of years, 330.
Legal theory, 44, 127.
Lentenearth, 282.

THE END.

www.ingramcontent.com/pod-product-compliance
Lightning Source LLC
Chambersburg PA
CBHW030532100426
42813CB00001B/227